# MAGILL'S
# SURVEY
# OF
# SCIENCE

# MAGILL'S SURVEY OF SCIENCE

## SPACE EXPLORATION SERIES

Volume 5
1917-2328
The Development of Spacesuits — Z
INDEX

*Edited by*

# FRANK N. MAGILL

SALEM PRESS
Pasadena, California   Englewood Cliffs, New Jersey

4p

**Library of Congress Cataloging-in-Publication Data**
Magill's survey of science. Space exploration series/
edited by Frank N. Magill
   p. cm.
   Bibliography: p.
   Includes index
   1. Astronautics. 2. Outer space—Exploration. I.
Magill, Frank Northen, 1907-
TL790.M24   1989                88-38267
629.4—dc19                          CIP
ISBN 0-89356-600-4 (set)
ISBN 0-89356-605-5 (volume 5)

06/12/92

PRINTED IN THE UNITED STATES OF AMERICA

# CONTENTS

# SPACE EXPLORATION

# THE DEVELOPMENT OF SPACESUITS

*Date:* Beginning May 5, 1961
*Type of technology:* Humans in space
*Country:* The United States

*Spacesuits initially provided astronauts with an emergency intravehicular backup system in case of the loss of spacecraft cabin pressure. Early spacesuit designs were based on the technology developed for high-altitude aircraft pressure suits. More complex spacesuit mobility systems now allow astronauts to venture beyond the protective limits of the spacecraft.*

*Principal personages*
JOHN SCOTT HALDANE, a British physiologist
MARK EDWARD RIDGE, an American balloonist
WILEY POST, an American aviator
RUSSELL COLLEY, a pressure suit designer
YURI A. GAGARIN, a Soviet cosmonaut
ALAN B. SHEPARD, an American astronaut
ALEXEI LEONOV, a Soviet cosmonaut
EDWARD H. WHITE, an American astronaut
NEIL A. ARMSTRONG, an American astronaut
JOSEPH KOSMO, Subsystem Manager, spacesuit development,
   NASA
HUBERT VYKUKAL, Senior Research Scientist, NASA

## Summary of the Technology

It has long been recognized that humans cannot survive the conditions of space without special protection. The development of spacesuits contributed significantly toward making space exploration possible.

In 1920, John Scott Haldane, a British physiologist, first proposed the use of a pressure suit to provide protection for flight crew members against the lack of oxygen at altitudes above 12,200 meters. This idea, however, was not tested until November 30, 1933, when American balloonist Mark Ridge donned a modified deep-sea diver's suit and was exposed to 25,600-meter altitude conditions in a low-pressure chamber.

In the same year that Ridge was testing the British-built "high-altitude" suit, Wiley Post, an American aviator, initiated the development of a full pressure suit. Post needed the pressure suit to help him break the existing world aircraft altitude record. Wearing a suit designed by Russell Colley of the B.F. Goodrich Company, Post made a number of high-altitude flights during 1934 and 1935. Unfortunately, because of problems with the recording barographs, no official altitude record could be verified. Unofficially, however, Post had reached altitudes in excess of

12,200 meters with the help of the full pressure suit. More important, the efforts made and risks taken by Ridge and Post proved that pressure suits were practical systems that would safely enable humans to fly at high altitudes and, in time, into space.

Before and during World War II, full pressure suits were developed by various European countries and the United States. All the early suits were very cumbersome to wear and, when inflated, caused serious mobility restrictions. These suits were primarily developed to protect high-altitude flight crew members from lack of oxygen, and as such, they were regarded as precursors of aircraft cabin pressurization systems. With the onset of World War II, the pressure cabin became standard in most aircraft, and from then on, pressure suit research focused on emergency situations in military and experimental high-altitude aircraft.

In 1961, the first men to wear full pressure suits in space were Russian cosmonaut Yuri Gagarin and American astronaut Alan Shepard. The pressure suits they used were worn uninflated in a pressurized cabin and would only have been inflated in the event of a failure of the Vostok or Mercury capsule pressurization system. The spacesuit configurations developed by the National Aeronautics and Space Administration (NASA) for the Mercury project and Gemini program originated from the earlier high-altitude aircraft full pressure suit.

The Mercury project and Gemini program spacesuits were essentially modified versions of existing military full pressure suits. The Mercury project utilized the Navy's Mark 4 full pressure suit, built by B.F. Goodrich Company, and the Gemini program spacesuit was derived from the Air Force's AP/22 full pressure suit, manufactured by David Clark Company. The early Soviet spacesuits also originated from military aircraft pressure suit technology. These early spacesuits lacked sophisticated mobility systems; because the suits served primarily as backup systems against the loss of cabin pressure, only limited pressurized intravehicular mobility was required.

The development of the mobile spacesuit was spurred by the requirement for astronauts to perform tasks outside the spacecraft. In 1965, cosmonaut Alexei Leonov, of Voskhod 2, and astronaut Edward White, of Gemini 4, performed the world's first "spacewalks." During this phase of the Gemini program, U.S. scientists recognized that astronauts needed improved mobility systems and protection from extravehicular environmental hazards.

The Apollo spacesuit was designed to function as an emergency intravehicular suit and as an extravehicular suit that would enable lunar surface exploration. A variety of prototype Apollo spacesuit configurations evolved between 1965 and 1970. The International Latex Corporation was responsible for the design, development, and fabrication of the A7L and A7LB Apollo spacesuits, which were selected for use. On July 20, 1969, Neil Armstrong, wearing an A7L spacesuit, was the first human to set foot on an extraterrestrial surface and collect data while being sustained in and protected from a hostile environment. Later Apollo astronauts wore the improved A7LB spacesuit when they explored the lunar surface. The Skylab program adopted the basic Apollo A7L spacesuit with minor modifications for use in various planned orbital extravehicular activities.

During the early 1960's, as spacesuits were being developed for the Gemini program and the planned Apollo and Skylab programs, Joseph Kosmo of the Johnson Space Center (JSC) and Hubert Vykukal of the Ames Research Center embarked on the development of advanced spacesuit mobility systems for potential future application. NASA long-range program planners had been studying the feasibility of establishing lunar surface bases and conducting manned Mars planetary exploration. In support of these envisioned post-Apollo operations, NASA initiated a series of spacesuit technology development programs.

The first of the JSC-sponsored advanced technology suit concepts was the rigid experimental suit assembly, or RX-1, developed by Litton Industries' Space Sciences Laboratory. The suit was a radical departure from the basic, soft-fabric spacesuits of early 1962. The RX-1 was developed to demonstrate the feasibility of low-force mobility joint systems in the arms and legs. Additional suit features included hard torso structure and an easily fastened single-plane body seal closure. (The Mercury, Gemini, and Apollo spacesuits used pressure-sealing zippers.) Between 1962 and 1968, numerous RX models were developed. Each version incorporated mobility joint and structural improvements made possible by evaluation and testing of the previous model. The RX-5A was the final configuration of the RX series.

In conjunction with the development of JSC's RX, Ames Research Center initiated investigations into a hard spacesuit that would use a combination of bearings and metal bellows for mobility joint systems. Between 1964 and 1968, two "Ames experimental" hard suit assemblies, identified as AX-1 and AX-2, were developed by Ames.

As the Apollo program matured, it became apparent that spacecraft payload weight and stowage volume limitations were constraints on the various hard suit concepts. This realization resulted in the initiation of new approaches to spacesuit design, and JSC produced a family of advanced spacesuit configurations representing a hybridization of hard suit and soft suit technologies. With the completion of the Apollo program, much of the advanced mobility system technology that had been developed earlier was shelved. In the 1970's and 1980's, various elements of the advanced spacesuit technology base were incorporated in the spacesuits designed for the U.S. space shuttle and space station programs.

Unlike previous flight program spacesuits, the shuttle spacesuit was designed for extravehicular use only. Emphasis was therefore placed on providing astronauts with a high degree of extravehicular operational capability, uncompromised by other requirements. The shuttle spacesuit incorporated a hard upper-torso shell of fiberglass, a horizontal single-plane body seal closure ring, pressure-sealed bearings in the shoulder, upper arm, and lower torso areas, and flat, all-fabric arm, waist, and leg joints. All these elements had evolved from earlier advanced spacesuit technology.

The space station program focused on expanding extravehicular activity (EVA) capabilities beyond those of previous space programs. The space station suit was to have a higher operating pressure—8.3 pounds per square inch—so that astronauts would not need to spend costly time prebreathing pure oxygen before performing an EVA. Previously, prebreathing operations served to wash nitrogen gas from an astronaut's bloodstream so that nitrogen bubbles would not form when the astronaut moved from the shuttle cabin, pressurized at 14.7 pounds per square inch, to the spacesuit, pressurized at 4.3 pounds per square inch. If, however, the spacesuit could operate at higher pressure, prebreathing could be eliminated and EVA operations would be able to be conducted more routinely. The core technology for advanced mobility systems established over the previous years enabled the development of higher operating pressure spacesuits. JSC's Mark 3 and Ames's AX-5, designs which eliminated the need for prebreathing, were developed in response to need of the space station program.

Minimizing energy expenditure by the astronaut, made difficult by the tendency of the volume of gas in joint elements to change during pressurized operations, continues to be the primary impetus behind research in improved mobility systems. The systems developed between 1960 and the 1980's have demonstrated the technical viability of certain design features and have served as a base for the development of future lunar and planetary exploration spacesuits.

## Knowledge Gained

As space missions became more complex, so did spacesuits. The experience gained from a variety of space missions has influenced spacesuit development.

From the manned EVAs of the Gemini program, it was learned that improved cooling techniques to remove astronaut-produced metabolic heat would be required if longer and more involved EVAs were to be conducted. As a result, NASA scientists developed an undergarment, to be worn inside the spacesuit, that contained small tubes through which water could be pumped. The liquid-cooled garment became a standard design feature of the Apollo spacesuit and all subsequent suits.

In the Apollo and Skylab programs, the spacesuit fulfilled two roles. It was worn at launch and during critical spacecraft docking operations, and its function during these phases was to provide a backup pressurized environment in case of cabin pressure failure. It also acted as a pressurized mobility system and a portable life-support system during orbital and lunar surface EVAs. The environmental hazards and hostile conditions of extended orbital operations and lunar surface exploration meant that scientists had to develop improved materials and designs to protect the spacesuited astronaut. The requirements of intravehicular versus extravehicular operations posed a number of design problems, including limitations on bulk, operational complexity, and mobility.

For the shuttle program, the spacesuit was designed for the single purpose of supporting manned extravehicular operations, and features were optimized for enhanced EVA performance and reduced cost. The shuttle spacesuit with its corresponding life-support system represented the first completely integrated extravehicular assembly. No cumbersome external life-support hoses, connections, or harness straps were required to allow an astronaut to leave the spacecraft.

Previously, each spacesuit was custom built to fit the astronaut and was used on only one mission. The shuttle spacesuit design featured modular components that could be combined in various ways, enabling both male and female astronauts to be fitted with a minimum number of spacesuits and reducing overall program cost.

Elimination of prebreathing operations through the development of spacesuit mobility systems which operate at higher pressure levels will make EVAs more routine and easier to perform. The modular design of the candidate space station pressure suits, being similar to that of the shuttle spacesuit, will enable the suits to be reused numerous times. In addition, in-orbit maintenance and replacement of various fabric components and the reuse of hardware components will reduce overall spacesuit and flight program costs.

## Context

Throughout the Mercury project and until the feasibility of EVAs was established on the Gemini 4 mission, spacesuits were simply backups for cabin pressure systems. The development of the true spacesuit occurred almost simultaneously in two separate parts of the world. In 1965, Soviet cosmonaut Leonov and American astronaut White performed independent spacewalks outside the confines of their respective spacecraft. The Gemini program provided the first EVA in the U.S. manned space effort.

The Gemini program's accomplishments were significant for spacesuit development. For the first time, spacesuits were used to allow humans to work in space. It was recognized that manned EVAs would increase spacecraft's capabilities and enable the development of new operational techniques. EVA technology from the Gemini program was incorporated wherever possible in the Apollo spacesuit. Improved body-cooling and mobility systems were direct results of the Gemini experiences.

Spacesuits make EVAs possible in three ways. First, in combination with a portable life-support system, the spacesuit maintains the physiological well-being of the astronaut, which includes supplying oxygen for breathing and ventilation and removing carbon dioxide and metabolic heat. Second, the spacesuit incorporates various mobility joint system features that enable the astronaut to perform tasks in the extravehicular environment. Finally, the spacesuit provides protection against the hazards of space, which include thermal extremes, meteoroid and debris particles, radiation, and, on the lunar surface, sand and dust. The pressure retention layer of the spacesuit is both a protective barrier and a structural foundation for various mobility systems. A separate outer garment comprising layers of various materials protects the astronaut from hostile environments.

None of the materials used in the early spacesuits were originally developed with space exploration in mind. As more complex spacesuit systems evolved, special needs were identified that required the development of new materials or combinations of materials to provide structural integrity and increased protection.

The space station created a need for a spacesuit that would operate at higher pressure, which in turn stimulated the development of improved mobility system technology. Extensive EVA experience has been accumulated in space environments ranging from near-Earth orbit to the lunar surface. In all cases, a spacesuit has been designed to accommodate the unique conditions encountered. As scientists plan future space missions that will encompass longer and more diversified EVAs, established spacesuit technology will form the foundation for the development of more advanced spacesuits.

## Bibliography

Cortright, Edgar M., ed. *Apollo Expeditions to the Moon*. NASA SP-350. Washington, D.C.: Government Printing Office, 1975. The personal accounts of eighteen men, including NASA managers, scientists, engineers, and astronauts, who directed, developed, and conducted the Apollo missions. Suitable for general audiences, it describes the various political events and engineering projects that influenced the Apollo program. Includes numerous illustrations and photographs covering the historical period of the Apollo program, along with pictures transmitted from Apollo spacecraft showing the use of spacesuits.

Faget, Maxime Allen. *Manned Space Flight*. New York: Holt, Rinehart and Winston, 1965. Describes some of the technical problems engineers are faced with in the building of manned spacecraft systems. Offers insights into the various scientific principles that were used to provide engineering solutions to those problems. Contains numerous charts and illustrations. Recommended for high school and college-level readers.

Machell, Reginald M., ed. *Summary of Gemini Extravehicular Activity*. NASA SP-149. Springfield, Va.: Clearinghouse for Federal Scientific Information, 1967. An official summary of the Gemini program extravehicular operations described from the developmental viewpoint. Discusses the systems used, the testing and qualification of those systems, the preparation of the flight crews, and operational and medical aspects of the missions. Contains numerous illustrations, charts, and photographs relating to the Gemini program. Suitable for advanced high school and college-level readers.

Mallan, Lloyd. *Suiting Up for Space: The Evolution of the Space Suit*. New York: John Day, 1971. Presents a historical perspective of the development of early pressure suits for high-altitude flight and the evolution of spacesuits from these beginnings. Contains numerous photographs of early prototype and flight model pressure suits and spacesuits. A highly accessible work.

Oberg, James E. *Mission to Mars: Plans and Concepts for the First Manned Landing*. Harrisburg, Pa.: Stackpole Books, 1982. Describes the feasibility of a manned Mars mission and discusses topics such as spaceship design, propulsion, life-support systems, spacesuits, Martian surface exploration, cost factors, and political and social issues relating to future plans for colonization. Contains photographs and illustrations. Suitable for general audiences.

Paine, Thomas O. *Pioneering the Space Frontier: The Report of the National Commission on Space.* New York: Bantam Books, 1986. Presents a programmatic view of the steps the United States must take to remain competitive with the Soviet Union for the next fifty years of space exploration. Discusses NASA's long-term goals. Contains photographs, charts, graphs, and illustrations related to future missions. Includes a glossary of technical terms and an extensive bibliography identifying a wide variety of space-related reference sources. Accessible to the layman.

Swenson, Loyd S., Jr., et al. *This New Ocean: A History of Project Mercury.* NASA SP-4201. Washington, D.C.: Government Printing Office, 1966. The official history of the Mercury project, this book details the elements of research, development, and operations that made up the program. Identifies and describes the importance of exploring the human factor in regard to spaceflight and records the beginning of the space age. Includes extensive footnotes and a thorough bibliography.

*Joseph J. Kosmo*

## Cross-References

Ames Research Center, 21; The Apollo Program, 28; Astronauts and the U.S. Astronaut Program, 154; Biological Effects of Space Travel on Humans, 188; The Commercial Use of Space Program Innovations, 253; Cosmonauts and the Soviet Cosmonaut Program, 273; The Gemini Program, 487; Johnson Space Center, 669; The Manned Maneuvering Unit, 829; The Mercury Project, 940; The Development of the Mercury Project, 947; The National Aeronautics and Space Administration, 1032; International Private Industry and Space Exploration, 1182; U.S. Private Industry and Space Exploration, 1187; The Skylab Program, 1285; The U.S. Space Shuttle, 1626; Space Shuttle Living Conditions, 1634; The Design and Uses of the U.S. Space Station, 1828; The Development of the U.S. Space Station, 1835; Living and Working in the U.S. Space Station, 1850; The Space Task Group, 1864.

# SPACEWATCH
## Tracking Space Debris

*Date:* Beginning October 4, 1957
*Type of issue:* Environmental
*Countries:* The United States, the Soviet Union, ESA nations, Brazil, China, Czechoslovakia, India, Indonesia, Japan, Mexico, and Saudi Arabia

*Artificial and natural objects in Earth orbit and interplanetary space have become a serious problem for national and international space programs; the number of objects capable of interfering with a spacecraft in orbit or threatening people on Earth has grown to more than seventeen thousand.*

### Principal personages
WERNHER VON BRAUN, Director of the Marshall Space Center and a rocketry pioneer
JAMES A. ABRAHAMSON, Director, Strategic Defense Initiative Organization
HARRY J. GOETT, the first Director of Goddard Space Flight Center
JOHN W. TOWNSEND, JR., Director, Goddard Space Flight Center
DALE W. HARRIS, Tracking and Data-Relay Satellite System Project Manager
ROBERT E. SPEARING, Director of Missions Operations and Data Systems, Goddard Space Flight Center

### Summary of the Issue

Just as pollution on Earth affects the environment and human beings' quality of life, so the mounting problem of debris in Earth orbit and interplanetary space threatens to hinder space travel. Moreover, Earth itself is endangered by the overcrowding of its celestial neighborhood.

There are both artificial and natural pieces of "debris" in orbit around the planet; more than seventeen thousand have been put there by the more than six hundred launches that take place each year. These objects vie for places in space with active, manned spacecraft, such as the Soviet Soyuz TM expendable ferries to the Mir and Salyut space stations, the reusable Soviet space shuttle *Buran*, and the American space shuttles *Atlantis*, *Discovery*, and *Columbia*. Active, unmanned spacecraft in Earth orbit include meteorological, communications, military surveillance, scientific, and commercial satellites used by nineteen countries.

Although these types of vehicle are the most important in terms of value to national and international space programs, they make up only a minority of all the objects in space. Inactive man-made objects in space include spent launch vehicles and upper-stage booster rockets that were used to place active satellites in orbit, trash ejected from manned vehicles, used equipment, "dead" satellites, and pieces of rockets, spacecraft, and other hardware that exploded in orbit. Almost all the inactive objects are in orbits and attitudes that cannot be controlled by flight managers on Earth, because the objects lack usable engines for maneuverability.

In addition to the artificial objects in space, there are an incalculable number of meteors and micrometeoroids that have been captured by Earth's gravitational pull. The total number of trackable objects in space changes daily, as objects reenter the atmosphere and burn up and others are launched from Earth or move into orbit from interplanetary space.

Even though space itself is imagined to be infinite, the area around Earth into which satellites can be placed for effective use is very limited. Each nation that places objects in space must move them into certain orbital planes in order to put them to use. U.S. satellites, for example, are frequently placed in orbit above the equator to allow maximal coverage of the United States and allied nations. Soviet satellites are placed in an orbital plane that affords optimal coverage of the Soviet Union and assures the best opportunity for reentry in Soviet territory so that other nations are prevented from studying the reentered vehicles. A satellite's orbital plane can be anywhere from approximately 130 kilometers above the planet's surface, for near-Earth observation, to 35,900 kilometers above the surface, the altitude used by geosynchronous communications satellites (satellites with twenty-four hour orbital periods). Some scientific satellites, such as the Active Magnetospheric Particle Tracer Explorers launched in 1984, fly in even higher orbits through and above the planet's magnetosphere and magnetosheath.

The problems relating to space debris are twofold. First and most threatening is the danger that inactive or uncontrolled objects present to active manned and unmanned spacecraft traveling in high-density orbits. Second is the less likely, but no less important, threat posed by objects' reentering Earth's atmosphere over populated areas.

Orbiting objects are dangerous to other spacecraft because of the speed at which they must travel to remain in orbit over the planet. A spacecraft must be accelerated to a velocity of approximately 28,200 kilometers per hour to balance Earth's gravitational pull and the centrifugal force created by the craft's own motion. When two or more objects travel at the same speed in the same orbital plane, their relative velocity is the same, and the danger of collision is eliminated. This fact was demonstrated in December, 1965, when Geminis 6A and 7 rendezvoused in orbit. Since both spacecraft moved in tandem, they appeared almost stationary relative to each other.

When two objects are moving in different orbital planes at the same orbital speed, however, they can strike each other with enormous and destructive force. A window on an American space shuttle was once damaged by a small paint chip left in orbit by another spacecraft. Experts note that as the number of objects in space increases, this sort of incident will become more and more likely.

Because inactive space objects do not have rocket engines with which to maintain their orbital velocity, gravity eventually overcomes centrifugal force and the spacecraft is pulled back through the atmosphere. The heat of reentry burns up small objects, but larger vehicles—such as the United States' Skylab, which weighed more than 80,000 kilograms, may survive reentry in one or more pieces and cause significant damage should they land in populated areas. This danger is increased by the nearly fifty unmanned American and Soviet satellites that contain, cumulatively, more than 900 kilograms of atomic materials. Upon reentry, these satellites would contaminate the upper atmosphere with a potentially high level of radioactivity.

When possible, and particularly with nuclear-powered spacecraft, flight managers will use a satellite's last fuel stores and orbital maneuvering capability to place the craft in a high Earth orbit that will take dozens, if not hundreds, of years to decay. Final disposal of dangerous payloads can also be accomplished by sending them on a collision course with the Sun.

Another danger created by the increase in space debris is the potential that reentering debris will be mistaken for an intercontinental ballistic missile (ICBM) launched by one of the superpower nations and will spur a counterattack. To protect against this possibility, the major spacefaring nations have constructed highly sophisticated monitoring systems in space and on Earth.

The North American Air Defense Command (NORAD) and the U.S. Space Command, both headquartered in the Cheyenne Mountains in Colorado, are charged with monitoring and identifying all objects larger than a few inches in diameter, both active and inactive, in Earth orbit. When any nation, particularly the Soviet Union, launches a rocket, the Space Command—in conjunction with the Deep Space Network, headquartered in Pasadena, California—studies the vehicle's size, shape, and trajectory and identifies its purpose. Once the object is in orbit, its orbital plane, along with that of any boosters and other debris that achieve orbit, is plotted and regularly monitored by NORAD and the Space Command. Should the paths followed by any of the objects intersect with those of other spacecraft, particularly manned missions or other active vehicles, warnings are issued and evasive actions are initiated. Collision projections are computed routinely before each American space shuttle mission, as well.

Goddard Space Flight Center, in Greenbelt, Maryland, regularly publishes a Space Objects Table listing objects that have entered, maintained, shifted, or left orbit. Objects too small to be tracked or that do not achieve orbit, such as sounding rockets and other scientific and military launch vehicles, are not included in the Space Objects Table.

NORAD commands a worldwide network of ground-based ballistic missile early-warning systems and radar detection stations that operate in cooperation with similar systems in Canada, the United Kingdom, France, and other nations. The five sites of the American Ground-Based Electro-Optical Deep Space Surveillance (GEODSS) system also play a part in the monitoring program by providing the capacity to collect images of satellites in orbit for identification. MIDAS and SAMOS surveillance satellites, equipped with radar and infrared sensors, are linked with the monitoring systems to provide comprehensive coverage of all rocket launches and spacecraft movements anywhere on Earth and in orbit. The Soviet Union is known to have a similar, if somewhat less sophisticated, monitoring system to detect Western spacecraft and launch vehicles.

The early-warning and monitoring systems put in place by both superpowers are central to the command and control structures that each nation uses as part of its ICBM and ballistic missile defense systems. In the United States, the politically controversial Strategic Defense Initiative, popularly known as "Star Wars," employs an early-warning monitoring system and an antisatellite defense program based on highly sophisticated technology to track space debris.

Natural debris—meteors, meteoroids, and micrometeoroids—is a phenomenon that caused concern in the early days of the space age. Scientists and mission planners worried that a shower of objects would destroy any man-made spacecraft placed in orbit. Consequently, space vehicle designers developed new materials to protect the vehicles, and spacesuits were constructed to protect astronauts and cosmonauts from the impacts of small or microscopic meteors during spacewalks and lunar excursions.

Experts predict that the space debris problem will continue to grow as more nations develop the capability to place satellites in orbit and as existing space programs launch more spacecraft each year. One reason for hope is that Soviet military surveillance satellites are now designed to have longer active lives—up to two or three months, instead of a few weeks as in the past—and will, therefore, not need to be replaced as often. Increasingly, however, space age nations will have to take the disposal of space hardware more seriously.

## Knowledge Gained

The problem of space debris, if it can be said to have a positive side, has encouraged the spacefaring nations to develop highly sophisticated systems for studying Earth's celestial neighborhood. Because of these systems, scientific knowledge extends far beyond the planet's surface and is reaching outward every year. Moreover, because of the space debris problem, both the United States and the Soviet Union have learned how to protect spacecraft and humans from the dangers presented by natural objects in space.

The need to detect space debris has forced the Soviet Union and the United States to develop extremely complex technology that has, according to many experts, lessened the possibility of a sneak attack with ICBMs. Both nations have had to cooperate with their allies in building worldwide tracking networks, and that has fostered a technological collegiality which has contributed to international stability.

For proponents of the Strategic Defense Initiative and other ballistic missile defense concepts, the detection systems developed to monitor space debris are crucial to the command and control structure that makes those concepts viable. Being able to detect launches immediately and to identify space vehicles gives both superpowers the capacity to make informed decisions about nuclear defense. The same intelligence will help each nation actively defend against attack by the other.

## Context

The problem of space debris both affects and is affected by the nuclear arms race and the use of space. The amount of debris is growing, and it is very likely that space debris will be the time bomb of the early twenty-first century.

Before the launch of Sputnik 1 in 1957, there was virtually no artificial debris in Earth orbit. Even after the United States and the Soviet Union began building their space programs, there were so few launches that the possibility of an active manned or unmanned spacecraft's colliding with space debris was extremely remote, even in the most frequently used orbital planes. The situation, however, has changed; today, there are literally thousands of objects in orbit around Earth at any given time, with several entering and leaving orbit regularly.

By the late 1980's, nations launching spacecraft, both manned and unmanned, had to take into account the potential for collision with orbiting objects before launching new vehicles. It has been noted that the United States has had to delay space shuttle launches because the Soviet Salyut 7 space station was over Cape Canaveral at the planned time of launch.

Because of the number of objects in space and the intensity of the nuclear arms race, the superpowers have had to develop extremely accurate early-warning systems, consisting of sophisticated radar and imaging equipment. These systems allow the United States, the Soviet Union, and their allies to detect any launch virtually anywhere on Earth within seconds after lift-off. Both nations have "eyes in space" that give them a comprehensive view of virtually every artificial object in orbit and every strategic location on Earth. This intelligence, in turn, has driven policymakers toward active missile defense strategies that are redefining nuclear warfare. Whether the world is safer or at greater risk is a source of much debate in the United States and around the world.

## Bibliography

Adragna, Steven P. *On Guard for Victory: Military Doctrine and Ballistic Missile Defense in the U.S.S.R.* Cambridge, Mass.: Institute for Foreign Policy Analysis, 1987. An overview of Soviet military policies regarding the Soviet Union's ballistic missile defense program. Written from a conservative viewpoint, but very informative.

Broad, William J., et al. *Claiming the Heavens: The New York Times Complete Guide to the Star Wars Debate.* New York: Times Books, 1988. This book, a compilation of an exhaustive series of articles on the Strategic Defense Initiative that appeared in *The New York Times*, is an essential resource for the beginner interested in learning basic facts about strategic defense.

Bussert, Jim. "Whose Phased-Array Radars Violate the ABM Treaty?" *Defense Electronics* (April, 1987): 116. Gives a good assessment of Soviet radar systems, their history, capabilities, and functions. Compares Soviet and U.S. radar systems and provides illustrations of them. Very accurate.

Gatland, Kenneth. *The Illustrated Encyclopedia of Space Technology: A Com-*

*prehensive History of Space Exploration*. New York: Crown Publishing Co., 1981. This well-illustrated volume contains chronologies of Soviet, American, and international space programs. It includes a chapter on early-warning satellite systems. Specific examples of successful applications of space technology in this area are cited. Contains an index.

Grey, Jerry, ed. *Space Tracking and Data Systems: AAS8*. New York: American Institute of Aeronautics and Astronautics, 1981. A report on the proceedings of a symposium on space tracking and data systems held in 1981. Provides an overview of activities and plans for the 1980's and 1990's. Describes tracking programs of the European, French, German, Japanese, Indian, and Soviet space agencies.

McAleer, Neil. *The Omni Space Almanac: A Complete Guide to the Space Age*. New York: Ballantine Books, 1987. A compendium of information about the major developments of the space age, with an emphasis on the developments of the 1980's and their import.

National Aeronautics and Space Administration. *An Overview of the Kaliningrad Spaceflight Control Center*. NASA TM-87980. Washington, D.C.: Author, 1986. This article is a translation of a Soviet document. Suitable for the general reader, it explains the operations that are carried out in Kaliningrad and the missions that are controlled from that facility. Includes good photographs of the center.

Turnill, Reginald, ed. *Jane's Spaceflight Directory*. London: Jane's Publishing Co., 1987. This is a concise, fact-filled listing of every space project and known phenomenon relating to spaceflight. Well written and interesting, it is one of the best books for the beginning space enthusiast.

U.S. Congress. Office of Technology Assessment. *SDI: Technology, Survivability and Software*. Princeton, N.J.: Princeton University Press, 1988. This is an unclassified version of a classified report on progress in the Strategic Defense Initiative through 1985. Somewhat technical in nature, it gives a clear picture of the technology required for strategic defense.

*Eric Christensen*

## Cross-References

The Apollo Program, 28; Attack Satellites, 167; Cape Canaveral and the Kennedy Space Center, 229; The Deep Space Network, 280; Early-Warning Satellites, 299; The Gemini Program, 487; Johnson Space Center, 669; The Mercury Project, 940; The National Aeronautics and Space Administration, 1032; Nuclear Detection Satellites, 1080; Saturn Launch Vehicles, 1240; The Soyuz-Kosmos Program, 1396; Space Centers and Launch Sites in the Soviet Union, 1592; Space Centers and Launch Sites in the United States, 1599; Space Law: Ongoing Issues, 1612; The Spaceflight Tracking and Data Network, 1872; The Soviet Spaceflight Tracking Network, 1877; Spy Satellites, 1937.

# THE SPUTNIK PROGRAM

*Date:* October 4, 1957, to April 6, 1960
*Type of program:* Unmanned Earth-orbiting satellites
*Country:* The Soviet Union

*With the Sputnik program, the Soviets launched the world's first artificial satellite (Sputnik 1), sent the first living passenger into Earth orbit (on Sputnik 2), and delivered the first long-duration geophysical observatory into orbit (Sputnik 3).*

### Principal personages

ANATOLI A. BLAGONRAVOV, a Soviet academician and space
  spokesman
VALENTIN P. GLUSHKO, a leading designer of Soviet rocket engines
M. V. KELDISH, President of the Soviet Academy of Sciences
NIKITA KHRUSHCHEV, Premier of the Soviet Union, 1956 to 1964
SERGEI KOROLEV, Chief Designer of the Soviet space program,
  1957 to 1966
LEONID SEDOV, Chairman of the Soviet Academy of Sciences
ALEXANDER VINOGRADOV, Vice President of the Soviet Academy
  of Sciences
MIKHAIL KUZMICH YANGEL, a leading engineer in the Soviet
  rocket program who eventually succeeded Korolev as Chief
  Designer

## Summary of the Program

Sputnik 1, launched by the Soviet Union on October 4, 1957, was the world's first artificial satellite. The official Russian name for the satellite was Iskustvennyi Sputnik Zemli, which translates as "fellow traveler of Earth." The 83.6-kilogram, 58-centimeter-in-diameter spherical satellite was launched from the Tyuratam space center by the A-class booster. Its initial orbit measured 228 by 947 kilometers with an inclination of 65.1 degrees and a period of 96.2 minutes.

The only instrumentation aboard Sputnik 1 was a special thermometer which altered the frequency of the satellite's two battery-powered radio transmitters as the temperature changed. Signals from the satellite lasted 0.3 second each with a 0.3-second break between, resulting in the famous "beep-beep-beep" Sputnik signature. The cricketlike 1-watt signal was transmitted at frequencies of 20.005 and 40.002 megahertz. The radio antennae on Sputnik 1 were four metal rods, 2.4 and 2.9 meters long, which were folded in at launch and folded out in space. For temperature control, Sputnik 1 was pressurized with nitrogen gas, which was circulated by a small fan.

Since American satellite tracking was done at 108 megahertz, the low frequency of the Sputnik radio signals created a mad scramble in the U.S. to find radio receivers to track the new satellite. The signals from Sputnik 1 were strong enough to be picked up by amateur radio operators all over the world. The Soviets requested that tape recordings of the signal be forwarded to the address "Sputnik, Moscow, U.S.S.R."

The signal from Sputnik 1 faded and was lost on October 22, 1957. The Sputnik 1 booster rocket reentered the atmosphere after sixty days. Soviet Premier Nikita Khrushchev stated that the booster had fallen in Alaska. Yet Robert Jastrow of the Naval Research Laboratory calculated that it fell in Outer Mongolia. The Sputnik 1 satellite had remained in orbit for ninety-four days before burning up upon reentry.

The first living creature to orbit Earth was the dog Laika (Russian for "little barker"), launched aboard Sputnik 2 on November 3, 1957. Laika, a female black-and-white fox terrier, was housed in a hermetically sealed cylindrical cabin which contained equipment for regenerating the air, regulating the temperature, and maintaining a food supply. No recovery was planned for Laika and Sputnik 2.

Launched by an A-class booster, Sputnik 2 had an initial orbit of 225 by 1,671 kilometers, inclined 65.3 degrees, with a period of 103.7 minutes. The 508.2-kilogram instrument section of Sputnik 2 remained attached to the booster rocket, resulting in a 7.79-metric-ton mass in orbit.

Prior to being placed in the cabin of Sputnik 2, Laika was bathed in a weak alcohol solution and groomed with a fine-tooth comb. The attachment points for biosensors were painted with iodine and streptocide. Laika was housed in a suit which allowed the monitoring of pulse, respiration, blood pressure, and heart rate. Food was provided in paste form, and waste was removed via a rubber reservoir attached to the dog. Laika survived the launch and subsequent space travel very well, and many data were returned. After one week in orbit, before the satellite's consumables were exhausted, Laika was euthanized by lethal injection.

While the living passenger aboard Sputnik 2 received the world's attention, the satellite also carried instruments to measure ultraviolet, X-ray, and cosmic radiation—as well as the impacts of micrometeors. The satellite power supply, temperature measuring devices, and radio transmitters were mounted in a spherical container above the dog's passenger cabin. Signals from Sputnik 2 were transmitted with 1 watt of power at 20.004 and 40.008 megahertz.

Signals from Sputnik 2 stopped on November 10, 1957. Sputnik 2 had remained in orbit for 162 days. The satellite was last photographed in orbit six hours before reentry by a Belgian amateur astronomer. Later, the Moonwatch team at Millbrook School in New York saw Sputnik 2 trailing a luminous stream of sparks. Minutes later, the Dutch tanker Mitra reported that Sputnik 2 plunged into the sea south of the Virgin Islands as a fireball trailing smoke and flames.

On May 15, 1958, the Soviets launched a massive geophysical observatory into a 226-by-1,881-kilometer orbit with an inclination of 65.2 degrees and an orbital period of 106 minutes. Known as Sputnik 3, the satellite weighed 1,327 kilograms and represented the maximum payload capability of the A-class booster without an additional upper stage. The spacecraft was cone-shaped, with protruding antennae, and measured 3.57 meters long and 1.73 meters wide at its base. Experiment and communications gear accounted for two-thirds of the satellite's weight.

Instrumentation aboard Sputnik 3 was designed to record data on Earth's radiation belts, solar radiation particles, atmospheric density, ionospheric properties, magnetic fields, cosmic rays, and micrometeorites. A self-orienting magnetometer also determined the orientation of the satellite at any given time. Sputnik 3 contained more instruments and experiments in one satellite than all the combined American satellites planned for the International Geophysical Year (an eighteen-month period in 1957 and 1958 designated for extensive international scientific Earth study).

This third satellite was far more sophisticated than its two predecessors, using solar cells for power and an elaborate system of sixteen movable louvers for temperature control. Observations in space were continuously recorded and played back to ground stations in the Soviet Union. Sputnik 3 contained a curious mixture of advanced solid-state electronic devices and off-the-shelf vacuum-tube electronics. A computer made entirely of solid-state devices, extremely advanced for its time, controlled the function of instruments in the satellite. An improved radio apparatus was carried by Sputnik 3 to provide an exact measurement of the orbital movement of the satellite. One radio transmitted by battery power at 20.004 megahertz, while solar cells powered a second transmitter at 40.008 megahertz. In spite of several advanced features on the satellite, studies of the construction of Sputnik 3 revealed the use of simple instrumentation, uncomplicated engineering, and a lack of technical detail in the fabrication of the satellite.

The booster used by Sputnik 3 was last seen in orbit by observers at Stanford University on December 3, 1958. The booster fell to Earth after 202 days in orbit. Sputnik 3 returned data from orbit during its entire 692-day lifetime. The satellite ceased transmitting just before reentry on April 6, 1960, between revolutions 10,035 and 10,036.

The final stage of the A-class booster which launched the first three Sputniks also went into orbit with the satellites. The booster casing, as long as a railroad car, was the object seen by most observers on Earth. Only Sputnik 2 remained attached to its booster rocket.

## Knowledge Gained

The primary benefit from Sputnik 1 was not scientific information, but rather a demonstration to the world that the space age had arrived. Sputnik 1 publicly drove home the fact that space travel was more than a science-fiction writer's fantasy. Indeed, it was to become a common part of twentieth century life.

As part of the Soviet effort for the International Geophysical Year, Sputnik 1 did return a limited amount of scientific information, in spite of carrying only a thermometer into space. Electron count in the ionosphere was studied by measuring the difference in the optical and radio rising times of Sputnik 1 as it cleared the horizon. Changes in the orbital altitude of Sputnik 1, as well as its eventual orbital decay, allowed study of the density of the upper atmosphere by applying mathematics of the known atmospheric drag on a sphere. The decay of Sputnik's carrier rocket was also used in atmospheric density studies.

While Sputnik 2 made geophysical measurements of the space environment, most public attention was on the well-being of the passenger on board, the dog Laika. Considerable biological data were returned on Laika's reaction to the forces of launch, subsequent weightlessness, radiation, and temperature changes. The Soviets reported that during launch acceleration, Laika's pulse rate rose to three times the normal rate but quickly stabilized after weightlessness. After prolonged weightlessness, Laika's heart rate dropped to below the normal rate. The instruments on Sputnik 2 also detected that, with the increase in orbital altitude and geomagnetic latitude, there was a corresponding increase in the flux of high-energy charged particles around the satellite. This effect was caused by the yet-undiscovered Van Allen radiation belts, fields of charged solar particles trapped in Earth's magnetic field.

Changes in the orbital parameters of Sputnik 3 also allowed studies of high-altitude atmospheric density. All three Sputniks showed that the atmospheric density at the satellite's altitude was ten times higher than expected at the time of maximum solar sunspot activity.

Sputnik 3 contributed to the studies leading to the discovery of the outer Van Allen radiation belt. Electrons with energies of 10 kilovolts were directly observed for the first time by Sputnik 3 between altitudes of 290 and 1,168 kilometers. Electron intensity was greater by day than by night. Data from Sputnik 3 showed that as the satellite entered the Van Allen radiation belt between 55 and 65 degrees latitude, north or south, there was a sharp increase in drag on the satellite. This increased drag was the result of bombardment by electrons with 100-kilovolt or greater energies in the Van Allen radiation belts.

In December of 1958, the Soviets released preliminary findings from the instruments on Sputnik 3. These findings included the observation that ions were detected at altitudes of up to 1,000 kilometers. Ion composition up to that altitude was mostly oxygen, with 3 to 7 percent being atomic nitrogen. No molecular forms of nitrogen were detected. A surprise reading from Sputnik 3 revealed that the temperature of electrons was higher than that of ions or neutral particles in the ionosphere. Also, electron gas field density was ten to one hundred times larger than expected. Magnetic field studies from Sputnik 3 suggested that a magnetic anomaly existed in the upper layers of Earth's crust in eastern Siberia.

## Context

The launching of the first Earth satellite by the Soviet Union was as much of a shock to the American public as had been the attack on Pearl Harbor sixteen years before. In the Cold War climate which existed between the Western and Communist nations in the years after the Korean War, a mixture of arrogance and ignorance caused Americans to regard the Soviet Union as being incapable of performing such a technical feat. Most Americans believed that the Sputnik 1 satellite was developed in secrecy. Actually, as early as August 2, 1955, Leonid Sedov of the Soviet Academy of Sciences was publicly predicting that the first Russian satellite would be launched within two years. He also accurately predicted the size of the orbits for the first Soviet satellites.

During 1957, in the seven months prior to the launch of Sputnik 1, the newspaper *Pravda* and Radio Moscow made repeated announcements about the forthcoming Soviet satellite launch. The Russian media provided descriptions of the size, weight, orbital inclination, and radio frequencies of the satellite—as well as the scientific experiments to be performed. Sputnik 1 was a surprise to the Western world because the West chose to regard Soviet predictions about the satellite as empty propaganda.

The Soviet success in launching the first satellite made such an impression on world opinion that the very name "Sputnik" became synonymous with any satellite in orbit. When the weight of Sputnik 1 was announced, some people thought that a decimal point had been misplaced. After Sputnik 2 was launched with a payload thirty-five times heavier than the American Explorer 1, some observers insisted, erroneously, that the Soviet Union had developed exotic fuels or atomic power for their boosters.

The launching of Sputnik was made possible by the development of the first Soviet intercontinental ballistic missile (ICBM) during the mid-1950's. Known in the West as the SS-6 Sapwood, this rocket was designed by Sergei Korolev and used engines designed by Valentin Glushko. The Sapwood was built to carry very heavy Soviet hydrogen bombs over intercontinental distances; with its 509,830-kilogram lift-off thrust, the Sapwood had great lifting capability compared to American rockets.

Though the construction of the first Russian satellite was complete in June, 1957, launch approval from Premier Nikita Khrushchev was not granted until twenty-four days after the first successful full range test of the Sapwood, August 3, 1957. An attempt was made to ready the satellite for launch within a month to celebrate the birthday of Konstantin Tsiolkovsky, the first theorist about spaceflight by rocket. The actual preparations took six weeks, however, and the launch was rescheduled for October.

The world reaction to the launch of Sputnik 1 caught Khrushchev unaware. He did not expect the tremendous outcry from Americans about their failure to place the first satellite in orbit. Khrushchev probably expected a stunned reaction, which would have allowed him to score a propaganda triumph over the West. Indeed, the Soviet propaganda machine used Sputnik to further a familiar theme: that Soviet success in space implies superiority on Earth.

After the initial panic had passed, Khrushchev detected a vigorous American reaction to "catch up" to the Russians. This effort triggered the technological boom of the 1960's and 1970's, which led to the Americans' surpassing of the Soviets in space technology. The greatest scare to the Western world created by Sputnik was the realization that if Russian rockets could orbit a satellite, they could deliver hydrogen bombs to the United States as well.

Buoyed by the success of Sputnik 1, Khrushchev used this space achievement for political purposes by threatening a missile attack on any nation which allowed American bases on their soil near the Soviet border. While this was a bluff, because Russian rocket production at the time could barely support space launches (let alone ICBM production), Khrushchev still managed to influence world politics with his military threats based on the Sputnik launch.

While the first Soviet satellites were technically crude, the launches of the Sputniks were an indication of Soviet space superiority over the West. The Soviets continued to dominate in the area of space exploration until the American Apollo program landed men on the Moon in 1969.

## Bibliography

Bergaust, Erik. *Wernher von Braun*. Washington D. C.: National Space Institute, 1976. An extensive biography of Wernher von Braun, the father of the American space program. Chronicles the development of rocket technology from pre-World War II Germany to the space shuttle. Gives insights into the Cold War political climate between the United States and the Soviet Union during the early days of the "space race." Provides details of the world reaction to the launching of the first Sputniks.

Caidin, Martin. *Man into Space*. New York: Pyramid Books, 1961. A review of the early American Mercury manned space program and the events leading up to the launch of the first American man in space. Several chapters are devoted to early Soviet space activities and chronicle the launch of Sputnik 1 and the flight of cosmonaut Yuri Gagarin.

Oberg, James E. *Red Star in Orbit*. New York: Random House, 1981. A comprehensive review of all phases of the Soviet space program, with equal emphasis given to both the problems in achieving Soviet spaceflight and the successes of ongoing research programs. Attention is given to behind-the-scenes personalities and politics of the Soviet space program. Includes an excellent overview of the canceled Russian man-to-the-Moon program.

Smolders, Peter. *Soviets in Space*. New York: Taplinger Publishing Co., 1974. A well-illustrated book on all aspects of the Soviet space program. Suitable for the general audience, it concentrates on the successful portions of the Russian space program as they were reported by the Soviet Union. The numerous diagrams and photographs illustrate the technical details of Soviet spacecraft and their missions.

Stafford, Walter H., and Robert M. Croft. *Artificial Earth Satellites and Successful Solar Probes, 1957-1960*. NASA technical translation, NASA TT D-601. Washington, D.C.: Office of Technical Services, Commerce Department, 1961. A presentation of information on all successful Earth satellites and space probes launched between 1957 and 1960. Provides a chronological listing of launchings, experiments, and orbital measurements of each satellite or probe. This 702-page volume includes photographs of the satellites, their launchers, and other illustrations.

Stoiko, Michael. *Soviet Rocketry*. New York: Holt, Rinehart and Winston, 1970. An overview of the Soviet space program, this book traces the evolution of Russian rocket development and satellite technology, leading to planetary exploration and manned spaceflight. Emphasizes the pre-Sputnik technology which led to advances in the Soviet space program. Speculates on future Russian space activities. A nontechnical narrative suitable for the beginner.

U.S. Congress. Senate. Committee on Commerce, Science, and Transportation. *Soviet Space Programs: 1976-1980*. Part 3, *Unmanned Space Activities*. Report prepared by Congressional Research Service, the Library of Congress. 99th Cong., 1st sess., 1985. Committee Print. This booklet features comprehensive descriptions of all phases of unmanned Soviet space programs. Provides a detailed overview of the technical development of Soviet unmanned space activities, scientific investigations, and results—as well as the political effects of Soviet space activities. Suitable for general audiences, this booklet is the standard reference for data on Soviet space programs.

Zaehringer, Alfred J. *Soviet Space Technology*. New York: Harper and Brothers, 1961. A compilation of all public information about the Soviet space program until the early 1960's. While some of the speculative information presented about Russian space activities was later shown to be incorrect, this book is still important, as it gives a picture of the development of Soviet rocket science from the time of the czars up to the early Sputnik and Luna launches. Suitable for the beginner.

*Robert Reeves*

## Cross-References

# SPY SATELLITES

*Date:* Beginning February 28, 1959
*Type of satellite:* Military
*Countries:* The United States, the Soviet Union, China, India, Israel, France, and
West Germany

*Spy satellites provide countries with an accurate and fast means of gathering sophisticated information where other means of reconnaissance are less effective and more dangerous. The United States and the Soviet Union have the most highly developed spy satellite programs.*

## Summary of the Satellites

Although reconnaissance airplanes had been in use since the outbreak of World War I, the development of antiaircraft weapons made the airplane increasingly vulnerable. It was not until the late 1950's that technology was advanced enough to permit an alternative method by which intelligence could be gathered.

In 1946, the Research and Development (RAND) Corporation published a report in which the feasibility of launching a reconnaissance satellite into orbit was discussed. Additional reports were published in 1956 and 1957. These reports played a large part in the eventual development and launching of spy satellites.

In 1958, President Dwight D. Eisenhower approved a reconnaissance program which was to be operational by 1959. Under this program, the Missile Defense Alarm System (MIDAS), Discoverer, and the Satellite and Missile Observation System (SAMOS) were developed.

MIDAS, later renamed Program 239A, was first launched February 26, 1960. Relying on an infrared scanner that was sensitive to the heat emitted by a rocket, it was to provide warnings of any intercontinental ballistic missile (ICBM) attack. The advantage of MIDAS over earlier warning systems, such as the Canadian Distant Early Warning System, was that it was capable of detecting ICBMs more quickly.

Discoverer 1 was launched on February 28, 1959, and Discoverer 38 on February 27, 1962. Of the thirty-eight launches attempted, twenty-six were successful. During the time that this program was in effect, emphasis was placed on the biomedical experiments conducted, such as the one involving the orbiting of the chimpanzee Pale Face.

The first United States photoreconnaissance satellite to be launched was Discoverer 14. The first twelve Discoverer enterprises had all ended in failure; finally, the successful launch of Discoverer 13 on August 10, 1960, convinced scientists that it was feasible to include a camera in Discoverer 14.

The average perigee of the Discoverer satellites was 220.3 kilometers. The perigee is that point at which a satellite makes its closest approach to Earth and, owing to increased gravitation, the point at which the speed is greatest. Photographs are therefore usually taken before or after the perigee. The apogee, or farthest point from Earth, was 706.3 kilometers. At a later stage, the resolution of the film was, according to the director of the program, on the order of 30.48 centimeters; in other words, the satellite was able to detect objects that were 30.48 centimeters or larger. This capability enabled the detection and identification of Soviet ICBMs. The lifetime of these satellites averaged 108 days.

Until the Kennedy Administration, the Discoverer program had had two sides, the public and the official. The public name for the program was Discoverer, and the official CORONA. President John F. Kennedy phased out the Discoverer program by simply removing the public name, after which essentially the same program continued for six more launches, but now under the name CORONA. CORONA was designated Keyhole (KH) 4, but commonly called Close Look. Six KH-4's were launched between March 7 and November 11, 1962. The perigee was reduced slightly, while the apogee now was only 337.63 kilometers. The lifetime was shortened to a mere 2.8 days.

SAMOS began as Weapon System-117L (WS-117L), with the code name Pied Piper, which was changed to Sentry and finally, during the Kennedy Administration, to KH-1. KH-1, which was operated by the United States Air Force, carried a conventional camera to photograph the target. The film was then developed and scanned by a fine beam of light, after which the signal was transmitted to a station on the ground, where it was used to construct a picture. Although this system was intended to pioneer spy activities, owing to unforeseen delays it was the last of the three to be launched. SAMOS was in operation from October 11, 1960, until November 27, 1963.

A second generation of U.S. spy satellites had been initiated with the launch of KH-5 on February 28, 1963, to replace SAMOS. On July 12, 1963, KH-6 replaced CORONA. The success rate of these new satellites was considerably greater than that of their predecessors, with forty-six of fifty KH-5's succeeding between February 28, 1963, and March 30, 1967, and thirty-six of thirty-eight KH-6's between July 12, 1963, and June 4, 1967.

In the summer of 1966, a new, third generation of satellites was introduced. On July 29, KH-8 was launched, followed almost immediately on August 9 by KH-7. The third-generation satellites supplemented their ordinary cameras with infrared scanners and with a new antenna that allowed a faster transmission rate. KH-7 satellites were phased out in 1972, but KH-8, with its excellent resolution, continued functioning until the early 1980's. It eventually became known that KH-8 was 7.3 meters long and 1.73 meters in diameter, with a weight of approximately 2,990 kilograms.

The more recent fourth generation of satellites consists of KH-9, KH-10, and KH-11. Of these, KH-9 is commonly dubbed Big Bird. KH-10 was to be a manned orbiting laboratory, but the success of KH-11, coupled with the growing cost of KH-10, resulted in the cancellation of the latter.

Big Bird was first launched on June 15, 1971. It weighed about 11,340 kilograms, was 15.25 meters in length, and had a diameter of 3.048 meters. The satellite was equipped with an ordinary camera and an infrared scanner. It was also believed to contain a multispectral camera, for use in detecting camouflage, and sensitive listening devices that would allow the Pentagon to intercept radio and microwave telephone signals as well as transmissions from Soviet satellites. On board there were four returnable film canisters. The average lifetime of KH-9 was 130 days. Its mean perigee was 166 kilometers and its apogee 269 kilometers.

KH-11 was the first satellite to report events in real time (as they occurred). This feat was achieved by using a charge coupled device (CCD), first developed in the New Jersey Bell Telephone Laboratory in 1970. A CCD is activated when light strikes a silicon sheet divided into millions of small pixels. The silicon sheet converts photons into electrons; the electrons in each pixel are counted, and the information is then transmitted to the ground. The greater the number of electrons, the greater the light intensity. Since the electrons are captured for only milliseconds before they drain away, the thousands of pictures transmitted each second can be put together in much the same way as films are.

The resolution of KH-11 was inferior to that of KH-8 but exceeded that of KH-9, in the range of 6.6 to 8.8 centimeters. KH-11 transmitted its information directly to a communications satellite and from there either to Fort Meade, Florida, or to Fort Belvoir, Virginia.

The KH-11 program received a severe setback when a technical manual was lost to Soviet intelligence in 1977. According to some, the Soviets had been completely unaware that KH-11 was a reconnaissance spacecraft (because of its indirect transmission methods), imagining instead that it was a "ferret" satellite (a term used to describe a spacecraft used to probe foreign radar and to detect microwave signals). Others disagree, arguing instead that the Soviets were aware of its nature but had simply underestimated its capabilities.

To replace KH-11, researchers designed KH-12. It was projected that this fifth-generation reconnaissance satellite would carry advanced versions of the KH-11 sensors, as well as extra fuel which would allow it to move from a low to a high orbit when not in use. Operating in fours, the new satellites would provide instant coverage of any locale within twenty minutes. When the fuel supply was exhausted, the satellite was to be refueled by the space shuttle.

Apart from the KH series, the United States placed three other types of reconnaissance satellites in orbit: electronic, ocean surveillance, and early warning. In the first, electronic devices pick up radio and microwave signals, which are used to determine what type of radar waves are sent out, so that correct methods can be used to penetrate them in the event of war. Ocean surveillance satellites play the same role as those that gather information over land. These satellites are used in detecting ships and submarines. Early warning satellites depend on infrared sensors to detect missile and rocket launches. Sophisticated radar then tracks each object until it becomes clear that it does not pose a threat to the United States.

Of the more than two thousand military satellites which had been launched as of the late 1980's, more than half were reconnaissance spacecraft. These reconnaissance satellites were usually launched by modified Titan rockets. It was projected that satellites would also be sent into orbit by the space shuttle. The loss of the Titan 34D rockets in August, 1985, and April, 1986, left the United States with only one KH-11 in orbit at that time.

The United States is not alone in launching spy satellites. On April 26, 1962, the Soviets launched Kosmos 4, their first photoreconnaissance satellite. Even in the 1980's, Soviet reconnaissance spacecraft were by American standards still fairly crude. While the United States preferred to employ a small number of handmade, state-of-the-art satellites, the Soviet Union has attempted to offset its lack of superior technology with sheer numbers. In 1985, the United States launched two KH-11 satellites, while the Soviets launched thirty-four camera-carrying spacecraft. Another major difference between Soviet and American satellites is the preparation time. Soviet satellites can be launched within a matter of hours, while an American launch follows months of preparation.

Several other nations have developed reconnaissance satellites that can be used for intelligence gathering, though that purpose is generally not overtly stated. Among these countries are China, India, Israel, France, and West Germany. France's SPOT, for Satellite Probatoire de l'Observation de la Terre (Satellite Probe for Earth Observation), despite its noncommittal title, is an example of an orbiting craft that can obtain information of military importance as well as data regarding weather and Earth resources.

## Knowledge Gained

Reconnaissance satellites regularly provide information on new Soviet airplanes, ships, and submarines. Such spying often encounters difficulties. For example, in order to stop satellites from monitoring the construction of their submarines, the Soviets placed netting over them. The Americans temporarily overcame this obstacle—until they inadvertently divulged their tactics during the Strategic Arms Limitation Treaty (SALT) II negotiations—by using slant photography to view the submarines from the side.

Reconnaissance satellites continually monitor troubled areas of the world. Photoreconnaissance is believed to have been used in 1967 during the Arab-Israeli conflict, for the attempted rescue in 1979 of the American hostages in Iran, and in 1986, in advance of the Libyan bombing and at the time of the nuclear accident at Chernobyl. The Persian Gulf War of the 1980's was presumably scrutinized by American satellites. When ships and submarines are at sea, infrared pictures allow their paths to be plotted.

Technology produced for spy satellites has had important ramifications for other space programs. For example, it is believed that military photographic technology was made available to the National Aeronautics and Space Administration (NASA) for its missions to Mars and the Moon.

Advanced radar has made it possible to plot the ground of the Soviet Union and other countries accurately. Shots of the same area taken at different times are subsequently fed into a computer, which removes similar objects and highlights the discrepancies by using a process known as electro-optical subtraction. The remaining objects either are identified and noted or, if they are blurred, are enhanced by digital restoration.

The CCD technology developed in Bell Laboratories for use in spy spacecraft is now used in many other fields, including astronomy, medical imaging, and plasma physics—even in video cameras. The Galileo spacecraft and the space telescope also rely on the CCD.

The Soviet Union has made use of its spy satellites not only in observing the Sino-Soviet border during the period of hostilities but also in attempting to trace the movements of the Afghan resistance. This last effort has met with mixed results.

An obvious use of reconnaissance photographs is to study cloud formations and weather around the world. It is possible that pictures of clouds are used by meteorologists at the Central Intelligence Agency (CIA) to determine the nature of the weather, and this information is then passed on to the armed forces.

## Context

In the years preceding the launch of the first U.S. reconnaissance satellite, it was widely believed that the Soviet Union had as many as two hundred ICBMs. As a result, millions of dollars were spent by the United States in an effort both to develop ICBMs and to modernize the airplanes that carried nuclear bombs. After the launch of the Discoverer spacecraft, the number of Soviet first-generation ICBMs was found to have been only around twenty. By exposing the true number of first-generation Soviet ICBMs, Discoverer saved millions of dollars on further U.S. military expenditures. It is possible that if Premier Nikita Khrushchev had not pushed the United States into the development of ICBMs with his constant hints that the Soviets would without hesitation use them on unfriendly countries, the United States might not have manufactured its own weapons for ten years, and the launching of reconnaissance spacecraft could well have been delayed by at least five years.

The significance of spy satellites to the United States can be gauged by the amount of money that is spent on the program. In March, 1967, President Lyndon B. Johnson told a small group of people that the total space-program expenditure up to that time was between $35 and $40 billion. At that time, the space program was less than twenty years old. He concluded that if nothing else had been achieved, the photographs from the spy satellites would have made the program worthwhile.

Since the beginning of the U.S. reconnaissance program, great advances have been made in photography. This photographic technology has been used in other programs, most notably in the space telescope, the Galileo spacecraft, and the probes sent to view the Moon and Mars. The excellent resolution of KH spacecraft cameras permits the identification of missiles and hence provides a means of verifying compliance with arms control treaties. In a political climate of mutual mistrust between the United States and the Soviet Union, spy satellites are relied on heavily to ensure that treaties are honored.

During the early years of the space program, the Soviet Union made strong condemnations of the intrusion into their air space of American satellites and threatened to shoot them down. The Soviets' rhetoric softened, however, after they began regular launches of their own reconnaissance spacecraft.

By the late 1980's, the United States had had one accident involving the reentry of a space satellite, while the Soviet Union had had two major mishaps in connection with spy satellites. In 1978, an area around Great Slave Lake in the Northwest Territories was littered with highly radioactive waste. Five years later, a nuclear reactor fell into the Indian Ocean.

### Bibliography

Burrows, William E. *Deep Black: Space Espionage and National Security*. New York: Random House, 1986. This carefully researched and well-written book documents the progression of the American reconnaissance satellite from the early years until the mid-1980's, presenting its strengths and weaknesses. Contains photographs and a list of references.

Jasani, Bhupendra. *Space Weapons: The Arms Control Dilemma*. London: Taylor and Francis, 1984. Features a chapter on reconnaissance satellites and antisatellite (ASAT) weapons. A bibliography is included.

Klass, Philip J. *Secret Sentries in Space*. New York: Random House, 1971. Klass has written one of the best books available on early spy satellites. He discusses their significance and use, covering reconnaissance spacecraft from their inception up to the ill-fated Manned Orbiting Laboratory. Klass also includes a chapter on the Soviet effort. Contains photographs.

Richelson, Jeffrey. *American Espionage and the Soviet Target*. New York: William Morrow and Co., 1987. The book gives a detailed view of how American espionage functions. There is a chapter on the Keyhole program, showing how the different methods of gathering information fit together. A large bibliography, a section on acronyms, and photographs are included.

_____ . "The Keyhole Satellite Program." *Journal of Strategic Studies* 7 (June, 1984): 121-153. This essay is probably the most complete analysis of the Keyhole program. Includes, among other things, sections on sensors and resolution. All satellites from CORONA to KH-11 are mentioned, and their contributions to the reconnaissance program are listed. Bibliography included.

Taylor, John W. R., ed. *Jane's All the World's Aircraft, 1978-1979*. London: Jane's Publishing Co., 1978. Contains a small section on the Big Bird satellite, giving dimensions and orbit specification. Directly below are notes on the Titan rocket which was used to launch KH-9.

*John Newman*

## Cross-References

The Chinese Space Program, 237; Early-Warning Satellites, 299; Electronic Intelligence Satellites, 361; The French Space Program, 461; Asian Launch Vehicles, 727; Soviet Launch Vehicles, 742; U.S. Military Telecommunications Satellites, 1012; Ocean Surveillance Satellites, 1085; The U.S. Space Shuttle, 1626; U.S. Passive Relay Telecommunications Satellites, 2009; Titan Launch Vehicles, 2036; Vandenberg Air Force Base, 2069; The West German Space Program, 2262.

# STELLAR EVOLUTION

*Type of phenomenon:* Stellar

*The life cycle of a star encompasses four stages: birth (the generation of stars in interstellar clouds), the main sequence (a long phase of hydrogen-burning), the red giant stage, and the star's demise. In the process of dying, the star becomes either a white dwarf or a supernova, then fades into either a neutron star or a black hole.*

Principal personages
MARTIN SCHWARZSCHILD and
FRED HOYLE, scientists who suggested theories and models of
    stellar evolution
WILLIAM A. FOWLER,
GEOFFREY R. BURBIDGE, and
MARGARET BURBIDGE, researchers of nuclear reactions

## Summary of the Phenomenon

For most of the twentieth century one of the primary goals of astronomers has been to determine how stars are born, how they live, and how they die. The years 1957 and 1958 set the stage for rapid advances in the ability to give detailed answers to these problems.

A long article by Margaret Burbidge, Geoffrey Burbidge, William A. Fowler, and Fred Hoyle titled "Synthesis of the Elements in Stars" (1957) helped to set the stage for progress. Subsequently, Marshall H. Wrubel published "Stellar Interiors" (1958), Halton C. Arp published "The Hertzsprung-Russell Diagram" (1958), and Burbidge and Burbidge published "Stellar Evolution" (1958). These three review articles were very important to further development in stellar evolution theory. Finally, Martin Schwarzschild's book *Structure and Evolution of the Stars* (1958) appeared and strongly stimulated research for the next decade. The year 1957 gains even more importance since the Soviet Union launched Sputnik, the first Earth satellite, in that year, thus opening the space age.

It is convenient to divide the life of a star into four periods. First, there is birth. The second stage is the main sequence stage, in which hydrogen is converted to helium in the core (central region) of the star. This is the longest stage in the life of a star, and it changes little during this phase. The third stage involves evolution to the red giant stage. The star is now much larger in radius and has a "cool" surface temperature, a mere 3,000 degrees Celsius or so. (For comparison, the Sun's surface temperature is just under 6,000 degrees Celsius.) The final stage, the death of the star, can lead to some of the most dramatic phenomena in stellar evolution. These phenomena will be discussed later. In the 1960's much progress was made in understanding stages two and three in the life of a star; some advances were made in understanding stage four, but little progress was made regarding stage one. These latter two stages were explored in more depth in the 1970's and 1980's.

Scientists generally express the mass, radius, and energy output of stars in relation to the Sun's measurements; for example, a given star might have a radius of ten solar radii or be ten times the size of the Sun. For reference, the mass of the Sun is $1.99 \times 10^{30}$ kilograms (330,000 times the mass of Earth), its radius is 696,000 kilometers (109 times larger than Earth's), and it has an energy output of $39 \times 10^{24}$ watts.

To study stage one, the formation of stars, infrared detectors are required. Infrared radiation is beyond red light, which is the longest wavelength the eye can see. Since stars are born in large gas and dust clouds (tens of light years in diameter) in interstellar space, and since these clouds are cold to warm ($-260$ to 500 degrees Celsius), infrared radiation is prominent (very hot objects emit ultraviolet or even X rays if temperatures reach millions of degrees, and cool to warm objects emit infrared). The first Infrared Astronomical Satellite (IRAS) was launched in 1985 and was very successful. Some infrared radiation can be observed from Earth as well. The combined results of ground-based and space-based research are improving researchers' understanding of star birth. In some parts of the Milky Way and other galaxies, stars are still being born. The interstellar clouds shrink and form "globs" of denser material, which shrink further, until eventually dozens to many thousands of stars are formed. As each of these protostars ("globs") contracts, it heats until, at about 10 million degrees Celsius, hydrogen burns in the center, and a main sequence star comes into being.

The main sequence is that stage of a star's existence when hydrogen-burning provides all the star's energy requirements. Hydrogen-burning is the fusing together of four protons (the proton is the nucleus or center of the hydrogen atom; an electron orbits the proton and the pair form the hydrogen atom) to make a helium nucleus. The helium nucleus consists of two protons and two neutrons packed together. Two of the four protons forming helium change into neutrons. The proton has about two thousand times as much mass as the electron. The electron has a negative electric charge and the proton has an equal but positive charge. The neutron has no charge and is nearly of the same mass as the proton. In hydrogen-burning, energy is released to heat the star and to provide the radiation it emits into space.

Astronomers have found that the main sequence phase takes up 80 to 90 percent of a star's life. More massive stars evolve through all of their evolutionary stages much more quickly than low-mass stars. For example, a star of 30 solar masses will be a main sequence star for 6 million years, but the Sun (one solar mass) will be a main sequence star for 10 billion years. The Sun has been a main sequence star for about 4.5 billion years already but still has more than 5 billion years to go.

During stage two, stars convert about 10 percent of their mass from hydrogen to helium (the core). Once this is accomplished, the star leaves the main sequence and begins stage three. The outer layers of the star expand greatly while the core heats. The star becomes a red giant, with a radius 10 to 100 times larger than that of the Sun, emitting energy at a rate of hundreds of times that of the Sun. Eventually, helium begins to burn in a small central core. Part of the helium core is converted to carbon. Soon (thousands to many millions of years later), the star runs out of burnable helium. It swells still further and becomes a red supergiant. Supergiants are hundreds or thousands of times larger than the Sun and up to 100,000 times brighter. Much mass loss (up to 80 percent) may occur in the giant and supergiant phases.

This mass loss is best detected at wavelengths shorter than violet rays, which are the shortest wavelengths which the human eye can detect. The shorter wavelengths are ultraviolet and X-ray radiation. Since Earth's atmosphere is opaque to ultraviolet and X-ray radiation, scientists use satellites to study these wavelengths. Quite a few such satellites have been placed in Earth orbit and have made remarkable discoveries.

The star now approaches its demise (stage four). The nature of its death depends on its initial (main sequence) mass. If the initial mass was less than about eight solar masses, the star loses all of its unburned "envelope" (main sequence stars are about 75 percent hydrogen, 22 percent helium, and 3 percent all other chemical elements), and the helium-carbon core becomes a white dwarf, cools, and dies. A white dwarf has about the same radius as Earth, and its matter is so compressed that a thimbleful would weigh 100,000 kilograms.

A star with more than eight solar masses will go through a series of nuclear fusion reactions. The central part of the star is eventually converted to iron. At this point, catastrophe occurs. The iron will not fuse and simply heats until, within seconds, it is disintegrated by its own heat. This disintegration requires energy, and the core cools. This cooling causes the core to collapse, compressing the matter immensely. This collapse, in turn, releases more energy in a few seconds than the star had generated in its entire lifetime. This burst of energy is called a supernova.

The star becomes as bright as a billion Suns for a few days and then gradually fades away as it cools and dies. All unburned material (one to thirty or more solar masses) is ejected into space at 5,000 to 30,000 kilometers per second. Dozens of these remnants, from explosions as long ago as 50,000 years and as recently as 1987, have been observed.

If the mass of the collapsed core is less than approximately three solar masses, it becomes a neutron star. A neutron star has a radius of only 15 kilometers and a density of 40 billion kilograms per teaspoon. Neutron stars have been detected with radio telescopes and X-ray satellites. If the collapsed core's mass is greater than three solar masses, however, the core becomes a black hole. The gravitational field of a black hole is so great that nothing, not even light, can escape from it. Consequently, a black hole cannot be "seen." Astronomers can only attempt to detect its effects, primarily through its gravity, on nearby objects. Several black hole candidates have been discovered, but certainty has not been established.

## Knowledge Gained

Stars are controlled hydrogen bombs throughout most of their lifetimes. Stars are also directly responsible for man's existence. As stars evolve, they convert hydrogen to helium, carbon, oxygen, and other elements, including iron. As massive stars undergo supernova explosion, the prodigious energy available creates all elements beyond iron and ejects this material back to its place or origin, the interstellar medium. Thus, this medium is enriched in atoms heavier than hydrogen.

If the big bang theory of the universe (according to which the universe originated in an unimaginable explosion from a minuscule volume and has been expanding ever since) is correct, only hydrogen and helium were present when the first stars formed, many billions of years before the Sun. Many of these stars created heavier atoms in their cores and became supernovae, creating even heavier elements, which were ejected into the interstellar medium. Consequently, the next generation of stars contained atoms heavier than helium. If this theory of nucleosynthesis (creation of heavier elements from lighter elements by nuclear fusion in stars) is correct, then every atom in human bodies other than hydrogen and helium (that is, all carbon, nitrogen, oxygen, and the like) was created during the evolution and supernova death of stars billions of years ago. Evolving stars are still enriching the interstellar gas with heavier elements.

The theory of stellar evolution has explained the existence of white dwarfs, which were discovered about 1880 and which defied explanation for many decades. It also predicted the existence of neutron stars, a prediction spectacularly verified when pulsars (rapidly rotating, highly magnetic neutron stars) were discovered in 1967.

The theory also predicts the existence of black holes. Strong evidence for their existence is found in several massive X-ray binaries such as Cygnus X-1. Massive X-ray binaries are pairs of stars orbiting each other, emitting powerful X rays and containing a neutron star or black hole.

In the far distant future, 5 billion years from now, the Sun will run out of hydrogen in its core. Its radius will increase over 100 million years, swallowing the planet Mercury and possibly Venus. At that point it will be a red giant, and temperatures on Earth will reach 1,200 degrees Celsius. In addition, a strong outward-flowing wind will form, carrying the Sun's unburned hydrogen envelope back into space. The Sun will then become a white dwarf, with perhaps one-half or two-thirds of its former solar mass. Initially, this white dwarf Sun will have a surface temperature of about 100,000 degrees Celsius. It will then cool, rapidly at first, then ever more slowly, a dying ember.

## Context

By the mid-1950's, astronomers had a qualitative understanding of the main sequence phase of the evolution of stars and an incomplete, sketchy comprehension of the rest of a star's life. This progress had been made possible by advances in nuclear physics in the 1930's and 1940's and by the hard work of both theoretical and observational astronomers. The year 1957 was important in two respects in this regard. Articles that laid the observational and theoretical foundations for further development of stellar evolution theory appeared in that year, and the first artificial satellite was put into Earth orbit by the Soviet Union, opening the age of space exploration and scientific development. Additional impetus was given to this work by the rapid advances made in computer technology. Without the high-speed computational abilities of computers, little progress in stellar evolution theory would have been possible.

In the decades since 1957, both ground-based research and scientific satellite studies have enabled researchers to gain a good general understanding of stellar evolution. Infrared studies are illuminating the cradles of star birth. For the first time, astronomers can begin to study embryonic stars and, even more important, embryonic planetary systems. The possibility of the existence of other solar systems—and of extraterrestrial life—will continue to be explored. In addition, an understanding of planet formation will teach scientists more about Earth's structure and point the way to more efficient use of its resources.

Satellite studies in the ultraviolet and X-ray regions of the electromagnetic spectrum have revealed that stars lose much more mass during their evolution than had been previously believed, and stellar evolution calculations are being revised to account for this discovery. Since white dwarfs are formed hot (about 100,000 degrees Celsius or more) and neutron stars are even hotter (millions of degrees Celsius), ultraviolet and X-ray satellites are the best means to study these objects.

Satellites are of extreme importance to astronomy, because Earth's atmosphere is opaque to gamma-ray, X-ray, ultraviolet, and most infrared radiation. Scientific instruments must be elevated above the atmosphere if hot objects, which emit gamma rays, X rays, and ultraviolet rays, and cool objects, which emit in the infrared, are to be studied. The wavelength regions provide critical information concerning the cool birth and the hot death of stars. Many fascinating objects such as gamma-ray bursts, X-ray binaries, X-ray novae, and stellar coronas (hot regions above the surface of many stars) were first discovered by means of scientific satellites.

To understand the world, the solar system, the Galaxy, and the universe is the goal of science. Such knowledge can only help man to understand himself and his place in the cosmos.

## Bibliography

Asimov, Isaac. *The Exploding Suns: The Secrets of the Supernovas*. New York: E. P. Dutton, 1985. An excellent book describing the death of massive stars. Asimov is the well-known author of many science-fiction stories and novels, popular science books, and publications in many other fields. The book discusses the evolution of stars and explains how some of them reach their ultimate fate— the cataclysm of a supernova explosion. A highly accessible treatment.

Chaisson, Eric. *Universe: An Evolutionary Approach to Astronomy*. Englewood Cliffs, N.J.: Prentice-Hall, 1988. An introductory textbook on astronomy. Many black-and-white figures, a few beautiful color plates, and numerous tables of pertinent data help to make this a fine book. Each chapter lists key terms, and a glossary is included for easy reference. Chapters 10-12 and 19-22 are most appropriate to the topic of stellar evolution.

Cohen, Martin. *In Darkness Born: The Study of Star Formation*. New York: Cambridge University Press, 1988. The author, a recognized authority in the field of star formation, has written the first general survey of the subject. The book discusses how stars form from interstellar material, and how astronomers can use both ground-based and space-based astronomical instruments to observe this intriguing process. This book is very well written and is appropriate for the person with little scientific background. Includes many black-and-white plates.

Cooke, Donald A. *The Life and Death of Stars*. New York: Crown Publishers, 1985. A general background to the subject is given, and a discussion of the overall picture of the Galaxy is included. There follow chapters on how stars form, how they shine and change as they burn up their fuel supply, and, finally, how they die as all energy sources are depleted. Written for the general reader.

Genet, Russell M., Donald S. Hayes, Douglas S. Hall, and David R. Genet. *Supernova 1987a: Astronomy's Explosive Enigma*. Mesa, Ariz.: Fairborn Press, 1988. The full story of the brightest supernova in almost four hundred years: supernova 1987a, discovered in March, 1987. This book discusses the evolution of this massive star from birth to its explosive demise in a supernova explosion. The book, which has more than one hundred illustrations, introduces the reader to the discoverers of supernova 1987a and explains how astronomers used both ground- and space-based observatories to study this event.

Greenstein, George. *Frozen Star*. New York: Charles Scribner's Sons, 1983. This book is devoted to neutron stars, pulsars, and black holes. The book is clearly written and contains many diagrams. The structure of a neutron star is clearly illustrated, and the discussion of black holes is very helpful. To illustrate these bizarre objects, the author takes his readers on an imaginary trip to a pulsar and discusses what would happen if the Sun became a black hole.

Henbest, Nigel, and Michael Marten. *The New Astronomy*. New York: Cambridge University Press, 1983. This book is a well-illustrated survey of then current understanding of the stars and universe. It boasts 170 color and eighty black-and-white illustrations. Emphasizes the knowledge that has been gained by scientists' use of satellites to observe the X-ray, ultraviolet, and infrared regions of the electromagnetic spectrum (of which the light humans detect with their eyes is just a small fraction).

Kaufmann, William J. *Universe*. 2d ed. New York: W. H. Freeman and Co., 1987. A beautifully illustrated textbook. Kaufmann, author of many other articles and books, has produced an excellent, well-written introduction to astronomy. The book has a complete glossary and is well indexed. Chapters 1 and 18-24 are directly related to the topic of stellar evolution.

Kippenhahn, Rudolf. *One Hundred Billion Suns: The Birth, Life, and Death of the Stars*. New York: Basic Books, 1985. Kippenhahn, who helped to pioneer the computer calculation of stellar evolution in the 1960's, has written an authoritative review of the subject of the life cycle of stars. The book is written in a delightful manner and is one of the best treatments of the subject. Well illustrated.

*George E. McCluskey, Jr.*

## Cross-References

The Big Bang Theory, 182; Black Holes, 211; Exobiology, 387; The Search for Extraterrestrial Intelligence, 447; The High-Energy Astronomical Observatories, 589; The Infrared Astronomical Satellite, 602; The International Ultraviolet Explorer, 625; The Orbiting Astronomical Observatories, 1092; Pulsars, 1209; The Solar Corona, 1323; The Solar Wind, 1382; Supernovae and Neutron Stars, 1970; Air and Space Telescopes, 2014; Ground-Based Telescopes, 2022; White Dwarf Stars, 2268.

# THE STRATEGIC DEFENSE INITIATIVE

*Date:* Beginning March 23, 1983
*Type of program:* Unmanned military defense
*Countries:* The United States and the Soviet Union

*The United States' Strategic Defense Initiative and similar efforts in the Soviet Union are multiphased programs designed to counter nuclear missile attacks. Both nations' projects involve the use of high-technology, space- and Earth-based, directed energy weapons to defeat intercontinental ballistic missiles.*

### Principal personages

RONALD REAGAN, fortieth President of the United States
EDWARD TELLER, Associate Director Emeritus, Lawrence
    Livermore National Laboratory
WILLIAM R. GRAHAM, JR., Director, Office of Science and
    Technology Policy
JAMES A. ABRAHAMSON, Director, Strategic Defense Initiative
    Organization
GEORGE A. KEYWORTH, former Science Adviser to the president

## Summary of the Program

The Strategic Defense Initiative (SDI), as first defined by U.S. president Ronald Reagan in 1983, is a research program designed to create an effective defense against nuclear missile attacks. SDI, or "Star Wars," as it is popularly termed, has been the subject of immense controversy in scientific and political circles and is expected to be a pivotal factor in both military planning and superpower relations into the twenty-first century.

On March 23, 1983, President Reagan used a nationally televised speech to announce a major research effort to discover ways to protect the United States from a strategic nuclear missile attack by the Soviet Union. The President stated his hope that technology developed through SDI could be used to make missile-delivered nuclear weapons obsolete in the twenty-first century. Achieving this end would require several advancements in existing technology and breakthroughs in hardware applications.

At the time of the president's announcement, both the superpowers were depending on the principle of mutual assured destruction (MAD) to prevent nuclear war. MAD is predicated on the belief that, since both the United States and Soviet Union possess enough nuclear weapons (six thousand for the United States, twelve thousand for the Soviet Union), to destroy each other several times over, and since neither nation could reasonably expect to survive a nuclear exchange, neither will be willing to risk its own destruction to defeat the other.

Strategic defense is based on the premise that high technology will allow the building of a defensive system to bear the brunt of a first-strike nuclear attack so that the defender nation would then be able to use its own weapons to counter-attack. The threat of such a counterattack would, according to the theory, be an adequate deterrent to a first strike.

For more than thirty years prior to the strategic defense program, both the United States and the Soviet Union had worked to find ways to defend against a nuclear missile attack. These efforts, known as BMD, for ballistic missile defense, provided impetus for the Anti-Ballistic Missile Treaty signed by President Richard Nixon and Soviet premier Leonid Brezhnev in 1972. The ABM Treaty allowed the two nations to build two anti-ballistic missile sites of no more than one hundred missiles each and to continue research into BMD. That research led to some of the major developments in SDI.

The Strategic Defense Initiative program will be deployed in three stages beginning in the 1990's and continuing through about 2115. It will consist largely of two types of technology: kinetic energy devices and lasers. When fully deployed, SDI will use these weapons systems and a complex array of sensors, relay satellites, and battle management computers to construct ground-based and Earth-orbiting "screens" to "filter out" intercontinental ballistic missiles (ICBMs) and their multiple nuclear warheads, known as reentry vehicles, before detonation.

Kinetic energy devices are nonexplosive projectiles that, when launched at an object, rely on their momentum, or kinetic energy, to destroy the target. Two types of kinetic energy weapon, space-based interceptors (SBIs) and the ground-launched exoatmospheric reentry interceptor system (ERIS), will be used in SDI. SBIs are weapons platforms to be placed in Earth orbit that will fire kinetic energy projectiles at just-launched ICBMs, destroying the missiles before the release of their multiple reentry vehicle payloads. ERIS interceptors launched from the ground will destroy reentry vehicles outside Earth's atmosphere after they have been released from an ICBM. High endoatmospheric interceptors will be employed at later stages to destroy warheads after they enter atmosphere but before they reach their targets and can inflict significant damage.

These kinetic energy weapons would be used in SDI's first phase of deployment, with refinements being put in place as development of the technology permitted. In 1984, the United States successfully conducted the first test of a ground-launched interceptor designed to destroy an ICBM, and 1995 was projected as a target date for the first phases of a ground-based kinetic energy defense system.

The second weapon to be used in SDI is the ground-based or space-based laser. Any or all of several types of laser, possibly including free electron lasers, nuclear powered X-ray lasers, chemical lasers, and laser guided particle beams, will be fired from bases on Earth at reflecting mirrors in Earth orbit that would reflect and enhance the beams, directing them toward incoming ICBMs or reentry vehicles. An experiment in which a harmless laser beam was aimed at the space shuttle *Discovery* was successfully completed in 1985.

Research is also being conducted into the possible use of particle beams as defensive weapons against nuclear missiles. Although this plan has numerous technological drawbacks, some scientists believe it will be possible to use beams of highly charged hydrogen protons to destroy an ICBM in flight.

It is also thought that orbiting platforms equipped with particle beam or laser weaponry for an advanced BMD program will be feasible at some point, perhaps as late as 2115.

In addition to the weapons systems, SDI will require a highly sophisticated command and communications system that will use massive satellites equipped with Earth-orbiting heat and radar sensors, ground-based sensors, aircraft, and specially launched sensor rockets. This complex network will detect, analyze, and relay information on incoming ICBMs to battle command centers and then relay and execute the commands of military and civilian leaders. So that those leaders can effectively recognize and react to a potential nuclear threat, command of the weapons systems and the sensor network will rely on a blend of computerized analysis and human judgment.

As originally conceived by the Reagan Administration, SDI serves at least two major military and diplomatic purposes. First, SDI is a defensive system designed to make the cost of a nuclear attack by either nation against the other prohibitive and its success uncertain, and second, from the United States' viewpoint, SDI gives the Soviet Union an added impetus to negotiate further arms control and disarmament agreements on every class of nuclear weapon. How successful SDI will be in bringing about either objective has been a matter of great controversy in the American and international political arenas since the program's inception.

Critics of SDI, who call the program "Star Wars," believe the concept to be too heavily dependent on uncertain technology to be fully or even reasonably effective. Since a full-scale missile attack might involve hundreds of missiles, thousands of reentry vehicles, and tens of thousands of decoy reentry vehicles launched simultaneously at hundreds of targets, there is considerable doubt whether a tremendously complex system such as SDI would work in the first minutes of an attack.

Some experts are concerned that, if the technology is deployed and is even partially successful, it may either provoke the Soviet Union into launching a preemptive nuclear strike or create the dangerous and false assumption among American leaders that a nuclear war could be survived and even won. Many European nations have also raised the question of how SDI will affect the balance of power between the United States and the Soviet Union, since the Soviet Union has a large numerical superiority in conventional military forces.

Opponents of the program also point out that space-based weapons or weapons-support systems are highly vulnerable to attack by a variety of different methods. This weakness, the critics argue, could render SDI useless and leave the United States more vulnerable to nuclear attack. Satellites in space can be destroyed by the detonation of a nuclear bomb above the atmosphere. They can be attacked by specially designed hunter-killer satellites that can be placed in orbit near the original satellites and used at the first sign of hostilities. Moreover, the same laser or particle beam technology that can be used to destroy an ICBM would be equally effective against satellites in Earth orbit.

The vulnerability of space-based weaponry has led SDI scientists and designers to include satellite defense and antisatellite weapons systems in the SDI blueprints. These systems, in turn, have made the whole SDI system more complex and, its critics suggest, more unreliable, because of the greater potential for technical problems and hardware failure.

Proponents of SDI, however, believe that SDI technology will enable the United States and the Soviet Union to control massive defense spending and that it will reduce the threat of nuclear war. They believe SDI to be more rational and moral than mutual assured destruction as a nuclear strategy for the twenty-first century.

## Knowledge Gained

The knowledge gained from SDI falls into two categories: scientific and political. As a scientific endeavor, SDI has significantly increased the funding and resources available to researchers working on directed energy (lasers and neutral and charged particle beams) and on satellite defense, communications, and support systems. Ways have been found to create free electron lasers and nuclear powered X-ray lasers, to guide a charged particle beam with a laser, and to accelerate neutrons into neutral particle beams, all of which have potential commercial and civilian applications.

Advances in kinetic weaponry can, regardless of how fully SDI is deployed in the future, help reduce the threat of nuclear war by making the effect and success of a first strike more uncertain. That, in itself, could make SDI an important part of the defensive structure of both the United States and the Soviet Union.

"Star Wars" has also changed the scope of political debate about the arms race. The Reagan Administration has used it as a bargaining chip; some observers claim that it helped bring about the 1988 Intermediate Nuclear Forces (INF) treaty, an agreement between the two superpowers to destroy a whole class of intermediate range nuclear missiles. SDI is also credited with helping to advance talks on the reduction of other classes of nuclear missiles.

SDI, by virtue of its high visibility and President Reagan's open and vocal support of the program, has also helped to increase public awareness of the arms race. Americans have gained a greater understanding of how, and how well, the nation is prepared to defend itself in the event of a nuclear war. This understanding, and the sentiment it has generated, may help to prevent a nuclear attack as effectively as the technology behind the SDI program.

## Context

The Strategic Defense Initiative was spurred by the desire to reduce the threat of nuclear war. When President Reagan proposed SDI, ballistic missile defense technology, particularly surface-to-air anti-ballistic missiles, had been under development for many years. BMD was the impetus for the ABM Treaty of 1972 between the Soviet Union and the United States. This treaty, in turn, created the avenue for

BMD research that led to President Reagan's announcement of the SDI program.

In a broader sense, SDI is an attempt to move the United States away from its reliance on mutual assured destruction—a primarily offensive strategy—and toward the defensive posture of SDI, which will ultimately eliminate the need for a first-strike capability.

From a political perspective, SDI was initiated in the context of a massive increase in defense spending on the part of both the United States and the Soviet Union. Some experts believe that SDI, as an effort to diminish the effect of nuclear weapons, will allow the two nations with the most nuclear weapons in their arsenals to reduce their stockpiles and divert the funds for those weapons systems to other productive uses.

Since SDI research is ongoing, it is likely to continue to affect American and Soviet strategic planning for several decades. The technology will grow more sophisticated, and it may dominate the arms race before the beginning of the twenty-first century.

SDI development is taking place alongside the development of more sophisticated nuclear and conventional weapons systems which, in turn, affect the course of research on ways to counter new weapons developments. SDI, then, is part of an upward technological spiral that will, its proponents say, lead to a lessening of military tension and a more stable global political structure.

## Bibliography

Adragna, Steven P. *On Guard for Victory: Military Doctrine and Ballistic Missile Defense in the U.S.S.R. Foreign Policy Report*. Cambridge, Mass.: Institute for Foreign Policy Analysis, 1987. An overview of Soviet military policies relating to the Soviet ballistic missile defense program. Written from a conservative viewpoint, but very informative.

Broad, William J., et al. *Claiming the Heavens: The New York Times Complete Guide to the Star Wars Debate*. New York: Times Books, 1988. A compilation of an exhaustive series of articles on SDI that appeared in *The New York Times*, this resource is essential reading for the beginner interested in learning the basics before going on to more complex aspects of the SDI controversy.

Codevilla, Angelo. *While Others Build: The Common Sense Approach to the Strategic Defense Initiative*. New York: Free Press, 1987. Codevilla, a noted expert on SDI, provides a strong, easy-to-read overview of the program and a critical look at its advantages and disadvantages from both a political and a technological viewpoint. The subject is presented mostly from a proponent's perspective, but the text is filled with interesting information.

Davis, Jacquelyn K., and Robert L. Pfaltzgraff. *Strategic Defense and Extended Deterrence: A New Transatlantic Debate*. Cambridge, Mass.: Institute for Foreign Policy Analysis, 1986. This booklet examines the debate among the United States' allies over the benefits and drawbacks of SDI from an international political perspective. It also examines the Soviet strategic defense program and the European defense structure. A scholarly work, yet understandable to the nonspecialist.

Godson, Dean. *SDI: Has America Told Her Story to the World?* Cambridge, Mass.: Institute for Foreign Policy Analysis, 1987. This brief treatise looks at how the United States has presented the arguments for SDI to the world community, particularly its European allies. Somewhat scholarly and technical, the work nevertheless provides a good geopolitical overview of a complex question.

Mikheyev, Dmitry. *The Soviet Perspective on the Strategic Defense Initiative: Foreign Policy Report.* Elmsford, N.Y.: Pergamon Press, 1987. This book, written by a former Soviet physicist, looks at the Soviet government's views on the SDI program. Provides interesting insights into Soviet military and political policies regarding strategic defense. Written from a conservative perspective.

U.S. Congress. Office of Technology Assessment. *SDI: Technology, Survivability and Software.* Princeton, N.J.: Princeton University Press, 1988. This is an unclassified version of a classified report prepared by the Office of Technology Assessment on SDI progress and feasibility as of 1985. Although somewhat technical in nature, the report gives a clear picture of "Star Wars" technology and reviews some of the arguments surrounding SDI.

*Eric Christensen*

## Cross-References

Attack Satellites, 167; U.S. and Soviet Cooperation in Space, 259; Early-Warning Satellites, 299; Electronic Intelligence Satellites, 361; U.S. Military Telecommunications Satellites, 1012; Nuclear Detection Satellites, 1080; The Outer Space Treaty, 1111; Space Law: Ongoing Issues, 1612; Spy Satellites, 1937.

# THE STRATOSPHERIC AEROSOL AND GAS EXPERIMENT

*Date:* Beginning February 18, 1979
*Type of satellite:* Scientific
*Country:* The United States

*The Stratospheric Aerosol and Gas Experiment (SAGE) instrument was designed to measure the concentration of some of the constituents of Earth's atmosphere. The SAGE satellite was one of the first remote-sensing satellites to provide estimates of the global distribution of stratospheric aerosols, ozone, nitrogen dioxide, and water vapor.*

*Principal personages*
M. PATRICK MCCORMICK, the principal investigator and
coordinator for SAGE 1 and SAGE 2, Langley Research Center
WILLIAM P. CHU, a researcher, Langley Research Center
THEODORE J. PEPIN, a researcher, University of Wyoming
DEREK M. CUNNOLD, a researcher, Georgia Institute of
Technology
ROYCE LANE, a researcher, University of Wyoming
PHILLIP B. RUSSELL, a researcher, Ames Research Center
GERALD W. GRAMS, a researcher, Georgia Institute of Technology

## Summary of the Satellites

The SAGE class of instruments was developed by the National Aeronautics and Space Administration (NASA) primarily through the efforts of M. Patrick McCormick of the Atmospheric Sciences Division at NASA's Langley Research Center in Virginia. The prototype to the SAGE experiments was conceived and built by Theodore J. Pepin of the University of Wyoming. This prototype was a small, manually operated instrument flown on the Apollo-Soyuz Test Project in 1975; it consisted of a handheld package containing a telescope, a Sun sensor, and an external electronics package. Its purpose was to measure the extinction of sunlight caused by aerosols in the atmosphere. The instrument was named the Stratospheric Aerosol Measurement (SAM) instrument and was operated by an astronaut as he pointed it directly at the Sun during a sunrise or sunset aboard a spacecraft.

It was shown that aerosols, which are small solid or liquid particles on the order of a micrometer in diameter, could be accurately measured in the atmosphere. After the successful results of SAM were revealed, SAM 2 was designed by NASA engineers and built at the University of Wyoming. SAM 2 was a much more sophisticated instrument than SAM and was built to fly aboard the unmanned Nimbus 7 spacecraft. SAM 2 was to measure atmospheric aerosols in the polar regions of Earth between the latitudes of 64 to 84 degrees south and 64 to 84 degrees north. SAM 2 began operation in November, 1978, and continues to operate long beyond its initial design lifetime.

The SAGE 1 and 2 instruments were even more sophisticated than the SAM 2 instrument. Their primary objectives were to determine the spatial distribution of not only stratospheric aerosols but also ozone, nitrogen dioxide, and water vapor on a global scale. The principle of operation of the SAGE instruments is identical to that of the SAM instruments. On a spacecraft that orbits approximately 600 kilometers above Earth, SAGE instruments receive sunlight that is focused onto a set of detectors. Depending on the point in the orbit, this sunlight enters the instrument unobstructed (full-Sun condition), enters the instrument partially obstructed by Earth's atmosphere (occultation), or does not enter the instruments because of Earth's being in the path between the instrument and the Sun (total occultation). Scientists call the sequence just described an "event."

The SAGE instrument makes measurements of solar irradiance during the full-Sun condition in order to obtain a reference value for the intensity of the Sun as it is viewed unobstructed by the atmosphere. The actual atmospheric measurement occurs during the time that the Sun's disk appears through the atmosphere. During this portion of the event, the instrument focuses on a very small area of the solar surface with a telescope. Simultaneously, a mirror sweeps the image of the Sun across the field of the telescope. The actual spatial extent of the solar disk as viewed from the instruments varies in size depending upon how high the Sun appears above Earth. As the Sun is viewed in the higher layers of the atmosphere, the vertical extent of the Sun is approximately 32 kilometers. As the solar disk appears to move lower into Earth's atmosphere, the disk becomes flattened because of the refraction by Earth's atmosphere. The entire event lasts approximately one minute.

Events are classified as being either sunrises or sunsets. Sunrise events are observed as the instrument orbits out from behind Earth and into the full sunlight, while sunset events are observed as the instrument orbits out of the full-Sun condition and into Earth's shadow. The small region on the surface of the Sun observed by the SAGE instrument during an event corresponds to a region in Earth's atmosphere that is approximately 1 kilometer high, 1 kilometer wide, and 200 kilometers long. This 200-kilometer-long volume of atmosphere lies along the line of sight joining the instrument and the Sun and, at any time during an event, is within 1 kilometer of a fixed altitude above the surface of Earth.

At the heart of the SAGE instruments is a grating, a flat plate on which are ruled closely spaced lines. This grating splits the incident sunlight into a rainbow of colors. Each color corresponds to a particular wavelength of light emitted from the Sun. The SAGE instruments measure the intensity of several of these wavelengths of light. As the sunlight is occulted by the atmosphere, each individual wavelength is diminished in intensity more or less independently of the other wavelengths being measured. The measure of intensity that a particular wavelength loses because of the intervening atmosphere is directly related to the type of aerosol or gas present in the atmosphere.

The presence of aerosols and gases in the atmosphere causes incident light to scatter or be absorbed. When a light ray is scattered, it is simply redirected from its incident direction into another direction. When light is absorbed, it is taken up by the molecules in a gas or aerosol and converted into energy. The conversion process may change the energy into molecular rotation or vibration, kinetic energy, or light at wavelengths different from the wavelength of the incident light. The processes of scattering and absorption are also called extinction. Very little absorption occurs for aerosols at the wavelengths where SAGE operates.

Basic principles of optics, atmospheric physics, and orbital mechanics are used to convert the relative instrumental quantities measured by the SAGE instruments into the absolute quantities of extinction and gas concentration. The information provided for experimenters by the SAGE 1 and SAGE 2 instruments comes in the form of vertical profiles of aerosol extinction and gas concentration. Each profile contains approximately sixty measurements, one measurement per kilometer, over an altitude range from cloud top to the top of the stratosphere. During any given day, fifteen sunrise and fifteen sunset measurements are made at equally spaced intervals around the world. Because the instruments take measurements at a local sunrise or sunset, the set of measurement profiles represent atmospheric conditions at the terminator, or the transition region on Earth that separates night and day.

On February 18, 1979, SAGE 1 was launched by NASA on the Applications Explorer Mission 2 (AEM 2). It operated successfully until November 18, 1981, when a spacecraft power problem caused the instrument to stop functioning. The mission provided more than thirteen thousand events from which atmospheric profiles of aerosol extinction, ozone, and nitrogen dioxide were retrieved. The latitudes over which measurements were made ranged from about 72 degrees south to 72 degrees north.

The SAGE 2 instrument was launched on October 5, 1984, on the Earth Radiation Budget Satellite (ERBS). Along with SAGE 2, the ERBS platform contains the Earth Radiation Budget Experiment. The ERBS is a key part of NASA's climate program. The SAGE 2 instrument makes atmospheric measurements from approximately 80 degrees south to 80 degrees north, depending on the season. It has recorded more than thirty-four thousand events from which scientists can retrieve profiles of extinction and gas concentration.

## Knowledge Gained
The long-term record of SAM 2 and SAGE 2 aerosol extinction data reveals periodic phenomena that occur in the Southern Hemisphere. The summertime aerosol extinction is relatively constant. During fall and winter, however, the temperatures decrease, and a large polar low pressure system with swirling winds at its boundaries, called the polar vortex, establishes itself over the Antarctic. When the stratospheric temperatures reach their lowest values in the year, polar stratospheric clouds form inside the vortex and persist throughout the winter and early spring. Such clouds are always detected by SAM 2 and SAGE 2 aerosol extinction sensors during the winter and early spring. A high degree of variability in the set of daily aerosol extinction values is recorded as SAM 2 measures inside and outside the vortex. This high variability is also observed in the SAGE 2 ozone, nitrogen diox-

ide, and water vapor measurements taken at this time. With the onset of springtime and the consequent evaporation of polar stratospheric clouds, the polar stratospheric aerosol extinction measurements reach very low values relative to the rest of the year. Furthermore, as the polar vortex is replaced by warmer springtime air, the values of aerosol extinction increase to levels more typical of the summertime.

During the periods immediately after the eruptions of volcanoes, the aerosol extinction data of SAGE 1, SAGE 2, and SAM 2 show high values of aerosol. Volcanic eruptions typically place large volumes of gas and dust high into the atmosphere. The newly injected material perturbs the background aerosol distribution which is normally hemispherically symmetric with a maximum above the equatorial latitudes. For some months after the volcanic injections, the aerosol extinction values continue to rise and eventually reach a maximum. This phenomenon is attributed to the conversion of gas to particles. That is, the large gas quantity emitted by volcanic eruption is converted to aerosols.

The SAGE 1 and 2 data reveal that the distribution of global ozone concentration is hemispherically symmetric with a maximum above the equator and minima near the polar latitudes. The temporal variation of the ozone in the midlatitudes is characterized by a strong annual cycle. Below 25 kilometers at these latitudes the ozone attains its maximum value of the year in summer, while between 25 and 37 kilometers the ozone attains its maximum value in winter. The temporal variation of the ozone at the equator is dominated by a semiannual cycle. Below approximately 60 kilometers there is no significant difference between sunrise ozone and sunset ozone. Above this altitude, the sunrise ozone is greater than the sunset ozone because of photochemical reactions. These types of reactions are controlled by the presence of sunlight. The chemical bonds of certain gases in the atmosphere break apart when light is absorbed.

The SAGE data reveal that the distribution of global nitrogen dioxide is essentially hemispherically symmetric. The temporal variation of the the nitrogen dioxide in the midlatitudes is characterized by a strong annual cycle. Over the altitudes from 20 to 45 kilometers at these latitudes, the maximum value of the year occurs in summer. Furthermore, the sunset nitrogen dioxide concentration is always greater than that for sunrise because of photochemical reactions.

Because the occultation method of measuring atmospheric constituents is dependent on sensing the solar disk as it rises or sets in the atmosphere, any cloud that might be along the line of sight from the satellite to the Sun affects the measurement. Thick clouds, such as cumulonimbus, tend to block the sunlight completely, whereas thin clouds, such as cirrus, may only partially obscure the sunlight. Thus, the global distribution of the frequency of occurrence of clouds and cloud altitudes may also be estimated from the SAM 2, SAGE 1, and SAGE 2 data.

## Context

A phenomenon called the ozone hole has been observed during the Antarctic springtime for more than a decade. The ozone hole is a decrease in the abundance of Antarctic ozone as sunlight returns to the pole in early springtime. Minimum monthly values of ozone concentration are observed in October. The ozone hole occurs inside the polar vortex and is believed to be related to chemical reactions that take place on the surface of polar stratospheric clouds. Man's industrial activities have caused chlorine compounds to be released into the atmosphere. The unique atmospheric conditions that exist inside the polar vortex during the Antarctic springtime cause the chlorine from these compounds to be released in a reactive form that destroys ozone. The SAGE 2 measurements have been shown to agree with ozone measurements taken by balloon-borne instruments in the same region. The large gradients in ozone concentration as one moves from outside the vortex to inside the vortex are recorded in the SAGE 2 data.

The SAGE instruments measured ozone in the midlatitudes more frequently than near the polar regions. In 1985, a report, based on satellite data, was presented to the United States Congress stating that large global ozone decreases had occurred since 1978. The satellite data set discussed was that of the solar backscattered ultraviolet (SBUV) instrument aboard Nimbus 7. It indicated that ozone had decreased by approximately 20 percent at 50 kilometers since 1978. An independent investigation of the SAGE ozone data sets over the same period revealed no trend at 50 kilometers and a small decrease ($-3$ percent) at 40 kilometers. The trend calculated from the SAGE data sets agreed more closely with theoretical predictions of ozone and temperature change than the trend computed from the SBUV data.

It is important to know the magnitude of any long-term decrease in the amount of ozone in the stratosphere because of the potential damage to life on Earth. The stratosphere contains most of the ozone in the atmosphere, with approximately 10 percent of the atmospheric ozone contained in the troposphere (even though man's activities generate ozone). Loss of ozone means that more solar ultraviolet light would penetrate the atmosphere to Earth's surface. Ultraviolet light is absorbed by stratospheric ozone and prevented from penetrating to the surface. The damage to humans, animals, and vegetation by unshielded solar ultraviolet light is potentially large.

The global distribution of aerosols mapped from the SAGE data shows that during volcanically active periods, gas and particles from eruptions are transported to different parts of the atmosphere by the general circulation. The data from the four aerosol extinction wavelengths measured by SAGE 2 have shown that it is possible to discriminate between the particle sizes injected into the atmosphere by a volcano. The aerosols emitted by volcanoes also act as tracers for the atmospheric circulation. In turn, researchers can further understand the dynamic motion of Earth's atmosphere.

The SAGE 1, SAGE 2, and SAM 2 satellite instruments have served as important tools in the understanding of Earth's atmosphere. Using their data, scientists have been able to map aerosol and ozone concentrations on a time scale shorter than major stratospheric changes; to locate stratospheric aerosol, ozone, nitrogen dioxide, and water vapor sources and sinks; to estimate long-term global ozone trends;

to study the Antarctic ozone hole; to monitor circulation and transport phenomena; to observe hemispheric differences; and to investigate the optical properties of aerosols and assess their effects on global climate.

## Bibliography

Anthes, Richard, A., Hans A. Panofsky, John J. Cahir, and Albert Rango. *The Atmosphere*. 2d ed. Columbus, Ohio: Charles E. Merrill, 1978. A nonmathematical introductory book on meteorology. Many illustrations and photographs show examples of tropospheric phenomena. Suitable for a general audience.

Craig, Richard A. *The Upper Atmosphere: Meteorology and Physics*. New York: Academic Press, 1965. Most of chapters 2 and 3 of this work are nonmathematical in nature and deal exclusively with the stratosphere. The emphasis is on historical discoveries and observed phenomena. Many charts and graphs illustrate the subject matter.

Scorer, Richard S. *Cloud Investigation by Satellite*. New York: Halstead Press, 1986. Provides six hundred satellite images of cloud structures of the Northern Hemisphere. Written for a general audience.

Wallace, John M., and Peter V. Hobbs. *Atmospheric Sciences: An Introductory Survey*. New York: Academic Press, 1977. An excellent introduction to physical and dynamical meteorology, this college-level book assumes a first-year calculus and chemistry background. The author alternates the subject matter in the chapters between dynamical meteorology and physical meteorology.

Watson, R. T., et al. *Present State of Knowledge of the Upper Atmosphere, 1988: An Assessment Report*. Reference publication 1208. Washington, D.C.: National Aeronautics and Space Administration, 1988. A publication geared toward those interested in the efforts of scientists to assess the ozone trend in 1987. All aspects of ozone measurement and trend estimation are discussed. Topics include satellite measurements, ground-based measurements, instrument calibration, the Antarctic ozone hole, stratospheric temperature, trace gases, chemical modeling, and aerosol distributions and abundances.

Young, Louise B. *Earth's Aura*. New York: Avon Books, 1979. Chapter 6 gives an interesting description of the ozone layer and the controversy concerning its destruction by man's activities. A historical account leading up to regulations on the use of certain chlorine compounds is given.

*Robert Veiga*

## Cross-References

The Apollo-Soyuz Test Project, 132; The Sun's Effect on Earth's Ozone Layer, 348; Atmosphere Explorers, 413; U.S. Meteorological Satellites, 999; Nimbus Meteorological Satellites, 1072.

# SUNSPOTS AND STARSPOTS

*Type of phenomenon:* Solar science

*The so-called spots seen on stars, including the Sun, are immense aggregations of cooler gases produced and transported via magnetic forces from deep within the stellar/solar body. Sunspots and starspots erupt on the surface, affecting the surrounding regions, magnetic fields, and even the weather of orbiting Earth-like planets.*

### Principal personages

ANDREW E. DOUGLASS, the astronomer who coined the term dendrochronology for research in dating prehistoric ruins by tree rings

JOHN A. EDDY, the scientist who found a correlation between "little ice ages" and sunspot minima

M. KOPECKY, an astronomer who discovered that solar activity has gradually increased since 1884

KARIN LABINSKY, a scientist who correlated solar activity and Earth's polar temperatures

E. W. MAUNDER, the scientist who correlated a sunspot minimum to the little ice age of 1645-1715

MILUTIN MILANKOVITCH, the scientist who developed the astronomical theory of ice ages

SAMUEL H. SCHWABE, an astronomer who discovered the periodicity of sunspots

GEORGE WILLIAMS, an interpreter of layering in Precambrian rock

OLIN C. WILSON, the astronomer who detected the first scientific evidence of starspots

RUDOLF WOLF, the solar astronomer who correlated sunspots and magnetic variations on Earth

## Summary of the Phenomenon

Although sunspots were first observed telescopically by Galileo in 1609, they were not considered to be a feature common to all stars until 1913, when certain emission lines of ionized calcium were detected in the chemical spectra of specific stars. Because these same features were already associated with sunspots, scientists theorized that stars and the Sun might have similar phenomena. This theory, however, was not proved until a systematic survey of several Sun-like stars was undertaken by Olin C. Wilson between 1966 and 1978, using the 2.5-meter telescope located atop Mount Wilson in California. Wilson's painstaking efforts revealed changes in the cycles of calcium emission comparable to those of sunspots and other solar phenomena, the first indirect evidence of starspots. Astronomers were then able to study the Sun and stars as common objects, thereby merging two aspects of astrophysics which had previously been separated.

By the 1950's, sunspots were known to be dark areas on the photosphere (the lowest visible level of the Sun's atmosphere). The central dark region is the umbra, with a temperature of some 4,000 Kelvins, or 1,800 Kelvins cooler than the photosphere. A region lighter in color, the penumbra, surrounds the umbra and is made up of thin fibrils radiating outward from the umbra. Sunspots generally form in pairs (the penumbras of both may actually touch), and each pair may belong to a group of sunspots in the same vicinity. Smaller sunspots, called pores, lack penumbras.

In the 1950's it was also understood that sunspots form in the high latitudes, 30 to 50 degrees north and south of the solar equator, moving from east to west as part of the Sun's daily rotation. Subsequent groups form ever closer to the equator. Each spot grows until reaching its full size after about one week, then the process reverses. The very largest sunspots, which are visible to the naked eye, may achieve diameters of 50,000 kilometers, although 10,000 kilometers is more typical. Sunspots tend to dissipate after about ten days, yet some have been known to survive for months.

Concurrent with this cycle is a larger one: Sunspots grow in number from virtually none at all to a maximum count of more than two hundred a day, this cycle averaging eleven years. Along with this eleven-year cycle is the similar pattern of an "active region," which sprawls several hundred thousand kilometers around each sunspot group. This activity takes the form of strong magnetic fields of between 500 and 4,000 gauss (a gauss is a unit of magnetic flux density) and produces visible currents of gas swirls and large patches of light gas called faculae. As the cycle progresses, more spots appear closer to the equator, culminating at 7 degrees from it in both hemispheres.

Not until the 1970's, however, did this relatively simple scenario begin to yield to a more complex understanding of sunspot cycles and the interrelationships of sunspot formation with the larger processes of internal solar dynamics. In 1979, "ephemeral regions" of bright faculae patches were discovered forming in latitudes well above 35 degrees immediately before a new sunspot maximum began. Furthermore, each new region exhibited a magnetic field with a polarity opposite to those of the new sunspots but the same as the preceding and following sunspot cycles. Then, in 1980, atmospheric currents were detected near the north and south poles of the Sun, drifting toward the equator over a period of twenty-two years, coincident with the solar magnetic cycle; the polarities of the leading spots reverse between hemispheres every eleven years, the full course running twice that time. In addition, observations of the solar corona (the outermost layer of the solar atmosphere) between 1975 and 1986 confirmed a thirty-year-old supposition that bright coronal emissions near the poles at the maximum of one sunspot cycle signaled the beginning of the next cycle.

By 1987, this new evidence indicated that sunspots were the final stage in an internal cycle which lasts between eighteen and twenty-two years. The process apparently begins deep within the convective zone of the Sun, that region which extends 200,000 kilometers below the photosphere (the diameter of the Sun is 1,392,000 kilometers). Solar radiation and convective motions propel circular eddies (perhaps resembling those on Jupiter) of hot plasma up from the interior. The cause of this convective activity may well be the rate of rotation of the Sun. Together, they may generate magnetic fields, for the rate of the rotation quickens at the poles in a torsional oscillation toward the equator in a twenty-two-year period, coincident with the sunspot and magnetic cycles.

The rising plasma loses heat and rolls over near the surface to move downward again—as in a boiling cup of soup. Such rolled eddies occur first near the poles, causing the atmospheric currents, and then break into giant cells, which begin to migrate toward the equator. Successive eddies and cells rotate in opposite directions, squeezing the downward-moving plasma between them, until the magnetic field is compressed enough to form the ephemeral regions at the higher latitudes and the sunspots below 35 degrees. Sunspots have large enhanced magnetic fields at least three times that of Earth, but because of the convective heat loss they appear darker than the photosphere.

Each spot group is formed when a magnetic "flux tube," or "rope," reaches the photosphere and breaks into two circular sections. These are seen as the leading and following sunspots. Meanwhile, individual strands, or fibers, break from part of the flux tube, still submerged, and then emerge between the spots above the photosphere as arc filaments. These filaments may precede the actual appearances of the spot group and remain present during its week-long period of growth. As the flux tube unravels, its individual fibers are dispersed by the surrounding upwelling gases of the photosphere's granules and supergranules (convection cells of five to ten minutes' duration). Magnetic polarities are mixed then squeezed by gas flows moving in opposite directions to cause magnetic elements called plages (faculae patches in the chromosphere, above the photosphere).

Such magnetic activity creates the active regions of the surface and solar atmosphere—namely, prominences (great filamentary eruptions that shoot out above the Sun), flares, and cool magnetic loops of plasma. Such activity also heralds the breakdown of the spots, seen as a "light bridge" that splits each spot. Smaller spots tend to join the larger ones. In 1982, the first spiral sunspot was observed.

The years of sunspot maxima dominate the magnetic aspects of the Sun and the solar system and have, apparently, affected climatic conditions on Earth. Although the effect of sunspot activity on Earth's climate was long disputed and even flatly denied by many astronomers, in the 1970's three Soviet scientists discovered correlations between increased sunspot activity and precipitation in certain areas of Earth over the twenty-two-year magnetic cycle. Droughts, for example, were shown to occur close to a sunspot maximum (the droughts in 1977 and 1988 supported this finding). Cross-analysis with tree-ring and geologic glacial dating suggested definite solar and especially sunspot influence on Earth's weather as far back as 680 million years and more precisely over the last 1,000 to 7,500 years.

The English scientist E. W. Maunder had detected a corresponding minimum of sunspot activity during the "little ice age" between 1645 and 1715 (when the average surface temperature of Europe dropped 1 degree Celsius), suggesting even longer sunspot cycles. Among others, the Czech astronomer M. Kopecky in 1958 used data between 1884 and 1958 to discover that solar activity has gradually increased. If his extrapolation proves correct, by the year 2030 activity on the Sun will reach its highest recorded level, presaging major droughts and forest fires throughout the world. According to the Australian George Williams, the opposite could be true; another "Maunder minimum" and extended cold period may ensue, since the 1980 solar maximum was less intense than the solar maximum in 1958.

Sunspots apparently affect other natural phenomena on Earth. Somehow, the spots cause interference with radio transmissions and generate geomagnetic storms. The aurora borealis (northern lights) and aurora australis (southern lights) are attributed to sunspot activity, and in 1987 astronomers produced evidence that a high sunspot level inhibits the cooling of the air above Earth's poles. Furthermore, because sunspots are an integral part of the internal processes of the Sun, they alone cannot explain the effects on Earth; their impact must be weighed alongside those of other solar activities.

The study of the surface features of stars proceeded more slowly than that of solar surface features. Knowing the basic characteristics of the Sun, scientists followed Olin Wilson's research during the 1970's and 1980's in examining stars like the Sun for hints of solarlike behavior. Using speckle interferometry, scientists tried to detect starspots by looking for variations in the total luminosity of Sun-like stars as they rotated. With this method, any traces of periodic fluctuations in their brightnesses must be separated from entirely normal changes such as their possibly being periodically eclipsed in binary (two-star) systems.

The best subjects for this kind of study were considered to be RS Canum Venaticorum variable stars—G2 "subgiants" some six times larger than the Sun but with cooler surface temperatures. Violent starspots of great intensity and related magnetic fields were detected on several such stars, except that the spots were one hundred times larger than sunspots, covering up to one-fifth of the star's surface (in contrast to 0.1 percent of the Sun being covered at a sunspot maximum). Also, the starspots seemed to exist in only one hemisphere and to migrate from the equatorial region toward the poles, the opposite of sunspot activity. In addition, they exhibited stronger magnetic fields and higher abundances of certain metals compared to the Sun. Their twenty- or thirty-year cycles, however, resembled the eleven-year sunspot cycle. Other classes of stars—M dwarfs and T Tauri—also indicate intense solar-type activity and spots.

So new were discoveries about internal solar and stellar dynamics that by the end of the 1980's major mysteries remained to be solved regarding sunspots and starspots. A major step forward was the creation of the new field of helioseismology to study the internal structure of the Sun and solarlike oscillations in the brightnesses of other stars.

## Knowledge Gained

By the end of the 1970's, the separate studies of the Sun and of similar solar-type stars came together as a common, interrelated science, which enabled sunspots and starspots to be understood as similar phenomena.

Sunspots were discovered to be the end result of a general internal mechanism of the Sun. Every eighteen to twenty-two years, radiation and convection currents deep within the Sun, perhaps stimulated by the Sun's rate of rotation, push hot plasma in the form of eddies toward the surface, or photosphere. The eddies are circular and roll over near the surface to become cells. Every other cell rotates in the opposite direction, squeezing the plasma, which becomes relatively cool after reaching the surface. Magnetic fields and flux tubes are generated in the process. When flux tubes break through the surface, they create the sunspots, usually in pairs.

The fact that sunspot and magnetic cycles coincide proves their interrelationship. Sunspot activity is first seen near the poles as atmospheric currents. Then, ephemeral regions (which gradually move closer to the equatorial area) are created. Finally, sunspot groups form below 35 degrees latitude. The flux tubes unravel after sunspot formation and interact with the surrounding granules of convection cells in the photosphere, causing the magnetic plages, prominences, and other associated phenomena of the solar atmosphere. This tremendous magnetic activity culminates in the dissolution of the sunspot groups, usually after two weeks.

These new data about solar cycles coincided with fresh, though imperfectly understood, related evidence regarding their possible impact on the weather and general climate of Earth. Longer solar cycles of 80 and 200 years were indicated by sunspot activity. This cycle has been interpreted variously as causing longer periods of either a cooler or a dryer climate—the former producing more glacial activity, the latter drought and wildfires.

Starspot activity apparently occurs on stars similar in makeup to the Sun. Research on stars larger than the Sun suggested the presence of immense spot regions, covering perhaps 20 percent of those stars' surfaces. Unlike those on the Sun, however, these spot groups have stronger magnetic fields, seem to be located in only one hemisphere, and move toward a pole rather than toward the equator. Their time cycles, however, do compare closely with those of the Sun.

## Context

The Sun is the ultimate source upon which life on Earth depends, but until the post-1950 period its features, including sunspots, were only crudely understood— and then often only as isolated phenomena. Largely through ground-based optical and radio telescopes and instruments on orbiting satellites, a more complete picture began to emerge during the 1970's. Sunspots then came to be appreciated as key manifestations of the "dynamo" which powers the Sun internally, probably a combination of the solar rotation and convective forces which produce magnetic fields. The eruption of the sunspots and related flares and phenomena in the photosphere generates the magnetic activity which affects the solar corona, the solar wind, and the interplanetary medium beyond, including that of Earth.

The possibility of sunspots influencing the climate and thus life on Earth was rejected until new statistical analyses and tree-ring and glacial dating established tentative links with the sunspot cycles of the past. Until long-term observations are possible, however, definite conclusions about the past and about future climatic conditions cannot be established. Clearly, the value of knowing whether to anticipate droughts or sustained cooler weather would be enormous.

Not until the 1970's, with the advent of increasingly sophisticated telescopic and spectroscopic instruments, could distant stars of the Milky Way begin to be examined for astrophysical characteristics akin to those of the Sun. As new knowledge of the Sun was gained, it was applied to possible scenarios accounting for the presence of starspots. The initial evidence revealed starspots of such immensity that they seemed to cover major parts of stellar surfaces. Data from these observations can be utilized for further solar research. What is more, the discovery of the properties of distant suns provides clues to their life-sustaining capacity and to the possible locations of distant solar systems and extraterrestrial intelligence. The combined study of the Sun and stars sets the stage for fresh perspectives on the nature of the universe and of the place of the human race in it.

## Bibliography

Frazier, Kendrick. *Our Turbulent Sun*. Englewood Cliffs, N.J.: Prentice-Hall, 1982. An excellent popular introduction to the Sun, including the controversy over the Maunder minimum relating to the seventeenth century. Unfortunately, the illustrations are poor.

Giampapa, Mark S. "The Solar-Stellar Connection." *Sky and Telescope* 74 (August, 1987): 142-146. A concise overview of the common physical and dynamic attributes of stars in general and the Sun in particular, with only a short treatment of sunspots and starspots.

Giovanelli, Ronald G. *Secrets of the Sun*. Cambridge: Cambridge University Press, 1984. A brief nonmathematical but otherwise technical summary of knowledge about the Sun through 1983, with three chapters devoted to sunspots and related topics. Theories of solar dynamics are presented succinctly and without bias, but the absence of a bibliography or even an index makes the work a poor vehicle for further research. The illustrations are magnificent.

Jordan, Stuart, ed. *The Sun as a Star*. NASA SP-450. Springfield, Va.: National Technical Information Service, 1981. A pioneering series of integrated essays on the methodological use of the Sun as a model for interpreting stellar physics in general. The chapter on the dynamics of the photosphere includes sunspots and, by extrapolation, starspots.

Kaler, James B. "Cousins of Our Sun: The G Stars." *Sky and Telescope* 72 (November, 1986): 450-453. An introduction to the study of stars similar to the Sun, focusing on their common spectra and chemical elements and internal mechanics, notably sunspots.

Robinson, Leif J. "The Sunspot Cycle: Tip of the Iceberg." *Sky and Telescope* 73 (June, 1987): 589-591. An account of discoveries between 1979 and 1987 which revealed sunspots to be but one manifestation of several in the dynamics of solar cycles and their suggested relationships with the climate of Earth. The graphics are particularly instructive of these processes.

Schove, D. Justin, ed. *Sunspot Cycles*. New York: Van Nostrand Reinhold Co., 1983. Forty technical papers summarizing two thousand years' worth of direct and indirect evidence treating the periodicity of sunspots. The book concludes that, although periods of eleven, eighty, and two hundred years occur, the evidence is too complex to offer definitive explanations.

Sturrock, Peter A., ed. *Physics of the Sun*. 3 vols. Norwell, Mass.: Kluwer Academic Publishers, 1986. Although this textbook is highly technical, it is valuable—even to the lay reader. Sunspots are an integral part of each multiauthored volume: *The Solar Interior*, *The Solar Atmosphere*, and *Astrophysics and Solar-Terrestrial Relations*.

Wallenhorst, Steven G. "Sunspot Numbers and Solar Cycles." *Sky and Telescope* 64 (September, 1982): 234-236. A condensed treatment of the debate over sunspot periods, their relationship to Earth's weather, and the arguments against the Maunder minimum theory.

Zeilik, Michael, et al. "The Strange RS Canum Venaticorum Binary Stars." *Sky and Telescope* 57 (February, 1979): 132-137. The initial evidence of huge starspots on one class of binary stars, showing them to be strong X-ray sources.

*Clark G. Reynolds*

## Cross-References

The Sun's Effect on Earth's Climate, 320; The Sun's Effect on Earth's Ionosphere, 334; The Sun's Effect on Earth's Ozone Layer, 348; The Search for Extraterrestrial Intelligence, 447; Heliospheric Physics, 583; The High-Energy Astronomical Observatories, 589; The Milky Way, 1018; The Orbiting Astronomical Observatories, 1092; The Skylab Program, 1285; Solar and Stellar Flares, 1315; The Solar Corona, 1323; The Solar Magnetic Field, 1344; Solar Radiation, 1359; The Solar Wind, 1382; The Solar X-Ray Region, 1390; Stellar Evolution, 1944.

# SUPERNOVAE AND NEUTRON STARS

*Type of phenomenon:* Intergalactic

A supernova is the explosion of a star which yields an increase in brightness by tens of millions. The complete destruction of a star in a double star system is called a Type I supernova. A Type II supernova, arising from a more massive star, may leave behind a neutron star, a collapsed star with the mass of the Sun but with a diameter of only about 20 kilometers.

*Principal personages*
WALTER BAADE and
FRITZ ZWICKY, researchers at the Palomar Observatory
JOCELYN BELL,
ANTONY HEWISH, and
FRED HOYLE, researchers at the University of Cambridge
WILLIAM FOWLER, a researcher at the California Institute of Technology
THOMAS GOLD, a researcher at Cornell University
L. D. LANDAU, a researcher at the Institute for Physical Problems, Moscow
KNUT LUNDMARK, a researcher at Stockholm University
RUDOLF MINKOWSKI, a researcher at Mount Wilson Observatory

## Summary of the Phenomenon

Supernovae are stellar explosions during which a star increases in brightness tens of millions of times. These stellar flares have been cataloged since the dawn of history; the most famous were those studied by Tycho Brahe (1572) and Johannes Kepler (1604) and one, recorded by Chinese astronomers (1054), that produced the Crab nebula. The Swedish astronomer Knut Lundmark first distinguished them from galactic novae, the flares from stars, which are much more common (several per year), much fainter (by a factor of ten thousand), and do not involve the nearly complete incineration of the star. Fritz Zwicky and Walter Baade, working at Palomar Observatory, atop Mount Palomar in Southern California, coined the name "supernovae" and undertook the first major search for them in other galaxies.

Supernovae are rare and bright. The last one seen in the Milky Way was Kepler's in 1604. The last two visible with the naked eye appeared in the Andromeda galaxy (August, 1885) and the Large Magellanic Cloud galaxy (February, 1987). It is estimated that in a galaxy such as the Milky Way, supernovae occur every thirty to one hundred years, but the majority of them are obscured by gas and dust and remain undetected. At their brightest, they shine with the light of 10 billion Suns, nearly the light of an entire galaxy. Within a few weeks, they begin to fade, virtually disappearing in one or two years.

In 1940, Rudolf Minkowski, examining records of supernova spectra, discovered that supernovae are of two general types, distinguished by the presence or absence of hydrogen. Spectra of Type I supernovae show either extremely weak or no hydrogen lines. Later it was realized, in addition, that Type I supernovae have a very characteristic "light curve," consisting of a sudden brightening, a quick decline in less than one month, and then a slower fading, with the supernova disappearing within one or two years. Type I supernovae also occur only in elliptical galaxies or in the nuclei or halos of spiral galaxies. They thus seem to be associated with older, low-mass stars (population II). On the other hand, Type II supernovae have strong hydrogen features in their spectra. They form a much less homogeneous class than those of Type I (their peak luminosity and light curve shape is variable) and occur only in the arms of spiral galaxies. They seem to be connected with young (population I) stars. The fact that they are often found within star-forming regions shows that they are massive stars, with greater than about 10 solar masses, since only such massive short-lived stars would have remained so close to their birthplaces.

When a star explodes, a nebula, or supernova remnant, is formed which rapidly expands, perhaps at a rate of 10,000 or more kilometers per second. This high expansion velocity distinguishes supernova remnants from planetary nebulae, which result from the almost evaporative loss of the outermost layers of low-mass stars late in their lives. The latter expand at the much slower rate of about 30 kilometers per second, which is characteristic of a hot gas rushing into a vacuum. Supernova remnants are clearly results of explosions of enormous power: Their total energy is the same as the entire visible light output of the Sun over its 10-billion-year lifetime.

Hundreds of thousands of years later, gas clouds ejected in such an explosion will be slowed as they rush into the ambient interstellar medium. In some cases, the gas will be heated and excited by high-energy particles produced in the aftermath of the explosion. (These particles may also be the source of extrasolar cosmic rays, bare atomic nuclei accelerated to velocities near the speed of light and emanating from all parts of the sky.) The gas then emits a peculiar synchrotron radiation, named after the light and radio emissions first observed from manmade particle accelerators (synchrotrons). The Crab nebula is an outstanding example of a supernova remnant in this stage, and it has powerful radio emissions. Later, the gas cools more, to a temperature of a few million degrees Celsius, and is compressed by the interstellar medium and magnetic fields into filamentary condensations. The Veil nebula, or Cygnus Loop, is a good example of a supernova in this phase. In 1970, a source of X rays was discovered from this remnant, which is to be expected from such a gas.

The mass of material ejected in a Type I supernova is about 1 solar mass; in a Type II supernova it can be many times larger. This ejected material is of enormous consequence for the Galaxy, and for that matter, human beings, because it is the source of the majority of the elements heavier than helium. (Hydrogen and most helium originated in the big bang.) Large amounts of carbon, nitrogen, and oxygen may be synthesized and ejected in red giant winds and nova explosions, but most of these biologically important elements probably are created in supernovae. Certainly most of the heavier elements, such as calcium, phosphorous, iron, and uranium, are created by supernovae.

Researchers believe that supernovae are connected with the deaths of stars. The association of Type I events with the older stellar population has led to the currently favored theory for their origin. It has long been apparent that stars which are born with less than 5 to 8 solar masses will end their lives as white dwarfs, compact objects containing a solar mass within an Earth-sized radius, after losing their outer stellar envelopes in a series of planetary nebula ejections. Occasionally, a white dwarf in a binary system will accrete, or pull, mass from its companion star. It is well known that a white dwarf's maximum mass is about 1.44 solar masses, the so-called Chandrasekhar limit, and should the accreting white dwarf mass approach this value, a nuclear instability will ensue. The carbon and oxygen which form the bulk of the white dwarf will thermonuclearly ignite and completely incinerate the star, resulting in the explosion and optical display seen as a supernova. The two remaining characteristics of Type I supernovae, their homogeneous nature and their lack of hydrogen, are explained by this model. It is not expected that a compact remnant, such as a neutron star, is produced in these supernovae.

More massive stars cannot peacefully retire as white dwarfs because they develop cores more massive than the Chandrasekhar limit, which eventually "burn" to iron, the most stable element. Further nuclear energy release is impossible and gravitational contraction begins, resulting in the formation of a neutron star. Type II supernovae originate from the conversion of the released gravitational energy into an explosion of the outer stellar layers. The predominance of hydrogen in the outermost layers explains the supernova's strength in the Type II spectra. Stars of different masses should result in a variety of light curves, because of variations in ejecta mass and explosion energies. Contrast this with the more homogeneous Type I supernovae, in which a fixed ejecta mass and explosion energy, thermonuclear in origin, is likely.

The implosion-explosion is possible because the collapsing core "bounces" when its density reaches nuclear density (the density found inside ordinary atomic nuclei, $3 \times 10^{14}$ grams per cubic centimeter). At this density, the pressure increases so rapidly that the core rebounds and creates an outgoing shock wave that ejects the outer envelope. The core itself does not reexpand; it stabilizes as a dense compact object which, as it cools, becomes a neutron star. More precisely, the core becomes a "proton-neutron star," because it is still 40 percent protons (iron is 46 percent protons, a neutron star is 5 to 10 percent protons). The conversion of a proton to a neutron involves the absorption of an electron and the emission of a neutrino, a massless, neutral, subatomic particle that reacts very weakly with matter. A shield of water more than 100 light-years thick is needed to absorb 50 percent of a beam of neutrinos. Nevertheless, a proton-neutron star is so dense, one thousand trillion times as dense as water, that the neutrinos cannot immediately escape. Several seconds must elapse before they finally diffuse, allowing the neutron star to form.

The supernova SN1987A observed in February, 1987, was very significant because three terrestrial neutrino detectors (in Japan, the United States, and the Soviet Union) observed it. The duration of the neutrino burst (10 seconds), the energies of the neutrinos, and the number observed were in complete accord with theoretical expectations of neutron star formation. Neutrinos from a supernova had never been seen before, because sufficiently large detectors did not exist before 1986. In addition, for the first time the progenitor star of this supernova was identified. Pre-outburst photographs, some taken as recently as one day before, revealed that it had been a massive star of 15 to 20 solar masses. Considering the rarity of supernovae, this event has nicely corroborated the general theory of Type II supernovae.

Neutron stars were first proposed, independently, by the Soviet physicist L. D. Landau and by Baade and Zwicky, shortly after the discovery of the neutron. They are highly condensed objects: Their average density is greater than that in an ordinary atomic nucleus, about 1 million times greater than that found in the densest white dwarfs. While white dwarfs are supported against gravitational collapse by the quantum-mechanical Fermi pressure of electrons, neutron stars are supported by nuclear forces and by neutron Fermi pressure. (Ordinary stars are supported by thermal gas pressure.) The discovery in 1967 of pulsars, stars that blink on and off with clocklike regularity, established the existence of neutron stars; the connection was first made by Thomas Gold of Cornell University. The additional discovery in 1968 of a pulsar in the Crab nebula conclusively proved the connection between neutron stars and supernovae. The immense magnetic fields of some neutron stars, coupled with their rapid rotation (1 to 1,000 times per second) and the highly ionized plasma expected to exist near their surfaces, lead to the pulsed radiation. Some compact X-ray sources also appear to be neutron stars in very close binaries which are accreting matter from their (ordinary) stellar companions. Altogether, more than three hundred neutron stars are now known.

At birth, neutron stars have interior temperatures greater than $3 \times 10^{11}$ degrees Celsius, but escaping neutrinos decrease the temperature to less than $10^{10}$ degrees Celsius within a few days. The temperature of the matter inside the neutron star is effectively zero degrees Celsius. The radius of a neutron star is about 10 kilometers, and the masses of neutron stars that have been measured are about 1.5 solar masses. The maximum mass a neutron star can have is uncertain and depends on the physics of ultradense matter, but it is certainly less than 3 solar masses. A compact object with a mass greater than this maximum mass will collapse further, eventually becoming a black hole, an object so dense that even light cannot escape from it.

The density of matter increases with depth in a neutron star. The outer crust contains bare nuclei in a sea of electrons, similar to terrestrial metals, and is about 1 kilometer thick. Below this crust is a layer of uncertain depth in which nuclei coexist with both electrons and neutrons which have been squeezed from the nuclei. Above this density, at greater depths, nuclei touch and merge into a uniform sea of neutrons, protons, and electrons. At even greater depths, other exotic subatomic particles such as muons, pions, and heavier baryons may exist as well; in addition, the matter might become superfluid. Finally, at densities in excess of $10^{15}$ grams per cubic centimeter, matter may dissolve into quarks, the elementary particles which are theorized to be the building blocks of neutrons, protons, and other baryonic matter.

## Knowledge Gained

Supernovae were recognized to comprise a separate class of objects during the 1920's. By 1960, their classification into two types was well established, and their origins were at least partially understood. The ideas that Type I supernovae originate in low-mass, evolved binaries, because of the explosion of an accreting white dwarf, and that Type II supernovae are the end products of the evolution of high-mass stars, were partially accepted. The 1960's saw several advances, both theoretical and observational, that fit this general scenario.

In 1962, T. Pankey of Harvard University suggested that the decay of radioactive nickel to cobalt and then iron was the source of the energy that distinguishes the light curves of Type I supernovae. The radioactivity has a half-life of 77 days, and 1 solar mass of it provides enough energy to explain the slow decline of the light curve. Spectral lines of cobalt and iron have since been seen in the spectra of Type I supernovae.

In 1948, John Bolton, an Australian, showed the first connection between a source of cosmic radio waves and a visible object, the Crab nebula. Later, in 1963, the Crab nebula was also discovered to be the first known source of X rays, a form of radiation like light, but a thousand times more energetic.

The discovery of pulsars by Jocelyn Bell and Antony Hewish of the University of Cambridge, in 1967, showed that neutron stars were not simply theoretical. The finding in 1968 that pulsars are located at the centers of the Veil and Crab nebulae, both supernova remnants, proved conclusively the connection between neutron stars and supernovae. In 1969, astronomers at the Steward Observatory in Tucson, Arizona, found optical pulses from the Crab nebula with the same period as the radio pulsar and were further able to identify, for the first time, the star that was emitting these pulses. Astronomers had finally identified the source of the high-energy particles that produce the nebula's synchrotron radiation. In 1975, the Small Astronomy Satellite detected gamma-ray pulses (these are even more energetic than X rays) from the pulsar in the Vela supernova remnant. In 1977, an Anglo-Australian team was able to detect optical pulses from this object as well. Still more pulsars are known to originate within supernova remnants.

In the 1960's and 1970's, evidence accumulated regarding the role of supernovae in element creation in the Galaxy. In 1957, Geoffrey and Margaret Burbidge and William Fowler of the California Institute of Technology, together with Fred Hoyle of Cambridge, put forth the first theories of how supernovae might be involved. By 1980, the supernova remnant Cassiopeia A was observed to have certain features with abnormally strong oxygen, sulfur, calcium, and argon lines. These elements are expected in matter ejected from the inside of a massive, evolved star. In addition, the Crab nebula also has peculiarities indicative of the production of heavy elements. The total mass of the Crab nebula is estimated at about 9 solar masses; thus it must have originated from the explosion of at least a moderate-mass star.

By far the most important development of the late 1980's was the observation of SN1987A in the Large Magellanic Cloud. On February 23, 1987, Ian Shelton of the University of Toronto discovered a naked-eye supernova in the southern sky from the Las Campanas Observatory in Chile. This supernova is particularly interesting because, for the first time, neutrinos from an extrasolar object were observed. The progenitor star of the supernova could be identified from archival photographs and had, in fact, been previously studied. The impact of this discovery on astrophysics and particle physics was enormous and is probably not yet fully realized. This supernova has been closely studied in the ultraviolet (with the International Ultraviolet Explorer satellite), in the radio, in the infrared, and in X rays.

Initially, the ultraviolet observations were confusing, because after the initial rapid fading of the supernova, as the result of the rapid cooling of the ejected outer layers of the progenitor star, residual ultraviolet light from two nearby blue stars remained. It appeared as though the progenitor star were still there. Careful positional measurements of archival photographs revealed, however, that there were originally three blue stars at the supernova's location. Thus, the identity of the progenitor star was clearly established as a blue supergiant. It was a surprise that the progenitor star was blue, but that did explain why this supernova was more than ten times fainter than expected.

Soon after the supernova was discovered, neutrino detectors in Europe, Japan, the United States, and the Soviet Union reported that they observed a neutrino burst on February 23. It was widely expected that a Type II supernova would give rise to a burst of neutrinos and that at the 160,000 light-year distance of the Large Magellanic Cloud a few such bursts might be detected. With the exception of the European detection, which was 4.5 hours earlier than the other three, these observations seemed to be in accord with theoretical predictions.

## Context

The supernova is the driving force behind the chemical evolution of the Galaxy. Supernovae eject heavy elements synthesized from the primordial hydrogen and helium in stellar cores throughout their lives; other elements, such as iron and heavier elements, are created during the explosions themselves. The fact that the light from SN1987A, after 180 days, faded exponentially with a half-life exactly that of cobalt 56, 77 days, proved such synthesis. In fact, models showed that about 0.07 solar mass of radioactive matter alone was created and ejected in this event. Evidence is accumulating that the most ancient meteorites bear traces of nuclear isotopes directly synthesized in a nearby supernova explosion that occurred prior to the formation of the solar system. It may even be that this presolar supernova triggered the collapse of the interstellar cloud, or presolar nebula, that eventually formed the Sun and its planets. Energy from supernova explosions dominates the physical and thermal structure of the interstellar medium; shock waves from events near dense clouds are observed to stimulate star formation. Such phenomena as starburst galaxies, in which stars are formed in large numbers, may result from a series of supernova explosions.

Supernovae produce, in some cases, neutron stars and black holes. Their remnants are among the brightest objects in the sky in radio and X-radiation. It is speculated that they are the dominant source of cosmic rays. Supernovae may be the largest producers of dust grains, which condense in the cooling, heavy-element-rich stellar layers, and, at the same time, they may be the single most effective destroyer of dust, which may be heated and vaporized as the supernova's powerful shock wave passes through the interstellar medium. In some interstellar clouds, as much as 99.99 percent of the more refractory, or condensable, elements, such as titanium, aluminum, and calcium, are "locked up" in dust.

Supernovae, and neutron stars, are the ultimate nuclear physics laboratory. In these formations, there exist conditions of extreme density and temperature that cannot yet be created in any accelerator. Neutrino observations of supernovae provide an especially crucial test of dense-matter physics, since neutrinos, unlike photons of optical or X-radiation, originate deep within the collapsed stellar core, inside the proto-neutron star. Neutron star masses, radii, and moments of inertia from observations of neutron stars in binary systems and from pulsars provide important information on the properties of dense matter.

The neutrino detection of a supernova in the Milky Way would facilitate research in this area greatly. Such an event would enable scientists to learn more about Type II supernovae in particular and high-density nuclear physics in general. Given the estimated time between supernovae in the Milky Way (thirty to one hundred years), astronomers may have to wait decades for that chance. Nevertheless, if SN1987A has left behind a neutron star, which is suggested by the energetics of the neutrinos, and if that neutron star becomes a pulsar, then this supernova may still help researchers learn much about the universe.

## Bibliography

Bethe, Hans A., and Gerry Brown. "How a Supernova Explodes." *Scientific American* 252 (May, 1985): 60-68. An up-to-date source for the most recent thinking on the mechanism for Type II supernovae. Includes a thorough discussion of various models. The authors are active researchers in problems concerning the interaction between nuclear physics and neutron stars and supernovae.

Clark, David H. *Superstars: How Stellar Explosions Shape the Destiny of Our Universe*. New York: McGraw-Hill Book Co., 1984. This book gives a general description of how supernovae affect the understanding of astronomy and how the Milky Way and the solar system may be shaped by supernovae. It contains, but goes well beyond, the simple description of what supernovae are and how they originate. There are many charts and figures as well as a useful bibliography.

Clark, David H., and F. Stephenson, eds. *The Historical Supernovae*. Elmsford,

N.Y.: Pergamon Press, 1977. A very readable text that traces the accounts of supernovae from Chinese and Korean records to the late 1970's. Contains extensive translations from original historical documents and results from computer simulations of the positions and brightnesses of ancient supernovae. Contains many figures and tables and an extensive bibliography. Contains some college-level material.

Moore, Patrick, and Iain Nicholson. *Black Holes in Space*. New York: W. W. Norton and Co., 1976. An introduction to black holes and ideas concerning their origin. Contains extensive discussions of supernovae and general relativity. Suitable for general audiences.

Murdin, Paul, and Lesley Murdin. *Supernovae*. New York: Cambridge University Press, 1985. A complete account of supernovae prior to SN1987A, this text is well illustrated and very readable. Contains accounts of historical supernovae, theories of supernovae and neutron star formation, and a description of element production in supernovae. Describes supernova remnants, cosmic rays, and black holes.

Page, T., and L. W. Page, eds. *The Evolution of Stars*. New York: Macmillan, 1968. This readable collection of articles from the favorite periodical of amateur astronomers, *Sky and Telescope*, describes star formation, the life cycles of stars, and the deaths of stars—including supernovae. The editors have contributed some material that bridges the gaps that inevitably arise in such compendiums, thereby maintaining a sense of continuity. There are extensive figures, tables, and bibliographies. Contains some college-level material.

Ruderman, Malvin A. "Solid Stars." *Scientific American* 224 (February, 1971): 12, 24-31. A readable introduction to white dwarfs, neutron stars, and ultradense matter. Some early ideas concerning the pulsar mechanism and neutron star X-ray sources are discussed. This article is now somewhat dated, but it is a good primer for further investigations.

Shklovskii, Iosif S. *Stars: Their Birth, Life, and Death*. Translated by Richard B. Rodman. New York: W. H. Freeman and Co., 1978. This very detailed but easy-to-read discussion of stars contains a wealth of information on star formation, stellar evolution, white dwarfs, supernovae, neutron stars and pulsars, X-ray binaries, and black holes. Contains an extensive bibliography and a multitude of figures, plates, and tables. There are some equations, and scientific notation is used.

*James M. Lattimer*

## Cross-References

Asteroids and Meteorites, 145; Black Holes, 211; Gamma-Ray Bursts, 481; The High-Energy Astronomical Observatories, 589; The International Ultraviolet Explorer, 625; The Mir Space Station, 1025; The New Astronomy and the Study of Cosmic Rays, 1059; The New Astronomy and the Study of Electromagnetic Radiation, 1066; Pulsars, 1209; Stellar Evolution, 1944; White Dwarf Stars, 2268.

# THE SURVEYOR PROGRAM

*Date:* May 30, 1966, to February 21, 1968
*Type of program:* Unmanned lunar probes
*Country:* The United States

*Surveyor 1 achieved the first lunar soft landing by a fully automated spacecraft. The Surveyor program developed the technology for soft-landing on the Moon, verified the compatibility of the design of the Apollo manned lunar-landing spacecraft with actual lunar surface conditions, and added to the scientific knowledge of the Moon.*

*Principal personages*
BENJAMIN MILWITZKY, Surveyor Program Manager at NASA
Headquarters, Office of Lunar and Planetary Programs
WALKER E. GIBERSON, Surveyor Project Manager at JPL from its
inception to 1965
ROBERT PARKS, Surveyor Project Manager at JPL from 1965 to
1966
HOWARD H. HAGLUND, Surveyor Project Manager at JPL from
1966 to 1968
R. G. FORNEY, Spacecraft Systems Manager at JPL
LEONARD JAFFE, Chairman, Surveyor Scientific Evaluation
Advisory Team
EUGENE M. SHOEMAKER, Principal Investigator, imaging
A. L. TURKEVICH, Principal Investigator, alpha scattering
RONALD F. SCOTT, Principal Investigator, soil mechanics surface
sampler

## Summary of the Program

In May, 1960, the National Aeronautics and Space Administration (NASA) approved a Surveyor program consisting of two parts: a lunar orbiter for photographic coverage of the Moon's surface and a lunar lander to obtain scientific information on the Moon's environment and structure. Before human beings could safely be sent to the Moon, the Surveyors were to provide spacecraft designers with information on the load-bearing limits of the lunar surface, its magnetic properties, and its radar and thermal reflectivity.

The Jet Propulsion Laboratory (JPL) was assigned project responsibility, and four Surveyor study contracts were awarded in July, 1960, to Hughes Aircraft, North American, Space Technology Laboratories, and McDonnell Aircraft. On January 19, 1961, NASA chose Hughes Aircraft's proposal for the Surveyor and began planning at JPL for seven lunar landing flights, the first of which was planned for launch on an Atlas-Centaur booster in 1963.

Because of development problems with the Centaur, early failures of the Ranger lunar impactor, and increasing demands for information on the lunar surface to support the Apollo program, the orbiter portion of Surveyor was dropped in 1962 and replaced by the Lunar Orbiter project, managed by NASA's Langley Research Center. Problems with the Centaur upper stage forced postponement of the first Surveyor launch and required a reduction in the spacecraft's weight—from an original 1,134 kilograms with a 156-kilogram payload to 953 kilograms carrying only 52 kilograms of instruments.

The Atlas-Centaur became operational in 1966, and Surveyor 1 was launched from Launch Complex 36A at Cape Kennedy, Florida, on May 30, 1966. Surveyor 1, the first test model of the series, carried more than one hundred engineering sensors to monitor spacecraft performance. No instrumentation was carried specifically for scientific experiments, but the spacecraft was outfitted with a survey television system and with instrumentation to measure the bearing strength, temperature, and radar reflectivity of the lunar surface.

After injection on a trajectory intersecting the Moon, the Surveyor spacecraft separated from the Centaur upper stage. Midcourse maneuvers, using vernier engines on the spacecraft, were performed to bring it within the desired target area. For the terminal descent, the main retro-engine was ignited, by command of an onboard radar altimeter, to provide most of the braking. After this retro-engine burned out, at about 10 kilometers above the lunar surface, it was jettisoned. A second radar, providing measurements of velocity and altitude, was used with the smaller vernier engines, in a closed loop under control of an onboard analog computer, for the final descent phase. To reduce the disturbance to the lunar surface, the vernier engines were extinguished by the computer when the spacecraft was about 4 meters above the surface and the descent rate was about 1.5 meters per second. At 0617 Greenwich mean time on June 2, 1966, Surveyor 1 soft-landed in the southwest portion of the Ocean of Storms, becoming the first U.S. spacecraft to soft-land on another celestial body.

During the next two lunar days (28 Earth days each) the Surveyor returned some 11,000 photographs of the surrounding terrain to Earth. Surveyor 1 completed its primary mission on July 14, 1966, but engineering interrogations were conducted at irregular intervals through January, 1967.

Surveyor 2, launched on September 20, 1966, had essentially the same configuration as Surveyor 1 and was intended to land in the Central Bay, another area of the potential Apollo landing zone. When the midcourse maneuver was attempted on September 21, one of the three vernier engines failed to ignite, and the unbalanced thrust caused the spacecraft to tumble. Although repeated commands were sent in an attempt to salvage the mission, Surveyor 2 crashed on the Moon on September 22, 1966.

Surveyor 3, though similar to the two earlier spacecraft, was equipped with two fixed mirrors to extend the view of its television camera underneath the spacecraft. A remotely controlled surface sampler arm, capable of digging trenches and manipulating the surface material in view of the television camera, was also added. The

Surveyor 3 spacecraft was launched on April 17, 1967, from Launch Complex 36B at Cape Kennedy—the first time the two-burn capability of the Centaur was used on an operational mission. After separation from the Atlas, the Centaur engine ignited and burned for approximately 5 minutes to place the vehicle into a 167-kilometer circular parking orbit. The Centaur coasted for 22 minutes, then reignited to place the spacecraft on a lunar-intercept trajectory. The use of a parking orbit greatly increased the fraction of the lunar surface to which the Surveyor could be targeted.

The midcourse correction maneuver and the firing and jettisoning of the retro-engine proceeded as planned. A few seconds before touchdown, however, the on-board radar lost its lock on the surface, apparently because of unexpected reflections from large rocks near the landing site. As a result, the spacecraft guidance system switched to an inertial mode, which prevented the vernier engines from extinguishing about 4 meters above the surface as planned. The spacecraft touched down with its vernier engines still firing, lifted off, touched down a second time, lifted off again, then touched down for a third time after receiving a command from Earth 34 seconds after the initial touchdown. The spacecraft had a lateral velocity of about 1 meter per second at the first touchdown, and the distance between the first and second touchdowns was about 20 meters, while there was a distance of about 11 meters between the second and third touchdowns.

The landing occurred on April 19, 1967, in the southeast part of the Ocean of Storms, a potential Apollo landing region. Surveyor 3 landed in a medium-sized crater and came to rest tilted at an angle of about 14 degrees. This location allowed the crater to be viewed from the inside, and the unplanned tilt permitted the camera to aim high enough to photograph an eclipse of the Sun by Earth, which would not have been possible if the landing had been on a level surface. The spacecraft returned 6,315 television pictures and operated its surface sampler for more than eighteen hours before transmissions ceased shortly after local sunset on May 3, 1967.

Surveyor 4, carrying the same payload as Surveyor 3 had, was launched on July 14, 1967. After a flawless flight to the Moon, radio signals from the spacecraft ceased abruptly during the final descent, approximately 2.5 minutes before touchdown and only 2 seconds before retro-engine burnout. Radio contact with the spacecraft was never reestablished, and Surveyor 4 crashed into the lunar surface, possibly after an explosion.

Surveyor 5 was launched from Cape Kennedy on September 8, 1967. Because of a helium regulator leak which developed during flight, a radically new descent technique was engineered, and the Surveyor 5 performed a flawless descent and soft landing in the Sea of Tranquillity on September 11, 1967. The spacecraft was similar to its two immediate predecessors, except that the surface sampler was replaced by an "alpha backscatter instrument," a device to determine the relative abundances of the chemical elements in the lunar surface material. In addition, a bar magnet was attached to one of the footpads to determine if magnetic material was present in the lunar soil.

During its first lunar day, which ended at sunset on September 24, 1967, Surveyor 5 took 18,006 television pictures, performed chemical analyses of the lunar soil, and fired its vernier engines for 0.55 second to determine the effects of high-velocity exhaust gases impinging on the lunar surface. On October 15, 1967, after exposure to the two-week deep freeze of the lunar night, Surveyor 5 responded to a command from Earth, reactivating, and transmitted an additional 1,043 pictures and data from the lunar surface.

The Surveyor 6 spacecraft, essentially identical to Surveyor 5, was launched on November 7, 1967, and landed on the Moon on November 10, 1967. The landing site, near the center of the Moon's visible hemisphere in the Central Bay, was the last of four potential Apollo landing sites designated for investigation by the Surveyor program. From landing until a few hours after lunar sunset on November 24, 1967, the spacecraft transmitted more than 29,000 television pictures, and the alpha back-scattering experiment acquired 30 hours of data on the chemical composition of the lunar soil. On November 17, 1967, Surveyor 6's vernier engines were fired for 2.5 seconds, causing the spacecraft to lift off from the lunar surface and move laterally about three meters to a new location. Television pictures showed the effect of rocket firings close to the lunar surface. When combined with images taken from the earlier landing site, the new photographs provided stereoscopic data of the surrounding terrain and surface features.

Since the previous Surveyors had completed the Apollo landing site survey, Surveyor 7 was targeted at the scientifically interesting rock-strewn ejecta blanket of the ray crater Tycho. Launched on January 7, 1968, the Surveyor 7 spacecraft landed less than two kilometers from its target on January 10, 1968. During the first lunar day, 21,046 pictures of the lunar surface were acquired, but the alpha backscatter package failed to deploy. The surface sampler arm was programmed from Earth to force the package into position and subsequently to move it to two additional sites. Laser beams from Earth were also detected by the television camera during a test. Forty-five more photographs and additional surface chemical data were obtained during the second lunar day of operation, before the spacecraft was deactivated on February 21, 1968.

Having met all the Apollo survey objectives, follow-on Block 2 missions were canceled because of budget constraints, and the Surveyor Project Office at JPL was closed on June 28, 1968.

## Knowledge Gained

The surface sampler arms on Surveyors 3 and 7 made measurements of how much weight the lunar surface soil could bear before being penetrated as well as how depth affected the bearing capacity and shear strength in trenches up to twenty centimeters deep. The strength and density of individual lunar rocks were also determined. Strain gauges on the shock absorbers determined the loads on the legs of the spacecraft during the touchdown on the lunar surface. The radar reflectivity and dielectric constant of the lunar surface material were determined by the landing radar system. Thermal sensors determined the surface temperatures, thermal inertia, and directional infrared emission at all five landing sites.

At the mare landing sites, firings of the vernier rocket engines on Surveyors 3, 5, and 6 and the attitude control rockets on Surveyors 1 and 6 against the lunar surface provided information on the permeability of the surface to gases, the cohesion of the soil, its response to gas erosion, and its adhesion to spacecraft surfaces.

The alpha backscattering experiments on Surveyors 5, 6, and 7 determined the abundances of the major chemical elements from carbon to iron on six surface samples and one subsurface sample at two mare sites and one highland site. These analyses indicated that the most abundant element of the lunar surface is oxygen (57 atomic percent, or 57 atoms per 100 representative atoms), followed by silicon (20 atomic percent), and aluminum (7 atomic percent). These are the same elements, and in the same order, that are most common in Earth's crust. The major chemical elements at the mare sites are generally similar to those found in terrestrial basaltic rocks. The similarity to basalts, as well as the morphology of the surface features determined from the Lunar Orbiter images, provides strong circumstantial evidence that some melting and chemical separation of the lunar material had occurred in the past. This surface composition is significantly different from primordial solar system material. It is also different from most known meteorites, indicating that the Moon is not a major source of the meteorites which hit Earth.

The magnets carried on Surveyors 5, 6, and 7 provided information on the magnetic particles at two mare sites and one highland site. The single highland site showed a lower abundance of iron and other chemically similar elements, demonstrating that the lunar surface is not homogeneous. These chemical differences were suggested as an explanation for the difference in "albedo," or surface reflectivity, between the highland and mare regions.

The five successful Surveyor spacecraft returned 87,700 television pictures of the lunar surface, Earth, the solar corona, Mercury, Venus, Jupiter, and stars to the sixth magnitude. The lunar surface images provided information on the size-frequency distribution of lunar craters ranging from a few centimeters to tens of meters in diameter. The observed distribution was consistent with the distribution predicted to be produced by prolonged bombardment by meteorites, and allowed the size distribution of the incoming meteoroids to be inferred.

Two and a half years after its landing, Surveyor 3 was visited by the Apollo 12 astronauts, who returned the video camera, some camera cable, aluminum tubing, and a glass filter to Earth. These Surveyor samples were analyzed to determine the extent of lunar weathering, micrometeorite impacts, and ion bombardment from the Sun.

## Context

Although the Soviet Union's Luna 9 spacecraft preceded Surveyor in soft-landing on the Moon, the Surveyors provided the first quantitative data on the bearing strength of the lunar soil, its radar reflectivity, and the variations in the lunar surface temperature. The Surveyors also demonstrated the existence of loose dust on the Moon.

Prior to Surveyor 1, the photographs of the lunar surface having the best resolution were taken by the Luna 9 spacecraft. Surveyor supplemented these with photographs from five additional sites, including one in the lunar highlands. A comparison of the highland surface at the Surveyor 7 landing site with that at the mare sites showed fewer craters larger than eight meters in diameter at the highland site, indicating that the Tycho rim material on which Surveyor 7 landed was much younger than the mare material. This provided a relative chronology for the Moon's different regions.

The computer-controlled soft landings of the Surveyor spacecraft on the Moon verified the soft-landing techniques planned for the Apollo lunar landing missions. Four of the Surveyors landed in potential Apollo landing regions and determined that the lunar surface was sufficiently strong to support the footpad loads planned for the Apollo spacecraft. They also provided information on the surface roughness and topography necessary for the Apollo flights.

## Bibliography

French, Bevan M. *The Moon Book*. New York: Penguin Books, 1977. Describes the explanations for the origin of the Earth-Moon system and places the contribution of the Surveyor program into the context of the entire lunar exploration program. Includes a thorough description and illustration on the alpha backscattering experiment and its results. Suitable for general audiences.

Hibbs, Albert R. "The Surface of the Moon." *Scientific American* 216 (March, 1967): 60-74. A well-illustrated article describing the results from the first nine spacecraft, including Surveyor 1, which provided close-up photographs of the lunar surface. Describes the various theories for the origin of the Moon in the context of scientific knowledge as it existed immediately after the landing of Surveyor 1.

Newell, Homer E. "Surveyor: Candid Camera on the Moon." *National Geographic* 130 (October, 1966): 578-592. A comprehensive collection of early Surveyor photographs and a description of the preliminary scientific interpretations of the video data.

Scott, Ronald F. "The Feel of the Moon." *Scientific American* 217 (November, 1967): 34-43. The principal investigator for the soil mechanics surface sampler describes the Surveyor spacecraft, emphasizing the sampler arm and the experiments to determine the strength of the lunar surface. Includes Surveyor images of the lunar surface and diagrams of the spacecraft and the sampler arm.

_____ . "Report on the Surveyor Project." *Journal of Geophysical Research* 72 (January 15, 1967): 771-856. In this series of articles, the scientists who participated in the Surveyor program report their original data and interpretations. Contains descriptions of the Surveyor instruments and a detailed account of the scientific results.

_____ . *Surveyor Program Results*. NASA SP-184. Washington, D.C.: Government Printing Office, 1969. This official program overview includes introductory articles summarizing each Surveyor mission and describing the principal scientific results. These are followed by individual articles on the imaging, surface mechanical and electrical properties, and temperatures experiments, and the chemical analysis. Document also contains a list of the program participants.

*George J. Flynn*

## Cross-References

The Apollo Program, 28; Apollo 12, 83; Cape Canaveral and the Kennedy Space Center, 229; The Jet Propulsion Laboratory, 662; U.S. Launch Vehicles, 749; The Luna Program, 764; The Luna Landings, 779; The Lunar Landscape, 809; The Lunar Orbiter, 816; Lunar Soil Samples, 823; The National Aeronautics and Space Administration, 1032; Space Centers and Launch Sites in the United States, 1599.

# NATIONAL TELECOMMUNICATIONS
# SATELLITE SYSTEMS

*Date:* Beginning November, 1972
*Type of satellite:* Communications
*Countries:* Australia, Brazil, Canada, China, Indonesia, Japan, Mexico, Thailand, and ESA countries

*National satellite systems allow countries to provide education, data relay, and telecommunications services to remote or sparsely populated areas and have reduced small nations' reliance on the space technology of the superpowers.*

## Summary of the Satellites

Among the most promising applications for space technology are satellite-based communications links. In the early 1960's, shortly after the rush to space began, large and small nations alike recognized satellites' ability to relay communications from even the most remote and inhospitable site to anywhere in the world, instantaneously. It is no wonder, then, that many nations began to plan for the time when they could operate their own satellite communications systems without having to rely on those controlled by the United States, the Soviet Union, and a handful of other nations. In 1964, a small group of nations became charter members of Intelsat, the International Telecommunications Satellite Corporation. Intelsat was originally managed by COMSAT, a U.S. government agency formed to oversee commercial exploitation of space technology developed by the National Aeronautics and Space Administration (NASA) and other agencies. During the 1970's and 1980's, individual nations began to develop and deploy satellites of their own to provide a variety of services.

The first nation to build its own domestic communications satellite system was Canada. The Canadian Telesat Corporation, a telephone and television conglomerate, launched Anik A1 in November of 1972, Anik A2 in April, 1973, Anik A3 in May, 1975, and Anik B1 in December, 1978. Since then, Anik C's and D's have been developed to provide telephone, data, and broadcast services to isolated regions of Canada into the twenty-first century.

Brazil has also emerged as a space nation with its Brazilsat system of communications satellites. Brazilsat 1 and 2 are used to connect the remote Amazon region with the more populous southern sector of the country, providing telephone, television, and data services.

In June, 1985, Mexico launched Morelos, its own telecommunications satellite. The first satellite to work simultaneously in both the C band and Ku band, Morelos has been able to satisfy all the demand for communications channels in Mexico from its geosynchronous orbit (an orbit with a twenty-four-hour period) above the equator. Built by Hughes Aircraft, it has twelve active and two redundant channels with a bandwidth of 36 megahertz in the C ba●d, and four active and two redundant channels in the Ku band. Morelos weighs 666 kilograms, and has a projected life span of almost ten years.

A second Morelos satellite was launched during the summer of 1986. Morelos 2 was scheduled to be activated in the early 1990's, when the first Morelos would begin to fail or when demand for channel access would outstrip the first satellite's supply of channels.

In Europe, some of the earliest communications satellites led the way to later generations of more powerful craft with greater capacity. France and West Germany collaborated on the development of the first successful European communications satellites, Symphonie 1 and Symphonie 2, which led to the European Communications Satellite (ECS). ECS was based on a design that had evolved from preoperational testing done on the European Orbital Test Satellite (OTS), launched in 1978.

France has played a major role in the development and deployment of communications satellites. A French space contractor, Aerospatiale, was contracted to build TDF-1, the country's first direct broadcast satellite, scheduled for launch during 1988. TDF-1 and West Germany's TV-SAT 1, also a direct broadcast satellite, were scheduled to be placed in geosynchronous orbit at longitude 19° west to provide service to 400 million households. Each satellite was equipped to broadcast five programs. France signed a contract for the construction of TDF-2 in 1987. The French Telecom satellite, launched in 1984, provides telecommunications circuits to the European community.

During the mid-1980's, Sweden committed itself to the development of Tele-X, a communications satellite that would provide direct broadcasting service to several Scandinavian countries, along with data and video circuits for business communications in that region. The project was developed under the direction of the Swedish Board for Space Activities (SBSA). No newcomer to space, Sweden had already launched Viking, its first satellite, in 1986. Viking, a scientific satellite, was designed to study the upper reaches of the atmosphere and to provide a low-cost alternative to other scientific satellites of its era.

Italsat, Italy's first telecommunications satellite, was to be launched in the early 1990's. Italsat was designed to provide twelve thousand telephone channels at a cost of $300 million. Italy planned to launch additional satellites during the early 1990's: Lageos 2, a geodesy satellite, and an astronomy satellite named SAX. The country's first military telecommunications satellite was scheduled for a 1994 launch.

In Asia, China has begun providing communications via the STW series of satellites. STW-4 was launched successfully during the spring of 1988 aboard the Chinese Long March 3 rocket. China is also developing two new launch vehicles, the CZ-3A and the CZ-4, to compete in the commercial space launch market.

Japan's NHK (Japan Broadcasting) and National Space Development Agency (NASDA) and the Telecommunications Satellite of Japan teamed up to provide broadcast service on the BS-2A satellite, launched in 1984, and the BS-2B, launched in 1986. In 1988, a BS-3 series was in development. Two transponders on the BS-2A failed immediately after the satellite was deployed, prompting NASDA to offer incentives to the BS-3 contractors to make sure all systems were functional.

Japan has also been active in other communications satellite programs. Its Sakura satellites entered a third series with the launch of Sakura 3b on September 16, 1988. Sakura 3b is the first satellite to be powered by a gallium arsenide battery, which is expected to give it a seven-year operating life, two years longer than the life spans of Sakura 2a and 2b. Sakura 3b is used by fourteen private and public organizations for communications and data relaying.

Australia entered the space era with the Australian Satellite System (Aussat), designed to provide long-distance education services. One program developed for the system is Schools of the Air (SOTA), which broadcasts programming nationwide for students at primary, secondary, and university levels. Aussat also provides video conferencing and information network links among schools and other institutions throughout Australia. Aussat has made the Australian communications infrastructure more reliable.

Indonesia has also exploited satellite technology to link remote and inaccessible regions of the country. A nation of thousands of islands where traditional telecommunications systems cannot be deployed efficiently, Indonesia became one of the first third-world nations to orbit a satellite when, in 1976, it launched Palapa A1. Since that time, four more Palapa satellites have been orbited.

In 1984, Palapa B2 was stranded in a useless orbit when a propulsion unit failed to fire. A U.S. space shuttle mission later retrieved it and returned it to Earth where it was refurbished in preparation for a 1990 launch. Indonesia has planned a C series of communications satellites to replace the B series; the C series is designed to be more powerful and to have a greater capacity for telecommunications and television transmission.

## Knowledge Gained

Satellites are an efficient solution to communications problems faced by countries that contain inaccessible, inhospitable, or sparsely populated areas difficult to reach by traditional means. Indonesia, for example, with its thousands of islands, was unable to provide efficient and convenient telephone service until Palapa 1 was orbited, allowing that Pacific rim nation to link the entire country for the first time. Canada, with its hundreds of thousands of square miles and a relatively small population, was also able to link the far eastern region of the country with the far western region. The same conditions exist in parts of the Middle East, served by Arabsat, a communications satellite that links several Arab nations.

Aside from meeting the basic need for communication among individuals, communications satellite systems provide opportunities for national educational programs like Aussat's Schools of the Air. By setting up special receiving sites in remote locations, the governments of many nations have been able to distribute information on subjects of all kinds, from agriculture to birth control to zoology.

Satellites have increased the number of telephone circuits and broadcast channels available internationally. The result has been more convenient, efficient, and economical communication among nations and their peoples. Indeed, this technology has had a dramatic effect on the relationships among nations and their governments.

Satellites have also improved the quality of electronic communications. Direct satellite-to-home broadcasts provide high-quality signal reception to all users, whether in urban or remote locations, and avoid the electromagnetic interference and range limitations common to terrestrial broadcasts. Increasingly powerful satellites with large channel capacities are capable of transmitting high-definition television signals that require a larger bandwidth than is available in the television broadcast frequency spectrum as allocated by the World Administrative Radio Conference.

Satellites often provide coverage beyond national boundaries, and that has stimulated political concerns in some quarters. Although satellite systems are highly efficient and economical, the availability of foreign programming to households in small, third-world countries, for example, is seen by some as a threat to cultural identity. Nevertheless, national communications satellite systems have also significantly reduced small nations' reliance on the space technology of larger nations, thereby internationalizing opportunities for exploitation of space for the public good.

## Context

The first effort to internationalize space for communications applications came in 1964 with the formation of Intelsat, the International Telecommunications Satellite Corporation. Although Intelsat has continued to grow and now provides more than one hundred nations around the world with satellite communications service, during its first decade the organization was operated almost exclusively by the United States through its semiprivate commercial space agency, COMSAT. From the start, member and nonmember nations alike voiced concerns about the substantial control over the system granted to the United States as a result of its leading funding and operational role. Intelsat's purpose was to provide access to satellite communications for any nation, regardless of its politics, size, or location, yet the major space powers dominated the industry. Shortly after Intelsat was formed, the Soviet Union proposed Intersputnik, an international communications satellite system that would compete with Intelsat.

Intersputnik never became the large organization that Intelsat did, but smaller nations began to recognize that the spectrum of frequencies for space communications was limited and that those nations not planning to put their own satellites into orbit ran the risk of being left out. Indeed, the United States and the Soviet Union may eventually use up all the geostationary satellite positions.

Many nations began to develop their own systems to ensure domestic control over vital communications facilities and to meet their own particular needs. Since all communications satellites that relay to stationary receiving stations must be in geosynchronous orbit above the equator, a satellite's location along that plane is critical to the quality of a satellite signal. In the early years, satellite positions were available on a first-come, first-served basis to those nations able to build and launch a satellite. Eventually, an international conference was held to negotiate an allocation arrangement that would suit the needs of all nations, not just the United States and the Soviet Union. That conference and others like it created expanded interest in satellite technology among many nations, the results of which are discussed above.

After the explosion of the space shuttle *Challenger* in January, 1986, the U.S. space program ground to a halt temporarily, allowing the emerging space programs of some smaller countries to gain a foothold among satellite users looking for launch opportunities. Among the nations that have offered launch services are France, China, and Brazil, each of which has an impressive list of successful satellite launches of domestic and foreign space hardware. As those programs develop and are joined by others, the exploitation of space for communications and science will continue to become internationalized.

## Bibliography

Anderson, Frank W., Jr. *Orders of Magnitude: A History of NACA and NASA, 1915-1980.* 2d ed. NASA SP-4403. Washington, D.C.: Government Printing Office, 1981. An illustrated history of the U.S. space program, written for the layperson. A small volume, it takes a broad approach with a focus on the political climate that prevailed during the height of the space program. Particular emphasis is placed on the manned programs, but Intelsat is described in the context of the exploitation of space science that proved beneficial to large segments of Earth's population. Included is a discussion of the events that led to what is described as "the new space program." Contains a bibliography and index.

Hirsch, Richard, and Joseph John Trento. *The National Aeronautics and Space Administration.* New York: Praeger Publishers, 1973. Describes the agency, its organization, its programs, and its relationship to other government agencies. Contains an interesting account of the relationship between NASA and the press during the most active years of the manned lunar exploration program. Also gives an early account of COMSAT's plans to launch satellites on the space shuttle as a way of cutting costs. Appendices include information—perhaps dated—on obtaining employment with NASA and a particulary useful list of U.S. and Soviet manned spaceflights launched between 1961 and 1971.

Ley, Willy. *Events in Space.* New York: David McKay Co., 1969. Contains summaries of all satellite programs, national and international, that were carried out during the 1960's. Particularly useful is a series of tables and glossaries that define space jargon and describe many of the decade's satellites and rockets. Also included are lists of satellite launches, complete with launch dates and other information on the satellites and the programs with which they were associated.

National Aeronautics and Space Administration. *NASA 1958-1983: Remembered Images.* NASA EP-200. Washington, D.C.: Government Printing Office, 1983. Traces various programs of the space agency from its beginnings. Included is a chapter on space sciences and another on Earth orbit applications, including communications. Illustrated with color photographs.

Paul, Günter. *The Satellite Spin-Off: The Achievements of Space Flight.* Translated by Alan Lacy and Barbara Lacy. Washington, D.C.: Robert B. Luce, 1975. A survey of the commercial scientific and communications applications that developed from the space research of the 1960's and early 1970's. Contains a comprehensive account of the early, politically charged days of Intelsat. This book is written from the perspective of the European community, which makes it necessary reading for those desiring a broader understanding of Intelsat than might be available from U.S. sources. In addition to communications applications, space medicine, meteorology, cartography, agriculture, and oceanography are discussed.

Shelton, William. *American Space Exploration: The First Decade.* Boston: Little, Brown and Co., 1967. Another historical account of the space program, with comprehensive listings of every American spaceflight launched between 1957 and 1967.

Sobel, Lester A., ed. *Space: From Sputnik to Gemini.* New York: Facts on File, 1965. A chronological history of international space activities up to the manned Gemini series. Does not feature Intelsat, but describes the technology that led to the first commercial communications satellites and describes in detail the launch of Early Bird (Intelsat 1).

Twentieth Century Fund. *Communicating by Satellite: Report of the Twentieth Century Fund Task Force on International Satellite Communications.* New York: Author, 1969. Contains a comprehensive and detailed history of the development of Intelsat and the issues that were being debated during the organization's early years. Describes COMSAT and the International Telecommunications Union and the roles each played in the early development of the commercial satellite system concept. Also presents ethical issues relevant to the development of such systems and suggestions for the equitable distribution, utilization, and management of the satellite frequencies spectrum.

*Michael S. Ameigh*

## Cross-References

# MARITIME TELECOMMUNICATIONS SATELLITES

*Date:* Beginning February 19, 1976
*Type of satellite:* Communications
*Countries:* The United States, the United Kingdom, Norway, Japan, the Soviet Union, and Canada

*A network of satellites designed to upgrade the communications capabilities of commercial and military maritime vessels was first proposed in 1972. In 1979, the International Maritime Satellite Organization was formed to create such a network. By 1985, the forty-three-nation consortium was using nine satellites to serve more than 3,200 vessels.*

## Summary of the Satellites

In 1972 a subgroup of the United Nations, the Intergovernmental Maritime Consultative Organization (IMCO), expressed an interest in using satellites in space for maritime purposes. IMCO represented the concerns of seafaring nations in areas such as distress systems, navigations and position determination, and operation of maritime mobile services. The tremendous growth of the international maritime industry after World War II indicated a serious need for improved communication methods. The American Institute of Shipping echoed this concern when it estimated that by 1980, the number of vessels on the high seas weighing more than 1.5 million kilograms could exceed fourteen thousand at any one time. Vessels were still using the inefficient "brass key" radiotelegraph method for their ship-to-shore communications.

In a report to the U.N. secretariat, IMCO proposed a satellite system that would allow the exchange of telegraph, telephone, and facsimile messages and improve navigation for maritime interests. A panel was formed to study the legal, financial, technical, and operational problems involved in creating an entity that would be responsible for such a system. An international convention was held in April and May of 1975, and delegates and observers from forty-five nations and fifteen international agencies attended. The conference concluded that an international organization was needed to administer a worldwide maritime satellite system, and by the end of the first session, the United States and thirteen other countries had agreed on the major elements of a system that would eventually be known as the International Maritime Satellite Organization (INMARSAT). It would be patterned after the International Telecommunications Satellite Organization (Intelsat), with some modifications for its unique maritime interests. INMARSAT would provide global telecommunications services for maritime commercial activities and safety.

After four years of study and debate, INMARSAT was formally chartered on July 16, 1979, in London. The organization comprised forty-three nation members, including the United States, Great Britain, Norway, Japan, the Soviet Union, and

Canada. The system was scheduled to become operational by the early 1980's.

Between 1976 and 1979, maritime communications were enhanced through the U.S. maritime satellite (Marisat) system. The Marisat system consisted of three satellites built by Hughes Aircraft Company for the Communications Satellite Corporation (COMSAT). Launched in 1976, the satellites formed the first maritime communications system in the world. The Marisats provided rapid, high-quality communications between ships at sea and home offices; they greatly improved communications of distress, safety, search and rescue, and weather reports.

All three Marisats were structurally identical. At lift-off they weighed 655 kilograms and were approximately 231 centimeters long with their antennae. A panel containing seven thousand solar cells supplied the craft with primary power. A "Straight-Eight" Delta rocket launched the satellites from Cape Canaveral, Florida, into geostationary orbits, wherein they would travel around Earth once every twenty-four hours. The payloads consisted of three ultrahigh frequency (UHF) bands, reserved for U.S. government use, and L-band and C-band channels. The latter were kept entirely separate from the UHF channels and were used to translate ship-to-shore signals. Each Marisat had a life expectancy of five years.

Marisat-A was launched on February 19, 1976, and was renamed Marisat 1 when it became operational over the equator at longitude 5° west. It served maritime traffic in the Atlantic. Marisat-B, later Marisat 2, was launched on June 9, 1976, and became operational in July. It served the major shipping lanes of the Pacific Ocean and covered a 120-million-square-mile area. It was stationed slightly west of Hawaii at longitude 176.5° west. On October 14, 1976, Marisat-C, the final satellite in the Marisat system, was launched. It was stationed over the Indian Ocean at longitude 73° east and was renamed Marisat 3 when it became operational. Initially, it served only the U.S. Navy, but it also acted as an in-orbit backup for Marisats 1 and 2.

Although the U.S. Maritime Administration and the U.S. Navy were early users of the Marisat system, the Marisats' main function was to provide communications services to ships of all nations. The satellites were owned by COMSAT, and the company reimbursed NASA for all administrative and launch costs.

Commercial satellite service to shipping continued to develop and expand during this period. Eight thousand ships were expected eventually to be equipped with satellite communications terminals. On February 15, 1979, the United States signed the convention on INMARSAT, in accordance with the International Maritime Communications Act of 1978. That summer, the existence of INMARSAT became official.

INMARSAT was to become operational by the early 1980's. It was expected to rely heavily on Intelsat 5 spacecraft for its first generation of satellites. Eventually, the system included the three U.S. Marisats, two Marecs leased from the European Space Agency (ESA), and four Intelsat 5's leased from COMSAT. All the craft were placed in geostationary orbits over the Atlantic, Pacific, and Indian Oceans.

Development of the Marecs portion of the INMARSAT system began in 1973 under the auspices of ESA. Initial funding came from Belgium, France, Italy, the

United Kingdom, Spain, and West Germany. Later, the Netherlands, Norway, and Sweden joined in the effort.

The Marecs satellite consisted of a service module, a derivative of the European Communications Satellite design, and a payload module. The payload contained a C-band to L-band forward transponder and an L-band to C-band return transponder incorporating a search and rescue (SAR) channel. The system was capable of operating without continuous ground control.

Marecs 1 was launched December 20, 1981, from the French Guiana polygon by an Ariane rocket; it was sent into a geostationary equatorial orbit at longitude 26° west. Marecs 2 was lost at launch because of the failure of the Ariane rocket. Its replacement, Marecs B2, was launched from the French Guiana complex on November 10, 1985; it orbited at longitude 177° east. The Marecs satellites had a life expectancy of seven years. The estimated cost of the Marecs program was $359.8 million.

Four Intelsat 5 satellites made up the remainder of the INMARSAT configuration. Each had a box-shaped housing and payload support system with a pair of winglike solar arrays. The three-axis stabilized satellites weighed about 1,950 kilograms at launch and about 860 kilograms in orbit. They were capable of being launched by the Atlas-Centaur rocket, the NASA space shuttle, and ESA's Ariane rocket. Ford Aerospace and Communications was the prime contractor for the Intelsat 5 series. The satellites were launched from 1980 through 1984 and had an expected life span of seven years.

The INMARSAT system has greatly improved communications between ships at sea and their land-based offices. There are more than 3,700 users of the system, and INMARSAT reports that new stations are being activated at the rate of about forty per week. More than 32,000 vessels of all types from about sixty nations receive navigation and communications services from the INMARSAT system. The largest users are the United States, Great Britain, Norway, Japan, the Soviet Union, and Canada.

Each INMARSAT user organization purchases its own terminal for installation on a ship or at a remote site. The INMARSAT charter is limited to providing services to users in the "marine environment," which includes ships, offshore oil rigs, Arctic research stations, and some remote inland temporary construction sites. There have been discussions, however, of expanding the charter to include aeronautics users.

## Knowledge Gained

INMARSAT has proved that the use of space-based satellites to enhance marine communications is both economically and technologically sound. Shipboard antennae link ships' telephone systems via INMARSAT satellites to coastal stations. Users can route their calls through any of the coastal stations within range of their transmissions. These Earth terminals are provided by the individual member countries; INMARSAT purchases or leases only the space-based portion of the system.

Although the agency does not provide the land-based stations for its members, it does control and monitor the specifications for the equipment at these stations. It therefore pays for technical consultancy services for its members. The need for these services is determined by the organization's monitoring commitments, which fluctuate. Purchasing the services allows INMARSAT to maintain its standards without the need for a large staff of employees.

The international agency is run along strictly commercial lines. There are no requirements as to the work share of each member nation and countries other than members can sell their goods or services to INMARSAT if they meet the specifications and have the best price.

INMARSAT also spends about $1 million a year on research and development programs. One program, planned to become operational in 1989 or 1990, is designed to install a distress beacon on every ship. The beacon could be activated automatically or by a crew member. It would report the ship's location and details to rescue agencies on shore rather than at sea. It has been shown that shore-based rescue operations are better equipped to respond quickly and effectively to a maritime emergency than are other vessels at sea.

There are already approximately 3,200 ships equipped with emergency pointing/ indicating radio beacon (EPIRB) systems, and this number is expected to increase dramatically by the time the system is fully operational. INMARSAT sees the program as a business venture; it will not purchase the EPIRBs but will assist in providing the technical specifications for the systems.

INMARSAT is also exploring the possibility of entering the television transmission and medical assistance fields. It is investigating a narrow-band video transmission system that would transmit a high-quality picture. INMARSAT has had some successes in a procedure whereby medical diagnosis is conducted from a remote location via television cameras and the INMARSAT system.

INMARSAT also conducts market research on future technical needs. One area of focus is the expansion of its technological services to include telex, computer links, remote control, automated reporting, and high-speed data transmissions.

The agency has also considered entering the aeronautical field, initially by providing air-to-ground communications. A change in the original charter that would permit INMARSAT to provide aeronautical and other nonmaritime services is being considered, since much of the technology developed by the agency can be applied to other fields.

## Context

When Arthur C. Clarke, British scientist and science fiction writer, suggested in a technical paper published in 1945 that communications satellites were feasible, the Soviet launching of Sputnik 1 was still twelve years in the future. It would be fifteen years before the National Aeronautics and Space Administration (NASA) launched Echo, the silvery balloon that orbited Earth every 118 minutes and reflected radio signals back to the surface. Echo was a passive satellite, but two years later NASA launched Relay, an active satellite that received signals, amplified them, and returned them to Earth.

With the launches of the early satellites in the late 1950's, many scientists and industry leaders recognized the potential for practical applications of the space program, especially in the area of communications. Even before any formal effort was made to utilize space technology, maritime interests were beginning to reap the benefits of satellite technology. The orbiting spacecraft were providing weather forecasts, storm tracking data, and information on iceberg locations with a degree of accuracy never before possible.

By the early 1960's, private companies were producing their own communications satellites, and in 1962 Congress authorized the Communications Satellite Corporation. COMSAT later became the U.S. representative in and manager of the International Telecommunications Satellite Corporation (Intelsat). As the satellites' ability to transmit voice, picture, and computer data grew, maritime interests began to investigate the possibility of using these technologies to improve and expand the outdated radiotelegraph technology that still handled most ship-to-shore communications on the high seas.

INMARSAT, the maritime equivalent of Intelsat, was formally chartered in 1979 after four years of study by a large group of nations and international maritime agencies. The space-based maritime communications system was dedicated to developing and implementing the latest in satellite and communications technology to enhance the worldwide marine communications network and to ensure the safety and efficiency of the international maritime industry. In the future, INMARSAT plans to expand its original charter to include aeronautical activities, services to remote land stations, improved rescue systems and devices, and long-distance medical diagnosis services.

## Bibliography

Caprara, Giovanni. *The Complete Encyclopedia of Space Satellites*. New York: Portland House, 1986. This volume presents short entries on both civil and military satellites of all nations. The book includes line drawings and an index. Suitable for general audiences.

Executive Office of the President. National Aeronautics and Space Council. *Aeronautics and Space Report of the President: 1979 Activities*. Washington, D.C.: Government Printing Office, 1979. A compilation in textbook format of all space-related activities carried on during 1979. Some technical data presented in general terms.

_____ . *Aeronautics and Space Report of the President: 1983 Activities*. Washington, D.C.: Government Printing Office, 1983. This book has the same format as the one above, but the information is for 1983. Suitable for general audiences.

Gregory, William H., ed. "Inmarsat." *Commercial Space* 1 (Summer, 1985): 55-57. This is an article in a quarterly publication that focuses on the commercial applications of space technology. The magazine contains about a dozen articles per issue and includes high-quality color photographs. Suitable for general audiences.

National Aeronautics and Space Administration. *NASA: The First Twenty-five Years*. NASA EP-182. Washington, D.C.: Government Printing Office, 1983. A brief chronological and topical history of NASA and the U.S. space program during its first twenty-five years, this book is designed for classroom teachers and features charts, graphs, drawings, color photographs, and suggested classroom activities. Topics include tracking and data-relay systems, space applications, aeronautics, and manned and unmanned missions. Suitable for general audiences.

Ritchie, Eleanor H. *Astronautics and Aeronautics 1976: A Chronology*. NASA SP-4021. Washington, D.C.: NASA, Scientific and Technical Information Branch, 1984. A compilation of U.S. space activities during the year 1976, this book presents technical information clearly for a general audience.

Rosenthal, Alfred, ed. *Satellite Handbook: A Record of NASA Space Missions 1958-1980*. Washington, D.C.: Government Printing Office, 1983. Brief summaries and documentation of all NASA manned and unmanned space missions undertaken between 1958 and 1980. Technical data on each mission includes descriptions of the spacecraft and launch vehicle, the payload, the mission's purpose, project results, and major participants. Suitable for a general audience.

Sherman, Madeline, ed. *TRW Spacelog: Twenty-fifth Anniversary of Space Exploration, 1957-1982*. Redondo Beach, Calif.: TRW, 1983. This is a booklet in magazine format that focuses on international space-related activities and programs. Contains brief summaries of various topics. Suitable for a general audience.

U.S. Congress. Office of Technology Assessment. *Civilian Space Policy and Applications*. OTA-STI-177. Washington, D.C.: Government Printing Office, 1982. An official publication that discusses the different policies and agencies that make use of space technology and applications. Contains technical material.

*Lulynne Streeter*

## Cross-References

The European Space Agency, 372; European Space Agency Satellites, 379; The Intelsat Communications Satellites, 613; The National Aeronautics and Space Administration, 1032; International Private Industry and Space Exploration, 1182; U.S. Private Industry and Space Exploration, 1187; U.S. Private and Commercial Telecommunications Satellites, 1997; U.S. Passive Relay Telecommunications Satellites, 2009.

# U.S. PRIVATE AND COMMERCIAL
# TELECOMMUNICATIONS SATELLITES

*Date:* Beginning August 12, 1960
*Type of satellite:* Communications
*Country:* The United States

*Since the early 1960's, communications satellites have been designed and built by private corporations to serve the needs of their customers. These commercial ventures in space have contributed to U.S. technological developments.*

Principal personages
RONALD REAGAN, the U.S. president who legalized a partial
    privatization of space for U.S. industry
HOWARD HUGHES, the corporate initiator of the Syncom satellite
    series
JOSEPH CHARTYK, a president of COMSAT
DEAN BURCH, Director General, Intelsat
GERARD K. O'NEILL, head of Geostar Corporation

## Summary of the Satellites

The satellite communications industry was born shortly after the first satellite was placed in orbit in the late 1960's. The usefulness of communications via satellite was obvious: An orbiting satellite's altitude allows it to transmit signals over very long distances; ground-based transmissions are limited by Earth's curvature. Since the microwaves that make up radio, television, and telephone signals travel in a straight line, ground relay stations must be placed about every 55 kilometers to compensate. Before satellites came into use, therefore, worldwide communications costs were prohibitive.

Scientists experimented with two types of communications satellites: the passive reflector and the active repeater. The passive reflector is typified by Echo 1, a "balloon" satellite, whose large surface was used to reflect radio signals from the ground. This sort of satellite had two advantages: Any transmitter could bounce a signal of any frequency off the reflective surface, and there were no parts to malfunction. The disadvantage was that the received signal was extremely weak. The first Echo was launched on August 12, 1960, and was useful for a little more than four months.

In 1962 the Telstar and Relay satellites were launched. These were active repeaters which received transmissions from ground stations, amplified them, and relayed them back to Earth. Telstar was designed and built by Bell Telephone Laboratories, and Relay was built by RCA. The early satellites were placed in relatively low orbits and moved rapidly across the sky, requiring elaborate tracking.

Telstar could handle one television channel, the equivalent of six hundred one-way voice channels. Because the satellite's signal was weak even after amplification, the ground station was located in the shelter of a ring of low mountains to reduce radio interference. A horn-shaped antenna with an opening 1,100 meters wide was used to focus the signal, which even then reached only a billionth of a watt.

Besides their usefulness as experimental communications satellites, Telstar and Relay also were important as probes of the space environment. They carried instruments which collected data on the Van Allen radiation belts, regions that encircle Earth and contain radioactive particles. The belts' existence was inferred from data returned by the first orbiting satellite, Sputnik.

Syncom, built by Hughes Aircraft for NASA, represented the next generation of communications satellites. Launched in 1963, it was placed in an orbit with a twenty-four-hour period and therefore matched Earth's rotation. Syncom was the first "geosynchronous" satellite. The main advantage of a geosynchronous satellite is that ground control is greatly simplified. Because the satellite remains over one area of Earth's surface, expensive and complex tracking equipment is unnecessary. The satellite is accessible to any ground station within its line of sight. A geosynchronous satellite must be placed directly over the equator to maintain its position relative to the surface; complex firings of gas jets are required to maneuver it into position. From its high altitude of about 35,900 kilometers, a geosynchronous satellite can transmit signals to nearly a third of Earth's surface. With a network of three such satellites, communications service can be provided to all populated areas of Earth. Although Syncom 1 failed and the network was not completed at that time, Syncom was the first step toward a global communications system.

Three Syncoms were launched. The first was lost when a high-pressure nitrogen bottle aboard the satellite burst. Syncom 2 was successful, and it set new records in long-distance communication. Syncom 3 transmitted the first television program (a relay of the Olympic Games in Tokyo) ever to span the Pacific via a geosynchronous satellite. Syncoms 2 and 3 remained in service until 1969.

The successes of Relay, Telstar, and particularly Syncom clearly demonstrated that communications satellites were moving away from experimental projects and toward commercial ventures. In 1963, the Communications Satellite Corporation (COMSAT) was created as a private company that would develop satellite systems. Half the corporation's stock was to go to the public; the other half, to large communications companies. COMSAT is part of Intelsat, the International Telecommunications Satellite Corporation, which was set up to provide a global communications network. COMSAT's first commercial satellite was Early Bird, launched in 1965. Early Bird relied heavily on technology from the Syncom satellites. This and other early commercial satellites demonstrated the feasibility of using geosynchronous satellites for commercial communications.

Private users of the satellites were communications common carriers, broadcasters, news wire services, newspapers, airlines, computer services companies, and television companies. At first, the satellites were used simply to receive television signals or telephone communications and relay them to one or several ground stations. It was foreseen that multipurpose satellites would eventually be built to serve the needs of various customers.

Early users of communications satellites would lease the services from one of a very few satellite owners. As the industry expanded, some large businesses began to own and operate their own satellites and lease excess capabilities to smaller businesses. Satellite capacity grew rapidly with new satellite technology. Satellites with multiple transponders (devices which, when triggered by a signal, transmit another signal at the same frequency) set at different frequencies began to support many customers simultaneously. In the mid-1960's, companies began building basic "production line" satellites; customers could choose one and then refine it to meet specific needs.

Western Union developed the first U.S. domestic satellite communications system. Westars 1 and 2 were launched in April and October of 1974, and Westar 3 was launched in August, 1979. Companies wishing to operate domestic satellite systems must obtain permission from the U.S. Federal Communications Commission (FCC), and Western Union was one of the first such companies to be licensed. The Westars were designed to relay voice, video, and data communications to the continental United States, Alaska, Hawaii, and Puerto Rico. The satellite can handle twelve color television channels or seven thousand two-way voice circuits simultaneously. The new generation of Westars—Westars 4, 5, and 6—were deployed by 1982 and had twice the capacity of the earlier satellites. They could also relay signals to the U.S. Virgin Islands.

Another domestic communications system, Satcom, was placed in orbit by RCA beginning in 1975. Satcom was the first satellite system devoted to relaying signals to cable television installations in the United States.

A third domestic communications satellite system was launched in 1976. Comstar is a telephone satellite system for long-distance calling throughout the United States; it was designed to handle increasing domestic telephone usage. Each Comstar satellite can relay more than eighteen thousand calls simultaneously. Four satellites were launched, and two were still operational in 1988. They are leased jointly by the American Telegraph and Telephone Company and GTE Satellite Corporation, a subsidiary of General Telephone and Electronics. In the early 1980's, AT&T launched a new series of Telstar satellites: Telstars 301, 302, and 303.

In March, 1981, Satellite Business Systems (SBS) began to offer satellite services for private business communications to large U.S. companies. The third SBS satellite to be deployed was the first commercial satellite launched by the U.S. space shuttle.

Although Hughes Aircraft had been designing and building satellites for other customers since the early 1960's, it was not until 1983 that it began launching the Galaxy series, owned by Hughes Communications. The Galaxy series was dedicated to the distribution of cable television programming. Hughes offered cable programmers the opportunity to buy, rather than lease, transponders on the satellite.

## Knowledge Gained

The major gains in knowledge made possible by private communications satellites have stemmed from advances in satellite technology and from the increased ease and speed of global and domestic communications.

The first satellites provided valuable information about the environment of Earth orbit. Technology improved almost immediately as the first satellites reported on the new conditions. Solar cells on Telstar 1 were damaged by radiation in the Van Allen belts, and satellite manufacturers learned new ways of compensating for radiation. Telstar 1 also returned valuable scientific data on the Van Allen belts as it passed through them. The densities and energies of free protons and electrons were measured, and the temperature and pressure within the satellite was recorded.

In 1959, an engineer working for Hughes Aircraft developed a satellite design that revolutionized the communications industry. Tiny rocket boosters were incorporated into the satellite to position it in a geosynchronous orbit. The rockets' periodic thrusts stabilize the satellite and orient it so that its communications antenna continually aims at Earth's surface. Hughes also developed spin-stabilized satellites. Spin-stabilization previously had been used to improve rockets' accuracy.

New technology was devised for the Comstars' antenna arrangement. A vertically polarized and a horizontally polarized antenna were used. Polarization changes the form in which signals are received and sent without changing the frequency, which allows the capacity of the system to be doubled.

Another Hughes development is the shaped beam. The microwave beam transmitted by the satellite is shaped to the contours of the receiving area, allowing a more concentrated and powerful transmission. Along with the new technology, the improvement of existing technology has allowed for increasingly longer satellite lifetimes and increased power output.

In 1981, the space shuttle began to be used for launching commercial satellites. Cargo space in the payload bay is limited, so satellite designs were modified with telescoping solar panels and folding antennae. Starting from a stowed size of about three meters high by two meters wide, a satellite can expand to the height of a two-story building when deployed in orbit.

Communications satellites function as channels for information. Knowledge must be distributed to be effective. It would be difficult to gauge the spread of knowledge that has resulted from improved communications. Satellites have helped bring a variety of educational programs to persons who were previously beyond the reach of educational systems. Engineering and technological programs are broadcast instantaneously to universities across the country, and businesses use satellites to provide training seminars for their employees.

## Context

The development of a country is related to its ability to communicate quickly and efficiently. Satellite communications have brought about a huge increase in the ability to transmit information economically and quickly. The transition from ground-based telecommunications to satellite telecommunications took place in less than twenty years. This growth is still taking place, not only in technologically advanced countries such as the United States, but all over the world. Many underdeveloped countries are using satellite systems to unite remote regions of the country. They are finding that the cost of employing satellite systems is far less than the cost of installing land-based relay stations. Educational systems can be improved and can compensate for teacher shortages.

Satellite usage primarily involves telephone and television transmission, but as the industry expands and costs become less prohibitive, new satellite uses evolve. Satellites regularly provide such services as computer-to-computer digital communications, video conferencing, monetary fund transfers, and air traffic control. Technology is being developed for mobile communications, and businesses are using satellite systems to handle electronic mail and data transfer.

The U.S. commercial satellite industry has been affected by unreliable launch systems. Because the shuttle program was suspended after the 1986 *Challenger* disaster and the revitalized program was slow to accelerate, satellite users were forced to use other, conventional launch systems. Some of those have proved unreliable, and several multimillion-dollar satellites have been lost. Insurance costs increase dramatically as the risk associated with a launch increases, and orders for new satellites slow as launch capability lessens. Many companies have looked to European launch facilities for reliable and timely deployment of satellites.

Some companies have argued that the federal government has not offered enough support to commercial space ventures. In the late 1980's, government support began to grow along with the perception that the United States was falling behind the rest of the world in the utilization of space. One way to increase a nation's space use is through the mobilization of the private sector.

Debris in space is also a growing problem. Hundreds of satellites are in geosynchronous orbit and satellite overcrowding is possible. For many applications, there are only a few suitable locations for signal transmission. Furthermore, satellites which are less than two degrees apart in orbit risk radio frequency interference.

Despite problems, the communications satellite industry has grown. Further technological developments may lead to communications satellites that can transmit power, rather than information, to Earth. It is conceivable that by 2025, one hundred power satellites could meet 30 percent of the United States' electrical needs.

There are four planets in the solar system with ring systems surrounding them. The deployment of geosynchronous satellites may produce a fifth. Earth's "ring system," however, would not be composed of dust, rocks, or ice, but of thousands of artificial satellites.

## Bibliography

*Aviation Week and Space Technology* 120 (June 25, 1984). This entire volume is devoted to prospects for the commercial use of space. It contains a series of authoritative articles that are readily understandable by laymen.

Braun, Wernher von, et al. *History of Rocketry and Space Travel*. New York: Thomas Y. Crowell, 1966. Reviews the entire history of spaceflight from the beginning of the concept to the sending of humans into space and to the Moon. Fully illustrated and easily understood.

Goldman, Nathan C. *Space Commerce: Free Enterprise on the High Frontier*. Cambridge, Mass.: Ballinger Publishing Co., 1985. Written for nonspecialists, this book provides a useful review of American commercial space enterprises. It is both synthetic and specific. Charts, tables, and a few photographs augment the text. Contains six appendices and an index.

Ordway, Frederick I., III, Carsbie C. Adams, and Mitchell R. Sharpe. *Dividends from Space*. New York: Thomas Y. Crowell, 1971. Explores the benefits to mankind that have directly resulted from the space program. Discusses products developed for mass consumption and advances in medicine, industry, research, and the study of Earth. Sparsely illustrated. Written for general audiences with an interest in space technology.

Paul, Günter. *The Satellite Spin-Off: The Achievements of Space Flight*. Translated by Alan Lacy and Barbara Lacy. Washington, D.C.: Robert B. Luce, 1975. A survey of the commercial scientific and communications applications that developed from the space research of the 1960's and early 1970's. Contains a comprehensive account of the early, politically charged days of Intelsat. This book is written from the perspective of the European community, and it is necessary reading for those desiring a broader understanding of Intelsat than might be available from the U.S. point of view.

Porter, Richard W. *The Versatile Satellite*. New York: Oxford University Press, 1977. This short book provides a fine introduction to the various uses of satellites. Chapter 4 deals with communications satellites.

Schwarz, Michiel, and Paul Stares, eds. *The Exploitation of Space: Policy Trends in the Military and Commercial Uses of Outer Space*. London: Butterworth and Co., 1986. Consists of highly readable and informed articles written by scholars but intended for laymen. Well illustrated. Notes and references conclude each article.

*Divonna Ogier*

## Cross-References

# SOVIET TELECOMMUNICATIONS SATELLITES

*Date:* Beginning April 23, 1965
*Type of satellite:* Communications
*Country:* The Soviet Union

*The successful orbiting of the first Molniya 1 on April 23, 1965, inaugurated Soviet communications satellite operations. The Molniya series of satellites, which traveled in highly elliptical orbits, were followed by geosynchronous satellites and a pair of low-orbiting Kosmos communications satellite networks. Amateur radio satellites, military satellites, and data-relay satellites were also developed.*

*Principal personages*
> N. D. PSURTEV, Soviet Minister of Communications, a Molniya
> program spokesperson
> I. V. KLOKOV, Soviet Deputy Minister of Communications, a
> Molniya program spokesperson
> W. HILTON and
> S. DAUNCEY, British space scientists who proposed the inclined
> twelve-hour elliptical orbit for the Molniya satellites

## Summary of the Satellites

Soviet communications satellite systems may be grouped into three separate families by the nature of their orbits. One family, the oldest and most successful, employs highly elliptical orbits. The second family is composed of two separate groups of satellites in low orbits; these are primarily used for military communications. The satellites in the last family travel in geosynchronous equatorial orbits.

The first Soviet communications satellites, those in the Molniya series, were placed in highly elliptical orbits between 400 and 40,000 kilometers above Earth. Their apogees were over the Soviet Union, and they remained accessible to Earth stations some eight hours daily. These satellites were said to be synchronous because their orbits took them over the same part of Earth every three hours, minimizing tracking operations. Eight such satellites with paths 45 degrees apart guaranteed continuous access to satellite communications throughout the Soviet Union. The weight of the satellites, which have an average lifetime of about two years, ranged from 1,750 to 1,800 kilograms.

Three series of satellites have been used in the Molniya program. The first satellite of the Molniya 1 series, Molniya 1-1, was launched April 23, 1965, by an A-2 rocket from Baikonur. Its orbit ranged from 538 to 39,300 kilometers and was inclined 65.5 degrees to the equator. Subsequent flights used the improved A-2e booster rocket, and, following the July 22, 1969, launch of Molniya 1-12, satellites in the series were orbited from Plesetsk. Molniya 1 satellites were tapered cylinders 1.6 meters in diameter and 3.4 meters in height; six solar planels and two

0.9-meter parabolic antennae extended from the base of the satellites, which carried 40-watt transmitters and television cameras used to monitor cloud cover. Seventy Molniya 1 satellites had been orbited by the end of 1986; there were no Molniya 1 missions in 1987.

The first Molniya 2 was launched on November 24, 1971. The satellites in this series had extensions attached to their six solar panels, extending their surface area by one-third and their generated power to 1,000 watts. Higher-frequency transmissions expanded the capabilities of the satellites, which were used to construct a Washington, D.C.-Moscow hot line. The series apparently ended with Molniya 2-17 on February 11, 1977.

Molniya 3-1 was placed in orbit on November 21, 1974. Satellites in this third series measured 0.8 meter longer than the Molniya 1 version and carried improved control systems. Like its predecessors, the satellites in the Molniya 3 series were stabilized on three axes. By 1988, thirty-one of these improved satellites had been orbited.

Two separate groups of military communications satellites, bearing numbers in the Kosmos series, were launched from Plesetsk aboard C1 launch vehicles into relatively low orbits inclined 74 degrees to the equator. The first group followed circular paths some 800 kilometers high; two sets of three satellites, weighing between 750 and 1,000 kilograms each and located on orbital planes 120 degrees apart, made up this system of satellites believed to be used for data relay. Satellites fitting this profile date at least to Kosmos 407 in April, 1971, and may trace back even further. Recent members of this group include Kosmos 1814, Kosmos 1850, and Kosmos 1898, all launched in 1987 roughly five months apart. They performed for an average of fourteen months before requiring replacement.

The second group of military communications satellites also followed circular paths, but at an altitude of almost 1,500 kilometers, where twenty-four satellites traveling in the same plane are required. Deployment of the satellites, believed to have weighed between 40 and 50 kilograms each, was in sets of eight aboard a single booster. The first eight-satellite launch, presumably part of this system, took place on April 25, 1970 (Kosmos 336 to Kosmos 343); subsequent eight-satellite sets were deployed on May 7, 1971 (Kosmos 411 to Kosmos 418), October 13, 1971 (Kosmos 444 to Kosmos 451), July 20, 1972 (Kosmos 504 to Kosmos 511), and November 1, 1972 (Kosmos 528 to Kosmos 535)—with some two or three sets launched yearly thereafter. Soviet low-altitude communications operations may have begun as early as July 16, 1965, with Kosmos 71 through 75 and subsequent sets of five Kosmos satellites launched on single C1 boosters from Plesetsk into somewhat lower orbits of 500 to 600 kilometers inclined only 56 degrees to the equator, according to American government officials.

Soviet utilization of geosynchronous orbit was slow in coming. Significant rocket power is required to achieve an equatorial orbit from the high latitudes of Soviet launch sites; thus a significant sacrifice in payload capability was necessary. No single geosynchronous satellite could simultaneously serve the vast east-west expanse of Soviet territory, and from the northernmost areas satellite in the geosynchronous belt would essentially be on the horizon. For these reasons, the Molniya system provided significant advantages for Soviet telecommunications needs.

The first Soviet flight to geosynchronous orbit was made by the 2,000-kilogram Kosmos 637 on March 26, 1974, from Baikonur aboard a D-1e Proton rocket. Two additional geosynchronous test flights, by Molniya 1S in 1974 and Kosmos 775 (probably not a communications satellite) in October, 1975, preceded operational flights by three types of satellites: Raduga (1975), Ekran (1976), and Gorizont (1978).

Raduga 1 was orbited on December 22, 1975, and weighed 5,000 kilograms, although later versions weighed closer to 2,000 kilograms. Twenty-one satellites in the series were orbited by 1988, primarily for telephone, telegraph, television, and newspaper page transmissions to remote areas of the Soviet Union.

Ekran satellites, primarily for television signals, began service on October 26, 1976. Weighing 2,000 kilograms, the satellites were cylindrical and measured 5 meters by 2 meters; a large rectangular antenna was mounted at the base and was outfitted with ninety-six helicoid elements. The 200 watts of power provided by two solar panels mounted on the sides was sufficient to allow reception by relatively simple and inexpensive receivers used by either small communities or individuals. By 1988, seventeen Ekran satellites had been launched, and more than three thousand receiving stations were in operation.

Gorizont satellites began flights on December 19, 1978, with a highly elliptical orbit inclined 14.3 degrees to the equator. Gorizont 2, launched on July 5, 1979, and subsequent satellites were geosynchronous. Fourteen Gorizont satellites, weighing some 2,000 kilograms each, had been orbited by 1988 as part of the Moskva domestic television relay system and the Intersputnik international telecommunications operation, the Soviet equivalent of Europe's International Telecommunications Satellite Corporation (Intelsat). Gorizont 7, part of the Washington, D.C.-Moscow backup hot line, was made available to American users through accords with Intelsat.

In addition to these three major families of communications satellites, the Soviet Union also operates an active program of data-relay satellites under the Kosmos name; two members of this group, Kosmos 1700 (1985) and Kosmos 1897 (1987), were launched into geosynchronous orbits. Satellites built by and for amateur radio enthusiasts have also been orbited by the Soviet Union under the names Radio (1978) and Iskra (1981); these were launched either piggyback, on rockets carrying other satellites, or by cosmonauts aboard the Salyut 7 space station.

## Knowledge Gained

Communications satellite systems introduced an entirely new technology to the world and initiated a revolution in education, entertainment, news, and information dissemination. The international nature of communications satellites, and their potential to influence both politics and business on a scale not previously known led to the establishment in the West of private national and international corporations charged with regulating satellite communications systems from construction to operation. While Soviet communications satellite development has provided little opportunity for commercial and business interactions, most scientific and technological advances brought by the resulting networks are put to use by Soviet industry.

Launch vehicles employed for communications satellite flights had been developed for other space missions. The unique demands placed on Soviet vehicles to achieve multiple-satellite launch and deployment for the families of low-orbiting communications satellites, and the maneuvers necessary to achieve geostationary equatorial orbits from launch sites above 45 degrees north latitude, posed a challenge to Soviet engineers and technicians.

Design technology was further enhanced by the construction of the satellites themselves. Knowledge obtained from the Molniya 1 series led to improved attitude control systems and expanded solar panel surface areas for the Molniya 2 and Molniya 3 satellites. The later families of geosynchronous satellites also benefited from experience gained in the construction and operation of their predecessors.

Linked directly to the establishment of communications satellite systems was the technology required for the associated ground stations necessary for relaying satellite communications. The Orbita/Orbita 2 Earth stations, numbering about one hundred and equipped with 12-meter rotating parabolic antennae, provided the major support for early Soviet communications satellite systems. Experience gained from the operation of these stations led to the development of new satellite components capable of sending signals to inexpensive receivers, receivers which could be made available to people far removed from major centers of population. The result was the Ekran geosynchronous television satellite and the distribution of more than six thousand Ekran receivers throughout Siberia which provide television reception quality equal to that enjoyed by people in major Soviet cities. The Moskva satellite television broadcasting distribution network was also established, primarily to transmit television programming to remote areas of the Soviet Union. In addition to telephone, radio, and television signals, the Soviet telecommunication system also transmitted newspaper pages directly to printing houses, allowing for more rapid dissemination of news to remote areas.

The development of an extensive communications satellite system has had a significant impact on Soviet technology and the lives of Soviet citizens. The system has begun the monumental task of unifying the people of a nation that stretches over more than half the globe and embraces more than a quarter billion people who speak some fifty different languages.

## Context

The Soviet Union was late entering the field of satellite telecommunications and was initially reluctant to participate in international cooperative ventures. The first U.S. active communications satellite, Project Score (December, 1958), was followed by the passive relay telecommunications balloon Echo 1 and military active-repeater Courier 1B—both launched in 1960. The 1962 launch of Telstar 1 inaugurated transatlantic television broadcasting, and two years later, the United States placed the first communications satellite into geosynchronous orbit.

By the time the Soviets launched their first Molniya, fourteen American communications satellites had been placed in orbit, two in geosynchronous orbit and three others designed exclusively for use by amateur radio enthusiasts. In addition, the private Communications Satellite Corporation (COMSAT) had been set up in the United States to oversee the orbiting of satellites for international communications, and European interests had formed Intelsat. Early Soviet interest in communications satellite technology centered on concerns that such systems could be used for propaganda purposes by other nations or by private businesses and could serve to promote United States strategic and political aims at the expense of the Soviet government. Nevertheless, the first joint U.S.-Soviet cooperative space program was conducted with the U.S. Echo 2 passive balloon satellite in 1964 (primarily involving tracking), and one-way limited communications experiments were carried out between Great Britain and the Soviet Union using Echo 2, which the Soviet press came to refer to as the "friendly Sputnik."

Concerns with the international implications of global satellite communications did not prevent Soviet space scientists from recognizing the importance of a nationwide network. The Soviets established an extensive domestic system capable of uniting the vast expanse of Soviet Asia and the diverse cultural heritages of its population with the Russian heartland. Linking the nations of the Socialist community into an international network independent of Western influences became another major objective for the Soviet communications satellite program.

Far from rejecting the prospects of future competition with Western communications satellite ventures, the Soviets boasted about the low cost to consumers of their own satellites over U.S. systems, both for television and telephone communication, almost immediately after Molniya began operations. Nevertheless, little real competition with Western commercial satellite organizations was evident from the Soviet systems as the 1980's drew to a close, and there would continue to be two largely independent communications satellite operations, one Western and one Soviet, with only limited interaction between the two.

## Bibliography

Caprara, Giovanni. *The Complete Encyclopedia of Space Satellites*. New York: Portland House, 1986. This lavishly illustrated volume describes the world's civil and military satellites, from the first Sputnik in 1957 to spacecraft launched in the mid-1980's. Line drawings as well as photographs of most satellites and their launch vehicles make this book an invaluable resource for the space enthusiast. Satellites are grouped by mission rather than in chronological order of launch date, making comparisons of national and international programs a simple task. A forty-page chapter is devoted to telecommunications satellites.

Johnson, Nicholas L. *Soviet Space Programs: 1980-1985*. San Diego: Univelt, 1987. This volume provides detailed analyses of both manned and unmanned Soviet space operations during a five-year period which saw the orbiting of two hundred communications satellites. Eighteen pages of the volume are devoted exclusively to Soviet communications satellite operations and include diagrams showing placement of Soviet geosynchronous satellites and illustrations of the various satellites in operation.

Shkolenko, Yuri. *The Space Age*. Moscow: Progress Publishers, 1987. The author's somewhat whimsical look at the impact of space exploration is rife with political connotations. It touches briefly on the uses and abuses of communications satellite technology from a Soviet perspective. This translation has some flaws but does convey a sense of the Soviets' view of humankind's future in space.

*The Soviet Year in Space: 1987*. Colorado Springs, Colo.: Teledyne Brown Engineering, 1988. Updated annually, this review of Soviet space activities contains an eleven-page section devoted to the year's communications satellites. Includes tables of planned geosynchronous satellites.

U.S. Congress. Senate. Committee on Aeronautical and Space Sciences. *Soviet Space Programs, 1962-1965: Goals and Purposes, Achievements, Plans, and International Implications*. Washington, D.C.: Government Printing Office, 1966. An extensive document of more than nine hundred pages. Covers the period of the first Soviet communications satellite and includes useful background information on Soviet attitudes toward U.S. and international satellite telecommunications activities.

*Richard A. Sweetsir*

## Cross-References

# U.S. PASSIVE RELAY
## TELECOMMUNICATIONS SATELLITES

*Date:* August 12, 1960, to June 7, 1969
*Type of satellite:* Communications
*Country:* The United States

*The United States' Echo satellite project included the first passive relay communications satellite launched into space and the first cooperative space venture between the United States and the Soviet Union. The satellites were inflated Mylar balloons that bounced radio signals between ground stations on Earth.*

Principal personages
WILLIAM J. O'SULLIVAN, JR., an aeronautical engineer at the
National Advisory Committee for Aeronautics
JOHN R. PIERCE, a researcher at Bell Telephone Laboratories

## Summary of the Satellites

The Echo passive relay communications satellite project was the first practical application of space technology in the field of telecommunications. The satellites were aluminum-coated Mylar spheres that were inflated in space. The concept was simple. The spheres passively reflected electromagnetic radio waves directed to them from a ground-based station at one location on Earth to a ground-based station at another location. They also provided information about the density of the upper atmosphere.

Echo was the first communications satellite project of the National Aeronautics and Space Administration (NASA). It was rooted in an earlier project conceived by William J. O'Sullivan, Jr., an aeronautical engineer at the Langley Aeronautics Laboratory, which was part of NASA's predecessor, the National Advisory Committee for Aeronautics (NACA). In 1956, O'Sullivan proposed that studies to measure Earth's atmosphere during the International Geophysical Year (IGY)—a period of intense scientific research set for July, 1957, to December, 1958—could be conducted more efficiently by using a low-density inflatable sphere that could be tracked optically. John R. Pierce of Bell Telephone Laboratories had proposed a similarly designed balloon in a 1955 article entitled "Orbital Radio Relays," but Pierce had wanted to use the orbiting inflatable spheres as reflectors for radio signals.

Several attempts to launch O'Sullivan's balloon with IGY payloads failed when the launch vehicles malfunctioned. Pierce proposed a cooperative communications experiment using O'Sullivan's inflatable spheres. According to O'Sullivan, it was a logical next step to consider using the balloons for communications purposes. In 1958, NACA's director, Hugh L. Dryden, told the U.S. Congress that the technology to orbit such a passive communications satellite existed—but certain design changes had to be made. It would be necessary to increase the size of the air-density balloon to provide a larger surface from which to bounce signals, and the surface would also have to be treated to increase its reflective capacities.

By 1959, the IGY project had become the newly formed NASA's passive communications satellite project. It was designated Project Echo. Technicians at NASA's Langley Research Center had three major requirements as they began designing a passive communications satellite that would inflate in orbit into a perfectly smooth-surfaced sphere: They needed a suitable material for the sphere, an inflation system, and a canister in which to launch the collapsed balloon.

It was decided that the balloon would be made from an aluminized polyester film manufactured by E. I. Dupont. Known as Mylar, the material was 0.5 millimeter thick. Another company cemented the Mylar into eighty-two flat gores that formed the Echo sphere. Benzoic acid was chosen as the inflating agent because it could change from a solid state to a gaseous state without going through the liquid stage. A spherical metal canister impregnated with plastic would carry the deflated balloon into space.

In October, 1959, the first test model was assembled and readied for testing. On the fourth attempt, in April, 1960, the balloon satellite was successfully inflated at an altitude of 375 kilometers. On May 13, 1960, a three-stage Thor-Delta rocket launched Echo A-10. During the vehicle's coast period, the attitude control jets on the second stage failed. The vehicle reentered the atmosphere and decomposed.

Three months later, on August 12, 1960, the world's first passive communications satellite was successfully launched from Cape Canaveral, Florida. Echo 1 was placed into space by a Thor-Delta three-stage rocket at an inclination of 47.28 degrees to the equator. The satellite measured 30.5 meters in diameter and weighed 76 kilograms. The inflatable portion was packed in a magnesium sphere and was released about two minutes after injection into orbit. In addition to the balloon, which was designed to transmit images, music, and voice signals from one side of the United States to the other, Echo carried two small radio beacons that assisted in locating and tracking the satellite. The beacons were mounted on small disks and attached to the balloon.

A pretaped message by President Dwight D. Eisenhower was the first voice signal to be bounced off Echo. It traveled from NASA's facility at Goldstone, California, to Bell Telephone's station at Holmdel, New Jersey. The first known two-way voice communication was bounced off Echo 1 on August 13, 1960, between Cedar Rapids, Iowa, and Richardson, Texas. The first reported image transmission via Echo 1 occurred on August 19, 1960, again between Cedar Rapids and Richardson.

For the next four months, Echo 1 was utilized by Bell Telephone Laboratories in New Jersey and the Jet Propulsion Laboratory in California. Eventually, micrometeoroids damaged the balloon's sensitive "skin," and its orbit was affected by solar winds. Yet it continued to reflect a variety of communications signals to and from Earth at ground stations all over the world. Echo 1 reentered Earth's atmosphere on May 24, 1968.

Echo 1 performed successfully, but it was apparent that some modifications of the design were necessary. In January of 1962, several suborbital tests of a modified Echo inflation system were conducted. Later that same year, plans were announced for the launch of two Echos to determine how smooth the surface area of an advanced Echo had to be. In December of 1962, the United States and the Soviet Union agreed to cooperate in the upcoming experiments planned for Echo.

Early in 1963, however, NASA officials announced that because of the formation of the Communications Satellite Corporation (COMSAT) and the Department of Defense's decision to cancel its Advent project, NASA would cancel its own plans for advanced passive and intermediate altitude communications satellite projects. In August, a private contractor was selected to build three second-generation Echos. This project was also eventually canceled.

On January 25, 1964, Echo 2 was launched from Vandenberg Air Force Base in California. Launched by a Thor-Agena B, the balloon was successfully placed in orbit at an inclination of 81.5 degrees. With a weight of 256 kilograms and a diameter of 41 meters, Echo 2 was somewhat larger than its predecessor. It was also more durable. The sphere was made up of 106 gores of Mylar, three layers thick, and bonded between two layers of a soft aluminum foil alloy. Its outer surface was coated with alodine, and its inner surface was coated with India ink. The improved satellite could maintain its rigidity for a longer period of time. Pyrazole crystals were used as the inflating agent. The crystals were positioned such that upon ejection from the canister into the sunlight they would gradually expand. It was estimated that with this method it would take about ninety minutes for the balloon to become fully inflated. That would permit higher pressures and produce a stronger structure and better reflecting power. Echo 2 also carried two beacon transmitters powered by solar cells and nickel-cadmium batteries.

Echo 2 had several objectives. It was to perform passive communications experiments with radio, telex, and facsimile signals, collect data concerning the spacecraft's orbital environment, and test the new inflation method. In addition, the Echo 2 spacecraft was used to conduct the first joint U.S.-Soviet space experiment, under the auspices of a 1962 cooperative space exploration experiment consisting of a communications link between stations at Jodrell Bank in Great Britain and the Zimenski Observatory at Gorki University, near Moscow. Echo 2 reentered Earth's atmosphere on June 7, 1969.

## Knowledge Gained

The Echo project proved that an inflatable sphere coated with aluminum to increase reflecting abilities could be successfully launched into space and placed into orbit. The balloon could be inflated in space and remain orbiting as it transmitted radio communications and images between distant points on Earth. It also provided a means of measuring such things as the density of the atmosphere. Echo 2 also carried out experiments on the pressure created by solar radiation. During both Echo missions the orbital parameters of the satellites underwent continual variation because of the pressure effects of solar radiation.

Passive relay communications satellites were soon replaced by more efficient and technologically advanced "active" communications satellites. The Echo satellites, however, did offer two advantages over the more sophisticated communications satellites which followed. They were extremely reliable, because of the simplicity of their design and the lack of electronic equipment, and they had multiple access capabilities.

## Context

Echo satellites constituted the first civilian telecommunications system set up in space. They were the beginning of a complex space-based communications network that could handle telephone, television, telex, facsimile, and radio signals. They represented the advent of communications systems that would eventually reach every portion of Earth, no matter how remote.

Passive communications satellites were not the most promising method of establishing space-based communications systems, and they were soon abandoned in favor of active systems. These active satellites were capable of receiving signals from Earth and then retransmitting them to another part of the planet. These satellites did not require the expensive ground-based stations necessary for the passive satellites.

Since it seemed clear that these so-called active-repeater satellites in synchronous orbits were more viable than the passive satellites for building a commercial communications system, NASA decided to direct its research to that area, and the agency abandoned further plans to upgrade the Echo project. In fact, Relay 1, an active-repeater satellite, was launched in 1962, two years before the flight of Echo 2.

At first, the use of space communications systems was an international effort through such organizations as the International Telecommunications Satellite Corporation (Intelsat), but soon more and more nations began launching their own satellites to reach remote areas. Such systems offer education, news, entertainment, and business and financial information to every citizen in possession of a receiver.

It is certain that as communications satellites become more advanced and efficient, their numbers will increase. It has even been suggested that widespread use will eventually result in overcrowding of frequencies and orbital positions. Yet whatever the future holds for communications satellites, the Echos, once visible to the naked eye as they traveled around Earth, are remembered as popular symbols of the peaceful and practical application of space research.

## Bibliography

Branigan, Thomas, ed. "Echo." *TRW Spacelog* 4, no. 2 (1964): 8-9. The magazine in which this article appears reports on and describes current international space research, development, and missions on a quarterly basis. This article features technical information, photographs, and charts. Written for a general audience.

Caprara, Giovanni. *The Complete Encyclopedia of Space Satellites*. New York:

Portland House, 1986. This volume contains a complete listing of every civilian and military satellite launched from 1957 to 1986. It contains color and black-and-white photographs, a bibliography, an index organized by country, a general index, and a table of contents. ·

National Aeronautics and Space Administration. *NASA: The First Twenty-five Years, 1958-1983*. NASA EP-182. Washington, D.C.: Government Printing Office, 1983. Designed for use by classroom teachers, this book features color photographs, charts, graphs, tables, and suggested activities. Topics include NASA history, programs, and missions.

Rosenthal, Alfred. *Satellite Handbook: A Record of NASA Space Missions, 1958-1980*. Greenbelt, Md.: Goddard Space Flight Center, 1981. This book contains detailed descriptions of major NASA satellite missions from 1958 to 1980. It includes a NASA launch record for those dates, a list of abbreviations and acronyms, an index, and photographs.

Van Nimmen, Jane, Leonard C. Bruno, and Richard L. Rosholt. *NASA Historical Date Book: 1958-1968*. NASA SP-4012. Springfield, Va.: National Technical Information Service, 1976. A complete history of NASA's programs and projects from 1958 to 1968. Contains much detailed information. Includes illustrations, charts, and tables.

Wells, Helen, et al., eds. *Origins of NASA Names*. Washington, D.C.: Government Printing Office, 1976. A brief report on the origins of NASA project names. Includes acronyms, abbreviations, and space terms. It also features the International Designation of Spacecraft, a list of major NASA launches from 1958 to 1974, reference notes, and an index.

*Lulynne Streeter*

## Cross-References

Amateur Radio Satellites, 14; U.S. and Soviet Cooperation in Space, 259; The Intelsat Communications Satellites, 613; Langley Research Center, 722; The National Aeronautics and Space Administration, 1032; International Private Industry and Space Exploration, 1182; U.S. Private Industry and Space Exploration, 1187; National Telecommunications Satellite Systems, 1985; U.S. Private and Commercial Telecommunications Satellites, 1997; Soviet Telecommunications Satellites, 2003.

# AIR AND SPACE TELESCOPES

*Type of technology:* Telescopes

*Telescopes, first invented in 1608, have undergone enormous diversification in the twentieth century, particularly as it has become possible to elevate them into and beyond Earth's atmosphere. They have played a vital role in the discovery and investigation of a wide variety of celestial bodies.*

### Principal personages

HANS LIPPERSHEY, the inventor of the telescope

GALILEO, the first person to use a telescope for study of the sky

SIR ISAAC NEWTON, the English physicist who made the first reflecting telescope

JOHANNES KEPLER, a German astronomer, the founder of modern optics

N. CASSEGRAIN, the inventor of the Cassegrain reflecting telescope

SIR WILLIAM HERSCHEL, the father of stellar astronomy

GEORGE ELLERY HALE, an astronomer who helped establish the Yerkes, Mount Wilson, and Mount Palomar observatories

ALVAN GRAHAM CLARK, the maker of many of the largest telescopes in the United States

GEORGE WILLIS RITCHEY, the director of photographic and telescopic research at the U.S. Naval Observatory

KARL AUGUST STEINHEIL, a German physicist

CHRISTIAAN HUYGENS, a Dutch astronomer, mathematician, and physicist

HEBER DOUST CURTIS, Director of the Observatory of the University of Michigan

## Summary of the Technology

Astronomy, one of the most ancient of sciences, was altered for all time by the invention of the telescope. The first such instrument was developed by Hans Lippershey of Middelburg, the Netherlands, in 1608; he discovered that a certain combination of concave and convex lenses worked to make distant objects seem nearer. Experimentation and refinement of technologies over the subsequent centuries made possible the proliferation of ground and space-based telescopes of the twentieth century.

Telescopes can be divided into two broad categories: optical telescopes and radio telescopes. Optical instruments collect light energy from a distant source and focus it into an image that can be studied by a number of different techniques. Those satelliteborne telescopes that are aimed at detecting celestial X rays or ultraviolet radiation are included in this category, since they operate according to the principles of geometrical optics. Radio telescopes are used in astronomical research to detect and measure radio waves coming from various parts of the Galaxy. These instruments consist of three complementary parts: a large reflecting surface that collects and focuses incident radiation, an electronic receiver that detects and amplifies cosmic radio signals, and a device which displays the information.

The diversity of modern telescope technology has its origins in the pioneering work of scientists such as Galileo, who in 1609 heard of Lippershey's "magic glass" and became fascinated with the idea of using it to study celestial bodies. The instrument that he developed consisted simply of a paper tube and a pair of appropriate lenses; it had the advantage of an erect image, but afforded only a small field of view. Johannes Kepler, Francesco Generini, and others experimented subsequently with variations on this design. Naturally, a principal goal was to increase the instrument's power, or magnification, which varies with the ratio of the focal length of the front (objective) lens to the focal length of the rear lens, or eyepiece. These early optical instruments, with two lenses centered on the same axis, are known as refracting telescopes.

In 1668, Sir Isaac Newton experimented with the use of a small, concave mirror in what became known as the reflecting telescope. Though his instrument was not particularly successful, its basic concept proved durable. The Frenchman N. Cassegrain produced a different type of reflecting instrument in 1672, with a convex mirror. These two types of reflectors, termed Newtonian and Cassegrain, remain in use in many large reflecting telescopes.

The simple, versatile Newtonian reflecting telescope is the most universally used type of telescope. It bends light rays by reflecting them from the surface of a concave mirror. Light from the object being viewed travels down the tube assembly and strikes the primary mirror; the light is then reflected toward a focal point that lies just outside the tube assembly. The focused rays are intercepted by a secondary diagonal mirror, which bends the rays at a ninety-degree angle to the incoming light. The light rays are then brought into contact with the eyepiece, which lies outside the tube plane. As a result of the bending of the light rays, the image is seen upside down, with some loss of light.

In the Cassegrain configuration, light is reflected by a hyperbolic mirror inserted in front of the prime focus, passes through a hole in a large parabolic mirror, and comes to a new focus on the back of the mirror. The Cassegrain telescope improved upon the Newtonian design through its use of a shorter focal length in its system. Its more compact formation requires a less massive mount for the same degree of stability. In addition, the eyepiece is placed more conveniently. Unfortunately, parabolizing the primary mirror to the required degree of accuracy is an expensive process.

Variations on these reflecting telescopes have been produced, each with its strengths and weaknesses. The Dall-Kirkham telescope uses an ellipsoidal primary mirror and a spherical secondary mirror. Its field of vision, however, is quite limited, and like the Cassegrain and Newtonian telescopes, it produces coma effects (a distortion in which points of light appear comet- or fan-shaped). The Ritchey-

Chrétien telescope uses a hyperboloidal primary mirror and an elliptical, convex secondary mirror. It reduces coma almost completely but suffers from astigmatism and a severe curvature of its field of vision. In general, because reflecting telescopes are not sealed, dust can accumulate on the mirrors; in addition, air turbulence within the tube can disrupt viewing.

Chromatic aberrations (false colors arising from the refraction of different wavelengths of light) are not a problem with reflecting telescopes, although low-expansion glass, which can resist the tendency of large mirror-surfaces to expand and contract differently in different areas, is a necessity. This type of telescope possesses considerable advantages in spectroscopic work and is particularly useful in the observation of faint objects, such as nebulae and galaxies.

Though for a time, with the success of reflecting-type telescopes their refracting counterparts became obsolete, eventual improvements in glass technology made possible a return to refracting instruments. By 1799, a Swiss craftsman had mastered the art of making flint glass that had the optical qualities required for refraction. Innumerable further refinements have led to the development of refracting telescopes that are mechanically simple, durable, and readily available.

The refracting telescope's closed-tube design eliminates the air currents that can degrade images. The objective lens is mounted at the far end of the apparatus; its diameter ranges from about 0.05 to 1 meter. This lens is focused on the image of a distant object, capturing light, which it then focuses onto a microscopic point. The eyepiece lens then concentrates that point of light onto the human eye. Refracting telescopes are especially useful for visual observations and astrometric measurements of stellar parallax and binary stars and for the visual and photographic determination of stellar positions.

The glass of the reflecting telescope's lens must be optically homogeneous and free of bubbles. The lenses require expensive material, and unless the correct combination of lenses and the proper focal length are used, chromatic aberrations arise. The flint lens of a refractor becomes increasingly opaque to wavelengths shorter than $4 \times 10^{-7}$ meter; it becomes useless in this spectral region.

Catadioptric telescopes, developed in the twentieth century, combine the best features of reflecting and refracting telescopes. These instruments have closed tubes, thus eliminating image-degrading currents and making the optics almost maintenance-free. These telescopes are portable and free of chromatic aberrations, and their additional optical elements allow users greater facility in correcting foci and surmounting the faults of the mirrors.

Various other telescopes have been developed for specialized functions. A heliostat, for example, is a telescope used to study the Sun; its flat moving mirror captures sunlight and feeds it to a fixed telescope with a stationary focal plane. A similar instrument used for observing stars is known as a siderostat. The zenith telescope has a fixed lens that points toward the zenith—that is, directly overhead. Incoming light is reflected from a mercury pool onto a photographic plate placed at the focus of the lens. Such telescopes are used for the precise determination of time.

Transit telescopes are refractors capable of moving in altitude but not in azimuth; they are particularly useful in making accurate observations of the stars as they cross the meridian. A chronograph is used to obtain photographs and film of the solar corona, even in daylight.

Despite all the refinements that increased the quality of the images produced by ground-based telescopes, astronomers realized that they suffered from an inherent limitation: the distortions produced by Earth's atmosphere. Earth's air absorbs essentially all ultraviolet radiation below a wavelength of $3 \times 10^{-7}$ meter, as well as much of the infrared spectrum between wavelengths of $1 \times 10^{-6}$ and $1 \times 10^{-3}$ meter. Moreover, the thermal currents in Earth's atmosphere deflect light and thus limit the sharpness of most Earth-based astronomical photographs.

It was a desire to observe the Sun that motivated early efforts to send telescopes into air and space. A balloonborne refractor sent aloft in 1956 and 1957 reached an altitude of between 6,096 and 7,620 meters and enabled astronomers from the University of Cambridge in England and the Meudon Observatory in France to obtain photographs of the granulation of the Sun.

Stratoscope 1, an American project, followed on the heels of the European refractor's launch. An unmanned balloon capable of lifting a payload of 635 kilograms to an altitude of 25,603.2 meters was designed. It carried a reflecting telescope that yielded an optical enlargement corresponding to an effective focal length of 60.96 meters. Several pairs of photodiodes acted as remote eyes to point the telescope toward the Sun's disk. A total of five flights of Stratoscope 1 were undertaken. The last flight furnished excellent photographs of solar granulation and sunspots, taken from an altitude of about 24,400 meters.

The success of these balloon experiments encouraged investigators to devise ways of observing other solar phenomena. Astronomers from Boulder, Colorado, organized the launch of the Coronascopes, special balloonborne telescopes whose purpose was to photograph the solar corona in full daylight. Coronascope 1 carried a small coronagraph with an aperture of 0.033 meter. It recorded images of the Sun automatically on a red-sensitive 0.035-meter spectroscopic film. Coronal streams between two and five times the solar radius from the Sun's center were detected.

Stratoscope 2 carried elaborate instruments to an altitude ranging from 21,641 to 25,603 meters. The first flight was on March 1, 1963; it was successful in obtaining measurements of a part of the infrared spectrum of Mars. Stratoscope 2's second flight took place on November 26, 1963; it returned images of the infrared spectra of about nine red stars and new data on Jupiter and the Moon.

Balloons could carry telescopes, however, only to the threshold of space. Further penetration into space required vehicles with greater lifting power. In response to this need, the first Orbiting Astronomical Observatory were launched into space on April 8, 1966. It carried eleven telescopes, four of which were coupled with ultraviolet vidicons to obtain maps of the sky. The other seven telescopes, in conjunction with two spectrometers and five photometers, were used to obtain spectral and energy distributions of numerous celestial objects.

A series of Orbiting Solar Observatories were launched beginning in 1962. These satellites were designed to return measurements of ultraviolet, X, and gamma radiation from the Sun. The Orbiting Geophysical Observatories, whose launches began in 1964, obtained measurements of radio noise and bursts of cosmic ray protons from the Sun.

Beginning in 1969, various probes—Mariners, Lunas, Voyagers, Rangers, Orbiters, Surveyors—were being launched in space with telescopes as standard equipment. Each craft carried a different type of telescope related to its function. By the late 1970's, these telescopes were being controlled by microcomputer.

With the May 14, 1973, launch of Skylab, a new era of space research began. Skylab carried eight separate solar telescopes on its Apollo Telescope Mount: two X-ray telescopes, an extreme ultraviolet spectroheliograph, an ultraviolet spectroheliometer, an ultraviolet spectrograph, a visible light coronagraph, and two hydrogen-alpha telescopes. These highly complex instruments gathered data on the Sun across the electromagnetic spectrum.

The first High-Energy Astronomical Observatory was launched on August 12, 1977; a series of such orbiting observatories were aimed at returning data on high-energy astrophysical processes. High-Energy Astronomical Observatory 2 carried the first X-ray telescope capable of providing focused images of X-ray objects in the sky.

In the meantime, scientists continued to find that telescopes mounted on aircraft could also return data of considerable value. The Kuiper Airborne Observatory C-141, for example, was mounted with a 0.90-meter telescope which was used to study the nature of extragalactic X-ray background radiation, distant quasi-stellar radio sources (quasars), X-ray sources in Galaxy M31, and X-ray emissions from other clusters of galaxies.

Certain Explorer satellites were designed to provide data on sources emitting ultraviolet radiation. The International Ultraviolet Explorer, an international venture undertaken by the National Aeronautics and Space Administration (NASA), Great Britain's Science Research Council, and the European Space Agency, was launched on January 26, 1978, into an eccentric geosynchronous orbit. It was mainly used to gather data on the transmission and absorption of radiation in the atmosphere of subluminous stars, in the interplanetary medium, and around other objects within the solar system.

The Infrared Astronomical Satellite, a cooperative project of NASA, the Netherlands, and Great Britain, carried a cryogenically cooled telescope system. It surveyed various celestial sources of infrared radiation.

The Solar Maximum Mission satellite, another telescope-bearing craft, was put into space to gather information on solar flares and the globular solar corona.

The first generation of orbiting telescopes—the Orbiting Solar Observatories, the Orbiting Geophysical Observatories, and the High-Energy Astronomical Observatory, for example—were automated telescopes revolving around Earth. Such telescopes function simply as search cameras or survey instruments. Eventually, plans were made for the design of manned orbiting telescopes, so that astronauts could go into space to do maintenance work on them; instruments could also be picked up by the space shuttle and returned to Earth for refurbishment and relaunch. After several years of study and refinement of the design principles, the Hubble Space Telescope became an approved NASA project. This high-resolution, 2.4-meter telescope was to be placed in orbit by June, 1989, as a joint venture of NASA and the European Space Agency. The Cassegrain telescope is accompanied by a high-resolution camera, a faint-object spectrograph, an infrared photometer, and guidance and protective equipment. The space telescope is designed to operate from wavelengths of 91.2 $\times$ $10^{-9}$ to about 1 $\times$ $10^{-3}$ meter—across the ultraviolet, optical, and infrared regions.

## Knowledge Gained

Almost all that is known regarding the Sun, the Moon, planets, stars, galaxies, and other celestial bodies has been gained with the aid of telescopes, ground-, air-, or space-based.

Galileo and other early telescope builders produced drawings of the sunspots that they observed, showing the presence of umbras (dark central regions) rimmed by penumbras (lighter areas). Scientists were able to observe and measure the sunspots' drifting motion across the Sun's face and thereby to show that the Sun rotates. Eventually, it was understood that the Sun goes through peaks (maxima) and valleys (minima) of sunspot activity in cycles of approximately eleven years. Telescopes carried by the Orbiting Solar Observatories, the Solar Maximum Mission satellite, and Skylab returned vital information regarding the sunspot cycle, coronal holes and loops, the solar wind, and much more.

With the help of his simple refractor, Galileo was able to observe the mountains and craters of the Moon's surface. He also discovered Jupiter's four large moons: Io, Europa, Ganymede, and Callisto. A dozen smaller Jovian satellites have been discovered. Jupiter's cloud belts have been found to be discontinuous and composed of a multitude of streamers and festoons. The 1955 discovery of radio waves being emitted from Jupiter led to the discovery of that planet's radiation belts. Mars's surface features, such as Syrtis Major and Mare Erythraeum, have been found to be discontinuous. That planet is known to be covered with volcanoes, canyons, and craters; Mercury, too, is highly cratered. Mercury and Venus were discovered to have unusual patterns of rotation. Telescopic examination has shown that Saturn has twelve concentric rings, as well as a red spot like that of Jupiter. Saturn also has some seventeen satellites of widely varying natures. Uranus, which was discovered by Sir William Herschel, has been found to possess only five moons. Rings have also been discovered around Uranus. Unexpected aspects of Uranus' orbital path led to the discovery of the planet Neptune, and distortions in Neptune's path in turn helped astronomers to locate tiny Pluto.

Halley's comet, whose periodicity was determined by Edmond Halley to be seventy-six years, has been studied telescopically during its three recurrences since

1758. Much has been learned about stars as well through the use of telescopes—for example, that there are many types of stars, including double, variable, and exploding stars. Quasi-stellar objects discovered in the 1950's with the aid of radio telescopes were dubbed quasars. Pulsars, celestial objects emitting rapid radio pulses, have also been discovered. With the aid of telescopic instruments, almost all the known galaxies, including the Milky Way, have been grouped into clusters. Large numbers of asteroids have also been discovered; most of them were found to move in solar orbits between the orbits of Mars and Jupiter.

Infrared emission from the planets has provided important information about the structure and evolution of planetary interiors. Various nebulae, such as the planetary nebulae, extragalactic objects, and some quasars, have been discovered to emit unexpectedly large amounts of infrared energy. Numerous quasars have been found to have a large redshift; thus, astronomers have discovered the rapid movement of those objects away from the Galaxy.

Radio observations of the interstellar medium have led to the discovery of complex molecules such as ammonia and formaldehyde, along with hydroxyl ions and water molecules.

## Context

The invention of the telescope provided mankind with a window on the universe. Subsequent refinements opened that window ever wider. Yet at the beginning of the twentieth century, much remained to be discovered. For example, knowledge of solar radiation extended only slightly beyond the visible-light spectrum, a range of $4 \times 10^{-7}$ to $7 \times 10^{-7}$ meter. Earth's atmosphere blocks out most of the shorter and longer wavelengths. Exotic, nonthermal radiations as well as the radiation emitted by very hot and very cold objects were beyond understanding.

Thus, the ability to raise telescopes into air and space led to a remarkable amplification of astronomers' knowledge of celestial bodies and their radiations. Observations of the planetary spectra by means of telescopes carried to Earth's stratosphere in jets, for example, are far superior to those obtained from ground-based facilities. In general, measurements obtained with Earth-orbiting telescopes are free from the interference from Earth's atmosphere. Deep space probes are able to carry telescopes even farther—and further open the window to knowledge of the universe.

## Bibliography

Brown, Sam. *All About Telescopes*. 5th ed. Barrington, N.J.: Edmund Scientific Co., 1981. This volume describes in detail the qualities of a good telescope and explains how to use a telescope and mount it for best viewing of the finer details of the sky. Suitable for high school and college-level students.

Fimmel, Richard O., James Van Allen, and Eric Burgess. *Pioneer: First to Jupiter, Saturn, and Beyond*. NASA SP-446. Washington, D.C.: Government Printing Office, 1980. This overview of the Pioneers' missions and data includes a brief introduction to telescopic study of the planets.

Kopal, Zdeněk. *Telescopes in Space*. London: Faber and Faber, 1968. This readable book covers the literature of the telescope. Illustrated.

Kuiper, Gerard P., and Barbara M. Middlehurst, eds. *Telescopes*. Vol. 1, *Stars and Stellar Systems*. Chicago: University of Chicago Press, 1960. This well-illustrated volume describes optical and radio telescopes and their accessories. There is a particular focus on the Hale telescope and the Lick Observatory.

Moore, Patrick, ed. *Astronomical Telescopes and Observatories for Amateurs*. New York: W. W. Norton and Co., 1973. This practical book for amateur astronomers contains detailed descriptions of many telescopes, along with illustrations.

Page, Thornton, and Lou Williams Page. *Sky and Telescope*. Vol. 1, *Wanderers in the Sky*, and vol. 4, *Telescopes*. New York: Macmillan, 1965-1966. Volume 1 describes various celestial bodies and defines key astronomical concepts. Volume 4, illustrated with more than 120 photographs, drawings, and diagrams, describes in detail the principles of telescope design and methods of fabrication. It also discusses some of the world's famous observatories and telescopes.

Pendray, Edward G. *Men, Mirrors, and Stars*. New York: Funk and Wagnalls, 1935. This history of the development of telescopes for space observation gives due recognition to the greatest names and foremost discoveries of astronomy.

Ronan, Colin A. *The Practical Astronomer*. New York: Macmillan, 1981. This book describes in detail the characteristics of the planets, their satellites, and other celestial objects. It is suitable for the general reader.

Sidgwick, J. B. *Observational Astronomy for Amateurs*. 4th ed. Hillside, N.J.: Enslow Publishers, 1982. This book presents observational techniques for various fields of amateur astronomy. It contains a vast amount of data collected by various deep space probes, suborbital vehicles, and ground-based facilities.

Traister, Robert J., and Susan E. Harris. *Astronomy and Telescopes: A Beginner's Handbook*. Blue Ridge Summit, Pa.: TAB Books, 1983. Traister and Harris survey optical telescopes, from the simple seventeenth century instruments to the most sophisticated telescopes of the 1980's.

*Raj Rani*
*Satya Pal*

### Cross-References

The High-Energy Astronomical Observatories, 589; The Infrared Astronomical Satellite, 602; The International Ultraviolet Explorer, 625; The Luna Program, 764; The New Astronomy and the Study of Electromagnetic Radiation, 1066; The Orbiting Astronomical Observatories, 1092; The Orbiting Geophysical Observatories, 1099; The Orbiting Solar Observatories, 1104; The Ranger Program, 1222; The Skylab Program, 1285; The Solar Maximum Mission, 1353; The Spacelab Program, 1884; The Surveyor Program, 1978; Ground-Based Telescopes, 2022.

# GROUND-BASED TELESCOPES

*Type of technology:* Telescopes

*Beginning in the 1960's, several large ground-based astronomical telescopes were built to be used, at least partly, as support instruments for the National Aeronautics and Space Administration's various space exploration missions.*

## Summary of the Technology

In the early 1950's, before space exploration became a reality, astronomers began preparing for it with a variety of ground-based programs using the world's principal optical and radio telescopes. In addition, plans were made to develop new telescopes specifically for the purpose of obtaining ground-based results to help with plans for space astronomy and to explore as much as possible from the ground objects that would be explored at greater expense from space. These activities helped to precipitate a dramatic increase in astronomical research, especially in certain branches of astronomy, such as solar system research and high-energy astrophysics.

Ground-based astronomy programs interacted with space exploration in its early days by helping to determine the atmospheric pressure of Mars. To plan a mission to Mars, especially one involving a lander, it was necessary to know at least the extent of its atmosphere. In the 1950's, the Martian atmosphere was known to be thin, and the best estimates, based on the intensity and polarization of Martian reflected light, indicated a surface pressure of 5 to 10 percent that on Earth. The makers of preliminary designs for Martian landers used this value when deciding whether a descent should be by balloon, glider, or downward-pointing rocket engine. Also, this much atmosphere suggested that Martian life might exist, as there would be enough air to breathe (if free oxygen were present) and enough protection from ultraviolet light and extreme temperature changes.

In the late 1950's, however, a University of California scientist, Hyron Spinrad, using ground-based telescopes, found evidence that the correct value might be very different. When he was able to obtain good high-dispersion spectra (photographs of the Martian light spread out into its various colors to allow identification of the gases in the atmosphere) with the Lick Observatory's 3-meter telescope in the early 1960's, he concluded that the true value for the surface pressure must be only about 5 millibars (1 bar is the surface pressure of Earth's atmosphere; a millibar is one-thousandth of a bar). This is only 0.5 percent of Earth's atmospheric pressure—a very small value. New designs had to be considered for Martian spacecraft, and it seemed less likely that anything remotely resembling terrestrial life could exist under such harsh conditions.

The largest optical telescope in the United States is the venerable Palomar Observatory's 5-meter Hale reflector. Completed in 1948, it stood for thirty years as the world's largest and was used primarily for deep space cosmology and stellar studies. With the advent of the space program and the accompanying renaissance of planetary astronomy, the Palomar telescope came to be used occasionally for solar system work. It was used, for example, to analyze the Martian atmospheric gases and, in the 1950's, to examine the Martian surface for signs of chlorophyll to see if the greenish areas might represent plant life (they did not). With infrared detectors, the telescope was used to make some of the first maps of the temperatures of Jupiter across its disk and to sample the temperatures of the surfaces of the other major planets.

More recently, the Palomar telescope has been used for other kinds of space-related research. For example, it was a prime source of information about the nature of many of the X-ray sources discovered by the various X-ray satellites (such as Uhuru and Einstein). Because of its large light-gathering power, it could detect many of the very distant X-ray quasars mapped from space, for example, and could search for and study faint stellar X-ray sources within the Galaxy.

Another area in which the Palomar telescope has played an important role in space research has been its exploration of objects that were identified by the Infrared Astronomical Satellite (IRAS) as being anomalous infrared sources. Many of these objects are obscured stars and interstellar clouds in the Galaxy, not easily detected and studied at optical wavelengths, but Palomar observers have used infrared detectors, working at short enough wavelengths to get through the atmosphere, to study the structure and to determine the nature of several galactic infrared objects. Similarly, the many infrared sources that, from their location in the sky, appear to lie outside the Galaxy have also been examined at Palomar. There is still a considerable amount of research to be done before the place of infrared-emitting galaxies in the general scheme of the extragalactic universe is understood thoroughly.

The second largest American telescope is located at the Whipple Observatory on Mount Hopkins in Arizona. It is called the MMT (for multimirror telescope): Instead of having a single large mirror or lens, it has six mirrors, all about 1.5 meters in diameter, arranged together with a common focus. It has the light-gathering power of a 4.5-meter single-mirror telescope. The MMT, built in 1976, is used almost exclusively for spectroscopy, mostly of stars and galaxies. At the same observatory is the much smaller 1.5-meter Tillinghast telescope, with which Robert Brown discovered the sodium cloud around Jupiter's satellite Io. This was an important precursor discovery to the later Voyager 1 and 2 discoveries and studies of Io's volcanism.

Third largest in size is the 4-meter Mayall telescope at the Kitt Peak National Observatory, which is part of the National Optical Astronomical Observatories. Completed in 1973, it was designed to be a multipurpose instrument, but, because of its high power and wide field, it was expected to be especially useful for photography of large, faint objects (nearby galaxies, such as the Andromeda Galaxy, and fields of distant galaxies and clusters). It has been used only rarely for night-time solar system work, but is sometimes available for daytime study of the planets. An important contribution, connected to the efforts to study Halley's comet by such space probes as Giotto, was Mayall telescope researchers' success in sighting the comet when it was still an extremely faint, distant dot in the outer solar system. Michael Belton and his colleagues at Kitt Peak first detected the incoming comet in 1985 and were still following it in 1988, two years after its pass close to the Sun in its slow retreat into the outer solar system.

The UKIRT (United Kingdom Infrared Telescope) is 3.8 meters in diameter and occupies a dome at the Mauna Kea Observatory, considered to be the best North American site for a ground-based observatory. The UKIRT was completed in 1979 and does not have direct ties to space projects, through some of its research is related to stellar and galactic problems for which space telescopes have played key roles.

Also on Mauna Kea is the slightly smaller 3.6-meter telescope operated by Canada, France, and the University of Hawaii and called the CFHT (Canada-France-Hawaii Telescope). Although primarily devoted to stellar and galactic research, it has been used for several programs related, for example, to cosmological questions precipitated by X-ray satellite maps of quasars and other very distant X-ray sources.

The Lick Observatory's largest telescope is the Shane 3-meter telescope, completed in 1959. It has been used by University of California astronomers to make numerous discoveries related to space research. An exotic example of such discoveries has to do with the planet Mercury. In 1961, there were reports from the Soviet Union that Mercury appeared to have an atmosphere (according to one Soviet astronomer, it was composed of hydrogen, but another report claimed that it was carbon dioxide). Space scientists were concerned about these reports. Because Mercury's surface was known to have high temperatures, astronomers had deduced that the planet should not be able to retain any appreciable atmosphere, because the gases would be so hot that they would escape out into space in a relatively short time. In 1962, to explore the question further, the Shane telescope was used to obtain high-dispersion spectra of Mercury (much more detailed data than those used by the Soviet astronomers). Because Mercury is always quite close to the Sun (never more than 28 degrees from it in the sky), the telescope was used during the daytime for these observations. The results, after analysis, were clear: The better data showed no sign whatsoever of an atmosphere. Years later, in 1979, Mariner 10 confirmed this conclusion by returning data that showed that the planet, because of its high temperature, does not have an appreciable atmosphere, but only retains temporarily a minute and tenuous envelope of hydrogen gas captured from the solar wind (the stream of very low-density gas that is ejected from the top of the Sun's atmosphere).

In 1979, the National Aeronautics and Space Administration (NASA) built a 3-meter infrared telescope to be used especially for space-related research. It was put on Mauna Kea to take advantage of the high altitude and lack of water vapor, and it has been employed successfully in a large number of infrared projects, including studies of asteroids, comets, planetary satellites, the galactic nucleus, and infrared-bright and active galaxies.

The 2.7-meter telescope of the McDonald Observatory in Texas was also built with NASA sponsorship (in 1968) and with the intent that it be used largely for space-related research. A particularly interesting example of this has been its lunar-ranging measurements. A powerful laser at its focal point is used to beam light to the lunar surface, and 2.5 seconds later the telescope detects the reflected light. The light's travel time can be measured so accurately that the distance to the Moon at that instant could be determined to an accuracy of about 2.5 centimeters (the distance to the Moon averages about 384,000 kilometers).

Large telescopes used to receive and analyze extraterrestrial radiation at radio wavelengths have been of great importance to the development of modern astronomy and space science. Most large radio telescopes have been one of three distinct types: large single dishes, interferometric arrays of dishes, and millimeter telescopes.

Centimeter-wavelength radio waves can best be detected by means of a very large parabolic reflecting surface (a "dish") that can move in position to follow the celestial object as it moves across the sky. The largest of these actually does not move, however, but instead has a moving receiver suspended above the dish. The 300-meter radio telescope of the Arecibo Ionospheric Radio Observatory was made by smoothing out a depression in the hills of Puerto Rico and lining it with a parabolic metal surface suspended a few feet above the ground. Three pylons rise from the rim of the valley and hold cables that span the depression and support the small laboratory, dangling above the center of the dish, that contains the receiver. Motors pull the receiver building from west to east to compensate for the diurnal motion of the image of the celestial object being observed. Only a limited range in position in the sky is available to the Arecibo telescope, but its immense collecting area and high resolution have made it an important instrument for many years.

A different type of single-dish antenna is the 100-meter radio telescope near Bonn, West Germany. In this case, the parabolic metal dish is fully movable; it can turn to any place in the sky and can follow celestial sources at the diurnal rate. Although it is smaller than the Arecibo telescope, its flexibility has made it useful for many projects that would have been impossible with a large, fixed dish. Similar, though smaller, single dishes that have been important are a 76-meter telescope at Jodrell Bank, England, a 64-meter telescope at Parkes, Australia, and a 43-meter one at Greenbank, West Virginia. A 90-meter transit-type radio telescope at Greenbank collapsed suddenly in 1988 and has not been rebuilt.

Resolution at radio wavelengths is hard to achieve. Resolution is proportional to wavelength; to achieve the same resolution afforded by an optical telescope, a radio telescope working at a long wavelength such as the 21-centimeter neutral hydrogen line must be many kilometers in diameter. This size would be impractical for a single-dish design, so radio astronomers have constructed giant arrays of radio dishes, connected electronically so that the signals received are blended and analyzed as if from an immense single telescope. These instruments are called "interferometric arrays" and range in size from 1 kilometer or so for the pioneer instrument in Cambridge, England, to intercontinental arrays.

The largest interferometers that are located in physical proximity are the VLA (Very Large Array) near Socorro, New Mexico, and the Westerbork Array in the Netherlands. The former consists of twenty 27-meter dishes spread in a circular pattern on the plains of St. Augustine, a dry lake bed; the latter consists of a linear array of telescopes. All radio interferometers of this type have at least some of their antennae on wheels and tracks so that the spacing can be adjusted according to the needs of different observing projects.

The Australia Telescope array was designed with some of the properties of both the VLA and Westerbork; a continental array of telescopes planned to span North America would permit extremely high resolution. Ad hoc interferometers, made up of existing single dishes that are coordinated to simulate an array, have utilized even larger baselines (for example, from Australia to Canada), achieving radio images that are more detailed than even optical telescopes can produce, using normal detectors. Spaceborne radio telescopes can achieve even wider separations, as large as the solar system.

Millimeter-wavelength radio telescopes tend to have characteristics midway between those of standard radio telescopes and those of optical telescopes. Most are housed in domes of some sort and are fully steerable. For example, the 9-meter millimeter telescope on Kitt Peak in Arizona has a dome-shaped housing with a large slit that can be opened for observing. The world's large millimeter telescopes are located in Hawaii (on Mauna Kea), in Japan, and in Massachusetts. They are especially powerful for detecting and analyzing emission from cool molecular gas in star-forming regions.

## Knowledge Gained

Ground-based telescopes have provided most of the basis for present astronomical research being conducted in space. Among the most important aspects of this ground-based support are the following: basic data on planetary celestial mechanics; the discovery and orbit determination of comets and asteroids; the mapping of galactic X-ray and infrared sources; the discovery of quasars and radio galaxies; and the detection of the cosmic background radiation.

For basic data on the orbits of the planets, ground-based telescopes are used for laser and radar ranging. In order to determine the continuously changing orbits of the planets well enough to make interplanetary spaceflight possible, it is important to map planetary positions very accurately. Laser ranging of the Moon, for example, allows astronomers with large ground-based telescopes to measure its distance at a given moment to within a few centimeters. Radar ranging measurements of the planets, especially Venus, Mercury, and Mars, have led to very precise determinations of their positions.

Spacecraft exploration of comets (such as Halley's comet, which was visited by spacecraft in 1986) depends on ground-based telescopes, to discover comets in the first place and then to monitor them in their somewhat unpredictable paths near the Sun and Earth. Exploration of asteroids by spacecraft similarly depends on ground-based telescopes for tactical support.

Most of the cosmic objects found at X-ray and infrared wavelengths by orbiting detectors in space would be unexplained were it not possible to study them at other wavelengths from the ground. For example, two of the objects thought to be black holes, LMC X-1 and Cygnus X-1, would merely be mysterious, unidentified X-ray sources if it had not been possible, using large ground-based telescopes, to discover that each is a binary star, with a normal star in orbit around a dark, massive object.

## Context

Much of space astronomy aims at a better understanding of cosmology; ground-based telescopes have provided the basic list of objects and phenomena (including quasars, radio galaxies, and cosmic background radiation) that allow astronomers to penetrate to the edge of the universe and the beginning of time. Spaceborne instruments, such as the Hubble Space Telescope, are designed to push farther into deep space and to determine the true story of how the universe came about.

Ground-based telescopes, then, have a twofold relationship with the space effort: They provide essential data on positions, motions, and the nature of bodies in space to which space probes are being sent, and they provide important backup information on the nature of celestial objects and phenomena discovered at exotic wavelengths by spaceborne detectors.

## Bibliography

Callender, John D. *Observatories*. Medina, Wash.: Russell-Winthrop Book Co., 1979. Describes fifty of the world's chief observatories, with a photograph of each and a map showing its location and road access. Lacks an index. Suitable for general readers.

_____ . *Telescopes*. Medina, Wash.: Russell-Winthrop Book Co., 1978. Describes the principle of the telescope and the various types of optical, radio, and space telescopes, and shows photographs of telescopes of many different designs. Suitable for general readers.

Kirby-Smith, Henry T. *U.S. Observatories: A Directory and Travel Guide*. New York: Van Nostrand Reinhold Co., 1976. A complete description of U.S. observatories, with some history and an account of the types of research and the equipment available. Notes on public availability for some are included. Suitable for general readers.

Kloeppel, James E. *Realm of the Long Eyes: A Brief History of Kitt Peak National Observatory*. San Diego: Univelt, 1983. A well-illustrated account of the development of the optical observatory on Kitt Peak, Arizona. Offers a complete history of the arguments for a national ground-based observatory and of the process of its establishment as one of the world's most productive scientific installations. Includes bibliography and an index.

Krisciunas, K. *Astronomical Centers of the World*. Cambridge: Cambridge University Press, 1987. A very thorough coverage of the world's major astronomical centers, including important historical installations. Includes material on advanced concepts, observatories of the future, and space observatories. Features useful tables and an index. Suitable for scientifically oriented general readers.

Kuiper, Gerard P., and Barbara M. Middlehurst, eds. *Telescopes: Stars and Stellar Systems*. Chicago: University of Chicago Press, 1960. A compendium of fairly technical chapters on various aspects of telescope design, with an emphasis on traditional large reflecting telescopes with equatorial mounts. Contains many tables, photographs, and graphs. Indexed. For college-level readers.

Marx, Siegfried, and Werner Pfau. *Observatories of the World*. Translated by C. S. V. Salt. Edited and revised by Simon Mitton. New York: Van Nostrand Reinhold Co., 1982. A comprehensive survey of the world's ground-based observatories. Includes detailed listings of instrument characteristics. Suitable for general readers and specialists.

Tucker, Wallace, and Karen Tucker. *The Cosmic Inquirers: Modern Telescopes and Their Makers*. Cambridge, Mass.: Harvard University Press, 1986. An excellent book about modern telescopes, including radio and space telescopes, and about the astronomers who brought them into existence. Includes narrative accounts and biographical data based on interviews with key people. For general readers.

*Paul Hodge*

## Cross-References

Comets, 245; Jupiter's Satellites, 704; Mariner 10, 871; The Martian Atmosphere, 916; Mercury's Landscape and Geology, 991; The National Aeronautics and Space Administration, 1032; Quasars, 1216; The Solar Wind, 1382; Air and Space Telescopes, 2014; The Viking Program, 2149; Voyager 1: Jupiter, 2227; Voyager 2: Jupiter, 2241.

# TIROS METEOROLOGICAL SATELLITES

*Date:* April 6, 1960, to September 17, 1986
*Type of satellite:* Meteorological
*Country:* The United States

*A TIROS satellite provided the first television picture from space on April 1, 1960. Thereafter, the satellites in this series would provide high-altitude views which have increased meteorologists' capability to forecast weather.*

Principal personages
WILLIAM G. STROUD, TIROS Project Manager
MORRIS TEPPER, TIROS Program Manager

## Summary of the Satellites

The first Television Infrared Observations Satellite, known as TIROS 1, was the earliest of a series of weather satellites designed to provide environmental data for the 80 percent of the globe that was not covered by conventional means. The purpose of these satellites is to measure temperature and humidity in Earth's atmosphere, the planet's surface temperature, cloud cover, water-ice boundaries, and changes in the flow of protons and electrons near Earth. TIROS satellites have the capability of receiving, processing, and transmitting data from balloons, buoys, and remote automatic stations.

The TIROS series was the first of four generations of polar-orbiting weather satellites launched and operated by the United States. The series included ten successful launches from Cape Canaveral between April, 1960, and July, 1965. The first eight spacecraft—18-sided polygons 106 centimeters in diameter, 56 centimeters high, covered by solar cells, and approximately 12 kilograms in weight—were in orbits inclined 48 and 58 degrees to the equator. With TIROS 9, engineers made the first attempt to place a satellite in polar orbit from Cape Canaveral, using a series of dogleg maneuvers over twenty orbits to reach that orbit. Similar maneuvers were used to achieve polar orbit with TIROS 10.

Initially, the TIROS spacecraft were equipped with two miniature television cameras, a tape recorder for each camera, two timer systems for programming future camera operations as set by a command from ground stations, and sensing devices for determining spacecraft attitude, environment, and equipment operations. As the program moved ahead, the satellites had progressively longer operational times and carried infrared measuring instruments (radiometers) to study the amount of radiation received and reradiated from Earth.

TIROS 8 had the first automatic picture transmission (APT) equipment, allowing pictures to be sent back to Earth immediately after they had been taken instead of being stored in tape recorders for later transmission. TIROS 9 and 10 were improved configurations; they led to the second generation of TIROS satellites, called ESSA after the government agency that financed and operated them, the Environmental Science Services Administration, later known as the National Oceanic and Atmospheric Administration (NOAA).

TIROS 1 through 10 enjoyed 6,630 useful days and provided 649,077 pictures. TIROS 1 proved television operation in space to be feasible. It had 89 days of useful life and transmitted 22,952 pictures. TIROS 2 studied ice floes and had 376 useful days, providing 36,156 pictures. TIROS 3 made the first hurricane observation and provided the first advance storm-warning. It had 230 days of useful life and sent back 35,033 pictures. TIROS 4 permitted the first international use of its weather data. It operated for 161 days and transmitted 32,593 pictures. TIROS 5 extended the coverage of weather satellites, operated for 321 days, and sent 58,226 pictures. TIROS 6 provided support for the Mercury 8 and Mercury 9 manned space missions, operated for 389 days, and provided 68,557 pictures.

TIROS 7 provided weather data to the International Indian Ocean Expedition, operated for 1,809 days, and sent back 125,331 pictures. TIROS 8 inaugurated the APT direct readout system, had a useful life of 1,287 days, and sent 102,463 pictures.

TIROS 9 and 10, with their improved configurations and near-polar orbits, improved global coverage. They had useful lives of 1,238 and 730 days respectively and sent back 88,892 and 78,874 pictures.

The ESSA satellites for the first time provided daily, worldwide observations without interruption in data. There were nine ESSA satellites. ESSA 1 was launched in February, 1966, operated for 861 days, and sent back 111,144 pictures. The average useful life of each of the nine ESSA satellites was nearly three years. Transmitting more than a quarter of a million television pictures, ESSA 8 lasted the longest, from December, 1968, until March, 1976. Altogether, ESSA 1 through 9 had 10,494 useful days and returned 1,006,140 television pictures.

In the 1970's, the third generation of meteorological satellites, known as the Improved TIROS Operational Satellite (ITOS), was developed. ITOS 1, launched in January, 1970, was the first of the TIROS system satellites equipped with television cameras for daytime coverage of the sunlit portion of Earth and infrared sensors sensitive to temperatures of the land, sea, and cloud tops for both daytime and nighttime coverage. A single ITOS spacecraft furnished global observation of Earth's cloud cover every 12 hours, as compared to every 24 hours with two of the ESSA satellites.

A second ITOS satellite was launched successfully in December, 1970. Following a launch failure in October, 1971, four ITOS satellites were launched successfully, the last one being ITOS H in July, 1976. When the Environmental Science Services Administration became the National Oceanic and Atmospheric Administration, the satellites were renamed: ITOS A became NOAA 1; ITOS D, NOAA 2; ITOS F, NOAA 3; ITOS G, NOAA 4; and ITOS H, NOAA 5. The ITOS (NOAA) satellites were launched from the Western Test Range at Vandenberg Air Force Base in California.

The TIROS-N/NOAA series is the fourth generation of the meteorological satellites built by RCA. These carry a wide variety of new and considerably more advanced sensors. Besides providing weather imagery data, these satellites transmit atmospheric and sea surface temperatures, water vapor soundings, measurements of particle activity surrounding Earth, and data gathered from balloonborne, ocean-based, and land-based weather-sensing platforms.

Sensor systems on the TIROS-N satellites include the TIROS operational vertical sounder (TOVS), which combines data from three complementary sounding units to provide improved temperature and moisture data from Earth's surface up through the stratosphere; the advanced very high-resolution radiometer (AVHRR), which gathers and stores visible and infrared measurements and images, permitting more precise evaluation of land, surface water, and ice as well as information on cloud conditions and sea surface temperatures; the space environment monitor (SEM), which allows the measurement of energetic particles emitted by the Sun over essentially the full range of energies and magnetic field variations in Earth's near-space environment (these measurements are tremendously helpful in determining solar radiation activities); and ARGOS, which permits the collection and transmission of environmental data from platforms on land, at sea, and in the air (ARGOS also determines the geographic location of platforms in motion on the sea surface or in the air).

The first satellite in the TIROS-N series was launched in October, 1978. It operated for twenty-eight months, twice its designed mission life. The second in the series, NOAA 6, was launched in June, 1979, followed by NOAA 7 in June, 1981. NOAA 8 was launched in March, 1983, NOAA 9 in December, 1984, and NOAA 10 in September, 1986. All these launches were from the Western Test Range in California using an Air Force Atlas launch vehicle.

These NOAA satellites operate in a near-polar, circular orbit at an altitude of 870 kilometers. In their operational configuration, two satellites are positioned with a normal separation of 90 degrees. One of the satellites operates in an afternoon ascending orbit, crossing the equator at 3:00 P.M. local solar time. The second operates in a morning descending orbit with an equator crossing at 7:30 A.M. local solar time. The satellites take 102 minutes to circle Earth.

These TIROS series satellites include instruments from the United Kingdom and France. The United Kingdom, through its Ministry of Defense Meteorological Offices, provides the stratospheric sounding unit, one of the three atmospheric sounding instruments on each satellite. The soundings provide three-dimensional observations of the atmosphere from the surface to approximately 65.5 kilometers. The two TIROS-N satellites provide roughly 16,000 timely soundings a day. The Centre National d'Études Spatiales of France supplies the data-collection and location system for the satellite (ARGOS) as well as the ground facilities to process data and make the information available to users. The French operate a receiving station for weather data at Lannion, on the English Channel, about 80 kilometers northeast of Brest.

The TIROS-N/NOAA satellites have been designed with sufficient space, power, and data-handling capability to allow additional instruments to be installed— including a search and rescue system made up of repeater and processor units, a solar backscatter ultraviolet radiometer for ozone mapping, and two Earth Radiation Budget Experiment instruments. NOAA 8, 9, and 10 have these instruments and are known as Advanced TIROS-N (ATN) satellites.

The search and rescue equipment installed on ATN enables detection of emergency transmissions from downed aircraft or ships in distress. The devices support an international search and rescue effort in which the principal partners are Canada, France, the Soviet Union, and the United States. From its beginning in September, 1982, until July, 1988, more than eleven hundred lives had been saved as a result of the program. NOAA, the National Aeronautics and Space Administration (NASA), the U.S. Air Force, and the U.S. Coast Guard are the principal U.S. agencies supporting this international program.

For more than a quarter century, these meteorological satellites have shown improvement in quality, quantity, and reliability. Since 1966, the entire Earth has been photographed at least once daily on a continuous basis. These data are considered almost indispensable for short-range weather forecasts by meteorologists and environmental scientists.

## Knowledge Gained

TIROS 1 demonstrated the practicality of meteorological observations from space and the ability to make observations with television. Observations from TIROS 1 confirmed and, in some cases, shed new light on the large-scale organization of clouds, showing that they were arranged in a highly organized pattern. The cloud vortex stood out dramatically. Meteorologists learned that these cloud vortices could be used to pinpoint accurately atmospheric storm regions. Of the nearly twenty-three thousand cloud-cover pictures transmitted by TIROS 1, more than nineteen thousand were usable for weather analysis. This opened a new era in weather observation by providing data that covered vast areas of Earth that previously had not been available to meteorologists.

Some storms were tracked for as long as four days, underscoring the value of television satellite pictures for weather forecasting. In one case, TIROS 1 observations of a storm near Bermuda in May, 1960, provided a series of pictures recording the degeneration of the storm. The weather maps drawn from conventional data were correlated with the pictures, affording a unique set of data on which to judge future pictures.

TIROS satellite data were used to establish, modify, and improve cloud analysis and to brief pilots on weather. Pictures of cloud cover, transmitted by teletype, were used to refine weather analysis in the region from Australia to Antarctica, and the Australian Meteorological Service used the data in conjunction with special research projects on storms over Australia.

Pictures of ice-pack conditions in the Gulf of Saint Lawrence proved that weather satellites could locate ice boundaries in relation to open seas. TIROS 2 observations were used in selecting proper weather conditions for the suborbital flight of Alan B. Shepard in May, 1961—America's first manned spaceflight.

The TIROS 3 satellite provided observations of all six of the major hurricanes in 1961. It detected Hurricane Esther two days before it was observed by conventional methods.

In 1963, three TIROS satellites (TIROS 5, 6, and 7) were in operation simultaneously and provided for the first time pictures of the cloud cover of various parts of the world on an almost continuous basis. These pictures formed the basis for adapting satellite data to forecasting methods and the use of numerical prediction models. Special projects surveying the Atlantic and Indian oceans brought clues to the origin and development of tropical cyclones. TIROS satellites have detected sandstorms in Saudi Arabia and have provided storm advisories in many areas of the world.

As a result of their analyses of the satellite pictures, meteorologists have been able to categorize cloud vortex patterns and to determine from those patterns the structure of moisture fields, the cloud structure of frontal zones, and the relationship of cloud patterns associated with jet streams. A series of atlases has been developed which are being used with the satellite data by research meteorologists to investigate a wide variety of theoretical conclusions.

## Context

Until the 1960's when meteorological satellites made their debut, the science of weather prediction left much to be desired. Meteorologists could not forecast with any great degree of accuracy the weather four or five days ahead. Forecasts can now be made for a number of days ahead, most of the time with great accuracy. A number of technological factors have contributed to this improvement. One was the development of the computer, which permits the analysis of millions of bits of information at high speeds so that the physical laws governing atmospheric motion can be calculated more accurately. The development of new communications links, enabling the rapid dissemination of meteorological data over great distances, is another.

Another advancement, equally important in the eyes of many, was the development of meteorological satellites. The development and operation of TIROS and other meteorological satellites have opened the inaccessible areas of the world to observation.

Improved weather forecasting extends to many daily activities of society. For example, improved forecasts are of inestimable value to agriculture. Better forecasting means better crop management and protection. A reliable forecast during the fruit-growing season in California or Florida could save fruit growers millions of dollars.

Improved forecasting offers benefits to transportation, to construction, to manufacturing, and to recreation. Better forecasts allow the routing of aircraft so that safety and comfort are enhanced. Thus, delays are avoided and money is saved as a result of improved fuel consumption. In construction, improved forecasting permits contractors to plan and schedule construction work as environmental conditions dictate. Improved forecasting also permits manufacturers to plan production, particularly when sales are sensitive to weather conditions.

Satellite pictures provide unique assistance to many. Images of the polar ice have helped vessels that otherwise would have been trapped find a way through the ice and have been used to assist ships that were caught in ocean storms. Weather services for Antarctica and for offshore oil-drilling platforms make it possible for activities in these locations to be undertaken in comparative safety. The infrared sensors can scan the ocean surface and determine the temperature, providing extremely useful information to the fishing industry, for example—temperatures can help locate schools of certain kinds of fish.

Meteorological support for humanity's daily activities on land, on sea, and in the air underscores the importance of continued measurements from space. Such measurements are being carried out on a global scale by all seafaring nations. Canada, France, Japan, India, the Soviet Union, the European Space Agency, the United States, and others all have active weather satellite programs.

## Bibliography

Grieve, Tim, Finn Lied, and Erik Tandberg, eds. *The Impact of Space Science on Mankind*. New York: Plenum Press, 1976. Contains edited summaries of papers presented at the Nobel Symposium in Spatind, Norway, in September, 1975. In a paper presented by Robert M. White, Administrator of the National Oceanic and Atmospheric Administration, the use of environmental satellites is described. The use of satellites and their benefits to mankind are outlined.

Jakes, John. *TIROS: Weather Eye of Space*. New York: Julian Messner, 1966. A nontechnical review of the significance of TIROS and the benefits of the meteorological satellites. Reviews history of meteorological research as well as the development of the TIROS payload. A list of accomplishments is given, underscoring the benefits of satellite observations.

National Aeronautics and Space Administration. *Significant Achievements in Satellite Meteorology, 1958-1964*. NASA SP-96. Washington, D.C.: Government Printing Office, 1966. This volume is one in a series which summarizes the progress made by NASA's Space Science and Applications Program from 1958 through 1964. It reviews NASA's meteorological program and its benefits. Describes TIROS, Nimbus, and the meteorological sounding-rocket program.

Rosenthal, Alfred. *The Early Years, Goddard Space Flight Center: Historical Origins and Activities Through December, 1962*. Washington, D.C.: Government Printing Office, 1964. Outlines the historical origins of the Goddard Space Flight Center and its development through 1962 and contains historical documents concerning the establishment of Goddard as a NASA center.

Widger, W. K., Jr. *Meteorological Satellites*. New York: Holt, Rinehart and Winston, 1965. As a member of the team that developed TIROS, the author provides an interesting overview of the TIROS program itself and a definitive account of the value of satellite information, the equipment that provides the satellite weather data, and early results of the scientific investigations obtained from TIROS.

*James C. Elliott*

## Cross-References

Environmental Science Services Administration Satellites, 367; ITOS/NOAA Meteorological Satellites, 648; Mercury-Redstone 3: *Freedom 7*, 953; U.S. Meteorological Satellites, 999; The National Aeronautics and Space Administration, 1032; Nimbus Meteorological Satellites, 1072.

# TITAN LAUNCH VEHICLES

*Date:* Beginning December 20, 1957
*Type of technology:* Rocket booster
*Country:* The United States

*The Titan series of rockets provided the United States with a means of launching satellites into orbit. During its early years, the Titan served as an intercontinental ballistic missile for the United States Air Force.*

### Principal personages

ALBERT C. HALL, director of technical activities for the Titan ICBM at Martin Marietta Corporation

OSMOND J. RITLAND, director of development for many early ICBMs, including the Titan

ROGER CHAMBERLAIN, manager of the Commercial Titan Program

J. DONALD RAUTH, Chairman and Chief Executive Officer, Martin Marietta Corporation

LAURENCE J. ADAMS, President, Martin Marietta Aerospace

CALEB B. HURTT, President, Denver Aerospace

## Summary of the Technology

During the years immediately following World War II, American officials had predicted that the Soviet Union would not have enough information to create an atomic bomb for at least another three years, and probably for five. It was, therefore, a great blow when in August, 1949, the Soviet Union detonated its first bomb. The Soviets again proved that they were an emerging superpower by performing intercontinental ballistic missile (ICBM) tests in 1957.

Although ICBMs were among the new weapons the United States decided to build in the postwar years, several factors prevented their production before 1954. The major cause can be traced to the lack of conviction on the part of many influential scientists that a rocket could possess enough accuracy, let alone enough strength, to make the system feasible. In addition, such an undertaking would have required enormous financial resources and skilled manpower, neither of which was available to the military until it had become clear that the United States was lagging behind the Soviets.

As a response to Soviet ICBMs, Americans designed several rockets. In this field the United States had a great advantage, for during the closing stages of World War II, many German rocket experts had surrendered to the Americans rather than face capture by the Soviets; these researchers became American citizens, willing to help their new country advance its weaponry.

The first American ICBM was the Atlas. It stood 24.4 meters tall and had two stages. During the early part of the program, both stages were ignited at lift-off to avoid having the rocket fail once the first stage had exhausted its fuel. The special

Air Force Strategic Missiles Evaluation Committee and the Research and Development (RAND) Corporation published reports in 1954 and 1955 in which they cited two reasons that Atlas should be replaced: the necessity of igniting both boosters at the same time and the unsuitable nature of a thin pressurized skin for high-acceleration lift-off.

President Dwight D. Eisenhower ordered the development of a new ICBM, to be called Titan, in mid-1955. The contract was awarded to the Martin Company (later the Martin Marietta Corporation). It was to have a range of approximately 11,000 kilometers. The total thrust produced at lift-off was to be 1,343 kilonewtons, while the weight of the rocket (including fuel) was to be 99,790 kilograms. Its height was to be 29.87 meters, its maximum diameter 3.048 meters.

Titan was to have two stages which would ignite separately, using a propellant of kerosene and liquid oxygen. Two huge tanks were located inside the first stage. The bottom tank housed the kerosene while the top housed the liquid oxygen. Two pumps pushed the liquids to the combustion chamber, where they were ignited. Once the fuel was consumed, the separation rocket fired and the first stage was freed. The second stage was much like the first, except that it contained, in addition to the main engine, four smaller rockets to guide it. Above the second stage were the nuclear warhead and the guidance systems.

After lift-off, Titan rose vertically for twenty seconds. It then arched into a curved trajectory for one hundred seconds, at a speed of 8,530 kilometers per hour. Its fuel exhausted, the first stage separated. The second stage ignited and propelled the rocket to a speed of up to 28,970 kilometers per hour. Four vernier engines (stabilizers) corrected velocity and trajectory. Once this had been accomplished, the second stage was released, and the nose cone fell toward Earth. As a missile, the Titan reached a height of 805 kilometers.

In the early 1960's, researchers realized that the Titan system had some flaws. For example, it was necessary to fuel the rockets immediately before the launch so that the liquid oxygen would not evaporate. Furthermore, the range of the Titan was considered insufficient. Martin Marietta and the National Aeronautics and Space Administration (NASA) were contracted to build a successor to Titan.

Titan 2 was completed in 1964. It stood 33.22 meters tall, with a diameter of 3.048 meters. It weighed 185,034 kilograms. For its fuel it used a combination of nitrogen tetroxide and Aerozine 50. The two stages together produced a total thrust of more than 2,223 kilonewtons.

When NASA built Gemini, a successor to the Mercury space capsule, the Titan was seen as the perfect launch vehicle, with one exception: The Titan suffered from what was known as the "pogo effect" (named for the "pogo stick"), violent, up-and-down motions as the rocket rose. These oscillations mattered little when the Titan carried warheads; for human passengers, however, the pogo effect would create unacceptable conditions. Designers were able to eliminate the worst of the pogo effect, and on April 8, 1964, using Titan 2, the first Gemini spacecraft was launched, followed on March 25, 1965, by the first manned launch.

The Gemini program as a whole was considered a success. The Gemini space-craft carried two astronauts, an improvement over the crowded, one-man Mercury capsule. During this program several records were set. The first docking with an-other spacecraft occurred, and the first American walked in space. For a time it was suggested that a variation of the Titan 2 vehicle should be used for the Apollo program. This plan was dropped in favor of using the more powerful Saturn launcher. Titan 2 was also intended to launch the ill-fated Dyna-Soar, a predecessor of the space shuttle.

From 1965 onward, Titan 2 was replaced by Titan 3. Titan 3, the modern-day heavy launch vehicle, can propel into orbit loads of 15,875 kilograms and handle as much as 3,175 kilograms for interplanetary missions. The core section of the rocket, sometimes known as Titan 3A, has two stages and is commonly flanked by boosters. The third stage, or transtage, contains the payload and the final fuel. Ti-tan 3 has four configurations commonly in use.

The Titan's first stage is 22.25 meters tall and provides approximately 2,356 kilo-newtons of thrust. The second stage measures slightly more than 7 meters and is capable of more than 445 kilonewtons of thrust. Both stages use nitrogen tetroxide and a mixture of unsymmetrical dimethylhydrazine (UDMH) and hydrazine. The transtage is of varying heights and can be as tall as 15.24 meters when launching Air Force payloads. It uses the same type of fuel as the first two stages. The two boosters are 26 meters long and use solid propellant.

The Titan 3B core has two stages and permits a variety of upper stages to be fitted, the most common being the Agena. It is not launched with boosters. Its cargoes have included Air Force reconnaissance satellites. The Titan 3B uses the standard inertial guidance system, which enables the satellite to maintain a pre-determined course.

The Titan 3C, first launched in 1965, has a takeoff thrust of 10,490 kilonewtons. Its height is 47.85 meters, and it carries two boosters that are 26 meters in length with diameters of approximately 3 meters. At takeoff, the two boosters are the only source of thrust. The core is ignited just before the boosters are released. The fuel consists of nitrogen tetroxide and Aerozine 50. Approximately 80 percent of the satellites launched by the United States into geosynchronous equatorial orbit use a Titan 3C rocket. A geosynchronous orbit is one that keeps precise pace with the rotation of Earth, thereby maintaining a stable position relative to any given site.

The Manned Orbiting Laboratory (MOL), which was to have undertaken recon-naissance projects, was slated for launch by the Titan 3C. Growing costs and the high performance of a previously launched spy satellite resulted in the cancellation of the project; yet, the Titan 3C has continued to launch signal intelligence (SigInt) satellites.

Although the Titan 3D is similar to the 3C in many respects, it does not have a transtage. Instead of depending on inertial guidance, it depends on radio guidance. Titan 3D is the rocket used to launch the so-called Big Bird satellite.

In February, 1974, the Titan 3E-Centaur, a modified version of the Titan 3D, was first tested. Although the test ended in failure, the Titan 3E-Centaur performed flawlessly when it launched the Viking spacecraft to Mars in 1975.

The Titan 34D, yet another model, lacks the traditional transtage and uses the Boeing Inertial Upper Stage instead (a stage originally developed for the space shuttle). Its first stage has been lengthened to 25.22 meters. Titan 34D was completed February 28, 1981; however, the program suffered from a series of failures in the mid-1980's. On August 18, 1985, after being launched from Vandenberg Air Force Base, the engine shut down prematurely, and the rocket fell into the Pacific Ocean. Disaster struck again on April 18, 1986. Mere seconds after launch, at 91.44 meters above ground, a Titan exploded, destroying a classified satellite.

The approximate cost of using a Titan 34D to launch a 12,700-kilogram satellite into a polar orbit of 185 kilometers is approximately $60 million if six are purchased at the same time. To place a satellite of 1,815 kilograms into geosynchronous orbit costs $125 million. In the event that only one launcher per year is ordered, the price would be raised by $121 million and $125 million respectively per flight. The average cost of the satellites that use the Titan 34D is more than $100 million.

In March, 1985, the U.S. Air Force awarded a $5 million contract to Martin Marietta to build a new and more powerful Titan rocket. The Titan 4's payload size is to be about the same as that of the space shuttle, and its height is to be 62 meters. The USAF's name for it is the Complementary Expendable Launch Vehicle (CELV).

## Knowledge Gained

The early Titan rocket served as a test vehicle. Various alternatives to the Atlas' thin casing were tested on the Titan, as were different fuels. Before a rocket is launched, thousands of modifications are made, ranging from the design of a better engine to the replacement of a first stage. The Atlas was designed so that both stages were ignited at once. When the Titan was built, a means of separating the first stage was devised. A system of igniting the second stage, after separation had occurred, was also designed.

In the process of choosing new propellants it was discovered that nitric acid and turpentine ignited upon contact. This fact proved to be very useful: Instead of having to reignite the fuel every time the rocket was started, it was possible by mixing the fuel to produce thrust once again. The combination of a fuel and an oxidizer that ignites spontaneously is called a hypergol.

For the Titan 2, a mixture of UDMH, hydrazine, and nitrogen tetroxide replaced the old mixture of kerosene and liquid oxygen. Before it could be placed in the rocket, many tests were performed. First, the pumps, which were designed to work well with liquid oxygen, had to be replaced with pumps that functioned at higher temperatures. The guidance system, containing some flaws, was replaced by an inertial system. Now that it was no longer necessary to add propellant a few minutes before launch, many of the ICBM silos could be simplified.

With the introduction of the even more powerful Titan 3, and the gradual phasing out of the Titan ICBMs in favor of more modern systems, Titan has become primarily a launch vehicle. As a launch vehicle, the Titan is required to do much more than propel a warhead into space and guide it back to Earth. For example, during the Gemini program the Titan had to boost the spacecraft into orbit, a job once likened to walking a mile with one's eyes shut and arriving no more than ten centimeters from one's destination. The job was made simpler during later flights by the use of an onboard computer which could be used to plot the flight path.

On interplanetary missions such as the Viking mission to Mars the Titan required a greater accuracy than on any of its previous missions. The distance from Earth to Mars is about 55,520,000 kilometers. The Titan vehicle benefited directly from the information gained from previous space missions.

When the Titan has reached the correct orbit with a satellite, a mechanism in the transtage allows it to separate from the satellite. The malfunction of this mechanism has resulted in the loss of many satellites. With the cost of spacecraft running into hundreds of millions of dollars, it has proved an expensive mistake.

## Context

Titan was the second American ICBM to be produced. The Atlas and Jupiter rockets had been built not out of necessity but by scientists who were interested in doing something new. Engineers soon became content with traditional V-2 rocket design. It was only when the need for ICBMs arose that progress was made.

The Titan provided engineers with a chance to put into use some new practices. Previously it was considered too risky to ignite a second stage after the first had been jettisoned. The use of alcohol and oxygen, though somewhat safer, was thought to provide less thrust than other fuels. Experimentation resulted in the discarding of Titan's first stage before the second stage was ignited, the use of oxygen and kerosene, and finally the mixture of UDMH, hydrazine, and nitrogen tetroxide as fuel.

During the Gemini program, the Titan was found to suffer from the pogo effect. Previously, the condition, though recognized, was regarded as unfortunate but unpreventable. Using the Titan in the manned space program prompted a rocket redesign. When the solution was found, it was applied to other rockets as well.

Until the 1980's, the Titan 3 rockets were used often in the U.S. space program. Yet, with the deployment of the space shuttle, an increasing number of companies showed an interest in the more advanced reusable orbiter as a launcher. The U.S. Air Force, however, had regarded the shuttle as too experimental. Expressing its confidence in the basic Titan design, the Air Force awarded Martin Marietta a contract for the successor to the Titan 3 series. With the explosion of the *Challenger* space shuttle in January, 1986, the Air Force's fears were realized, and the Titan was once again in demand for the launching of satellite payloads. After the *Challenger* explosion, all satellites which carry volatile fuel were banned from the shuttle. This ban created a new market for the Titan.

## Bibliography

Binder, Otto O. *Victory in Space*. New York: Walker and Co., 1962. One of the best books written in its period, *Victory in Space* answers many key questions that were being asked during the early part of the space program. The author does not set out to write about the Titan rocket, but it is mentioned in the context of other subjects.

Emme, Eugene M., ed. *The History of Rocket Technology*. Detroit: Wayne State University Press, 1964. This collection of essays provides a useful survey of the U.S. space program as a whole. Essays on the Atlas, Thor, Titan, and Minuteman ICBMs are followed by a concluding essay on the Titan 3C. Includes a bibliography.

Ley, Willy. *Events in Space*. New York: David McKay Co., 1969. This book includes sections covering the beginning of satellites and rockets. Ley covers Titan, Titan 2, and Titan 3C. It should be noted, however, that the primary topic is space exploration, not the Titan series.

Newlon, Clarke. *One Thousand and One Questions Answered About Space*. New York: Dodd, Mead and Co., 1962. Newlon answers some of the questions most frequently asked about the Titan ICBM and Titan 2. Information is also given about Titan's contemporaries. Capsule biographies of important people in the field of rocketry are included.

Peterson, Robert W. *Space: From Gemini to the Moon and Beyond*. New York: Facts on File, 1972. This volume shows the involvement of the Titan launcher in the American space program. The Gemini project, MOL, and various other payloads are discussed. Suitable for high school and college reading.

Sobel, Lester A., ed. *Space: From Sputnik to Gemini*. New York: Facts on File, 1965. Gives additional information on the use of the Titan rocket as a launching vehicle during the beginning of the space program. The book ends with the introduction of the Titan 3C.

Taylor, John W. R., ed. *Jane's All the World's Aircraft, 1981-1982*. London: Jane's Publishing Co., 1981. Written for a general audience, this volume includes information on the later series of Titan rockets.

*John Newman*

## Cross-References

Atlas Launch Vehicles, 160; The Gemini Program, 487; U.S. Launch Vehicles, 749; Saturn Launch Vehicles, 1240; The U.S. Space Shuttle, 1626; Spaceplanes, 1912; Vandenberg Air Force Base, 2069.

# TRACKING AND DATA-RELAY COMMUNICATIONS SATELLITES

*Date:* Beginning April 4, 1983
*Type of satellite:* Communications
*Countries:* The United States and the Soviet Union

*Both the United States and the Soviet Union have developed and begun implementation of separate communications satellite systems, which are designed to improve tracking and data-relay capabilities from low-Earth-orbiting manned and unmanned spacecraft. Scheduled to be fully operational by the end of the 1990's, both systems have been hampered by payload losses, malfunctions, and delays.*

### Principal personages

DALE W. HARRIS, the Tracking and Data-Relay Satellite System
Project Manager at Goddard Space Flight Center
CHARLES M. (CHUCK) HUNTER, TDRSS Deputy Project Manager

## Summary of the Satellites

As manned and unmanned missions in both the U.S. and the Soviet space programs increased in number and complexity, it became apparent that former tracking and data-relay systems were becoming obsolete. Based on expensive, complicated networks of ground stations, communications ships, and outmoded equipment, the old systems only provided minimal contact with manned spacecraft. They also were unable to process and relay the enormous volumes of data generated by a new era of scientific applications satellites. Upgrading and expanding the old systems was economically unfeasible and inefficient for the task at hand.

In December of 1976, the National Aeronautics and Space Administration (NASA) contracted with the Space Communications Company (Spacecom) to develop and implement a tracking and data-relay system that would be able to transmit data efficiently and continuously from low-Earth-orbiting manned and unmanned spacecraft and maintain almost uninterrupted contact with manned crews. Spacecom, a joint venture between Continental Telecom and Fairchild Industries developed the Tracking and Data-Relay Satellite System (TDRSS). Its basic design consisted of two operational satellites, one in-orbit spare, and a ground station. The satellites would function as repeaters, neither processing nor altering any communications. The uplink channels would receive transmissions from the ground, amplify them, and transmit them to the spacecraft. The downlink channels would receive, amplify, and transmit signals from the craft to the ground station. When completely operational, the system could provide almost continuous contact with manned space vehicles such as Skylab and the space shuttle. Data transmitting equipment could transfer the entire contents of a medium-sized library in seconds. It would be the largest and most advanced space tracking and data-relay system ever developed. TDRSS would form a vital link between Earth and near space.

The TDRSS ground terminal is located at White Sands Test Facility in southern New Mexico. TRW Defense and Space Systems Group designed, built, and tested the three satellites and integrated the ground terminal equipment. By 1983, the first satellite was ready for launch and the ground station, with its three 18-meter-diameter dish antennae, was completed. The New Mexico location was chosen for its arid climate and clear line of sight to the relay satellites. All transmissions to and from TDRSS pass through the White Sands station.

On April 4, 1983, at 1:30 P.M. eastern standard time (EST), space shuttle mission STS 6 was launched at Cape Canaveral, Florida. After the first of the three TDRSS satellites, TDRS-A, was launched from the *Challenger* payload bay and proper orbit was achieved, it became known as TDRS 1. The satellite, weighing 2,250 kilograms, measures 17 meters across at the two winglike solar panels. The panels provide the craft with electrical power. The design of the satellite consists of three modules. The equipment module, located in the lower part of the core hexagon, encompasses the subsystems that control and stabilize the satellite. It also contains the equipment that stores and manages the power supply and the machinery that operates the telemetry and tracking equipment. The communications payload module is in the upper portion of the hexagon, just below the multiple-access antenna elements. It contains electronic equipment that regulates the flow of transmissions between the various antennae and other communications functions. Finally, the antenna module consists of a platform holding various antennae, including thirty helices of the multiple-access phased array.

An Inertial Upper Stage (IUS) booster rocket was to place TDRS 1 in a geostationary orbit (an orbit in which a satellite revolves around Earth once every 24 hours). A malfunction in the IUS left the satellite tumbling in a 35,317-by-20,273-kilometer orbit, forcing ground controllers to separate the satellite from the IUS, and the craft stabilized itself in an elliptical orbit.

A NASA/TRW team devised a way to use the tiny onboard attitude control thrusters (designed for minor station-keeping duties) to nudge the satellite into its proper orbit through a series of controlled firings. The maneuver took extensive engineering and technical analysis and thirty-nine separate burns to get the spacecraft into its appointed orbit of 67 degrees west longitude on June 29, 1983. Following checkout, it was moved to its operational position of 41 degrees west. In its position 35,690 kilometers above the equator on the northeast coast of Brazil, TDRS 1 is considered the "east" station in the TDRSS network.

With the launch of TDRS 1, the new system became partially operational. The satellite, assisted by a few of the remaining ground stations from the Spaceflight Tracking and Data Network (STDN), began transmitting data to White Sands. Eventually, TDRS 1 would be replaced by another satellite and moved to 79 degrees west to function as the in-orbit spare for the system.

On January 28, 1986, at 11:40 A.M. EST, TDRS-B, which would have become TDRS 2 and the "west" link in the TDRSS network, was destroyed when the space shuttle *Challenger* exploded during launch at Cape Canaveral. The *Challenger* disaster caused many delays in the U.S. space program, and these included the TDRSS launch schedule. It finally moved forward when TDRS-C (after launch, TDRS 3), designated to replace the destroyed satellite, was launched from the space shuttle *Discovery* on mission STS 26 on September 29, 1988. The satellite was placed in orbit at 151 degrees west for testing and support of shuttle mission STS 27. After STS 27 completed its mission, TDRS-C (TDRS 3) would be moved to a final position of 171 degrees west over the Pacific Ocean. It would become the "west" station in its geostationary orbit southwest of the Hawaiian and Gilbert Islands.

With the successful launch of TDRS-D (TDRS 4) from STS 29, and the replacement of TDRS 1 as an in-orbit spare, TDRSS would become fully operational. In 1988, expansion was already under way at the White Sands Ground Station, and TDRS-E, -F, -G, and -H launches were scheduled through 1993. Contracts were awarded in 1987 for the development of an advanced TDRSS.

In 1983, the same year the United States launched its first phase of TDRSS, the Soviets announced their plans to develop and implement an advanced satellite tracking and data-relay system known as the Satellite Data-Relay Network (SDRN). Confronted with many of the same problems that the United States was having with its outmoded system, the Soviets had the additional pressure of the sophisticated Mir space station and its proposed Kvant science module with which to deal. Both would collect vast amounts of data, and the old very high frequency (VHF) network of ground stations and communications ships was unable to handle the volume efficiently. The strain on manned space missions under the old system was becoming excessive. Opportunities for communications between Soviet manned missions and the ground were of short duration and irregular frequency under the old system. For example, communications both to and from Mir and the ground were only possible for about four hours each day. The Soviets considered this unsafe and a serious impediment to a smooth work pattern.

Apparently the system would be similar to TDRSS and feature two geostationary repeater satellites, one in-orbit spare, and a ground station. The first satellite was designated as "Luch." Observers believe that Luch, or Kosmos 1700, was launched sometime in early 1986. Listeners to the Mir VHF downlink detected a new signal that indicated that Mir was connected to a geostationary satellite. Later it was noted that Kosmos 1700 was in geostationary orbit over the equator at 95 degrees east. It had the capabilities of communicating with Mir for a forty-minute session during every orbit and had wideband microwave links capable of handling much more data than the very restricted VHF downlinks.

Observation showed that Kosmos 1700 provided television and data relay from Mir to the ground from March, 1986, to February, 1987. At that time, it was noted that the Mir crew had begun to use the old VHF system again, and certain signals indicated that the Mir/satellite hookup was no longer operational. It is believed that the satellite failed and drifted off-station. As of July, 1987, it appeared that the Soviets had abandoned trying to transfer the tremendous amounts of data collected by the Kvant science module until they could get the satellite functioning again.

It also appeared that the Soviets were having other problems implementing SDRN. It is suspected that the system's deployment was further delayed when the Soviets lost the payload launched on a Proton rocket on January 30, 1988, from the Baikonur cosmodrome. Observers believe that the satellite was stranded in a short-lived, low orbit because of a failure of the upper stage of the launch vehicle. Soviet authorities, however, have not reported the loss of any satellite with a Kosmos designation.

In spite of their losses, the Soviets are expected to press forward with the development and deployment of a sophisticated tracking and data-relay network for Mir, Kvant, and subsequent low-Earth-orbiting missions.

## Knowledge Gained

Although the United States TDRSS network is only partially operational, it has already improved and enhanced the U.S. space program's tracking and data-relay capabilities for low-orbit spacecraft. Before the launch of TDRS-C, with only one satellite in orbit and the ground station operational, TDRSS had significantly influenced U.S. space research and operations. Alone, the first satellite and ground station had stretched communications between Earth and the space shuttle from 15 percent to 50 percent of mission time. Augmented with fifteen STDN ground stations, TDRS 1 and its ground station allowed the astronauts on STS 9, launched in November, 1983, to be the first U.S. shuttle crew to enjoy almost continuous communications with Earth. The European-built orbital research module Spacelab, carried in STS 9's cargo bay, was able to transmit volumes of data to scientists on Earth instantaneously. Researchers were able to respond to project results while many experiments were still ongoing. On that mission, more data were retrieved through space-to-ground communications than on all other previous U.S. space-flights combined because of the partially operational TDRSS. Fifty times more information was transmitted on Spacelab's ten-day mission than on Skylab's twenty-four-day mission a decade before. TDRS 1 also returned outstanding pictures from the Landsat 4 satellite, in what was the first satellite-to-satellite-to-Earth data relay.

The potential of TDRSS is vast. The deployment of TDRS 3 increased the communications capability to 85 percent. The completed system was designed to allow almost uninterrupted voice and data exchange between Earth and U.S. manned spacecraft. The only ground station involved will be the New Mexico TDRSS station. All other STDN stations, except those used during shuttle launches and those used to track satellites incompatible with TDRSS, will shut down. A fully operational TDRSS will also enable almost continuous command and telemetry communications between the ground control centers and unmanned, automatic research and applications spacecraft orbiting several thousand kilometers above Earth. Its ability to transmit vast amounts of data also eliminates the necessity to send additional bulky equipment aboard these craft for data storage.

A "typical" message from a low-orbiting research spacecraft would be transmitted to the proper TDRSS satellite. The TDRS would then relay that data instantly to the ground station at White Sands. From there, it might be sent back up to a commercial communications satellite and relayed to Goddard Space Flight Center (GSFC) in Greenbelt, Maryland. TDRSS is under the aegis of GSFC, and all data are transmitted there for processing and further routing or storage.

At GSFC, the message might again be relayed to another commercial satellite and sent to an appropriate data center such as the Payload Operations Control Center (POCC). This is where researchers can obtain instant results from their research equipment in space. Many POCCs are located at the home laboratories of researchers on university campuses or in research centers in the United States and abroad. The amount of information transmitted and the information gained under the partially operational TDRSS is more than impressive. The completed system will revolutionize the United States' abilities to increase and develop the commercial, scientific, and industrial potentials of space.

Certainly, the Soviets have gained some information and data from their short-lived Kosmos 1700 satellite. The potential gains that their system will provide once it is operational mirror those of the United States.

## Context

The Goddard Space Flight Center has played a pioneering role in both manned and unmanned spacecraft tracking and data communications since the earliest days of the U.S. space program. From the first minitrack system to the Spaceflight Tracking and Data Network, GSFC has played a prominent role in keeping track of and communicating with U.S. spacecraft. Until the mid-1970's, these systems consisted of a number of complex, sometimes overlapping networks of ground-based antennae, tracking stations, and communications ships.

In 1972, the STDN was founded when the Space Tracking and Data Acquisition Network (STADAN) merged with the Manned Space Flight Network (MSFN). The move to update and streamline the old system resulted in a network of fifteen international stations. Twelve of the stations tracked manned and unmanned Earth orbital and suborbital missions, and three were used to support the infant space shuttle program. During the 1970's, STDN was continually upgraded to provide greater data processing capabilities and increase manned flight communications time. Most of the STDN equipment had been installed in the mid-1960's to support the Apollo program. Obsolescence and maintenance difficulties continued to increase.

With the advent of the Space Transportation System program and its schedule of frequent flights and the increasing sophistication of unmanned applications and research satellites, it became apparent that either STDN would have to go through a major upgrade or a new system would have to be developed. Studies revealed that it would be less expensive and more efficient to devise a new system using the latest technological advances than to attempt to refurbish the outmoded STDN. Plans were initiated for a new Space Network that would provide global coverage for U.S. spacecraft using a low-Earth orbit. The system would be able to support the ambitious projects scheduled for the future. The key component of the Space Network would be TDRSS. The system would be cost effective, provide almost uninterrupted coverage, and be able to transmit mountains of data. It would also eliminate the need to go through the political maneuvers necessary to maintain or set up additional ground stations in foreign countries.

The full deployment of the TDRSS and the completion of the $18.5 million ground terminal backup facility would make the Space Network a vital link between Earth and space. Each TDRSS satellite has a functioning life expectancy of about ten years and costs about $100 million. Total cost for the TDRSS program through 1993 is an estimated $3.1 billion.

Some of the projects that would benefit from the Space Network included shuttle missions, space stations, commercial satellites, research and data-gathering satellites, and the Hubble Space Telescope. Although the Air Force would make some use of TDRSS, the system does have some disadvantages from a military point of view: The lack of security equipment and the fact that NASA only leases the satellites are two reasons for the armed forces' reluctance to make use of them.

Plans for a Soviet geostationary tracking and data-relay system grew out of similar problems with an outmoded and inefficient system and the need to have a network that would handle the increased activity from the manned and unmanned programs.

## Bibliography

Branegan, John. "Mir Communications in 1987." *Spaceflight Magazine* 30 (March, 1988): 108-112. The article reports observed communication signals both to and from the Soviet space station Mir. It also relates some background on the old Soviet tracking and data system and the new geostationary Satellite Data-Relay Network. College-level material.

Froelich, Walter. *The New Space Network: The New Tracking and Data Relay Satellite System.* NASA EP-251. Washington, D.C.: Government Printing Office, n.d. A booklet published by NASA that describes the Tracking and Data-Relay Satellite System and the Space Network. Presents technical information in terms comprehensible to the layman. Includes color photographs, graphs, charts, and illustrations. Suitable for general audiences.

Karas, Thomas. *The New High Ground: Strategies and Weapons of Space-Age War.* New York: Simon and Schuster, 1983. An in-depth look at the latest in space-age military weapons and systems and their proposed deployment in space. The book briefly discusses the role of TDRSS in military applications. Some technical material written for a general audience. Contains an index, notes, and acknowledgments.

National Aeronautics and Space Administration. *Goddard Space Flight Center.* Washington, D.C.: Government Printing Office, 1987. A pamphlet describing the history and programs of the Goddard Space Flight Center.

_____. *NASA: The First Twenty-five Years, 1958-1983.* NASA EP-182. Washington, D.C.: Government Printing Office, 1983. A chronological history of NASA and the U.S. space program during its first twenty-five years. Designed for use by teachers in the classroom, it features color photographs, charts, graphs, tables, and suggested classroom activities. Topics include tracking and data-relay systems, applications, aeronautics, manned and unmanned spacecraft, and missions. Suitable for a general audience.

Rosenthal, Alfred, ed. *A Record of NASA Space Missions Since 1958*. Washington, D.C.: Government Printing Office, 1982. Brief summaries and documentation of all NASA manned and unmanned space missions since 1958. Technical data include descriptions of the spacecraft and launch vehicle, payload, purpose, project results, and major participants and key personnel. Suitable for a general audience.

Thomas, Shirley. *Satellite Tracking Facilities: Their History and Operation*. New York: Holt, Rinehart and Winston, 1963. A somewhat dated text, which is useful for its history of early spacecraft tracking and data-relay systems and the relationship to the early U.S. space program. Contains an index and footnotes. Suitable for a general audience.

*Lulynne Streeter*

## Cross-References

Goddard Space Flight Center, 563; The Mir Space Station, 1025; The National Aeronautics and Space Administration, 1032; The Skylab Program, 1285; Space Shuttle Mission 6: *Challenger*, 1684; Space Shuttle Mission 9: *Columbia*, 1705; Space Shuttle Mission 25: *Challenger*, 1813; Space Shuttle Mission 26: *Discovery*, 1822; The Spaceflight Tracking and Data Network, 1872; The Soviet Spaceflight Tracking Network, 1877; The Spacelab Program, 1884.

# THE UNITED STATES SPACE COMMAND

*Date:* Beginning September 23, 1985
*Type of organization:* Military space agency
*Country:* The United States

*Space technology has developed to the point that systems first devised for exploration have become essential to national defense, providing critical functions. A unified command across all armed services now provides the needed operational focus, consolidating control of space assets and activities in support of nonspace missions.*

*Principal personages*
RONALD REAGAN, President of the United States, 1981-1989
CASPAR W. WEINBERGER, Secretary of Defense
KEN KRAMER, Representative from Colorado

## Summary of the Organization

Military space systems are critical elements in national defense. The military applications of space technology were recognized very early in the space age. As American policy expanded to include national defense as well as scientific concerns, the need became apparent for a space command, unified across all armed services, to provide an operational focus. The need intensified as plans for the Strategic Defense Initiative (SDI) became more concrete.

The U.S. Air Force had consolidated its space-related efforts in the Air Force Space Command (AFSC), formed in September, 1982. The parallel Naval Space Command was established in October, 1983. President Ronald Reagan's announcement in March, 1983, that he would endorse plans for the development of SDI once again focused public attention on the military uses of space. The Joint Chiefs of Staff began to consider the formation of a unified space command. After studying a June 7, 1983, proposal from the Air Force Chief of Staff, the Joint Chiefs recommended the establishment of a unified space command to Secretary of Defense Caspar Weinberger on November 8, 1983. Also, Representative Ken Kramer presented a letter, signed by fifty-three congressmen, to President Reagan on November 18, 1983, recommending that a unified space command be a vital part of the SDI organization.

On November 26, 1983, Secretary Weinberger presented the Joint Chiefs' proposal to the National Security Council, recommending that President Reagan approve it. The Joint Chiefs created the Joint Planning Staff for Space (JPSS) in February, 1984, to plan the transition. On November 20, 1984, President Reagan announced activation of a unified space command by October, 1985. The JPSS worked from late 1984 through 1985 establishing organizational roles and relationships and assigning missions for the U.S. Space Command.

One concern of the planners was the North American Air Defense Command (NORAD). The United States and Canada had formed NORAD to provide early warning of invasions by bombers and centralized operation of air defense forces. As the Soviet danger evolved to ballistic missile and antisatellite capabilities, NORAD's atmospheric early-warning line and jet interceptors became less valuable. (Canada participates in the U.S. missile warning and space surveillance system but declines to participate in missile defense research and development.)

The Joint Chiefs addressed Canada's concerns by specifying that the U.S. Space Command would not be a component of NORAD but would provide NORAD with space surveillance and missile warning capabilities. NORAD is responsible to the National Command Authorities of both the United States and Canada for warning of any aerospace attack on the North American continent but does not have any responsibility for ballistic missile defense.

The Joint Chiefs of Staff approved the NORAD commander in chief as the commander in chief of the U.S. Space Command. NORAD headquarters is located at Peterson Air Force Base, with key warning operations inside Cheyenne Mountain, sixteen kilometers to the west, near Colorado Springs, Colorado. The U.S. Space Command headquarters is also at Peterson. The commander in chief is directly responsible to the President through the Joint Chiefs and the Secretary of Defense. The Joint Chiefs of Staff completed assignment of responsibilities and missions in August, 1985. On August 30, President Reagan gave final approval, with the proviso for a one-year review.

The U.S. Space Command, activated September 23, 1985, has three components: the Air Force Space Command, the Naval Space Command, and the Army Space Command. The Air Force Space Command operates most military space systems for the U.S. Space Command, with headquarters at Peterson and other facilities at Cheyenne Mountain Air Force Base and the Consolidated Space Operations Center at Falcon Air Force Base, fourteen kilometers east of Peterson. The Air Force Space Division, another subgroup, is not part of the U.S. Space Command but part of the Air Force Systems Command. It serves the Department of Defense, planning activities concerning the space shuttle's military use. Its staff also researches, develops, and performs in-orbit testing of Air Force satellites prior to their operation by the Air Force Space Command.

The Naval Space Command, based in Dahlgren, Virginia, has a senior liaison staff at the U.S. Space Command headquarters and two major space-oriented units: the Naval Space Surveillance System (NSSS), based in Dahlgren, and the Navy Astronautics Group (NAG), based in Point Mugu, California. The NSSS functions as a dedicated space-tracking sensor forming an electronic "fence" extending 1,609 kilometers out from both the Pacific and Atlantic coasts, and 4,827 kilometers across the Gulf Coast. It reaches 24,139 kilometers into space and disseminates information to forces at sea. The NSSS also acts as the Alternate Space Defense Operations Center and Alternate Space Surveillance Center. The NAG operates Transit, the oldest operational satellite system.

The Army Space Command, activated on August 1, 1986, as an agency (and as a command in April, 1988), is based at Peterson. It provides military satellite communications and space surveillance support to the U.S. Space Command and support to Army field forces.

The staff of the U.S. Space Command spent most of its first year organizing and hiring new personnel, initiating its planning and operations responsibilities, and establishing relationships with its component commands. These activities included transferring to it the space mission areas of Aerospace Defense Command before the latter's deactivation (NORAD was assigned the air defense responsibilities).

The Joint Chiefs conducted the required review in October, 1986. Besides approving the continuation of one commander in chief for both the U.S. Space Command and NORAD, the Joint Chiefs authorized the U.S. Space Command's deputy commander in chief to be NORAD's vice commander in chief. This ensured continuity of responsibility in supporting NORAD.

On August 14, 1987, the commander in chief reported that the U.S. Space Command Center had reached initial operational capability. The center monitors space events globally, around the clock. It transmits to the National Command Authorities both information and warnings. In the fall of 1987, the Army Space Agency took operational control of space-tracking radar functions and the Defense Satellite Communications System, beginning its transformation into the Army Space Command. Also in 1987, the Army Space Command trained personnel in the use of Global Positioning System (GPS) terminals. These employees received data on position and navigation that allowed speedy, precise response.

During that same year, the Air Force Satellite Control Facility was transferred to the Air Force Space Command from the Air Force Space Division. The satellite control network consists of the Consolidated Space Operations Center (CSOC); the Satellite Test Center in Sunnyvale, California; seven worldwide tracking stations; and worldwide ground stations for the Navstar GPS, Defense Meteorological Satellite Program, and Defense Support Program. Automation of the Air Force Space Command tracking stations, completed in 1988, allows CSOC and satellite test centers to control the stations remotely.

The U.S. Space Command employs fewer than twelve thousand men and women. The headquarters staff employed more than six hundred people in 1988; the composition of the staff was approximately 50 percent Air Force, 30 percent Navy and Marines combined, and 20 percent Army in that year. The U.S. Space Command has responsibility in three broad areas: space operations, space surveillance and warning, and ballistic missile defense planning. Space operations covers space control, directing space support operations, and operating space systems in support of other commands.

Space control, the primary mission of space operations, includes ensuring interference-free access to and operations in space; denying an enemy the use of space-based systems supporting hostile forces; protecting space-related assets; and surveilling space objects.

Ensuring access to space includes the U.S. Space Command's effort to devise requirements for a space launch infrastructure. Denying an enemy the use of hostile space-based systems occurs when needed. Research and development in antisatellite (ASAT) systems technology is ongoing.

Protection of the space-related assets of both the United States and its allies involves passive protection, including such measures as adding maneuvering fuel and hardening electronics, and the U.S. Space Command's Space Defense Operations Center, or Spadoc. Spadoc, located in the Cheyenne Mountain Air Force Base, monitors space activities, detects and verifies potentially hostile acts, and warns space systems owners and operators so they can take appropriate defensive measures if necessary.

The surveillance of space objects is managed by the Space Surveillance Center, also at Cheyenne. The center makes daily observations, predicts approximately where and when man-made objects will reenter the atmosphere, and warns of possible collisions between space objects. With its Space Surveillance Network, it makes thirty to fifty thousand observations daily, detecting, identifying, tracking, and cataloging more than seven thousand man-made orbiting objects. The network uses Earth-based sensors such as nonmechanical phased-array radars which track multiple satellites simultaneously, cameras with telescopes which can detect satellites more than 32,000 kilometers away, and the ground-based electro-optical deep space surveillance system, linked to video cameras to enable transmission to the Space Surveillance Network in minutes.

The second function under the category of space operations, directing space support operations and supporting launch and in-orbit requirements, consists of satellite support and terrestrial support. Satellite support includes both action in support of spaceborne forces and operation of satellite systems. Actions consist of launch; telemetry, tracking, and commanding; in-orbit maintenance; crisis operations planning; and recovery. Operations incorporates the transit satellite operation, the Defense Meteorological Satellite Program (DMSP), and the Satellite Early-Warning System (SEWS). Transit's successor is the Navstar GPS, a twenty-one-satellite radio navigation network designed to provide precise navigation and positioning information for both civilian and military use. The Air Force Space Command operates those GPS satellites already in place. The DMSP, a two-satellite network operated by the Air Force Space Command, provides oceanographic, meteorological, and solar-geophysical data to the Navy, the Air Force, and worldwide weather terminals. SEWS monitors the oceans and known ballistic missile sites worldwide for missile attacks.

Terrestrial support, parallel to satellite support, involves command control communications; surveillance from space; navigation; warnings and indications, including the ballistic missile early-warning system of large stationary radars and phased-array radars; and environmental monitoring for all sea, air, and land forces.

Another aspect of space operations, operating space systems in support of other commands, embraces "force-enhancement" support of communications, navigation, and surveillance for both U.S. and allied ground-based forces.

Space surveillance and warning, the second major responsibility of the U.S. Space Command, involves support to NORAD through providing space surveillance and missile warning data and to commanders in chief needing warnings of attacks for areas outside North America. The third responsibility of the command is ballistic missile defense planning. The U.S. Space Command develops requirements and plans for engaging attacking missiles.

The staff of the U.S. Space Command acts as both operational support and headquarters management. For example, the systems integration, logistics, and support director has important acquisition functions in supporting the Air Force Space Command and ensures operation of command electronics and communications. The intelligence director provides intelligence support to both command headquarters and the space operational intelligence watch crews, who identify space objects and supply strategic-launch warning information. The operations director supports several operational centers in Cheyenne and the U.S. Space Command Center, also providing for the worldwide component operational plans, coordination, and guidance.

The U.S. Space Command performs many other functions. Its deputy director for ballistic missile defense planning devises requirements and interacts with the SDI organization. The Center for Aerospace Analysis provides the U.S. Space Command and other defense agencies with analyses of space systems, air-breathing defense, and missile warning and defense. The command enhances the support provided to operational commanders by space systems and improves support to combatant commanders by codifying operational requirements for such areas as communications, wide-area surveillance, precision navigation, and environmental information.

The U.S. Space Command has established a space annex for other commands' contingency and operational plans and developed procedures to allow theater commanders to request tactical data support. It has devised worldwide requirements for missile warning information and created procedures to distribute this information quickly. The command has also deployed a mobile command control system designed to survive an attack and provide jam-resistant tactical warning and assessment, as well as data on missile events.

Since its inception in 1985, the command has integrated its components. For example, GPS operational crews come from the Army, and Naval Transit experience shape GPS operational techniques. Also, critical early-warning sites include Navy personnel. In short, the U.S. Space Command is well established to protect the United States in space.

## Context

President and former Army General Dwight Eisenhower formulated the first space policy, maintaining that space should be used for peaceful, scientific activities. He favored using space satellites for "open skies" reconnaissance, instead of high-flying U-2 aircraft, which the Soviets successfully attacked. Eisenhower's emphasis on peace led to the United States' early separation of military from civilian space programs. The first proposal for a unified command of military space activities came in 1959; it had been developed by the Chief of Naval Operations but was basically ignored by the other services.

Each service developed different space interests. The Army focused on launch and booster vehicles; the Navy, high-altitude rockets and early satellite technology, growing into space-based fleet-support communications and navigation systems; and the Air Force, intercontinental ballistic missiles at first, and then extensive satellite applications in communications, surveillance, meteorology, and navigation.

President John F. Kennedy did not want the deployment of reconnaissance satellites publicized, and he had classified military launches by 1962. Yet all services were allowed to conduct space research; the Air Force became responsible for research and development and testing of all Department of Defense space projects.

The United States ratified three space treaties under President Lyndon B. Johnson: the Nuclear Test Ban Treaty, prohibiting nuclear explosions in space; the Outer Space Treaty, banning the orbiting of mass-destruction weapons; and the Astronaut Rescue and Return Agreement. To further his Great Society programs, programs aimed at expanding government's role in social welfare, Johnson emphasized the commercial and domestic benefits of space. Better capabilities in communications and meteorology resulted, aiding both civilian and military uses. The Air Force received some funding (in short supply because of the demands posed by the Vietnam War) for research on the Manned Orbiting Laboratory, a potential surveillance post which was later canceled.

Major space policy changes began with President Jimmy Carter's Presidential Directive DD-37. It stated the objective of cooperating with other nations to ensure the freedom to pursue activities in space which enhance mankind's security. It also shifted policy by pursuing the survivability of space weapons systems, creating a program to identify which civilian space resources would be incorporated into military operations during national emergencies, and researching ASAT capabilities permitted by international agreements.

President Reagan built on Carter's foundation with National Security Decision Directive (NSDD) 42, issued in July, 1982. It stated that the United States would conduct national security space activities (including communications, navigation, surveillance, warning, command and control, environmental monitoring, and space defense), develop and operate ASATs, and deny enemies the use of space-based systems in support of hostile forces. Reagan also supported the space shuttle, giving priority to national security missions.

President Reagan's NSDD 85, issued on March 25, 1983, announced his plans for the development of SDI, with a goal of defending against missile attack. Reagan promulgated a national space strategy on August 15, 1984. The shuttle would be the primary launch vehicle for national security missions. The Department of Defense was required to implement the 1982 policy and SDI, ensure access to space by supplementing the shuttle with expendable launch vehicles, and emphasize advanced technologies to provide new capabilities and improve space-based assets.

## Bibliography

Covault, Craig. "Ground Troops to Benefit from Army Space Command." *Aviation Week and Space Technology* 128 (April 25, 1988): 80-82. Discusses the formation of the Army Space Command and its work with the U.S. Space Command. Also discusses the Army astronauts at Johnson Space Center.

_____ . "New Space Operations Center Will Improve Threat Assessment." *Aviation Week and Space Technology* 126 (May 25, 1987): 50, 52. This article offers a description of Spadoc's facilities and operations.

_____ . "NORAD: Space Command Request System for Surveillance of Soviet Weapons." *Aviation Week and Space Technology* 126 (April 6, 1987): 73-76. Discussion of the request for development of space-based intelligence and surveillance systems to counter a range of new Soviet strategic weapons.

_____ . "Space Command: NORAD Merging Missile, Air, and Space Warning Roles." *Aviation Week and Space Technology* 122 (February 11, 1985): 60-62. Includes explanations of how NORAD and the U.S. Space Command will co-operate the new strategies to be implemented, and what the command will control.

_____ . "U.S. Space Command Focuses on Strategic Control in Wartime." *Aviation Week and Space Technology* 126 (March 30, 1987): 83-84. Descriptions of various operations centers in the U.S. Space Command.

_____ . "USAF Initiates Broad Program to Improve Surveillance of Soviets." *Aviation Week and Space Technology* 122 (January 22, 1985): 14-17. This article describes the Air Force Space Command before the U.S. Space Command was formed and the surveillance systems the Air Force operated. Offers information on Soviet space activity as monitored by the Air Force.

McDougall, Walter A. . . . *The Heavens and the Earth: A Political History of the Space Age*. New York: Basic Books, 1985. This scholarly text provides the history, especially the political history, of space exploration. The military uses of space are thoroughly covered.

Michaud, Michael A. G. *Reaching for the High Frontier: The American Pro-Space Movement, 1972-1984*. New York: Praeger Publishers, 1986. The prospace movement (more than fifty advocacy groups, involving more than 200,000 Americans) has developed since the end of the Apollo program. Michaud traces key groups, identifying their origins and goals and telling how they have influenced space policy—however subtly. Includes a bibliography, with many sources on military space activity.

"Several U.S. Military Spacecraft Operating on Final Backup Systems." *Aviation Week and Space Technology* 126 (March 30, 1987): 22-23. A description of what the U.S. Space Command is doing to maintain its surveillance in the light of several military satellites operating without backups.

Smith, Bruce A. "Air Force Supports Demonstration of Surveillance Technology in the 1990's." *Aviation Week and Space Technology* 128 (March 14, 1988): 93, 95. Two examples of space-based surveillance technologies are surveillance of space objects from a space platform and a space-based radar system. The Air Force Space Division is working with U.S. Space Command to define operational requirements. In this article, details are given on these and other ongoing similar projects.

_____ . "USAF Readies Vandenberg: Colorado Center for Military Shuttle Operations." *Aviation Week and Space Technology* 122 (March 18, 1985): 125-126. Discussion of what would be done at the U.S. Space Command once construction was completed and how it would interact with Vandenberg Air Force Base.

"Space Command Completes Acquisition of Pave Paws Warning Radar Installations." *Aviation Week and Space Technology* 126 (May 18, 1987): 128-129. A description of Pave Paws (Phased-Array Warning System), which tracks intercontinental and submarine-launched missiles as well as space objects for the U.S. Space Command.

*Patricia Jackson*

## Cross-References

Attack Satellites, 167; Early-Warning Satellites, 299; Electronic Intelligence Satellites, 361; U.S. Military Telecommunications Satellites, 1012; Nuclear Detection Satellites, 1080; Ocean Surveillance Satellites, 1085; The Outer Space Treaty, 1111; Space Centers and Launch Sites in the United States, 1599; Space Law: 1968-1979, 1606; Space Law: Ongoing Issues, 1612; Spy Satellites, 1937.

# URANUS' ATMOSPHERE, RINGS, AND MOONS

*Type of phenomenon:* Planetary science

*Uranus, discovered in 1781 by Sir William Herschel, is the seventh planet from the Sun and one of the most unusual planets in the solar system. Much of the information on Uranus was gathered in 1986 as a result of the Voyager 2 flyby.*

## Summary of the Phenomena

Uranus is one of the four gas giants of the solar system, with an atmosphere that is thousands of kilometers deep. The large sheath of gas surrounding Uranus prevents detailed studies of the planet by remote-sensing methods. Therefore, the Voyager 2 spacecraft, equipped with eleven experiments, had to rely solely on output signals from the Uranian system during its flyby in January of 1986.

The Uranian system is the most unusual planetary system in its orientation with respect to the Sun. Essentially, it is as if the whole planetary system—the planet, its moons, and its rings—had been knocked on its side, very much like a top that falls over but remains spinning. A number of theories have been promoted to explain this unusual orientation; most suggest a major impact with some sort of external object. These theories are supported by the current physical condition of the planetary system, manifested especially in the surface features of the Uranian satellites.

It takes Uranus about eighty-four years to revolve once about the Sun. Because of the planet's sideways orientation, each of its poles points toward the Sun for approximately half of each circuit. (Currently, the south pole is pointing toward the Sun.) The planet appears to lack a large internal source of heat; only about 30 percent of its heat seems to come from the interior. The interiors of Jupiter and Saturn supply 70 percent of their heat, whereas the inner planets, such as Earth, have centers which provide less than 1 percent of their heat.

The dark side of the planet, at 1,000 Kelvins, is hotter than the light side, because the latter is only about halfway through its lit phase. Conversely, the dark side had been heating for twice as long as it has been cooling. A tenuous gas, such as that which makes up the upper portions of the Uranian atmosphere, does not cool itself efficiently; once heated, it remains so for a long time.

The atmosphere of Uranus has low visual contrast and appears in all the direct photographs returned by Voyager as a filmy, blue-green sphere. Uranus, like the other planets in the solar system, reflects the Sun's light. The planet appears blue-green because the hydrocarbons in its atmosphere absorb the red wavelengths of sunlight and reflect most of the blue and green light.

The tropopause is the upper boundary of the lowest layer of the atmosphere, or the troposphere. In the troposphere, the temperature generally declines with height. The atmosphere is coldest (about 52 Kelvins) at the tropopause; in the extreme upper atmosphere, the temperature increases to 750 Kelvins. The temperature also varies as a function of latitude. At approximately 30° latitude in both hemispheres, there is a drop of a few degrees. This dip is known as the latitude collar and may be caused by cold gas currents welling up from below.

Approximately 83 percent of the Uranian atmosphere is molecular hydrogen. Molecular helium represents approximately 15 percent. Models of planet formation are heavily dependent on the amount of helium in the planet's atmosphere, and the helium fraction is particularly important in reconstructions of the history of the four gas giants—Jupiter, Saturn, Uranus, and Neptune. The other major constituent of the Uranian atmosphere is the gas methane.

The upper atmosphere is composed almost exclusively of atomic and molecular hydrogen. The lower atmosphere contains methane and acetylene. Acetylene results from the breakdown of methane by the ultraviolet portion of the Sun's light. The sunlight reacting with the methane in the atmosphere contributes to the haze at the planet's poles, known as the "polar smog."

There are winds on Uranus similar to the jet stream on Earth; they always blow from the west, in the direction of the planet's rotation on its axis, so they are referred to as prograde winds. The velocities of these winds increase at higher altitudes and higher latitudes. Meteorological theory did not predict the direction of the winds, and scientists were surprised at the information returned by Voyager. They deduced that Uranian atmospheric circulation is dominated by forces associated with the planet's rotation.

There are four discrete clouds that lie deep in the atmosphere. These clouds are moving with a velocity of 100 meters per second, a speed equivalent to a violent tornado's, and are similar to Earth's thunderheads. The tracking of these clouds provided the first unambiguous measurements of the Uranian atmosphere. Their rotational periods vary from fourteen to seventeen hours; the ones closest to the equator have the longest periods. The variations mean that the clouds are not propelled simply by the planet's rotation. (Uranus takes 17.24 hours to spin once on its axis.)

Uranus' sunlit south polar region appears dark in violet light, which implies that there is some sort of haze (the polar smog) that absorbs violet light. Long exposures of the planet's dark northern hemisphere supplied no evidence of lightning, as was discovered in the Jovian system. Voyager 2 detected some auroral emissions, however, at the planet's dark north pole. The aurora rotates at the same rate as the planet.

A planet's ionosphere is that layer of its atmosphere where the amount of free electrons becomes significant. In the Uranian atmosphere, there appear to be two distinct, narrow ionospheric layers at altitudes between 2,000 and 3,500 kilometers above the planet's surface. In comparison, Earth's ionosphere is 80 to 120 kilometers above sea level.

In the past, the only planet thought to have rings was Saturn. As telescope technology improved, fainter and smaller objects began to be detected, and scientists discovered that Jupiter and Uranus also have rings. Voyager 2 was able to study these rings in detail.

Before Voyager's encounter with Uranus, nine distinct rings had been deduced from Earth-based measurements. (This ring system was first discovered in 1977 by

James Elliot and his colleagues.) The method of determining quantitative details of individual rings relies on stellar occultation, the process of measuring variations in the light from stars (two stars, in the case of Uranus) as they are repeatedly obscured by material in the rings. The Voyager 2 spacecraft data yielded detailed information on the nine known rings and provided evidence for at least two additional rings and some ring arcs, or incomplete rings.

The rings tend to be almost circular and are concentric with respect to the planet. The eleven identified rings, from the innermost to the outermost, are 1986U2R, 6, 5, 4, α, β, η, γ, δ, 1986U1R, and ε. (The strange nomenclature associated with the ring system is the result of two different groups' naming the rings. One group started naming rings from the inside out, using Greek letters, and the other group started from the outside, using Arabic numbers. The two Voyager rings are named for the year of their discovery.) The width of the rings increases in proportion to their distance from the planet.

The material that makes up the Uranian ring system has very little mass and is very dark, with a total reflectivity of only 1.6 to 2 percent. Its reflective power, or albedo, is similar to that of the minor Uranian satellites detected by Voyager. Photographs taken with different filters show that the γ and η rings' coloration is different from that of the ε, δ, β and α rings. The system's extreme darkness may be caused either by carbonaceous material in the rings or by high-energy proton bombardment of methane trapped in the icy surfaces of the rings. Irradiation of methane is known to darken the surfaces, and there is a radiation cloud surrounding the Uranian system which is more intense than the one surrounding the Saturnian system. This radiation process, as modeled in terrestrial laboratories, tends to cause darkening and reddening of surfaces, however, and there is no apparent reddening of the Uranian ring material or satellites.

The ε ring is the outermost and most dominant ring of the system; it represents 70 percent of the system's surface area. This ring has been extensively studied, and astronomers have found that it, like the other Uranian rings, lacks particles smaller than a few tenths of a centimeter in diameter. In fact, most of the particles in the ε ring are larger than one meter in diameter. The Uranian ring system is much closer to the parent planet than Saturn's rings are to Saturn, and the planet's extended hydrogen corona, or atmosphere, sweeps up any small particles. As a result, there is only 10 percent as much dust in Uranus' rings as there is in Saturn's most tenuous ring, and all the dust in the Uranian ring system would make a ball no more than 100 meters in diameter.

The images returned by Voyager revealed new details of the rings that had been discovered from ground-based observations. It was found that the α ring is composed of four strands, the β ring of three strands, and the δ ring of a single strand in one portion of its orbit but three strands elsewhere. (The Uranian ring system is similar to the Saturnian ring system in that there are both distinct rings and rings that change their character in different portions of their orbit.) The γ ring is very narrow, measuring only 600 meters across, and very thin, whereas the η ring is broad.

Orbital velocity is the speed with which an entity moves about a central body. The rings' orbital velocity decreases as they proceed outward from the planet, a phenomenon caused by the decrease in the planet's gravitational pull. Ring 6 has an orbital velocity of 12 kilometers per second; the $\epsilon$ ring has an orbital velocity of less than 11 kilometers per second. (Earth's orbital velocity about the Sun is approximately 30 kilometers per second, or 108,000 kilometers per hour.)

Two of Uranus' moons confine the $\epsilon$ ring's particles to their orbit. The path of the moon 1986U7 is between the $\delta$ and 1986U1R rings, and the path of the moon 1986U8 is outside the $\epsilon$ ring. There are no other detectable "shepherd" moons in the main body of the ring system.

Before the Voyager 2 flyby, five Uranian moons had been observed from Earth. Voyager detected an additional ten. Uranus' five major moons range from 484 to 1,610 kilometers in diameter; the ten minor moons range from 40 to 170 kilometers. The large moons take from 33.9 to 323.1 hours to orbit the planet and have albedos of from 19 to 40 percent. The smaller ones, because they are closer to Uranus, have orbital periods which range from 8 to 18.3 hours; they are also quite dark, with albedos of less than 10 percent. All the Uranian moons, with the exceptions of Phoebe and the dark regions of Iapetus, are darker than the Saturnian moons. The surface material of the Uranian moons absorbs both ultraviolet and infrared light.

The orbits of the Uranian satellites are nearly circular. With the exception of Miranda, the moons travel in Uranus' equatorial plane. The two moons closest to the planet have orbits inside the Roche radius, the region in which a planet's tidal forces prevent the growth of large satellites. These two moons, 1986U7 and 1986U8, are the shepherd moons for the $\epsilon$ ring.

The fifteen moons, from innermost to outermost, are 1986U7 (Cordelia), 1986U8 (Ophelia), 1986U9, 1986U3, 1986U6, 1986U2, 1986U1, 1986U4, 1986U5, 1985U1, Miranda, Ariel, Umbriel, Titania, and Oberon. The moons' orbital periods increase as the distance from the planet increases. For each of the moons detected by Voyager, the first four digits of the name are the year of discovery. The year is followed by the letter *U*, for Uranus, and a counter to designate the moon's order of discovery within the year. Thus, 1986U5 is the fifth Uranian moon discovered in the year 1986.

The major Uranian moons have undergone some degree of differentiation, a process whereby some of the dense rock settles toward the central portion of a moon and some of the lighter, brighter ice rises to the surface. For differentiation to occur, there must be an internal heat source, which in turn requires a critical satellite mass.

The four outermost moons—Ariel, Umbriel, Titania, and Oberon—have significantly higher densities than all but one of the Saturnian satellites of comparable size. This relatively higher density implies a smaller fraction of water ice in the Uranian moons than in their Saturnian counterparts. Water ice has been detected on each of the five major moons of Uranus, whereas methane has not been detected on any. All the major moons have densities which rule out a cometary origin.

Oberon, discovered in 1787 by Sir William Herschel, appears to be undergoing a late-stage, global-scale tectonic episode. The most prominent feature of this outermost moon of the Uranian system is a large mountain which rises approximately 20 kilometers above the moon's limb. Oberon's diameter, density, color, and albedo are very similar to Titania's, but the two satellites' cratering records are quite dissimilar; Titania has many fewer craters wider than 10 kilometers than Oberon. The presence of a large number of impact craters on Oberon and Umbriel implies that these moons represent some of the oldest surfaces of the Uranian satellite system. There are dark patches on the crater floors, which are an indication of icy volcanic activity but little tectonic activity. The Tsiolkovsky crater in the highlands of Earth's Moon is similar to these dark-floored craters.

Umbriel, discovered in 1851 by William Lassell, is the darkest of the major satellites, with an albedo of 10 percent. It has the lowest contrast across its surface and appears dull gray. These qualities suggest a young surface, but the moon's crater topography suggests an ancient surface which seems to have remained unchanged for billions of years. The combination of young and old characteristics indicates that the moon may recently have been coated with a uniform blanket of dark material.

Titania, also discovered in 1787 by Herschel, is distinguished by an extensive network of faults, similar to that on Earth's Moon, which covers half the satellite's surface. These extensional faults may have formed when water in the interior froze and expanded, shattering the crust above. Titania's youngest features are its bright craters, whose abundance is consistent with the impact of occasional comets over the last three to four billion years. This neutral gray moon is covered with craters 10 to 50 kilometers in diameter and exhibits only a few larger craters.

Ariel, discovered by Lassell in 1851, has the youngest surface of the outer moons, with an extensive system of faults, but is the least cratered. Ariel's fault valleys lie along its equator. Craters larger than 50 kilometers are absent. The youngest features are bright-rimmed craters and bright deposits on the surface. (Ariel is the brightest of the Uranian satellites.) This active moon is about one-third the size of Earth's Moon.

Miranda was discovered in 1948 by Gerard Kuiper. Its most notable feature is a dominant chevron-shaped fault with sharp corners, postulated to be the result of an external impact or of internal forces. The terrain on the high side of the fault is thought to have been subjected to compressional forces. Miranda is the smallest and innermost of the major Uranian moons and has a surface temperature of only 86 Kelvins. It is about one sixth the size of Earth's moon. The surface is marked by old, heavily cratered terrain and by young, complex terrain consisting of bright and dark bands, scarps, and ridges. The scarps are higher than the walls of the Grand Canyon. Large impact craters are absent.

## Knowledge Gained

Detailed data on the temperature, pressure, and makeup of the layers of Uranus' atmosphere were acquired by a number of different instruments aboard the Voyager 2 spacecraft. These data provided scientists with new information about this icy, remote world.

The breakdown, or dissociation, of molecular hydrogen into atomic hydrogen was first measured by Voyager during the flybys of the Jovian and Saturnian systems, but it was not recognized as a new process until it was observed at Uranus, where it is more intense. This phenomenon, known as the electroglow, could be caused by the interaction of atmospheric winds with the ionosphere. Low-energy electrons in the ionosphere interact with the atmosphere's molecular hydrogen, and this interaction yields atomic hydrogen and releases energy. The energy creates a glow which dominates the ultraviolet portion of the spectrum and produces an auroral region centered on the planet's magnetic pole. (The magnetic pole is tilted 55 degrees with respect to the rotational pole.) Approximately half the atomic hydrogen dissipates away from Uranus and contributes to the extended hydrogen corona about the planet.

Voyager detected two rings around Uranus that had not been observed from Earth. They are very different in size. The first is 1986U1R, which is only one or two kilometers wide. Between this ring and the δ ring is a dark, nearly empty lane which defines the orbit of one of the Uranian moons, 1986U7. The second ring is a broad, diffuse band of material inside ring 6; it is approximately 2,500 kilometers wide. The Voyager data include other observations which may indicate additional rings and ring arcs. The presence of numerous ring arcs, of which at least ten are exceedingly narrow, implies a young, dynamic system and suggests that the ring system may have formed after the planet. Ring arcs were also seen in Voyager images of Saturn's ring system.

Micron-sized particles struck the Voyager spacecraft at a rate of thirty per second near Miranda, which is 75,000 kilometers beyond the ε ring. Dust so far outside the ring system was unexpected.

Voyager 2 provided scientists with detailed geological knowledge of the major Uranian moons. It also tripled the number of known moons in the system.

Voyager photographed Oberon and Titania numerous times to calculate the exact positions required for the flyby. These images, in turn, were used to compute the two moons' masses. Their mass and size imply that Oberon and Titania are 40 to 65 percent rock, a considerably higher rock content than that of the Saturnian moons of comparable size. This result was unexpected, because normally a moon contains more ice the farther it is from the Sun.

The largest of Uranus' minor moons is 1985U1, which was detected by Voyager more than a month before the actual flyby. Because 1985U1 was discovered prior to the probe's close approach, the planned imaging sequence was reprogrammed to include a close-up of it. It is spherical, which is unusual for a moon this small; typically, small moons are quite irregularly shaped. It is nearly ten times the size of the other minor moons but only a third as large as Miranda. Very few craters mark the surface, and all of them were caused by comet impacts over the past several billion years. The moon 1985U1, unlike Uranus' major moons, probably consists of a homogeneous mixture of ice and rock.

Voyager photographed only the southern hemispheres of the Uranian moons, and because its trajectory was such that it made its closest approach to all the moons almost simultaneously, there was little time for close-ups. Perturbations of the δ and γ rings had suggested the presence of a 100-kilometer-wide satellite in their vicinity, but no such satellite appeared in any of the Voyager images.

## Context

Uranus, the first planet to be detected after the invention of the telescope, is twice as far from the Sun as Saturn; its discovery, in 1781, doubled the size of the known solar system. Nineteenth-century scientists were puzzled by anomalies in Uranus' orbit, and to explain these anomalies, several astronomers postulated an eighth planet and made precise predictions of its position. In 1846, the discovery of Neptune proved the predictions correct. Subsequent Earth-based observations revealed that Uranus and Neptune are very similar in volume and mass.

The first successful planetary flyby was achieved in 1962, when the United States launched Mariner 2 on a trajectory toward Venus. Pioneer 10, the first spacecraft to fly by Jupiter, was launched in 1972. By the late 1980's, three other probes had traveled beyond Mars to the outer planets. Pioneer 11 and Voyager 1 returned data on Jupiter and Saturn; Voyager 2 was sent on a tour of all four gas giants.

There were some technical problems early in the Voyager 2 mission, but the spacecraft performed well in its encounters with Jupiter, Saturn, and Uranus. Launched in late 1977, it arrived at Uranus eight years later, on January 24, 1986, within seventy seconds of the predicted arrival time. Flight engineers at the National Aeronautics and Space Administration's Jet Propulsion Laboratory were already planning for the probe's journey to Neptune, which would take another three years.

## Bibliography

Beatty, J. Kelly. "A Place Called Uranus." *Sky and Telescope* 71 (April, 1986): 333-337. Presents an overview of the icy, remote world of Uranus as scanned for the first time in detail by the Voyager spacecraft. Illustrated with some of the processed images returned by Voyager which yielded detailed data on the clouds and rings. Suitable for general audiences.

Chaikin, Andrew. "Voyager Among the Ice Worlds." *Sky and Telescope* 71 (April, 1986): 338-343. An overview of the moons of Uranus as observed by the Voyager spacecraft. Presents some of the photographs that Voyager took of the major moons of the system. Suitable for general audiences.

Cuzzi, Jeffrey N., and Larry W. Esposito. "The Rings of Uranus." *Scientific American* 257 (July, 1987): 52-54. Summarizes the scientific information on the Uranian ring system learned from the analysis of the Voyager 2 data. Presents theories on the formation of the ring system and includes illustrations and photographs of the rings. Written for the layperson.

Ingersoll, Andrew P. "Uranus." *Scientific American* 256 (January, 1987): 38-45. Summarizes the scientific information on Uranus and its atmosphere deduced from data returned by Voyager 2. Describes how the data relate to standard atmospheric models. Includes good illustrations and photographs of the planet and its clouds.

Johnson, Torrence V., et al. "The Moons of Uranus." *Scientific American* 256 (April, 1987): 48-60. Discusses the Uranian moon system and the relevant Voyager 2 data. Explains scientists' theories on the formation of the moon system. Includes photographs of the six largest moons.

*Theresa A. Nagy*

## Cross-References

The Jovian System, 677; Jupiter's Atmosphere, 683; Jupiter's Satellites, 704; Neptune and Its Moons, 1053; Planetary Evolution, 1159; Comparative Planetology, 1168; Saturn's Atmosphere, 1246; Saturn's Moons, 1261; Saturn's Rings, 1268; The History of the Solar System, 1367; The Voyager Program, 2219; Voyager 1: Jupiter, 2227; Voyager 1: Saturn, 2234; Voyager 2: Jupiter, 2241; Voyager 2: Saturn, 2248; Voyager 2: Uranus, 2255.

# THE VAN ALLEN RADIATION BELTS

*Type of phenomenon:* Earth science

*The Van Allen radiation belts are concentrated rings of electrified particles in Earth's magnetosphere. The intensity of their radiation is capable of demagnetizing Earth's magnetic field. Detailed study of the radiation belts led to an understanding of certain phenomena occurring in the ionosphere and the determination of the physical properties of the exosphere.*

*Principal personages*
JAMES A. VAN ALLEN, Explorer Project Scientist
GEORGE H. LUDWIG,
CARL E. MCILWAIN, and
ERNEST C. RAY, members of the Explorer 1 scientific team
SERGEI VERNOV and
ALEXANDER CHUDAKOV, members of the Sputnik 3 scientific team

## Summary of the Phenomena

The Van Allen radiation belts are concentrated, torus-shaped regions of electrified particles in Earth's magnetosphere. The particles, made up of protons, electrons, and neutrons, spiral about in great numbers between Earth's magnetic poles. The magnetic and charged particles within the Van Allen belts can be divided into four regions: the Van Allen geomagnetically trapped radiation region, the auroral region, the magnetosheath, and interplanetary space. The inner and outer belts are part of the Van Allen geomagnetically trapped radiation region. In discussions of the Van Allen belts, the magnetic storm is often referred to as a third radiation belt.

The intensity structure of the inner zone stretches from about 1,000 to more than 5,000 kilometers above Earth. It is mainly independent of time. Its composition is nearly consistent with that expected for the decay products of cosmic-ray-produced neutrons in the atmosphere (a neutron is an elementary, neutral particle of mass); this zone is of cosmic ray origin. The radiation in the middle of the inner zone is composed of electrons with energies exceeding 40 kiloelectronvolts and protons with energies greater than 40 million electron volts. (Electrons are elementary particles of mass with a negative charge; protons are positively charged particles.) In the inner belt, many of the high-energy protons are capable of penetrating several inches of lead. At the edge of the inner zone in the region of geomagnetic latitudes 35 to 40 degrees, particles of low-energy electrons are found. The decay of albedo, or light-reflecting, neutrons gives rise to high-energy protons. Beyond Earth's magnetic field, the mean ionizing capacity is two and one-half times higher than the minimum ionizing capacity. Particles in the inner zone are stable and exist for a long period of time.

The intensity structure of the outer zone stretches about 15,000 to 25,000 kilometers above Earth. This zone undergoes very large temporal fluctuations appearing to be caused by solar activity and auroras, atmospheric heating, and magnetic storms. The outer belt contains soft particles; it is of solar origin. The outer zone contains electrons with more than 40 kiloelectronvolts of energy and protons with more than 60 million electron volts of energy. The outer zone has greater geophysical significance than the inner zone. According to the comparison of E. V. Gorchakov, the boundaries of the outer zone coincide with isochasms (lines of equal probability of auroras). The trapped particles introduce magnetic effects in the outer radiation belt. This effect was measured by Luna 1. The increase in ionization of the outer zone is unstable: The particles exist for a short period of time compared with those of the inner belt.

It is believed that a third radiation belt is produced by magnetic storms. The protons are transported from the Sun in a corpuscular stream and are injected by magnetic field perturbations into Earth's field. The charge exchange with neutral hydrogen in Earth's exosphere is the fastest mechanism of removal and about a hundred times faster than scattering from ions in the exosphere. With the exception of trapped radiation, the entire region in the magnetic cavity is known as the auroral region. The auroral particles, the islands or pulses in the long tail and spikes at high latitudes of 1,000 kilometers, are phenomena which occur in the auroral region. The electrons of uniform angular distribution have a roughly constant intensity between 100 and 180 kilometers in altitude.

The magnetosheath lies between the shock front formed by the solar wind and the magnetic cavity. Electron islands have been observed in the magnetosheath. At its widest, the magnetosheath is about four times the radius of Earth. It contains a compressed, disorderly interplanetary magnetic field. The interplanetary field connected to the Sun is predominantly in the ecliptic plane. The field terminates when the solar wind undergoes a shock transition to subsonic flow.

The lifetime of trapped particles decreases with distance from Earth. The lifetime of electrons with energies greater than one million electron volts at a distance of 1.2 to 1.5 times Earth's radius is about a year. The lifetime of the same electrons reduces to days and months at a distance of 1.5 to 2.5 times Earth's radius. At even greater distances, the lifetime of the particles is measured in minutes. Because Earth is enclosed in the Sun's outer atmosphere, its geomagnetic field does not decrease indefinitely with increasing distance, as does the field of a bar magnet in a vacuum. The solar wind pushes Earth's magnetic field and is deflected by it. At about ten Earth radii, the radiation belt ends abruptly.

Particles of trapped radiation may be lost in two ways. During a magnetic storm, the magnetosphere may lose or gain particles. This occurs at distances of 1.0 to 1.5 times Earth's radius. The other mechanism occurs at distances greater than eight times Earth's radius. The small, rapid variation in the magnetic field at such distances scatters the trapped particles, dumping them into the atmosphere.

Beautiful auroral displays occur when the charged particles are dumped into Earth's upper atmosphere. Solar flares (huge masses of incandescent gas) are ejected into space. Streams of high-energy protons and electrons erupt within the flares. When these beams of high-energy particles are directed toward Earth, Earth's magnetic field is partially disrupted. Particles trapped within the field lines can escape downward toward Earth at the lower ends of the crescent radiation belts. The high-energy particles, reinforced with particles from the Sun, energize the upper atmosphere, causing luminous and often colorful auroras.

## Knowledge Gained

With the data returned by Explorer 1, America's first man-made satellite, a high-energy radiation belt was detected by James A. Van Allen and his assistants, George H. Ludwig, Carl E. McIlwain, and Ernest C. Ray. The same observations were made by Explorer 3, launched by the U.S. Army on March 26, 1958, and Sputnik 3, launched by the Soviet Union on May 15, 1958.

Later, a satellite was launched as part of project Argus, which studied the location, height, and yield of electron blasts. This project was carried out by the Advanced Research Projects Agency. The belt of electrons produced by the Argus nuclear explosions occurs at a distance of twice Earth's radius. Explorer 4, launched on July 26, 1958, carried four Geiger counters to handle high levels of radiation. One of these Geiger counters was shielded with a thin layer of lead to keep out most of the radiation. The satellite reached a height of 2,200 kilometers and registered an intensity of high-energy radiation. From the data returned, scientists concluded that Earth is surrounded by belts of high-energy radiation consisting of particles originating from the Sun and trapped in the lines of force of Earth's magnetic field. These were named "Van Allen radiation belts." Probes to Mercury, Jupiter, Saturn, and Uranus have discovered radiation belts similar to Earth's Van Allen belts.

Explorer 4 obtained a kidney-shaped intensity contour of the inner belt. Data from early Pioneer spacecraft suggested a solar origin of soft particles populating the outer zone. All three Pioneer probes and Luna 1 discovered the crescent-shaped intensity contours of the outer belt. Sputnik 3 data helped identify the bulk of the outer belt particles as low-energy electrons (10 to 50 kiloelectronvolts).

Several more man-made belts were produced in 1962. The Starfish project, an American venture, created a belt much wider than the Argus belt. Decay of some of the particles took several years in low altitudes. In the same year, the Soviets created at least three similar belts.

## Context

In the earliest days of space exploration, gauging the intensity of Earth's radiation belts with unmanned spacecraft was crucial as a first step in manning space. Both the United States and the Soviet Union had a vested interest in the results of early investigations of the magnetosphere.

The Van Allen belts are potentially hazardous to Earth-orbiting spacecraft. They threaten electronics systems and instrumentation and can interfere with radio transmissions. In the late 1950's, it was not known just how hazardous the radiation surrounding Earth would prove to humans.

The relationship between auroras and the Van Allen belts is not completely understood. Scientists do know that most bright auroras are produced by electrons dumped into Earth's atmosphere by solar flares. The auroral particles are the electrons escaping from the outer Van Allen radiation belt. The average kinetic energy of the electrons is 32 kiloelectronvolts. The leakage of corpuscular radiation into the auroral zones is the most important loss of corpuscular radiation from the outer Van Allen belt.

## Bibliography

Donn, William L. *Meteorology*. 4th ed. New York: McGraw-Hill Book Co., 1975. A brief description of the Van Allen radiation belts is presented. The paths of magnetic lines of force and of the electrified particles are clearly depicted.

Haymes, Robert C. *Introduction to Space Science*. New York: John Wiley and Sons, 1971. This book discusses both the composition and sources of the trapped radiation in the magnetosphere. Illustrated.

Kallmann-Bijl, Hildegaard, ed. *Space Research: Proceedings of the First International Space Science Symposium*. New York: Interscience Publishers, 1960. A detailed explanation of the theory behind the nature, origin, and composition of the inner, outer, and third radiation belts is provided. A somewhat technical, but useful, treatment. Illustrated.

Ronan, Colin A. *The Practical Astronomer*. New York: Macmillan, 1981. Provides a brief description of the Van Allen belts. Valuable for its beautiful illustration of the phenomena.

Roy, A. E., and D. C. Clarke. *Astronomy, Structure of Universe*. 2d ed. Bristol: Adam Hilger Publishers, 1982. The authors include a description of the Van Allen belts. The shapes of the belts and the movement of the charged particles are shown.

Sullivan, Walter. *Assault on the Unknown*. New York: McGraw-Hill Book Co., 1961. Sullivan describes the discovery of the Van Allen belts in great detail.

Van Allen, James A. "Radiation Belts Around the Earth." *Scientific American* 200 (March, 1959): 39-47. A very interesting article by the discoverer of the Van Allen belts. Well illustrated.

White, R. Stephen. *Space Physics*. New York: Gordon and Breach, 1970. This volume describes Earth's radiation belts; included are sketches of the energy spectrum. Also presents a discussion of the lifetime of electrons. A list of references is provided for further study.

*Satya Pal*

## Cross-References

Earth's Magnetosphere, 341; Jupiter's Magnetic Field and Trapped Radiation, 697; The Luna Program, 764; Pioneer Missions 1-5, 1116; Solar and Stellar Flares, 1315; The Solar Magnetic Field, 1344; The Sputnik Program, 1930; Sunspots and Starspots, 1963.

# VANDENBERG AIR FORCE BASE

*Date:* Beginning October 4, 1958
*Type of facility:* Military base and launch site
*Country:* The United States

*Vandenberg Air Force Base has served as the site for more than five hundred orbital and one thousand nonorbital launches of American rockets and ballistic missiles. Between 1965 and 1969, a launch complex for the Manned Orbiting Laboratory was built at Vandenberg. From 1979 to 1986, these facilities were expanded to form a West Coast launch complex for the space shuttle.*

*Principal personages*
DAVID WADE, Commander of VAFB
AUBREY B. SLOAN, initial planner of the space shuttle facility at
VAFB and the first commander of the 6,595th Shuttle Test
Group
FORREST S. MCCARTNEY, Commander of Air Force Space
Division
ORLANDO SEVERO, Manager, space shuttle operations at VAFB
GEORGE A. STETZ, Deputy Director, space shuttle operations at
VAFB
RICHARD C. HENRY, Space and Missile Systems Organization,
Los Angeles Air Force Station

## Summary of the Facility

Because of its ideal position for launching satellites into polar orbits, Vandenberg Air Force Base (VAFB) has become a prime lauching site for orbital payloads. As a military facility, Vandenberg has seen the launching of most American reconnaissance satellites and the firing of ballistic missiles for test purposes. In the early 1980's, the base underwent massive construction for a planned West Coast launch and landing site for the space shuttle.

In January, 1956, the U.S. Department of Defense (DOD) had decided that the United States needed a facility to train the men who were handling intercontinental and intermediate range ballistic missiles (ICBMs and IRBMs). On June 7, 1957, the DOD allocated to the U.S. Air Force the northern two-thirds of Camp Cooke, an inactive World War II Army training camp located along forty kilometers of the Pacific Coast just eighty-eight kilometers northwest of Santa Barbara, California. The portion of the land south of the Santa Ynez River fell to the Navy, which installed the Naval Missile Facility, Point Arguello. The Air Force made its new base the headquarters of the First Strategic Aerospace Division and integrated it into the Strategic Air Command.

On October 4, 1958, the Air Force's land was officially dedicated as Vandenberg

Air Force Base, and on December 16, 1958, the first Thor missile was launched, thus making Vandenberg the first operational ICBM facility in the United States.

The Air Force, however, had even more ambitious plans than the testing of missiles, since the location of Vandenberg made it ideal for launching satellites into polar orbit. Flying from pole to pole, a satellite will pass over every part of Earth while the planet rotates beneath it. Because VAFB is situated on a promontory jutting west from the California coastline into the Pacific, a rocket which has been launched toward the South Pole from VAFB will not fly over land until it reaches Antarctica. The risks involved for such a launch are low, because fallout from failed missions will not hit inhabited areas.

In cooperation with the National Aeronautics and Space Administration (NASA) and the United States Navy, the Air Force immediately constructed control centers and pads for the launching of satellites from Vandenberg. The first of these facilities was erected on a small, round peninsula extending west into the Pacific Ocean, situated near the base's airport. Vandenberg, together with the Navy's Point Arguello, became the Western Test Range of the Space and Missile Test Organization (SAMTO), an umbrella organization for Pacific and Atlantic aerospace test ranges.

On February 28, 1959, the first successful lift-off of a launch vehicle took place at Vandenberg: A Thor-Agena A rose from launchpad 75-3-4 (now Space Launch Center 1 West, or SLC 1W) and ejected its payload, Discoverer 1, the first American satellite to reach polar orbit. Soon, the first of the powerful Atlas launch vehicles arrived at Vandenberg, where facilities grew and military and scientific personnel began to populate the village of Lompoc, east of the base.

The Discoverer series carried data capsules which were designed to fall back to Earth to be recovered and analyzed by Air Force specialists. It took one and a half years before the capsule ejected from Discoverer 13 was recovered from the Pacific Oean west of Vandenberg. Eight days later, the Air Force succeeded in retrieving the data capsule of the next Discoverer in midair. From that point onward, the military was able to launch payloads at Vandenberg or Point Arguello and safely recover the data packs; throughout the years, about three-quarters of all the midair recovery attempts have been successful.

In 1960 and 1961, a new class of reconnaissance satellites was launched from the Western Test Range. Enthusiastically promoted as "spy-in-the-sky-satellites" by General Bernard A. Schriever, then Head of Air Force Systems Command, this hardware forced a closer cooperation between the Air Force and the Central Intelligence Agency (CIA) at Vandenberg. As a military base, Vandenberg had a higher-level security classification than did other American space facilities. Yet, the introduction of the new payloads of spy satellites was not kept a secret at first. Both the failure of the first Samos (Satellite and Missile Observation System) satellite, which was launched from Point Arguello on October 11, 1960, and the relative success of Samos 2 were publicized. Similarly, the MIDAS, or Missile Defense Alarm System, satellites were announced publicly at first.

Late in 1961, however, a shroud of secrecy descended on Vandenberg. Military reconnaissance satellites were no longer given names, but a CIA code—KH (for "keyhole") and a number—was applied to them. Discoverer 38 was the last named spy satellite to reach orbit from Vandenberg, in March, 1962. Thereafter, Air Force and Navy officials would not release any information other than the standard statement, "A classified payload went into orbit today."

In 1963 and 1964, the Air Force developed plans for a military Manned Orbital Laboratory (MOL). Riding atop a new Titan 3C (later revised to Titan 3M) rocket, the modified Gemini capsule would be launched from VAFB and circle Earth for thirty days. The main goal of the MOL was to test how well manned spacecraft could perform military space operations. The predecessors of the launch vehicle for the MOL, the Titan 1 and 2 series, had already been test-fired from Vandenberg in their military applications as ICBMs.

In 1964, the Naval Missile Facility at Point Arguello became an integral part of Vandenberg; since then, the facility has been divided into North Vandenberg and South Vandenberg. The combined base encompasses 476 square kilometers, making Vandenberg the third largest base operated by the Air Force. A year later, the DOD authorized the Air Force to build Space Launch Complex 6 (SLC 6 LE-1, or "Slick Six"—as Air Force officials called it) for the MOL on South Vandenberg territory, and construction began immediately.

On February 13, 1969, President Richard M. Nixon established his Space Task Group, which recommended that MOL be canceled and the facilities which had already been erected mothballed. This left SLC 6 with a launchpad, a mobile service tower, and a launch control center in the immediate vicinity.

Throughout the 1960's, Vandenberg had served as the prime launching site for both military and scientific satellites. ICBMs were tested and stored in silos at the northwestern edge of the base. Some of the older pads were decommissioned as advanced facilities were constructed. The Air Force cooperated closely with NASA for many successful launches of rockets delivering communications and scientific satellites such as Echo 2 and the Explorer series.

The 1970's brought new excitement after the frustration over the cancellation of MOL. On June 15, 1971, the first Big Bird (KH 9) Air Force reconnaissance satellite was successfully launched atop the first known Titan 3D-Agena rocket. Before the end of the program in 1984, Vandenberg saw nineteen launches of this type of classified satellite. The base also facilitated launching the more recent KH 11, the maiden launch of which occurred on December 19, 1976.

In April, 1972, the Shuttle Launch and Recovery Board chose Vandenberg as the western shuttle launch and landing site, and in 1975 it was recommended that SLC 6 be used as the core for the new facilities. Construction started in 1979. Originally planned to be completed in 1985 at a cost of $850 million, the shuttle complex was subjected to continuous delays; more ambitious plans for total shuttle processing capability were gradually downscaled. By July, 1986, about $3.3 billion had been spent on the facilities, which were almost sufficient to accommodate a shuttle launch.

To equip Vandenberg with a landing strip for the shuttle orbiter, the runway at Vandenberg's airstrip was expanded to 4,500 meters. To transport the orbiter on the ground, a mobile orbiter lifting frame was developed. Finally, a special maintenance facility was built. In this facility, the shuttle is placed on seismic jacks, designed to protect the orbiter from the effects of an earthquake (since VAFB lies in an earthquake-prone area). Curtains hanging from the ceiling provide a clean environment (known as the "clean room") from the orbiter's nose to the rear end of its cargo bay. A sixty-ton bridge crane was designed to lift payloads from the shuttle into a pit sixteen meters below the ground.

Because of cost overruns, Vandenberg was only equipped to perform minor repairs or service the shuttle after an aborted launch. Normally, the shuttle is prepared for launching at the Kennedy Space Center.

Plans to build a facility for the refurbishment and subassembly of the solid-fueled rocket boosters, and a related installation for the refurbishment of their parachutes, never reached the construction stage. Also, the building reserved for processing of the external tank has only been used as a storage area; one empty tank was stored there in 1984.

From its checkout stand, the refurbished orbiter is placed on a special seventy-six-wheel, self-leveling transporter and sent on a three- to four-hour journey of 25 kilometers to the launch complex. There, in a procedure different from that at Kennedy Space Center, the final assembly of shuttle, payload, external tank, and solid-fueled rocket boosters occurs directly on the launchpad.

The modified SLC 6 launchpad harbors the old mobile service tower. Since the Vandenberg area is subject to gusty winds and occasional fog, a 71-meter-tall mobile weather shelter was built after 1981. Called the shuttle assembly building, the shelter—together with the mobile service tower—forms a protected working area around the launchpad.

Payloads for a shuttle mission are prepared in the payload preparation room, from which they are lifted into the mobile payload "changeout" room. This structure stands 52 meters tall and can roll the 250 meters to the shuttle assembly building. There, payloads are put into the cargo bay of the shuttle.

Once the shuttle is fueled on the launchpad, warm air is blown over the liquid hydrogen section of the external tank to prevent icing. The air comes from two jet engines which are housed in a concrete shack thirty-three meters away. The hot air is ducted around and away from the tank, warming its surface but not contaminating it. During lift-off, the exhaust gases from the boosters and the liquid fuel engines escape through two exhaust ducts.

Since 1979, the launch control center of the abandoned MOL program has been transformed into a modern facility of 13,800 square meters. Its outer walls consist of a solid structure sixty-five centimeters thick. Electronic equipment is protected from possible seismic shocks and potential overpressure during launch.

In January, 1985, Vandenberg's shuttle launch facilities underwent a verification check with the test flight orbiter *Enterprise*. The *Enterprise* was guided through the various stations, from the orbiter lifting frame to the launchpad. While still hoping for a more active role in an actual shuttle mission after the tragic explosion of the *Challenger* space shuttle in January, 1986, the base suffered from a new accumulation of financial and technical difficulties. A design flaw was discovered in the two exhaust and flame ducts at the launchpad. In those ducts enough hydrogen could be trapped to cause an explosion which could destroy the orbiter on the pad. The safest redesign required radical alteration of the ducts at a cost of millions of dollars. During the ensuing shuttle program delays, more safety concerns were expressed. Fog and occasional temperatures of below 10 degrees Celsius at Vandenberg could stress the reliability of some critical systems of the shuttle. Some quality control personnel believed that the distance of 350 meters between the pad and the launch control center was not enough to safeguard the delicate electronic equipment from vibrations during lift-off, or even protect the center itself in case of a shuttle explosion on the launchpad.

Finally, in July, 1986, after an intense debate about the need for a West Coast launch center for the shuttle program, the Air Force recommended mothballing Vandenberg's shuttle complex. President Ronald Reagan adopted the most extreme option outlined by Congress: All shuttle-related facilities at Vandenberg were to be shut down until at least the mid-1990's.

In the meantime, launches of orbital payloads as well as missile tests continued. In January, 1988, Congress cut the budget for the shuttle complex at Vandenberg to $40 million and recommended cancellation of the Air Force's shuttle plans. Instead, some of the existing facilities at Vandenberg would be used for the Strategic Defense Initiative (SDI), the Advanced Launch System (ALS, an unmanned alternative to the space shuttle), the Titan program, and minor NASA missions.

By 1988, forty-eight different types of launch vehicles, sounding rockets, and missiles had been launched from fifty-one different pads at Vandenberg. The base houses more than one thousand different buildings which are connected by more than 830 kilometers of roads. After layoffs in 1986, it was estimated that more than ten thousand workers, both military and civilian, were employed there. While most launching activity has been redirected to South Vandenberg, North Vandenberg harbors eighteen vertical silo launchers for Minuteman 3 and Titan 2 ICBMs.

## Context

Vandenberg Air Force Base has served well in its dual function as testing site for ballistic missiles and as launching base for military and scientific satellites. Because of its geographical position, the base has a natural edge over Kennedy Space Center, where solid land to the north and south prohibits direct launches into a polar orbit. Thus, during the 1960's, more satellites were launched from Vandenberg than from Cape Kennedy (later, Cape Canaveral), and the American space program achieved splendid results from the California launches.

Despite their being military satellites, the Discoverers, the first satellites launched from Vandenberg, conveyed a series of important scientific findings about the dynamics and mechanics of atmospheric reentry and space radiation. These findings were crucial to the discovery of the Van Allen radiation belts and the commencement of the Mercury manned orbiting program, a program which put the first American into space.

Together with their Soviet counterparts, the Kosmos series satellites, the reconnaissance satellites which were launched mostly from Vandenberg have helped to make the world a safer place by providing each superpower with the means of gathering more exact knowledge of the other's military and nuclear capabilities. Samos 2, launched from Vandenberg on January 31, 1961, stayed in orbit for one month and proved with its photographs that the United States had vastly overestimated the so-called missile gap between itself and the Soviets and that there was far less to fear from Soviet ICBM superiority.

Also, during grave international crises such as the Arab-Israeli wars and the gulf war between Iraq and Iran, both superpowers rapidly launched reconnaissance and surveillance satellites to gather reliable information about the areas of concern. Then, the Big Birds launched from Vandenberg helped American politicians and military officials to make informed decisions and avoid haphazard guesswork. In terms of verification of arms accord treaties, spy satellites were equally helpful in the years before on-site inspections became politically possible.

In cooperation with NASA, Vandenberg has made possible the launch of the Landsat and Seasat satellites. Both programs have delivered invaluable data about the geography of Earth and have made remote sensing a reliable tool for the geological sciences. Agricultural projects can be assessed more easily, flood warnings can be served very quickly, and the effects of natural and man-made changes on the face and structure of Earth can be studied from a sharp bird's-eye view.

A predecessor to Skylab and the U.S. Space Station, the Manned Orbiting Laboratory also allowed Vandenberg to become part of the ambitious shuttle program. During the years of rebuilding SLC 6, new knowledge gained from the experience with the shuttle at Kennedy Space Center was continually applied to the engineering of the facilities at Vandenberg. As a result, these installations became the most modern, though incomplete, shuttle complex.

In the future, Vandenberg's geographical advantages will guarantee the base its share of launch traffic. Furthermore, missile testing will remain an integral part of the base's function as a part of the Strategic Air Command of the United States. As home to the headquarters of the First Strategic Aerospace Division of the Air Force, Vandenberg's military and scientific contributions to the exploration of space will continue into the next millennium.

## Bibliography

De Ste. Croix, Philip. *Space Technology*. London: Salamander, 1981. An exhaustive look at space exploration, with many cross-references to specific points of interest such as spy satellites, launch vehicles, and ballistic missiles. Places Vandenberg in the context of the U.S. space effort. Informative, ideal for a general audience, with many color and black-and-white photographs and a detailed bibliography.

Diamond, Edwin. *The Rise and the Fall of the Space Age*. Garden City, N.Y.: Doubleday and Co., 1964. An early critique of the military's role in space and the relationship of NASA to the military-industrial complex. Describes and criticizes the programs situated at Vandenberg and places them in a national and international context. Argumentative but informative and readable. Contains no illustrations, but a few tables.

Klass, Philip J. *Secret Sentries in Space*. New York: Random House, 1971. Promilitary, this text emphasizes the technology behind spy satellites. It stresses the importance of these satellites for global safety. Klass is very good at placing Vandenberg in the broader context of an international espionage race. Includes photographs of the satellites, related hardware, and what they detect. For the technically inclined reader.

Sharpe, Mitchell R. *Satellites and Probes*. Garden City, N.Y.: Doubleday and Co., 1970. Close description and analysis of the international development of unmanned spaceflight. Stresses the contribution of the Vandenberg launch facilities to the success of U.S. military and scientific satellites. Compares this facility with its worldwide counterparts. Includes color and black-and-white photographs.

Shelton, William Roy. *American Space Exploration: The First Decade*. Rev. ed. Boston: Little, Brown and Co., 1967. Chronicles the history of U.S. spaceflight and provides good background information about the first decade at Vandenberg. Full of relevant anecdotes and biographies of persons important to the space effort. Written in a very readable, journalistic style, this book includes illustrations.

Sloan, Aubrey B. "Vandenberg Planning for the Space Transportation System." *Astronautics and Aeronautics* 19 (November, 1981): 44-50. A detailed description of the original, ambitious plan for the Vandenberg shuttle complex. Written by the man who was largely responsible for overseeing the development of this facility in its early stages. Good history of the decision-making process involved in bringing the shuttle complex to Vandenberg. Supplemented with illustrations, diagrams, and a useful bibliography for further, more specialized studies.

Stockton, William, and John Noble Wilford. *Space Liner: "The New York Times" Report on the Columbia Voyage*. New York: Times Books, 1981. A journalistic account of the space shuttle program from its conception to the first flight of the orbiter *Columbia* in April, 1981. Delineates the planned role of VAFB for further missions and talks about the decision to create a shuttle program with two major facilities in the eastern and western regions of the United States. Anecdotal and easy to read, with some fine black-and-white illustrations.

*Reinhart Lutz*

## Cross-References

Attack Satellites, 167; Cape Canaveral and the Kennedy Space Center, 229; Early-Warning Satellites, 299; Electronic Intelligence Satellites, 361; Funding Procedures of U.S. Space Programs, 468; Military Meteorological Satellites, 1006; U.S. Military Telecommunications Satellites, 1012; The National Aeronautics and Space Administration, 1032; Nuclear Detection Satellites, 1080; Ocean Surveillance Satellites, 1085; Space Centers and Launch Sites in the United States, 1599; The U.S. Space Shuttle, 1626; The Space Shuttle Test Flights: *Enterprise*, 1641; Space Shuttle Mission 25: *Challenger*, 1813; The Strategic Defense Initiative, 1951; The United States Space Command, 2049.

# THE VANGUARD PROGRAM

*Date:* September 9, 1955, to September 18, 1959
*Type of technology:* Rocket booster
*Country:* The United States

*Destined to be remembered for its failed attempts to launch the first U.S. man-made satellites, the Vanguard program generated important developments in rocket propulsion, satellite design, and satellite telemetry and tracking and eventually succeeded in launching three Vanguard satellites.*

Principal personages
JOHN P. HAGEN, Vanguard Program Manager
JAMES A. VAN ALLEN, Professor of Physics, Iowa State University
WILLIAM H. PICKERING, Director, Jet Propulsion Laboratory
MILTON W. ROSEN, Vanguard program Technical Director
DONALD J. MARKARIAN, a Vanguard program engineer with the
     Glenn L. Martin Company
T. K. GLENNAN, NASA Administrator

## Summary of the Technology

Project Vanguard consisted of fourteen multistage launches, including test vehicles, with the stated purpose of placing the United States'-first man-made satellite into Earth orbit.

In the early part of the twentieth century, Robert H. Goddard designed, tested, and successfully launched both liquid- and solid-fueled rockets. Rocket designers in the United States, the Soviet Union, Germany, and Austria were busy throughout the 1920's, 1930's, and 1940's developing the skills and technology that would later be used by rocket scientists of the post-World War II era. After World War II, a global awareness of the effective use of rockets forced the U.S. military to alter the scope and direction of its ballistic missile research. After the May, 1945, surrender to the Allies of roughly 120 German rocket scientists at Peenemünde—led by Wernher von Braun—the academic research community, industry, and military of the United States became engaged in dissecting, modifying, and eventually using German V-2 rockets for basic research. The U.S. Army, Air Force, and Navy were independently developing sounding rockets (rockets capable of suborbital flight) and spacecraft capable of orbital flight (research satellites). Because of the outbreak of the Korean War, however, military research was largely aimed at accurate delivery of nuclear or conventional weapon payloads.

On September 9, 1955, with the backing of President Dwight D. Eisenhower, the Department of Defense authorized the Naval Research Laboratory (NRL) to administrate a far-reaching program to design, build, and launch at least one artificial satellite during the International Geophysical Year, or IGY—a period of a year and a half running from July 1, 1957, to December 31, 1958. The United States' participation in the IGY, an international peacetime research effort, was problematic, because only military agencies had the hardware, financial backing, and manpower necessary to launch a satellite. Nevertheless, with the support of the Department of Defense, the Bureau of Aeronautics, the Office of Naval Research, the National Academy of Sciences, and the National Science Foundation, the NRL began implementing Project Vanguard. The NRL was backed by the Glenn L. Martin Company (GLM), Aerojet General Corporation, Grand Central Rocket Company (GCR), Allegany Ballistics Laboratory, General Electric (GE), International Business Machines (IBM), Minneapolis-Honeywell, and myriad U.S. universities and research facilities.

The planning and construction of the Vanguard launch vehicle's main stage was facilitated with testing in the late 1940's of the Viking rocket built by GLM for the NRL. Nurturing a working association with one of the nation's largest rocket builders, it was only natural that the NRL turn to GLM for help with the development and deployment of Vanguard test vehicles and satellite launch vehicles. Unfortunately, GLM also won a contract with the Air Force to construct the Titan missile, thus diluting the manpower it could expend on the Navy's Project Vanguard.

Despite these problems and others involving questions of responsibility and decision making, the NRL and GLM effort was successful. Rocket design specifications were completed by February, 1956, but again, disagreement between the NRL and GLM resulted in amendments and delay. The early Vanguards, Viking M-15's manufactured by GLM, were modified Viking M-10 missiles with a GE first stage motor, an Aerojet Aerobee-Hi liquid-propellant second stage, and a GCR solid-fueled upper stage. The specter of the military dissipated, as the Viking missile was a renowned research vehicle that had long been used for atmospheric sounding.

Kerosene and liquid oxygen were used for the first stage of the Vanguard rocket, which generated 120,096 newtons of thrust. The fuel and oxidant were supplied to the engines by a hydrogen peroxide decomposition technique, which produced superheated steam and oxygen to drive turbine-driven fuel and liquid oxygen pumps. Helium gas supplied pressure for the fuel tanks. The second stage produced 33,360 newtons of thrust with a mixture of white fuming nitric acid and unsymmetrical dimethylhydrazine, an explosive rocket fuel. The third stage was powered by a solid-propellant motor and generated roughly 13,344 newtons of thrust.

With the development of the transistor and miniaturized electronic circuitry, satellite instrumentation design programs at the NRL, Jet Propulsion Laboratory (JPL), and university campuses swung into full gear. Satellites were built under the directorship of the National Academy of Sciences. Meanwhile, NRL telemetering and tracking systems were in advanced stages of development. The deployment and success of the Minitrack system was a result of rigorous testing and research; this highly accurate tracking system formed the backbone of satellite tracking during and after the Vanguard era. GLM developed computer programs that balanced weight against anticipated flight trajectory. IBM offered the NRL free computer time at the Massachusetts Institute of Technology. Because of loans and contracts, both optical and electronic tracking and telemetry stations were built and manned largely by civilian personnel.

As originally planned, Vanguard test vehicles—numbered TV 0 through TV 5—would precede the production of Vanguard model satellite launch vehicles that would be used for missions SLV 1 through SLV 6; there would be a total of twelve launches. Because of engineering changes in payload shape, weight, and size, a moderate degree of launch failure, and the globally transmitted 20- to 40-megahertz beep of Sputnik 1, the original Project Vanguard firing schedule was accelerated and ultimately expanded to fourteen attempts with the launches of two backup test vehicles, TV 3BU and TV 4BU. In all, three highly successful satellites were placed into Earth orbit, and abundant new geophysical, atmospheric, and near-space data were gathered for processing and analysis.

The first Vanguard launch, TV 0, occurred on December 8, 1956, and successfully tested the Viking 13 first stage and the telemetry and tracking systems, which reached an altitude of 203.5 kilometers and a range of 157 kilometers. TV 1, or Viking 14, followed on May 1, 1957, and after a test of third-stage propulsion reached a range of 726 kilometers with a 195-kilometer peak altitude. Sputnik 1, launched October 4, 1957, interrupted the proposed Vanguard test launch schedule; TV 2 restored confidence in the project with a better-than-expected performance, involving the three-stage Vanguard prototype with inert second and third stages, on October 23, 1957. The Soviet Union launched the dog Laika into space on Sputnik 2 on November 3, 1957. The Vanguard TV 3, a three-stage missile complete with the United States' first artificial satellite, was fired on December 6, 1957, but to the amazement of all spectators, it toppled and exploded on the launchpad. This failure was a crushing blow to American pride, but it was also a stimulant for more careful engine system tooling and rocket construction techniques by GE and GLM, respectively, in preparation for future Vanguard firings.

In the interim, the Army Ballistic Missile Agency (ABMA) at the Redstone Arsenal in Huntsville, Alabama, had been researching modified German V-2 rockets with the assistance of the California Institute of Technology's Jet Propulsion Laboratory. On January 31, 1958, the ABMA-JPL team launched the Juno 1, a four-stage version of the Jupiter C rocket, which carried the first U.S. satellite, Explorer 1. Project Vanguard's second attempt, with TV 3BU, ended in failure on February 5, 1958, when a control system problem resulted in loss of attitude control and eventual breakup of the TV 3BU Vanguard after fifty-seven seconds of flight.

Finally, on March 17, 1958, TV 4 placed Vanguard 1 into orbit with an apogee (the point farthest from Earth) of 3,966 kilometers and a perigee (the point nearest to Earth) of 653 kilometers. Vanguard 1 was designed to measure Earth's shape and atmospheric density. It is expected to orbit, with its third-stage motor casing, for more than two centuries. The 25.8-kilogram, 16.26-centimeter spacecraft fulfilled the Project Vanguard goal of launching an artificial satellite within the IGY. The TV 5 launch attempt on April 28, 1958, failed to orbit a 50.8-centimeter, spherical,

9.8-kilogram X-ray and environmental satellite because of second-stage shutdown problems.

The first production version of a satellite launch vehicle, SLV 1, was, on May 27, 1958, to carry a satellite nearly identical to that destroyed during the TV 5 attempt. Again, during second-stage burnout, attitude control problems arose that resulted in firing of the third stage at an angle unsatisfactory for orbit. On June 26, 1958, SLV 2 encountered second-stage propulsion system shutdown after eight seconds. Failure to achieve orbit also plagued the SLV 3 launch on September 26, 1958, when the second stage underperformed.

With passage of the Space Act of 1958, the civilian National Aeronautics and Space Administration (NASA) was created to direct the U.S. space program. Vanguard 2 was successfully placed into orbit by NASA on February 17, 1959, with the launch of SLV 4. Weighing a total of 32.4 kilograms, the 10.7-kilogram payload and 21.7-kilogram third-stage motor casing attained an initial orbital apogee of 3,319 kilometers and a perigee of 556.7 kilometers. The Vanguard 2 payload, destined to orbit for roughly two hundred years, is a 50.8-centimeter spherical satellite that measures cloud distribution and the terrestrial energy cycle budget.

SLV 5 was fired on April 13, 1959; it attempted to launch a 33-centimeter satellite magnetometer and a 76.2-centimeter expandable sphere. Problems arose during the separation of the second stage and resulted in an aborted flight. SLV 6 was fired on June 22, 1959, but again, a second-stage failure sabotaged the launch with a rapid drop in fuel tank pressure, faulty ignition, and explosion of the helium tank because of overheating. The 50.8-centimeter satellite on board, designed to measure solar radiation and its reflection from Earth, failed to orbit.

NASA decided to use a spare backup launch vehicle, TV 4BU, in a final attempt to launch a third Vanguard satellite. Using a new solid-propellant third-stage motor, built by Allegany Ballistics Laboratory, the rocket successfully launched Vanguard 3 on September 18, 1959. The final Vanguard weighed 42.9 kilograms and included a 23.7-kilogram payload and 19.2-kilogram motor casing. The initial orbital apogee was 3,743 kilometers, and the perigee was 510 kilometers. The payload included a magnetometer, an X-ray device, and environmental measuring systems. In large part, Vanguard 3 fulfilled the agenda of previous unsuccessful Vanguard launch attempts.

## Knowledge Gained

With the end of NRL control of Project Vanguard in late September, 1958, and the creation of NASA in October, many key Vanguard personnel joined the NASA staff. As such, the knowledge gained during the Vanguard era was applied toward all subsequent U.S. space ventures. Growth in the fields of vehicle engineering, construction, fueling, and launch were predictable outcomes of Project Vanguard. The three Vanguard satellites that were successfully launched investigated energy fields in the boundary between Earth's atmosphere and space and carried out Earth-directed research.

Vanguard 1 achieved a high-apogee orbit and provided a tracking signal until 1965 thanks to its pioneering use of solar cells. By analyzing changes in orbital acceleration, the satellite detected a bulge in the atmosphere caused by solar heating and recorded a bulge in the Southern Hemisphere of Earth itself, thus confirming that Earth is nonspherical and Earth's interior is inhomogeneous.

Vanguard 2 performed an experiment that measured variations in cloud-top reflectivity. The results were not conclusive, but they contributed some data and perfected meteorological techniques used in later missions. Vanguard 3 was a 50.8-centimeter sphere with sensors for solar X-ray and Lyman-alpha radiation measurements, environmental sensors, and a 66-centimeter projection supporting a magnetometer. Because of the Van Allen radiation belts, the radiation detectors were overloaded and failed to provide accurate data, but accurate temperature monitoring was accomplished over seventy days. Measurements of interplanetary cosmic dust showed a variable but significant influx of particulate matter estimated at 9,072,000 kilograms per day. The magnetometer provided accurate measurements of Earth's magnetic field, plus data on magnetic disturbance events and upper atmosphere lightning ionization.

## Context

The technological impact of Project Vanguard has permeated every aspect of manned and unmanned space exploration and discovery. First and foremost, Project Vanguard developed budgeting, command, and scheduling techniques for effective launching of missiles. Advances in missile guidance, tracking, telemetry, and antennae systems, developments in electronic miniaturization, and solar cell and mercury cell use in satellites were made possible by Project Vanguard. The use of fiberglass casings and the eventual design of the Air Force Thor-Ablestar booster and NASA's highly successful Delta and Atlas launch vehicles are all direct descendants of Viking and Vanguard technology.

In addition, the Vanguards provided new views of Earth's geologic cycles, thus promoting environmental awareness. The subsequent research in electronics, computers, communication, and optics has changed the quality of human life. Finally, Project Vanguard demonstrated that the American military-industrial-academic complex was capable of far-reaching outer space missions.

## Bibliography

Bergaust, E., and W. Beller. *Satellite!* New York: Hanover House, 1956. Details for the layperson the planning for satellite launches during the International Geophysical Year (IGY) and includes detailed drawings of the Vanguard missile. Dated by post-IGY satellite development, this volume discusses the visionary goals of project scientists for the Vanguard and early Explorer missions.

Braun, Wernher von, et al. *History of Rocketry and Space Travel.* Rev. ed. New York: Thomas Y. Crowell, 1969. Includes a comprehensive, superbly illustrated history of post-World War II rocket research and abundant tables of data on missiles, missions, satellites, and manned spacecraft. It contains a detailed bibliography and is recommended to rocketry enthusiasts. A new edition, entitled *Space Travel: A History*, was published in 1985 by Harper & Row, New York.

Caidin, Martin. *Vanguard! The Story of the First Man-Made Satellite*. New York: E.P. Dutton, 1957. A layperson's account of the developmental history of Project Vanguard up to, but not including, the launch of Vanguard 1. This well-illustrated but somewhat dated volume details missile development during Project Vanguard and traces the development of payloads, tracking, and telemetry.

Green, Constance M., and Milton Lomask. *Vanguard: A History*. NASA SP-4202. Washington, D.C.: Government Printing Office, 1970. This is a detailed history of Project Vanguard describing the people, agencies, and administrative programs that led to the launchings of Vanguard missiles and satellites. Contains numerous photographs and diagrams. Mission goals and successes are described in detail. The appendices contain flight summaries for the Vanguard and Explorer programs and IGY satellite launches.

Hall, R. Cargill, ed. *Essays on the History of Rocketry and Astronautics*. NASA Conference Publication 2014. 2 vols. Washington, D.C.: Government Printing Office, 1977. A compilation of papers and memoirs written by active participants, this work traces international efforts in rocketry. Volume 2 concentrates on liquid- and solid-propellant rocket research before and after World War II. Accounts of the early phases of the Vanguard and Explorer projects are noteworthy.

*Charles Merguerian*

## Cross-References

The Sun's Effect on Earth's Climate, 320; The Sun's Effect on Earth's Ionosphere, 334; Explorers 1-7, 394; U.S. Launch Vehicles, 749; U.S. Meteorological Satellites, 999; The National Aeronautics and Space Administration, 1032; The Van Allen Radiation Belts, 2065.

# THE VENERA PROGRAM

*Date:* Beginning February 4, 1961
*Type of program:* Unmanned deep space probes
*Country:* The Soviet Union

*The Venera space probes to Venus represent the Soviet Union's most successful venture in interplanetary exploration. These missions provided scientists with an abundance of data on the surface and atmospheric conditions of Venus. Eight of the · Venera spacecraft succeeded in soft-landing on the Venusian surface, and four survived long enough to transmit pictures of the surrounding landscape.*

### Principal personages

VALERI BARSUKOV, Director of the Vernadsky Institute of Geochemistry and Analytic Chemistry, Soviet Academy of Sciences, the chief scientist for much of the Venera program

ALEXANDER BASILEVSKY, deputy chief of Barsukov's fifteen-member team of radar image analysts

LEONID KSANFOMALITI, the chief scientist in charge of Venusian thunderstorm experiments

YURI SURKOV, of the Vernadsky Institute, a scientific investigator for the Venera program

MIKHAIL MARKOV, of Moscow State University, a physicist at the Institute of Atmospheric Physics, Soviet Academy of Sciences, another scientific investigator for the Venera program

SERGEI KOROLEV, the designer of the Venera space probes

M. V. KELDISH, a leading theoretician of the Soviet space program

ROALD SAGDEYEV, Director of the Institute for Space Research, Societ Academy of Sciences, the leading scientist for the Venus-Halley (Vega) project

### Summary of the Program

Venera (the Russian word for "Venus") is the Soviet Union's nearly quarter-century-long, highly ambitious program of interplanetary investigation of the planet Venus. Between 1961 and 1983, the Soviets launched sixteen Venera space probes to Venus. While early missions were merely "flybys," one mission in the late 1960's resulted in the first successful landing of a spacecraft on another planet. Other landings soon followed in the early 1970's and continued until the 1980's. It was obvious to scientists that landing a probe on Venus and returning rock samples to Earth (as in the case of the Moon) would be prohibitive. M. V. Keldish, a leading theoretician of the Soviet space program, had previously suggested analyzing samples in a landing module. With this in mind, Sergei Korolev began Venera designs for Venusian surface conditions expected to be in the ranges of 60 to 80 degrees Celsius and 1 to 5 Earth atmospheres (15 to 75 pounds per square inch). As the missions progressed, these designs were continually modified as conditions on Venus were revealed to be much more severe than initially estimated. In charge of many of the scientific experiments for the Venera program was Valeri Barsukov, Director of the Vernadsky Institute of Geochemistry and Analytic Chemistry in Moscow. Alexander Basilevsky, a planetary geologist, was chosen to head Barsukov's team of radar image analysts. Other participants included Mikhail Markov, an expert on the dynamics of atmospheric processes on Earth and other planets, and Leonid Ksanfomaliti, also involved with atmospheric studies, who designed experiments to study Venusian storms.

On February 12, 1961, the Soviets launched the first of the Venera probes from the Baikonur (Tyuratam) cosmodrome missile complex. With a payload of 643 kilograms, Venera 1 was one of the largest and most sophisticated spacecraft of that time. Cylindrical in shape, with large solar panels extending like wings from its body, the probe was lost after it was about 500,000 kilometers from Earth. The spacecraft was estimated to have passed Venus at a distance of 100,000 kilometers on May 19, 1961. After several years of unsuccessful attempts at launching Venera-type space probes, the Soviets launched Veneras 2 and 3 in 1965 within a span of four days. Venera 2 was launched November 12 and passed within 24,000 kilometers of Venus. Unfortunately no planetary data were received, and the probe eventually entered solar orbit. Venera 3, launched November 16, 1965, also failed to send back planetary data, but it did succeed in penetrating the Venusian atmosphere. Crushed by extreme atmospheric pressures during its descent, Venera 3 nevertheless was the first man-made spacecraft to land on another planetary body (March 1, 1966).

Venera 4 was a milestone in planetary exploration and the first real success in the Soviet Venusian space program. Launched on June 12, 1967, and weighing about 1,100 kilograms, the Venera probe arrived at Venus on October 18, 1967. A 382-kilogram capsule, separating from the main cylindrical bus, parachuted down through the atmosphere and made a soft landing on the surface of Venus. During its 94-minute descent, the Venera capsule made direct measurements of the gas content, density, and pressure of the Venusian atmosphere. Doppler shift measurements to determine wind velocities were performed. Data from the capsule were transmitted to the bus above and then relayed back to Earth. On board the bus were cosmic ray detectors, a magnetometer, gas detectors, and charged particle sensors.

Venus launch windows occur approximately every nineteen months. Because scientists wish to take maximum advantage of the launch time available, multiple launches at the beginning of the interval are not uncommon. Thus, as they had done in 1965, the Soviets launched two Venera probes in 1969 within days of each other. Venera 5 was sent up on January 5, 1969; Venera 6 on January 10. Arriving at Venus on May 16, 1969, Venera 5 collected data for 53 minutes as it parachuted through the Venusian atmosphere. Venera 6, almost identical in construction to Venera 5 and more rugged than it predecessors, arrived at Venus a day later and transmitted data for approximately 51 minutes before communications ceased. Later calculations showed that the two spacecraft did not survive long enough to transmit from the surface. Like Venera 3, they also were crushed by the tremendously high atmospheric pressure present near the Venusian surface.

Venera 7, weighing 1,179 kilograms, was more successful. Launched on August 17, 1970, the lander (weighing 495 kilograms) became the first spacecraft to transmit data from the surface of another planet. After landing on Venus on December 15, 1970, the capsule succeeded in sending pressure and temperature data for 23 minutes before dying out. This triumph came as a result of a different design for the Venera lander: It was made in the shape of a perfect sphere, and there were no holes in the shell which might give rise to weakened points upon its descent to the surface. Sensors on the probe were exposed only at the time of parachute deployment when the hatch was blown off. In addition, a smaller parachute was used to minimize the descent time to the surface (thus increasing survival time while on the ground) and shock absorbers were added to the lander. On March 27, 1972, the Soviets launched Venera 8, which was nearly identical to its immediate predecessor. It succeeded in transmitting data for 50 minutes from the surface of the day side of Venus, including measurements of temperature, pressure, illumination, and soil and rock compositions.

The first direct photographs from a spacecraft on the surface of another planet were received from the Venera 9 and Venera 10 missions. Launched on June 8, 1975, with a payload of 5,000 kilograms, Venera 9 transmitted data and pictures for 53 minutes after it landed on October 22, 1975. Communication with the lander then ceased. While it was in operation, Venera 9 managed to photograph a plateau region called Beta Regio, revealing the presence of many stones with sharp edges. Data on soil conditions and wind velocities at the surface were also collected. Venera 10, launched June 14, 1975, landed 2,200 kilometers to the south of Venera 9 on October 25, 1975. Mission 10 transmitted data and television pictures for 65 minutes from the surface. The Venera 9 and 10 buses were inserted into Venusian orbit at the time of their respective lander touchdowns. Temperature measurements and recordings of the radiation emanating from the cloud layer were carried out, and an experiment to measure the deuterium-to-hydrogen ratio in the Venusian atmosphere was performed. Data were also collected on magnetic field strengths and the solar wind (a stream of ionized particles from the Sun). As the orbiters passed behind Venus, measurements of radio occultation (that is, the eclipse of the light or signal from one object as it passes behind another) were performed to determine the structure of the cloud layer.

Veneras 11 and 12 were launched on September 9, 1978, and September 14, 1978, respectively. Venera 11 transmitted data for 110 minutes after landing on Venus on December 21, 1978. Reaching the Venusian surface four days later and about 820 kilometers from Venera 11, Venera 12 sent data back to Earth via its bus for the same duration. Unlike missions 9 and 10, which utilized an orbiting bus and lander, probes 11 and 12 each consisted of a flyby and lander with a combined weight of 4,990 kilograms. They were also slightly lighter than the probes used in preceding missions, since the energy requirements to reach Venus in the 1978 launch window were much greater than for the 1975 probes. Surface experiments from both missions 11 and 12 included temperature and pressure measurements. Acoustical sensors recorded local noise levels. Unfortunately, the imaging systems on board both landers failed, preventing the transmission of pictures. During their respective descents, each landing capsule sampled the Venusian atmosphere to determine the chemical composition of the clouds and atmosphere and the degree of electrical discharge (lightning) present.

In 1981, the Soviets again launched a pair of probes to Venus: Venera 13 on October 30 and Venera 14 five days later, on November 4. Landing on the surface on March 1, 1982, and March 5, 1982, respectively, the two spacecraft returned color photographs from a highland region named Phoebe Regio. Venera 13 transmitted data to its flyby bus for 127 minutes; Venera 14 for slightly more than 60 minutes. As usual, data from the buses were relayed back to Earth. In addition to standard temperature and pressure measurements, each lander was able to acquire core samples of the surrounding soil. X-ray fluorescence and electrical conductivity measurements were performed on these samples, which led to the identification of the material as mostly volcanic basalt, a type of rock indicative of solidified lava. Prior to landing, the Venera landers monitored the composition of the Venusian atmosphere and recorded data on lightning strokes.

The last of the Soviet Venera series, Veneras 15 and 16, were launched on June 2, 1983, and June 7, 1983, respectively. These probes, unlike those of the preceding missions, were not intended as landers but were equipped with radar to map the northern surface areas of Venus from highly elliptical orbits. Data collected over several months by both orbiters indicated the presence of several hot spots with temperatures in excess of 700 degrees Celsius. In December of 1984 the Soviets launched two more spacecraft, Vegas 1 and 2, to study Comet Halley. These are considered by some to be Veneras 17 and 18, respectively, since part of their mission was to study Venus on the way to the comet. Dubbed the Venus-Halley project, the *Ve* in Vega comes from the first two letters in "Venera," while the *ga* corresponds (in Russian) to the *Ha* in Halley.

## Knowledge Gained

Surface temperature and pressure measurements by the Venera landers repeatedly revealed that Venus, though approximately the same size as Earth, is dramatically different from it. The surface pressure has been found to be a crushing 90 times that of Earth, while the temperature averages close to 482 degrees Celsius (900 degrees Fahrenheit). Wind velocities near the surface are relatively mild: between 2 and 4 kilometers per second, as recorded by landers 9 and 10. Although at one time it was thought that the thick cloud cover surrounding Venus would prevent sunlight from reaching the surface, television pictures show that enough light penetrates the atmosphere to make the illumination equivalent to that of an overcast day on Earth. One surprising observation made by Venera 11 is the frequency and intensity of the lightning strikes that are present near the surface: as many as 25 per second were detected at an altitude of only 1 mile. Acoustical sensors on board also detected noise levels that suggest accompanying thunder.

Television pictures, combined with radar images of the surface, reveal that the Venusian surface consists primarily of rolling plains. The rocks near both the Venera 9 and 14 modules appeared to be sharp-edged and in a region devoid of dust and soil. In contrast, Veneras 10 and 13 showed rocks that are rounded and that are accompanied by areas of loose dust and soil. Venera 8 inserted a probe containing a gamma-ray spectrometer into the soil in an area near Phoebe Regio and found a high radioactivity content in the rocks suggestive of granites. On the other hand, Veneras 9 and 10 found heavy concentrations of basalts such as those found in terrestrial seabeds. The X-ray fluorescence experiments of Veneras 13 and 14 also revealed regions rich in basalts. As a result, Soviet scientists speculate that Venus may be 70 percent basaltic on its surface.

All the Venera probes carried scientific payloads to study in detail the atmosphere of Venus. The Venera 4 mission was the first to provide a profile of both the temperature and pressure of the Venusian atmosphere at different altitudes. Data revealed temperatures ranging from −43 degrees Celsius at the cloud tops to +483 degrees Celsius near the surface. Later missions essentially confirmed these results. The atmosphere was found to be nearly 97 percent carbon dioxide, while the clouds, 24 kilometers (15 miles) thick and extending down to a base of approximately 50 kilometers (30 miles) above the surface of Venus, were found to be composed of sulfuric acid. Early Venera missions suggested, incorrectly, that a large amount of water vapor was present in the atmosphere. Later experiments by the Venera 11 and 12 probes measured a small quantity of water vapor (0.01 percent), which, when combined with an abundant concentration of sulfur dioxide, forms the sulfuric acid clouds. One surprising result of the air sampling experiments was the amount of argon 36 present compared to radioactive argon 40: two hundred times the ratio found on Earth. This suggests that the formation of the Venusian atmosphere has probably taken place differently from that of Earth. Pressure readings of nearly 1,350 pounds per square inch at the Venusian surface (90 times that of Earth) were consistently recorded, providing dramatic evidence for the thickness of the Venusian atmosphere.

The Doppler shift measurements to measure wind velocities were first carried out by Venera 4 and were repeated by succeeding missions. The most surprising discovery was the rapid rotation of the upper atmosphere. Although Venus rotates extremely slowly, with a rotation rate of 243 Earth days, the upper winds on Venus traverse the planet in 4 Earth days at 400 kilometers per second (or 250 miles per hour). On the other hand, surface wind velocities are moderate and calm. Magnetometers and plasma detectors on board Venera spacecraft (especially probes 9 and 10) measured, respectively, a weak magnetic field near Venus and a permanent bow-shaped shock wave around the planet which prevents the solar wind from reaching the Venusian surface. Other measurements suggest that Venus has no magnetic field of its own but indicate instead that the magnetic field present is a result of the solar wind.

## Context

Over the eighteen years of the Venera series many firsts in interplanetary exploration have been realized and much of the early speculation about Venus has proved to be false. Among their many accomplishments, the Venera space probes were the first to make soft landings on another planet and the first to transmit pictures of its surface to Earth. Little was known about the atmosphere, and nothing about the surface conditions of Venus, until Veneras 4 and 7. Previous telescopic observations from Earth showed Venus to be a featureless disk. Flybys by the U.S. Mariner 2 in 1962 indicated high temperatures. Not until Venera 4 entered the Venusian atmosphere were the magnitudes of the planet's temperature and atmospheric pressure made apparent. An atmosphere of mostly carbon dioxide with a layer of sulfur dioxide (smog) above it were shown to be present. These findings led scientists to conclude that Venus suffers from the "greenhouse effect," in which heat is trapped on the planet by the heavy carbon dioxide concentration in the atmosphere. As a result, the temperatures on the planet are extremely high, greater than on any other planetary body in the solar system. Venus thus represents for scientists an ideal laboratory for studying the role of both sulfur dioxide and carbon dioxide in an atmosphere and their subsequent effects upon a planetary climate. This is important for Earth climatology, since the burning of fossil fuels contributes to a greenhouse effect on Earth. The discovery of the rapid wind patterns at the top of the Venusian cloud layer, combined with the vertical wind velocity measurements made by descent modules, are also valuable in providing comparative data on other planetary weather systems. The argon measurements on Venus revealed that its atmosphere may be the remnant of the initial solar nebula, unlike Earth's, which is primarily the result of outgasing from the terrestrial interior.

In contrast to its atmosphere, the Venusian morphology (the surface properties indicating its planetary evolution) is confusing, in part because the landers were able to survey only a small portion of the Venusian surface. In the areas where Veneras 10 and 13 landed, the surface contained rounded rocks and loose soil, indicating an erosive, older terrain. The other lander missions found a younger, less weathered terrain. Radar images suggest that Venus is mostly a rolling, relatively smooth plane with mountains representing only 10 percent of the surface. In contrast to Earth, Venus may lie on a single tectonic plate. Consistent with the heavy concentration of basalts observed by the Venera landers, Venus appears to be dominated by volcanism. The location of hot spots from radar imaging further suggests the presence of volcanoes. They may also explain the lightning which occurs near ground level. Rather than coming from clouds (found to be too insignificant in the area), the discharges may result from explosions of dust particles ejected from nearby volcanic vents.

The ratio of deuterium to hydrogen found in the atmosphere of Venus is even greater than that found in seawater on Earth, suggesting that, early in the formation of the solar system, Venus may have had as much water as Earth. As the Sun's heat increased, this water probably boiled away. Carbon dioxide, vented from volcanoes, would not have been returned to the surface by rainwater to form carbonates as it is on Earth. As a result, it is theorized, the carbon dioxide remained in the atmosphere and a runaway greenhouse effect ensued. Thus Venus, once thought to be like Earth because of is nearly identical size and proximity, has been revealed to be exceedingly hostile to life and to have evolved at a much slower rate than its sister planets Earth and Mars.

## Bibliography

Beatty, J. Kelley, et al., eds. *The New Solar System*. New York: Sky Publishing Corp., 1982. A summary of what is known about the planets and other members of the solar system from the perspective of space exploration, starting with the beginning decades and continuing to the early 1980's. Well illustrated with many color photographs. Suitable for general audiences.

Burgess, Eric. *Venus: An Errant Twin*. New York: Columbia University Press, 1985. Describes all the exploratory missions to Venus (U.S. and Soviet) and the scientific results obtained from them. This volume, suited for the general public, is perhaps the best source for a concise description of the Venera program. Chapter 3 is devoted entirely to the Soviet effort, and an appendix at the back presents a brief summary of each mission. Nearly a hundred black-and-white illustrations are included.

Chapman, Clark R. *Planets of Rock and Ice: From Mercury to the Moons of Saturn*. Rev. ed. New York: Charles Scribner's Sons, 1982. This easy-to-read text focuses on the solid objects of the inner solar system, although some effort is devoted to the outer planets. Chapter 7 is devoted to the planet Venus. Contains fifty black-and-white photographs three of Venus.

Greeley, Ronald. *Planetary Landscapes*. London: Allen and Unwin, 1985. Describes the surface features of the solid planets and other satellites of the solar system. A morphologic interpretation of the surfaces is presented. Extremely well illustrated, with numerous references included, this volume is intended primarily for college-level and advanced audiences.

Hunt, Garry E., and Patrick Moore. *The Planet Venus*. London: Trinity Press, 1982. An excellent overview of the planet Venus, this volume divides its subject matter into what was known about Venus before the space age and what has been learned about it as a result of space exploration. Contains about ten black-and-white photographs and fourteen line diagrams, and many references, mostly from scientific journals. Suitable for general audiences.

Hunten, D. M., et al., eds. *Venus*. Tucson: University of Arizona Press, 1983. Part of the publisher's Space Science series, this book contains thirty papers dealing mainly with the Venera and Pioneer missions. After an introductory chapter on the history of Venusian study, the papers include the results of the Venera 8, 9, and 10 missions and preliminary findings of Veneras 13 and 14. Technical in nature and intended for researchers in the field, it is suitable for a college-level audience. Many scientific figures, tables, and maps are presented, and a voluminous bibliography of technical journals (with more than twelve hundred entries) is included.

Kaufmann, William J., III. *Exploration of the Solar System*. New York: Macmillan, 1978. Although somewhat dated, the chapter on Venus discusses the results of the Venera missions up to and including mission 10. Black-and-white photographs of the Venusian surface are included. Written primarily for the liberal arts major at most colleges.

Powers, Robert M. *Planetary Encounters*. Harrisburg, Pa.: Stackpole Books, 1978. Describes the exploration of the solar system by unmanned space probes and, in the case of Venus, up through the Venera 10 mission. Numerous black-and-white photographs and about ten color prints. Suitable for general audiences.

*David C. Sousa*

## Cross-References

The French Space Program, 461; Halley's Comet Probes, 569; Mariner 1 and 2, 835; Mariner 5, 849; Mariner 10, 871; Pioneer Venus 1, 1145; Pioneer Venus 2, 1152; Planetary Evolution, 1159; The History of the Solar System, 1367; The Solar Wind, 1382; Space Centers and Launch Sites in the Soviet Union, 1592; Venera 1-6, 2091; Venera 7 and 8, 2098; Venera 9 and 10, 2105; Venera 11 and 12, 2112; Venera 13 and 14, 2119; Venera 15 and 16, 2126; Venus' Atmosphere, 2132; Venus' Landscape and Geology, 2138; Venusian Soil Samples, 2143.

# VENERA 1-6

*Date:* February 4, 1961, to May 17, 1969
*Type of mission:* Unmanned deep space probes
*Country:* The Soviet Union

*The early phases of the Soviet Venera program saw the launching of the first interplanetary probe and the impacting of the first artificial object on another planet.*

### Principal personages
G. N. BABAKIN, Corresponding Member of the Soviet Academy of
    Sciences and Chief Designer of the Venera design team
ANATOLI A. BLAGONRAVOV, Chairman of the Commission for the
    Exploration and Use of Outer Space, Soviet Academy of
    Sciences
S. DOLGINOV, a researcher at the Institute of Earth Magnetism and
    Radiowave Propagation, Soviet Academy of Sciences
K. GRINGAUZ, a researcher at the Institute of Space Research,
    Soviet Academy of Sciences
M. V. KELDISH, President of the Soviet Academy of Sciences
SERGEI KOROLEV, Chief Designer of the Soviet space program,
    1957 to 1966
MIKHAIL KUZMICH YANGEL, Chief Designer of the Soviet space
    program, 1966 to 1971
LEONID SEDOV, Chairman of the Commission for Interplanetary
    Communications
ALEXANDER VINOGRADOV, Vice President of the Soviet Academy
    of Sciences

## Summary of the Missions
Soviet planetary exploration began on February 4, 1961, with the attempted launch of a Venus probe by the Sputnik 7 satellite. Placed into a 223-by-327-kilometer orbit by an A-2 booster from the Tyuratam space center, Sputnik 7 weighed a record 6,482 kilograms. A faulty rocket design prevented the reignition of the fourth stage, and the Venus probe payload was trapped in Earth orbit.

Eight days later, the launch of the 6,474-kilogram Sputnik 8 placed the Venera 1 probe into a 198-by-318-kilometer parking orbit around Earth. This time, the upper stage reignited in orbit and propelled the world's first planetary probe into a heliocentric trajectory. The 643.5-kilogram Venera 1 crossed the orbit of Venus 100,000 kilometers from the planet three months later. The 2-meter-long Venera 1 had no midcourse correction capability. The probe's final targeting was determined by the booster's guidance and cutoff velocity.

Instruments aboard Venera 1 included a magnetometer, charged particle detectors, a plasma analyzer, and a micrometeor counter. As the probe approached Venus, a high-gain directional antenna was to unfold to transmit data to Earth.

To track Venera 1 in deep space, the Soviets built a huge steerable antenna on a state farm in Yevpatoriya (in the Crimean Oblast). The antenna consisted of eight separate 12-meter dishes mounted on a common frame which weighed 907,200 kilograms. The Soviet deep space probes of the early 1960's used very powerful transmitters to make up for the lack of sensitive tracking and receiving antennae on Earth. The high power required to transmit from deep space required the Venera probes to limit data transmission to brief periods each day when the Soviet ground station was in view. When Venera 1 was 7,560,000 kilometers from Earth on February 27, 1961, contact with the probe was lost.

On June 9, 1961, a British radio telescope 78 meters in diameter was made available to the Soviets in an attempt to reestablish contact with Venera 1. On June 11 and 12, 1961, two Soviets, with the aid of Bernard Lovell, succeeded in picking up very weak signals from the area where the Venera 1 probe was supposed to be. Yet the signals were so weak that nothing of their nature could be determined.

During 1962, there were three unannounced Soviet launch attempts toward Venus. All three achieved Earth orbit, but again the upper stage failed to reignite and the probes were stranded. An attempt was made to diagnose the problem of continuing planetary launch failures. On November 11, 1963, another flight failed to leave Earth orbit. It was known as the Kosmos 21 satellite. The following year saw still more launch attempts toward Venus. Boosters, however, failed again. One probe, launched on March 27, 1964, remained in Earth orbit, becoming the Kosmos 27 satellite. The eighth attempted Soviet Venus probe, launched on April 2, 1964, finally succeeded in leaving Earth orbit and was named Zond 1. Communications with Zond 1 were lost on May 14, 1964.

Finally, planetary launches on November 12 and 15, 1965, placed the Veneras 2 and 3 on course toward Venus. (A third Venera launch on November 23, 1965, exploded in Earth orbit and was designated Kosmos 96.) Veneras 2 through 6, launched by the A-2 booster from Tyuratam, were all of similar design—being about 3 meters long, 1 meter in diameter, and powered by solar cells. The craft consisted of a cylindrical section which housed the communications and navigation equipment, power supply, and course correction rocket. Attached to this section was a Venus atmospheric entry capsule, 1 meter in diameter, which accounted for about one-third of the vehicle's weight.

Venera 2 was to fly past Venus and transmit television photographs, while Venera 3 was to land an instrument capsule on the planet to measure atmospheric temperature and pressure. Because of uncertainty over the nature of the Venusian surface, the Venera 3 lander carried instruments which could distinguish between land and ocean surfaces. Veneras 2 and 3 both carried instruments to measure interplanetary magnetic fields, cosmic rays, charged particles, solar plasma, micrometeors, and long wavelength cosmic radio emanations.

The initial trajectory of Venera 2 was so accurate that no further course corrections were required. Immediately before the Venus encounter, however, telemetry showed an unexplained increase in the probe's internal temperature before communications failed. On February 27, 1966, Venera 2 silently passed the planet at 24,140 kilometers.

During the planetary landing attempts of Veneras 3 through 6, Venus was always between Earth and the Sun, so as the spacecraft approached the planet, they were on the nightside of Venus. A midcourse correction on December 26, 1965, placed Venera 3 on a trajectory so accurate that it impacted the nightside of Venus only 450 kilometers from the visible center of the planet. Prior to the encounter, on March 1, 1966, communications with Venera 3 also failed. Thus, no data were returned. Venera 3 was the first man-made object to impact another planet.

Up to this point in Soviet planetary exploration there had been a total of eighteen launches to Venus and Mars without a single success. These failures prompted Sergei Korolev and G. N. Babakin to redesign the planetary probes used by the Soviet Union. The result was a heavier spacecraft, weighing 1,100 kilograms. The vehicles had an improved temperature control system and upgraded instrumentation in the landing capsule.

The new design was flown with the Venera 4 launch of June 12, 1967, which carried a 383-kilogram atmospheric entry capsule designed to withstand a gravitational force of 300 upon reentry. (Venera 4 had a twin probe launched June 17, 1967, which never left Earth orbit and was called Kosmos 167.) The Venera 4 spacecraft bus carried a magnetometer, a cosmic ray counter, particle detectors, and oxygen and hydrogen traps. The landing capsule carried two thermometers, a barometer, a radio altimeter, an atmospheric density gauge, and eleven gas analyzers.

After a flight of 128 days, Venera 4 arrived at Venus on October 18, 1967, and ejected its landing capsule, which entered the Venusian atmosphere at coordinates 19 degrees north and 38 degrees west. During aerodynamic braking, the capsule slowed to 300 meters per second. The drogue and main parachutes slowed it further, to 10 meters per second. The parachutes on Venera 4 were designed to withstand temperatures of 450 degrees Celsius. At a preset atmospheric pressure, the instruments were activated, and they transmitted data for 96 minutes as the capsule sank through the Venusian atmosphere. At the time, it was thought that the capsule had reached the surface, but later it was determined that the signals had stopped at an altitude of 26 kilometers, where, to the surprise of project scientists, the probe was crushed by the high pressure of Venus' atmosphere.

The results of the Venera 4 mission suggested that the surface pressure on Venus may be as high as 100 Earth atmospheres, but some Soviet scientists did not accept this possibility. Regardless, there was insufficient time to redesign the lander to withstand that pressure before the next Venus launch period in 1969. It was decided to make minor improvements on the Venera 5 and 6 landers and concentrate on building better landers for the 1970 Venera mission.

The spacecraft buses of Veneras 5 and 6 were essentially the same as that of Venera 4, but the landers were more heavily insulated, reinforced to withstand pressures to 27 Earth atmospheres and built to withstand atmospheric gravitational forces of 450 during deceleration. In addition, to allow the 405-kilogram landers' instruments to reach lower altitudes before high temperature destroyed them, the landers of Veneras 5 and 6 were equipped with parachutes only one-third as large as the parachute on Venera 4. In case the lander was intact when it reached the surface, the instrument compartment had a special liquid shock-absorbing mechanism.

Veneras 5 and 6 were launched on January 5 and 10, 1969. The Venera 6 launch was unusual in that it occurred in heavy snow, conditions which Western officials believed were unsafe for launching spacecraft.

On May 16, 1969, after a 121-day flight, the Venera 5 landing capsule separated from the spacecraft bus at an altitude of 37,000 kilometers above Venus. The lander entered the planet's atmosphere at a speed of 11.18 kilometers per second. After slowing to 210 meters per second, the parachutes deployed and further slowed the capsule's descent. Data were returned for 53 minutes until, at an altitude of 24 kilometers, the lid on the instrument compartment was crushed by an atmospheric pressure twenty-seven times greater than that on Earth.

One day later, the Venera 6 capsule separated from the spacecraft bus 25,000 kilometers above Venus and also entered the planet's atmosphere. Data were returned for 51 minutes until, at an altitude of 10 kilometers, it too was crushed by Venus' heavy atmosphere. The spacecraft buses for Veneras 3, 4, 5, and 6 all entered the Venusian atmosphere on the dark side of the planet and were destroyed.

## Knowledge Gained

Communication was lost with the first three Venera probes prior to their arrival at Venus, and no planetary data were returned. Venera 4 was the first to return data from inside the Venusian atmosphere. Launched June 12, Venera 4 was an interplanetary success merely because it was still functioning when it encountered Venus on October 18. Thus, Venera 4 became the first success after a total of nineteen planetary flight attempts.

Instruments on Venera 4's spacecraft bus detected a weak hydrogen corona 10,000 kilometers above the nightside of the planet. Additionally, a team headed by S. Dolginov measured a magnetic field of only 10 gammas at a 200-kilometer altitude—five thousand times weaker than Earth's magnetic field. Venera 4's instruments detected no planetary radiation belts similar to Earth's Van Allen radiation belts. Measurements by the charged particle traps designed by a team headed by K. Gringauz showed that the lack of a magnetic field allowed Venus' bow shock (the buildup of solar particles ahead of the planetary magnetic field) to be much closer to the planet than Earth's bow shock is to Earth.

Venera 4's experiments showed that the nighttime ionosphere above Venus is variable and irregular. Measurements by the descending lander showed the atmospheric temperature had risen to 280 degrees Celsius when the lander was destroyed by an atmospheric pressure twenty times greater than that on Earth at an altitude of 26 kilometers. Analysis of Venera 4 data showed that the Venusian atmosphere consisted of 98.5 percent carbon dioxide, 0.4 to 0.8 percent oxygen, and less than 2.5 percent nitrogen. Water vapor was 1 to 8 milligrams per liter at a pressure of 0.6 Earth atmosphere. Gaseous carbon monoxide, hydrogen chloride, and hydrogen fluoride were also found in trace amounts.

The major components of Venus' atmosphere were later confirmed by the entry of probes released by Veneras 5 and 6. The new readings at two separate altitudes revealed that the atmosphere consisted of 93 to 97 percent carbon dioxide, 2 to 5 percent nitrogen, and a maximum of 0.4 percent oxygen. Water vapor measured 4 to 11 milligrams per liter at a pressure of 0.6 Earth atmosphere.

Extrapolation of the atmospheric readings taken during the parachute descent of Venera 5 showed that the surface temperature on Venus is 530 degrees Celsius with a pressure of 140 Earth atmospheres. These figures correlate with actual readings obtained from later surface landers. Data from Veneras 5 and 6 revealed that there is more water vapor in the Venusian atmosphere than there is in Earth's. If all the water vapor in Venus' atmosphere were to take the form of precipitation, however, the total depth of rainwater would be less than 0.5 meter.

After Veneras 5 and 6, Soviet scientists finally accepted the high surface temperature and pressure implied by the earlier Venera 4 mission and took steps to design future landers to survive pressure of 180 Earth atmospheres.

## Context

Of all the early Soviet space programs, the Venera program was perhaps the least politically motivated. Other Soviet manned, lunar, and Mars space programs were heavily accented with the Soviet-American Cold War political and propaganda rhetoric for which Premier Nikita Khrushchev had been famous. The Venera program, however, remained relatively apolitical.

On the other hand, the Venera program was one of the Soviet Union's most productive space research projects. Although by the time Venera 6 reached Venus there had been fifteen Soviet Venus probe attempts without one landing on the planet, the program represented a building-block approach to planetary exploration; the Soviets analyzed past mistakes and corrected them to progress further with the next mission.

The Venera program represented a tremendous technical undertaking by the Soviet Union. The project flourished with the full political backing of the Soviet government and was not subject to the whims of Congress and succeeding administrations, as were American planetary programs. Soviet efforts to explore Venus undoubtedly suffered from an overbearing bureaucracy, but at least the program enjoyed the continuing support of the Soviet government. The planners of the Venera program displayed extreme determination. Through the use of large boosters and design innovations, Soviet probes finally reached Venus.

After a slow beginning, the Venera program eventually changed scientists' entire conception of the planet Venus. Prior to the Venera atmospheric probes, very little was known about the mysteries beneath the Venusian cloud tops. Even something as simple as the mass of Venus was unknown, because the planet has no natural satellite from which scientists might learn about its gravitational fields.

Limited data from Earth-based radio observations and a microwave scan by the American Mariner 2 probe had shown the possibility of a very hot surface temperature on Venus. This idea was controversial at the time of the Venera probes. Planetary specialists argued that these high readings might reflect the temperature of the upper cloud structure only and that the surface might be relatively cool, even Earth-like. Some leading planetary scientists thought that there might even be a great swamp under Venus' cloud cover, while others argued that the surface was a vast desert. Astronomer Carl Sagan was one of the first to propose that the dense carbon dioxide atmosphere of Venus would act like the glass on a greenhouse and trap solar radiation within the Venusian atmosphere, creating the extreme surface temperatures postulated by some astronomers.

The arrival of the early Venera probes started to dispel some of the myths about Venus. By the time Veneras 5 and 6 had completed their missions, scientists had a good understanding of the planet's dynamics. The proponents of the theory of a hot surface covered by a high pressure atmosphere found that they were correct: Venus' surface conditions are far from Earth-like, with an average temperature of 480 degrees Celsius and a pressure of 100 Earth atmospheres. Almost everything scientists know about the surface and atmosphere of Venus had its roots in the first phase of the Venera program.

## Bibliography

Burgess, Eric. *Venus: An Errant Twin*. New York: Columbia University Press, 1985. Written for the general audience, this book summarizes scientists' knowledge of Venus into an easily readable package. Emphasis is on spacecraft exploration of Venus, with an entire chapter devoted to Soviet Venera exploration. Provides a chronology of the evolution of knowledge about Venus, detailing the step-by-step process of learning about another planet by remote spacecraft exploration.

Fimmel, Richard O., et. al. *Pioneer Venus*. NASA SP-461. Washington, D.C.: Government Printing Office, 1983. Concentrates on the development of the Pioneer Venus spacecraft, its mission, and scientific results, but this book also has a large section relating to the scientific results of Soviet Venera missions to Venus. Written for the advanced reader.

Gatland, Kenneth. *The Robot Explorers*. London: Macmillan, 1972. A chronology of Soviet and American lunar and planetary space exploration programs. Contains numerous color illustrations providing insights into the design and functions of American and Soviet lunar and planetary spacecraft. The descriptive narrative provides details and results of all Soviet and American lunar and planetary exploration spacecraft and their missions. Suitable for general audiences.

Short, Nicholas M. *Planetary Geology*. Englewood Cliffs, N.J.: Prentice-Hall, 1975.

Summarizes the accomplishments and scientific results of both American and Soviet lunar and planetary space programs. Stresses the chemical nature of the Moon and inner planets, their geological similarities and differences, and their origins. Illustrated with many diagrams and photographs taken during the space missions discussed.

Smolders, Peter. *Soviets in Space*. New York: Taplinger Publishing Co., 1974. A well-illustrated narrative on all aspects of the Soviet space program. Suitable for the general audience, it concentrates on the successful portions of the Russian space program as they were reported by the Soviet Union. Contains numerous diagrams and photographs illustrating the technical details of Soviet spacecraft and their missions.

Turnill, Reginald. *The Observer's Spaceflight Directory*. London: Frederick Warne, 1978. A lavishly illustrated summary of spaceflight activities by all nations. Lists chronologies of major manned and unmanned space missions. Technical narrative describes worldwide space activities by nation and program, providing details of spacecraft, mission summaries, and program results. One-third of this directory is devoted to Soviet programs. Suitable for readers at the high school and college levels.

U.S. Congress. Senate. Committee on Commerce, Science, and Transportation. *Soviet Space Programs: 1976-1980*. Part 3, *Unmanned Space Activities*. 99th Cong., 1st sess., 1985. Committee Print. This booklet offers a comprehensive review of unmanned space activities for a four-year period. Scientific investigations aboard the Soviet missions are detailed.

*Robert Reeves*

## Cross-References

Halley's Comet Probes, 569; Soviet Launch Vehicles, 742; Mariner 1 and 2, 835; Mariner 5, 849; Mariner 10, 871; Pioneer Venus 1, 1145; Pioneer Venus 2, 1152; Planetary Evolution, 1159; Comparative Planetology, 1168; Space Centers and Launch Sites in the Soviet Union, 1592; The Venera Program, 2083; Venera 7 and 8, 2098; Venera 9 and 10, 2105; Venera 11 and 12, 2112; Venera 13 and 14, 2119; Venera 15 and 16, 2126; Venus' Atmosphere, 2132; Venus' Landscape and Geology, 2138; Venusian Soil Samples, 2143; Zond 1-8, 2275.

# VENERA 7 and 8

*Date:* August 17, 1970, to July 22, 1972
*Type of mission:* Unmanned deep space probes
*Country:* The Soviet Union

*Veneras 7 and 8, whose missions were separated by twenty months, were the first and second spacecraft from Earth to achieve soft landings on another planet.*

### Principal personages

MIKHAIL KUZMICH YANGEL, Chief Designer of the Soviet space program, 1966-1971
G. I. PETROV, Director of the Institute of Space Research, Soviet Academy of Sciences
LEONID SEDOV, Chairman of the Commission for Interplanetary Communications
BORIS PETROV, Director of the Department of Mechanics and Control Processes

## Summary of the Missions

Venera 7 was one of a pair of probes to Venus that the Soviet Union launched when Venus passed close to Earth in the latter part of 1970. Its sister craft, which would have been designated Venera 8 if it had successfully begun its journey, bears instead the designation Kosmos 359.

Although in outward appearance very similar to the Venera 4, 5, and 6 craft and consisting of a cylindrical carrier bus and a spherical descent module, Venera 7 and its sister craft were redesigned when Venera 4 reported Venus' astounding temperatures and atmospheric pressure; the craft's descent modules were prepared for these conditions. In place of a boxlike instrument container, the new modules utilized a spherical pressure chamber to contain the instruments. Soviet engineers likened these containers to the bathyscaphes used in undersea exploration, and indeed their designed tolerance was 180 atmospheres (one atmosphere is the pressure exerted at sea level by Earth's atmosphere).

Other changes were aimed at helping the instruments survive the planet's searing heat for as long as possible. This included heavy passive insulation and heat shielding, as well as an apparatus that injected cold gas into the instrument package prior to descent, chilling it to $-8$ degrees Celsius. The descent parachutes were made smaller to expedite the module's journey through the Venusian atmosphere so that it could spend more of its expected 90-minute life span reporting from the surface. To ensure that the descent module actually separated from the carrier bus at the right moment, there were four redundant separation systems.

The net effect of these changes was to make Venera 7 and its sister craft the heaviest Venus probes yet. Each weighed 1,180 kilograms, with 495 kilograms attributed to the descent modules. Nevertheless, this was still within the launch capabilities of the A-2 booster, which was the standard interplanetary launch vehicle for the Veneras up to that time.

Venera 7 was launched from Tyuratam's cosmodrome on August 17, 1970, and successfully achieved a parking orbit around Earth. One hour and 21 minutes later, the booster's special interplanetary kick stage thrust the probe out of Earth orbit and into its Venus intercept trajectory. On August 22, the sister craft underwent a similar successful launch, but its interplanetary kick stage failed to operate properly, sending the probe into a useless elliptical Earth orbit and earning for it the designation Kosmos 359 in an apparent attempt to disguise the failure. The fate of the second probe was an all too familiar scenario in the Soviet interplanetary program up to that time. Western experts believe that the two August, 1970, launches to Venus were actually the eighteenth and nineteenth Venera-type missions attempted. Of these, eight had failed for exactly the same reason as Kosmos 359.

En route to Venus, the Venera 7 probe received midcourse correction commands on October 2 and November 17, while instrumentation on the carrier bus collected data on the solar wind (the ionized particles flowing out from the Sun) and other high-energy phenomena of the inner solar system. The descent module remained dormant until December 12, when a command was sent that began the "cold soak" (chilling the instrument package down to $-8$ degrees Celsius) and started charging the battery pack.

The encounter with Venus occurred on December 15. At 8:02 A.M. Moscow time, the descent module separated from the carrier at an altitude of 135 kilometers per second. Atmospheric friction alone slowed the craft rapidly and at an altitude of 60 kilometers, traveling at 200 meters per second, the parachutes deployed. By 8:35 the lander was safely on the surface at a location on the nightside of Venus.

On impact, the spherical lander either rolled over or was pulled by its spent parachutes into a position that blocked its antenna and seriously impaired communication with Earth. Initial reports that the signal was lost on impact resulted in a widespread misimpression that the landing was unsuccessful. Fortunately, the Soviet tracking facilities were able to determine that a signal only 1 percent of the predicted strength was being received, and subsequent computer enhancement of the recordings of this transmission yielded 23 minutes of data from the surface before the instruments failed because of the intense heat.

From its first Venus flyby attempt in 1961, the Soviet Union had never let a favorable opportunity for a Venus mission pass without attempting to send at least a pair of spacecraft toward the planet. Preparations for the March, 1972, launch window were strongly influenced by the information supplied by the Venera 5, 6, and 7 successes and the new questions raised by the results of these missions. Two more probes were readied, and their descent modules were extensively redesigned. For one thing, Venera 7's data showing that the atmospheric pressure on the surface was approximately ninety times that of Earth convinced the engineers that the "bathyscaphe" instrument package, designed to withstand much greater pressure, could be redesigned. The new container was built to tolerate only 105 atmospheres, saving space and weight for the addition of more instruments. Among these was a device to measure the amount of sunlight that penetrated the clouds, using a series of photoresistors to take light readings during descent and on the surface. The ammonia content of the clouds was to be studied as the descent module passed through them by observing a change in the color of a reagent material if the gas was detected. Wind speed detectors were also added to obtain information about air circulation at various altitudes, and a gamma-ray spectrometer was included to study the composition of the planet's crust.

Various engineering changes were also made. Best known among these was the inclusion of a backup antenna that was to eject from the probe on impact with the surface, so that a signal loss like that experienced by Venera 7 would not be repeated. To extend the lander's resistance to the high surface temperatures, it was fitted with a two-stage parachute system designed to reduce the descent time. The effects of the injection of cold gas into the instrument package before separation from the bus were prolonged by the addition of a small refrigeration unit in the descent module.

Venera 8 embarked on its journey with a dawn launch on March 27, 1972. After completing one circuit of Earth, its kick stage fired successfully and injected the probe into a 312,225,000-kilometer intercept trajectory with Venus. The sister craft was launched on March 31, but, like so many before it, the kick stage misfired and the probe remained in Earth orbit, causing it to receive the designation Kosmos 482.

En route to Venus the Flight Control Center interrogated the Venera 8 carrier bus eighty-six times to check the status of onboard systems and gather data from the interplanetary experiments it carried. Among these were instruments to measure the level and consistency of solar radiation in interplanetary space and to detect the presence of gamma radiation.

When Venus is close enough to offer attractive launch windows, its sunlit side is largely turned away from Earth. Consequently, all previous data from the Venus probes concerned conditions encountered on the nightside of the planet. Scientists were anxious to obtain comparative information from a point experiencing daylight. At the same time, it was important that a landing occur at a point that would keep the line of sight to Earth as high as possible above the local horizon to ensure good radio communication. These requirements dictated that the target zone for Venera 8's landing be an area only 500 kilometers in diameter, centered on a narrow crescent of the daylight side presented to Earth. A midcourse correction executed on April 6 was so precise that no further trajectory adjustments were required.

The spacecraft arrived at Venus on July 22, and at 9:40 A.M. the descent module separated from the carrier bus, almost one hour prior to atmospheric entry. Plunging at more than 10 kilometers per second, the descent module caused friction that heated and ionized the atmosphere around it, preventing radio communications with it until it had been slowed by aerodynamic resistance to about 10 kilometers per minute. Signals from the descent module began to be received at 10:38 A.M., and the drogue parachute was deployed at about the same time. This maneuver was followed by release of the main parachute in a 70 percent reefed condition, so that the descent module fell swiftly until it emerged from the bottom of the cloud deck. At about 30 kilometers above the surface, the main parachute blossomed to full deployment, and at 11:29 A.M. the descent module came to rest near the center of its targeted landing zone, at a spot about 500 kilometers beyond the terminator (the line between daylight and darkness).

In the early morning of a long Venusian day, the scientific package collected data and relayed its findings for 50 minutes before succumbing to surface temperatures hot enough to melt lead. It would later be determined that the Venera 8 descent module came to rest on ancient crustal terrain and that the landscape around it was probably a gently rolling plain.

## Knowledge Gained

Venera 7's all-important task was to obtain direct measurements of the atmospheric pressure and temperature conditions at the surface of Venus. It reported the temperature to be approximately 475 degrees Celsius and the atmospheric pressure to be about ninety times greater than that of Earth. The value for the temperature was consistent with indirect measurements obtained by earlier spacecraft and by Earth-based studies, but the atmospheric pressure had been highly uncertain up to that time, as evidenced by the fact that the Venera 7 lander had been designed to withstand up to twice the pressure it actually encountered.

Temperature and pressure measurements were recorded throughout the journey down through the Venusian atmosphere and were correlated with the altitudes obtained by the craft's radio altimeter. As a result, the investigating scientists were able to discover the distribution of pressure and temperature within the atmosphere, which was important for theoretical modeling of the atmosphere's properties and dynamics. It was found that, unlike the temperature on Earth, the temperature on Venus is strictly a function of altitude and increases linearly below an altitude of 100 kilometers.

Venera 7 sampled the gases of the atmosphere twice during the descent: once when the main parachute opened and again several minutes later. It reconfirmed the earlier findings that carbon dioxide accounts for 97 percent of the atmosphere and that the planet appeared to be almost totally lacking in water vapor.

Venera 8 refined the knowledge of surface temperature and pressure still further, providing readings of 470 degrees Celsius and 90 atmospheres. These measurements came from the daylight side of the planet yet were virtually identical to those recorded by Venera 7 at its night landing site, implying that powerful forces were at work to circulate the atmosphere. Indeed, Venera 8's wind detectors discovered a very high altitude wind blowing at about 350 kilometers per hour about 50 kilometers above the surface. As the atmospheric pressure increased, however, the wind diminished, until air movement at the surface could scarcely be detected.

One of Venera 8's most intriguing discoveries came from the light-metering experiment. It showed that the Venusian clouds, which occur very high in the atmosphere (above 50 kilometers), reduce the incident sunlight by 50 percent. This was not as much as many had expected, but the probe further reported that the air below the clouds, which is clear and transparent, nevertheless reduces the sunlight reaching the surface drastically through its density alone. Only 1 percent of the sunlight striking the cloud tops actually reaches the surface; since Venus is closer to the Sun than is Earth and experiences more incident light from the beginning, however, this illumination is equivalent to a heavily overcast day on Earth.

The gamma-ray spectrometer detected radioactive potassium (4 percent), uranium (0.002 percent), and thorium (0.00065 percent) in the Venusian soil. These proportions of trace elements correspond fairly closely to Earth's granite but are significantly different from the lunar rocks. The probe's landing site seemed to be a very low density soil of 1.5 grams per cubic centimeter. Normal sandy soil on Earth is almost twice that dense.

## Context

Veneras 7 and 8 and their two unsuccessful sister craft were the last of a score of fairly similar Russian Venus probes launched between 1961 and 1972. During the same interval, the United States had launched three Venus probes. Of this armada of interplanetary craft sent to Earth's mysterious neighbor, only five Soviet and two American probes successfully returned data. In part this illustrates the difficulty of the challenge, but is also shows the determination with which the Soviets faced the inherent difficulties.

No other area of Soviet space exploration experienced more setbacks and reversals than did the Venus program. Opting not for the easier flyby missions, the Soviets boldly and doggedly tackled the problems of atmospheric penetration and soft landing on a world that was extraordinarily inhospitable, even to machines. Even before the Venera 7 mission, William Shelton noted (in *Soviet Space Exploration: The First Decade*, 1968) that the Soviets' "very boldness invited both failure and success." After many failures and a few qualified successes, Venera 7 made the first successful soft landing on another planet, aside from lunar exploration.

The Soviets' fascination with Venus has always puzzled Americans. After Mariner 2 showed the planet to be unlikely to harbor life or be explorable by manned expeditions, the National Aeronautics and Space Administration (NASA) turned what interest and resources it had for planetary studies almost exclusively toward Mars and the outer solar system. In contrast, the Soviet Academy of Sciences' relentless program of Venus exploration has been marked by an almost passionate curiosity that to most Western observers seems compulsive, even irrational. Research shows that this goal is, in fact, consistent with a widely held view among the Soviet population, who have taken deeply to heart the proclamation of rocketry pioneer Konstantin Tsiolkovsky: "Man will not stay on Earth forever, but in the pursuit of life and space will . . . advance until he has conquered the whole of circumsolar space." The average Soviet citizen regards the space frontier with a sense of "manifest destiny" not unlike the view that Americans held of their western frontier a century and more ago. It was from this popular infatuation that the Venera program derived its energy.

By the time Venera 8's radio fell silent, it had reported all the elementary information that could be expected from such a probe, but as with all scientific inquiry the new answers only led to new questions. The composition of the clouds themselves remained in much doubt, as was the cause or causes for Venus' heavily heated, high-pressure atmosphere. Man's visual sensitivity made the inability to see the surface beneath the clouds frustrating, and the desire to obtain images of Venusian landscapes was a high priority. There was still much uncertainty concerning the composition of the surface and virtually nothing was known about its topography. Although it was clear that there could be no oceans or other bodies of water, the almost total absence of even water vapor was still a mystery.

Such questions would require much more sophisticated spacecraft to answer. The second-generation Veneras were already on the drawing board but would not be ready in time for the next launch window, which occurred in the fall of 1973.

## Bibliography

Burgess, Eric. *Venus: An Errant Twin*. New York: Columbia University Press, 1985. The definitive work for laymen interested in what is currently known about Venus, how it was learned, and what the current research questions are. The Venera missions are treated in a full chapter. The book contains nearly one hundred illustrations.

"Dual Antenna Used by Soviets to Transmit Venus-Earth Data." *Aviation Week and Space Technology* 97 (July 31, 1972): 18. This fact-filled report summarizes the design improvements and details the mission events of the Venera 8 flight up to the time of its successful landing. Results of the onboard experiments were not known when the article was published.

Hunt, Garry E., and Patrick Moore. *The Planet Venus*. London: Trinity Press, 1982. A comprehensive book organized in two parts, the first treating what can be known about the planet from Earth observation and the history of how this knowledge was acquired. The second part deals with the atmosphere, surface, and interior of Venus as revealed by spacecraft studies. Details of the spacecraft themselves are limited.

Johnson, Nicholas L. *Handbook of Soviet Lunar and Planetary Exploration*. San Diego: Univelt, 1979. A forty-page section of this work is devoted to the Venera missions, presenting details of spacecraft design and flightplans, instrumentation, and general results of the missions. The information is readable and the drawings and photographs are helpful. It does not discuss the development of knowledge about Venus in a clear and organized way.

Shelton, William. *Soviet Space Exploration: The First Decade*. New York: Washington Square Press, 1968. Although predating the Venera 7 and 8 missions by several years, this book is valuable for its insights into the Soviets' fascination with Venus exploration. Shelton helps the reader to understand the Soviets' persistent efforts in spite of severe obstacles and many setbacks.

*Richard S. Knapp*

## Cross-References

Mariner 1 and 2, 835; Mariner 5, 849; The Mars Program's Technical Development, 885; Planetary Evolution, 1159; Comparative Planetology, 1168; Solar Radiation, 1359; The Solar Wind, 1382; The Venera Program, 2083; Venera 1-6, 2091; Venera 9 and 10, 2105; Venera 11 and 12, 2112; Venus' Atmosphere, 2132; Venus' Landscape and Geology, 2138; Venusian Soil Samples, 2143.

# VENERA 9 and 10

*Date:* June 8, 1975, to October, 1976
*Type of mission:* Unmanned deep space probes
*Country:* The Soviet Union

*The first spacecraft to orbit Venus and return data about the planet, Veneras 9 and 10 also sent landers to its surface and returned the first close-up images of Earth's twin.*

*Principal personages*
ROALD SAGDEYEV, Director of the Institute for Space Research,
   Soviet Academy of Sciences
DMITRI GROGORYEV, Chairman of the International Commission
   on Space Mineralogy
BORIS NOPOKLONOV, the chief Venusian topographer
V. AVDUYEVSKY,
V. ISHEVSKY,
M. MARANOV, and
VASILY MOROZ, project scientists
K. GRINGAUZ,
VADIM ISTOMIN,
MIKHAIL MAROV,
LEV MUKHIN, and
YURI SURKOV, scientific investigators

## Summary of the Missions

Part of a second generation of heavier Soviet Venus probes designed during the three-year gap between launch windows, Veneras 9 and 10 were to carry a much larger cargo of planetary and surface exploration experiments. The new probes also differed from their predecessors in that the spacecraft buses were planetary orbiters instead of flyby vehicles. Four times heavier than the earlier probes, the new spacecraft had to be launched with the larger Proton booster rocket.

Venera 9 was launched from the Baikonur cosmodrome on June 8, 1975, and Venera 10 followed on June 14, 1975. During Venera 9's 300-million-kilometer, 136-day flight to Venus, the spacecraft observed the interplanetary medium. Venera 10 performed similar interplanetary observations. Instead of relying on commands from ground controllers, the spacecraft carried digital computers which carried out many of the navigational calculations en route to Venus. Two course corrections were required to aim each of the Veneras toward an orbit around Venus. The first placed the spacecraft on an intercept trajectory with the planet to allow the lander to enter the atmosphere, while the second directed the spacecraft bus into an orbit around the planet after the lander separated.

The Venera 9 lander and bus arrived at Venus on October 22, 1975, and the space-craft bus entered a 1,300-by-112,000-kilometer orbit around the planet. Venera 10 arrived three days later and entered a 1,400-by-114,000-kilometer orbit. The craft had orbital periods of 48 hours, 18 minutes, and 49 hours, 23 minutes, respectively.

The Venera 9 lander entered the atmosphere at a velocity of 38,558 kilometers per hour and an angle of 20.5 degrees. Aerodynamic braking reduced the lander's speed to 899 kilometers per hour. Venera 10 performed a similar maneuver later. The landers were protected by a 2.4-meter-diameter spherical heatshield, which the Soviets said could withstand pressures as great as 272,160 kilograms and a tempera-ture of 2,000 degrees Celsius.

To prevent the planet's high temperatures from prematurely destroying the land-ers' electronics during a lengthy atmospheric passage, Veneras 9 and 10 had a new descent system designed to allow a rapid drop to the surface. Despite its complexity the procedure worked perfectly, and the landers returned the first images of the planet before being destroyed by the heat and pressure. The 1,560-kilogram landers used a series of six parachutes with a total surface area of 180 square meters. At a height of 65 kilometers above the surface and a velocity of 250 meters per second, the first parachute deployed, reducing the lander's descent speed to 150 meters per second. Then a small parachute pulled off the upper portion of the spherical heatshield. This in turn activated a pilot chute, which deployed a braking parachute, slowing the lander to a speed of 50 meters per second. Next, three main parachutes were deployed, lowering the lander to an altitude of 50 kilometers, where they were cut loose.

Final descent to the surface was accomplished by a broad aerobraking ring which surrounded the upper portion of the spherical landers much like a hat brim. This braking ring used the thick Venusian atmosphere to slow the craft. Ballast and a low center of gravity stabilized the descending landers. At touchdown, when the craft were traveling at a velocity of 24 kilometers per hour, the landings were cushioned by a ringlike apparatus which acted as a shock absorber.

The first signals from the Venera 9 lander were received five minutes after its atmospheric entry. Descent through the atmosphere took one hour and fifteen minutes, with landing occurring at 8:13 A.M. Moscow time on October 22, 1975, at Venus coordinates 32° north latitude, longitude 291° west. The Venera 10 lander touched down three days later at 8:17 A.M. Moscow time on October 25, 1975, at Venus coordinates 15° north latitude and longitude 295° west. Both landers touched down immediately east of what is now known as Beta Regio. Venera 9 transmitted data for 53 minutes, while Venera 10 remained in contact with Earth for 65 minutes.

The identical Venera landers incorporated special features to help them survive the harsh Venusian conditions. The instrument sections were spherical to help combat the crushing pressure of the atmosphere and were covered with a thick layer of insulation. To further help the landers survive the intense surface heat on Venus, their interiors were chilled in space to −10 degrees Celsius, while the external instruments were chilled to −100 degrees Celsius. These temperature control features worked so well that the landers' internal temperatures had climbed only 60 degrees before signal relay was lost as the orbiters passed out of view.

Each lander was equipped with two scanning telephotometers for planetary surface photography. Each camera unit had a field of view of 40 by 180 degrees and took 20 minutes to scan a picture. Despite the extra unit, only one camera on each lander was used. Because scientists believed that the illumination through the atmospheric clouds would be too dim for the taking of pictures, the landers were equipped with 10,000-lux floodlights. Fifteen minutes after landing, the Venera 9 lander returned the first photograph taken from the surface of another planet. Venera 10 relayed another shortly after it landed three days later. In addition, both landers performed analyses of the planet's surface using gamma-ray spectrometers to determine the radioactive elements in the rocks and soil.

The orbiters also remained active. After relaying data from the initial lander experiments, they studied the structure, temperature, and radiation of the Venusian cloud layers using spectrometers, radiometers, and photopolarimeters. The orbiters also studied the weak planetary magnetic fields and particles in the stream of the solar wind.

The Venera 9 and 10 missions also marked the first interplanetary cooperation by the Soviet Union and France. A large-scale composite image of the Venusian cloud cover was accumulated using a French ultraviolet spectrometer. The instrument also studied the ratios of hydrogen and deuterium in the Venusian atmosphere.

## Knowledge Gained

The Venera 9 and 10 landers demonstrated that a harsh environment awaits any spacecraft landing on Venus. Venera 9 recorded surface atmospheric conditions of 460 degrees Celsius, with a pressure of 90 Earth atmospheres and a surface wind speed of 2 kilometers per hour. Venera 10, landing 2,200 kilometers away, recorded a 465-degree-Celsius surface temperature with a pressure of 92 atmospheres and a surface wind velocity of 12 kilometers per hour. While the wind speed at the surface of Venus might not seem very great compared to winds on Earth, it must be remembered that the Venusian atmosphere has a density one-tenth that of water. Thus, 12-kilometer "breezes" on Venus have the force of an ocean wave on Earth driven by 80-kilometer-per-hour winds. Venera 9 and 10 data were in close agreement with those of previous probes, which had showed that the atmosphere of Venus is composed of 97 percent carbon dioxide and 2 percent nitrogen, with traces of argon, carbon monoxide, and water vapor.

In an unprecedented technical achievement each lander transmitted one photograph of the planetary surface. Although the Sun's elevation at the Venera 9 landing site was 54 degrees, some scientists had thought that the planetary cloud cover would prove to be so thick that surface illumination would be too dim for photography. Thus, they were pleasantly surprised when the images showed shadows cast under surface rocks. One spacecraft designer remarked that the sky appeared as bright at the Venera 9 site as it was at noon in Moscow on a cloudy summer day.

The Venera 9 surface photograph, in which detail was visible up to 100 meters away, showed that the lander had come to rest at the base of a hill in the midst of the remains of a rock slide. The image showed a surface littered with sharp-edged rocks as large as 40 centimeters in diameter. The sharp, angular rocks and lack of dust and sand destroyed forever the idea that the Venusian surface was a sandy desert created by wind, sand, and heat erosion. The lack of old, blunted rocks showed that the surface is young, evolving, and tectonically active, with the surface rocks having been created by geologically recent seismic or volcanic activity. The local horizon was too close to determine whether the predicted superrefractive effects of the high-pressure Venusian atmosphere made the horizon appear concave. The Venera 10 surface photograph, taken three days later at a site 2,200 kilometers away, showed flat, slablike rocks with dark markings. These rocks were eroded and proved that the surface could be radically different from spot to spot.

The appearance of the Venusian surface as suggested by the Venera 9 and 10 photographs is similar to that of a terrestrial sea bottom with all the organic material removed. Apparently, Venus' extremely dense atmosphere acts like an ocean, shaping the landscape with currents instead of winds, even moving boulders across the surface.

Boris Nopoklonov, the chief Venusian topographer, described the Venera 9 landing site as a young mountainscape, while the Venera 10 landing area was "a landscape of old mountain formations." Nopoklonov also summed up the scientists' surprise at the appearance of the Venera 9 site: "We thought there couldn't be any rocks on Venus [because] they would all be annihilated by constant wind and temperature erosion, but there they were, with edges absolutely not blunted. This picture makes us reconsider all our concepts of Venus."

Using a gamma-ray spectrometer, the landers measured surface radioactivity, thus allowing scientists to infer the composition of the Venusian surface. Analyses of both sites showed the rocks to contain 0.3 percent potassium, 0.0002 percent thorium, and 0.0001 percent uranium, with a rock density of 2.7 to 2.9 grams per cubic centimeter. These measurements are consistent with those found in terrestrial basalt. Earlier Venera 8 measurements, however, had shown readings similar to those of terrestrial granite.

During their descent to the surface, the Venera 9 and 10 landers performed atmospheric and cloud studies. These measurements revealed that there are three layers of clouds surrounding Venus. The upper layer extends from 57 to 70 kilometers, the middle layer extends from 52 to 57 kilometers, while the lower layer extends from 49 to 52 kilometers. The cloud particles were also found to be of three types. Widespread large particles about 7 micrometers in size make up 90 percent of the cloud mass, while there are medium-sized particles 2 to 2.5 micrometers in size and small particles averaging 0.4 micrometer in size as well. The large particles were found in all three cloud layers, while the smaller particles were found only in the upper two layers. Wind measurements during descent showed that there are high winds in the clouds with a large wind shear at the base of the clouds. Below the clouds, however, the wind slowly diminishes to about one meter per second at the surface. Both spacecraft detected what were believed to be lightning flashes in the nightside clouds.

The orbiters determined that the clouds of Venus are not thick, like terrestrial clouds, but are merely a slight haze. Venera 9 found the visibility within the clouds to be 1 to 2.5 kilometers. Other studies proved that the clouds did not contain water, but were made of some other liquid. The temperature at the upper boundary of Venus' cloudtops was measured by Veneras 9 and 10 at −35 degrees Celsius. The temperature of the clouds on the nightside of the planet, however, was found to be ten degrees higher because of the radiating material carried to high altitudes by convection streams on the dayside. The Venera 10 orbiter also surveyed the surface of the planet with a bistatic radar and determined that the elevation under the orbital track varied by only a few kilometers. The two orbiters detected a constant night-time airglow caused by chemical reactions in the upper atmosphere and confirmed the occasional existence of the mysterious "ashen light" phenomenon on the dark side of the planet.

Venera orbiter measurements showed that the weak magnetic field around Venus is not natural to the planet but instead is induced by currents flowing in its convective ionosphere. These currents are caused by the solar magnetic field carried past Venus by the solar wind (the outward flow of plasma from the Sun). The strength of this induced magnetic field at the surface is no greater than 5 gammas. The lack of a strong magnetic field around Venus allows the ionopause (the boundary between the solar wind and the planet's ionosphere) to compress against the planet. The height of the ionopause is dependent upon the solar elevation; where the Sun is overhead, it is only 250 to 280 kilometers above the planet.

Other orbiter studies showed that Venus has a plasma tail with features similar to Earth's tail. Bundles of magnetic field lines were separated by a layer similar to the neutral sheet in Earth's tail. The tail boundary was shown to have two different types of plasma, one coming from the planet and the other from the solar wind.

## Context

The Venus launch opportunity following the flight of Venera 8 was bypassed in order to allow time for a major structural redesign of the Venera spacecraft and its planetary lander to adapt them to the Venusian environment. The resulting generation of Venera spacecraft, led by Veneras 9 and 10, remained the basic Soviet planetary exploration design for thirteen years. The success of Veneras 9 and 10 culminated a fourteen-year effort by the Soviets to explore Venus. The Venera program had demonstrated the Soviets' ability to overcome technical problems encountered in earlier attempts and develop a step-by-step plan for exploring the planet. Each succeeding mission was modified by applying what was learned from the previous flight until Veneras 9 and 10 became the showcase for Soviet planetary exploration. Indeed, the Venera 9 and 10 missions were so important that the Soviet government built a new 70-meter-diameter receiving antenna at their deep space communications facility to ensure contact with the planetary orbiters.

In a departure from past practices, the missions of Veneras 9 and 10 were the least propagandized major spaceflights yet carried out by the Soviet Union. Up to that time, with the exception of three U.S. Mariner spacecraft, the Soviets had had a virtual monopoly on the exploration of Venus. This twin flight was the chance to show the West that Soviet space technology and planetary science was equal to that of the West. Venus was clearly Soviet territory, but the interest shown in the Soviet press was primarily scientific.

Considering the harshness of the hot, high-pressure Venusian atmosphere and the difficulty in designing instruments to survive and work in such conditions, Soviet space engineers had reason to be proud of their planetary exploration program. The huge success of the Venera 9 and 10 effort did much to improve the morale of the people involved in the Soviet space program after the deaths of the Soyuz 11 crew four years earlier.

## Bibliography

Burgess, Eric. *Venus: An Errant Twin*. New York: Columbia University Press, 1985. Written for the general audience, this book summarizes current knowledge of Venus. Emphasis is on the exploration of Venus, with an entire chapter devoted to Soviet Venera explorations. Provides a chronology of the evolution of knowledge of Venus, detailing the step-by-step process of learning about another planet by remote spacecraft exploration. Illustrated.

Fimmel, Richard O., et al. *Pioneer Venus*. NASA SP-461. Washington, D.C.: Government Printing Office, 1983. This work concentrates on the development of the Pioneer Venus spacecraft, mission, and scientific results, but also has a large section relating the scientific results of the Venera missions. Contains numerous graphs and illustrations.

Kopal, Zdenek. *The Realm of the Terrestrial Planets*. New York: Halstead Press, 1979. A compilation of data about the rocky planets in the solar system. Written for the intermediate-level reader, this volume describes the atmospheres, surfaces, interior geologies, and physical properties of Earth-sized planets. Presents an overall view of planetary understanding as gained from observations from Earth, theoretical deduction, and remote spacecraft investigations.

Turnill, Reginald. *The Observer's Spaceflight Directory*. London: Frederick Warne, 1978. A beautifully illustrated summary of all spaceflight activities worldwide, this work lists major manned and unmanned space missions. The technical narrative provides details of spacecraft, mission summaries, and program results, including those of the Soviets.

_____, ed. *Jane's Spaceflight Directory*. London: Jane's Publishing Co., 1987. A comprehensive listing of facts, figures, and statistics related to all American, Soviet, and international spaceflights and programs, launch sites, control centers, astronauts, and cosmonauts. Illustrated with many photographs, this volume summarizes mission results and is a renowned authority for spaceflight data.

U.S. Congress. Senate. Committee on Commerce, Science, and Transportation. *Soviet Space Programs: 1976-1980*. Part 3, *Unmanned Space Activities*. Report prepared by Congressional Research Service, the Library of Congress. 99th Cong., 1st sess., 1985. Committee Print. Comprehensive descriptions of all phases of the unmanned Soviet space programs are provided. Includes a detailed overview of space activities, scientific investigations, and results, as well as the political effects of the Soviet activities. The standard reference for the Soviet program.

*Robert Reeves*

## Cross-References

Halley's Comet Probes, 569; Soviet Launch Vehicles, 742; Mariner 1 and 2, 835; Mariner 5, 849; Mariner 10, 871; Pioneer Venus 1, 1145; Pioneer Venus 2, 1152; Planetary Evolution, 1159; Comparative Planetology, 1168; The History of the Solar System, 1367; Space Centers and Launch Sites in the Soviet Union, 1592; The Soviet Spaceflight Tracking Network, 1877; The Venera Program, 2083; Venera 1-6, 2091; Venera 7 and 8, 2098; Venera 11 and 12, 2112; Venera 13 and 14, 2119; Venera 15 and 16, 2126; Venus' Atmosphere, 2132; Venus' Landscape and Geology, 2138; Venusian Soil Samples, 2143; Zond 1-8, 2275.

# VENERA 11 and 12

*Date:* September 9 to December 25, 1978
*Type of mission:* Unmanned deep space probes
*Country:* The Soviet Union

*Veneras 11 and 12 were part of a four-vehicle international fleet of probes which investigated Venus in 1978. Both of these craft achieved their intended soft landings, but their accomplishments were overshadowed by the American Pioneer Venus 1 and 2 missions.*

### Principal personages
VLADIMIR N. CHELOMEI, Chief Designer of the Soviet space program
ROALD SAGDEYEV, Director of the Institute of Space Research, Soviet Academy of Sciences
LEONID SEDOV, Chairman of the Commission for Interplanetary Communications
LEONID KSANFOMALITI, a senior project scientist with the Space Research Institute

### Summary of the Missions

Soon after Veneras 9 and 10 introduced the Soviets' second-generation Venus probe design, it was announced that the Soviets intended to pass up the 1976-1977 launch window in order to allow more time to evaluate the data and incorporate appropriate design improvements into the Venera 11 and 12 spacecraft. This decision was notable because it marked only the second time in fifteen years that the Soviets had chosen not to avail themselves of a Venus launch opportunity, which occurs at approximately nineteen-month intervals. Apparently weighing heavily in this decision was a French proposal to supply an experiment to Veneras 11 and 12 that would release balloon-borne instrument packages into the atmosphere during descent; this idea was subsequently postponed, however, and the Venera 11 and 12 spacecraft did not differ radically from their immediate predecessors.

The Venus launch window of 1978 was a particularly unappealing one in terms of the greater than average distance separating Earth and Venus at that time. That it was also the target launch date for U.S. Venus orbiters and multiprobes designated Pioneer Venus missions 1 and 2, which had been delayed because of funding problems, illustrates that political and economic realities often outweigh nature, even in space exploration. The extra effort required to reach Venus at this time caused Soviet designers to sacrifice the equipment needed to make the carrier buses become Venus orbiters, as they had been with Veneras 9 and 10. Venera 11, weighing 4,500 kilograms at launch, was 436 kilograms lighter than Venera 9. Venera 12 weighed 33 kilograms less than Venera 10 and was 5,000 kilograms at launch.

Among the design changes incorporated in the descent modules, none is better known than the "Groza," or lightning experiment. Scientists suspected that strong static electrical discharges pulsed through the Venusian atmosphere, so both vehicles were equipped with antennae sensitive to frequencies in the 10, 18, 36, and 80 kilohertz ranges and microphones responsive to frequencies from 200 to 5,000 hertz.

Measurements of the atmospheric content made by Veneras 9 and 10 were suspect because of a design error which had placed the intake ports for the mass spectrometers in the slipstreams of the vehicles. The result was contamination of the experiment with gases emitted by the superheated exteriors of the modules themselves. The new descent modules relied on a sophisticated scanning spectrometer and added a gas chromatograph to verify the results using an alternative experimental approach.

Only Venera 12 carried a nephelometer, an instrument with which to assay the particles which formed the clouds. It utilized special filters to capture the particles and an X-ray fluorescent spectrometer to analyze their chemical content.

Telephotometer imaging systems such as those used successfully on Veneras 9 and 10 to send images from the surface were also included. When no pictures were received, there was speculation that perhaps these instruments had been deleted, but portions of their lens systems can be clearly seen in prelaunch photographs of the probes.

The carrier buses, in addition to their principal roles as support and communications links for the descent modules, were equipped with instrumentation to gather data about conditions in interplanetary space. Among these experiments was a French instrument which recorded gamma-ray bursts detected in deep space. Other devices collected data on solar radiation and the "solar wind," a flow of highly charged particles from the Sun.

Venera 11 was launched from the Tyuratam cosmodrome on September 9, 1978, atop a D-1 (Proton) booster fitted with an additional interplanetary kick stage. Following the standard Soviet planetary mission format, it made one full circuit of Earth in a low parking orbit before the kick stage was fired to inject the vehicle into a Venus intercept trajectory. Venera 12 followed the same sequence of events on September 14. Trajectory refinements were made on the flight path of Venera 11 on September 16 and then not again until December 17. Venera 12's flight path was refined on September 21 and again on December 14.

The two U.S. Pioneer Venus probes were launched about three weeks ahead of the Veneras and would arrive at Venus in early December. The Veneras would arrive about Christmastime. Soviet and American scientists had cooperated successfully in exchanging data from the Venera 9 and 10 and Viking 1 and 2 (Mars) missions, and an agreement between the two nations called for a similar exchange following the forthcoming encounters. Trajectory information had already been exchanged, allowing the investigating teams to compare simultaneous observations by all four craft in an effort to understand how the energy fields of the Sun vary at different points in interplanetary space. In accordance with this agreement, Veneras 11 and 12 were also commanded to make long-range measurements of Venus on December 4 and 9, the dates when the two American craft arrived.

During the journey to Venus, Venera 12 overtook Venera 11 as a result of trajectory differences caused by the relative positions of Earth and Venus on the crafts' respective launch dates. On December 19, a command was sent to Venera 12 to separate the descent module from the carrier bus and begin its entry. The carrier continued on course, passing 35,000 kilometers from Venus while acting as a communications relay during the operational life of its descent module.

Venera 12's descent module, encased in a spherical entry shield, entered the atmosphere of Venus on December 21, 1978. At the Flight Control Center outside Moscow, the time was about 5:30 A.M. Friction and aerodynamic braking, or drag, slowed the vehicle from 11.2 kilometers per second to about 250 meters per second. When the probe reached an altitude of 64 kilometers, the upper hemisphere of the entry shield was jettisoned, revealing a large helical antenna, the instrument package, and a disk-shaped "air brake" which would provide additional drag in the lower atmosphere. A drogue parachute was deployed in the process. This was followed by the deployment of three main parachutes and jettisoning of the lower hemisphere of the entry shield. At an altitude of 40 kilometers, the main chutes were discarded and the probe completed its descent in "free fall," slowed only by the air brake. Impact with the surface occurred at a speed of 7 meters per second (about 25 kilometers per hour) and special shock absorbers and a collapsing impact bumper provided the necessary cushioning.

Contact with the surface came at 6:30 A.M. in a location about thirty-five hundred kilometers west of the Venera 8 landing site and two thousand kilometers south of where Venera 10 rested. This location was well inside the daylight area of the planet at that time. Some immediate problems occurred, chief among them being the failure of the telephotometer imaging system. The external temperature sensors had also failed during the last minutes of the descent, but other sensors recorded a temperature of 460 degrees Celsius at the landing site. The X-ray fluorescent spectrometer, intended to provide a soil analysis, also failed, apparently on impact. All other instrumentation survived and worked properly, and data were still coming from the surface to the carrier bus for relay to Earth when the bus passed behind Venus and its signal was blocked at 8:20 A.M., 110 minutes after landing.

Scientists gathered in the Flight Control Center again in the early morning hours of Christmas Day as Venera 11's descent module approached its rendezvous with Venus and began atmospheric entry at about 5:25 A.M. The probe followed the same descent scenario, using parachutes only between the altitudes of 64 and 40 kilometers and relying on atmospheric drag to provide the rest of the braking. Curiously, this probe's external temperature sensors also failed in the final minutes before surface contact.

Venera 11 landed at 6:24 A.M. at a spot about eight hundred kilometers southeast of its sister craft. This location was also in daylight, and a temperature of

446 degrees Celsius was reported. Again the telephotometer imaging system failed to return the expected panoramic surface pictures, and again the soil analysis X-ray fluorescent spectrometer failed on impact. All other instruments supplied data for 95 minutes, until they too were silenced when the carrier bus passed behind Venus and lost radio contact with Earth.

## Knowledge Gained

Both probes carried the most sophisticated equipment yet for determining the chemical composition of the Venusian atmosphere. The scanning spectrometers alone were reported to have returned five hundred spectra, from which the Soviets deduced the content to be carbon dioxide (95 percent), nitrogen (between 3 and 4 percent), water vapor (0.03 percent), argon (0.01 percent), neon (0.001 percent), and krypton (0.0005 percent). Both landers also reported detecting carbon monoxide in the lower atmosphere. In this respect, the data they gathered differed sharply from those obtained by the Pioneer Venus entry probes, which did not detect this gas.

Soviet and American data also disagreed regarding the amount of water vapor present. The Venera findings showed so little water that if all of it could be condensed on the surface of Venus, it would cover the planet only to a depth of one centimeter. The Pioneer Venus data suggested that water vapor, while not plentiful, was considerably more abundant—perhaps as much as ten times more than the Veneras reported. Soviet planetologists stood by their own findings, arguing that the American results could not be correct unless the planet were some 200 degrees Celsius hotter than measurements had shown.

One of the surprises detected by the probes of both nations was the very high ratio of argon 36 to argon 40 relative to that found on Earth. All data agreed that argon 36 and argon 40 were present in about equal amounts, whereas on Earth there is three hundred times more argon 40 than the lighter isotope. Although the total percentage of argon present is seemingly small, the significance of the discovery lies in explanations of the argon's original source. Argon 36 is thought to be a remnant of the primordial nebula from which the Sun and planets condensed, and it is difficult for theorists to explain how Venus might possess so much more of it than other locales within the solar system.

The lightning experiments on both probes detected a pulse electromagnetic field in the Venusian atmosphere that extended from 32 kilometers down to 2 kilometers above the surface. Its strength was equivalent to that of a distant thunderstorm (200 to 1,000 microvolts per meter), but the discharges surged through the atmosphere much more frequently. The microphones also detected sounds akin to thunder (one clap rumbled for fifteen minutes), but in other respects the phenomena bore no relationship to a terrestrial thunderstorm, and the cause of the discharges could not be determined.

Venera 12's cloud experiment showed that the main constituent of the eternal veil around Venus is concentrated sulfuric acid, which exists in small droplets in a zone from 50 to 70 kilometers above the surface. Here it lies like a fog, within which the visibility limit was estimated to be 1 kilometer. Reports circulated that the Veneras had detected sulfuric acid rain, but those reports were based on a misunderstanding of the Soviets' announcement of these data.

The ambient light levels were measured by spectrophotometers that could discriminate the angular distribution of the light. They showed that the clouds not only filter out 50 percent of the sunlight but also diffuse it so effectively that below the cloud deck the location of the Sun could be determined only as a general area of increased brightness in the sky.

## Context

The significant contributions made to planetary science by Veneras 11 and 12 were eclipsed in the West because the U.S. Pioneer Venus 1 and 2 probes preceded them and the Voyager 1 and 2 encounters with Jupiter followed in March and July, capped by Pioneer 11's encounter with Saturn in September. The Jupiter and Saturn encounters were clearly of enormous significance, but Soviet planetologists were defensive about the Venus encounters, believing that the Americans were late-comers to Venus exploration and that their spacecraft and experiments were inferior to the Veneras. To some extent that was true. The U.S. journal *Chemical and Engineering News* featured an article on the Pioneer Venus missions in its December, 1978, issue in which it was admitted that the Venera 9 and 10 missions had already answered many of the questions Pioneer Venus 1 and 2 would investigate. Harvard University's Richard Goody, one of the Pioneer Venus planners, also admitted that the Soviets had already answered "about a third" of the questions for which he and his colleagues were designing the probes.

Whether the Venera 11 and 12 craft were technically superior to the Pioneer Venus was argued in the international press, with the Soviets pointing to advanced analytical instrumentation and the engineering sophistication that allowed soft landings while U.S. scientists touted the ability of their multiprobe mission to gather atmospheric data simultaneously from four different locations on Venus. The failure of both Veneras' imaging systems and soil analysis experiments made the value of the soft landings somewhat moot in this case and denied the Soviets the information that was of greatest popular interest and was clearly beyond the scope of the American missions.

Of much more consequence than these arguments was the opportunity that the nearly simultaneous missions provided to compare data. It was fortunate that the missions occurred during a period of détente, during which a series of scientific meetings between both nations took place. These contacts set the stage for a major meeting of the U.S./U.S.S.R. Working Group on Near-Earth Space, the Moon, and the Planets, held in Innsbruck, Austria, in June, 1978. A protocol was signed regarding the exchange of data from these flights and steps were taken toward greater cooperation in future missions, but subsequent world events brought about the end of détente and, with it, a retreat from such cooperation.

From a practical standpoint, the investigations of Venus may be of profound significance for the future of Earth. The behavior of Earth's atmosphere is still not well understood, and theories concerning it are extremely difficult to test. A major unknown is to what extent the burning of fossil fuels and the use of fluorocarbons alter the atmosphere's role in maintaining Earth's heat balance. In the Venusian atmosphere, the carbon-dioxide-induced "greenhouse effect," a trapping of the Sun's heat, has run wild. Scientists seeking to understand how this process has occurred on Venus will gain a valuable understanding of Earth as well. As Fredric Taylor of the Jet Propulsion Laboratory has warned, "I think we ought to look at Venus and be scared stiff."

## Bibliography

Burgess, Eric. *Venus: An Errant Twin*. New York: Columbia University Press, 1985. This is an authoritative work for laypersons wanting to know what has been learned about Venus and how it was discovered. The Venera missions are discussed in a full chapter. The book contains nearly one hundred high-quality illustrations.

Hunt, Garry E., and Patrick Moore. *The Planet Venus*. London: Trinity Press, 1982. This comprehensive book discusses the knowledge that can be gained about Venus from Earth observation in its first half, and deals with the results of spacecraft exploration in the second. Its focus is on the planet rather than on the spacecraft. The illustrations and bibliography are useful.

Johnson, Nicholas L. *Handbook of Soviet Lunar and Planetary Exploration*. San Diego: Univelt, 1979. Forty pages are devoted to the Venera missions, with emphasis placed on the spacecraft hardware and mission highlights. The information is brief and general, not technical. There are only a few illustrations of the Venera spacecraft, but these are helpful.

Ksanfomaliti, Leonid V. "Soviet Probes Explore Venus." *Space World* P-8-190 (June, 1979): 28-29. This article is included in a monthly feature entitled "Russian Report" contributed by Novosti Press Agency. The author, a senior project scientist and member of the Venera 11 and 12 investigating team, discusses the Soviet findings and presents interpretations of discrepancies between Venera and Pioneer Venus data.

U.S. Congress. House. Committee on Science and Technology. *1980 NASA Authorization*. Vol. 1, part 3. 96th Cong., 1st sess., 1979. This document is a transcript of the testimony of Noel Hinners, a top NASA administrator. The subject of international cooperation in planetary studies is addressed, and Hinners comments on the meetings of the U.S./U.S.S.R. Working Group on Near-Earth Space, the Moon, and the Planets.

*Richard S. Knapp*

## Cross-References

# VENERA 13 and 14

*Date:* October 30, 1981, to June, 1982
*Type of mission:* Unmanned deep space probes
*Country:* The Soviet Union

*The Venera 13 and 14 planetary landers sent back the first color photographs of the Venusian surface and completed a complex program of drilling into and chemically analyzing the Venusian surface.*

*Principal personages*
ROALD SAGDEYEV, Director of the Institute for Space Research,
Soviet Academy of Sciences
YURI SURKOV, Vernadsky Institute, X-ray fluorescence
spectrometer investigator
BORIS NOPOKLONOV, the chief Venusian topographer
VALERI BARSUKOV, Director of the Vernadsky Institute of
Geochemistry and Analytic Chemistry
MIKHAIL MAROV, a researcher at the Soviet Institute of Applied
Mathematics
K. GRINGAUZ, a researcher at the Institute for Space Research,
Soviet Academy of Sciences
VLADIMIR N. CHELOMEI, Chief Designer of the Soviet space
program

## Summary of the Missions

The primary purpose of Veneras 13 and 14 was to land a drilling apparatus on Venus to obtain rock samples. The material gathered during the drilling was to be studied by means of an X-ray fluorescence spectrometer in a miniature laboratory within the lander. The Venera 13 probe was launched by a Proton booster rocket from the Baikonur cosmodrome on October 30, 1981, while the Venera 14 probe followed on November 4, 1981. Planetary-escape-stage rockets propelled both probes out of Earth orbit into a trajectory toward Venus. En route to Venus, both Veneras studied gamma-ray bursts with Soviet- and French-made instruments, while an Austrian-made magnetometer gathered data on the interplanetary magnetic field. American cooperation on the Venera missions began when Harold Masursky of the U.S. Geological Survey provided the Soviets with Pioneer Venus radar data. These data allowed the Soviets to land the Venera craft on both Venusian lowland and highland areas in order to study geologically diverse areas. After arriving near Venus, the Venera 13 lander separated from its spacecraft bus on February 27, 1982, in preparation for its March 1, 1982, landing on the planet. Later, the spacecraft bus was commanded to miss the planet by 36,000 kilometers. Prior to atmospheric entry, the landers were cooled in space to −10 degrees Celsius to help them cope with the high temperatures on the surface.

Externally, both planetary landers were similar to the new design initiated by the earlier Veneras 9 and 10, consisting of a spherical instrument section supported below by a ring-shaped shock-absorbing mechanism and with a circular atmospheric braking disc above. The landers were enclosed in a special spherical heatshield which could withstand a force equivalent to 250 times Earth's gravity during its entry through the atmosphere. The heatshield, parachutes, and lander weighed a combined 1,480 kilograms. After jettisoning the heatshield and parachutes, the lander weighed 751 kilograms.

Venera 13 entered the Venusian atmosphere at a velocity of 39,845 kilometers per hour. After aerodynamic braking, the lander released its first parachute at an altitude of 65 kilometers. Later, after slowing to 125 meters per second, a series of parachutes deployed to further slow the lander's descent and the return of scientific data was initiated. At a height of 48 kilometers, the parachutes were jettisoned and the spherical lander continued a free-fall descent to the surface, using only the braking ring above the lander to control its drop through the thick Venusian atmosphere. Its landing speed was 8 meters per second. During the descent, atmospheric measurements were made by a mass spectrometer, a gas chromatograph, an optical spectrophotometer, a hydrometer, a nephelometer, and an X-ray fluorescence spectrometer.

The Venera 13 lander touched down at 6:57 A.M. Moscow time, after a 62-minute descent through the atmosphere, in an area known as Phoebe Regio on the sunlit side of the planet. Immediately after landing, the probe's surface photography experiment began to scan around the touchdown site. Eight color images—the first such photographs taken of Venus—were returned before contact was lost. The lander survived for 127 minutes in the Venusian heat—four times longer than expected.

Venera 14 touched down on March 5, 1982, landing 960 kilometers east of Venera 13's site; the new landing site was apparently on a hillside. This second lander also returned color images of the Venusian surface during the 57 minutes it remained in contact with Earth.

Each lander carried two imaging photometers. The smaller pixel size of the new Venera cameras allowed nearby details only 4 millimeters in size to be seen. Color photographs were taken by combining successive exposures taken through red, blue, and green filters. The spacecraft deployed a color scale on the surface for color calibration. Each color photograph took 14 minutes to scan.

Thirty-two seconds after landing, Venera 13 began drilling into the Venusian rock for a period of 12 minutes, reaching a depth of 30 centimeters. A 1-cubic-centimeter surface sample was transferred into a hermetically sealed chamber within the lander where it was analyzed. Four days later, Venera 14's probe performed similar surface experiments.

The Venera landers faced a severe problem in sealing out the harsh, high-pressure Venusian atmosphere during the sample analysis. The experiment was done in a sealed chamber where the pressure was reduced to 50 millimeters of mercury (one two-thousandth that of the normal surface pressure) and the temperature held at 30 degrees Celsius (compared to 457 degrees Celsius outside the lander). The drill mechanism consisted of a hollow pipe with two blades inside to penetrate the surface. The sample chamber had a capacity of 10 liters, in case the soil was loose or sandy. Since bare rock was the main component of the Venera 13 landing site, only a 1-cubic-centimeter sample was drilled after 12 minutes. To reach the analysis chamber, the rock sample traveled through a series of chambers which had progressively lower pressure. The walls of the chambers were blown apart by flare cartridges, which created a suction, drawing the sample into the chamber. Once the sample was inside the chamber, the pressure was reduced to 50 millimeters of mercury.

Both landers also carried a spring-powered penetrometer to determine the capacity of the local Venusian surface to bear loads and a uniaxial seismometer to search for seismic disturbances. Wind speed at the planet's surface was measured by acoustical sensors.

The Venera 13 and 14 spacecraft buses were not designed to be planetary orbiters as were those of Venera 9 and 10. This was to allow them to remain aligned with the landers for a greater period of time, permitting a longer period for relaying signals to Earth.

## Knowledge Gained

During their interplanetary cruises, Veneras 13 and 14 recorded more than twenty gamma-ray bursts; ten of the bursts were associated with solar flares. Atmospheric studies performed during descent by both landers confirmed readings from previous probes by showing that the Venusian atmosphere consisted of 96 percent carbon dioxide and 4 percent nitrogen, with other trace gases present. Surface environment measurements by Venera 13 correlated those of previous probes, showing a temperature of 457 degrees Celsius and an atmospheric pressure 89 times greater than that of Earth.

The Venusian surface as photographed by Venera 13 showed an area of rolling foothills covered with sharp rocks and fine dust and sand. Large gray boulders were also seen. This contrasted sharply with the Venera 14 views, which showed a flat plain covered with flat cracked rock, a characteristic of cooled basalt. In one area of the Venera 14 view was a pile of rocks showing evidence of gases having bubbled up through molten rock, which then solidified.

The Venera 13 and 14 surface photographs are reminiscent of a terrestrial ocean floor and suggest that Venus' extreme atmospheric pressure acts in a similar fashion. Initially, the color image from Venera 14 showed that the local area was brown, but later analysis showed that the surface was really yellowish orange, with some green areas. In a discovery which the Soviets described as one of the most striking results of the mission, the Venera color images showed that the Venusian sky is orange, apparently reflecting the surface color.

The Venera 13 and 14 landers carried a more sensitive mass spectrometer than previous missions had. It determined that the ratio of isotopes of neon 20 to neon 22 was 11.8, less than had been detected by the U.S. Pioneer Venus Multiprobe. This ratio is higher than that of the terrestrial atmosphere but less than that of the solar wind (the outward flow of plasma from the Sun). These atmospheric readings are important because they show that Venus and Earth could not have been made up of the same combinations of volatile materials taken from the solar nebula at the time of planetary creation. The makeup of the planets is slightly different and suggests that Earth formed from the solar nebula before Venus did. Measurements at Venus also showed it to have less argon 40 than Earth. Argon 40 is formed by the radioactive decay of potassium 40, and it requires tectonic activity or volcanism to bring it to the surface, where it can enter the atmosphere. Since the abundance of potassium and the ratio of potassium to uranium found in the Venus rocks has been Earth-like, the reduced amount of argon 40 at Venus leads to the conclusion that Venus is not as tectonically active as Earth.

The two craft's spectrometers found the krypton readings to be confusing; they were considerably different from those detected by previous probes. Traces of xenon were found in the atmosphere of Venus as well as carbonyl sulfide and hydrogen sulfide, compounds which were not detected by the Pioneer Venus Multiprobe. Atmospheric data also showed that most ultraviolet radiation is absorbed at an altitude of 60 kilometers.

During descent, cloud particles were examined by X-ray fluoroscopy. As expected, sulfur was the primary element, with smaller amounts of chlorine present. This observation was the opposite of that returned by the Venera 12 lander several years earlier. The water vapor content of the Venusian atmosphere was also quite different from readings taken by previous probes. Venera 13 and 14 measurements suggested that water was being removed from within the clouds and released at the cloud base. The presence of sulfuric acid could explain the absorption of water within the clouds, but the reason that water vapor decreased progressively closer to the surface remained a mystery.

The wind speed measured at the Venera 13 and 14 landing sites was one-half meter per second. These speeds in the thick Venusian atmosphere have been shown to be sufficient to transport the fine material eroded off surface rocks. X-ray fluorescence analysis of the Venera 13 highland surface sample showed it to be like terrestrial leucite basalt, rich in potassium and magnesium. This is rare on Earth but is found in the Mediterranean volcanic area. Analysis five days later of Venera 14's lowland area sample showed a similarity to oceanic tholeitic basalts; the sample had much less potassium than the Venera 13 site. Because of the lack of secondary soil changes in the Venera 13 and 14 landing areas, scientists concluded that the areas were relatively young. On Earth, an area which resembles those found by the Venera craft would be the region around Hawaii. The lowland Venera 14 samples are similar to lava on the ocean floor, while the Venera 13 highland sample is similar to the volcanic mountainsides of the islands.

The spacecraft data confirmed that rocks on Venus do not weather by the same processes as they do on Earth. Rocks on Venus undergo several other types of weathering; chemical weathering by the atmosphere would decompose olivines, pyroxenes, quartz, and feldspars into magnesite, tremolite, dolomite, sulfates, and sulfites, while mechanical weathering would disintegrate rocks by spalling (breaking rock off in chips) and preferential weathering and by wind erosion.

The mechanical strength of the Venusian soil was measured by the landers using a rod penetrometer. The Venera 13 site had a soil strength range of 2.6 to 10 dekanewtons per square centimeter. The Venera 14 site tested at 65 to 250 dekanewtons per square centimeter, but the Soviets admitted that Venera 14 suffered a partial equipment failure and the reading might have been abnormally high.

Seismic activity at the two landing sites was also measured using uniaxial seismometers, which could study only vertical movement. While Venera 13 recorded no seismic events, Venera 14 recorded two. The Soviets said that the two readings may have been caused by the wind and no firm conclusion could be drawn about seismic activity on Venus.

After completion of the surface activity on Venus, both spacecraft buses continued to perform experiments in heliocentric orbit. By June, 1982, a total of eighty-nine cosmic-ray bursts and more than three hundred solar flares had been recorded.

## Context

"Venera" is the Russian word for Venus, but with the successes of the Venera space probes the word has come to represent a series of highly successful planetary exploration spacecraft. While people worldwide believed that the Venera program was a stunning success after overcoming early technical adversity, by the time the flights of Venera 13 and 14 were completed some Soviet space scientists were openly grumbling that they felt "sentenced to the exploration of Venus" because there were no other active Soviet planetary exploration programs.

In spite of these complaints, Soviet space engineers had created a mechanical marvel: The Venera 13 and 14 spacecraft were then the only planetary landers, with the exception of the American Viking Mars landers, to ingest soil directly into the lander for chemical analysis. Considering the corrosive harshness, extreme pressure, and heat of the Venusian atmosphere, Soviet planetary scientists had reason to be proud of their success. Harold Masursky, a leading American space geologist, examined the Venera 13 and 14 surface drilling and sampling apparatus and described it as a "technical masterpiece."

The study of Venus is assuming critical importance to the preservation of life on Earth. Two major ecological disasters which may affect future generations were discovered as a result of the exploration of Venus: the greenhouse effect, which uses atmospheric carbon dioxide to trap solar heat and raise the temperature of the atmosphere, and holes in Earth's ozone layer, which shields the planet from excess ultraviolet radiation.

The data returned by Veneras 13 and 14 help in understanding the exact planetary evolution mechanism which allowed Venus and Earth, planets which formed in similar ways, to take two divergent paths. The underlying scientific question is why Venus became a high pressure oven while Earth became a life-sustaining garden.

## Bibliography

Burgess, Eric. *Venus: An Errant Twin*. New York: Columbia University Press, 1985. Authoritative yet readable, this work provides an extensive overview of all knowledge that was gained about Venus through observation from Earth and planetary exploration through the early 1980's. An entire chapter is devoted to the Venera missions. Includes chronologies, illustrations, and indexes.

Fimmel, Richard O., et al. *Pioneer Venus*. NASA SP-461. Washington, D.C.: Government Printing Office, 1983. Although primarily concerned with the Pioneer Venus mission, this volume also considers the contributions made by the various Soviet Veneras. A table of launch and landing information, extensive illustrations, and an index help the reader to compare Soviet and American achievements.

Johnson, Nicholas L. *Handbook of Soviet Lunar and Planetary Exploration*. San Diego: Univelt, 1979. Although its account does not extend to the Venera 13 and 14 missions, this study of the Soviet efforts devotes considerable time to the Venera program as a whole. Much of the information relates to the spacecraft hardware and some of the highlights of the earlier missions. Intended for the general reader. Illustrated.

Smolders, Peter. *Soviets in Space*. New York: Taplinger Publishing Co., 1974. This well-illustrated overview considers the successes of the Soviet space program as they were officially reported to the world. Diagrams and photographs detail the technical information about the craft and their missions.

Turnill, Reginald, ed. *Jane's Spaceflight Directory*. London: Jane's Publishing Co., 1987. This extensive volume comprehensively lists all known data about the various international space programs. Illustrated with photographs, diagrams, and various tables.

U.S. Congress. Senate. Committee on Commerce, Science, and Transportation. *Soviet Space Programs: 1976-1980*. Part 3, *Unmanned Space Activities*. Report prepared by Congressional Research Service, the Library of Congress. 99th Cong., 1st sess., 1985. Committee Print. This detailed overview of the unmanned Soviet space programs is considered the standard reference work. Considers the development, investigations, and political effects of the various Soviet missions.

*Robert Reeves*

## Cross-References

Halley's Comet Probes, 569; Soviet Launch Vehicles, 742; Mariner 1 and 2, 835; Mariner 5, 849; Mariner 10, 871; Pioneer Venus 1, 1145; Pioneer Venus 2, 1152; Planetary Evolution, 1159; Comparative Planetology, 1168; The History of the Solar

System, 1367; Space Centers and Launch Sites in the Soviet Union, 1592; The Soviet Spaceflight Tracking Network, 1877; The Venera Program, 2083; Venera 1-6, 2091; Venera 7 and 8, 2098; Venera 9 and 10, 2105; Venera 11 and 12, 2112; Venera 15 and 16, 2126; Venus' Atmosphere, 2132; Venus' Landscape and Geology, 2138; Venusian Soil Samples, 2143; Zond 1-8, 2275.

# VENERA 15 and 16

*Date:* June 2, 1983, to November, 1984
*Type of mission:* Unmanned deep space probes
*Country:* The Soviet Union

*Unlike the previous spacecraft in the Venera series, these two vehicles were not intended to land on the surface of Venus. They were designed to detect major landscape features through the thick Venusian clouds using radar.*

### Principal personages
ROALD SAGDEYEV, Director, Institute for Space Research, Soviet Academy of Sciences
YU. N. ALEXANDROV, a researcher at the Institute of Radioengineering and Electronics
VALERI BARSUKOV, Director, Vernadsky Institute of Geochemistry and Analytical Chemistry
ALEXANDER BASILEVSKY, Chief, Comparative Planetology Laboratory, Vernadsky Institute
S. A. KADNICHANSKI, a researcher at the Central Research Institute of Geodesy, Aerosurvey, and Cartography
E. L. AKIM, a researcher at the Institute of Applied Mathematics

## Summary of the Missions

The main structure of the Venera 15 and 16 spacecraft was similar to the previous, second-generation spacecraft used in the Soviet Union's extensive Venus exploration program (Veneras 9 through 14). The vehicle's distinctive external components were designed to serve the unique goals of Venera missions 15 and 16. Chief among these components were the huge radar antennae, which opened from a folded configuration to a rectangular area of 8.6 by 1.4 meters. The antennae were mounted atop the orbiter, in the same position as the spherical descent module on the previous Veneras. Also prominent was a large parabolic dish antenna mounted to the cylindrical body of the orbiter and hinged to swing toward Earth when in use. There was one other obvious difference distinguishing this spacecraft from its predecessors: two rings of spherical propellant tanks for the attitude control engines. These tanks encircled the orbiter at both ends and provided the fuel to allow the spacecraft to control its orientation throughout the eight-month mapping period.

Each vehicle was equipped with an 8-centimeter-wavelength synthetic aperture radar (SAR) with which to image the surface terrain. SAR operates in a manner fundamentally different from visual imaging but can produce images that appear strikingly similar to optical photography. It does not require the presence of light, so it can obtain images at night as well as during the day. Furthermore, the SAR can detect land features through clouds, as if the clouds were transparent. No lenses are involved, and resolution is not dependent on distance from the surface; thus, theoretically, a given SAR system can detect as much from 2,000 kilometers away as from 200 kilometers away. The resolution of the Venera radars was in the 1- to 2-kilometer range, which is sufficient to reveal craters, hills, ridges, and major fractures.

An SAR system works by sending bursts of microwave energy toward the planet and then carefully recording the strength of the signal on its return bounce from the surface (the "return bounce" is also known as the "echo"), the time delay in receiving the return bounce of the signal, and the frequency change (the Doppler shift) in the return signal. This information is gathered simultaneously for different points in the target area. When considered together, the time delay and frequency change yield the true distance to each data point (pixel) in the picture and remove the effect of the motion of the spacecraft itself. The echo's strength gives information on the angle of the surface (ground slope) and may also help in determining the composition of that surface.

Both vehicles also carried radar altimeters to measure the heights of various topographic features to within 50 meters. The radar altimeters were pointed straight down on the terrain over which the spacecraft was passing, while the imaging radars were aimed 12 degrees to the side of the spacecraft's vertical axis. Both vehicles carried cosmic ray counters for further studies during the interplanetary voyage to Venus, and Venera 16 was also equipped with an infrared spectrometer for additional atmospheric studies of the planet. An improved telemetry system permitted a data rate of 100,000 bits per second, a substantially larger data rate than had been possible with the earlier Veneras.

Venera 15 was launched from Tyuratam by the massive four-stage D-1e booster at 2:38 A.M. Moscow time on June 2, 1983. Venera 16 followed it into orbit five days later. After initial test orbits of Earth, the fourth-stage engines boosted the vehicles into trans-Venusian trajectories. Their 130-day flights to Venus were uneventful, and each spacecraft required only two midcourse corrections. At 6:05 A.M. on October 10, 1983, Venera 15 executed a braking maneuver and swept into a highly elliptical near-polar orbit that brought it to within 1,000 kilometers of the surface at the nearest point and more than 65,000 kilometers at the farthest point. Venera 15 spent the next few days undergoing a systems test. Venera 16 arrived at 9:22 A.M. on October 14 and entered a virtually identical orbit, as planned. Venera 15 commenced mapping operations on October 16, and Venera 16 began its work on October 20.

The two spacecraft were operated in shifts to reduce the data flow to the tracking stations and to allow time for each to recharge its batteries after a mapping pass. As each spacecraft lowered itself over the surface, its radar altimeter took readings at 3-kilometer intervals on the height of the ground directly below the spacecraft. Simultaneously, the SAR system was gathering imaging information for a swath of the surface 150 kilometers wide by 9,000 kilometers long. With the antenna's pointing angle slightly offset from the vertical, the area examined by the SAR was centered on a line parallel to but 12 degrees to the side of the spacecraft's ground track. That meant that the altimeter data for a given pass were received before the SAR data for the same area, and the two sets of results had to be brought together at a later stage in the image processing. Venus' very slow axial rotation caused the ground tracks and radar paths to shift eastward by 1.5 degrees each day, so the altimeter data led the SAR data by eight orbits. Using the rotation of the planet to provide the scanning coverage of the surface also meant that over an eight-month operational life the two spacecraft could provide complete coverage of the northern hemisphere of the planet to within 18 degrees of the equator. While the radar instruments were mapping the topography of the surface, the other instrumentation was mapping surface temperature distribution and the composition of the atmosphere.

The amount of data collected in a single mapping pass was too great to be relayed to Earth in real time, even with the higher telemetry rates and larger communications antennae used on these spacecraft. Moreover, the Veneras were not equipped to process the data completely as it was received. The radar echoes were recorded on board the Veneras during the mapping pass and then replayed to Earth at a slower rate during the hours preceding the next time the radar was activated. Sophisticated mathematical processing to correct for the motion of the spacecraft and to assemble meaningful images was accomplished by a special digital signal processor back on Earth. This procedure also made the best use of the limited electrical power aboard the spacecraft. It is a procedure similar to data management techniques used with many U.S. interplanetary spacecraft. Once the raw radar data were received on Earth, they were subjected to computer enhancement to refine the images represented. This process caused a delay of many weeks in the release of high-quality images from the missions.

Veneras 15 and 16 both operated beyond their designed lifetimes. Venera 15 continued to send images from Venus until July, 1984, and Venera 16 remained operational until November of that year. The Soviets considered but eventually abandoned plans to shift the orbits of the two spacecraft so as to begin mapping of the southern hemisphere. The volume of data transmitted was so great that image processing continued for more than a year after the last mapping pass was completed.

## Knowledge Gained

Although scientists had already speculated about most of the features revealed by the spacecraft, Veneras 15 and 16 portrayed these features with enough detail to permit planetary geologists to begin constructing theories on how they were formed. Valeri Barsukov, Director of the Vernadsky Institute of Geochemistry and Analytical Chemistry, was quick to announce that the manifestations of very intense tectonic activity could be observed in the first images received on Earth. Harold Masursky of the U.S. Geological Survey later proclaimed that the images revealed a "wonderfully complicated and complex geology."

The Venusian surface was seen to be generally flatter than that of other terrestrial planets. Some 60 percent lies within 800 meters of Venus' mean radius, and only 10 percent is regarded as highlands. The low relief was offset in one mapped area by a continent-sized mass of elevated terrain larger than Australia, called Ishtar Terra. Its average elevation is several kilometers above the mean radius of the planet, and it contains a mountain, Maxwell Montes, that rises 1,525 meters higher than Mount Everest. Within the Ishtar Terra region are mountain ranges that appear to have been formed by horizontal compression forces in a process similar to the formation of the Himalayas and Appalachians. Not far away is another region where the surface appears to have been torn in a manner similar to the Rift Valley of East Africa. These are only some of the more dramatic examples revealing that the Venusian crust has undergone extensive tectonic deformation and, in terms of its history and evolution, is much more like Earth than Mars.

With millions of square kilometers imaged, only a few score of impact craters were detected—further evidence that the surface described by the Venera space-craft is a relatively recent one. Current theories ascribe the heavily cratered faces of Mercury and Earth's Moon to a period of intense bombardment in the early history of the solar system. When that era ended, about 4 billion years ago, all the ter-restrial planets looked like the Moon and Mercury still do. Geologic activity and erosion have erased all traces of this era from Earth, and apparently also from Venus. The craters which can be seen in the Veneras' radar images are the result of sporadic impacts in the much more recent past. By comparing the number of craters in a given area with the rate at which such impacts occur, scientists can approx-imately date the surface. On this basis, the Soviets fixed the age of the Venusian rolling plains (about 70 percent of the area studied) at not more than 1 billion years.

The radar findings also support theories that extensive volcanism has occurred on Venus in the geologically recent past. There is evidence of volcanic domes, conic mountains capped by calderas, and lava that has flowed in sheets into valleys and low areas. Whether Venus is volcanically active today could not be clearly ascer-tained from the Veneras' data, but that possibility is one of the most dramatic and controversial to grow out of the missions. It also could not be determined whether erosion processes are or have been significant factors in shaping the landscape, because the resolution of the radar was not high enough to reveal the effects of erosion.

## Context

The Venera 15 and 16 missions were not the first successful efforts to employ radar to penetrate the clouds of Venus. Earth-based radio telescopes operating as radar systems had attempted the same thing as early as the 1960's, and the Ameri-can Pioneer Venus mission of 1978 had already successfully returned radar images while orbiting the planet. Yet the resolution of these systems had been too poor to furnish more than a hint of what the major landscape features might be. Pioneer Venus, for example, had a limiting resolution of 25 kilometers. The Veneras' radars were designed to provide ten times better resolution.

During the summer of 1983, before the Venera missions could return data, they were "scooped" to some extent by a U.S. project that modified the gigantic Arecibo radio telescope in Puerto Rico. The Americans were able to obtain radar images of Venus with a resolution almost identical to that of the Venera radar images. Still, the Arecibo telescope could only obtain high-resolution images for a small area in the southern hemisphere of Venus; so the two efforts were complementary. Nevertheless, many U.S. space scientists expressed surprise that the Venera radars were not capable of better resolution, considering that their antennae were so large.

The Soviet Venera missions also drew criticism from the West for the slowness with which the results were made available. In the months following the encounters, only a few images were made public, and these were usually not accompanied by geodetic information that would explain where the features were located. Western researchers were surprised by the Soviet's unwillingness to share data because excellent international cooperation had characterized the Venera 13 and 14 missions. All of that changed in the spring of 1984, when a delegation of Soviet scientists were the star attraction at a lunar and planetary sciences conference in Houston, where they reported details of the Venera 15 and 16 results. It seemed that computer processing and enhancement of the images had taken the Soviets much longer than expected and had only been completed for the first set of images the week before the conference. Venera project scientists showed dozens of high-quality photographs, contour maps, and profiles and promised that additional information would be forthcoming.

Even as the data from the Venera 15 and 16 spacecraft were being received, the Soviet Union was involved in preparations for an advanced Venus/Halley's comet mission named Vega. An altogether new spacecraft design was planned; the science experiments required a return to the instrumented descent module, and balloon-borne instrumentation would be released into the atmosphere.

At about the same time that the Venera mapping operations were coming to an end, Roald Sagdeyev, Director of the Soviet Academy of Science's Institute for Space Research, acknowledged that the Soviet scientific community was strongly divided on the value of continuing the Venus exploration program, and it appears that subsequently a decision was made to shift the emphasis toward Mars. The two Vega craft would be the final missions in a twenty-five-year series, during which the Soviets seldom intentionally missed an opportunity to send several space probes to Venus whenever the planet came within range. What is surprising is that, having come so far in unlocking the secrets of the mysterious planet, the Soviets stopped short of combining the image quality of the Veneras with the global coverage of Pioneer Venus. Thus, the way was left open for the United States to continue its plans for Magellan, an advanced radar mapper intended to furnish images of virtually the entire surface of Venus to a resolution limit of 0.15 kilometer.

## Bibliography

Alexandrov, Yu. N., et al. "Venus: Detailed Mapping of Maxwell Montes Region." *Science* 231 (March 14, 1986): 1271-1273. Prepared for U.S. publication by the Soviet scientific team that was responsible for the radar imaging experiments on the Veneras. Although this article requires a fairly good technical vocabulary and understanding on the part of the reader, it is one of the few readily accessible sources that attempts to explain specifically how the data were collected and presented for interpretation.

Beatty, J. Kelly. "Radar Views of Venus." *Sky and Telescope* 67 (February, 1984): 110-112. A useful article for the information it provides on the Venera 15 and 16 spacecraft and their mission operations. Offers excellent descriptions of the problems with the information first released to the West.

Burgess, Eric. *Venus: An Errant Twin*. New York: Columbia University Press, 1985. The definitive work for the lay reader wanting to know what has been learned about Venus and how it has been learned. The Venera missions are treated in a full chapter. The book contains 160 pages and nearly one hundred high-quality illustrations.

Johnson, Nicholas L. *Soviet Space Programs: 1980-1985*. San Diego: Univelt, 1987. This volume is a compilation and synthesis of information published annually by Teledyne Brown Engineering. The book provides an excellent overview of the Soviet space program.

Kobrick, Michael. "SAR Imaging: Seeing the Unseen." *Sky and Telescope* 63 (February, 1982): 139-140. The technology of synthetic aperture radar is briefly explained and illustrated with photographs and diagrams based on an SAR experiment flown aboard the U.S. space shuttle. The information is suitable for a technically literate lay reader. The author comments that the technology "is more or less perfected" but that scientists are still learning how best to interpret the data.

Register, Bridget Mintz. "Venus Shines at Rockfest '84." *Space World* U-7-247 (July, 1984): 17-18. This article records the presentation of findings from the Venera 15 and 16 missions along with the results of Arecibo telescope research. The discussion is nontechnical and focuses on the highlights of this research.

*Richard S. Knapp*

## Cross-References

# VENUS' ATMOSPHERE

*Type of phenomenon:* Planetary science

*For more than twenty-five years, a series of planetary probes sent out by the United States and the Soviet Union has provided new information about the atmosphere of Earth's closest planetary neighbor, Venus. Once considered its twin, Venus has proved very different from Earth.*

## Summary of the Phenomenon

Venus is often called Earth's twin because of its comparable size, mass, and mean density. From an atmospheric perspective, however, Venus is very different from Earth in several important ways. Venus' surface is hot, about 460 degrees Celsius, while Earth's is only about 15 degrees Celsius. Venus' atmosphere is massive, with an atmospheric surface pressure about ninety times greater than that of Earth. The overwhelming constituent of the Venusian atmosphere is carbon dioxide, which makes up about 96 percent by volume of the atmosphere. In Earth's atmosphere, carbon dioxide is only a minor constituent, making up about 0.035 percent by volume. The thick, unbroken Venusian cloud cover does not permit direct observation of the planet's surface. These clouds are believed to be composed of droplets of sulfuric acid. The clouds in Earth's atmosphere are much thinner, cover only about 50 percent of the surface at any given time, and are composed of water vapor.

Much of the information about the Venusian atmosphere resulted from a series of flybys, orbiters, and entry probes beginning with the Soviet Venera 1 in 1961. From 1961 to 1984, the Soviet Union launched sixteen Venera flybys, orbiters, and hard- and soft-landers, as well as two Vega probes. Also during that time, the United States launched three Mariner probes and two Pioneer Venus spacecraft to Venus.

Prior to the landings of these planetary probes, little was known about Venus or its atmosphere. In the mid-1960's, high-resolution spectroscopy from Earth indicated that carbon dioxide was the dominant constituent of the Venusian atmosphere. Spectroscopic measurements in the 1960's also indicated that the concentration of water vapor in the atmosphere was extremely low and variable, in the range of a few hundredths percent by volume or less. In Earth's atmosphere water vapor is much more abundant. During this same period, measurements with Earth-based radio telescopes suggested that microwave emission from Venus was much greater than was expected. The high microwave emission was the result of either a very hot surface or hot electrons in a dense ionosphere. If the high microwave emission, which corresponded to a surface temperature of more than 450 degrees Celsius, originated at the surface of Venus, it was the result of a very efficient "greenhouse effect." (The greenhouse effect is the process by which certain atmospheric gases trap or absorb the heat or infrared energy radiated by a planet's surface and prevent this radiation from escaping into space and thus cooling the surface of the planet. The trapped or absorbed heat energy is then reemitted by the greenhouse gas. The downward-directed component of the reemitted heat energy results in additional heating of the planetary surface.) Carbon dioxide is an efficient greenhouse gas. Venera 4, the first successful Venus entry probe (launched June 12, 1967, and reaching Venus in October) provided the first direct evidence that carbon dioxide was indeed the major component of the atmosphere of Venus, and Veneras 4 through 8 (launched between 1967 and 1972) all indicated that carbon dioxide constitutes about 96 percent of the atmosphere. Microwave measurements obtained by Mariner 2 indicated that the surface of Venus was very hot and thus was the source of the microwave emissions. Venera 7 obtained the first direct measurement of the planet's surface temperature; it was found to be in excess of 450 degrees Celsius.

Mariner 10 obtained detailed ultraviolet spectra of the Venusian atmosphere. These spectra confirmed the Earth-based spectroscopic findings that carbon monoxide and atomic oxygen were present in surprisingly low concentrations. Both carbon monoxide and atomic oxygen are products resulting from the photodissociation, or "breakdown," of carbon dioxide by solar ultraviolet radiation. In the daytime upper atmosphere (above 100 kilometers), carbon dioxide is readily photodissociated, with a photochemical atmospheric lifetime of only about one week. Thus, photodissociation could easily convert the entire concentration of carbon dioxide in Venus' atmosphere to carbon monoxide and atomic and molecular oxygen in about 4 million years—geologically a short period of time for a planet 4.6 billion years old. It is now believed that the carbon dioxide must be reformed from carbon monoxide and oxygen through various chemical reactions involving hydrogen and chlorine in the planet's atmosphere.

The Pioneer Venus and Venera 11 and 12 spacecraft sampled the Venus atmosphere both above and below the cloud level with mass spectrometers and gas chromatographs. The following atmospheric gases were identified by these instruments: molecular nitrogen, carbon monoxide, sulfur dioxide, water vapor, helium, neon, argon, and krypton. These instruments also provided tentative evidence for the presence of molecular oxygen, hydrogen sulfide, and carbonyl sulfide.

The ionosphere of Venus was also studied by the Pioneer Venus ion mass spectrometer, which found the atomic oxygen ion to be the dominant ion above about 200 kilometers and the molecular oxygen ion dominant below 180 kilometers. The ionosphere on Venus is well developed, with a peak electron density of about $3 \times 10^5$ electrons per cubic centimeter at an altitude of about 150 kilometers on the dayside. Nightside electron densities at 150 kilometers are about 30 times greater than those on the dayside.

The atmospheric compositions of Venus and Earth are very different. Carbon dioxide, which is the overwhelming constituent of Venus' atmosphere, makes up only 0.035 percent of Earth's atmosphere. Nitrogen, the second most abundant gas in the atmosphere of Venus (about 4 percent), is the major constituent of Earth's atmosphere (78.08 percent). Oxygen, the second most abundant gas on Earth (20.95 percent), is at a concentration on the order of only about one-thousandth of

1 percent on Venus. In Earth's atmosphere, water vapor is variable but may range up to several percent. The atmosphere of Venus is very dry with water vapor also quite variable, but in the range of only about one-hundredth of 1 percent.

Veneras 9 and 10 (launched in June and July of 1975 and reaching Venus in October) carried instrumentation to measure the distribution of cloud particles in Venus' atmosphere. These measurements indicated that the cloud base was at an altitude of about 50 kilometers and that the cloud particle number densities ranged from 50 to 500 particles per cubic centimeter. Previous theoretical calculations had predicted a similar cloud base altitude and similar particle number densities if the clouds were composed of concentrated sulfuric acid droplets. The clouds appear to resemble a stratified low-density haze.

The vertical mass distribution of the cloud particles was investigated with the Pioneer Venus particle-size spectrometer. Three distinct cloud particle types were identified: aerosols (about 0.3 micrometer in diameter), called "mode 1" particles; spheres (about 2 micrometers in diameter), termed "mode 2" particles; and large particles (about 7 micrometers), which may be crystalline and are designated "mode 3." The total extinction optical depth of the clouds in visible light is about 29, with modes 1, 2, and 3 contributing approximately 3, 10, and 16 optical depths. (For each optical depth, the incoming solar radiation is reduced by about 36 percent.) The extinction of visible light in the atmosphere of Venus is almost totally the result of scattering by the cloud particles as opposed to particle or gaseous absorption. The reflective properties of the Venus clouds enable Venus to have the highest albedo (reflectivity) of any planet in the solar system; its albedo is about 77 percent, compared to about 30 percent for Earth. Despite its greater proximity to the Sun, Venus actually absorbs less solar energy than does Earth. As already noted, the efficient carbon dioxide greenhouse effect on Venus more than adequately accounts for the high surface temperature, even though Venus absorbs less solar energy than does Earth. The mode 2 particles, the cloud particles visible from Earth, are composed of concentrated sulfuric acid droplets. The other cloud particles, modes 1 and 3, may also be composed of sulfuric acid, elemental sulfur, or perchloric acid crystals. The sulfuric acid cloud droplets most probably result from the chemical transformation of atmospheric sulfur gases, such as sulfur dioxide, hydrogen sulfide, and carbonyl sulfide.

The atmospheres of Venus, Earth, and Mars are believed to have resulted from the outgassing of volatiles (removal of gases) trapped in the solid planet during the formation of the planets. It is also believed that Venus and Earth formed with approximately the same volatile inventory of water vapor, carbon dioxide, and nitrogen, the three most abundant volatiles that have outgassed over geological time. On Earth, the outgassed water vapor condensed out of the atmosphere, forming Earth's vast oceans. The outgassed carbon dioxide dissolved in the oceans and subsequently reacted with ions of calcium and magnesium in the seawater, forming carbonates. Outgassed nitrogen, which did not condense out of the atmosphere or dissolve in the ocean, as did carbon dioxide, built up in the atmosphere to become the major constituent of Earth's atmosphere.

If Venus and Earth were formed with comparable concentrations of volatiles, then Venus must have lost about 300 bars of water vapor (1 bar is the equivalent of 1 atmosphere, the pressure exerted by Earth's atmosphere at sea level). The loss of such a large quantity of water may have resulted from the "runaway" greenhouse effect. Because of the planet's slightly shorter distance from the Sun, and thus its slightly warmer surface temperature, its outgassed water vapor could never have condensed out of the atmosphere as it did on Earth. The continuing buildup in the atmosphere of Venus of outgassed water vapor and carbon dioxide, both very efficient greenhouse gases, would have resulted in a runaway greenhouse effect, in which the temperature of the atmosphere was always too high for water vapor to condense out of the atmosphere. Without liquid water on its surface, carbon dioxide could not leave the atmosphere via dissolution followed by carbonate formation. Thus, carbon dioxide was destined to build up in the atmosphere and become the overwhelming atmospheric component, with a surface pressure about 90 times greater than Earth's. Over the history of Venus, the outgassed water vapor remained in the atmosphere, where it eventually was photodissociated by solar radiation. The photodissociation products of water vapor are atomic hydrogen and atomic oxygen. Atomic hydrogen, the lightest element, could easily have escaped from Venus' gravitational field into space, and oxygen, in either its atomic or its molecular form, would have combined with minerals in the crust of Venus, forming a highly oxidized surface. Thus, over its history, Venus may have lost about 300 bars of water. Alternately, it is possible that Venus formed without the substantial concentration of water with which Earth formed, and hence, there would be no reason to invoke Venus losing such a massive amount of water.

## Knowledge Gained

More than twenty-five years of exploration and discovery of Venus by U.S. and Soviet flybys, orbiters, and landers have provided a new picture of the atmosphere of Earth's closest planetary neighbor. The surface of Venus was found to be very hot, about 460 degrees Celsius (the temperature of Earth's surface is about 15 degrees Celsius). The atmosphere of Venus is massive; its atmospheric surface pressure is about 90 atmospheres (the surface pressure of Earth's atmosphere is 1 atmosphere). The overwhelming constituent of Venus' atmosphere is carbon dioxide, which makes up about 96 percent of the atmosphere (carbon dioxide is a minor constituent of Earth's atmosphere, constituting only about 0.035 percent). The clouds in the atmosphere of Venus are thick and unbroken and are composed of sulfuric acid droplets. The clouds in Earth's atmosphere are thin, broken, and composed of water droplets. Venus is a dry planet, whereas Earth is a water-covered planet.

## Context

Understanding the divergent paths of the same outgassed volatiles (water vapor, carbon dioxide, and nitrogen) on Venus and Earth has provided new insights into the biogeochemical cycling of elements on global scales. The exploration of Venus by planetary probes has also provided a better understanding of several environmental problems facing Earth: The increasing atmospheric concentrations of carbon dioxide and other greenhouse gases on this planet may lead to a global warming, the depletion of ozone in Earth's stratosphere (the atmospheric region between the altitudes of about 15 and 50 kilometers), which is controlled by chlorine chemistry, and the formation of acidic precipitation, of which sulfuric acid is the major component.

Levels of carbon dioxide in Earth's atmosphere are increasing because of human activities, such as the burning of fossil fuel, particularly coal, and deforestation by burning. An increase in carbon dioxide will cause global warming. Venus is the ultimate example of the impact that a carbon dioxide greenhouse can have on the temperature of a planet.

The chemistry and photochemistry of chlorine and chlorine compounds in the atmosphere of Venus were first studied in the early 1970's. These investigations took place several years before it was discovered that these compounds can lead to the chemical destruction of stratospheric ozone. In Earth's atmosphere, stratospheric ozone absorbs solar ultraviolet radiation and shields the surface of the planet from the biologically lethal radiation. It is now generally believed that the more than 50 percent depletion in stratospheric ozone over the Antarctic during the 1980's, the Antarctic ozone "hole," has been caused by chlorine compounds.

Studies of the oxidation of sulfur compounds in the atmosphere of Venus have provided new information on the chemical production of sulfuric acid. Sulfuric acid is the major component of the clouds on Venus and the major component of acid precipitation in Earth's atmosphere. In all these examples, studies of the atmosphere of Venus have provided important new information with which to assess important environmental problems on Earth.

## Bibliography

Fimmel, Richard O., et al. *Pioneer Venus*. NASA SP-461. Washington, D.C.: Government Printing Office, 1983. A detailed and readable account of the exploration of Venus; particularly emphasizes the Pioneer Venus missions.

Hunten, D. M., et al., eds. *Venus*. Tucson: University of Arizona Press, 1983. The authors of most of the articles included in this collection are from either the United States or the Soviet Union, and their papers primarily consider the results of their countries' missions to Venus. College level.

Levine, Joel S., ed. *The Photochemistry of Atmospheres: Earth, the Other Planets, and Comets*. Orlando, Fla.: Academic Press, 1985. Nine chapters cover the atmospheres of Venus, Earth, Mars, the outer planets, and the comets. Includes detailed chemical discussions and an index.

Lewis, John S., and Ronald G. Prinn. *Planets and Their Atmospheres: Origin and Evolution*. Orlando, Fla.: Academic Press, 1983. A college textbook covering

Venus, Mercury, Earth, Mars, the outer planets and their satellites, and the asteroids. Provides an index.

National Aeronautics and Space Administration Advisory Council. Solar System Exploratory Committee. *Planetary Exploration Through Year 2000: A Core Program.* Washington, D.C.: Government Printing Office, 1983.

——————— . *Planetary Exploration Through Year 2000: An Augmented Program.* Washington, D.C.: Government Printing Office, 1986. These two volumes provide a detailed plan for the exploration of the solar system through the end of the century as well as summaries of the accomplishments of the American space program.

*Joel S. Levine*

## Cross-References

Mariner 1 and 2, 835; Mariner 5, 849; Mariner 10, 871; Pioneer Venus 1, 1145; Pioneer Venus 2, 1152; Planetary Evolution, 1159; Comparative Planetology, 1168; The History of the Solar System, 1367; The Venera Program, 2083; Venera 1-6, 2091; Venera 7 and 8, 2098; Venera 9 and 10, 2105; Venera 11 and 12, 2112; Venera 13 and 14, 2119; Venera 15 and 16, 2126.

# VENUS' LANDSCAPE AND GEOLOGY

*Type of phenomenon:* Planetary science

*Twenty successful missions have been flown to Venus, fifteen by the Soviet Union and five by the United States. In spite of the large number of successes, a complete map of the surface still does not exist, and as a result the geologic history of the planet is not understood. Nevertheless, these missions have obtained important surface data, including low-resolution maps of 65 percent of the planet (obtained by the Pioneer Venus Orbiter altimetry experiment) and maps of 25 percent of the northern hemisphere at a resolution of 1 to 3 kilometers (produced by the Soviet Venera 15 and 16 radar experiments).*

## Summary of the Phenomenon

The surface of Venus is perpetually hidden from the view of earthbound telescopes and conventional satellite imaging systems because of its all-encompassing clouds. For this reason, there had been wild speculations about the surface conditions and the possible existence of water or life on the planet until the development of an imaging system enabled scientists to penetrate the thick clouds and discover familiar landforms. Moving from speculation to fact has happened gradually, starting with the Soviets' unsuccessful Venera 1 mission in February of 1961 and culminating in the launch of the Soviets' successful Vega 2 on December 21, 1984. In those twenty-three years, both the United States and the Soviet Union flew successful missions which revealed enticing information about Venus' surface conditions, atmospheric dynamics, composition, temperature and pressure, internal structure, and magnetic field, as well as photographs from the surface, chemical analyses of the surface rocks, and data on the interactions of the solar wind with the Venusian atmosphere. Surprisingly, the accumulation of all these data has not produced the most basic tool of exploration, a map. If a sufficiently complete map is created, it may provide the basis for a unified interpretation of the history of that planet.

The Venusian landscape is decidedly different from Earth's. Venus is smoother, although the highest mountain, Maxwell Montes (63.8° north latitude, longitude 2.2° east), stands 2.3 kilometers higher above the mean planetary radius than does Mount Everest (whose elevation is 8.85 kilometers) above sea level. The lowest known elevation on Venus is in a trench called Diana Chasma (14° south latitude, longitude 156° east), and it is only about one-fifth as deep as Earth's Mariana Trench (11 kilometers). The total relief on Venus (about 13 kilometers) is approximately two-thirds of Earth's (nearly 20 kilometers). The surface of Venus is also smooth compared with those of the Moon and Mars.

Three provinces have been defined for Venus' surface based upon topography: upland rolling plains (65 percent of the surface), highlands (8 percent of the surface), and lowlands (27 percent of the surface). If there were water on the surface of the planet, the lowlands would be the site of vast oceans. Harold Masursky, Don Hunten, and other members of the Pioneer Venus project have speculated on various geological processes that could account for the global smoothness of Venus. An efficient erosional mechanism could have relocated material from the highlands to the lowlands with the early halt to large-scale tectonic movement (the movement of continent-sized land masses; this process tends to create mountains). Widespread deposition of lava could have filled depressions, as could have active eolian (wind) erosion. Finally, incoming meteors could have been blocked by the dense atmosphere, thus preventing widespread cratering and the production of ejected material. Since Pioneer Venus, ground observations acquired by the Arecibo radio telescope in Puerto Rico and by the Soviet Venera 15 and 16 missions have substantiated the existence of volcanic flow morphologies, sparsely populated impact features, porous and fine materials covering 27 percent of the surface, rock exposures covering most of the surface, aligned linear features that suggest at least regional crustal movement, and the existence of a number of ovoid features ranging in size from 150 to 600 kilometers.

Volcanic activity may be ongoing. The existence of sulfur dioxide in the upper atmosphere, in the form of sulfuric acid droplets, suggests that a replenishing source of sulfur would be necessary to maintain this concentration. Typical sources of sulfur are volcanic vents. Another source could be the decomposition of the mineral pyrite, a common iron sulfide mineral on Earth and a candidate for widespread exposure at the Venusian surface. Gordon H. Pettengill and Peter Ford have identified areas of high elevation on Venus that exhibit both low surface emissivity (low natural radiation emanating from the surface at a given radar wavelength) and unusually high reflectivity at the same wavelength. This implies a surface material with high electrical conductivity, which pyrite has.

Ronald Greeley at Arizona State University has conducted experiments in a "Venus simulator" in an attempt to explain this anomalously high reflectivity at high elevations by demonstrating that winds can concentrate pyrite on the surface as a lag deposit, that the mineral is stable at high elevations, and that it is unstable at the lower elevations, where high surface temperatures and pressures exist. At lower elevations, pyrite readily converts to hematite while losing sulfur to the atmosphere. Unfortunately, Raymond F. Jurgens and his colleagues Martin A. Slade and R. Stephen Saunders at the Jet Propulsion Laboratory (JPL) have reported anomalously high reflectivity material in low-elevation regions as well.

The Soviets' Vega 2 lander returned analyses of a surface sample indicating that the rocks at that site are similar in chemical composition to a common Earth rock. After extrapolating the appearance, the natural emissions, and the reflectivity as seen from orbit to other areas of Venus, the Soviets have suggested that most of the planet's surface materials are probably of the same general type as those at the Vega 2 site.

Present studies are limited to those that utilize large-scale surface and subsurface features to speculate on forces, either past or present, that caused the observed feature. The smaller the feature, the more likely it will be interpreted differently by different investigators. There is even disagreement over the interpretation of large-scale features; for example, is the northern circular feature, known as Cleopatra Patera, a volcanic caldera or an impact crater? Geologists from the U.S. Geological Survey in Flagstaff, Arizona, and the Soviet Vernadsky Institute in Moscow disagree on the object's origin. Higher resolution radar photographs should resolve the issue.

Another large feature with an uncertain origin is the highland region at the Venusian equator known as Aphrodite Terra. Is this enormous elevated landmass a series of volcanic constructs akin to the Hawaiian Islands or is it a series of mountains upthrust by the intersection of moving plates within the Venusian crust? (The latter process is known as "plate tectonics.") Possibly a combination of the two processes has been at work. Another possibility, and the one favored by James W. Head III and Larry S. Crumpler of Brown University in Providence, Rhode Island, is that Aphrodite Terra represents a spreading center similar to the mid-Atlantic fracture zone from which oceanic plates diverge. These planetary geologists have studied the topography of the region in detail, discovering the existence of fracture zones with offset domains possessing bilateral symmetry from a central rise. They have identified linear features, such as ridges and troughs, arrayed parallel to the rise crest, linear scarps, and other features that look sus-piciously similar to features found along the mid-Atlantic ridge. The similarity of features, they claim, suggests that Aphrodite Terra represents a region under tension and that regions at higher latitudes appear to exhibit evidence of compression. If these assumptions are true, then Venus evolved in a fashion similar to Earth, with plate tectonics being responsible for many features found at the surface today.

This thesis is by no means universally accepted. A. T. Basilevsky of the Ver-nadsky Institute, Moscow, has claimed, for example, that plate tectonics as they occur on Earth apparently do not exist on Venus. This conclusion comes as a result of analyses of the Venera 15 and 16 data by many Soviet planetary scientists. American scientists, including R. Stephen Saunders of JPL, also share this view. The Soviets, however, have identified several features which they have attributed to tectonism: linear zones of subparallel ridges and grooves covering large expanses on Maxwell Montes (although they have not speculated on the probable mechanism of formation); "parquet terrain," a rough surface created by the intersection of sub-parallel series of ridges and grooves, which is speculated to be the result of a thin crust moving in relation to a somewhat plastic subsurface discontinuity; and con-centric oval features, dubbed "coronae," thought to be created when domelike upwellings subside back onto themselves. More information of higher quality is needed before a serious attempt can be made at unraveling the geologic history of Venus.

## Knowledge Gained

Venus has no moon or any measured magnetic field; it rotates on its axis in the opposite direction from Earth and most of the other planets. Venus rotates once every 243 Earth days, while it takes only 225 Earth days to make one revolution around the Sun. The planet's solar day lasts 117 Earth days. The atmospheric pressure at the surface is 90 times greater than that at Earth's surface, equivalent to the pressure at a depth of 800 to 900 meters in the ocean. The dynamic atmosphere is stratified and consists predominantly of carbon dioxide, with virtually no water vapor. The upper reaches of the atmosphere contain droplets of sulfuric acid. Temperatures reach a scorching 470 degrees Celsius, hot enough to melt lead. Processes presently active at the surface which are responsible for modifying landforms may be different from those that operated in the geologic past. There is some evidence of tectonic movement. Volcanism existed sometime in the past and may still be active. The massive atmosphere is probably responsible for buffering incoming meteors so that only the larger objects could make their way to the surface to create impact features. The surface does not resemble any of the other terrestrial planets at comparable scales.

## Context

Venus and Earth have been referred to as sister planets because of their similarity in size, density, and proximity to the Sun. The "Morning Star" (which is also confusingly known as the "Evening Star") becomes even more intriguing when its differences are considered. A primary goal of any future mission is to improve the knowledge of Venus' geologic history. The surface structure and electrical properties, and the processes that control them, should be analyzed. The study of the volcanic and tectonic histories could help unravel what may be complex and interrelated geological processes that have led to today's surface characteristics. Another goal would be to increase the knowledge of the geophysics of Venus, principally the distribution and dynamics of concentrations of mass within the planet. This objective could be achieved by tracking subtle changes in a spacecraft's orbit as it circumnavigates the globe.

An altimetry experiment could result in elevation profiles of the surface. A radiometry experiment could measure the natural thermal radiation emitted from the surface; from these data brightness temperatures could be derived. Gravity data, combined with the results from the Pioneer Venus Orbiter, would refine the concept of Venus' gravity field.

The Venusian landscape, like the landscape of any planetary body, is the surface expression of its geologic past. Interior forces, like plate tectonics and volcanism, tend to shape and enhance the surface relief. Exterior forces, like meteoritic bombardment and wind and water erosion, tend to modify or diminish the relief. The dominant force or forces responsible for the present Venusian landscape and geology will not be known until a future mission successfully accomplishes these goals.

## Bibliography

Burgess, Eric. *Venus: An Errant Twin*. New York: Columbia University Press, 1985. A skillful science writer, Burgess has created a beautifully illustrated, informative overview of the most important Venusian discoveries, including those of the Soviet and American probes.

Fimmel, Richard O., et al. *Pioneer Venus*. NASA SP-461. Washington, D.C.: Government Printing Office, 1983. This volume provides an account of Pioneer Venus, the knowledge available about the planet prior to the 1978 mission, and the spectacular results of the orbiter and the multiprobe.

Greeley, Ronald. *Planetary Landscapes*. London: Allen and Unwin, 1985. Greeley introduces the reader to the landforms of the planets and satellites of the solar system. He explains the general physiology of Venus and discusses the geological processes which may have developed the various features.

Hunten, D. M., et al., eds. *Venus*. Tucson: University of Arizona Press, 1983. A collection of thirty articles, this volume details knowledge of Venus through 1983. The definitive work for the serious student; chapters 6, 9, and 10 deal with Venusian landscape and geology.

Sagan, Carl, et al. *Planets*. New York: Time-Life Books, 1969. An introductory discussion of the many broad areas of disagreement about the planets' origins, compositions, atmospheres, and surface features. Considers the possibility of extraterrestrial life.

*Neil L. Nickle*

## Cross-References

Ames Research Center, 21; The Jet Propulsion Laboratory, 662; Pioneer Venus 1, 1145; Pioneer Venus 2, 1152; Plate Tectonics and Geodetic Mapping, 1175; The Venera Program, 2083.

# VENUSIAN SOIL SAMPLES

*Date:* Beginning 1970
*Type of phenomenon:* Planetary science
*Countries:* The United States and the Soviet Union

*An understanding of the geology of the other planets in the solar system is important for understanding the geologic past and future of Earth. Venus holds many clues to this understanding, including its surface geology, which appears to be mostly igneous and basaltlike in nature.*

*Principal personages*
JOHN SIMPSON LEWIS,
MICHAEL MALIN, and
RONALD STEPHEN SAUNDERS, American scientists
CARL SAGAN, an American astronomer
YURI SURKOV, the Soviet scientist who built the X-ray
fluorescence device for the Vega lander

## Summary of the Phenomenon

The planet Venus is considered one of the terrestrial, or Earth-like, planets because of its position in the solar system, planetary diameter, geology, and other characteristics. Despite being called Earth's twin because of these similarities, Venus is actually very different, although the study of the planet has been at best difficult because of its heavy cloud cover.

The best information on the Venusian surface and its soils comes from the Soviets, who have focused on exploring the planet, successfully landing six spacecraft on the surface. Even though these craft have operated for only limited amounts of time because of the planet's extreme temperatures and the pressure of its atmosphere, the data provided from them have given astronomers and geologists important clues to the soils on Venus. Much of the information obtained by the Soviets can be compared with that known about Earth and to the data obtained from firsthand examination of the lunar rocks and soils. In addition, scientists can use similar information gained from the U.S. Viking probes to Mars for comparisons. For example, photographs can be useful in examining the appearances of the soil and rocks and the distribution of the rocks. Images taken by Venusian landers can be compared with photographs of similar materials found on Earth and the Moon.

The first of the Soviet landers to provide clues to the Venusian soils was Venera 8, which made the first soft landing on Venus, on July 22, 1972, in a region generally thought to be like the rolling plains of Earth. The probe analyzed the surface with a device called a gamma-ray spectrometer, which can be used to determine the chemical composition of material. In this case, that included the surface and the soils directly underneath the spacecraft.

Results showed that the soils under the Venera 8 were igneous (igneous rock is one of the three classes of rock; as its name, which refers to molten rock, suggests, igneous rock is often volcanic in origin). The layer was found to be approximately 4 percent potassium, approximately 200 parts per million uranium, and approximately 650 parts per million thorium. The layer was also determined to have a density of approximately 1.5 grams per cubic centimeter (in comparison, water has a density of 1 gram per cubic centimeter at a temperature of 4 degrees Celsius). From these data, astronomers and geologists were able to ascertain not only that the soils under Venera 8 were igneous but also that they were probably similar to the granites or basalts found on Earth.

In 1975, Veneras 9 and 10 provided an even better look at the Venusian soils. Each lander transmitted an image which showed the soil and rocks surrounding it. These photographs showed rocks that were on the average 20 centimeters wide, about 50 to 60 centimeters long, and slablike in appearance. A few of the rocks showed evidence of volcanic origin. Many of the rocks had jagged edges, which demonstrates little erosion, although some did show signs of weathering.

This relative lack of erosion surprised many astronomers and geologists, who had believed that, because of the planet's extremes in temperature, atmospheric pressure, wind velocity, and chemical composition, the photographs would show well-eroded landscapes. Astronomer Carl Sagan, among others, hypothesized that low wind velocities at the surface levels of Venus produce little effect on the rock. Apparently, the Venusian surface temperature stays fairly constant and thus does not create much wind.

Chemical analysis of the rocks again showed the elements potassium, uranium, and thorium. Nevertheless, the sites differed in the type of rock material. At one Venera lander site, the rocks were basaltlike in appearance, similar to those lining Earth's oceans. At the other site, the rocks were more like granite, similar to that found in Earth's mountains. The rocks appear to be relatively young in age. This would indicate that the planet is geologically active. The Venusian soil in the areas observed photographically appeared to be loose, coarse-grained dirt. One thing is evident from the photographs: Venus (or at least parts of it) is a dry and dusty planet.

The Soviets continued their studies of the Venusian surface with two additional spacecraft, Veneras 13 and 14. These two spacecraft performed similar examinations but in a much more complex manner. Rather than single images, near-panoramic views of the landing sites were produced. The photographs showed somewhat similar rocks to those found at the Venera 9 and 10 landing sites. Rocks also showed evidence, however, of what appears to be thin layering, ripple marks, and fracturing, especially around Venera 14. Some rocks showed evidence of erosion. On Earth, rocks that show layering are usually sedimentary (rocks that form by the layering of sediments; examples include sandstone and limestone). Based on the photographs and measurements made by the spacecraft, several Soviet scientists have suggested that these also might be sedimentary rocks.

The possible cause of the erosion remains unknown. In the absence of water, several possibilities have been suggested. These include chemical weathering or erosion caused by nearby volcanism and its resulting ash, dust, and lava. Chemical weathering seems the most likely explanation.

Both spacecraft collected a cubic centimeter of Venusian soil for analysis. The probes utilized an X-ray source to stimulate emissions from the collected soil samples. This chemical analysis revealed that the samples were similar to basalt in composition, although the basalts differed at the two sites. Near the Venera 13 landing site, the type of basalt found is referred to as leucitic high-potassium basalt, while near the Venera 14 landing site, a tholeiitic basalt, similar to that found on the ocean floors on Earth, was found.

The soil itself appeared fine-grained, and the photographs revealed many small rocks. It has been speculated that this also indicates that weathering processes of some type are at work, breaking down larger rocks into smaller ones, finally reducing them to soil.

Another Soviet probe, the Vega spacecraft, landed in June, 1985. Its results revealed a Venusian soil and surface that are again similar to basalt. Nevertheless, the new data also revealed a surface rich in the element sulfur, which is usually associated with volcanism. This presence has provided another clue to the surface and geology of Venus.

Venera 8 landed about 5,000 kilometers east of an area referred to as the Phoebe region. Veneras 9, 10, 13, and 14 all landed between 900 and 3,000 kilometers east of the raised areas known as Beta Regio and Phoebe Regio. Even though the craft landed on and took samples from an area that could be of the same or similar geologic makeup, they have given astronomers and geologists a good idea of the planet's surface composition.

The probes produced mostly photographic data, although some chemical analysis was conducted on site. Thus, any discussion of soil samples is based on the evidence reported by these spacecraft, since, as of 1988, no samples had been returned to Earth for detailed study. Nevertheless, these spacecraft data have enabled astronomers and geologists to begin to understand not only the surface of the planet Venus and its chemical makeup but also the planet's evolutionary path.

## Knowledge Gained

It appears that Venus is still an active planet geologically. Scientists have inferred from the discovery of high concentrations of sulfur that Venus is volcanically active. Thus, its soils, for the most part, must be considered with that fact in mind.

The analysis of Venusian rocks around the landers provided scientists with interesting but sometimes confusing data. For example, the fact that most of the rocks appear to lack signs of erosion at first seemed puzzling. An understanding of the weather patterns on Venus and the planet's atmospheric chemistry, however, has led to the development of theories relating the small-scale erosion to a low wind velocity at the surface because of its unchanging temperature.

The rocks themselves appeared to be mostly igneous in nature. Most of these igneous samples appeared to be similar to basalt, much like those rocks and materials that line Earth's ocean floors. Some of the rocks resembled granite, like those which form Earth's mountains. Yet despite these apparent volcanic origins for Venus' crust, some specimens appeared to be sedimentary. This led to further questions. Although the sedimentation process on Earth is usually accomplished by water, present-day Venus has no water, nor is there any evidence of water in its near past. Thus, the origins of this phenomenon remain unknown.

The analyzed samples varied slightly from site to site, as was expected by geologists, since samples on Earth also differ. In fact, the variation of Earth samples is greater than that of Venusian ones. Nevertheless, potassium—a key element in igneous and especially basaltic materials—was detected, as were uranium and thorium. Geologically, the rocks are young, presenting additional evidence that Venus is a planet that is experiencing continuous changes. Fine-grained soils were found at some sites, while coarser soils appeared at others. At one site, at least, smaller rocks led scientists to theorize that erosion does occur on the planet, thus producing soil.

## Context

When the planets of the solar system are categorized, one usually finds two major groupings—the terrestrial, or Earth-like, planets, and the Jovian, or Jupiter-like, planets. Venus, because of its relative size, atmosphere, position within the solar system, and surface, is among the terrestrial planets.

An understanding of other planets in the solar system increases scientists' understanding of Earth and its past, present, and future. An understanding of the nature of the terrestrial planets, their atmospheres, planetary geologies, and soils can give astronomers and geologists clues to the past of these worlds, revealing not only how these planets were formed and what geological changes they have undergone, but also how these worlds might be related. Venus holds many clues to the formation of the solar system. Unfortunately, observations of the planet's surface are impossible from Earth because of the dense atmosphere that surrounds the planet. Orbiting spacecraft could provide information regarding the general geologic contours on the surface—the planet's mountains, valleys, craters, and the like—but hard evidence of the nature of the surface, in particular soil and soil compositions, must come from the surface of the planet. Prior to the landing of Soviet probes on the Venusian surface, no information about the surface existed.

The materials sampled and photographed in the vicinities of the Soviet landers proved to be mostly igneous in nature. Additional on-site chemical analysis showed these materials—both rocks and soils—to be similar to granite or basalt. Basalt-type materials are not unique to the second planet from the Sun. These materials have been found on Mars in the vicinities of the American Viking landers and in samples brought back from the Moon by the American Apollo crews and by unmanned Soviet spacecraft.

As Soviet spacecraft have become more sophisticated and knowledge of the harsh Venusian environment has grown, landers have been able to provide additional data on the surface of Venus, among other things. Additional information may provide scientists with clues to the past of the terrestrial planets, part of which is hidden in the Venusian surface and soil. Perhaps more important, Venusian soil information may provide clues to Earth's future, particularly regarding our planet's fragile environment.

## Bibliography

Chaisson, Eric. *Universe: An Evolutionary Approach to Astronomy*. Englewood Cliffs, N.J.: Prentice-Hall, 1988. In this thorough text, the author discusses light and its properties, the atom, the equipment and systems of measurement used in astronomy, the solar system—with an emphasis on Earth and the Moon—stellar astronomy, galactic astronomy, cosmology, evolution, and extraterrestrial life.

Corliss, William R., ed. *The Moon and the Planets*. Glen Arm, Md.: Sourcebook Project, 1985. This book is a discussion of many solar system phenomena that cannot be easily explained by prevailing scientific theories. Each anomaly is defined, substantiating data are presented, and the challenge the anomaly presents to astronomers is explained. Examples and references are also listed.

Frazier, Kendrick. *Solar Systems*. Rev. ed. Alexandria, Va.: Time-Life Books, 1985. This text contains outstanding color photographs, diagrams, and coverage of the planets of the solar system.

Hartmann, William K. *Moons and Planets*. 2d ed. Belmont, Calif.: Wadsworth Publishing Co., 1983. This volume provides a general overview of the planets and their satellites, celestial mechanics as applicable to the solar system, the formation of the solar system, meteoritics, planetary interiors, surfaces, and atmospheres. Includes summaries at the end of each chapter. College level.

Morrison, David, and Tobias Owen. *The Planetary System*. Reading, Mass.: Addison-Wesley Publishing Co., 1987. The authors provide a detailed description of the members of the solar system, with details on each of the planets and other bodies. Some coverage of general astronomy and chemistry is included in introductory chapters. College level.

Snow, Theodore P. *The Dynamic Universe*. Rev. ed. St. Paul, Minn.: West Publishing Co., 1988. A general introductory text on astronomy. Covers historical astronomy, equipment used in astronomy, the solar system, stellar astronomy, galactic astronomy, cosmology, and life in the universe. Featured in the book are special inserts, guest editorials, and a list of additional readings at the end of each chapter. College level.

*Mike D. Reynolds*

## Cross-References

823; Mariner 10, 871; Martian Landscape and Geology, 922; Pioneer Venus 1, 1145; Pioneer Venus 2, 1152; Planetary Evolution, 1159; Comparative Planetology, 1168; The Venera Program, 2083; Venera 1-6, 2091; Venera 7 and 8, 2098; Venera 9 and 10, 2105; Venera 11 and 12, 2112; Venera 13 and 14, 2119; Venera 15 and 16, 2126; Venus' Atmosphere, 2132; Venus' Landscape and Geology, 2138; The Viking Program, 2149; Viking 1 and 2, 2155.

# THE VIKING PROGRAM

Date: August 20, 1975, to November 13, 1982
Type of program: Unmanned deep space probes
Country: The United States

The Viking program, using a pair of heat-sterilized landers, acquired the first data from the surface of Mars. Relay communications equipment on the landers and orbiters enhanced the ability to send high-rate data to Earth and improved the scientific value of these first landings.

Principal personages
JAMES S. MARTIN, JR., Project Manager
HOWARD WRIGHT,
ISRAEL TABACK, and
HARPER E. (JACK) VAN NESS, deputy project managers
GERALD A. SOFFEN, Project Scientist

## Summary of the Program

Plans to conduct unmanned missions to Mars were initiated shortly after the National Aeronautics and Space Administration (NASA) was established in the fall of 1958. At that time, the Jet Propulsion Laboratory (JPL) was a U.S. Army laboratory operated by personnel from the California Institute of Technology (Caltech). JPL was transferred by executive order from the Army to NASA on December 3, 1958. JPL and NASA had reached agreements that the laboratory would be principally involved in unmanned exploration of the Moon and the planets.

The JPL staff started to plan a series of missions; the early ones involved small spacecraft, with larger, more complicated craft intended for subsequent missions, when more powerful launch vehicles were scheduled to be available. The initial goals were to demonstrate to the country that NASA was an aggressive organization and that it was not necessary to use the military to conduct the civil space program. The lunar and planetary missions included Ranger missions to the Moon and a series of Mariner spacecraft for exploration of Venus and Mars. The Mariners were to be followed by Voyager spacecraft that would require the development of Saturn launch vehicles before they could be flown.

During the early 1960's, developmental problems in the improved launch vehicles and launch failures resulted in the postponement of the earliest missions and deferred the more complicated ones.

The Mariner 2 spacecraft in 1962 and the Mariner 5 spacecraft in 1967 were sent to Venus. The Mariner 4 probe was successfully sent to Mars in 1964. Ambitious plans were supported by NASA for large Mars landers and orbiters to be launched by a single Saturn 5 in 1973. Yet on August 30, 1967, the Voyager project was canceled—because of the lack of adequate support from the Congress, which at that time was concerned about the war in southeast Asia. At the time, a dual flyby mission to Mars for 1969 was under development at JPL. A subsequent deep space mission to Jupiter, Saturn, and Uranus, launched in 1977, was designated by NASA as Voyagers 1 and 2.

For several years prior to the cancellation of the Mars Voyager program, both the Langley Research Center and JPL had been planning unmanned missions to Mars. The research center was interested in the technical challenge of the landing vehicles' passing through the thin Martian atmosphere and in the opportunity to develop and manage an important flight project following Langley's successful role on the Lunar Orbiter project. The design studies that had been performed by the Voyager staff (NASA, JPL, and contractors) were of considerable value in preparing plans for a Mars landing mission at a cost considerably lower than estimates had been for the canceled Voyager project. In December, 1968, NASA supported a soft-lander mission with a ninety-day surface lifetime goal along with a Mariner 1971-class orbiter to be launched in 1973 to continue the exploration of Mars. The project's responsibility was assigned to Langley. NASA assigned the responsibility for the development of the soft-lander system to Langley Research Center, the development of the orbiter system and the tracking and data acquisition system to JPL, and the development of the Titan-Centaur launch vehicle systems to the Lewis Research Center. Further, the control of the flights, following launch from Cape Kennedy, Florida, was to be conducted from JPL facilities in California.

In the spring of 1969, the Viking project office at Langley issued a request for proposals for the development of the Viking lander. The Martin Marietta Corporation's Aerospace Division in Denver, Colorado, won the contract and immediately set about developing the state-of-the-art lander system.

Following the successful Apollo landings on the Moon in 1969, there was an anti-technology furor and a subsequent shortage of federal funds, causing the Bureau of the Budget to make substantial cuts in the NASA budget for fiscal year 1971. To operate with these fiscal restraints, NASA slipped the Viking project from a launch in 1973 to 1975, when the next launch window opened. At Langley, James Martin made the decision to slow the work on the Viking Orbiter substantially, since the risks associated with its development were considered lower than those of the new lander system. The JPL project staff was reduced by almost two hundred people in less than a month to be able to apply the available funds to the new technology. (It was fortunate that JPL was able to reassign these people to the Mariner 8, 9, and 10 projects.)

The Viking lander was considerably more complex than the Surveyor spacecraft that had successfully landed on the Moon. The Viking lander had to use the thin Martian atmosphere to slow it initially so that it could successfully open a large parachute which carried the vehicle to within 1,400 meters of the surface, where the terminal descent engines took over to soft-land the craft. Additionally, all the equipment contained on the lander had had to be sterilized to ensure that the life-detection instruments on the lander did not detect life-forms that it had carried from Earth to Mars. The lander had to survive a sterilization cycle of 40 hours in which the minimum temperature in the lander was 112 degrees Celsius. This included all the scientific and electronic equipment, parachutes, liquid propellants, and a radioactive power source.

During the 1975 launch window, the flight time to Mars was greater than it would have been in 1973, and the spacecraft would be farther from the Sun and Earth. Thus, larger solar panels were necessary, along with a larger high-gain antenna to communicate with Earth. Some additional redundancy of engineering subsystems was included to increase the chance of success during the longer flight.

The Viking project was the most complicated unmanned mission in space conducted by NASA. Activities at four NASA centers—Langley and Lewis research centers, JPL, and Kennedy Space Center—had to be coordinated. The Titan 3E Centaur launcher was used on the two Viking flights. Four separate spacecraft were flown (two orbiters and two landers). Communication links were established between Earth and each of the four spacecraft; in addition, radio links were provided between the orbiters and landers to recover high-rate data from the landers when they were on the surface of Mars.

To ensure that all elements of the project were efficiently coordinated, the project's manager, James Martin, established a management council that met every month at Langley. The managers of each of the systems developed for the project spent roughly two days a month describing the progress and problems of their systems along with plans for activities currently under way. Martin also instituted a "Top Ten Problem List" to highlight the most significant problems which might put the program's success at risk. These difficulties were reviewed in detail at each management council meeting, and Martin had to be satisfied that each problem had been resolved before it could be removed from the list. A total of forty were identified and eventually resolved during the developmental phase of the project.

In a few cases, Martin supported the parallel development of competing designs to ensure that suitable equipment would be available for the mission. The opportunity to fly to Mars occurs roughly every twenty-five months, and if some part of the flight systems were not available, the project would miss its launch opportunity during August-September, 1975. Ensuring that costs were not overrun was a challenge. Viking had been NASA's most expensive unmanned project to date; even so, it was necessary to reduce the number of available subsystems to cut costs.

As a further step to reduce costs, NASA conducted extensive joint tests with structural models of the lander and orbiter and several separate interface tests of the prototype equipment that provided either data or electrical power to the lander or orbiter. The first full physical and operational tests utilizing complete landers and orbiters did not occur until the flight systems had been delivered to the Kennedy Space Center for the final launch preparations. Fortunately, the project manager had included schedule reserves of roughly one month for planned activities at the Cape to ensure that the first Viking would be launched on time. This reserve became vital when a severe thunderstorm activated the electrical power of the initial orbiter on the launchpad and the flight orbiter and lander had to be switched with those intended for the second launch to replace the discharged batteries.

## Knowledge Gained

The Viking mission provided the first and second soft landings on the surface of Mars. Observations and measurements of the surface and atmospheric conditions were obtained for far longer than the three months for which the landers had been designed. The two orbiting spacecraft also operated significantly beyond their design goals; as a consequence, substantially more scientific and visual data were obtained from Mars than had been originally expected.

The flight operations activities were complicated. More than five hundred people were required to conduct these operations during the prelanding and initial post-landing operations. A large team of scientists was present at the JPL operations center, along with personnel from the Viking project office, lander technical specialists from Martin Marietta, and orbiter and tracking and data acquisition personnel from JPL.

The primary mission ended on November 15, 1976, during the solar conjunction (when Mars was on the opposite side of the Sun from Earth and no communications were possible with any of the spacecraft). When communications were again possible in mid-December, 1976, an extended mission was originated. On April 1, 1978, the extended mission was concluded and project management responsibility was transferred from Langley to JPL for a continuation mission which was designed to acquire scientific information as long as the spacecraft continued to operate.

Viking Orbiter 2 developed leaks in its attitude control gas equipment, and its operations were terminated on July 25, 1978. Viking Lander 2 was shut down on April 12, 1980. Orbiter 1 was silenced on August 7, 1980. Communications with Lander 1 became limited to a once-a-week transmission to Earth at a low data rate, and limited science data were produced. A total of 51,539 orbiter images and more than 4,500 lander images had been returned to Earth.

## Context

The Viking missions were the fifth and sixth to visit Mars and the first two soft landings on the surface that provided data. The Soviets had tried earlier, but with minimal success. In 1971 the Soviets launched two identical missions to Mars with orbiters and landers which weighed eight times more than the U.S. orbiter Mariner 9, which was also flown in 1971. The Soviet Mars 2 crashed on Mars on November 27, 1971. The Mars 3 lander landed on December 3, 1971, but communicated with its orbiter for only twenty seconds. The large dust storm on Mars at that time outlasted the Soviet orbiters' lifetimes and little useful data resulted. The Soviets also received some preliminary data from their Mars 6 probe in 1974.

Mariner 4, launched in 1964, had provided the first flyby views of Mars. In 1969, Mariners 6 and 7 conducted flyby missions which supplied roughly two hundred times more imaging data than had been acquired by Mariner 4. In 1971,

Mariner 9—the first American Mars orbiter—was successfully flown. When Mariner 9 arrived at Mars on November 13, 1971, a severe dust storm was in progress which obscured all surface features. After several days, the peaks of the four large volcanic craters on Mars appeared above the pall of dust. In February, 1972, the dust cleared at the lower altitudes, which were of particular interest for Viking landing sites, and useful photographs were obtained. In all, Mariner 9 provided 7,329 pictures covering 85 percent of the Martian surface. As a result, an initial mapping of Mars became possible.

The Mariner missions had showed that Mars has a small magnetic field. Its atmospheric density, altitudinal variations, and surface and atmospheric temperatures had also been determined by the Mariner probes. Before the Viking program, Mars was known to have volcanoes, and water was observed in its polar caps. It was known that the atmosphere consisted principally of carbon dioxide, but the Viking lander determined that a small amount of nitrogen was also present. The 4,000-kilometer-long Valles Marineris had been photographed by Mariner 9.

The scientific instruments on the lander were intended to determine whether life existed on Mars. As a result of the Viking mission, scientists concluded that life does not exist at the two locations where the spacecraft landed. The severe ultraviolet radiation on the planet's surface would have destroyed any organic compounds. It is probable that the severe radiation has highly oxidized chemicals on the surface of Mars. Nevertheless, several scientists still believe that the possibility for life on Mars exists, either farther below the surface of the planet or nearer the polar regions, where it is clear that more water is present than exists at the Viking landers' equatorial locations.

A considerable amount of water must have been present long ago to form the channels that have been observed on Mars. The question is, where did the water go? There is frozen water in the polar caps, but is there also water below the surface? The current atmospheric density is so low that liquid water cannot exist on the surface of Mars. Continued study of the planet's atmosphere and meteorology may be helpful in improving the understanding of processes occurring on Earth.

## Bibliography

Baker, Victor R. *The Channels of Mars*. Austin: University of Texas Press, 1982. Includes many illustrations obtained by the Viking orbiters and landers along with a few obtained by Mariners 4, 6, 7, and 9. This text includes a chapter about the existence of water, or water ice, on Mars.

Corliss, William R. *The Viking Mission to Mars*. NASA SP-334. Washington, D.C.: Government Printing Office, 1975. Suitable for high school and college levels. Contains a description of the spacecraft and launch vehicle used along with information on the scientific exploration accomplished during the mission.

Ezell, Edward Clinton, and Linda Neuman Ezell. *On Mars*. NASA SP-4212. Washington, D.C.: Government Printing Office, 1984. The official history of the Viking missions. Written by historians, this work is suitable for high school and college levels. Contains substantial background information on earlier missions to Mars along with numerous illustrations, photographs of the Viking staff and spacecraft, and pictures returned from the mission.

Kopal, Zdenek. *The Realm of the Terrestrial Planets*. New York: John Wiley and Sons, 1979. This book deals principally with what has been learned about the inner planets (Mercury, Venus, Earth, and Mars) and the Moon through space exploration. Excellent illustrations are included.

Pollack, James B. "Mars." *Scientific American* 233 (September, 1975): 16, 106-117. Contains an excellent overview of pre-Viking knowledge of the evolution of Mars and its atmospheric and surface characteristics.

Sagan, Carl. "The Solar System." *Scientific American* 233 (September, 1975): 16, 22-31. Suitable for both high school and college audiences. Describes each of the planets of the solar system and briefly discusses the then-current or planned missions for planetary exploration.

*Henry W. Norris*

## Cross-References

Cape Canaveral and the Kennedy Space Center, 229; The Jet Propulsion Laboratory, 662; Langley Research Center, 722; U.S. Launch Vehicles, 749; Lewis Research Center, 757; Mariner 1 and 2, 835; Mariner 3 and 4, 842; Mariner 5, 849; Mariner 6 and 7, 856; Mariner 8 and 9, 862; The Mars Program, 878; Mars 6 and 7, 903; The Martian Atmosphere, 916; Martian Landscape and Geology, 922; Titan Launch Vehicles, 2036; Viking 1 and 2, 2155; The Voyager Program, 2219.

# VIKING 1 and 2

*Date:* August 20, 1975, to November 13, 1982
*Type of mission:* Unmanned deep space probes
*Country:* The United States

*The Viking mission to Mars was the first long-duration, intensive exploration of the surface of another planet. Vikings 1 and 2 each consisted of a soft-lander which examined the physical and chemical properties of the Martian surface and atmosphere and an orbiter which extensively surveyed Mars from orbit and served as an Earth-Mars transport vehicle and communications relay for its lander.*

Principal personages
JAMES S. MARTIN, JR., Project Manager
A. THOMAS YOUNG, Mission Director
GERALD A. SOFFEN, Project Scientist
B. GENTRY LEE, Director of Science Analysis and Mission Planning
CONWAY W. SNYDER, Orbiter Scientist, primary mission, and Project Scientist, extended mission
HAROLD MASURSKY, Team Leader, landing site certification
THOMAS A. MUTCH, Team Leader, lander imaging
MICHAEL H. CARR, Team Leader, orbiter imaging
KLAUS BIEMANN, Team Leader, molecular analysis
HAROLD P. KLEIN, Team Leader, biology

## Summary of the Missions

Vikings 1 and 2 each consisted of an unmanned soft-lander and an orbiter which carried the lander to Mars and served as a communications relay station from Mars orbit. The Viking mission's primary objectives were to investigate the physical characteristics of Mars and to search for Martian life. To this end, the Viking spacecraft carried the experiments of thirteen teams of scientists who throughout the mission maintained remote control over their experiments from the mission control center at the Jet Propulsion Laboratory (JPL) in Pasadena, California.

Since Viking was to be the first attempt by the National Aeronautics and Space Administration (NASA) at soft-landing a craft on another planet, the spacecraft designs required tremendous technological advances over previous vehicles. In addition to the usual scientific tasks, the orbiters would carry the landers to Mars, hold them in orbit while certifying the preselected landing sites as safe, position and release the landers for descent to the surface, and serve as relay stations for communications between the landers and Earth. To meet these ends, the highly successful Mariner design—a flat, octagonal body with four protruding rectangular solar panels—was adopted, enlarged, and considerably modified for the task. Compared to their Mariner predecessors, the resulting Viking Orbiters were larger (9.75 meters across the extended solar panels) and heavier (2,328 kilograms launch weight), and they carried vastly superior computer command systems (two redundant 4,096-word computers, either of which could operate the craft independently from pre-programmed instructions or from commands sent from Earth).

The landers were essentially a new design. Hidden beneath a panoply of protruding scientific instruments, cameras, and antennae was a flat (0.457-meter-high), hexagonal body (1.494 meters across) with alternately long (1.1-meter) and short (0.56-meter) sides. A shock-absorbing landing leg extended from each of the three short sides, while inside the body were self-contained, miniaturized laboratories for analyzing the Martian soil and looking for signs of microbial life in it.

To avoid bringing to Mars any terrestrial organisms which might interfere with the Vikings' search for life there (or, worse yet, inadvertently contaminate Mars), each lander was sterilized prior to launch and then sealed inside a contamination-proof bioshield capsule, where it would remain until safely outside Earth's atmosphere. Since the orbiters were not sterilized, the initial launch trajectories were set so the Vikings would miss Mars altogether (rather than crash-land there) if the craft proved uncontrollable after launch. Once in flight and proved directable, they would be redirected toward Mars.

Both Vikings were to be launched on Titan 3E Centaur launch vehicles from Cape Canaveral's Launch Complex 41, the first scheduled for August 11, 1975, and the second ten days later. As the launch dates approached, a faulty thrust vector control valve (one of twenty-four valves which give fine guidance control over the thrust direction), followed by an accidental battery draining, caused the two craft to be switched. The first launch, designated Viking 1, occurred nine days late on August 20 at 2:22 P.M. Pacific standard time. The original craft was then repaired and prepared for launch as Viking 2. After the thrust vector control valve had been repaired, further repair work on its S-band (low-frequency) radio receiver was required. Viking 2 finally lifted off on September 9 at 11:39 A.M., only three minutes before an approaching storm would have canceled the launch. To compensate for these launch delays, minor course connections were made so that Viking 1 would reach Mars only one day behind its original schedule and Viking 2 would arrive on schedule.

On May 1, 1976, Viking 1's sensors first detected Mars—a calibration picture was taken from a distance of eleven million kilometers. Beginning six weeks later, a series of color photographs taken of Mars during approach showed that the dust storms which had hampered Mariner 9 were absent: The 4,500-kilometer-long Valles Marineris (Valley of the Mariners) and the 27-kilometer-high volcano Olympus Mons (Mount Olympus) were clearly visible, as were water-ice fogs and various surface and atmospheric brightenings.

Even as these images were being planned and taken, a leaking pressure regulator was found to be threatening to overpressurize the Viking Orbiter 1 rocket propellant tanks. The pressure was relieved by ordering two unscheduled engine burns (on June 10 and 15), which slowed Viking 1 by 4,000 kilometers per hour and delayed its arrival at Mars by some six hours. Finally, on June 19, a 38-minute engine burn—the longest burn to date in deep space—expelled 1,063 kilograms of propellant and placed Viking 1 into Mars orbit.

An orbit trim maneuver two days later settled Viking 1 into a highly elongated, synchronous orbit (an orbit in which the craft's orbital period is identical to the rotation period of the planet below—in this case 24 hours, 39 minutes, and 36 seconds). With each orbit Viking 1 dived to a periapsis (closest approach to the planet) of only 1,514 kilometers—directly above its intended landing site—and then ascended to an apoapsis (farthest point from the planet) of 32,800 kilometers. The initial periapsis passage (on June 19) was designated "P0," the next "P1," and the others followed in this sequence; the historic first Mars landing was scheduled for P15, which (not coincidentally) would occur on July 4, 1976—the American Bicentennial.

The primary landing target (designated "A1" for "mission A, site 1") was at 19.5° north latitude and longitude 34° west in Chryse, a now-dry delta region in the outflow pattern of an ancient flood channel. This site was selected because it was at a low elevation (where the higher atmospheric pressure made landing easier), close to the equator (as required by the lander's approach angle), relatively level and devoid of high winds (which made landing safer), and showed evidence of past water (which enhanced the chances of finding life).

The first detailed photographs of A1, taken on P3 and P4, showed spectacular image quality but frightening details. What Mariner 9's cameras had picked up as a smooth plain was revealed to be a confusion of craters, depressions, knobs, and islands—apparently too hazardous a terrain in which to attempt a landing. This assessment was complicated by the fact that, despite their impressive quality, the Viking orbiter photographs could not reveal objects less than 100 meters in size; the greatest hazard to the Viking landers would be from objects 0.1 to 1 meter in size.

In the interest of safety, the planned landing was postponed, and the Viking flight team began feverishly looking for an alternative landing site. Orbiter 1 was directed to photograph areas immediately to the south and northwest of A1 as well as the Viking 2 primary target site B1 (44° north latitude, longitude 10° west) in Cydonia and the alternative site C1 (6.5° south latitude, longitude 42.75° west) in Capri. Viking geologists, assisted by a tireless team of undergraduate interns, worked around the clock assessing the potential landing hazards suggested by these photographs. Leonard Tyler, a member of the Radio Science Team, analyzed data from the Arecibo and Goldstone radio observatories on Earth which, through the pattern of radar signals reflected from Mars, could be used to estimate the average surface roughness resulting from centimeter-sized objects scattered over large areas of the Martian surface. All this information was used by the Landing Site Certification Team, led by astrogeologist Harold Masursky, to form geologic models from which estimates of the landing hazards presented by the unobservable meter-sized objects could be made.

In the end, the leader of the Magnetic Properties Team Robert B. Hargraves suggested looking farther "downstream"—that is, northwest—from A1, where the ancient floods might have deposited fine-grained sediments and left a relatively smooth surface. On July 8, Viking 1's orbit was altered to bring its periapsis point over a newly designated A1-NW site, 300 kilometers northwest of A1. After further evaluation of the area, a site 240 kilometers due west of A1-NW was selected as the final landing target. This target lay at 22.4° north latitude and longitude 47.5° west, just within the western edge of Chryse Planitia (the Plains of Gold). The landing was set for July 20, 1976; coincidentally, this would be the seventh anniversary of the first manned lunar landing, a date now known as Space Exploration Day.

On the morning of July 20, Mars was 360 million kilometers from Earth. At that distance, one-way radio communication took 19 minutes—too long for flight controllers on Earth to intervene in the landing. Viking would have to land on its own. At 1:51:15 A.M. Pacific daylight time, Viking Orbiter 1 released Viking Lander 1; a 20-minute burn of the lander's own engines then nudged it out of orbit to begin a long, looping descent toward Mars. At 5:03 A.M., Lander 1 entered the top of the Martian atmosphere at a shallow 16-degree angle; it would need to travel nearly horizontally for a thousand kilometers in that thin atmosphere before its speed decreased sufficiently for landing. Radar monitored the descent while other instruments collected data on the composition and physical characteristics of the atmosphere and radioed them back to Earth. At 5:10 A.M., at an altitude of 5,906 meters, Lander 1 opened its parachute. Forty-five seconds later, at an altitude of 1,462 meters, the parachute was jettisoned, and three terminal descent engines, which exhausted sterile propellants in an outward fan-pattern to avoid contaminating or disturbing the landing site below, immediately burst into life. They slowed the lander to a scant 2 meters per second (5 miles per hour) at which speed it soft-landed at 22.46° north latitude, longitude 47.82° west—within 20 kilometers of the targeted site.

Immediately upon landing, the rate at which Viking Lander 1 was transmitting data back to Earth automatically increased from 4,000 bits per second to 16,000 bits per second. Nineteen minutes later, at 5:12:07 A.M., mission controllers at JPL received that increased bit rate as the first indication of Viking's safe landing. Their immediate shout of "Touchdown. We have touchdown," echoed to the cheers of eight hundred Viking team members at JPL.

On Mars, it was late afternoon (4:13:12 P.M. local lander time upon landing), and Lander 1 was busy. Some 25 seconds after touchdown, it began taking the first photograph—an image of the ground around its right front footpad. During that 4-minute exposure, the lander also erected and aimed a high-gain antenna at Earth and deployed a weather station. Within 15 minutes, a second photograph was completed; both were transmitted to Earth, where they were processed immediately.

By 5:54 A.M. excitement mounted at JPL as the first of these photographs—the first successful picture ever taken from the surface of another planet—appeared on the laboratory monitors. The image was incredibly sharp and clear. Small rocks, up to 10 centimeters in size, littered the area. On the right, the circular footpad was clearly visible; it had barely penetrated the ground, indicating that the surface was solid. On the left, dust still settling from the landing had left dark streaks on the photograph. Undeniably, Viking Lander 1 was on Mars.

The second photograph showed a 300-degree panorama of the Martian landscape. A series of ridges and depressions led to a horizon 3 or 4 kilometers in the distance. Boulders, perhaps meters in size, and smaller rocks were strewn about everywhere. In all, the scene was remarkably Earth-like—reminiscent of a Southwestern desert—except that nowhere was there any visible sign of vegetation or any other form of life.

The first color picture, taken on SOL 1, mistakenly showed a delightfully blue Earth-like sky. (A SOL is a Martian day as defined by one rotation of Mars—equal to 24 hours, 40 minutes of Earth time. The day of the landing was designated SOL 0 and the next SOL 1.) Subsequent corrections to the color balance revealed a salmon-pink Martian sky (made so by dust particles suspended in the atmosphere) overlooking a rusty, reddish-orange landscape. Meteorology team leader Seymour Hess made history by issuing the first weather report from another planet: "Light winds from the east in the late afternoon, changing to light winds from the southwest after midnight. . . . Temperature range from −122 degrees Fahrenheit, just after dawn, to −22 degrees Fahrenheit. . . . Pressure is steady at 7.70 millibars."

On SOL 3, the remaining 60 degrees of landscape was scanned, and a field of large sand dunes with a huge boulder, affectionately dubbed "Big Joe," was found. Viking scientists were struck by the realization that if Lander 1 had come down on Big Joe, it would have never survived the landing. (On SOL 12, a picture of the left front footpad revealed yet another surprise: The footpad was buried several centimeters deep in soft sediment.)

Also on SOL 3 an attempt was made to extend a 3-meter-long surface sampler arm intended to dig up and collect soil samples; the arm stalled upon retraction. Viking engineers, using duplicate Landers on Earth, concluded that a locking pin used to stow the sampler arm during flight had failed to release. They then "repaired" it by sending a sequence of extension and rotation commands which caused the pin to drop free. On SOL 8, the arm successfully dug trenches and delivered soil to biology, inorganic chemistry, and molecular analysis instruments inside the Lander body. Early responses from the biology instruments were suggestive of life having been found. In a climate of utter hopefulness coupled with scientific caution, it gradually became clear that the responses were most likely the result not of biota but of chemical reactions in the Martian soil. The next week and a half was spent attempting to make further repairs to the sampler arm, the molecular analyzer, and a radio transmitter, while obtaining more surface samples, photographing the surroundings in detail, and puzzling over results.

Viking 2 entered Mars orbit flawlessly on August 7, immediately adopting an orbit which would allow its periapsis point to "walk" around the planet, passing over the entire 40- to 50-degree north latitude band every eight days. With assistance from Orbiter 1, Orbiter 2 carefully surveyed Lander 2's prime landing site

(B1) in Cydonia, its backup landing site (B2) near Alba Patera, and a hastily chosen additional backup site (B3) in Utopia Planitia. After much analysis, and with some misgivings, the B3 site at 47.9° north latitude and longitude 225.8° west was picked by a Viking crew too exhausted to consider further searching.

On September 3, 1976, Viking Lander 2 headed for a suspenseful landing. When it separated from its orbiter, flight controllers temporarily lost contact with the orbiter. Unable to receive progress reports relayed from the lander, they could only sit and wait as Lander 2 landed automatically and, miraculously, sent home the high-transmission-rate direct signal which indicated a safe landing. Touchdown was recorded at 3:58:20 P.M.

The scene at Utopia was remarkably reminiscent of that at Chryse: A desolate, red, rock-and-boulder-strewn landscape was seen. There were, however, differences in detail: Utopia was generally flatter than Chryse, and it had perhaps twice as many rocks. Most of them were irregularly broken and laced with pits and holes. Apparently, the unphotographable back leg of Lander 2 had, in fact, come down on top of one of those rocks: The Lander was tilted about 8 degrees from the upright position. Lander 2 set about a science analysis sequence similar to that followed by Lander 1. It also set another precedent in planetary exploration: It used its sampler arm to push aside a rock and sample the soil beneath.

Throughout all this, scientific activities with Viking 1 continued unabated. The harried Viking flight team had four spacecraft—two orbiters and two landers—with which to conduct scientific studies simultaneously. Each of the thirteen teams of scientists had cooperated closely in designing their instrumentation to fit and operate in the close confines of the Viking craft. Now they cooperated in sharing the available resources of the craft (for example, data storage and transmission and electrical power capabilities), and in making sure that each of the various investigations complemented the efforts of the others. These goals were all amply met as science investigators followed a hectic routine.

Each day at noon, the scientists met to share the findings of the previous twenty-four hours, discuss their significance, and plan future activities. Every two days, on average, a new set of instructions for future operations was laid out and "uplinked" (sent by radio telemetry) to the craft on Mars. Thus, while the Vikings always had in their onboard computers complete instructions for operating automatically in case the uplink capability was lost, the instructions were continually updated to meet the ongoing needs of the project. This updating capability contributed immeasurably to the mission's success as experimental procedures were altered in response to unexpected findings. Also—and perhaps more important—problems with the craft themselves were continually analyzed and in some cases repaired by remote control.

In an unprecedented acknowledgment of public interest in Viking, Viking scientists reported daily their findings and progress to the more than one hundred members of an international press corps resident at JPL. So close was the cooperation with the press that on one occasion the Viking biology team actually performed an experimental sequence suggested by reporter Jonathan Eberhart of *Science News*. From the seeming chaos of these day-to-day operations, a new picture of Mars gradually began to emerge.

The routine continued until November 15, 1976, when the orbit of Mars was about to take it behind the Sun. Radio communications with the Vikings would then be impossible, so the primary mission was declared ended. In mid-December, Mars reemerged from behind the Sun, and an extended mission began, mostly with replacement personnel.

On February 12, 1977, Orbiter 1's orbit was altered to bring it within 90 kilometers of the Martian moon Phobos for high-resolution photography. On March 11, 1977, its periapsis was lowered to 300 kilometers, allowing photographic identification of features on Mars as small as 20 meters across. On September 25, 1977, Orbiter 2's orbit was altered to bring it within 22 kilometers of the other moon, Deimos; on October 23, 1977, its periapsis was also lowered to 300 kilometers. Both craft continued observing and mapping Mars from orbit until an entire Martian year had elapsed. Then, on July 25, 1978, with nearly sixteen thousand photographs to its credit, Orbiter 2 was powered down when a series of leaks exhausted its steering gas. Orbiter 1 continued observing Mars until July 14, 1980, when it took the last of its more than thirty-four thousand photographs. Almost out of steering propellant, the orbiter was then used in a series of tests to determine exactly how close to empty the tanks could get before control of the craft was lost. This provided information crucial to the design of future space missions. After these tests, Orbiter 1 was finally deactivated on August 7, 1980.

On Mars's surface, Lander 2 had observed ground frost in mid-August of 1977, late in the Martian winter. It continued monitoring its surroundings until April 12, 1980, when, apparently because of battery failure, it stopped transmitting information to Earth. Meanwhile, Lander 1 was programmed to take photographs automatically and to monitor the Martian weather through 1994. On January 7, 1981, it was designated by NASA as the Thomas A. Mutch Memorial Station, dedicated to the Viking Imaging Team leader after his untimely death in a tragic mountain-climbing accident. The Mutch Station continued returning photographs from Mars until November 13, 1982, when its radio transmitter unexpectedly fell silent. A heroic effort to revive the craft was mounted, but after five unsuccessful months the effort was abandoned and the Viking mission was at long last officially terminated. Lander 1's career, however, was not yet finished. On May 18, 1984, ownership of the Mutch Memorial Station was transferred to the National Air and Space Museum of the Smithsonian Institution to begin a new career as the most distant landed historical marker of human civilization.

## Knowledge Gained

Each Viking orbiter carried two vidicon cameras (similar to television cameras), with a 475-millimeter telephoto lens and filters allowing color photography. In total, 51,539 pictures were returned, covering the entire planet at a resolution of

200 meters and much of it at resolutions as small as 8 meters. Pictures of the Martian moons, Phobos and Deimos, were also taken; those of Deimos were the highest-resolution pictures ever taken of a planetary body from a flyby or orbiting spacecraft.

Mars was revealed as a planet with a tremendous variety of land features. Of greatest interest were those that gave clear evidence of past water flow: Broad, dry flood channels, apparently formed by episodes of catastrophic flooding two or three billion years ago, and smaller, dry networks of runoff channels generally more than three and a half billion years old were commonly seen. Such features were surprising because the Martian atmosphere is too thin and the climate too cold for liquid water to exist. Indeed, no signs of liquid water, nor any past or present ocean or lake basins, were seen. The water was apparently underground, frozen in a 1- to 3-kilometer-thick layer of permafrost. As evidence, some meteorite impact craters resembled giant mud splats, apparently created when heat from the impact had melted subsurface ice. Other areas showed large-scale polygonal features or fretted terrain (smooth, flat lowlands bounded by abrupt cliffs) perhaps caused by the activity of ground ice. The polar regions consisted of alternating layers of water ice (as verified below) and entrapped dust; apparently, these were the regions where the underlying ice breached the surface.

Volcanism was also apparent. Large shield volcanoes (in which the lava flows out through cracks), including Olympus Mons and others in the Tharsis region, were seen, as were composite volcanoes (which sometimes erupt explosively). Unique to Mars were the low, broad volcanic vents known as pateras. Pedestal craters (craters sitting atop raised plateaus) were revealed by Viking to be similar to Icelandic table mountains (shield volcanoes erupting beneath thick ice sheets). Some volcanoes showed evidence of having been active within the last few hundred million years.

Valles Marineris, a 4,500-kilometer-long system of steep-walled canyons up to 9 kilometers deep, was apparently formed by large-scale faults. Subsequent slumping (in-falling or landsliding) of the canyon walls was easily visible, as were horizontal sedimentary rock layers in the canyon walls.

Other features seen included numerous meteorite impact craters and basins, bright streaks indicative of wind-blown dust, dark streaks interpreted as erosion scars, atmospheric haze caused by airborne dust, and carbon-dioxide condensate clouds and fogs. Spectacular clouds routinely formed around Olympus Mons and other large volcanoes in the late morning. Two global dust storms and several dozen localized dust storms were observed during the extended mission.

High-resolution pictures of the Martian moon Phobos revealed sharp, fresh-looking impact craters and a peculiar system of parallel linear grooves, apparently formed during the impact which created Phobos' large crater Stickney. The other moon, Deimos, was seen to be saturated with impact craters and covered, apparently, with a layer of dust.

An infrared spectrometer on board each orbiter measured the concentration of water vapor suspended in the Martian atmosphere. The amounts found were highly variable, ranging from zero parts per million during the Martian winter to eighty-five parts per million near the poles during the Martian summer. Over the northern polar cap in mid-Martian summer, the atmosphere was saturated (held as much water vapor as possible without condensation occurring), strongly suggesting that the polar cap itself contained water ice. In total, the equivalent of 1.3 cubic kilometers of water ice was found in vapor form in the atmosphere.

A radiometer on each orbiter mapped the surface of Mars in infrared light (heat rays); from the amount of infrared radiation being given off, the temperature of the surface could be determined. The most significant finding was that the temperature of the permanent northern polar cap was −73 to −58 degrees Celsius—too warm to be frozen carbon dioxide (dry ice); it therefore had to be made of water ice. A layer of carbon-dioxide ice apparently settled over the water ice in the winter but evaporated in the summer. The southern polar cap was much colder, suggesting that it was a mix of water and carbon-dioxide ice with a year-round cover of carbon-dioxide frost. The global temperature extremes ranged from −140 degrees Celsius at the winter poles to 20 degrees Celsius at the noonday equator.

The radio communications and radar instruments on board Viking were used for a number of experiments auxiliary to their primary purposes. When Mars went behind the Sun, the Sun's gravity was observed to slow the transit time of radio signals passing near it. This was in accord with predictions made by Albert Einstein's general theory of relativity and it provided new confirmation of that theory. Also at that time, radio signals passing through the solar corona yielded information on the small-scale structure of the corona. Other radio data led to improved measurements of the planet's size, orientation, spin rate, orbital characteristics, and distance from Earth, finding the exact location of the landers on Mars (to 11-kilometer accuracy), and information on the electrical properties of the Martian surface.

During the descent to the surface, instruments on board the Viking landers examined the properties of the atmosphere. The upper atmosphere was found to be mostly carbon dioxide, with small amounts of nitrogen, argon, carbon monoxide, oxygen, and nitrogen monoxide. The concentration of nitrogen 14 (normal nitrogen) relative to that of nitrogen 15 (a nitrogen atom with one extra neutron) was found to be lower than it is expected to have been early in the planet's history. Since nitrogen 14 escapes from the Martian atmosphere more rapidly than does nitrogen 15, there must have been much more nitrogen 14 present in the past. This suggests that Mars had a much denser atmosphere sometime in the past—perhaps one dense enough to have allowed the flow of liquid water.

Each lander carried two facsimile cameras—cameras in which the field of view is divided into a grid of small squares which are scanned one at a time to produce the whole picture. The horizon around Lander 1 showed meter-sized boulders and a crater 500 kilometers in diameter at a distance of 2.5 kilometers fronting a ridge 10 kilometers distant. The near surface was duricrust (a coinage for the hard, cemented Martian soil) littered with small rocks. Throughout the field were numerous ventifacts (angular, multifaced blocks shaped by winds), a ubiquitous litter of blocks thought to be either debris from impact craters or deposition from past floods, sediment drifts (probably of silt and clay), and outcrops of bedrock. The drifts were stable; in fact, the only sign of movement observed was a small slumping of soil around Big Joe (significant, nevertheless, as the first observation of geologic change ever made on another planet). During the extended mission, darkening of the sky and softening of shadows were observed during two global dust storms.

The horizon around Lander 2 showed gently undulating plains with much less relief than at the Lander 1 site; the terrain was almost undoubtedly formed by ejecta (debris) from the impact crater Mie, 160 kilometers to the east. Like the terrain around Lander 1, there were a duricrust surface, ventifacts, and a litter of blocks and boulders. Most of the Lander 2 blocks, however, were vesicular (pitted and porous-looking), probably the result of gas bubbles trapped in cooling volcanic lava, but some were smoother, typical of finer-grained volcanic rock. Signs of wind erosion included the ventifacts, wind-scalloped blocks, and wind-sculpted pedestals under some boulders. A linear trough, 10 to 15 centimeters deep and more than 10 meters long, was seen as part of a polygonal network near the lander; it may have been formed by seasonal freezing and thawing of groundwater. The frost observed was probably water ice or clathrate (a mixture of carbon dioxide and water); the ambient temperatures were too high for the existence of frozen carbon dioxide alone.

Other activities of lander imaging included monitoring the sampler arm, the soil sample collection, and the magnetic properties experiment. Lander imagery also proved invaluable as an aid to diagnosing problems with other parts of the space-craft. Some astronomy—photographs of Phobos, the Sun, and the shadow of Phobos during a solar eclipse—was also done. A few pictures, particularly those of the American flags on the landers and of the spectacular sunsets and sunrises, were taken primarily for their aesthetic value. In total, more than 4,500 lander photo-graphs were taken.

Data compiled from photographs, the forces exerted by the ground on the landing legs and sampler arm, and other such clues were used to understand properties of the Martian surface material. The surface was generally firm (with the exception of the area under Lander 1's left footpad) and adhesive (meaning that it stuck to things such as parts of the lander), but only weakly cohesive (meaning that it did not stick well to itself; instead, it crumbled like a clod of dirt).

An array of magnets attached to the collector head of each sampler arm picked up any magnetic materials in the soil. Photographs of the magnets then revealed the material and allowed determination of its abundance and magnetic properties. Roughly 10 percent of the soil was found to be magnetic, most likely maghemite (a compound of iron and oxygen similar to rust). If so, then the planet's surface is red because it is, quite literally, rusty.

Each lander carried a seismometer designed to detect "Marsquakes." During the first five months at Utopia Planitia, no major disturbances were detected, although data believed to indicate a small quake (2.8 on the Richter scale) were recorded on SOL 80. Analysis of the underground reflections of that disturbance indicated that the crust in the region near Lander 2 was 15 kilometers thick. An analysis of the structure of the planet's deep interior, the primary goal of this investigation, was not possible because the seismometer on Lander 1 failed to unlock from its stowed position after landing. The Lander 2 seismometer routinely picked up spacecraft vibrations resulting from winds and the activities of other instruments on board the craft. It was unexpectedly pressed into use as a wind monitor to supplement the meteorology instruments.

A complete weather station, including air temperature, pressure, and wind condition sensors, occupied the end of a boom extending 1 meter from each lander. Subsequent reports collected during six years on Mars provided data important for understanding both global and local atmospheric circulation patterns. Lander 1 recorded temperatures ranging from −88 degrees Celsius to −12 degrees Celsius. Winds were mild—generally only a few meters per second—although they did exceed 50 meters per second during violent storms. The atmospheric pressure was observed to vary by some 30 percent as carbon dioxide from the atmosphere froze onto or sublimated from the polar caps with the seasons.

The chemical composition of Martian soil samples was analyzed by an X-ray fluorescence spectrometer, a device that identifies various chemicals through their absorption and reemission of X rays. The soil was basically an iron-rich clay. Its composition was 5 percent magnesium, 3 percent aluminum, 20.9 percent silicon, 3.1 percent sulfur, 0.7 percent chlorine, less than 0.25 percent potassium, 4 percent calcium, 0.51 percent titanium, and 12.7 percent iron, with traces of rubidium, strontium, ytterbium, and zirconium; the remainder consisted of elements which could not be identified by the spectrometer.

A gas chromatograph mass spectrometer (essentially a sophisticated, miniaturized version of a breath alcohol content analyzer) on board each lander identified organic molecules by breaking them down into their constituent elements. Their primary finding was that the Martian soil contained no organic compounds in quantities which could be detected—making the probability of finding life there extremely unlikely. This instrument was also used to analyze the chemical composition of the Martian atmosphere. It corroborated the atmospheric composition found by the entry science experiments (95 percent carbon dioxide, 2.7 percent nitrogen, 1.6 percent argon, 0.13 percent oxygen, and smaller amounts of other constituents), and it revealed an underabundance of argon 36 (argon with four fewer neutrons than normal) relative to argon 40 (normal argon) of 10 percent, compared to Earth's atmosphere. This observation provided vital clues to models suggesting that early in its history Mars had a substantially warmer and denser atmosphere which might have allowed liquid water to exist on its surface.

Three experiments designed to detect microorganisms in the Martian soil were on each lander. Controversy over their results continued throughout the mission.

In the gas exchange experiment, a soil sample was placed in an artificial atmosphere of helium, krypton, and carbon dioxide humidified with a liquid nutrient. The presumption was that if microorganisms were present, they would reveal themselves by metabolizing the nutrient and then emitting hydrogen, nitrogen, oxygen, methane, or carbon dioxide. Surprisingly, the first run on Lander 1 produced copious amounts of oxygen, suggesting the presence of life. Subsequent experiments—particularly the demonstration that heat sterilization did not prevent the release of oxygen—indicated that the reaction was not indicative of life but of a peculiar physical chemistry process in the Martian soil. Apparently, ultraviolet light from the Sun had bound oxygen to material in the soil, creating compounds known as peroxides (or perhaps variants known as superoxides or ozonides). Water vapor from the nutrient apparently released that bound oxygen, mimicking a biological response. Similar results were obtained by Lander 2.

In the labeled release experiment, a soil sample was moistened with a liquid nutrient seeded with radioactive carbon 14 (which served as an easily monitored "label" or tracer of the nutrient). The presumption was that if any microorganisms were present, they would take in the nutrient and expel carbon dioxide or other gases containing the carbon 14 labels. In fact, labeled carbon dioxide was released, again mimicking a biological reaction. When more nutrient was added to the sample, however, the carbon dioxide release did not increase (as it would if organisms were releasing it); instead, it decreased, consistent with the premise that the nutrient had been decomposing peroxides to create the carbon dioxide. Heat sterilization here prevented carbon-dioxide production completely, a result consistent with either biological or physical chemistry explanations.

In the pyrolytic release experiment, a soil sample was exposed to normal Martian air which had been labeled with radioactive carbon monoxide 14 and carbon dioxide 14. The sample was then incubated under simulated sunlight, with the presumption that if any plantlike microorganisms were present, they would take in the radioactive gases. After prolonged incubation, the sample was vaporized (by heating, hence the term "pyrolytic") and the vapors examined for radioactive carbon. In the first run on Lander 1, a substantial amount of radioactive carbon was found—again suggesting life. Subsequent runs, however, failed to confirm that result.

Experiment designer Norman H. Horowitz concluded that the chance of the results being caused by biological activity was negligible in that the first high carbon reading could not be reproduced, adding water vapor had no effect on the reactions, turning off the light had no substantial effect on the reactions, and laboratory simulations on Earth could reproduce the results through the interaction of the labeled gases with iron oxide compounds such as maghemite (which the magnetic properties experiment had suggested was prevalent on Mars).

In the final analysis, virtually all the Viking scientists agreed that although a biological basis for the results could not be completely ruled out, it was extremely unlikely. The lack of organic compounds in the soil argued strongly against a biological explanation, and scientists had shown that all the results could be explained by purely physical chemistry processes. Labeled release experiment designer Gilbert V. Levin continued to argue for the minute possibility that life might nevertheless have been found.

## Context

Before the space age, Mars was a fantasy place. From Edgar Rice Burroughs' tales of John Carter on Mars to Percival Lowell's scientific speculations about Mars as an "abode of life," the Western world equated "Martians" with "extraterrestrial life." The Mariner missions replaced those fantasies with orbital photographs of Moon-like craters and Earth-like volcanoes, valleys, and flood channels; the surface landscape itself, however, remained a matter of speculation. When Viking 1 touched down on Mars, all that changed: The entire world saw the barren, red, rock-strewn desert landscape of Chryse Planitia. Instantly, Mars became real.

Project Scientist Gerald Soffen has often said that in Viking's first month on Mars, more was learned about Mars than had been previously learned in the entire history of humanity. The complete absence of detectable organic compounds in the soil and the failure to find confirmable signs of life there was disappointing, even as the copious evidence for a history of flowing water was tantalizing. What allowed that water to flow in the past? Was there once a warm, dense atmosphere on Mars? Where has that water gone? Theorists analyzing the Viking data now suspect that there indeed was once such an atmosphere, and that the water is now locked in a kilometers-thick layer of ice-laden permafrost which undergirds the entire surface of the planet and emerges at the polar caps. This planetary picture—a once-hospitable, now dry, cold, and lifeless world—contrasts with the sulfuric acid-laden hothouse of Venus and leaves scientists astounded at the temperate, water-rich world called Earth.

It is easy to argue that Viking was the pinnacle of unmanned exploration of the solar system. Certainly, the task of simultaneously operating four craft in the vicinity of Mars while landing two of them successfully on the surface was an unprecedented challenge for mission controllers. At the time, the ability of the Vikings to operate either completely automatically or upon continually updated instructions from Earth made them the most versatile and sophisticated deep space craft ever flown. The spectacular operational lifetime of Viking Lander 1 of 6 years, 3 months, and 24 days on Mars set a long-lasting record for continual scientific operations on the surface of another planet.

Subsequent exploration of Mars did not resume until July, 1988, when the Soviet Union launched Project Phobos, two craft intended to examine Phobos at close range and land probes upon the Martian moon for which they are named. The American Mars Observer, a long-duration mission to continue mapping and monitoring Mars from orbit, was scheduled for launch by the space shuttle sometime after resumption of flights following the *Challenger* accident. Beyond that, there remained the desire for further Mars landings, including a Mars rover and a Mars sample return mission, and the firm belief that someday human beings would themselves walk on Mars.

## Bibliography

Baker, Victor R. *The Channels of Mars*. Austin: University of Texas Press, 1982. A detailed analysis and summary of Martian geomorphology as revealed by Viking, focusing on water-cut channels and other evidence of water on Mars. Extensive references and numerous illustrations. Advanced college level.

Burgess, Eric. *To the Red Planet*. New York: Columbia University Press, 1978. A good, chronological summary of the Viking missions, beginning with historical perceptions of Mars and continuing through the early Viking results. Some illustrations; written for general audiences.

Carr, Michael H. *The Surface of Mars*. New Haven, Conn.: Yale University Press, 1981. A comprehensive survey by the leader of the Orbiter Imaging Team of physical processes affecting the surface of Mars. Also includes illustrations, a chapter on the search for life on Mars, and a chapter on the Martian moons. Advanced college level.

Cooper, Henry S. F., Jr. *The Search for Life on Mars: Evolution of an Idea*. New York: Holt, Rinehart and Winston, 1980. A masterful account by *The New Yorker*'s premier science writer. Covers the history and chronology of the Viking biology experiments in exquisite detail, with much attention to the human side of the experimenters. Accurate and easily accessible for general audiences.

Eberhart, Jonathan. "Operation Red Planet." *Science News* 109 (June 5/12, 1976): 362. This article and its accompanying special reports began an extensive series of articles on Viking which continued in subsequent issues throughout the mission. Eberhart, the undisputed dean of space science reporters, is lucid, insightful, and accessible to all audiences.

Ezell, Edward Clinton, and Linda Neuman Ezell. *On Mars: Exploration of the Red Planet, 1958-1978*. NASA SP-4212. Washington, D.C.: Government Printing Office, 1984. NASA's official history of the Viking program. Includes extensive administrative, political, financial, and scientific background on the development of the U.S. Martian exploration program. Also contains an in-depth review of Viking landing-site selection and certification procedures and an overview of Viking science results. Detailed appendices and references; suitable for general audiences.

Horowitz, Norman H. *To Utopia and Back: The Search for Life in the Solar System*. New York: W. H. Freeman and Co., 1986. An authoritative, firsthand analysis of the search for life in the solar system, written by one of the principal Viking biologists. Covers biological background, development of Viking biology experiments, and the Viking mission itself. Clear and accurate; college level.

Moore, Patrick. *Guide to Mars*. New York: W. W. Norton and Co., 1977. Great Britain's celebrated astronomer and writer presents a tourist's guide to Mars, beginning with basic introductions to the solar system and telescopes, continuing with a history of Mars exploration, and culminating with Viking and a look toward future exploration. Highly accessible and informative for all audiences.

National Aeronautics and Space Administration, Viking Lander Imaging Team. *The Martian Landscape*. NASA SP-425. Washington, D.C.: Government Printing Office, 1978. Viking Lander Imaging Team leader Thomas Mutch's anecdotal account of the conception, design, building, and operation on Mars of the lander cameras, followed by more than two hundred of the best and most representative photographs taken by the Viking landers—some in color, some in stereo, all with explanatory text. Stereo viewer included. For all audiences.

*Science* 193/194 (August 27, October 1, and December 17, 1976). These three issues are dedicated to the Viking missions; the overview was written by Gerald Soffen and Conway Snyder, two members of the various Viking teams (see entry below).

Soffen, Gerald A., and Conway W. Snyder. "The First Viking Mission to Mars." *Science* 193 (August 27, 1976): 759. This overview begins the first of three special issues of *Science* dedicated to the Viking missions (see entry above). Advanced college level.

Spitzer, Cary R., ed. *Viking Orbiter Views of Mars*. NASA SP-441. Washington, D.C.: Government Printing Office, 1980. The Viking Orbiter Imaging Team's public report on their findings. Contains brief introductions to Viking and Mars, followed by spectacular photographs—some in stereo (viewer provided)—illustrating all the major landforms and atmospheric phenomena observed by the Viking orbiters. Includes detailed photographs of the Viking landing sites. The extensive captions are college level; the photographs are enthralling to all audiences.

Washburn, Mark. *Mars at Last!* New York: G. P. Putnam's Sons, 1977. An engaging, popularized (though sometimes scientifically misleading) account of Viking. The first half focuses on the cultural and mythological motivations for going to Mars; the second half covers the Mariner and Viking missions. Suitable for general audiences.

*Philip J. Sakimoto*

## Cross-References

The Jet Propulsion Laboratory, 662; Mariner 8 and 9, 862; The Mars Program, 878; The Martian Atmosphere, 916; Martian Landscape and Geology, 922; Martian Moons, 928; Planetary Evolution, 1159; Comparative Planetology, 1168; The History of the Solar System, 1367; The Viking Program, 2149.

# THE VOSKHOD PROGRAM

*Date:* October 12, 1964, to March 20, 1965
*Type of program:* Manned Earth-orbiting spaceflights
*Country:* The Soviet Union

*During Voskhod, the follow-up program to Vostok, the Soviet Union achieved two important firsts: multiple-passenger manned spacecraft and extravehicular activity. The Voskhod program marked the end, however, of the Soviet space spectaculars that were characteristic of the early days of the space age.*

*Principal personages*
VLADIMIR M. KOMAROV, Voskhod 1 commander
KONSTANTIN P. FEOKTISTOV, Voskhod 1 cosmonaut-scientist
BORIS B. YEGOROV, Voskhod 1 cosmonaut-physician
PAVEL I. BELYAYEV, Voskhod 2 commander
ALEXEI LEONOV, Voskhod 2 flight engineer and the first man to
    walk in space
SERGEI KOROLEV, Chief Designer of Soviet spacecraft
NIKITA KHRUSHCHEV, Soviet Communist Party Chairman
LEONID BREZHNEV, President of the Soviet Union

## Summary of the Program

Western observers anxiously awaited the next Soviet step in manned spaceflight following the conclusion of the Vostok series of space spectaculars; there were no Soviet manned spaceflights for well over a year after the landing of Vostok 5 in mid-June, 1963. Vostok cosmonauts had accumulated thirteen days more in-flight experience than the U.S. Mercury astronauts. A next-generation Soviet spacecraft was expected to widen the gap between the American and Soviet manned space efforts.

Voskhod 1 ended sixteen months of no Soviet manned spaceflights when it was launched atop an A-2 (SL-4) launch vehicle on October 12, 1964, at 10:30 A.M. Moscow time, from the Tyuratam cosmodrome. On board the world's first multiple-passenger spacecraft were Vladimir Komarov (age thirty-seven), Konstantin Feoktistov (age thirty-eight), and Boris Yegorov (age twenty-seven). The launch vehicle propelled these cosmonauts into an orbit with an apogee of 392 kilometers, a perigee of 272 kilometers, a 65-degree inclination, and a period of 91 minutes. Voskhod 1 completed sixteen orbits during the 24-hour, 17-minute, 3-second flight and landed in the Soviet Union approximately 310 kilometers northeast of Kustanai.

Vladimir Mikhailovich Komarov was the command pilot for Voskhod 1. He had served as backup pilot for Vostok 4, and he later died during flight as the lone pilot of Soyuz 1 on April 23, 1967. Born on March 16, 1927, in Moscow, Komarov had attended Moscow Air Force School, Third Sassov Air Force School, Serov Flying School, and the Zhukovski Air Force Engineering Academy and ultimately achieved the rank of colonel. Komarov had joined the cosmonaut corps in 1960.

Boris Borisovich Yegorov was the physician for Voskhod 1. His career as a cosmonaut was a brief one; he joined the cosmonaut corps in 1964 and returned to practicing medicine shortly after his flight aboard Voskhod 1. Yegorov was born in Moscow on November 26, 1937. A 1961 graduate of the First Medical Institute, he earned a doctor of medicine degree in 1965 from the Humboldt University of Berlin. Yegorov achieved the title of medical lieutenant in the Soviet Air Force.

Konstantin Petrovich Feoktistov served as flight engineer on Voskhod 1. Born February 26, 1926, in Voronezh, Feoktistov had been graduated from the Bauman Higher Technical School in Moscow with a master of science degree in engineering in 1949; he later received the degree of doctor of technical sciences. Feoktistov was deeply involved in the design of the Voskhod spacecraft in which he was ultimately to fly. Feoktistov joined the cosmonaut corps in 1964, flew on Voskhod 1, and then returned to high-level spacecraft engineering work in connection with the Salyut space stations.

During their flight these cosmonauts performed a number of minor astronomical and geophysical experiments and spacecraft maneuvers. They observed thunderstorms raging over Africa. "Glenn-like fireflies" (frozen ice crystals) were reported floating about the spacecraft at sunrise. Yegorov investigated the human vestibular apparatus response in weightlessness and assessed the hygienic conditions of the spacecraft. Psychological compatibility studies were carried out to determine how amiably several cosmonauts would live and work together within the confined cabin space. Considering the mission's brevity, the amount of psychological data of any value must have been meager. Reports indicate that Feoktistov and Yegorov did not respond well to weightlessness. Komarov, who had trained far longer, suffered no ill effects. Experiments to observe the behavior of confined gas-liquid fluid systems were conducted.

Essentially an upgraded Vostok, the Voskhod spacecraft weighed 4,800 kilograms and consisted of a pressurized cabin and instrument compartment. To provide space and weight for three cosmonauts and their required life-support consumables, the ejection seats and reserve parachute were removed from the Vostok design. Now too heavy to return to land safely under one parachute, Voskhod was designed with a reentry section that included a pair of retro-rocket systems, one to deorbit and one to fire just prior to touchdown to reduce descent speed essentially to zero. Sufficient consumables (water, air, and food) for only two days were included, one day's worth as an emergency supply. Voskhod 2 had only two seats, which allowed the addition of a small, collapsible air lock and two pressure suits. Both versions of the Voskhod spacecraft had been tested in a series of unmanned flights which had verified their ability to execute planned missions safely.

Voskhod 2 was launched at 10:00 A.M. Moscow time on March 18, 1965 (just days before the launch of Gemini 3) from the Tyuratam cosmodrome. The spacecraft, carrying cosmonauts Pavel Belyayev (age thirty-nine) and Alexei Leonov (age thirty), was inserted into an orbit having an apogee of 493 kilometers, a perigee of 173 kilometers, a 65-degree inclination, and a 90-minute period. Voskhod 2 completed seventeen orbits during the 26-hour, 2-minute, 17-second flight before returning to the Soviet Union, landing 960 kilometers off target in the snow-covered forests of Perm.

Pavel Ivanovich Belyayev, a colonel in the Soviet Naval Air Force, was the command pilot of Voskhod 2. Born on June 26, 1925, in Chelishchevo, Vologda, he had attended the Zhukovski Air Force Engineering Academy, ultimately joining the cosmonaut corps in 1960. Voskhod 2 was Belyayev's only spaceflight, for in 1970 he developed complications following an operation for a stomach ulcer and died, becoming the first of the astronauts/cosmonauts to die of natural causes.

Alexei Arkhipovich Leonov served as copilot and flight engineer of Voskhod 2. Born on May 20, 1934, in Listvayanka, Altay, he had been graduated from the Chuguyev Air Force School and the Zhukovski Air Force Engineering Academy and reached the rank of major general. Leonov had joined the cosmonaut corps in 1960. Ten years after his Voskhod flight, he would participate in the Apollo-Soyuz Test Project, flying as the command pilot of Soyuz 19. Following that assignment, Leonov became Deputy Director of the Gagarin Cosmonaut Training Center.

Soon after orbital insertion the cosmonauts prepared to attempt an extravehicular activity (EVA). Leonov attached a life-sustaining backpack to his suit, while Belyayev activated the collapsible, nearly meter-wide air lock. The air lock was depressurized to allow Leonov to open the outer hatch. Leonov exited the air lock head first, attached to Voskhod 2 by his 5-meter-long tether. Drifting away from the hatch, Leonov quickly reached the end of this tether. The cosmonaut maneuvered about by tugging on the tether; he had no other means for movement control. During the EVA Leonov experienced great difficulty positioning himself, expending significant amounts of energy in the process. After performing several somersaults, as television and an automatic camera recorded his historic steps, Leonov attempted to reenter the air lock to terminate the EVA.

Leonov's suit was pressurized to 6 pounds per square inch (sea level pressure is 14.7 pounds per square inch). Bending motions in his restrictive suit were difficult. In addition, Leonov's helmet visor had become partially fogged. These two conditions combined to hinder his attempt to insert his feet into the air lock, bend, and pull the rest of his body inside. Leonov's respiration and heart rates increased dramatically as he struggled to gain safe entry. To increase suit flexibility, he lowered his suit pressure to 4 pounds per square inch, although this move risked the onset of the bends (nitrogen narcosis). Now Leonov managed to slip back into the air lock feet first. After struggling with a release mechanism to retrieve the automatic motion-picture camera, Leonov closed the outer hatch, having been out of the cabin for more than twenty-three minutes, ten of which were spent floating free of the air lock. Later the air lock was jettisoned.

Because the spacecraft's autopilot suffered a sensor malfunction, the retro-rocket firing to deorbit was postponed for one full revolution. Manual control of the reentry had to be assumed by Belyayev, the first cosmonaut to do so. A combination of factors—orbit and some manual control errors—caused Voskhod 2 to plunge to

Earth far from the intended landing zone. Belyayev and Leonov landed gently in deep snow, not in the flat steppes of the Kazakhstan as planned, but in a thick birch forest in the Ural Mountains, nearly one thousand kilometers away from the rescue teams. To complicate matters, Voskhod 2's telemetry antenna was damaged, making aerial reconnaissance more difficult. Voskhod 2 landed about noon; a helicopter located the spacecraft two and one-half hours later. Because the thick forest terrain ruled out a helicopter rescue, the cosmonauts settled back for a long wait, keeping their spacesuits on and building a small fire to keep warm. As night fell, a band of hungry wolves approached the cosmonauts' campsite. Leonov and Belyayev quickly abandoned the relative comfort of their campsite for the safety of the spacecraft, only to find that the hatch was damaged, preventing complete closure. The cosmonauts spent several hours fending off the wolves before a ski patrol arrived, just before dawn. After a change of clothes and some food, the cosmonauts skied out to a waiting helicopter.

Voskhod 2 had indeed been an ordeal. Western observers were unaware of the true nature of its end-of-mission difficulties. The long delay with no Soviet report of a safe recovery of Leonov and Belyayev was mistakenly interpreted as signaling a disaster.

Over the next year, observers in the West speculated on the date and nature of the next Voskhod flight. It was suggested that such a flight would be of a long duration (between a week and ten days) and that it might incorporate a rendezvous. European amateur radio observers detected Voskhod-like signals briefly on July 3, 1965, leading to speculation that a manned launch had failed. There is no supporting evidence, however, for such an event. Because of what has come to light about the basic nature of Voskhod, it is clear that a long and complex flight would have been beyond Voskhod's capabilities.

## Knowledge Gained

Voskhod showed that it was possible to send humans into space without bulky spacesuits, given sufficient confidence in spacecraft cabin pressure integrity. Voskhod 1 astronauts were reported to have emergency pressure suits available, but this seems unlikely, because the principal reason the cosmonauts did not wear suits was for spacecraft weight reduction. On Voskhod 2, with only two cosmonauts, pressure suits were carried to support the EVA by Leonov.

Voskhod cosmonauts used conventional sextants to investigate problems in celestial navigation. Feoktistov was easily able to identify dozens of constellations and individual stars. He believed that optical star sightings would be possible as a future navigational aid on later long-duration flights. Visual acuity and color perception did not appear to diminish during day-long spaceflights.

Yegorov conducted preliminary space motion-sickness experiments, directing Voskhod 1 cosmonauts to shake their heads while in orbit. Dizziness and a sensation of general discomfort were observed, different from cosmonaut reactions to similar tests performed both pre- and postflight. Blood samples were periodically drawn to be tested later for sugar content, cholesterol, protein, chlorides, and blood-cell count. Galvanic currents stimulated cosmonaut inner-ear systems; orbital results were compared to ground-based data. Measures of radiation levels at Voskhod orbital altitudes showed no threat to cosmonaut health. Cosmonauts were able to sleep for three to five hours and reported sound, dreamless sleep.

Stability of contained gas-liquid fluid systems experiments indicated that gas bubbles in liquids are unstable. Slight shocks will break such bubbles down into smaller bubbles, which do not reform back into larger gas bubbles. Liquid bubbles in gases, however, are stable against external disturbances. Liquids tend to spread along the walls of a gas-filled vessel.

Voskhod demonstrated the utility of television systems on manned spacecraft. Voskhod cameras used 625 lines and 25 frames per second, a significant improvement over Vostok television systems (400 lines and 10 frames per second). The spacecraft was reported to have an exterior television system, mounted near the heatshield, in addition to an interior television system for showing cosmonaut activity. Television provided views of Leonov during his EVA.

Cosmonauts attempted to control cabin temperatures by rolling Voskhod spacecraft at about one revolution per minute. (Such a roll was clearly discernible during Leonov's televised EVA.) Temperatures remained comfortable at 21 to 24 degrees Celsius. (Such a "barbecue-roll" would later be used as a passive cooling mode during Apollo lunar flights.)

Leonov performed a series of maneuvers during his EVA to assess motor reactions in a weightless environment and cosmonaut-to-spacecraft dynamics during EVA operations. Leonov reported that Voskhod 2 was very sensitive to his touch and that he could easily perturb its attitude. Leonov had considerable difficulty positioning himself and remaining stable against rotation. He reported that his tether, or umbilical line, worked against him when he was trying to maneuver.

The apparent ease of his EVA was deceptive; Leonov actually experienced a strenuous work load. His vision was hindered when his helmet visor fogged up because his suit cooling system could not adequately handle his overexertion. Had designers at the National Aeronautics and Space Administration (NASA) known of Leonov's degree of exertion during EVA work, difficulties encountered by astronaut Eugene A. Cernan during his Gemini 9 EVA might have been averted.

## Context

Both the Soviet Union and the United States concluded their initial man-in-space programs, Vostok and Mercury respectively, in 1963. Both programs had demonstrated man's ability to survive the rigors of ascent, orbital flight, and reentry. Soviet cosmonauts had accumulated far more time in orbit, however, than had the Mercury astronauts. The Soviet Union held a commanding lead in manned spaceflight, and both NASA and Lyndon B. Johnson's administration anxiously awaited the next Soviet program while preparations for the American follow-up program, the two-man Gemini series, left astronauts earthbound for nearly two years. The primary goals of the Gemini program, openly stated to be rendezvous and docking, long-duration flights, walking in space outside the spacecraft, and controlled reentry, were key to acquiring the skills and confidence necessary for attempting to fulfill President John F. Kennedy's goal of a manned lunar landing. With limited intelligence information, NASA could only guess at the nature of the next Soviet step in space.

Nikita Khrushchev ordered Chief Designer Sergei Korolev to devise a means to counteract the American Gemini program immediately rather than await the Soyuz program, which was not likely to begin flight operations before 1966. Korolev's response was Voskhod, something Khrushchev could use to obtain further space spectaculars, multiple-passenger flight and spacewalking, prior to Gemini attempts at similar feats. Safety was at a minimum in this spacecraft. It was a technological dead end, with achievement of space firsts as the only justification for its development.

Internal Communist Party politics played a central role in the Voskhod program. Voskhod was set into motion under the direction of Khrushchev. The Khrushchevian approach to spaceflight was to use spectacular space achievements to "prove" Soviet technological and ideological superiority. With this approach, the Soviets amassed a lengthy list of firsts at great expense and risk, giving Khrushchev a maximum political return.

Khrushchev greeted the Voskhod 1 cosmonauts in orbit. When the cosmonauts returned to Moscow, a different set of leaders greeted them; Khrushchev had been ousted by the new Brezhnev-Kosygin regime. Khrushchev became an "unperson"; his haphazard leadership of the Soviet space program was over. Voskhod 2, however, already in development, proceeded as planned. It would be the final Khrushchev-style space spectacular. Under Leonid Brezhnev, the Soviet space program was allowed to proceed more logically under the direction of Sergei Korolev. Voskhod was abandoned following Leonov's historic spacewalk in favor of work on the more advanced Soyuz spacecraft and the large Proton rocket. Unfortunately, Korolev died early in 1966, but before his death he was able to redirect the course of Soviet spaceflight.

Voskhod's effects on NASA were profound. As a result of Voskhod, NASA requested applications from the scientific community for scientist-astronauts, and EVA was attached to an early Gemini flight plan. Gemini astronauts quickly surpassed the achievement of the Voskhod cosmonauts. Not a single cosmonaut would fly in space during the course of the Gemini program. Instead of constituting a step toward future space achievements, Voskhod (which translates as "sunrise," although in the archaic sense its meaning is, ironically, identical with that of *Vostok*, "east") closed the first chapter in Soviet spaceflight.

## Bibliography

*Aviation Week* 81/82 (October 19, 1964; October 26, 1964; November 23, 1964; March 22, 1965; March 29, 1965; April 5, 1965; April 12, 1965; May 24, 1965;

June 21, 1965; June 28, 1965). These technical reports were written as Voskhod program events occurred and provide readers with historical background of Western reactions to Voskhod. Detailed information is accompanied by photographs.

Dmitriyev, A. Yu., et al. *From Spaceships to Orbiting Stations.* 2d ed. NASA technical translation, NASA TT F-812. Washington, D.C.: Government Printing Office, 1973. Although most of this report deals with Soyuz and Salyut operations, there is a presentation of the Soviet perspective on the Vostok and Voskhod programs in the overall development of Soviet cosmonautics. Curiously, this report asserts that Leonov's return to Voskhod 2's cabin at the conclusion of his spacewalk occurred without surprises.

Furniss, Tim. *Manned Spaceflight Log.* Rev. ed. London: Jane's Publishing Co., 1986. Gives a concise summary of both American and Russian manned spaceflights. In addition to describing Earth-orbital and lunar flights, it reports on X-15 "astro-flights." Interesting photographs accompany flight accounts. Suitable for all readers; a must for serious spaceflight observers.

Oberg, James E. *Red Star in Orbit.* New York: Random House, 1981. Provides an excellent overview of Soviet spaceflights, stressing internal politics as well as technical achievements. Of particular interest is the treatment of Nikita Khrushchev's impact on the early days of Soviet space programs. Suitable for all readers. Photographs shed light on the secrecy and disinformation policy employed by the Soviets during early space programs.

Riabchikov, Evgeny. *Russians in Space.* Edited by Nikolai P. Kamanin. Translated by Guy Daniels. Garden City, N.Y.: Doubleday and Co., 1971. The period from Sputnik 1 to Soyuz 11/Salyut 1 is covered from the official Soviet viewpoint. The book proves to be interesting reading, but it must be recognized as the propaganda that it is. Predictably, there is a remarkable difference in interpretation of events between Riabchikov and Oberg.

U.S. Congress. House. Committee on Science and Technology. *Astronauts and Cosmonauts Biographical and Statistical Data.* Report prepared by Congressional Research Service, the Library of Congress. 99th Cong., 1st sess., rev. ed. 1985. Committee Print. Includes brief biographical sketches of both American astronauts and Soviet cosmonauts. New editions of this work are published as the astronaut/cosmonaut ranks change.

*David G. Fisher*

**Cross-References**

The Apollo-Soyuz Test Project, 132; Biological Effects of Space Travel on Humans, 188; Cosmonauts and the Soviet Cosmonaut Program, 273; The Gemini Program, 487; Gemini 3, 494; Gemini 4, 501; The Development of Spacesuits, 1917; The Vostok Program, 2177.

# THE VOSTOK PROGRAM

*Date:* Early 1959 to June 19, 1963
*Type of program:* Manned Earth-orbiting spaceflights
*Country:* The Soviet Union

*The Vostok program launched the first human passenger into orbit, accomplished the first manned full day in orbit and the first group flight of two manned spacecraft, and put the first woman in orbit.*

### Principal personages
ANATOLI A. BLAGONRAVOV, Chairman of the Commission for the
Exploration and Use of Outer Space, Soviet Academy of
Sciences
NIKOLAI KAMANIN, Commander of the Cosmonaut Corps,
1960-1971.
NIKITA KHRUSHCHEV, the third Premier of the Soviet Union
SERGEI KOROLEV, Chief Designer and head of the Soviet space
program, 1957-1966
MITROFAN NEDELIN, Chief of all Soviet rocket forces, 1957-1960
LEONID SEDOV, Chairman of the Interdepartmental Commission
of Interplanetary Communications, Soviet Academy of
Sciences
YURI GAGARIN, Vostok 1 cosmonaut, the first man to orbit Earth
GHERMAN TITOV, Vostok 2 cosmonaut
ANDRIAN NIKOLAYEV, Vostok 3 cosmonaut
PAVEL R. POPOVICH, Vostok 4 cosmonaut
VALERI BYKOVSKY, Vostok 5 cosmonaut
VALENTINA TERESHKOVA, Vostok 6 cosmonaut, the first woman
in space

## Summary of the Program
The Vostok program was the Soviet Union's first manned spaceflight program. The Vostok spacecraft has the historical distinction of having been the first to carry a human passenger into space and return him safely. The flight of the first Soviet cosmonaut, Yuri Gagarin, caused as much worldwide sensation as did the orbiting of the first Russian satellite, Sputnik 1, less than four years earlier.

When the Vostok program ended in June, 1963, there had been a total of six manned flights, whose achievements include the first full day in orbit, a pair of group flights by two spacecraft simultaneously, and the flight of the first woman in space, Valentina Tereshkova.

The spacecraft's name, the Russian word *vostok*, has been translated into English as "east," along with the political connotations of that name. *Vostok* also means "an upward flow," however, and thus the name suggests the upward flow of humanity into the universe.

The exact date of the beginning of the Vostok program is unknown in the West, but it can be assumed that planning and hardware fabrication began in early 1959. The Vostok was designed by the anonymous "Chief Designer" of the Soviet space program. It was not until after his death in 1966 that it was revealed that the Chief Designer had been Sergei Korolev.

The Vostok spacecraft weighed more than 4,700 kilograms and consisted of two main sections. The spherical reentry cabin section, 2.3 meters in diameter, housed the cosmonaut and his life-support equipment. The other section consisted of an instrument section/retro-rocket module which was attached to the spherical cabin.

Three factors led to the selection of a spherical shape for the reentry cabin section of Vostok: its simplicity of design, its aerodynamic properties, and its efficiency (the sphere has maximum volume in relation to external area).

The cabin section of Vostok weighed 2,400 kilograms and was covered with a metal foil to insulate it from solar heat while in orbit and an ablative material to help it survive the heat of reentry. The Vostok air-conditioning system provided for humidity regulation, concentration of oxygen, and temperature control within a range of 12 to 25 degrees Celsius. Humidity and carbon dioxide were controlled by one unit which was a dehumidifier using silica gel impregnated with lithium hydroxide and activated charcoal to control the level of harmful gases in the cabin. The Vostok used an automatic orbital orientation system with a manual backup and used both gyroscopic and optical sensors to stabilize the spacecraft.

The reentry cabin had three large round hatches: an entrance hatch, a parachute hatch, and an auxiliary access hatch. Three heat-resistant glass portholes allowed the cosmonaut to see outside the spacecraft. The center porthole housed an optical orientation device which the cosmonaut could use to orient the spacecraft for retrofire in case the orbital guidance system failed.

For stability during reentry, the spherical cabin had an offset center of gravity so that upon atmospheric deceleration, it would automatically roll around, making the pilot's back and the heaviest portion of the heatshield face the direction of travel.

The instrument/retro-rocket module, which resembled two cones placed base to base, was attached to the rear of the Vostok's spherical cabin. The instrument package housed the retro-rocket, telemetry equipment, part of the scientific payload for studying cosmic and solar radiation, and orbital guidance and heat-regulation equipment.

The Vostok retro-rocket utilized amine/nitrous oxide propellants and fired with a thrust of 1,614 kilograms. In anticipation of the possibility of retro-rocket failure, Vostok was deliberately placed in a low orbit, guaranteeing that the orbit would decay naturally before the spacecraft's ten-day supply of consumables was depleted.

The limited allowance in the Vostok design and flightplan for the cosmonaut to control the spacecraft and its systems reduced the Vostok to little more than an automated satellite which happened to carry a human passenger. Because the

Vostok spacecraft had numerous redundant and automatic systems and was capable of completing its mission totally by preprogrammed sequencer, the basic Vostok vehicle became the standard design for many Kosmos military reconnaissance flights as well as Kosmos biological specimen flights.

A total of 800 kilograms of equipment could be carried inside the Vostok reentry cabin. This included the cosmonaut's ejection seat, materials for in-cabin experiments, and consumables for sustaining the cosmonaut.

The Vostok spacecraft was launched by an A-1 booster, which consisted of a modified SS-6 Sapwood intercontinental ballistic missile forming the first and second stages. The third stage was the same as that used for the early Luna flights to the Moon. All Vostok launches were from the Tyuratam Space Center.

Vostok was designed primarily for recovery on land; the spacecraft was so heavy, however, that a parachute landing was hazardous for a cosmonaut remaining within the reentry cabin. This dictated the need for ejection and separate landing from the descending reentry cabin. The ejection seat body also housed the spacesuit ventilation system, parachute systems, and ground survival kit.

The cosmonaut's ejection sequence began at 7,000 meters, when the entrance hatch was automatically jettisoned. Two seconds later, the seat fired and its parachute system was triggered. At 4,000 meters, the seat fell free and the cosmonaut descended with his personal parachute. A survival kit and an automatically inflated rubber dinghy were suspended below the parachuting cosmonaut on a 15-meter cable. The cosmonaut's touchdown speed was 6 meters per second.

On the first two Vostok flights, meals consisted of mashed foods squeezed from tubes. On the final four flights, meals consisted of prepackaged food similar to a normal meal. In addition to the cosmonaut, later Vostok flights also carried biological specimens, including fruit flies, human cancer cells, and seeds.

The Vostok precursor flights began with suborbital testing of the reentry capsule on January 20 and January 31, 1960. Four months later, on May 15, 1960, the launching of Sputnik 4, or Korabl Sputnik 1 (Spaceship Satellite 1), performed the first orbital testing of the Vostok. The unmanned four-day test flight showed that the basic design of the spacecraft was sound, but an error in orientation during retrofire accidentally pushed the reentry cabin into a higher orbit instead of lowering it into a descent trajectory.

Sputnik 5 (Korabl Sputnik 2) was launched on August 19, 1960, for a one-day test flight. This time, the Vostok reentry cabin contained two dogs, Strelka and Belka, housed in containers attached to the ejection seat. Two television cameras observed the dogs' reactions to the space environment.

A third orbital test of the Vostok spacecraft was carried out on December 1, 1960, when two more dogs were flown as passengers aboard the Vostok prototype, Sputnik 6 (Korabl Sputnik 3). The recovery of the dogs, Pchelka and Mushka, the following day was unsuccessful when the reentry cabin entered the atmosphere at too steep an angle and was burned beyond recovery.

Sputnik 9 (Korabl Sputnik 4) was launched on March 9, 1961. The single live passenger, a dog named Chernushka, and a dummy cosmonaut were successfully recovered after one Earth orbit.

Sixteen days later, the final Vostok test flight carried the dog Zvezdochka for one orbit aboard Sputnik 10 (Korabl Sputnik 5). The successful recovery of the dog and a dummy cosmonaut cleared the way for the first manned Vostok launch to follow eighteen days later.

The first human passenger to fly in space was launched on April 12, 1961, aboard Vostok 1. Major Yuri Alekseyevich Gagarin gained a place in history for himself and the Soviet Union for having flown the first manned spaceflight. Gagarin's one-orbit flight was completed without incident. While in orbit, he made visual observations of Earth, ate and drank, wrote in a log book, operated his radios, and monitored the spacecraft's instruments. The successful flight of Vostok 1 laid to rest doctor's fears that man could not function in the weightless environment.

Vostok 2 was the first manned spacecraft to spend a full day in orbit. Launched on August 6, 1961, it carried Major Gherman Titov on a seventeen-orbit flight. Titov was the first man in space to experience the vestibular disorientation, or spacesickness, which would eventually affect half of all space travelers.

Launched August 11, 1962, and August 12, 1962, Vostoks 3 and 4 carried Major Andrian Nikolayev and Lieutenant Colonel Pavel R. Popovich on four- and three-day space flights respectively, during the first group flight of two manned spacecraft. Medical observations aimed at determining the cause of Titov's spacesickness were a major medical objective for these flights.

Vostoks 3 and 4 were launched into a co-orbit and at one time were within 6.5 kilometers of each other. Neither craft had maneuvering or docking ability, so no rendezvous was possible.

On the joint flight of Vostoks 5 and 6, launched June 14, 1963, and June 16, 1963, Lieutenant Colonel Valeri Bykovsky and the first woman in space, Lieutenant Valentina Tereshkova, flew five- and three-day space missions, respectively. Bykovsky, aboard Vostok 5, performed further medical observations on the effects of spaceflight on the human organism and performed astronomical and geophysical observations.

## Knowledge Gained

Proof that man can survive without impairment and perform useful work in space was one of the Vostok program's greatest scientific achievements. The passengers aboard the Vostok flights laid to rest the concerns of some leading space-medicine authorities of the day that man would be incapacitated by the spaceflight experience, possibly hallucinating or losing self-control. The postflight health of the Vostok passengers showed that the short-term, near-Earth orbit exposure to the space environment poses no direct threat to the well-being of space travelers.

One of the early medical discoveries from the Vostok flights was of vestibular disturbances during weightlessness which cause nausea and disorientation. These symptoms were first observed by Gherman Titov on the one-day flight of Vostok 2. Titov reported that nausea started about two hours after lift-off and reached a maximum six hours after launch, then diminished after he had slept. Further studies of this spacesickness phenomenon by Dr. Vladimir Yazdovsky showed that it was caused by the lack of gravity on the otoliths, small bones in the inner ear which pass on information about balance and posture to the brain. Studies have shown that nearly half of all space travelers temporarily suffer from this effect after entering space. Another medical observation pioneered by the Vostok program was the discovery of temporary cardiovascular irregularities which persisted for up to two weeks after return to Earth from the weightless environment. Additional biological data gained from the Vostok flights include observations of reproductive experiments on drosophila, or fruit flies.

Comparison of the effects of spaceflight on women to its effects on men was one of the goals of Valentina Tereshkova's Vostok 6 flight. Soviet space doctors were given the added bonus of being able to study the offspring of male and female space travelers when Tereshkova married Vostok 3 cosmonaut Andrian Nikolayev and bore a healthy daughter in 1964.

The Vostok series provided Soviet space technicians with valuable experience in the perfection of manned spaceflight techniques, including control of two manned spacecraft simultaneously. The production experience gained in fabricating the Vostok has led to the development of a highly reliable automated spacecraft which has been adapted to a number of different roles, including the early Kosmos military photoreconnaissance spacecraft and the Kosmos biological experiment carrier.

The Vostok program also provided Soviet launch controllers with experience in the rapid turnaround and reuse of launch facilities with the flights of Vostoks 3 and 4 and Vostoks 5 and 6 from the same pad. Perfection of Vostok spacecraft recovery techniques proved useful not only in later manned programs but also in the military applications of the Vostok-type spacecraft used for photoreconnaissance.

## Context

All over the world, the flight of Yuri Gagarin aboard Vostok 1 was recognized as the single most important development in the space age since Sputnik 1. The flights of the Vostok and its cosmonaut passengers must, however, be viewed not only from their historical and scientific standpoint but also as one of the tools used by Soviet Premier Nikita Khrushchev to influence Soviet-American Cold War politics during the early 1960's.

The post-World War II and Korean War era spawned the political Cold War between the West and the Soviet Union. The Cold War was highlighted by games of one-upmanship which were carried to extremes by Premier Khrushchev in his attempts to portray the Soviet system as superior to Western democracy. Khrushchev became a master at using the Soviet space program as a propaganda tool in pursuit of this aim. Khrushchev was especially sensitive to world opinion that the Soviet Union was still technologically backward and primitive in the decade following World War II. He saw the Soviet space program as a way to prove that Soviet science was superior to that of the West. Khrushchev's rationale was that the Soviet scientific and technical achievements would provide evidence of the superiority of the Soviet Communist system of government.

The history of the Vostok manned space program was dominated by the political goals of Khrushchev in his quest for more space "firsts." To a large degree, the Western space program as well was shaped by Khrushchev because of the United States' race to be first in placing a man on the Moon. The launching of the first man into space by the Soviet Union so captured the world's imagination that President John F. Kennedy started the manned Apollo program to compete with Soviet space achievements.

The Soviets managed to conceal the fact that their spacecraft were little more than spherical ballistic capsules, products of the crude, heavy technology of the 1950's. These vehicles were barely adequate to the job of carrying passengers into space and returning them alive. The fact that the cosmonauts aboard the Vostok flights were little more than passengers in a technologically simple vehicle was not known in the West.

An ironic legacy of the early Soviet manned space program—and of Khrushchev's attempt to use it for propaganda purposes—is that the Soviets' space achievements constituted the most important motivation for the American push into space, with all the resulting technological gains by the West.

## Bibliography

Gatland, Kenneth. *Manned Spacecraft*. Rev. ed. New York: Macmillan, 1976. A chronology of worldwide events leading to the development of manned spaceflight by both the United States and the Soviet Union. Contains numerous illustrations detailing the design and functions of American and Soviet manned spacecraft. Descriptive narratives provide details of all manned spacecraft and their missions. Suitable for general audiences.

Johnson, Nicholas L. *Handbook of Soviet Manned Space Flight*. San Diego: Univelt, 1980. A technical chronology of Soviet manned spaceflight. Contains many drawings and illustrations detailing Soviet manned spaceflight hardware. Aimed at the advanced reader, this handbook emphasizes the technical details of the Soviet manned programs and summarizes the mission results. One of the most authoritative sources of information on Soviet manned space programs.

McDougall, Walter A. . . . *The Heavens and the Earth: A Political History of the Space Age*. New York: Basic Books, 1985. A political history of the space age. This well-researched and heavily footnoted historical text describes and analyzes the decisions by the leaders of both the United States and the Soviet Union and their effects on the respective space programs. Heavy emphasis on the key political and technological leaders of the time. Relates how the American and Soviet space programs became an integral part of Cold War politics. Suitable for general audiences.

Oberg, James E. *Red Star in Orbit*. New York: Random House, 1981. Comprehensive review of all phases of the Soviet space program, with emphasis given to both the problems and failures in achieving Soviet spaceflight and the success of ongoing research programs. Attention is given to the behind-the-scenes personalities and politics of the Soviet space program. An excellent overview of the canceled Soviet man-to-the-Moon program. Suitable for general audiences.

Smolders, Peter. *Soviets in Space*. New York: Taplinger Publisher Co., 1974. A well-illustrated narrative of all aspects of the Soviet space program. Heavy emphasis is placed on manned activities. Suitable for general audiences, it concentrates on the successful aspects of Soviet space missions as they were reported by the Soviet government. Contains numerous diagrams and photographs illustrating the technical details of the spacecraft and their missions.

Turnill, Reginald. *The Observer's Spaceflight Directory*. London: Frederick Warne, 1978. A lavishly illustrated summary of spaceflight activities by all nations. Includes chronologies of major manned and unmanned space missions. Technical narrative describes worldwide space activities, classified by nation and program, providing details of spacecraft, mission summaries, and program results. One-third of the directory is devoted to Soviet programs. Suitable for readers with some background in the subject.

U.S. Congress. Senate. Committee on Commerce, Science, and Transportation. *Soviet Space Programs: 1976-80*. Part 2, *Manned Space Programs and Space Life Sciences*. Report prepared by Congressional Research Service, the Library of Congress. 98th Cong., 2d sess., 1984. Committee Print. Comprehensive descriptions of all phases of Soviet manned spaceflight. Provides a detailed overview of the technical development of Soviet manned space activities, scientific investigations, space medicine research and results, and the political effects of Soviet space activity. Suitable for general audiences.

*Robert Reeves*

### Cross-References

# THE VOSTOK TEST FLIGHTS

*Date:* May 15, 1960, to March 25, 1961
*Type of program:* Unmanned spacecraft test flights
*Country:* The Soviet Union

*Sputnik missions 4, 5, 6, 9, and 10 were unmanned test flights of the Vostok spacecraft which later carried the first human passenger into orbit. Vital spacecraft engineering data, spaceflight experience, and biological data from animal passengers were gained prior to launching human passengers aboard the Vostok.*

*Principal personages*
ANATOLI A. BLAGONRAVOV, Chairman of the Commission for the Exploration and Use of Outer Space, Soviet Academy of Sciences
M. V. KELDISH, President of the Soviet Academy of Sciences
NIKITA KHRUSHCHEV, the third Premier of the Soviet Union
SERGEI KOROLEV, Chief Designer and head of the Soviet space program, 1957-1966
MITROFAN NEDELIN, Chief of all Soviet rocket forces, 1957-1960
G. I. PETROV, Director of the Institute of Space Research, Soviet Academy of Sciences
LEONID SEDOV, Chairman of the Interdepartmental Commission of Interplanetary Communications, Soviet Academy of Sciences

## Summary of the Program

Only one month after the launching of the first Earth satellite, Soviet space scientists demonstrated their interest in future manned spaceflight by launching the first living passenger into orbit, the dog Laika, carried aboard the Sputnik 2 satellite on November 3, 1957. Encouraged by the medical success of Sputnik 2, Soviet space officials began plans to send men into orbit. In 1959, designs for the manned satellite which would become known as the Vostok were completed, and under the direction of the then-anonymous "Chief Designer," Sergei Korolev, actual hardware fabrication began.

The Vostok spacecraft took shape as a 2,400-kilogram spherical reentry cabin, 2.3 meters in diameter, which contained life-support equipment to sustain a passenger. This was attached to an instrument/retro-rocket module, which brought the total spacecraft weight to more than 4,700 kilograms. The instrument/retro-rocket package resembled two cones placed base to base and contained a liquid-fueled retro-rocket assembly and telemetry, heat regulation, orbital guidance, and radiation monitoring equipment.

The spherical reentry cabin of the Vostok was covered with an ablative heatshield to allow it to survive atmospheric heating, which reached a temperature of 10,000 degrees Celsius in the shock wave which preceded the descending cabin.

During reentry, the Vostok was oriented with the heaviest portion of the heatshield facing the direction of travel by offsetting the spacecraft's center of gravity. When atmospheric resistance was encountered, the spacecraft automatically rolled over until the heatshield was properly positioned.

Unlike early American manned spacecraft, which were parachuted into the ocean, Soviet spacecraft were returned to Soviet territory and touched down on land. The extreme weight of the 2,400-kilogram Vostok reentry cabin resulted in a very hard parachute landing. To accomplish a softer landing speed for the Vostok passengers, an ejection seat was provided to allow the cosmonauts to descend under a personal parachute. The ejection seat was fired from the descending spacecraft at 7,000 meters. At 4,000 meters, the seat fell free and the cosmonaut's personal parachute completed the recovery. The reentry cabin parachute also deployed at 4,000 meters.

The Sputnik test flights of the Vostok were launched by the A1 booster, which consisted of a modified SS-6 Sapwood intercontinental ballistic missile for the first two stages, while the third stage was the same as that developed to boost the early Luna missions toward the Moon. All Vostok launches were from the Tyuratam launch complex. Suborbital reentry tests of the Vostok spacecraft were performed on January 20 and January 31, 1960.

The first orbital test of the Vostok was Sputnik 4, launched on May 15, 1960, into a 312-by-369-kilometer orbit. The Soviets called the test satellite Korabl Sputnik 1 (Spaceship Satellite 1). Sputnik 4 carried a dummy cosmonaut and tested the spacecraft's life-support system during its planned four-day flight. Extensive prerecorded communications and telemetry were returned. In case of a mishap during the Sputnik 4 test flight, and to prevent Western claims that a man was carried aboard the spacecraft and lost, the Soviets used a tape of a Russian choral group instead of a prerecorded pilot's voice during communication tests.

After sixty-four orbits, the retro-rocket on Sputnik 4 was fired to return the passenger cabin to Earth. A malfunction in the spacecraft attitude control system oriented the retro-rocket at the wrong angle and boosted the reentry cabin into a higher 290-by-675-kilometer orbit instead of a reentry trajectory. After retrofire, Sputnik 4 broke up into eight pieces.

After 844 days in space, the instrument section/retro-rocket module from Sputnik 4 reentered on September 5, 1962. A nine-kilogram fragment of the instrument package was discovered embedded in the asphalt of a Manitowoc, Wisconsin, city street. Chemical analysis of the recovered fragment showed two rare minerals, wustite and akaganeite, which had previously been seen in recovered meteorites. The reentry cabin finally decayed from orbit on October 15, 1965.

A second orbital test of the Vostok was unsuccessful in July, 1960, when the carrier rocket exploded in flight. Sputnik 5 (Korabl Sputnik 2) was the first successful test of the Vostok. Launched August 19, 1960, into a 305-by-339-kilometer orbit, the flight of Sputnik 5 was shortened to one day to minimize the probability of control failure.

Sputnik 5 was the first satellite to carry living creatures into orbit and return them safely to Earth. A wide variety of specimens was carried, including two dogs (Strelka and Belka), two rats, forty mice, and various insects and plants. Particular attention was paid to the dog passengers aboard Sputnik 5: Two television cameras monitored their reaction to the weightless environment. Additional experiments carried on Sputnik 5 included human skin samples and nuclear photographic emulsions to study cosmic rays. The living passengers aboard Sputnik 5 were housed in a special pressurized container which was attached to the ejection seat. After their recovery, Strelka and Belka were national heroes in the Soviet Union and were put on extensive public display. The two dogs apparently suffered no ill effects from the flight and later produced several litters of healthy puppies.

While the early U.S. space program made use of chimpanzees as biological test specimens, the Russians chose to use dogs, for they are very intelligent and well suited to the training required for the Vostok test flights. The heart and blood vessels of dogs are similar enough to man's to allow for valid medical comparisons.

Had it been successful, Sputnik 6 (Korabl Sputnik 3) would probably have been the final test of the Vostok system before it was committed to manned flight. Launched December 1, 1960, into a 186-by-265-kilometer orbit, Sputnik 6, which carried two more dog passengers, Pchelka and Mushka, performed well for one day in space. The orbital parameters of this flight were deliberately lower than on previous flights to allow for the possibility of retro-rocket failure; thus, the orbit would decay automatically before the ten-day supply of spacecraft consumables were depleted.

The Soviets let it be known that a new computer-operated spacecraft control system was being tried on the Sputnik 6 flight for the first time. Apparently, this new spacecraft control computer malfunctioned. During retrofire, the Sputnik 6 reentry cabin was placed on an improper trajectory and descended at too steep an angle into the atmosphere, where it was burned beyond recovery. Pchelka and Mushka thus became the first important casualties of spaceflight. The day after the unsuccessful recovery, the Chief Designer, Sergei Korolev, had a heart attack.

The Sputnik 6 failure prompted the cancellation of plans for an immediate manned launch aboard the next Vostok flight. The recovery failure of Sputnik 6 was not immediately revealed to the Vostok cosmonaut trainees. Soviet psychologists were concerned about the cosmonauts' reactions to the failure.

A second Korabl Sputnik launch attempt in December, 1960, was also unsuccessful when the booster failed to achieve orbit.

To expedite the first manned flight, the designers of the Vostok program eliminated their goal of a one-day stay in orbit for the first manned shot and limited the subsequent tests to one orbit only. These adjustments were made in an effort to prevent the control problems which had plagued previous Vostok recoveries. While the first two Vostok dog flights could be considered flying biological laboratories, the final two were engineering flights to prove the Vostok system capable of recovering human passengers from spaceflight.

The next Vostok test was Sputnik 9, or Korabl Sputnik 4 (Sputniks 7 and 8 were Venus probe attempts), launched March 9, 1961, into a 183-by-250-kilometer orbit; it made a single revolution of Earth before being successfully recovered. The ejection seat of Sputnik 9 carried a dummy cosmonaut dressed in an operational spacesuit. The single dog passenger aboard, Chernushka, landed inside the reentry cabin and was not ejected during recovery.

Only sixteen days later, the final flight test of the Vostok was successful. Sputnik 10 (Korabl Sputnik 5) was launched on March 25, 1961, for a single 178-by-246-kilometer orbit of Earth. The dog Zvezdochka was carried in the cabin, while another dummy cosmonaut rode in the ejection seat.

Eighteen days later, the first man in space, Yuri Gagarin, flew an identical one-orbit mission.

## Knowledge Gained

The Sputnik 4, 5, 6, 9, and 10 flights enabled Soviet technicians to gain valuable spaceflight experience to man-rate the Vostok hardware prior to committing a human passenger to spaceflight.

Though the recovery of Sputnik 4 was unsuccessful, that flight validated the basic design of the Vostok spacecraft, as the cabin life-support system functioned in orbit for eight days.

The flight of Sputnik 5 was an extensive biological test of the reactions of various forms of animal life to the space environment. Soviet space scientists regarded cosmic radiation as the chief obstacle to manned spaceflight. To study the effects of radiation, Sputnik 5 carried nuclear photographic emulsion packs. These consisted of strips of photographic film stacked together; when they were disassembled and developed, they allowed a tracing of the paths of cosmic particles through the emulsion stack and the study of secondary nuclear particles created by the collisions of cosmic rays with the atoms in the film packs. Black mice were also flown aboard Sputnik 5 because their color changes rapidly when they are exposed to radiation.

Another biological radiation experiment involved human skin tissue samples donated by Drs. Kapichnikov, Rybakov, and Novikov of the Moscow Institute of Experimental Biology. Some of the samples were flown aboard Sputnik 5, while other comparison samples were kept in a laboratory. After the Sputnik 5 mission, both flight and comparison samples were then regrafted to the donors to study the effect of space exposure on human tissues. Both samples began to knit back onto the donors, but the flight samples took longer than the comparison samples.

Soviet space scientists were encouraged when they determined that the rats and mice aboard Sputnik 5 had eaten well in spite of weightlessness. This showed they had adapted to the space environment. The overall medical results from the Sputnik 5 biological flight showed that a man could travel into space and return with no apparent ill effects.

The final two flights, Sputniks 9 and 10, were concerned less with space biological experiments than with the safety and successful return of the spacecraft. Procedural changes and design improvements were tested prior to committing a human passenger to spaceflight aboard Vostok.

Engineering experience gained in the Vostok flight operations of the Sputnik precursor flights was applied not only to the manned flights which followed but also to the military version of the Vostok spacecraft, which was used extensively for photoreconnaissance.

The design of the Vostok spacecraft eventually proved so reliable that the same spacecraft is still used today for biological flights in the Kosmos series.

## Context

In order to understand the true reasons that the Sputnik precursor flights for the Vostok were carried out, one must be aware of the type of rivalry that existed between the United States and the Soviet Union during the early 1960's. Throughout the years of the Sputnik test flight program to man-rate the Vostok, Cold War tensions between the United States and the Soviet Union were very high. Hostile confrontations included the May, 1960, U2 espionage airplane incident over the Soviet Union, Soviet Premier Nikita Khrushchev's famous temper tantrums in September of 1960 at United Nations-sponsored talks, and, finally, the American-backed Cuban invasion at the Bay of Pigs.

In the midst of all these political conflicts between the Soviet Union and the United States, both nations were intensely engaged in a technological race to be the first to orbit a man around Earth. The United States and the Soviet Union alike were using their space programs, particularly their manned space programs, as propaganda tools against each other. Soviet Premier Nikita Khrushchev was intent on using his space program to challenge the scientific superiority of the Western world. Khrushchev's aim was to beat the United States to all major space goals and use these space firsts as propaganda ploys in his attempt to convince the world that the Communist system of government was superior to that of the Western democracies.

Actually, the Soviet manned spaceflight hardware designs were much simpler and less sophisticated than those of the United States, and the Soviets were also less ambitious in their overall goal. The Soviets simply wanted to place a man in space at the earliest opportunity. Khrushchev's goal with the first Vostok manned flight was not so much a scientific as a propaganda victory over the United States. The Sputnik precursor flights leading to the Vostok manned flights were stepping-stones toward achieving this goal.

In spite of Khrushchev's political propaganda aims, the voyages of Sputniks 5, 9, and 10 did prove that living creatures can survive the rigors of spaceflight and return to Earth in good health. This basic knowledge was very helpful to American as well as Soviet space planners.

Up to early 1961, there were still many space medicine specialists who were concerned that weightlessness, cosmic radiation, and the spaceflight experience could be too much for a human passenger to withstand, so that manned spaceflight might be impractical from a medical standpoint. The flights of Sputniks 4 through 10 did much to dispel this thinking and showed that the space environment was safe for human passengers in near-Earth orbit.

## Bibliography

Gatland, Kenneth. *Manned Spacecraft.* Rev. ed. New York: Macmillan, 1976. A chronology of the development of manned spaceflight by the superpowers. Its numerous illustrations detail the design and functions of the various American and Soviet manned spacecraft. Gatland also provides descriptive narratives with details of the development and subsequent missions of all manned spacecraft. Appropriate for the general reader.

Johnson, Nicholas L. *Handbook of Soviet Manned Space Flight.* San Diego: Univelt, 1980. Johnson's chronology of Soviet manned spaceflight emphasizes technical aspects, with many drawings and illustrations detailing flight hardware. This focus makes the book suitable only for the knowledgeable reader. Summaries of the mission results are provided. One of the most authoritative sources of information on Soviet manned space programs.

Oberg, James E. *Red Star in Orbit.* New York: Random House, 1981. All phases of the Soviet space program are covered, with a careful examination of not only the successes of ongoing research programs but also the failures of some early attempts. Oberg shows how personalities and political considerations played into the development of the Soviet space program. Includes an informative discussion of the aborted Soviet plan to land a man on the Moon. Suitable for general audiences.

Smolders, Peter. *Soviets in Space.* New York: Taplinger Publishing Co., 1974. Manned spaceflight programs are the primary emphasis of this study, which is an accessible overview, less critical than Oberg's in that it tends to give primary attention to the officially reported successes of the Soviet space program. Diagrams and photographs illustrate the technical details of Soviet spacecraft and their missions.

Stoiko, Michael. *Soviet Rocketry.* New York: Holt, Rinehart and Winston, 1970. An overview of the Soviet space program, tracing the evolution of rocket development and satellite technology leading to planetary exploration and manned spaceflight. Emphasis on the pre-Sputnik technology development leading to the current space program. Speculates on future Soviet space activities. Nontechnical narrative suitable for the beginner.

Turnill, Reginald. *The Observer's Spaceflight Directory.* London: Frederick Warne, 1978. This summary of spaceflight activities by all nations is notable for its abundant illustrations. Chronologies of major space missions, manned and unmanned, are provided. Organized according to nation and program, the text includes details of spacecraft, mission summaries, and program results. The discussion of Soviet programs makes up one-third of the book. Readers with some basic familiarity with the subject will find the volume accessible.

U.S. Congress. Senate. Committee on Commerce, Science, and Transportation. *Soviet Space Programs: 1976-1980.* Part 2, *Manned Space Programs and Space Life Sciences.* Report prepared by Congressional Research Service, the Library of Congress. 98th Cong., 2d sess., 1984. Committee Print. This report examines in detail the technical development of Soviet manned space activities, experiments and medical research, and political aspects of the space program. A comprehensive overview, accessible to the general reader.

*Robert Reeves*

## Cross-References

# VOSTOK 1

*Date:* April 12, 1961
*Type of mission:* Manned Earth-orbiting spaceflight
*Country:* The Soviet Union

*The Vostok 1 manned spaceflight mission was the world's first spaceflight in which a human being was lofted into space beyond Earth's atmospheric envelope and returned safely. The first human in space, cosmonaut pilot Yuri Gagarin, completed one Earth orbit, broadcast live voice transmission from space, and proved that a human could not only survive such a flight but also function normally inside a closed spacecraft container.*

### Principal personages
YURI A. GAGARIN, the cosmonaut who piloted the spacecraft
SERGEI KOROLEV, Chief Designer of the Soviet space program
GHERMAN S. TITOV, the backup pilot
NIKOLAI KAMANIN, the trainer of the cosmonauts
YEVGENI ANATOLYEVICH, the chief physician to the cosmonauts
    and Gagarin's personal doctor
YEVGENI KARPOV, the assistant physician to the cosmonauts

## Summary of the Mission

The Soviet Vostok 1 manned mission carried the first human being into space and returned him safely to Earth after completing one orbit. Up to this time, the Soviets had orbited a number of unmanned spacecraft identified by the Soviets as precursor flights from May, 1960, through March, 1961. The research flights operated under the name Korabl Sputnik Satellite Ships (not to be confused with the Sputnik 1 satellite) and carried a total of seven dogs—Laika, Belka, Strelka, Pchelka, Mushka, Chernushka, and Zvezdochka—over the ten-month period. Some of the Korabl missions also carried dummy human forms for research purposes. The considerable engineering and biological data from these experiments led to the decision to attempt a manned flight in 1961.

By the time Yuri Gagarin made his historic flight, the Soviet Union had launched the world's first satellite (Sputnik 1 in October, 1957) and had conducted two successful unmanned experiments involving lunar photography and a lunar landing. Luna 2 became the first artificial object to impact the lunar surface, and Luna 3 the first craft to photograph the lunar far side (the side of the Moon which always faces away from Earth). These successful missions implemented the technology that would ensure future successes in manned flight.

The Vostok 1 spacecraft weighed 4,725 kilograms. It was made of two parts. The first part, in the shape of a large sphere, was designed to enclose and support a human being during spaceflight with a minimum of instrumentation and pilot control and to serve as the mission reentry vehicle carrying the cosmonaut to a safe landing. The pressurized ball had an outer covering of asbestos, underneath which were several layers of special metals. The sphere contained three small portholes through which the pilot could see outside the craft, as well as four antennae for various kinds of communication between the craft and the ground control station. In all, the Vostok 1 capsule carried about eight instruments, including a radio, in-flight automatic camera, air conditioner, telegraph key, attitude control handgrip, television camera, oxygen capacity/consumption indicators, and a cosmonaut couch-ejection seat set on a sliding track and capable of turning 360 degrees inside the cabin. The sphere was referred to as the "cosmonaut cabin" and was mated to the front of an instrumentation-and-mechanics section that looked like two cones fixed head-to-head. Inside this mechanical section were located the chemical batteries, orientation motors, main retrograde engines, and support equipment. A series of spherical gas bottles were attached in a ring around the outside of the two craft, at the juncture of the cosmonaut cabin and the mechanical section.

These two modules together sat atop the main booster rocket, which consisted of five clusters of four rocket motors in each cluster (a total of twenty motors). The configuration was designated the SS-6 Sapwood rocket (surface-to-surface) by the United States military and was actually a Soviet intercontinental ballistic missile (ICBM) rocket which came to be referred to in the West as A-1. During launch, all the motors fired simultaneously for maximum thrust. Four of the five spent clusters then fell away, while the Vostok 1 continued upward, propelled by the central sustainer cluster, which was also spent before the Vostok 1 reached orbit. The remaining distance to orbit was covered by the thrust of the Vostok 1's upper-stage motors, which reached orbit still attached to the mechanical stage of the spacecraft. When this upper stage was spent, it was jettisoned and left to tumble through space until its own orbit decayed and the motor burned during reentry.

The Vostok spacecraft was the rocket's payload. At launch, the two sections of the Vostok configuration were completely surrounded by a protective metal cylinder known as a shroud. The shroud protected the Vostok from any damaging effects during the launch-to-orbit sequence. The connected cosmonaut cabin and mechanical section sat at the very top of the rocket itself and could only be reached by a tall launchpad elevator which the cosmonaut rode in order to climb into his craft. The base of the spherical cosmonaut cabin/reentry module was weighted so that after reentry the module would automatically right itself. This way, the cosmonaut would descend in a position upright relative to Earth's surface.

The Vostok-type spacecraft (there were six of them all together) was designed by the Soviet Chief Designer, Sergei Korolev. As Chief Designer, Korolev had enormous influence in the Soviet Union at this time and was the Soviets' most qualified space technologist. He also engaged in much cosmonaut training, especially as regarded actual spaceflight and the operation of spacecraft. Korolev and Gagarin became fast friends. The designer was constantly at Gagarin's side throughout his training, even up to the last several minutes before Gagarin rode the elevator up to the waiting Vostok craft just before launch on April 12, 1961. Other cosmonauts, particularly backup pilot Gherman Titov, also worked closely with Gagarin.

Although their space programs were kept confidential, Soviet cosmonauts and American astronauts were required to complete very similar types of training—with one major exception. The Soviet manned space program was designed to land a human on land at the end of the flight; American spaceflights featured water landings. Since Soviet cosmonauts were limited to land landings, they were obliged to undergo a long period of parachute training. The cosmonaut couch in the Vostok was designed as an ejection seat in case of an emergency, at which time the pilot would have to land via parachute. As a Red Air Force pilot, Gagarin had made several parachute practice jumps; before the Vostok flight, however, his parachute training became intense.

There were other types of training as well, in astronautics, astronomy, and engineering—and with a soundproof isolation chamber, a centrifuge, and a spacecraft simulator. Cosmonauts learned about the characteristics of spaceflight and were briefed on the space environment. Intensive physical training was also required, including gymnastics, swimming, and running—even boxing and workouts with free weights. Throughout cosmonaut training, the main participants in the process were cosmonaut chief physician Yevgeni Anatolyevich, assistant physician Yevgeni Karpov, and the training program director, Red Air Force general Nikolai Kamanin.

It is not known when the Soviet manned space program started; some estimates indicate that it began as early as the early 1950's. Certainly Korolev had been thinking about manned flight for many years. When the first cosmonauts were chosen in 1960, the spacecraft had already been designed and was in production. Only very minor changes in instrumentation were needed for the Soviets to launch the first human into space. As with all Soviet scientific programs, the space program came under the overall direction of the Soviet Academy of Sciences with its multitude of bureaucratic committees and departments, and the academy was subservient to the Central Committee of the Communist Party. For the manned space program, however, all matters also came under the direct jurisdiction of Premier and Party Chairman Nikita Khrushchev—presumably because of the immense domestic and international political implications and because Khrushchev was seeking to bolster his own career.

Gagarin did not train specifically to be the first cosmonaut into space; in fact, he learned that he had been chosen only several days before the launch date. A government board gave final approval on April 8 for the mission to proceed; the date chosen was April 12. At that meeting, General Kamanin suggested Lieutenant Yuri Alekseyevich Gagarin as the first pilot. After some discussion, the board gave its formal consent: The cosmonaut pilot would be Gagarin. The young pilot himself was told of the decision the following day by General Kamanin, who made an informal announcement at a party at the general's home.

The government board met again at 6:00 A.M. Moscow time on April 12 and signed the official papers for the mission. At 6:50 A.M., Gagarin and fellow cosmonaut Titov stepped out of the blue cosmonaut transfer bus onto the concrete launchpad at the Tyuratam cosmodrome in Kazakhstan. As required by the board, Gagarin then made the following statement to the press:

> In a few minutes a powerful spaceship will carry me to the expanses of outer space. What can I tell you in these last moments before takeoff? My entire life looks to me as one wonderful moment. I have lived and worked all my life for the sake of this moment. . . .
> To be the first to do what generations have dreamed of, the first to blaze man's trail to the stars. . . . Name a task more complex than the one I am facing. I am not responsible to one man, or only to a score of people, or merely to all my colleagues. I am responsible to all the Soviet people, to all mankind, to its present and future. And if, in the face of it all, I am still ready for this mission, it is only because I am a Communist, inspired by the examples of unsurpassed heroism of my countrymen— the Soviet people.

Vostok 1 left the Tyuratam launch complex at 9:07 A.M. Moscow time; by 9:26, Gagarin, whose in-flight code name was Cedar, reported by voice radio that his condition was normal and that the flight was proceeding according to plan. He also commented on what he saw out the spacecraft windows: "I can clearly see mountain ranges, shaded areas, large forests, islands and sea coastlines. I saw the Sun, clouds and light shadows on my dear far Earth. . . . The flight is going as planned. Normal reaction to free fall. I feel fine. All equipment and systems functioning normally." At 9:57 A.M., the pilot announced that he was passing over America; at 10:25 A.M., Vostok's retro-rockets began braking for descent and reentry, slowing the swiftly speeding sphere for a precise angle for reentering Earth's atmospheric envelope. The cosmonaut sphere landed at 10:55 A.M. Moscow time in a field near the village of Smelovka.

## Knowledge Gained

As a recognizable public achievement, the flight of Vostok 1 is one of the most outstanding events in the recorded history of civilization. It proved conclusively that spaceflight was altogether possible, and it paved the way for numerous subsequent manned spaceflights of astronauts from many nations across the globe. The Gagarin accomplishment also propelled the Soviet Union into a new and unprecedented category of world leadership of which Kremlin politicians took immediate advantage over the following several years. World opinion about Soviet capabilities improved, and the United States' image around the globe was considerably diminished in comparison.

As purely a technological event, the Vostok 1 flight does not seem to match the politics or the public acclaim associated with it. Yuri Gagarin was a captive passenger in a vehicle over which he had no control and had only eight instruments to monitor. The only maneuvers he commanded were attitude control of the Vostok craft (keeping the craft right side up and in a level flight path) and pilot escape. Vostok 1 was entirely controlled by ground technicians; the mission sequence from takeoff to landing had been decided long before the flight took place, and the pilot had no individual initiatives or alternative actions he could take. It is necessary to examine the goals and objectives of the technology and the event without detracting from the character of the pilot or the physical consequences of the deed.

## Context

There were six Vostok flights altogether. The spacecrafts for all six were essentially identical in design, and all the Vostok cosmonauts had the limited responsibility that Gagarin had. In fact, the cosmonauts' extensive training had been largely unnecessary because they had nothing to do while in space except keep calm, look out the window, and talk on the voice radio. Valentina Tereshkova, the world's first woman in space (she flew in Vostok 6), had been a textile worker and was taken out of the factory and put through a cursory training program emphasizing parachute tactics in case she had to bail out toward the end of the mission.

The design of the Vostok craft was so simple that it endangered the lives of its passengers. In comparison, the United States Mercury spacecraft contained some 136 instruments, including backup mechanisms in case the primary systems failed. The Mercury astronauts had a total spacecraft control option which came to be known in space jargon as "fly-by-wire" (referring to an astronaut's control over the craft by manipulating the main instruments). This option was used by all the Mercury astronauts except Alan B. Shepherd, Jr., during the first American manned spaceflight.

Gagarin, in contrast, had only two options: It was possible for him to override the automatic ground control command by means of a mechanism operated with his right hand and to abort the mission by blowing off the escape hatch of the cosmonaut cabin and firing his "sled-couch" out that opening by a mechanism operated with his left hand. These options were installed in the Vostok primarily in the event of a life-threatening launch emergency.

The man-in-space achievements of both the United States and the Soviet Union have always been compared. While the technological foundations of these first flights are not comparable, the public will always remember that the Soviet Union did in fact send the first human into space. Thus the profound significance of Gagarin's flight is greatest in a political sense and not in a technological or scientific sense. On April 12, 1961, the Soviet Central Committee issued a worldwide statement:

> We, Soviet people building Communism, have had the honour of being the first to penetrate into outer space. We consider successes in the conquest of space as belonging not to our people alone, but to all mankind. We are happy to put them at the disposal of all in the name of the progress, happiness, and welfare of all peoples on

earth. We are putting our achievements and discoveries not at the service of war, but at the service of peace and the security of nations.

On March 27, 1968, at 11:10 A.M., an aircraft piloted by Yuri Gagarin crashed into a wooded area near Moscow. Gagarin and one of his countrymen died in the accident.

## Bibliography

Daniloff, Nicholas. *The Kremlin and the Cosmos*. New York: Alfred A. Knopf, 1972. This book is an excellent review of the Soviet political structure as it relates to the national space program. Readers will find fascinating explanations of human behavior based on political imperatives. Nikita Khrushchev, Sergei Korolev, Yuri Gagarin, and many other Soviet personalities from the manned flight era are discussed. Suitable for high school and college readers as well as the general public.

Shelton, William. *Soviet Space Exploration: The First Decade*. New York: Washington Square Press, 1968. This well-written and authoritative account of the first ten years of the Soviet space program is an in-depth survey of the political, scientific, and technological events which came together to assure the Soviets the position of being first in space technology during this period. Written by a professional journalist and researcher, the book includes many authentic anecdotes and insights. The book also contains an excellent bibliography and a chronology of Soviet space events. The volume is suitable for high school and college readers.

Stoiko, Michael. *Soviet Rocketry: Past, Present and Future*. New York: Holt, Rinehart and Winston, 1970. Written by an accomplished aerospace engineer, this book surveys all the "nuts and bolts" of Soviet space technology, including the first generations of manned spacecraft. Excellent photographs, numerous tables and charts, and detailed illustrations make this an invaluable book for anyone interested in Soviet space technology. Suitable for high school and college students, as well as the general public.

Tsymbal, Nikolai, ed. *First Man in Space: The Life and Achievement of Yuri Gagarin, a Collection*. Moscow: Progress Publishers, 1984. Written entirely by Soviet authors and biographers, this oversized book tells the life history of Yuri Gagarin, from his earliest years to his death in 1968. Contains many rare photographs of Gagarin, his colleagues, and Soviet space hardware and facilities. Although the narrative is sometimes propagandized, it offers an unusual insight into the Soviet mind and daily life, as well as some examples of how the Soviet bureaucracy works.

U.S. Congress. Senate. Committee on Commerce, Science, and Transportation. *Soviet Space Programs: 1976-80*. Part 1, *Supporting Facilities and Launch Vehicles*. Report prepared by Congressional Research Service, the Library of Congress. 98th Cong., 2d sess., 1982. Committee Print. Part 1 of a three-part overview of the Soviet space program, this paperback volume is the "official" reference. Filled with charts, diagrams, and authoritative information collected by the best American researchers, the book provides data about everything from cosmonaut training to launch sites and the development of rockets. Although somewhat technical, it is accessible to most high school students.

_____ . *Soviet Space Programs: 1976-80*. Part 2, *Manned Space Programs and Space Life Sciences*. Report prepared by Congressional Research Service, the Library of Congress. 98th Cong., 2d sess., 1984. Committee Print. Contains excellent illustrations of many manned spacecraft, from Vostok 1 to the Salyut space station. An overview of past space projects includes good references on the first years of the manned program.

*Thomas W. Becker*

## Cross-References

Biological Effects of Space Travel on Humans, 188; Cosmonauts and the Soviet Cosmonaut Program, 273; The Mercury Project, 940; Mercury-Redstone 3: *Freedom 7*, 953; Space Centers and Launch Sites in the Soviet Union, 1592; The Sputnik Program, 1930; The Voskhod Program, 2170; The Vostok Program, 2177; Vostok 2, 2198; Vostok 3 and 4, 2205; Vostok 5 and 6, 2212.

# VOSTOK 2

*Date:* August 6 to August 7, 1961
*Type of mission:* Manned Earth-orbiting spaceflight
*Country:* The Soviet Union

*Vostok 2 was the second manned spaceflight. Its purpose was to test the effects of the space environment on a human pilot while making multiple orbits of Earth.*

### Principal personage
GHERMAN S. TITOV, the Vostok 2 pilot

## Summary of the Mission

While Vostok 1 had established that a man was able to withstand the accelerations of launch and landing encountered during the course of a spaceflight, the single-orbit mission provided few data on the effects of the space environment itself. The second flight in the Vostok program would address this question.

The second man to orbit Earth was Gherman S. Titov. Titov was born in Siberia. He joined the Soviet air force and was one of the first to be selected to the cosmonaut corps. After more than a year of training, he was chosen as the backup commander of the first manned spaceflight. Titov accompanied Yuri A. Gagarin to the launchpad on the day of his historic mission, then met the senior cosmonaut at the Vostok 1 landing site. Titov officially learned of his assignment to Vostok 2 upon Gagarin's return. At twenty-five years of age, Titov was the youngest person ever to travel into space.

During the summer of 1961, as the time for the second Vostok flight approached, astronomers predicted a large outburst of activity on the Sun. Such activity would produce large amounts of radiation near Earth—radiation that would be dangerous to a cosmonaut, unprotected by Earth's atmosphere. The anticipated August mission might have been delayed had the solar storm not occurred in July, allowing conditions in space to return to normal before the scheduled Vostok departure date.

Vostok 2 was launched from Tyuratam, a secret site 370 kilometers southeast of Baikonur, four months after Vostok 1. Lift-off occurred as planned on August 6, 1961, at 9:00 A.M. Moscow time. The 4,730-kilogram Soviet spacecraft, 2.3 meters in diameter, was almost identical to Vostok 1 and was placed into orbit by the same Semyorka launch vehicle. This orbit ranged from 178 to 257 kilometers in altitude and was inclined to Earth's equator by 64 degrees, 56 minutes of arc. Vostok 2 made one revolution every 88.6 minutes.

Titov would make seventeen orbits of Earth, staying in space 25 hours and 18 minutes. An improved air-conditioning system and radiation detector were incorporated into the spacecraft for a flight to last 23.5 hours longer than Gagarin's. Some of the minor modifications in Vostok 2 had been suggested by Titov himself.

The jump from one to seventeen revolutions between Vostok 1 and Vostok 2 was necessary because of the inclinations of the Vostok orbits. Only at that interval would the spacecraft be in the best position to land within Soviet territory, a mission requirement. Thus, Titov became the first person to spend a day in space. He was also the first to observe multiple sunrises and sunsets through his window over the course of a single day.

During launch, Titov was subjected to a force equal to five times that of Earth's gravity at sea level. Once the booster engines had shut down, however, he was plunged into a weightless condition. The sudden change caused Titov at least a minute of spatial disorientation. He had difficulty seeing his instrument panel. After the flight, Titov described the sensation as one of flying upside down. Later, during the fifth orbit, the cosmonaut began to experience nausea. He was also dizzy when he moved his head in a certain fashion. These symptoms were unexpected and concerned physicians on the ground, but researchers now know that Titov was the first person to suffer from spacesickness. The Vostok 1 pilot recovered and had accustomed himself to the environment of free-fall around Earth by the thirteenth orbit.

The flightplan called for the cosmonaut to experiment with eating in space during the third orbit. Titov had little appetite but complied. Lunch consisted of drawing water and pastelike food out of tubes—a form of dining, like so many other aspects of the flight, that he had practiced aboard aircraft. In space, some juice droplets escaped Titov's mouth, and he watched them drift about the cabin.

Though Vostok was designed to be fully automated, it was equipped with manual controls. Although Gagarin had not used them, his mastery of these manual controls was important if he needed to initiate reentry at an unexpected point in the spacecraft's orbit. Beginning in his fourth orbit, Titov was able to pilot his vehicle on several instances during the flight for up to twenty minutes at a time. This task consisted of maintaining the spacecraft in its proper attitude using small rockets controlled by a hand stick. An experienced jet aircraft pilot, Titov performed this maneuver with ease.

Titov conducted other experiments dealing with human ability to function in space. These tests investigated muscle sensitivity and coordination and were executed at regular intervals during the flight. In addition, Titov was called upon to monitor gauges on his instrument panel and make general observations. A tape recorder provided him with the opportunity to make remarks when he was out of range of Soviet radio communications stations. Titov also kept a written log.

One fundamental question to be answered was whether it was possible to sleep in space. Fatigued at midflight, Titov was certainly willing to try to do so. On his first attempt, though, he found that his arms kept rising up and floating above him. To avoid this disturbance, he tucked his hands in his seatbelt. That done, he managed to sleep almost continuously for eight hours and seven minutes. In fact, he slept more than half an hour longer than scheduled. (After Titov awoke, he found that his arms had broken free and were hovering above him.)

Titov photographed the stars and Earth with a motion-picture camera through the three Vostok portholes (enlarged since Vostok 1), producing the first film made in space. Because of the inclination of Vostok 1's orbit and the length of its flight, the cosmonaut was able to fly over most of Earth's surface, a fact not lost on American intelligence-gathering agencies. In addition to automatic telemetry and voice radio, the Vostok transmitted televised pictures of Titov from a camera mounted beneath his instrument panel.

The frequencies of the radio signals from Vostok 2 were publicized so that they could be received around the world. People on Earth could hear Titov's articulate flight commentary, the first public broadcasts from space. They served not only to monitor the cosmonaut's condition but also to lessen skepticism regarding the authenticity of the Soviet manned space program, skepticism first voiced during the Vostok 1 mission. (Vostok transmitted on very high-frequency channels when over Soviet territory but was also equipped for longer-range shortwave transmission.) Among the messages sent from Earth to space were best wishes from the only veteran space traveler, Yuri Gagarin. While still aboard Vostok 2, Titov received word of his promotion to the rank of major.

After prolonged exposure to space, would the Vostok's reentry system function? The large payload capacity of the Vostok booster allowed provisioning of the spacecraft with food, water, oxygen, and electrical power for ten days; because of the Vostok's low altitude, its orbit might decay naturally, and these provisions would allow the cosmonaut some possibility of returning to Earth even if the reentry system failed.

This precaution proved unnecessary. At the prescribed time on the seventeenth orbit, the flight of Vostok 2 was automatically ended when a computer successfully oriented and fired retro-rockets, thereby slowing the spacecraft and causing it to fall to Earth. (Titov was prepared to activate this sequence manually if required.) The Vostok instrument compartment was detached, and Titov soon saw himself surrounded by flame through open viewports as the insulated Vostok reentry body was heated by friction created by the reencounter with Earth's atmosphere. Ablative material coating the spherical craft carried the heat away and protected the cosmonaut inside. Indeed, the cabin temperature remained constant throughout most of the flight.

Soon, Titov watched objects that had been left floating about the cabin settle to the floor as the force of Earth's gravity once again began to affect the spacecraft. He had left space behind. In total, Vostok 1 had traveled 700,000 kilometers in its elliptical journey through space.

After being slowed by the vehicle's parachute, Titov used the ejection seat into which he had been strapped throughout the mission to separate himself from the Vostok at an altitude of 7 kilometers. Cutting away the chair and hanging from his own parachute, he was able to watch the falling spacecraft descend beneath him. Titov landed lightly on his feet, saving himself the jarring landing he would have experienced had he remained inside the heavy Vostok all the way to the ground.

Vostok 2 landed at 10:18 A.M. Moscow time on August 7. The landing site was a plowed field in the Saratov region of the Soviet Union, near the Volga River and not far from where Gagarin had touched down. Titov was first found by passersby on motorcycles, who enthusiastically greeted the overnight celebrity. In the nearby village of Krasny Kut, Titov was met by his backup pilot, Andrian G. Nikolayev, who had quickly flown to the area from the launch complex.

Titov praised his Vostok spacecraft then and later. Only after returning did he make the full extent of his inflight medical problems known, and they were not revealed publicly for several months. (He was hospitalized briefly.) Titov experienced inner-ear trouble for some time after the mission; he never flew in space again.

## Knowledge Gained

Vostok 2 demonstrated that a cosmonaut could both work and rest for many hours in space despite the effects of weightlessness. Operating controls, maintaining effective communications, performing experiments, exercising, eating, and drinking were all possible there. Like that of Vostok 1, the flight of Vostok 2 confirmed that launch and atmospheric reentry, while less than pleasant, were endurable. For example, a cosmonaut could still speak while experiencing the high forces of acceleration. Furthermore, the Vostok systems designed to provide vital electricity, climate control, and oxygen all performed well for a second time. The reentry procedure and landing technique were perfected. Not only could a cosmonaut be recovered, but he could be recovered at a specific time and place.

Gherman Titov experienced no serious lasting effects from the flight. His motion-related problems were attributed to violent movements of his head that affected his sense of balance. Titov's sleeping and his attempt to control his head motions during the latter portion of the flight helped alleviate the nausea. The cosmonaut's spacesickness was deemed an individual response. Aboard Mercury 6 six months later, John Glenn had no such problems during orbital flight.

Unlike the American Mercury capsule, the Vostok was spin-stabilized. The cosmonaut training program involved some brief simulations of weightlessness in a jet aircraft on a parabolic trajectory but was changed after Vostok 2 to include special exercises involving rapid head turns while the body was rotated about multiple axes. This training proved effective, as no later Vostok pilot complained of serious spacesickness. (Two crew members of Voskhod 1, who had had limited training, did experience the symptoms, as have numerous astronauts and cosmonauts, to a greater or lesser extent, ever since.)

The automated biomedical telemetry reported no other physiological problems during Titov's flight. Titov's pulse rate, respiration, and electrocardiogram remained consistent with their preflight values, when he was both awake and asleep. His heart rate was greatest, as expected, at launch; at that point, it reached 132 beats per minute.

That Titov could sleep for a normal duration while whirling about Earth, despite the stress and excitement associated with such an adventure, surprised even the most optimistic observers. The pilot's ability to relax so completely was a testament to the confidence he and others had developed in the automated life-support system and other safety systems aboard Vostok. The isolation of space, something for which the cosmonauts had spent days and weeks preparing inside an austere sound-proofed isolation chamber, proved to be less stressful than the simulation.

Rumors of the use of hypnosis and sleeping pills during the flight did not detract from the propaganda victory for the Soviet Union resulting from a Vostok flight that was successful in accomplishing all of its major objectives. The multiorbit mission made the suborbital spaceflights of the United States appear unsophisticated and unexciting in comparison.

## Context

Titov was welcomed back to Moscow with news conferences, a hero's parade in Red Square, and congratulations from the Soviet Union's foremost space promoter, Nikita Khrushchev. Sports commissioners quickly certified his spaceflight duration record for the International Astronautic Federation.

Major Titov remained involved with the Soviet space program; he was its popular spokesman for more than a decade. He also served as flight controller for the Salyut 3 mission in 1974. The former cosmonaut eventually attained the rank of lieutenant general.

After the flight of Vostok 2, space would no longer be considered a fundamentally hostile environment fit only for brief forays by the brave and strong. Indeed, Gherman Titov returned with a counterproposal: that space travel might actually be enjoyable.

Much of what is known of the Vostok 2 flight comes from Titov's popular book *"I Am Eagle!"* (1962). The book, whose title refers to his mission call sign, was written with the help of a ghostwriter and based on numerous interviews with the cosmonaut. Part autobiography, part propaganda, and somewhat removed from the actual words of the "author," it nevertheless provided the West's first detailed look at a Soviet manned space mission at a time when flight specifics were closely guarded.

It would be several years until an actual Vostok spacecraft would be displayed publicly and American astronautics experts would get an inside view of how their Eastern counterparts had solved the engineering problems involved in manned orbital spaceflight. Then they would learn that the Soviet technical innovations were often quite similar to those used to perfect their own spacecraft.

While Yuri Gagarin's flight had come as a shock to the American space program, some dismissed it as a stunt performed with crude engineering and brute rocket force. Late in 1961, a Soviet cosmonaut successfully traveled over most of the United States during seventeen orbits of spaceflight; at the same time no American had so much as circled the globe once. It could not be ignored that the Soviet Union had achieved a technical sophistication in space that the United States had not exhibited. While some personnel from the famous German rocketry program of

World War II had been brought to the East, the "cream" of the German rocket scientists had ended up working on the American space program—a fact which made the Soviet successes even more impressive.

As more and more Soviet accomplishments in space became known, morale within the astronautics community in the United States dropped. It was in this atmosphere that President John F. Kennedy gave direction to the American program with his goal of landing a man on the Moon. This act drew attention away from the sprint to space, a race the Soviets had clearly won, and toward a longer, more significant competition in which only the first steps had been taken.

## Bibliography

Blaine, James C. *The End of an Era in Space Exploration: From International Rivalry to International Cooperation*. San Diego: Univelt, 1976. This chronicle of the early years of space exploration places the Vostok missions in proper chronological perspective with other manned and unmanned programs. Relatively few pages are devoted to the individual Vostok flights themselves; the book's merit lies in the fact that mission highlights are printed in italics for quick reference. The reading level is nontechnical. Illustrations are included, but there are none covering the Vostok program. This work is published as volume 42 of *Science and Technology*, edited by H. Jacobs.

Cassutt, Michael. *Who's Who in Space: The First Twenty-five Years*. Boston: G. K. Hall and Co., 1987. This series of biographies sketches the life of every space traveler from Yuri Gagarin through 1986. Each biography is approximately one page long, and most include a photograph of the cosmonaut or astronaut. Those who participated in the Soviet space program are allotted coverage equal to that given to the Americans. Each alphabetical entry is written in a standard biographical format.

McAleer, Neil. *The Omni Space Almanac: A Complete Guide to the Space Age*. New York: Pharos Books, 1987. This general-audience history of space travel is well formatted for easy reference. A description of the flight of Vostok 2 appears in a section titled "Life Above Earth: The First Year."

Nicholson, Iain. *Sputnik to Space Shuttle: The Complete Story of Space Flight*. New York: Dodd, Mead and Co., 1985. As its name implies, this book compares the histories of the manned space programs of the United States and the Soviet Union. Its liberal use of quotations should be particularly interesting to the lay reader. A good photograph of a complete Vostok spacecraft is provided.

Riabchikov, Evgeny. *Russians in Space*. Edited by Nikolai P. Kamanin. Translated by Guy Daniels. Garden City, N.Y.: Doubleday and Co., 1971. The author's role as a documentary cinematographer for the Vostok and subsequent Soviet spaceflights makes this a unique, though not totally objective, resource. It is written from a personal point of view, and the author's style seems to have survived translation into English. Folios of photographs are inserted occasionally in the text; many of these are rarely published prints.

Shelton, William. *Soviet Space Exploration: The First Decade*. New York: Washington Square Press, 1968. Shelton was a Time-Life correspondent assigned to cover the early days of space exploration. His research, both in the United States and in the Soviet Union, makes this a most comprehensive review of the first ten years of Soviet spaceflight. The material is detailed, but Shelton's journalistic style should make it understandable enough to satisfy the serious reader regardless of his or her background. Twenty-six photographs and a bibliography complement the book.

Titov, Gherman S., and Martin Caidin. *"I Am Eagle!"* Indianapolis: Bobbs-Merrill, 1962. The title refers to Gherman Titov's radio call sign aboard Vostok 2. It is written in the first person, but this "autobiography" was actually assembled by well-known science writer Martin Caidin. Its significance is discussed in the text of this article. *"I Am Eagle!"* remains the only book about an individual cosmonaut and Vostok mission readily available in the United States. Illustrations are included.

Turnill, Reginald, ed. *Jane's Spaceflight Directory*. London: Jane's Publishing Co., 1987. The format is that of a spaceflight yearbook. The Jane's series is known for its accuracy, objectivity, and readability. New editions are published frequently. There is an article on Vostok and its missions. Photographs include views of Vostok reentry bodies both in the field immediately after landing and in more pristine conditions, on display at the Paris Air Show.

*Thomas Hockey*

## Cross-References

The Apollo Program, 28; Biological Effects of Space Travel on Humans, 188; Cosmonauts and the Soviet Cosmonaut Program, 273; Soviet Launch Vehicles, 742; The Mercury Project, 940; Mercury-Redstone 3: *Freedom 7*, 953; Mercury-Redstone 4: *Liberty Bell 7*, 960; Mercury-Atlas 6: *Friendship 7*, 967; The Solar Wind, 1382; Space Centers and Launch Sites in the Soviet Union, 1592; Spy Satellites, 1937; The Voskhod Program, 2170; The Vostok Program, 2177; Vostok 1, 2191.

# VOSTOK 3 and 4

*Date:* August 11 to August 15, 1962
*Type of mission:* Manned Earth-orbiting spaceflights
*Country:* The Soviet Union

*Vostok 3 and Vostok 4 were the first manned vehicles to orbit Earth simultaneously. The missions investigated spacecraft control, communications, and crew health during spaceflights lasting longer than one day.*

Principal personages
ANDRIAN G. NIKOLAYEV, the Vostok 3 pilot
PAVEL R. POPOVICH, the Vostok 4 pilot

## Summary of the Missions

Vostok 3 and Vostok 4 were assigned to examine two key problems of space travel: First, was it possible to operate two independent spacecraft in orbit at the same time, maintaining three-way communications between the two vehicles and the ground? Second, was spacesickness a necessary consequence of prolonged exposure to weightlessness? Thus, the joint Vostok 3 and Vostok 4 mission was a test of both man and machine.

After one year and five days of quiescence in its manned space program since the successful flight of Vostok 2, the Soviet Union launched Vostok 3 at 11:30 A.M. Moscow time, August 11, 1962, with Andrian G. Nikolayev, the backup pilot for Vostok 2, on board. What amazed the world was that Vostok 4 was launched not a year or months later but a day after Vostok 3: on August 12, at 11:02 A.M. Moscow time, while Vostok 3 was still in space on its seventeenth orbit. The pilot of Vostok 4 was Pavel R. Popovich, also a former member of the Vostok 2 team (as the cosmonauts' in-flight radio liaison with Gherman S. Titov). With Popovich's launch, the Soviet Union became the first country to fly more than one man in space at the same time.

There was concern before the twin launches about the potential effects of radiation released by the then-common high-altitude tests of nuclear explosives. An American test of this nature shortly before the launches prompted an unmanned satellite in the Kosmos series to be sent up first in order to test radiation levels. The Soviet Union requested that the United States abstain from such explosions while cosmonauts were in orbit. The United States replied that it intended to do nothing to endanger the crews of orbiting spacecraft. (The Soviets later said that the third and fourth Vostok launches were actually delayed because of residue radiation in near space from the last American nuclear test.)

Lift-off for Vostok 3 took place at the Tyuratam launch site. Pilot Nikolayev was placed in an orbit with its closest point to Earth (its perigee) at an altitude of 183 kilometers and its farthest point away from Earth (its apogee) at an altitude of

251 kilometers. The orbit was inclined to Earth's equator by 64 degrees, 50 minutes of arc, with a period of 88.3 minutes. All these parameters were quite similar to those for the Vostok 2 mission, as were those for Vostok 4. Popovich's Vostok left Tyuratam and went into an orbit with an apogee of 254 kilometers and a perigee of 180 kilometers. This path yielded a slightly longer period (88.4 minutes) than Nikolayev's. The inclination of the Vostok 4 orbit was close to 65 degrees. Physically, the spacecraft were nearly identical to the earlier Vostoks. Vostok 3 and Vostok 4 weighed 4,722 kilograms and 4,728 kilograms, respectively.

The team that had now assembled in space consisted of individuals with very different backgrounds. Nikolayev was a lumberjack from the Soviet Chuvash Republic who had been drafted into the army. Eventually, he was allowed to undergo flight training and discovered his skills as a pilot. Popovich, a Ukrainian, had once been a shepherd. As a youth, he suffered under German occupation. Afterward, he became an amateur pilot and volunteered for the Soviet air force in order to pursue his hobby as a career. In temperament, the pilots also differed greatly. The more introverted Nikolayev was a man of quintessential military demeanor. His coolness under stressful and dangerous conditions was almost legendary. Popovich, on the other hand, was a more gregarious sort; he typically engaged in light conversation. Whether intentionally or not, the Soviets had devised an experiment that would simultaneously test the effects of the extraordinary space experience on two very different personalities.

In the West, the first thoughts about this mission were that the Soviets might attempt an actual rendezvous, even a docking, of the two manned vehicles. Rendezvous and docking were considered to be vital capabilities for any sustained future human presence in space and for carrying out journeys of exploration to the Moon and beyond. In a few years' time, the American Gemini program would practice these skills many times. It is unlikely, however, that the technological ability to perform such activities existed anywhere in the world in 1962. Vostoks 3 and 4 did not attempt to rendezvous. The slight differences in their orbits were enough to preclude this, and neither spacecraft possessed maneuvering rockets to alter its orbit after the booster stages had shut down. (The Vostok retro-rockets were not designed to raise an orbit.) Was this a failed experiment? Were the two orbits dissimilar because of launch error? Soviet statements that the objective of the two Vostoks was to establish a "direct link" added to the confusion.

It eventually became clear that no rendezvous or docking exercise was ever planned for Vostok. The Vostok spacecraft lacked both a radar range finder for negotiating rendezvous and any mechanism for physically coupling two craft. The "direct link" evidently referred only to radio communication between the two vehicles.

Even though the orbits of Vostoks 3 and 4 did not cross, the two spacecraft came within 6.5 kilometers of each other shortly after Vostok 4 was launched. This launch was timed so that it occurred just as tracking data indicated that Vostok 3 was passing over the launch site. The two vehicles would have come even closer to each other if Vostok 4's speed had been slightly less, but as this close a flyby was the result solely of precision launching it was a legitimate feat. Reportedly, the synchronized launches were both within one second of those called for in the flightplan. For a brief time the two cosmonauts had visual contact with each other's vehicle. Each spacecraft looked like a small moon to the occupant of the other. While both were in orbit, the cosmonauts maintained regular radio communication with each other. (The farthest separation between the two Vostoks was 3,000 kilometers.) Nikolayev's radio call sign was Sokol (meaning "falcon"); Popovich's was Berkut (meaning "golden eagle"). Their exchanges were not always work-related; on at least one occasion they sang a song together.

During the time they were both in space, Nikolayev and Popovich followed the same schedule. Their ability to communicate with each other enabled them to perform the same activities at the same time. The purpose of this parallel routine was to test to what extent spacesickness was an individual reaction. Under duplicated circumstances, would the independent sources of medical data respond differently? Particularly, would either of the cosmonauts report vertigo or nausea in their sixth or seventh orbit, as Gherman Titov had aboard Vostok 2? In the case of Vostoks 3 and 4, there was no difference in response. Neither cosmonaut reported any such symptoms during any orbit of the lengthy flights (though Popovich later mentioned some mild disorientation).

Popovich, on Vostok 4, spent a total of 71 hours in space, far surpassing Titov's record on Vostok 2. This would have established a new record except for the fact that Nikolayev, on Vostok 3, spent 94 hours and 20 minutes in space—four times longer than Titov's flight. Much of the cosmonauts' time in orbit was occupied by the same activities that had been hastily performed by the pilots of Vostok 1 and Vostok 2 on their brief voyages. Detailed logs were kept, and radio reports were transmitted regularly. Observations, films, and still photographs were made of stars, the Moon, and Earth. The cloud formations below them particularly held the attention of the two men.

Multiple live television broadcasts took place for the first time. The new Vostoks came equipped with two television cameras: one that looked directly at the seated cosmonaut and one that obtained a profile view. Nikolayev and Popovich performed tricks with articles floating in their cabins in order to demonstrate the effects of a weightless environment to the audience back on Earth.

While previous Vostok crews had remained strapped in their seats, these cosmonauts unfastened themselves in order to stretch and exercise during their multiday missions. Nikolayev was the first to do so; he floated free in his spacecraft cabin for more than three hours. Also, unlike those of Vostoks 1 and 2, the crews of Vostoks 3 and 4 were able to take off their protective but cumbersome spacesuits for intervals of time. Cosmonaut Popovich made forty-eight circumnavigations of Earth, a distance of 1,981,100 kilometers. He was far outdistanced by Nikolayev's 2,639,600 kilometers during sixty-four orbits.

On August 15, 1962, both Nikolayev and Popovich returned to Earth. Both Vostok spacecraft fired their retro-rockets while over Africa and parachuted to the ground east of the Ural Mountains. The landing sites were in the Karaganda region of Kazakhstan, 2,400 kilometers southeast of Moscow: Vostok 3 in the vicinity of Karkaralinsk and Vostok 4 near Atasu. In an incredible demonstration of flight control efficiency, the vehicles came to rest 193 kilometers apart within six minutes of each other. (Both men elected to use the alternate landing method of ejecting from the Vostok reentry body just before touchdown and parachuting to the ground separately from their craft.)

Andrian Nikolayev, the new record holder for spending the longest time in space, went on to command the Soyuz 9 mission in 1970, which lasted nearly eighteen days. Between flights he was head of the cosmonaut team. Pavel Popovich commanded Soyuz 14, which docked with the Salyut 3 space station for sixteen days. He was also the flight controller for other Salyut missions. Both men became actively involved in the training of other cosmonauts, and both eventually attained the rank of major general.

## Knowledge Gained

The duet in space that was the Vostok 3 and Vostok 4 mission demonstrated a capability for precision launching and recovery in manned spaceflight. The ability to put more than one Vostok in approximately the same orbit brought nearer to reality the possibility of putting components of complex spacecraft and space stations into orbit and then bringing them together there for final assembly. As space assembly of a vehicle was one route to implementing a manned mission to the Moon, the Soviets seemed to be nearer that goal with the successful completion of the joint mission of 1962. Hints continued to reach the West that this was indeed the Soviet Union's objective. At the same time, the Soviets were also demonstrating a military capability: Putting one vehicle in space near another meant that satellite interception was possible and that antisatellite weapons could reach their targets.

The pilots of Vostok 3 and Vostok 4 retained all of their abilities to perform necessary tasks during prolonged weightlessness and extended flight. They ate well, slept soundly, and enjoyed the scenery out their windows during off hours. All the while, biomedical telemetry remained normal.

For flights of three and four days' duration, cosmonaut food had transcended the paste and liquid stage. By and large, the men ate natural foods: meat pies, chicken fillets, caviar sandwiches, roast veal, fresh fruit, and dessert candies, for example. All these items were cut into small pieces and wrapped in cellophane packages. In turn, several small packages were placed in a container that represented a single meal. The foods were augmented by vitamins. The cosmonauts gave their space cuisine high marks.

The cosmonauts' water supplies were individualized. Water from the man's geographical home region was provided for him, treated only for preservation. Filtered drinking water was always available on demand through a tube and mouthpiece at the touch of a button. The water, too, tasted completely natural to the cosmonauts, despite the presence of bactericidal and deodorizing agents.

One article that did not accompany the cosmonauts was the toothbrush. A special gargling solution took its place. Washing was satisfactorily accomplished with a cloth soaked in a soaplike solution.

Debilitating spacesickness became less of a worry to space physicians after Vostok 3 and Vostok 4. The side-by-side physiological analysis of the two pilots further showed that adaptation to space was an individual response that could be enhanced by proper training. As spaceflights became more sophisticated, it was becoming clear that people could actually live in space and not merely exist there. While Nikolayev and Popovich were physically isolated during their missions, their ability to see each other's spacecraft and converse by radio had a positive psychological effect. At least one thing was clear: that future space exploration would and should be a corporate endeavor.

## Context

During the Vostok flights, the Soviet space program had remained secretive. Announcement of the existence of Vostok 3 came seventy minutes after lift-off, though days before the launch there had been rumors of some impending Soviet space spectacular. Experts in the West had expected it to be merely an extension of Gherman Titov's space endurance record, not a joint flight.

The Vostok 3 mission did accomplish a medium-duration flight in impressive fashion. Though the United States had managed to place two Mercury capsules into orbit since Vostok 2—John Glenn (Mercury 6) and Scott Carpenter (Mercury 7) had both undertaken three-orbit flights—Andrian Nikolayev's four-day record for the Soviet Union contrasted dramatically with the American one of five hours. It would not be until 1963 that an American—L. Gordon Cooper, aboard Mercury 9—would spend more than a single day in space. A journey to the Moon would last several days and, in 1962, the Soviets seemed to be ahead in the technological race to get there.

The major Soviet space achievement of 1962, the simultaneous orbits of the Vostok 3 and Vostok 4 spacecraft, was interpreted as a prelude to proper rendezvous and docking in space. These maneuvers were expected soon—perhaps on the very next pair of flights. The military implications of this latter feat, even more than the perfection of long-duration space trips, helped to encourage the channeling of more money into the American space program. Ironically, it would be the Americans who would first rendezvous and dock manned spacecraft. Yet these events would not occur until 1965 and 1966, respectively.

Meanwhile, the successful Vostok missions continued to be touted by the Soviets as evidence of the success of the Communist system. New postcolonial nations of the Third World were especially targeted for this message, and the overflight of these countries by manned Soviet spacecraft provided a splendid propaganda opportunity. The fact that Vostok was a spin-off of a major weapons delivery system— the intercontinental ballistic missile (ICBM)—was downplayed (as was the similar connection between Project Mercury and the Atlas ICBM by the United States).

Easily forgotten in the attention given the Vostok program during 1962 was the increasing momentum of the Soviet unmanned space program taking place simultaneously. In that year alone, the Semyorka rockets that lifted Vostoks 3 and 4 into space also carried eighteen satellites and space probes into space. These missions included a successful first-time flyby of the planet Mars. Working anonymously as far as the rest of the world was concerned, the brilliant Chief Designer, Sergei Korolev, and his colleagues continued to produce the hardware necessary to extend the presence of the hammer-and-sickle emblem further into space.

## Bibliography

Blaine, James C. *The End of an Era in Space Exploration: From International Rivalry to International Cooperation*. San Diego: Univelt, 1976. A chronicle of the early years of space exploration, this volume places the Vostok missions in proper perspective, in the context of other manned and unmanned programs. Relatively few pages are devoted to the individual Vostok flights themselves, but the book serves as a useful reference for mission highlights, which are printed in italics. Includes illustrations (although none cover the Vostok program). Written in nontechnical language.

Cassutt, Michael. *Who's Who in Space: The First Twenty-five Years*. Boston: G. K. Hall and Co., 1987. This series of biographical sketches covers the lives of every space traveler through 1986. Each one-page biography includes a photograph of the cosmonaut or astronaut. The Soviet space program receives coverage equal to that given the American space program.

Lewis, Richard S. *From Vinland to Mars: A Thousand Years of Exploration*. New York: Times Books, 1976. Though not obvious from its title, *From Vinland to Mars* contains more material on the early Soviet manned spaceflights than do some texts dedicated strictly to the history of space exploration. The Vostok 3 and Vostok 4 missions, which are often slighted in accounts of the Vostok program, are given much the same coverage as more sensational flights such as Vostok 1 or Vostok 6. The book is intended for a general audience. It is illustrated and includes a bibliography.

McAleer, Neil. *The Omni Space Almanac: A Complete Guide to the Space Age*. New York: Pharos Books, 1987. A general history of space travel, this volume is organized with various column headings and subheadings, making it easy to follow. Contains a description of the flights of Vostoks 3 and 4. Illustrated.

Nicholson, Iain. *Sputnik to Space Shuttle: The Complete Story of Space Flight*. New York: Dodd, Mead and Co., 1985. This book compares the histories of the manned space programs of the United States and the Soviet Union. Quotations are used liberally, making this volume especially interesting for the layman.

Riabchikov, Evgeny. *Russians in Space*. Edited by Nikolai P. Kamanin. Translated by Guy Daniels. Garden City, N.Y.: Doubleday and Co., 1971. The author, a documentary cinematographer for the Vostok and subsequent Soviet spaceflights, offers a unique though not totally objective perspective. Written from a personal point of view and translated into English. Folios of rarely reproduced photographs are inserted periodically in the text.

Shelton, William. *Soviet Space Exploration: The First Decade*. New York: Washington Square Press, 1968. William Shelton, a Time-Life correspondent assigned to cover the early days of space exploration, researched this book both in the United States and in the Soviet Union; it is a most comprehensive review of the first ten years of Soviet spaceflight. Although the material is detailed, Shelton makes it understandable to the general reader. Contains twenty-six photographs and a bibliography.

Turnill, Reginald, ed. *Jane's Spaceflight Directory*. London: Jane's Publishing Co., 1987. The Jane's spaceflight yearbook series is known for its accuracy, objectivity, and readability. There is an article on Vostok and its missions. Photographs include views of Vostok reentry bodies both in the field immediately after landing and in more pristine condition on display at the Paris Air Show.

*Thomas Hockey*

## Cross-References

The Apollo Program, 28; Biological Effects of Space Travel on Humans, 188; Food and Diet for Space Travel, 454; Gemini 6A and 7, 514; Gemini 8, 520; Soviet Launch Vehicles, 742; Mars 2 and 3, 891; Mercury-Atlas 6: *Friendship 7*, 967; Mercury-Atlas 7: *Aurora 7*, 973; Mercury-Atlas 9: *Faith 7*, 985; Soyuz 9, 1431; Soyuz 14 and 15, 1454; Space Centers and Launch Sites in the Soviet Union, 1592; The Sputnik Program, 1930; Venera 1-6, 2091; The Vostok Program, 2177; Vostok 1, 2191; Vostok 2, 2198; Vostok 5 and 6, 2212.

# VOSTOK 5 and 6

*Date:* June 14 to June 19, 1963
*Type of mission:* Manned Earth-orbiting spaceflights
*Country:* The Soviet Union

*Vostok 5 and Vostok 6 continued the investigations begun during previous Vostok missions in spacecraft control, communications, and crew health during spaceflights lasting longer than one day. The effects of the space environment on both male and female biology were compared for the first time.*

Principal personages
VALERI F. BYKOVSKY, the Vostok 5 pilot
VALENTINA V. TERESHKOVA, the Vostok 6 pilot

## Summary of the Missions

In June, 1963, two Vostok spacecraft were launched into space. This joint mission was a more sophisticated version of that conducted by Vostok 3 and 4 one year before. The major interest in Vostok 6 lay in its crew. For the first time, a woman traveled into space.

Valentina Vladimirovna Tereshkova was a textile worker from Yaroslavl, a small city on the Volga River. Her hobby was parachute jumping. Upon hearing of Yuri Gagarin's first manned spaceflight, she resolved to become a cosmonaut herself and boldly wrote to Moscow describing her qualifications. Fortuitously, Moscow was looking for the first group of female cosmonauts. There were few female pilots in the Soviet Union at the time, so women with parachute experience (and thus familiarity with free-fall) were especially valued. Tereshkova was chosen for cosmonaut training along with three other women. She was subjected to all the tests that the men had undergone—Tereshkova was the first woman to ride in a centrifuge designed to simulate the strong forces encountered during launch and reentry—and also received fundamental aircraft flight training that eventually included the flying of jets. She was commissioned a junior lieutenant in the Soviet air force.

Eventually, Tereshkova was assigned to pilot Vostok 6. Her radio call sign would be Chaika (meaning "seagull"). Chaika was launched at 12:30 P.M. Moscow time on June 16, 1963, while Vostok 5, on its thirty-first revolution, passed overhead. Vostok 5 was piloted by Yastreb (meaning "hawk"), Valeri Fyodorovich Bykovsky of the Soviet air force. Bykovsky was a native of a Moscow suburb. He had been a pilot since secondary school. Following the pattern established during previous Vostok missions, Bykovsky had been Andrian Nikolayev's backup for Vostok 3.

Vostok 5 had been launched at 3:00 P.M. on June 14, 1963, after a one-day delay, reportedly the result of high winds at the launch site. Vostok 5 traveled in an orbit varying between 181 and 235 kilometers above Earth. It went around Earth once every 88.4 minutes on an elliptical path inclined 65 degrees to Earth's equator. A slightly shorter period would have matched that of Vostok 6 (88.3 minutes). This small difference in elliptical paths caused analysts to wonder whether a launch error had preempted an attempt to rendezvous two spacecraft in the same orbit. Such a rendezvous would have been theoretically possible with the thousandth-of-a-second launch precision obtainable by Soviet ground controllers, but a rendezvous was never part of the official Vostok 5/Vostok 6 flight plans.

Instead, a mission very similar to that performed by Vostoks 3 and 4 was flown. Vostok 6 was placed in an orbit inclined similarly to that of Vostok 5, 183 kilometers high at its perigee and 233 kilometers high at its apogee. The two spacecraft were within 5 kilometers of each other on Vostok 6's first orbit, but this distance increased as the flights progressed. The Vostok 5 spacecraft weighed 4,720 kilograms; Vostok 6 was 7 kilograms lighter.

Bykovsky and Tereshkova settled in for what was by now a routine mission of scientific experiments, observations, reports, regular exercise, rest, and meals. Some of these tasks varied from those of previous missions only in complexity; many of the onboard experiments conducted by the cosmonauts required considerable dexterity. The two cosmonauts communicated with each other frequently by radio. Television and radio transmissions were sent back to Earth. During her fourth orbit, Tereshkova spoke with Soviet Premier Nikita Khrushchev. Over North America, Bykovsky sent a special greeting to citizens of the United States.

Tereshkova remained strapped in her seat throughout her mission, though the chair slid on tracks to any orientation required to conduct business about the Vostok cabin. Bykovsky left his seat for a period of ninety minutes on each day of his flight. On his eighteenth orbit, he put on a special "performance" for the television audience in which he and other objects floated freely past the onboard cameras.

The cosmonauts continued tests of the manual controls in their spacecraft that had begun during the Vostok 2 flight. They monitored and operated internal systems. Earth's surface, the Moon, stars, and the spectrum of the Sun were photographed. Motion pictures were made. Automatic telemetry broadcast biomedical information about the two cosmonauts. All told, Vostoks 5 and 6 produced more scientific and technical data than did any previous mission.

Much of this information was medical in nature. The cosmonauts underwent physiological and psychological testing directed from the ground. These tests included specific experiments that they performed on themselves to study the effects of a weightless state on the inner ear, where the body's sense of balance is maintained. Indeed, medical experiments were the focus of the Vostok 6 mission. Would space travel affect a woman's body differently from the way it affected a man's? The space adaptation of Tereshkova was directly compared to that of Bykovsky in Vostok 5. Her reactions to all experiments and situations were carefully observed by physicians on Earth.

As the Vostok 5 and 6 flights were to be the longest yet undertaken, more time had been spent engineering the Vostok cabin for comfort. Further alterations had had to be made to accommodate female anatomy. Radiation dose accumulation was especially monitored as both missions proceeded. Tereshkova was originally scheduled to spend one day in space. Her mission went smoothly enough, though, that a request for a two-day extension was quickly granted. The Vostok 6 pilot spent 70 hours and 50 minutes in space. During this time, her spacecraft made forty-eight orbits of Earth and traveled a distance of 2 million kilometers.

On June 19, Vostok 6 parachuted to a site 620 kilometers northeast of the city of Karaganda in northern Kazakhstan, 2,000 kilometers southeast of Moscow. Tereshkova, who ejected from the Vostok reentry body just before reaching the ground, landed only 400 meters away from her spacecraft. She sustained a slight bruise on her nose during the fall. The cosmonaut was greeted by a crowd that included many children from the nearby countryside. Later, she would be met by the recovery crew and whisked off to Moscow for the now-traditional meeting with Khrushchev and a ceremony and reception at the Kremlin.

The attention given Valentina Tereshkova almost eclipsed the flight of Vostok 5. The joint flight had lasted almost three days, yet at the time of Vostok 6's landing at 11:20 A.M., Valeri Bykovsky was still in space. Almost without notice, he was establishing a new space endurance record of 119 hours and 6 minutes—nearly five days. This record would stand for two more years, until the flight of Gemini 5. No one would spend as much time alone in space as Bykovsky did. In eighty-one orbits, he covered more than 3 million kilometers by himself. Even so, the Vostok 5 pilot requested, but was denied, permission to extend his mission.

The Vostok 5 odyssey ended five hours and forty-six minutes after that of Vostok 6. Bykovsky and his spacecraft landed 540 kilometers northwest of Karaganda, 800 kilometers from the Vostok 6 landing site. Like each cosmonaut since Yuri Gagarin, Bykovsky avoided a hard landing by ejecting from the Vostok before it hit the ground and parachuting down separately. He was uninjured.

With Bykovsky back on Earth, the Vostok program came to an end. In total, Vostok spacecraft had made 259 orbits of the globe, and their crews had accumulated more than 382 hours in space. Bykovsky was scheduled to command a test flight of the new Soyuz spacecraft in 1967, but Soyuz 2 was canceled as a manned mission after the fatal crash landing of Soyuz 1. Also, he was to be involved with a manned flight around the Moon, but that mission, too, was canceled—as was the Soviet program for manned lunar exploration. Bykovsky was the backup pilot for Soyuz 13 in 1973 and training director for the Apollo-Soyuz Test Project flown in 1975.

Although Bykovsky's activities in the Soviet space program were ground-based for more than a dozen years following his Vostok assignment, he spent more time in space during a two-year period in the latter 1970's than he did while setting the endurance record aboard Vostok 5 in 1963. Bykovsky commanded Soyuz 22 in 1976 and Soyuz 31 in 1978. In his three spaceflights, Bykovsky accrued a total of twenty-one days in orbit.

Tereshkova did not remain with the Soviet space program. Despite rumors that she had originally been the backup pilot for Vostok 6 and only took her place in history when the more experienced primary pilot failed to pass her last preflight physical examination, and despite rumors that Tereshkova suffered disorientation and was spacesick for much of her mission, the Vostok 6 pilot became an instant heroine in the Soviet Union and abroad. She made frequent public appearances after her return to Earth, traveled extensively, and, though she still spoke of future spaceflights to the Moon and beyond, eventually left astronautics for the world of politics. Tereshkova became a member of the Supreme Soviet in 1966 and was named to the Central Committee in 1971.

## Knowledge Gained

The last two Vostoks continued the engineering tests of Soviet manned space hardware begun two years earlier. Life-support, communications, and control systems all held up well. Confidence in the Soviet ability to operate two craft in space at the same time was solidified with these successful flights. Launch and recovery accuracy now seemed routine.

The spaceflight-to-spacecraft radio link worked as expected and proved especially important to the cosmonauts. They would otherwise have been completely isolated when outside the Soviet radio receiving network, which at that time extended only over the vicinity of Europe and Asia.

The amount of scientific data generated by the two missions introduced the concept of orbiting laboratories with human experimenters functioning efficiently. Foremost, Vostok 5 and Vostok 6 continued the study of the effects of space on the human body undertaken during the previous four Vostok missions. Female biology in space was examined aboard Vostok 6, while long-term space exposure was the emphasis of Vostok 5. Neither radiation nor weightlessness appeared to be detrimental to either man or woman, and plans for even longer missions were approved because of the success of these two flights.

Late in 1963, a long-suspected love affair between Valentina Tereshkova and Vostok 3 pilot Andrian Nikolayev proved to be true. The two celebrities were married on November 3 in a large state wedding. The event was covered by the world press, and Nikita Khrushchev gave away the bride. Tereshkova gave birth to a daughter the next year. This opportunity to study the effect of space on human reproduction in a case where both parents had made lengthy orbital flights was enough of a medical coup to inspire cynics to suggest that the romance had actually been encouraged by the government. (The couple were divorced in 1982.)

Nevertheless, the question to be answered was a real one: Would the cosmic radiation to which both Nikolayev and Tereshkova had been subjected affect genes? Apparently, the cosmic radiation did not affect the pilots' genes. The baby girl, named Yelena Andrianovna, was born after a routine pregnancy and weighed a healthy 3 kilograms. In every respect she was a perfectly normal child.

While Valentina Tereshkova's presence in space was not intended solely as an experiment in human reproduction, her ability to bear healthy offspring soon after a spaceflight helped to lessen yet another fear about the potentially harmful effects of space. Her relative lack of training demonstrated the trust placed in the Soviet space program's new technology.

## Context

No other woman from the group with whom Tereshkova trained ever flew in space. The next female cosmonaut did not become a space traveler until 1982. For a while, it seemed that after it had been established that female physiology was not affected by space travel in any unforeseen way, women were no longer of interest to Soviet space science and the early cosmonaut program. Yet in sending a woman into space, the Soviets were motivated by the long-range goals of the Soviet space program.

While the Americans were hastily heading for the Moon, the Soviets were methodically proceeding toward a more distant future that involved a permanent human presence in space aboard space stations and, eventually, human inhabitation of the planets. Within colonies established on the Moon or Mars, women and entire families would have roles to play. Indeed, people with a variety of characteristics and abilities would be needed to make such ventures successful. The philosophy embodied in these long-range goals helps to explain the importance placed on group psychology in cosmonaut crew selection as well as the Soviet scientists' continual monitoring of human interaction in space. Indeed, this interest makes ideological sense in the light of the importance placed on cooperation in a Marxist state.

Clearly, Valentina Tereshkova's flight had enormous propagandistic value. It spotlighted the reality of the prominent role of women in most aspects of Soviet society. Feminist groups around the world pointed to a greater equality between the sexes in the Soviet Union that seemed to be exemplified by that country's space program. In the West, many tried to relegate cosmonaut Tereshkova to token status; yet two decades later, much attention would be given to the flight of the first American female astronaut.

The Vostok program had successfully sent six people individually into space and returned them safely. (Claims of amateur radio operators to have heard the cries of cosmonauts stranded or lost beyond Earth made garish news for tabloid presses but were unfounded.) Following the Vostok flights, more than a year elapsed before Soviet manned space missions resumed. Vostok's successor, Voskhod, was actually a modified Vostok spacecraft that could carry more than one cosmonaut. Solo spaceflights of the kind seen in the Vostok and Mercury programs would eventually become a thing of the past, as the operation of and demands made on vehicles in space became more complicated and dependent on control by their crews.

The next series of Soviet spaceflights built upon the pioneering work done by the Vostok program. Valeri Bykovsky's activities while unconfined in his cabin were preparatory to actually sending a man outside his spacecraft to float freely as an independent Earth satellite during a spacewalk. Such an event was forthcoming; it was performed for the first time by Alexei Leonov, a member of the Voskhod 2 crew, in 1965. Furthermore, the improvement in spacecraft maneuvering skills demonstrated during these flights would be relied on when manned vehicles would begin to rendezvous with each other in space, also beginning in 1965.

## Bibliography

Blaine, James C. *The End of an Era in Space Exploration: From International Rivalry to International Cooperation*. San Diego: Univelt, 1976. Blaine places the Vostok missions in their proper perspective, together with other manned and unmanned programs from the early years of space exploration. A valuable reference, the book features the inclusion of mission highlights printed in italics. Written for the layman.

Cassutt, Michael. *Who's Who in Space: The First Twenty-five Years*. Boston: G. K. Hall and Co., 1987. This series of sketches profiles every space traveler from Yuri Gagarin to those of 1986. Each biography is approximately one page long, and photographs accompany most of them. Participants in the Soviet space program are covered as thoroughly as those in the American program.

McAleer, Neil. *The Omni Space Almanac: A Complete Guide to the Space Age*. New York: Ballantine Books, 1987. A general history of space travel. Well organized, this volume describes the flights of Vostoks 5 and 6. Includes some illustrations.

Nicholson, Iain. *Sputnik to Space Shuttle: The Complete Story of Space Flight*. New York: Dodd, Mead and Co., 1985. A comparative history of the manned space programs of the United States and the Soviet Union. Its liberal use of quotations makes it especially accessible for the layman.

Riabchikov, Evgeny. *Russians in Space*. Edited by Nikolai P. Kamanin. Translated by Guy Daniels. Garden City, N.Y.: Doubleday and Co., 1971. Written from a personal point of view by a documentary cinematographer for the Vostok flights, this volume is a unique resource. Reproductions of rare photographs are inserted periodically in the text.

Shelton, William. *Soviet Space Exploration: The First Decade*. New York: Washington Square Press, 1968. A Time-Life correspondent assigned to cover the early days of space exploration, Shelton researched his book in both this country and the Soviet Union, making it a most comprehensive review of the first ten years of Soviet spaceflight. Detailed material, but Shelton's journalistic style should appeal to the general reader. Twenty-six photographs and a bibliography complement the text.

Smolders, Peter L. *Soviets in Space*. Translated by Marian Powell. New York: Taplinger Publishing Co., 1974. This recounting of the Soviet space program gives proportionately more attention to the flights of Vostoks 5 and 6 than to earlier missions. The author writes assuming no specialized knowledge on the part of the reader. Illustrated.

Turnill, Reginald, ed. *Jane's Spaceflight Directory*. New York: Jane's Publishing Co.,

1987. A spaceflight yearbook known for its accuracy, objectivity, and readability. Photographs include views of Vostok reentry bodies before and after launch.

*Thomas Hockey*

## Cross-References

The Apollo Program, 28; The Apollo-Soyuz Test Project, 132; Biological Effects of Space Travel on Humans, 188; Cosmonauts and the Soviet Cosmonaut Program, 273; Gemini 3, 494; Gemini 6A and 7, 514; Soviet Launch Vehicles, 742; The Mercury Project, 940; The Salyut Space Station, 1233; Soyuz 1, 1403; Soyuz 2 and 3, 1410; Soyuz 13, 1447; Space Centers and Launch Sites in the Soviet Union, 1592; The Vostok Program, 2177; Vostok 1, 2191; Vostok 3 and 4, 2205.

# THE VOYAGER PROGRAM

*Date:* Beginning August 20, 1977
*Type of program:* Unmanned deep space probes
*Country:* The United States

*The Voyager probes executed the first Grand Tour in planetary exploration by successively encountering Jupiter, Saturn, Uranus, and Neptune. Such a tour, using the "planetary-gravity-assist" technique to travel from planet to planet, is possible only once every 175 years.*

### Principal personages

MICHAEL A. MINOVITCH, the inventor of the gravity-assist concept
GARY A. FLANDRO, the discoverer of the 175-year period between Grand Tour alignments of the outer planets
EDWARD C. STONE, Voyager Project Scientist
CHARLES E. KOHLHASE, Principal Mission Designer
ELLIS D. MINER, Assistant Project Scientist
ANDREI B. SERGEYEVSKY, Principal Trajectory Designer for the Neptune encounter
BRADFORD A. SMITH, Principal Investigator, imaging science
G. LEONARD TYLER, Principal Investigator, radio science
HARRIS SCHURMEIER, Voyager Project Manager from project inception through development
JOHN R. CASANI, Voyager Project Manager from before launch through Jupiter-encounter preparations
RAYMOND L. HEACOCK, Voyager Project Manager for the Jupiter and Saturn encounters
RICHARD P. LAESER, Voyager Project Manager for the Uranus encounter
NORMAN R. HAYNES, Voyager Project Manager for the Neptune encounter

## Summary of the Program

Voyager conducted the first planetary Grand Tour in history. Two Voyager spacecraft were launched from Earth in 1977; Voyager 1 encountered Jupiter in 1979 and Saturn in 1980, and Voyager 2 encountered Jupiter in 1979, Saturn in 1981, and Uranus in 1986; it was projected to encounter Neptune in 1989. It is this latter sequence of planetary encounters that is called the Grand Tour.

The Voyager spacecraft used the "planetary-gravity-assist" technique to move from one planet to the next. Concepts of using gravity to propel a spacecraft from one body to another have existed since the 1920's. The actual technique of executing a gravity assist was not well understood, however, until Michael Minovitch developed it in the early 1960's.

With twentieth century technology, it is not possible to accomplish a Grand Tour unless the gravity-assist technique is used. The fuel requirements of a nongravity-assist tour are vastly beyond the existing technology. To illustrate, Voyager saved 1.5 million kilograms of fuel by using Jupiter's gravity to propel it toward Saturn. Similar amounts of fuel were saved at Saturn (using gravity assist to reach Uranus) and at Uranus (using gravity assist to proceed to Neptune).

The outer planets must be properly aligned or the tour is not possible. In 1966, Gary Flandro discovered that this alignment occurs only every 175 years, that the last alignment had occurred in 1802, and that the next time the planets would be properly aligned for a Grand Tour launch would be in 1977. The Voyager mission was designed to take advantage of that opportunity.

The National Aeronautics and Space Administration (NASA) authorized the Jet Propulsion Laboratory (JPL) in 1972 to start the Voyager project. Initially, only a four-year mission to Jupiter and Saturn, with a launch date in 1977, was funded. This circumstance led to the original name of the project: Mariner Jupiter Saturn 77 (MJS77). In 1977, the name of the project was changed to Voyager.

Two spacecraft were to visit Jupiter, then Saturn. If the Voyager 1 encounter with Saturn was successful, then Voyager 2 would be permitted to go on to Uranus and then Neptune. The Uranus option was authorized in 1981, the Neptune option in 1986.

The Voyager spacecraft, which were identical, used the Mariner spacecraft's decagonal shape. The ten bays housed electronics boxes. In the middle was a fuel tank for the propulsion system. Attached to one end was a large communication antenna for receiving spacecraft commands from Earth and for transmitting data back to it. Also attached were two deployable booms. At the end of one lay the three nuclear power plants that provided the electrical power to run the spacecraft. Along the sides and at the end of the other boom lay various scientific instruments.

The Voyager Grand Tour mission was one of scientific exploration. Each space-craft carried the same eleven instruments; the complete package included sensors that point at an object (target body instruments) and ones that make *in situ* mea-surements (field, particle, and wave instruments). The target body sensors included wide-angle and telephoto cameras, an infrared telescope, an ultraviolet telescope, an instrument to measure certain characteristics of light, and a radio transmitter to send radio signals through planetary atmospheres and rings back to Earth. The *in situ* sensors included a magnetic field sensor, a radio receiver, a plasma wave sensor, and three particle detectors.

The two spacecraft were to be launched from Titan-Centaur launch vehicles, approximately three weeks apart. The first spacecraft would be on a slower path to Jupiter and Saturn; the second would be on a faster path to the planets and thus would arrive first. As the order in which the spacecraft would encounter each planet was far more important than the order of launch, Voyager 2 was launched first, at 10:29:45 A.M. eastern daylight time on August 20, 1977, and Voyager 1 was launched second, at 8:56:01 A.M. on September 5, 1977.

Each spacecraft orbited Earth several times and then was injected onto a Jupiter-encounter path by a solid-fueled rocket. After burnout, all deployable booms were extended, and the spacecraft were thoroughly checked. Thirteen days after launch, Voyager 1 turned its telephoto camera toward Earth and shuttered the first image in history to contain both Earth and the Moon.

The Voyagers' first planetary encounter was with Jupiter. Two spacecraft had preceded the Voyagers there: Pioneers 10 and 11. Pioneer 10 had encountered the planet in 1973, and Pioneer 11 a year later. Neither spacecraft had an imaging camera, although each had an imaging photopolarimeter which could (and did) take rather crude photographs. It was left to Voyager to provide the first high-quality images of the solar system's largest planet.

Voyager 1 took exactly eighteen months to reach Jupiter, making its closest approach on March 5, 1979. Voyager 2 made its closest approach on July 9, 1979. Jupiter was known to have four huge moons (discovered by Galileo in 1610 and named "the Galilean satellites" in his honor) and nine smaller ones. The planet itself and the four large Galilean satellites were the main targets of interest; thus, the Voyager trajectories were designed to permit a close encounter with each of these five main bodies.

The planetary-gravity-assist technique was used by both Voyagers at Jupiter to propel the spacecraft on to Saturn. Before the Voyagers executed the gravity assist, they had been in an elliptical orbit about the Sun and Jupiter. After the maneuver, the spacecraft had enough energy to escape the gravitational pull of the Sun permanently. It was the gravity assist at Jupiter that started Voyager 2 on the Grand Tour.

The Voyagers' second planetary encounter was with Saturn. One spacecraft had preceded Voyager to Saturn: Pioneer 11, which had encountered Saturn on September 1, 1979. After a little more than twenty months of interplanetary cruising from Jupiter, Voyager 1 made its closest approach to Saturn on November 12, 1980. Voyager 2 followed nine months later, making its closest approach on August 25, 1981.

Saturn was known to have nine moons of varying sizes. Between the two spacecraft, close encounters with seven of the nine were made. One of the moons, Titan, which is much larger than the others, was known to have an atmosphere. Thus, there was the possibility of an environment capable of supporting life. For these reasons, Voyager 1 was targeted to pass within 4,000 kilometers of Titan's surface. Unfortunately, this close passage flung the spacecraft out of the plane of the ecliptic (the plane in which the planets orbit the Sun) at about a 35-degree angle, costing Voyager 1 the opportunity to encounter Uranus, Neptune, and Pluto.

Voyager 2's third planetary encounter was with Uranus, which had not yet been encountered by any spacecraft. After a four-year, four-month interplanetary cruise, Voyager 2 made its closest approach to Uranus on January 24, 1986. This planet is tilted on its side. As it orbits the Sun, first its northern pole, then its equator, then its southern pole, and then its equator points toward the Sun. When Voyager 2 encountered Uranus the planet's southern pole was pointed at the Sun.

Five moons were known to orbit Uranus about its equator. As Voyager 2 approached the southern pole, the five moons appeared to orbit the planet in concentric circles, creating a bull's-eye effect. Because of this geometric pattern, Voyager 2 could pass close to only one moon. Fortunately, the gravity assist required at Uranus for the trip to Neptune allowed the spacecraft to pass close to Miranda, the moon closest to Uranus.

The final Voyager 2 planetary encounter was to be with Neptune, and the spacecraft was projected to make its closest approach to the planet on August 25, 1989. Neptune is known to have one large moon, Triton, and one small one, Nereid. Of the two, Triton is known to have an atmosphere, and thus scientific interest in it is high. Voyager 2 was to come close to both bodies, receiving a final gravity assist at Neptune to bend the spacecraft's path by almost 45 degrees so that it could pass within 40,000 kilometers of the surface of Triton. This dual encounter would mark the end of the Grand Tour and begin Voyager's interstellar mission.

### Knowledge Gained

The Voyager mission provided the first high-quality visual study and the most comprehensive scientific investigation of the Jovian system until that time. The outer atmosphere of Jupiter is now known to be made up of about 89 percent hydrogen, about 11 percent helium, and trace amounts of many elements. Cloud-top lightning was observed at all latitudes on the dark side of the planet. At the place in the atmosphere where the pressure is the same as that at Earth's surface, the temperature is about $-108$ degrees Celsius. Voyager discovered a set of rings, no more than thirty kilometers thick, composed of fine particles.

For the first time, humanity knows what the surfaces of Jupiter's four major moons look like. On Io, nine volcanoes in the process of eruption were observed. Europa was observed to have the smoothest known surface in the solar system, with a difference in altitude between the highest peak and the lowest valley of two hundred meters or less. Ganymede proved to be the largest known moon in the solar system. Three new Jovian moons were discovered.

Jupiter's magnetic field is the largest of all the planets in the solar system. (The magnetic field of the Sun is larger.) At times Jupiter's magnetic field stretches beyond the orbit of Saturn. An electric current of more than five million amperes flows between Io and Jupiter.

Voyager also provided the first high-quality visual images and a highly comprehensive scientific study of the Saturnian system. The outer atmosphere of Saturn is now known to be made up of about 94 percent hydrogen, about 6 percent helium, and trace amounts of many other elements. Saturn radiates about 80 percent more energy than it receives from the Sun. Lightning was observed at low latitudes on the dark side of the planet. At the place in the atmosphere where the pressure is the same as that at Earth's surface, the temperature is about $-139$ degrees Celsius. Saturn's day is 10 hours, 39 minutes, and 15 seconds long.

Each of Saturn's three great rings (the A-, B-, and C-rings) actually contains many hundreds of thousands of ringlets. Pioneer 11's discovery of the thin F-ring was confirmed, and Voyager discovered two new rings: the diffuse D- and G-rings. Two small moons, one on either side of the thin F-ring, were discovered; the existence of these moons had been predicted before Voyager 1's encounter with Saturn.

An enormous crater, one-third Mimas' diameter, was discovered on Saturn's innermost major moon, Mimas. An even larger crater, 400 kilometers in diameter, was observed on Saturn's moon Tethys. The moon Enceladus has the second smoothest surface in the solar system. The moon Iapetus is half light and half dark, giving it the largest light-to-dark ratio of any body in the solar system. Voyager 1 established that Saturn's largest moon, Titan, is the second largest in the solar system. Titan's atmosphere has a near-surface pressure 1.5 times that of Earth, has a temperature of −179 degrees Celsius, and is composed of 90 percent nitrogen, with methane, argon, and trace carbon and hydrocarbon compounds making up the remaining 10 percent. Three new moons were discovered: the two moons on either side of the F-ring and a moon just outside the A-ring.

Saturn's magnetic field is aligned with its north pole to within one degree. A torus of hydrogen and oxygen ions that orbits Saturn is probably provided by the moons Tethys and Dione. Titan provides its own orbiting torus of neutral hydrogen atoms.

As another first, Voyager provided the first encounter of any kind with the Uranian system. The quality of the visual imagery obtained and the completeness of its scientific investigation there were comparable to those attained at Jupiter and Saturn. For the first time, the appearance of the planet Uranus, its eleven rings, and its five major moons became known. The outer atmosphere of Uranus is now known to be made up of 85 percent hydrogen, about 15 percent helium, and trace amounts of many hydrocarbon compounds. Unlike Saturn, Uranus radiates only about one-third as much energy as it receives from the Sun. Lightning was also detected in Uranus' atmosphere. The Uranian day is 17 hours, 14 minutes, and 40 seconds long.

Voyager 2 discovered two new rings, both of them very thin. All eleven of Uranus' rings are thin (no more than 100 kilometers wide). Two moons, one on either side of the outermost (and thickest) Uranian ring, the epsilon ring, were discovered. These moons help confine the epsilon ring particles. Ten new moons (including the two discussed above) were discovered. The surface of Uranus' innermost major moon, Miranda, revealed nearly every type of geological process observed anywhere else in the solar system.

Voyager 2 discovered that Uranus has a magnetic field. The field is tilted by 58.6 degrees with respect to Uranus' north pole. In contrast to any other planet that has been explored, the magnetic field's center is offset from the center of Uranus by nearly one-third of the planet's radius.

The color of Neptune has already been determined to be almost the same as that of Uranus: aqua. Neptune's largest moon, Triton, appears to have an orange color.

## Context

Voyagers 1 and 2 were the third and fourth spacecraft to encounter Jupiter, and the second and third to encounter Saturn. Voyager 2 was the first spacecraft to encounter Uranus and was to be the first spacecraft to encounter Neptune. It was also the first spacecraft to go on the Grand Tour of the outer solar system.

The solar system contains one star, nine planets, more than fifty moons, thousands of asteroids, and hundreds of comets. Together, the two Voyager spacecraft used the planetary gravity assist a total of six times to encounter five of the nine planets and fifty-one moons. Voyager provided the first high-quality visual imagery of Jupiter and Saturn and the first imagery of any kind of the moons of Jupiter, the rings and moons of Saturn, the planet Uranus and its rings and moons, and the planet Neptune and its rings and moons. An extensive scientific investigation of the four gas giants' systems was conducted.

Voyager conducted the first scientific reconnaissance of the entire outer solar system, contributing greatly to the understanding of the characteristics of the solar system's parts that is necessary before a full-fledged theory of the solar system can be developed. Such a theory would explain the creation and evolution of the entire system and each of its parts. The theory might then permit accurate predictions regarding the system's future evolution. The inhabitants of Earth have a vested interest in knowing what will happen to their planet. A well-supported theory of the solar system might also allow accurate predictions to be made of the density and characteristics of solar systems in the Galaxy and beyond.

## Bibliography

Beatty, J. Kelly, et al., eds. *The New Solar System*. Cambridge, Mass.: Sky Publishing, 1982. Gives a comprehensive description of the solar system, using the results of planetary exploration missions from all countries. Each of the twenty-one chapters is written by a pioneer in planetary exploration. Contains many illustrations and reproductions of images returned by planetary spacecraft. Suitable for general audiences.

Fimmel, Richard O., William Swindell, and Eric Burgess. *Pioneer Odyssey*. NASA SP-396. Washington, D.C.: Government Printing Office, 1977. Discusses the state of knowledge of the Jovian system before the Pioneer 10 and 11 encounters, the history of the Pioneer 10 and 11 missions, and the knowledge gained from the two spacecraft. Contains many illustrations, a list of project participants, and recommendations for further reading.

Fimmel, Richard O., James Van Allen, and Eric Burgess. *Pioneer: First to Jupiter, Saturn, and Beyond*. NASA SP-446. Washington, D.C.: Government Printing Office, 1980. This book is an update to *Pioneer Odyssey*, covering the Pioneer 11 encounter with Saturn and the mission after the planetary encounters. A more mature discussion of the knowledge gained from the Jupiter encounters is also provided. Contains many illustrations, images from both Jupiter and Saturn, a listing of project participants, and a bibliography.

Frazier, Kendrick. *Solar System*. Alexandria, Va.: Time-Life Books, 1985. Considers the state of knowledge about the solar system, starting with the Sun, working out to the inner terrestrial planets and the outer gas giants, and ending with the comets and asteroids. Also discusses what little is known about the beginning and evolution of the solar system and the galaxy. Contains many color illustrations, photographs, and charts.

Gallant, Roy A. *Our Universe*. Washington, D.C.: National Geographic Society, 1980. Treats the state of knowledge of the solar system, the Galaxy, and the rest of the universe. Also discusses the future of manned spacecraft. Contains many color illustrations and reproductions of images returned from various exploratory spacecraft.

Morrison, David. *Voyages to Saturn*. NASA SP-451. Washington, D.C.: Government Printing Office, 1982. Examines the state of knowledge of the Saturnian system before Pioneer 11 and gives an account of the Pioneer 11 encounter, the history of the Voyager mission, and the Voyager encounters. Contains many images returned by the Pioneer 11 and Voyager spacecraft, a list of Voyager project personnel and suggestions for additional reading.

Morrison, David, and Tobias Owen. *The Planetary System*. Reading, Mass.: Addison-Wesley Publishing Co., 1988. This is one of the most helpful books on planetary science; it was designed to be used in an introductory college course for nonscience undergraduates. Discusses the entire solar system, making reference to fundamental concepts from physics, astronomy, geology, and atmospheric science when necessary.

Morrison, David, and Jane Samz. *Voyage to Jupiter*. NASA SP-439. Washington, D.C.: Government Printing Office, 1980. Discusses the state of knowledge of the Jovian system before any of the spacecraft encounters; proceeds to give an account of the Pioneer encounters, the history of the Voyager project, the Voyager encounters, and the prospects for a return to Jupiter. Reproduces many images returned by the Pioneer and Voyager spacecraft and includes a list of the Voyager project personnel and suggestions for additional reading.

Trefil, James S. *Space, Time, Infinity: The Smithsonian Views the Universe*. New York: Pantheon Books, 1985. Explores the history of astronomy and the state of knowledge of the solar system, of the Galaxy, and of the universe. Predictions regarding the future of astronomy and the evolution of the solar system, the Galaxy, and the universe are made. Illustrated. Suitable for a general audience.

Yeates, C. M., et al. *Galileo: Exploration of Jupiter's System*. NASA SP-479. Washington, D.C.: Government Printing Office, 1985. Discusses the state of knowledge of the Jovian system and the design of the Galileo spacecraft (which was projected to orbit Jupiter), scientific instruments, and trajectory. Includes many photographs of parts of the Jovian system, a list of Galileo project personnel, and a list of references. Suitable for general audiences.

*William J. Kosmann*

**Cross-References**

# VOYAGER 1
## Jupiter

*Date:* March 5 to April 15, 1979
*Type of mission:* Unmanned deep space probe
*Country:* The United States

*Voyager 1 collected detailed information on the planet Jupiter, its rings, satellites, and surrounding environment, including detailed photographs of the four Galilean satellites: Io, Europa, Ganymede, and Callisto. Voyager 1 demonstrated the viability of building a complex, semiautonomous spacecraft capable of lasting more than a decade.*

*Principal personages*
HARRIS SCHURMEIER, the first Voyager Project Manager
RAY HEACOCK, Voyager Project Manager for the Jupiter encounter
EDWARD C. STONE, Voyager Project Scientist
ROCHUS E. VOGT, Principal Investigator, cosmic ray experiment
RUDOLF A. HANEL, Principal Investigator, infrared experiment
BRADFORD A. SMITH, Principal Investigator, imaging experiment
S. M. (TOM) KRIMIGIS, Principal Investigator, low-energy charged
   particle experiment
NORMAN F. NESS, Principal Investigator, magnetometer
   experiment
HERBERT S. BRIDGE, Principal Investigator, plasma science
   experiment
CHARLES W. HORD, Principal Investigator, photopolarimetry
   experiment
JAMES W. WARWICK, Principal Investigator, planetary radio
   astronomy experiment
FREDERICK L. SCARF, Principal Investigator, plasma wave
   experiment
G. LEONARD TYLER, Principal Investigator, radio science
   experiment
A. LYLE BROADFOOT, Principal Investigator, ultraviolet
   spectrometer experiment

## Summary of the Mission

The story of Voyager 1 began in 1966 at the Jet Propulsion Laboratory (JPL) in Pasadena, California, where a team of scientists and engineers conceived the idea of a Grand Tour of the outer planets. A spacecraft can use the gravity of one planet to speed up and deflect its trajectory toward another planet—a technique called gravity assist. In the late 1970's, Jupiter, Saturn, Uranus, and Neptune were all positioned in an arc on the same side of the Sun, making possible a gravity-assist trajectory from one planet to the next. This special alignment of planets occurs only once every 175 years.

To study the feasibility of a mission to the outer planets, the thermoelectric outer planet spacecraft (TOPS) group was formed. The TOPS group considered many problems posed in designing a spacecraft for the outer solar system. For example, the spacecraft would have to function at greater distances from the Sun and Earth than had any other spacecraft. Since a mission to the outer planets would take about ten years to complete, all parts in the spacecraft had to be designed to last that number of years or have a failproof backup system. The spacecraft needed to be more automatic and more independent than any previous spacecraft. Because the outer planets are so distant from Earth, it would take hours for engineers to correct a spacecraft malfunction.

When some of the more significant questions were answered, the Space Science Board, a group of appointed scientists, carefully studied the recommendations of the TOPS group. In 1969, a series of five separate outer planet missions to visit Jupiter, Saturn, Uranus, Neptune, and Pluto were recommended. At the same time, many other missions were competing for funds within the National Aeronautics and Space Administration (NASA) in Washington, D.C. Because of budget constraints in 1972, Congress approved a revised plan to build only three spacecraft. Voyager 1 would fly by both Jupiter and Saturn. If the Voyager 1 mission was a success, then Voyager 2 would be targeted to fly by not only Jupiter and Saturn but Uranus and Neptune as well. The third spacecraft would be built as a ground spare. To provide advance knowledge about the environments around both Jupiter and Saturn, two additional less complex spacecraft, Pioneer 10 and Pioneer 11, were separately funded and launched in 1972.

JPL was selected to implement the mission. The Mariner Jupiter Saturn 77 (MJS77) project, later renamed Voyager, began on July 1, 1972, under the management of Harris Schurmeier. When funds were authorized for the mission, NASA issued an "announcement of flight opportunity" to select the scientific instruments for the craft. Eventually, eleven instruments were built for Voyager 1. Edward C. Stone was selected as Project Scientist and charged with coordinating scientific activity. For Voyager 1's Jupiter flyby, Ray Heacock was Project Manager.

The Voyager 1 spacecraft was modeled on the Mariner spacecraft series, which had flown earlier to Venus and Mars. The spacecraft was about the size of a compact car. It weighed 825 kilograms, including 117 kilograms of scientific instruments. Voyager 1 was not a spinning spacecraft; it was stabilized on all three axes, using one sensor locked on the Sun and a second sensor locked on a star. Voyager 1 was a ten-sided aluminum structure, containing its key electronic elements inside its inner walls. The center of the structure contained a spherical propellant tank filled with hydrazine fuel. The fuel was used for trajectory corrections and to control the orientation of the spacecraft so that the high-gain antenna, 3.66 meters in diameter, pointed toward Earth.

The spacecraft was powered by three nuclear power sources, radioisotope thermal generators (RTGs) that produced about 400 watts of electrical power. A digital tape recorder could store about 500 million bits of information—equivalent to about one hundred images. The spacecraft was controlled by six onboard computers (two of each kind): the attitude and articulation control subsystem, the flight data subsystem, and the computer command subsystem. The attitude control subsystem controlled the stability and orientation of the spacecraft and the scan platform. The flight data subsystem provided instrument control for the scientific instruments and digital tape recorder and formatted the scientific and engineering data before they were sent to the ground. The computer command subsystem provided primary control of the spacecraft. These Voyager 1 computers could accept precoded sets of instructions that could provide autonomous operation for days or even weeks. These systems also included detailed instructions to detect and correct problems without human intervention.

On Labor Day, September 5, 1977, Voyager 1 was launched from Cape Canaveral, Florida, at 8:56 A.M. eastern daylight time, five days after the launch window had opened. The launch vehicle was a Titan 3E-Centaur rocket. Unexpectedly, the Titan main engine shut down early during the launch, and the Centaur stage had to make up the difference during the trajectory-insertion burn. After completing the insertion burn, the Centaur stage shut down with less than five seconds' worth of fuel left in its tank. If the launch had proceeded five days before, as scheduled, the thrust from the remaining fuel would not have been enough to allow Voyager 1 to reach Jupiter. With a little bit of luck, Voyager 1 was on its way to Jupiter.

During the autumn of 1977, a series of small problems challenged the JPL engineers. Attitude control thrusters fired at the wrong times, and sometimes the computer control systems overrode the commands from the ground. The onboard computers had been programmed to be too sensitive to slight changes on the spacecraft, and some reprogramming of the computers was necessary.

On February 23, 1978, the scan platform malfunctioned and prematurely stopped. This platform contained important remote-sensing instruments, and full mobility of the platform during the planetary flybys was essential. At JPL, tests were run on an exact copy of the scan platform. Slowly and carefully, the spacecraft platform was commanded to move, and normal operation was resumed. Engineers suspected that some material caught in the platform gears had been moved out of the way or crushed.

On January 4, 1979, the science-intensive Jupiter encounter began. Voyager 1 was now transmitting information not obtainable from Earth. For the next three months, Voyager 1 carried out a scientific survey of Jupiter, its satellites, and its magnetosphere. More than 30,000 images were transmitted to Earth during the encounter with Jupiter. Throughout the month of January, the Voyager 1 cameras sent back a series of images every two hours. The images were then turned into a color "motion picture" of Jupiter's weather patterns.

On February 28, Voyager 1 crossed Jupiter's bow shock—the boundary between the solar plasma that flows from the Sun (solar wind) and the planet's magnetosphere. Six hours later, the solar wind had pushed the magnetosphere back toward Jupiter, and Voyager 1 was once again in the solar wind. Over the next several days, variations in the solar wind pressure allowed Voyager 1 to cross the bow shock five times in all, as the Jovian magnetosphere repeatedly expanded and contracted.

A single eleven-minute imaging exposure of space, just above the equatorial cloud tops, was taken as the spacecraft passed through the plane of Jupiter's equator on March 4. Faint rings circling the planet were discovered. Close-range observations of the four Galilean satellites—Io, Europa, Ganymede, and Callisto—were made between March 4 and March 6. The closest flyby distances from each satellite were Io, 22,000 kilometers; Europa, 734,000 kilometers; Ganymede, 115,000 kilometers; and Callisto, 126,000 kilometers.

Voyager 1's closest approach to Jupiter took place on March 5, 1979, at 4:05 A.M. Pacific standard time. Thirty-seven minutes later, at 4:42, the signals from the spacecraft reached Earth. At 8:14, the spacecraft passed out of sight behind Jupiter, and the radio occultation of the Jovian atmosphere began. As the spacecraft flew behind Jupiter, the varying strength of the radio signal was used to probe the cloud structure in the atmosphere. Two hours later, Voyager 1 safely reappeared.

On March 5, during the period when it was closest to Jupiter, harsh radiation from the planet caused problems on the spacecraft. The main spacecraft clock slowed a total of eight seconds, and two computers were out of synchronization with the flight data subsystem computer. Some of the best images of Io and Ganymede were out of focus because the spacecraft started to move before the camera's shutter closed. Once the spacecraft moved farther away from Jupiter, this problem was corrected. On March 20, Voyager 1 crossed the Jovian bow shock, leaving Jupiter's magnetosphere and once again entering the solar wind. After a spectacular encounter with Jupiter, Voyager 1 was on its way for an encounter with Saturn on November 12, 1980.

## Knowledge Gained

Voyager 1's pictures of Jupiter provide details of a turbulent colorful atmosphere unlike any seen before. Images of Jupiter's Great Red Spot, a feature whose diameter is three times that of Earth and which is more than three hundred years old, reveal a huge hurricane-like storm towering above the surrounding clouds. White oval-shaped features about the size of Earth are other storms similar to the Great Red Spot.

Images of Jupiter reveal a stable zonal pattern of east-west winds. This planet-wide flow is more fundamental than the shifting cloud patterns within the east-west alternating belts (dark, deeper atmospheric regions) and zones (light, higher atmospheric regions). Within the belts and zones reside dark, brownish regions known as hot spots, holes in the uppermost cloud tops. These regions are warmer than the surrounding atmosphere, and both water vapor and germanium were discovered there. The minimum temperature on Jupiter was 110 Kelvins at 0.1 bar (on Earth, the surface pressure is typically 1.0 bar).

Cloud-top lightning bolts, similar to superbolts on Earth, were photographed, and radio-frequency emissions associated with the lightning were observed by the instrument for the planetary radio astronomy experiment. Auroral emissions in the polar region were seen in both the ultraviolet and the visible spectra.

With the imaging system, eight active sulfur volcanoes were discovered on the surface of Io, with plumes extending 250 kilometers above the surface. Tidal heating as a result of interactions with the other satellites and with Jupiter's powerful gravity melts the interior of Io, producing spectacular volcanoes. The moon's surface is uncratered and young because the volcanoes bring about continual resurfacing. The infrared instrument discovered hot spots on the surface of the satellite, and infrared scientists independently concluded that volcanoes existed there. Infrared measurements identified sulfur dioxide gas over the volcano named Loki.

Imaging observations showed numerous intersecting, linear features on the surface of Europa. Two distinct types of terrain, craters and grooves, characterize the surface of Ganymede. Ganymede was the the first body other than Earth to display evidence of tectonic activity. Callisto displays a heavily cratered surface.

Voyager discovered rings of material orbiting Jupiter, with an outer edge about 128,000 kilometers from the center of the planet. The rings consist of small, dusty particles. Two newly discovered satellites, Metis and Adrastea, are embedded in the rings and are probably the source of the tiny ring particles.

An electric current of more than one million amperes flows in a magnetic flux tube linking Jupiter and Io. An Io torus—an invisible "doughnut" containing ionized sulfur and oxygen circling Jupiter at Io's orbit—was discovered. Jupiter has unusual radio emissions at the kilometer wavelength which may be generated by plasma interactions with the Io torus.

Pioneer had shown that the magnetic field of Jupiter was dipolar, with a tilt of 11 degrees, and Voyager verified it. Both Pioneer and Voyager measurements showed that the magnetosphere of Jupiter is large. If viewed from Earth, it would be twice the size of the Moon at its fullest.

## Context

Voyager 1 was the third spacecraft to fly through the Jovian system and the first to take high-resolution pictures of all four Galilean satellites. Voyager 2 followed four months later. The flybys five years earlier had both been U.S. missions as well, Pioneer 10 and Pioneer 11.

In the late 1960's, Earth observations had established that Jupiter had an internal heat source. Pioneer investigations had confirmed this finding: Jupiter is still cooling from its initial collapse and formation. Infrared instruments aboard Pioneer had provided the first measurement of the ratio of hydrogen to helium on Jupiter, and Voyager was able to refine this value further. This ratio, roughly ten hydrogen atoms for every helium atom, is comparable to the value for the Sun, supporting the idea that Jupiter and the Sun have similar compositions.

Observations of Jupiter are important for the understanding of the origin and evolution of the solar system. Jupiter has an extremely large mass. Had it been roughly one hundred times more massive it would have formed a star. With the same basic composition as the Sun, Jupiter constitutes a sample of the original material from which the solar system formed.

The four large Galilean satellites form a miniature planetary system. Ranging in size from just larger than the planet Mercury (Ganymede and Callisto) to just smaller than the Moon (Io and Europa), these satellites decrease in density with increasing distance from Jupiter, as do the planets in the solar system with increasing distance from the Sun. With the exception of Callisto's, the surfaces on the other Galilean satellites are in general much younger than expected. Cratering records showed multiple periods of bombardment, interspersed with resurfacing.

Plans for a return to Jupiter focused on the Galileo spacecraft, a combined orbiter and probe. Galileo's projected launch date was spring or summer of 1989; it was to reach Jupiter about six years later. The probe would be sent into the atmosphere of Jupiter, and the orbiter was to circle the planet, recording data, during the two years of its prime mission. One final opportunity for a Jupiter flyby was to come with the Cassini mission to Saturn. The planned year of launch was 1996, with a Jupiter flyby in the year 2000. The gravity of Jupiter would be used to speed up and deflect the Cassini spacecraft toward Saturn.

Voyager established the viability of building a spacecraft to last a decade or more. Scientists expected that this technology would play a major role in the design of spacecraft for extended missions to the outer planets, craft that would relay information to Earth for many years.

Both Voyager and Pioneer expanded the frontier of the outer solar system. With the pictures and information sent back by Voyager, the Galilean satellites were transformed from pinpoints of light into tiny worlds. Jupiter's turbulent atmosphere provides a model against which Earth's circulation patterns can be compared. Still, Voyager 1 only began to address fundamental questions about the formation and evolution of Jupiter and planets in the outer solar system.

## Bibliography

Beatty, J. Kelly, et al., eds. *The New Solar System*. Cambridge, Mass.: Sky Publishing, 1982. Twenty chapters by distinguished researchers synthesize knowledge of the solar system. Findings on the Sun, the planets, the satellites, and the medium between are clearly discussed, with an emphasis on the discoveries of space probes such as Voyager.

Eberhart, Jonathan. "Jupiter and Family." *Science News* 115 (March 17, 1979): 164-165, 172-173. Highlights of Voyager 1's Jupiter encounter, particularly the discovery of volcanoes on Jupiter's moon Io, are described in this article published less than two weeks after the closest approach to Jupiter. Color photographs of Jupiter and its moons are included.

Gore, Rick. "Voyager Views Jupiter's Dazzling Realm." *National Geographic* 157 (January, 1980): 2-29. This readable article describes the findings of the Voyager

Jupiter flybys. Includes quotes from key individuals involved in the mission. Beautiful color images of Jupiter and the Galilean satellites are included.

Lauber, Patricia. *Journey to the Planets.* Rev. ed. New York: Crown Publishers, 1987. The history and physical character of the nine planets and their moons are described, including their differences and similarities. Photographs and observations from space probes, including Voyager, are discussed. Suitable for general audiences, including junior high school students.

Poynter, Margaret, and Arthur L. Lane. *Voyager: Story of a Space Mission.* New York: Macmillan, 1981. Relating stories of the people behind the scenes during the Voyager encounters with Jupiter, this book describes the process leading to mission selection and funding. The interactions between the scientists and engineers in building and flying the Voyager spacecraft are discussed, culminating in an inside look at the excitement and wonder of new discoveries about Jupiter. Suitable for junior high school and high school levels.

Simon, Seymour. *Jupiter.* New York: William Morrow and Co., 1985. This well-written book summarizes knowledge of the planet Jupiter in a format suitable for elementary levels and older. Twenty color photographs taken during the Voyager encounters highlight this introduction to Jupiter.

Soderblom, L. "The Galilean Moons of Jupiter." *Scientific American* 242 (January, 1980): 88-100. The four Galilean satellites, Io, Europa, Ganymede, and Callisto, are discussed in detail in this journal article. Physical characteristics of the satellites and the parameters of the Voyager flybys of each satellite are detailed. Possible evolution scenarios and cratering rates are outlined. Suitable for high school and college students.

*Linda J. Horn*

## Cross-References

Volcanic Activity on Io, 643; The Jet Propulsion Laboratory, 662; The Jovian System, 677; Jupiter's Atmosphere, 683; Jupiter's Great Red Spot, 690; Jupiter's Magnetic Field and Trapped Radiation, 697; Jupiter's Satellites, 704; Pioneer 10, 1130; Pioneer 11, 1138; Planetary Evolution, 1159; Comparative Planetology, 1168; The History of the Solar System, 1367; The Voyager Program, 2219; Voyager 1: Saturn, 2234; Voyager 2: Jupiter, 2241; Voyager 2: Saturn, 2248; Voyager 2: Uranus, 2255.

# VOYAGER 1
## Saturn

*Date:* November 12 to December 15, 1980
*Type of mission:* Unmanned deep space probe
*Country:* The United States

*On its second planetary flyby, Voyager 1 encountered Saturn and sent back to Earth information on the planet's rings, satellites, and atmosphere. In the process, the probe helped demonstrate that a complex spacecraft could last more than a decade while operating in space semiautonomously.*

*Principal personages*

HARRIS SCHURMEIER, the first Voyager Project Manager
RAY HEACOCK, Voyager Project Manager for the Saturn encounter
EDWARD C. STONE, Voyager Project Scientist
ROCHUS E. VOGT, Principal Investigator, cosmic ray experiment
RUDOLF A. HANEL, Principal Investigator, infrared experiment
BRADFORD A. SMITH, Principal Investigator, imaging experiment
S. M. (TOM) KRIMIGIS, Principal Investigator, low-energy charged particle experiment
NORMAN F. NESS, Principal Investigator, magnetic fields experiment
HERBERT S. BRIDGE, Principal Investigator, plasma science experiment
ARTHUR L. LANE, Principal Investigator, photopolarimetry experiment
JAMES W. WARWICK, Principal Investigator, planetary radio astronomy experiment
FREDERICK L. SCARF, Principal Investigator, plasma wave experiment
G. LEONARD TYLER, Principal Investigator, radio science experiment
A. LYLE BROADFOOT, Principal Investigator, ultraviolet spectrometer experiment

## Summary of the Mission

The Grand Tour of the outer planets in the solar system was conceived by a team of engineers and scientists working at the Jet Propulsion Laboratory (JPL) in Pasadena, California. A plan to build three spacecraft for a mission to the outer planets was approved by Congress in 1972. One of those spacecraft was Voyager 1; its trajectory took it past both Jupiter and Saturn. Jupiter's gravity was used to increase the spacecraft's velocity and divert its trajectory toward Saturn, shortening the travel time to Saturn from 6 years to 3.3 years.

JPL was chosen to implement the mission. The Mariner Jupiter Saturn 77 (MJS77) project, later renamed Voyager, began on July 1, 1972, under the management of Harris Schurmeier. When funds were authorized for the mission, the National Aeronautics and Space Administration (NASA) began the process of selecting the scientific instruments that would be installed on the craft. Eventually, eleven instruments were built for Voyager 1. To coordinate the scientific activity, Edward C. Stone was selected as Project Scientist, and Ray Heacock was Project Manager for the Saturn flyby.

There were two groups of Voyager instruments. The first group comprised the remote-sensing instruments. Most of these were mounted on a movable scan platform and obtained data on remote targets. The second group included *in situ* instruments, those that made direct measurements of the surrounding charged particles, magnetic field, and plasma waves.

The remote-sensing instruments were mounted on a movable scan platform at the end of a 2.3-meter science boom. The scan platform could move in two axes, scanning all the sky except for the region blocked by the spacecraft itself. The instruments mounted on the scan platform included the infrared interferometer spectrometer and radiometer, two imaging cameras, a photopolarimeter, and an ultraviolet spectrometer. Together, these instruments measured the properties of the objects they detected in wavelengths from the infrared through the visible to the ultraviolet.

Attached at the midpoint of the science boom were two *in situ* instruments, the cosmic ray experiment and the low-energy charged particle experiment. The plasma experiment was an *in situ* instrument farther out on the science boom, near the scan platform. These instruments measured the distribution of energetic charged particles such as electrons, protons, and ions.

The planetary radio astronomy and plasma wave experiments shared an antenna. The antenna consisted of two thin metal rods, each 10 meters long, set at right angles to each other. These rods were extended from the spacecraft after launch. The planetary radio astronomy experiment was a remote-sensing instrument, and the plasma wave experiment took samples *in situ*. The *in situ* magnetic field experiment consisted of four three-axis magnetometers, two high-field sensors attached to the spacecraft, and two low-field sensors mounted at the end of a 13-meter boom. This boom was packed tightly in a canister during launch; once in space, the canister opened, and the boom extended automatically.

The final Voyager instrument, the radio science experiment, used the dish-shaped high-gain antenna. The high-gain antenna was the radio communications links between Earth and Voyager, relaying data from the outer science instruments as well as making remote-sensing measurements of various atmospheres as the spacecraft passed behind planetary bodies.

On Labor Day, September 5, 1977, Voyager 1 was launched from Cape Canaveral, Florida, at 8:56 A.M. eastern daylight time, five days after the launch window opened. The launch vehicle was a Titan 3E-Centaur rocket. The Titan main engine cut out early, forcing the Centaur stage to make up the difference during the trajectory insertion burn. After completing its burn, the Centaur stage shut down with very little fuel left in its tank. If the launch had not been delayed, the thrust from the remaining fuel would have been insufficient to allow Voyager 1 to reach first Jupiter and then Saturn.

During the one-and-one-half-year cruise period between the Jupiter and Saturn encounters, Voyager 1 continued to measure the solar wind. On January 1, ten months before the Voyager 1 encounter, the planetary radio astronomy instrument discovered very long wavelength radio bursts from Saturn. These bursts were highly regular, allowing calculation of the rotation rate for Saturn's interior, which proved to be 10 hours and 39.4 minutes.

In the fall of 1980, the science-intensive Saturn encounter began. Voyager 1 performed a detailed survey of Saturn, its ring system, and its satellites—including a close flyby of the large moon Titan. More than 18,000 images were transmitted to Earth during the encounter with Saturn.

On October 6, an extensive set of images of Saturn's rings revealed unexpected and detailed structure in the rings. As a result of this observed structure, the spacecraft was reprogrammed, and on October 25 the spacecraft cameras pointed toward one ansae (end) of the rings and imaged the rings every five minutes for ten hours. These images were used to produce a "film" of ring activity which highlighted the "spokes," dark fingers of material extending radially outward over a portion of the rings. In images from this film, two tiny satellites, Prometheus and Pandora, were first discovered. They orbit on each side of the narrow F-ring.

On November 11, Voyager 1 crossed the Saturn bow shock, the boundary between the solar plasma which flows from the Sun (solar wind), and Saturn's magnetosphere. Just inside the bow shock, a boundary called the magnetopause separates the turbulent area between the bow shock and the actual magnetosphere. The location of the magnetopause changes dynamically with variations in solar wind pressure. Five magnetopause crossings occurred during the period of one hour before Voyager 1 entered the magnetosphere for the final time.

The closest approach to Titan took place on November 11, within 4,000 kilometers. Infrared measurements of varying atmospheric levels were performed from the edge of Titan's north pole. As Voyager 1 passed behind Titan, the varying strength of its radio signal probed Titan's atmosphere (a technique known as radio occultation), measuring its pressure and temperature as a function of distance above the surface. The ultraviolet instrument on board the spacecraft observed the sunset on Titan (solar occultation), and another measurement of Titan's atmosphere was made. About fifteen minutes later, the spacecraft safely reappeared from the shadow of Titan. As Voyager 1 was passing close to Titan, it simultaneously passed through the Saturn ring plane, which passes through Saturn's equator and through the known rings. No damaging particles hit the spacecraft during this passage.

November 12, 1980, was encounter day. Voyager 1's closest approach to Saturn took place at 6:45 P.M. eastern standard time, only 124,000 kilometers above the cloud tops. At 7:08 P.M., the spacecraft passed behind Saturn, and the structure of the clouds in the planet's atmosphere was probed by measuring the varying strength of the radio signals sent to Earth. A solar occultation by the atmosphere was simultaneously observed. The spacecraft reappeared briefly as it reached the other side of Saturn, and then it passed behind Saturn's rings, where it measured the distribution of ring material in the main rings by using the variation in the strength of the radio signal. Almost forty-five minutes after the occultations ended, Voyager 1 crossed the ring plane again, at the orbit of the satellite Dione, called the Dione clear zone, where the risk of collision with a ring particle was less likely. Observing the sunlight shining through them, Voyager 1 spent twenty-three hours underneath the rings photographing views never before seen from Earth.

Close-up views of five of the major Saturnian satellites were obtained on November 12. The closest flyby distances to each satellite were Mimas, 88,000 kilometers; Enceladus, 202,000 kilometers; Tethys, 416,000 kilometers; Dione, 161,000 kilometers; and Rhea, 74,000 kilometers. The images with the highest resolution were of Rhea. To obtain sharp images, the entire spacecraft was turned to keep Rhea motionless in the cameras.

By the end of November, Voyager 1 had crossed the Saturn bow shock to leave Saturn's magnetosphere and enter the solar wind for the final time. No further planetary encounters were possible for Voyager 1. In order to bring it close to the satellite Titan, the spacecraft trajectory, using Saturn's gravity, was bent out of the plane containing the orbits of the major planets. Voyager 1 is outward bound on a path leaving the solar system. Perhaps in several hundred thousand years Voyager 1 will fly close to another star. Mounted on the spacecraft is a gold-plated recording of the sights and sounds of planet Earth. Should a distant civilization find Voyager 1 and decode the recording, greetings from Earth spoken in fifty-three languages and various sounds of the world will be heard. One hundred fifteen images will display the diversity of life and culture on Earth. With its departure from Saturn, Voyager 1 was only beginning a journey of epic proportions.

**Knowledge Gained**

Images of Saturn reveal alternating east-west belts (darker bands) and zones (lighter bands) similar to those in the Jovian atmosphere, although on Saturn they are considerably more muted. Saturn's equatorial jet stream blows four times harder (about 500 meters per second) around Saturn's equator than Jupiter's winds blow around Jupiter. Measured temperatures in Saturn's atmosphere include a minimum temperature of 80 Kelvins at 0.1 bar (on the surface of Earth the average atmospheric pressure is 1.0 bar).

Voyager 1's data revealed that Titan is hidden by an atmosphere thicker than Earth's, and that it may possess hydrocarbon oceans. A thick, smoglike haze covers Titan and creates a greenhouse effect, warming the surface. Voyager 1 provided the first measurements of the near-surface atmospheric pressure (1.6 bars) and temperature (95 Kelvins) on Titan. The main constituent of Titan's atmosphere was found to be nitrogen. Infrared measurements detected trace amounts of various hydrocarbons in the atmosphere. Nitriles—molecules composed of hydrogen, nitrogen, and carbon—were discovered also.

Images from the Voyager 1 cameras revealed three new, tiny satellites. Atlas orbits just outside the outer edge of the main ring system; Prometheus and Pandora fall on either side of the narrow F-ring, located 3,000 kilometers outside the main ring system. The F-ring appears braided and clumpy as a result of gravitational interactions with these satellites.

Using the imaging system, the sizes of the seventeen known satellites were determined for the first time, thus permitting a more accurate estimate of their densities. On Mimas, a huge crater, 130 kilometers in diameter and one-third the diameter of Mimas itself, was discovered. Enceladus is the brightest satellite in the solar system; some regions of its bright surface are almost devoid of craters, indicating a young surface. An enormous canyon, covering nearly three-quarters of its circumference, engulfs Tethys. Both Dione and Rhea display a dark surface overlaid with bright, wispy terrain, possibly a product of internal processing. Iapetus has an unusual distribution of light and dark material on its surface: It is bright on one side and completely dark on the other. The light material is approximately ten times brighter than the dark material.

Voyager 1 revealed a ring system of structural complexity and variety. The rings are not bland sheets of material, as originally thought prior to the Voyager 1 flyby, but possess detailed structures on scales smaller than a kilometer. The rings are composed of particles in a wide range of sizes, from tiny pebbles to giant boulders, including a sprinkling of fine dust. Spokes and elliptical as well as discontinuous ringlets were discovered in the main ring system by Voyager 1. A new ring, the tenuous G-ring, was discovered between the orbits of Mimas and two coorbiting satellites.

Voyager 1's instruments confirmed that, unlike Earth, Saturn has a magnetic dipole axis that is closely aligned with the planet's spin axis. The relative tilt between the magnetic dipole axis and the spin axis is only 0.7 degree for Saturn, compared to a tilt of 11.5 degrees for Earth. The number of charged particles in Saturn's magnetosphere is much smaller than the number measured at Jupiter. The rings are effective particle absorbers in the inner magnetosphere.

### Context

Voyager 1 was the second spacecraft to fly through the Saturn system and the first to take high-resolution images of Saturn, Titan, the icy satellites, and the rings. Voyager 2 followed nine months later. One year earlier, Pioneer 11, another U.S. mission, had also conducted a flyby.

Saturn, the sixth planet from the Sun, is second in size only to Jupiter. Studies of the Saturn system have contributed to the understanding of the origin and evolution of the solar system. Earth-based observations established that Saturn has an internal heat source, and infrared measurements by both Pioneer 11 and Voyager 1 confirmed it. Primordial cooling from Saturn's initial formation and collapse should be complete; thus, an excess of heat was unexpected. Voyager 1 also measured the hydrogen-to-helium ratio of Saturn's upper atmosphere: roughly thirty hydrogen molecules for every helium molecule. Saturn has suffered a threefold depletion of helium relative to the solar abundance value. The mechanism responsible for this depletion in the upper atmosphere may also generate the excess heat.

With the exception of the Jovian satellite Ganymede, Titan is the largest satellite in the solar system, and it is the only one known to possess a substantial atmosphere. At a greater distance from the Sun than Ganymede, it is much colder and richer in ices. Some of the chemical reactions occurring in Titan's atmosphere provide possible analogues to some of the prebiotic chemistry that took place on primitive Earth to form the nucleic acids found in living organisms.

An interesting puzzle is the apparent youth of the ring system, only $10^7$ to $10^8$ years, much shorter than the solar system age of $4.5 \times 10^9$ years. Understanding the evolution of planetary rings may also lead to a better understanding of planetary accretion from the disk of material originally surrounding the Sun.

Plans for a return to Saturn focused on the Cassini mission, a combined U.S. and European project consisting of an orbiter and a probe. The planned launch date was in 1996, with arrival at Saturn in 2002. The probe was to be released into the Titan atmosphere, and measurements were to be taken during its descent to the surface. The orbiter was to circle Saturn, recording data for four years.

Voyager 1 established the possibility of building a spacecraft to last for more than a decade. Sophisticated engineering for Voyager 1's Saturn flyby utilized complex maneuvers to track the limb of the planet during the radio occultation and to compensate for the rapid motion of Rhea during the close flyby. Both Voyager 1 and Pioneer 11 extended the frontier of the outer solar system. With images and information relayed to Earth, a wealth of new knowledge was provided about the Saturnian system.

## Bibliography

Beatty, J. Kelly, et al., eds. *The New Solar System*. Cambridge, Mass.: Sky Publishing, 1982. Well-known scientists have provided a useful overview of the solar system, including discussions of the Sun, the planets and their satellites, and the medium between the various bodies.

Branley, F. *Saturn, the Spectacular Planet*. New York: Thomas Y. Crowell, 1983. This clear, straightforward book presents current information on Saturn and its satellites and rings. Simple diagrams illustrate basic concepts about the Saturn system, enhanced with photographs from the Voyager flybys. Suitable for general audiences, including junior high school students.

Cooper, H. *Imaging Saturn*. New York: Holt, Rinehart and Winston, 1981. The Voyager mission is chronicled in a day-by-day description of events that occurred during the Saturn encounters. Accounts of key individuals, in particular the Voyager imaging team members, are detailed. Suitable for general audiences.

Eberhart, Jonathan. "Secrets of Saturn: Anything but Elementary." *Science News* 120 (September 5, 1981): 148-158. Highlights of the Voyager Saturn encounters are described in this article with a focus on Saturn's rings. Several photographs from the encounter are included. Suitable for general audiences.

Gore, Rick. "Voyager 1 at Saturn." *National Geographic* 160 (July, 1981): 2-31. This readable article describes the results of Voyager 1's Saturn flyby and includes statements from key individuals involved in the mission. Beautiful color images of Saturn, Titan, the icy satellites, and the rings are included.

Lauber, Patricia. *Journey to the Planets*. Rev. ed. New York: Crown Publishers, 1987. Lauber describes the history and nature of the planets, noting their resemblances and differences. Includes photographs and information from the Voyager missions.

Morrison, David, and Jane Samz. *Voyages to Saturn*. NASA SP-451. Washington, D.C.: Government Printing Office, 1982. The official account of the Voyager encounters with Saturn. Well illustrated. Includes appendices of information about the personnel involved in the Voyager missions as well as a list of suggested reading material.

Poynter, Margaret, and Arthur L. Lane. *Voyager: The Story of a Space Mission*. New York: Macmillan, 1981. Provides a behind-the-scenes account of the missions during all phases, from planning to the planetary encounters.

Simon, Seymour. *Saturn*. New York: William Morrow and Co., 1985. This easy-to-read book surveys knowledge of the planet Saturn. Includes twenty large color photographs taken during the Voyager encounters.

*Linda J. Horn*

## Cross-References

The Jet Propulsion Laboratory, 662; Pioneer 10, 1130; Pioneer 11, 1138; Planetary Evolution, 1159; Comparative Planetology, 1168; Saturn's Atmosphere, 1246; Saturn's Magnetic Field, 1254; Saturn's Moons, 1261; Saturn's Rings, 1268; The History of the Solar System, 1367; The Voyager Program, 2219; Voyager 1: Jupiter, 2227; Voyager 2: Jupiter, 2241; Voyager 2: Saturn, 2248; Voyager 2: Uranus, 2255.

# VOYAGER 2
## Jupiter

*Date:* August 20, 1977, to July 11, 1979
*Type of mission:* Unmanned deep space probe
*Country:* The United States

*The Voyager 2 flyby of Jupiter provided vital information about the Jovian system, in spite of a number of technical problems and equipment failures. Complementing the Voyager 1 flyby, this mission helped map Jupiter's moons, collected valuable data on the magnetic and radiation fields surrounding Jupiter, and monitored atmospheric phenomena.*

*Principal personages*
RAY HEACOCK, Project Manager
EDWARD C. STONE, Project Scientist
BRADFORD A. SMITH, imaging science team leader
RUDOLF. A. HANEL, Principal Investigator, infrared interferometry
A. LYLE BROADFOOT, Principal Investigator, ultraviolet
  spectroscopy
C. R. LILLIE and
CHARLES W. HORD, principal investigators, photopolarimetry
JAMES W. WARWICK, Principal Investigator, planetary radio
  astronomy
NORMAN F. NESS, Principal Investigator, magnetic fields
HERBERT S. BRIDGE, Principal Investigator, plasma particles
FREDERICK L. SCARF, Principal Investigator, plasma waves
STAMATIOS (TOM) KRIMIGIS, Principal Investigator, low-energy
  charged particles
ROCHUS E. VOGT, Principal Investigator, cosmic ray particles
VON R. ESHLEMAN, radio science team leader

## Summary of the Mission

Voyager 2 was launched on August 20, 1977, sixteen days before the launch date of its twin, Voyager 1. The flight paths of the two spacecraft were such that between the orbits of Mars and Jupiter, in the asteroid belt, Voyager 1 overtook Voyager 2 and arrived at Jupiter four months and four days before Voyager 2. The differences in these two flight paths allowed the two spacecraft to complement each other, so that Voyager 2 obtained data on features of the Jovian (and Saturnian) system that Voyager 1 was unable to probe. Voyager 2's flight path was designed to carry it past Uranus and Neptune, while Voyager 1 would leave the plane of the solar system after its encounter with Saturn.

The data and pictures sent back to Earth by Voyager 2 are remarkable not only for their quality and uniqueness but also because of the number of problems which were overcome to obtain them. Even before launch, failures in two of the computer subsystems of the VGR77-2 spacecraft (which later became Voyager 1) delayed its launch and forced the substitution of the identical VGR77-3 spacecraft, now known as Voyager 2. Also just before the August 20 launch, the low-energy charged particle instrument had to be replaced. During launch, Voyager 2 behaved as if it had been jolted or bumped, switching to backup systems and losing telemetry signals. Flight engineers later determined that the attitude and articulation control subsystem (AACS) had experienced some electronic gyrations. Just after launch, the lock on the scientific instrument boom failed to signal that the boom was extended, even though it was. During the fall of 1977, Voyager 2 continued its erratic behavior. Finally, it was determined that the spacecraft's systems had been programmed to be too sensitive to environmental changes; after reprogramming, the erratic behavior subsided.

A more serious problem soon developed. The Voyager spacecraft are equipped with two receivers, a primary and a secondary or backup, through which commands are received from Earth. In late November, 1977, Voyager 2's primary receiver began losing power; it failed in late March, 1978. The failure would have caused no major difficulty if the backup receiver had been working properly, but when the spacecraft's computer command subsystem (CCS) switched to the backup receiver seven days after it received its last communication from Earth, Voyager 2 still did not respond properly. Twelve hours later, on April 5, 1978, the CCS switched back to the primary receiver, which worked for half an hour before a power surge blew its fuses and permanently disabled it. During the next seven days, flight engineers devised a way of communicating through the faulty secondary receiver. The problem with the backup receiver was that it had lost its ability to compensate for slight frequency changes in signals from Earth, so that now only the most accurate signals could be recognized. Slight changes in frequency and receiver response result from Earth's rotation (Doppler shift), temperature fluctuations caused by electronic components switching on and off, and environmental factors, such as the magnetic and electric fields near planets and the associated radiation to which the spacecraft is subjected. Now all these fluctuations had to be accounted for when a signal was beamed from Earth, which made programming Voyager 2 from Earth much more difficult. On June 23 and October 12, 1978, Voyager 2 was programmed for backup automatic missions at Saturn and Jupiter in the event that the faulty backup receiver should fail completely. In August, 1978, it was again reprogrammed to ensure better scientific results during its Jupiter encounter. In particular, Voyager 2 was instructed to compensate for motions caused by its tape recorder. These motions would cause time-exposed television images to blur and lose details. Throughout the Voyager 2 mission, the faulty backup receiver was used repeatedly to reprogram the spacecraft. This reprogramming was crucial to the amount and quality of information sent back to Earth.

A serious fuel shortage also threatened the mission. Course corrections took 15 to 20 percent more fuel than had been expected because the maneuvering jets were partially blocked by the struts that had connected the spacecraft to its last booster rocket. To reduce the number and duration of course corrections, Voyager 2 was tipped upside down. In this attitude the spacecraft was not as easily blown off course by the solar wind (charged particles streaming from the Sun), but its attitude control system had to be reprogrammed to steer by different guide stars. Another major fuel-saving maneuver was accomplished only two hours after Voyager 2's closest approach to Jupiter. Flight engineers determined that about 10 percent of the original fuel load could be saved by rescheduling a major course correction to that time. Executing this course correction so close to Jupiter made it much more difficult to monitor. In fact, just as the spacecraft began the 76-minute thruster firing which would send it on to Saturn, communication with Earth was lost. Afterward, once the interference from the Jovian magnetosphere (the region dominated by Jupiter's magnetic field instead of the Sun's) was penetrated, the flight controllers found that Voyager 2 had executed its new programming perfectly and was headed toward Saturn, with enough fuel to redirect it toward Uranus and beyond.

In spite of all these problems, Voyager 2 began sending back information about interplanetary space days after launch. During its cruise to Jupiter, the spacecraft's instruments were being calibrated and tested. Not only did this provide ground controllers and investigators with a better understanding of the instruments' behavior, but it also provided a chance to study infrared and ultraviolet radiation, magnetic fields, solar flares, and the solar wind far from Earth's influences. Unlike the Pioneer missions, Voyager 2 was not equipped to analyze the particulates of matter in the asteroid belt. Fortunately, the passage through this "shooting gallery" was uneventful, and by October, 1978, Voyager 2 had passed through the asteroid belt and was slightly more than halfway to Jupiter.

The July 9, 1979, encounter with Jupiter was planned so that Voyager 2 could photograph the unseen sides of Jupiter's largest moons. (Because of Jupiter's tremendous gravitational and tidal pull on its satellites, one side of these bodies always faces Jupiter and the other side is turned out toward space.) When Voyager 2 passed through the Jovian system, the moons were encountered first, so that their spaceward sides were facing the Sun and Voyager 2's cameras. The flight path followed by Voyager 2 brought it near enough to Europa to resolve features as small as four kilometers across. In contrast, the best Voyager 1 pictures of Europa revealed only features 33 kilometers across or larger. Even though Io was always more than one million kilometers away from Voyager 2, the volcanoes discovered with the help of Voyager 1 data had so fascinated project scientists that a ten-hour "Io volcano watch" was planned. Just after its closest approach to Jupiter, Voyager 2 turned its cameras and instruments toward Io and the glowing gases which surround its orbit about Jupiter.

Because Voyager 2 was scheduled to go to Uranus and Neptune, it could not come as close to Jupiter as Voyager 1 had. In spite of this, Voyager 2 data revealed a moon (later dubbed Adrastea), closer to Jupiter than Amalthea, and took spectacular pictures of Jupiter's rings. Voyager 2 data also showed that the magnetosphere and radiation belts surrounding Jupiter had enlarged and intensified since Voyager 1's flyby. Jupiter's radiation belts resemble Earth's Van Allen belts, except that they can be ten thousand times stronger. Their radiation is generated by energetic charged particles which are trapped by Jupiter's magnetic field. Voyager 2's closest distance from Jupiter was nearly twice Voyager 1's closest distance, yet Voyager 2 instruments detected radiation levels that were three times stronger than those detected by Voyager 1 (a circumstance which may explain the communication interruption at closest approach). Furthermore, Voyager 2 first encountered Jupiter's bow shock (where the solar wind collides with a planet's magnetosphere) at a greater distance than Voyager 1 had four months earlier. Jupiter's bow shock flutters in the solar wind, however, so that in three days Voyager 2 passed through the bow shock ten times.

Another important aspect of the Voyager 2 flyby of Jupiter was the information it returned on Jupiter's meteorology. Six weeks after the first Voyager flyby, Voyager 2 turned its cameras toward Jupiter and began to document the cloud movements of Jupiter. A series of pictures were taken which were combined into a motion picture of the dynamics of Jupiter's atmosphere. Throughout the encounter, the spacecraft took pictures of Jupiter itself; scientists hoped thereby to detect changes in cloud patterns, lightning flashes, or auroras.

## Knowledge Gained

The information returned by Voyager 2 dealt with three basic aspects of the Jovian system: Jupiter's atmosphere, satellites and rings, and magnetosphere. This information permitted important comparisons with Voyager 1's data or provided detailed images and measurements of phenomena documented only briefly by Voyager 1. Not only did Voyager 2 confirm many of the sightings of Voyager 1, but it also supplied significant new information.

The motions of Jupiter's upper atmosphere were revealed in a series of photographs taken by Voyager 2. High-altitude jet streams were shown to form bands at constant latitudes and alternate with Jupiter's belts (dark bands) and zones (light bands). The jet stream velocities varied slightly from those measured by Voyager 1. At the boundaries of Jupiter's belts and zones can be found turbulence and storms. Some of these storms are very persistent; the Great Red Spot, for example, has lasted more than four centuries, and three white ovals have been studied since 1939. Voyager 2 revealed that these ovals, like the Great Red Spot, are all anticyclonic (rotating counterclockwise in the southern hemisphere and clockwise in the north). This finding indicates that these ovals, and four other white spots identified by Voyager 2, are sites of upsurging material. In the four months between the Voyager flybys, a protrusion formed to the east of the Great Red Spot, blocking the circulation of small structures about it. During the Voyager 2 flyby, a white region covered a brown oval in the north, showing that the brown ovals are actually breaks in the higher-altitude clouds of white ammonia crystals. Ultraviolet studies of Jupiter by

Voyager 2 revealed an absorbent layer of haze above the cloudtops, precipitation of charged particles from the magnetosphere, and auroras near the poles. The high-latitude auroras are induced by charged particles from Io and play a part in the atmospheric chemistry of Jupiter, as does lightning, which produced eight flashes detected by Voyager 2.

Jupiter's moons and main ring were also scrutinized by Voyager 2's cameras and instruments. The smooth surface of Europa was photographed with unprecedented resolution, so that the moon was shown to have uniform, bright terrain crisscrossed by dark lines and ridges and almost no features resembling craters. In contrast, Callisto's outward face, like its inward face (which is always turned toward Jupiter), is heavily cratered and very ancient. Ganymede, between Callisto and Europa, exhibits a variety of surface features such as the old and cratered surface of Regio Galileo, discovered by Voyager 2, and ancient parallel mountain ridges, nearly the size of Earth's Appalachian Mountains. Six of Io's volcanoes were still active at the time of the Io volcano watch. The Pele volcano, which had been the most violent, was now quiet, but its surrounding terrain had been visibly altered since the time of the Voyager 1 images; the plume of the volcano Loki was much larger than it had been. High-resolution images of Jupiter's ring were obtained, revealing a bright, narrow segment with a slightly brighter center surrounding a broader, dimmer disk—all surrounded by a halo of very fine particles. The outer edge of the ring is sharp, and two moons orbit just outside the edge. The inner disk of the ring probably extends all the way down to the cloud tops of Jupiter.

The outer edge of Jupiter's magnetosphere was observed to fluctuate considerably as Voyager 2 crossed it several times. In spite of the boundary's instability, it was clear that the magnetosphere had changed shape since the first Voyager probed it, protruding more toward the Sun and narrowing in its long tail. Inside the magnetosphere, a hot plasma (a gas so hot that its atoms cannot keep their electrons) of hydrogen, oxygen, and sulfur was slowly spiraling outward. The amount of oxygen and sulfur had decreased, though, since the Voyager 1 passage, suggesting that these heavier atoms were slowly settling back toward Jupiter and that Io was producing less of them. These heavier atoms of sulfur and oxygen are most likely injected into the magnetosphere by the volcanoes on Io and first collect in a plasma cloud that surrounds Io's orbit. During the Voyager 2 encounter, this plasma cloud was glowing twice as bright with ultraviolet radiation as it had four months before, yet its temperature had decreased. It was also determined that the auroras observed on Jupiter were caused by Io's plasma cloud. Data from Voyager 2 also revealed that Ganymede swept up some of the charged particles from the magnetosphere's plasma, producing a plasma wake similar to the wake of a speedboat on a calm lake. A similar effect had been detected near Io by Voyager 1.

## Context

Voyager 2 was the fourth spacecraft to encounter Jupiter. The first two, Pioneers 10 and 11, principally showed that the later Voyager missions were possible.

Voyager 2's design and flight path were altered after these two Pioneer missions supplied measurements of Jupiter and its moons, permitted identification of certain problems—such as the intense radiation surrounding the planet—and suggested interesting phenomena for study. Some Voyager discoveries had been hinted at by Earth-based observations. Radio signals from Jupiter suggested that electrical current was flowing between Io and Jupiter, but the current proved much stronger than had been imagined.

Data from Voyager 1 provided the most guidance for the second Voyager flyby of Jupiter. For example, theories had predicted that Jupiter could not have a ring, because gravity would pull the material into Jupiter's atmosphere; yet Voyager 1 found a ring. The ring could not be studied carefully at the time, because the discovery was unexpected. The presence of the ring could be explained by Io's volcanoes, which were subsequently detected by Voyager 1. Some of the material ejected by Io may find its way down toward Jupiter, where it could replace precipitating material. Another possible explanation is that the rings are renewed by collisions between high-velocity particles and Jupiter's nearest moons, Adrastea and Metis, which undoubtedly shape the ring even if they do not regenerate it. In any event, much of the information Voyager 2 collected about the rings, Io's volcanoes, and Adrastea would have been undiscovered if data from Voyager 1 had not pointed the way.

Another surprise of the Voyager mission to Jupiter was the smooth surface of Europa. The lack of large impact craters suggests a relatively new surface, and the smooth regions between intersecting lines resemble an aerial photograph of Arctic ice crossed by pressure ridges. If this interpretation is correct, Europa may be covered by a frozen ocean. How thick the ice is and whether liquid water lies underneath is still speculative; more information is needed. Without the Voyager 2 images, however, the idea of a recently frozen surface would seem very unlikely.

The information from Voyager 2's flyby of Jupiter has taken years to analyze, and some of the mysteries cannot be solved without another mission. The Galileo mission has had to wait for a number of difficulties to be resolved. In this next step, a spacecraft would not merely pass by Jupiter but would become another satellite of that planet, providing long-term observations of phenomena that Voyager instruments could detect only briefly.

## Bibliography

Beatty, J. Kelly, et al., eds. *The New Solar System*. Cambridge, Mass.: Sky Publishing, 1982. A collection of articles by noted experts. Chapters 11, 12, 13, 14, and 19 are particularly relevant for readers who wish to learn more about Voyager 2's flyby of Jupiter.

Couper, Heather, and Nigel Henbest. *New Worlds: In Search of the Planets*. Reading, Mass.: Addison-Wesley Publishing Co., 1986. Includes a summary of the explorations of the Jovian system. Accessible to the general reader.

Editors of Time-Life Books. *The Far Planets*. Alexandria, Va.: Time-Life Books,

1988. This volume is notable not only for its photographs and informative illustrations but also for its lively and complete account of the Voyager 2 mission. This is a volume in the Voyage Through the Universe series.

Hunt, Garry E., and Patrick Moore. *Jupiter*. New York: Rand McNally and Co., 1981. A succinct yet complete treatment of almost all aspects of Jupiter and the Voyager missions to Jupiter. Its maps of the Galilean satellites are notable.

Morrison, David, and Tobias Owen. *The Planetary System*. Reading, Mass.: Addison-Wesley Publishing Co., 1987. A very complete summary of all the Sun's satellites by two members of the Voyager imaging team. Contains photographs and information never before published.

Morrison, David, and Jane Samz. *Voyage to Jupiter*. NASA SP-439. Washington, D.C.: Government Printing Office, 1980. The official summary of the Voyager missions to Jupiter. This volume is notable for its chronological approach to both Voyager flybys of Jupiter, its summaries, its photographs and tables, and its maps of Jupiter's moons.

Murray, Bruce C., ed. *The Planets*. New York: W. H. Freeman and Co., 1983. This collection of reprints of *Scientific American* articles includes articles on Jupiter, its Galilean moons, and its planetary rings.

Smoluchowski, Roman. *The Solar System*. New York: W. H. Freeman and Co., 1983. A well-written and well-illustrated summary of man's understanding of the solar system. The discussion of Io is particularly fascinating.

Snow, Theodore P. *Essentials of the Dynamic Universe: An Introduction*. 2d ed. St. Paul, Minn.: West Publishing Co., 1987. A well-written introduction to astronomy and astrophysics. Intended for nonscientists. The chapter on Jupiter contains a summary of the Voyager missions.

*Larry M. Browning*

### Cross-References

Volcanic Activity on Io, 643; The Jovian System, 677; Jupiter's Atmosphere, 683; Jupiter's Great Red Spot, 690; Jupiter's Magnetic Field and Trapped Radiation, 697; Jupiter's Satellites, 704; Mariner 10, 871; Pioneer 10, 1130; Pioneer 11, 1138; The Van Allen Radiation Belts, 2065; The Voyager Program, 2219; Voyager 1: Jupiter, 2227; Voyager 1: Saturn, 2234; Voyager 2: Saturn, 2248.

# VOYAGER 2
## Saturn

*Date:* June 5 to September 4, 1981
*Type of mission:* Unmanned deep space probe
*Country:* The United States

*The Voyager 2 flyby of Saturn produced high-resolution images of Saturn's ring system and of the satellites Iapetus, Hyperion, Enceladus, and Tethys. In addition, this second Voyager mission to Saturn collected valuable data on the magnetic and radiation fields surrounding that planet and observed atmospheric phenomena on Saturn.*

*Principal personages*
ESKER DAVIS, Project Manager
EDWARD C. STONE, Project Scientist
BRADFORD A. SMITH, imaging science team leader
RUDOLF. A. HANEL, Principal Investigator, infrared interferometry
A. LYLE BROADFOOT, Principal Investigator, ultraviolet spectroscopy
ARTHUR L. LANE, Principal Investigator, photopolarimetry
JAMES W. WARWICK, Principal Investigator, planetary radio astronomy
NORMAN F. NESS, Principal Investigator, magnetic fields
HERBERT S. BRIDGE, Principal Investigator, plasma particles
FREDERICK L. SCARF, Principal Investigator, plasma waves
STAMATIOS (TOM) KRIMIGIS, Principal Investigator, low-energy charged particles
ROCHUS E. VOGT, Principal Investigator, cosmic ray particles
G. LEONARD TYLER, radio science team leader

## Summary of the Mission

The Voyager 2 mission to Saturn was the last formal objective for the Voyager program, but the flight controllers knew that with careful planning and a little luck, Voyager 2 could be sent to Uranus and Neptune on a "grand tour" of the outer solar system. Voyager 2's flight path took the probe only 32,000 kilometers from the edge of Saturn's F-ring, through the region where Pioneer 11 nearly collided with the satellite now known as Janus. This trajectory was chosen so that Saturn's gravitational pull would assist in sending Voyager 2 toward a 1986 encounter with Uranus. The timing of Voyager 2's passage through the Saturnian system was also planned to optimize measurements of the moons Iapetus, Enceladus, and Tethys, as well as of the rings, which were better illuminated by the Sun than they had been during Voyager 1's flyby. Other satellites would also be photographed and compared with data returned by Voyager 1, which had achieved very close encounters with the moons Mimas, Rhea, and Titan.

During its approach to Saturn, Voyager 2 monitored the solar wind, the charged particles that stream from holes in the Sun's corona. This information warned Voyager 1 flight controllers and scientists of gusts or other changes in the solar wind which would affect the boundary of Saturn's magnetosphere (the region surrounding a planet that is dominated by that planet's magnetic field). The data were useful in interpreting information sent from Voyager 1 as it crossed Saturn's bow shock. (A planet's bow shock is the region where the solar wind first encounters the planet's magnetic field and loses most of its energy.)

In February of 1981, Voyager 2 passed through the tail of Jupiter's magnetosphere. It was expected that in August of 1981, during Voyager 2's Saturn encounter, Jupiter's magnetosphere would extend over Saturn, shading Saturn from the solar wind. That did not happen, however, and Saturn's magnetosphere was subjected to the solar wind's full fury, robbing Voyager 2 of the opportunity to study the collision of Jupiter and Saturn's magnetospheres.

Ten weeks before periapsis (closest approach), Voyager 2 began taking a series of pictures which were later combined into films showing the motion of Saturn's atmosphere and rings. The atmospheric films showed banding and turbulence similar to those on Jupiter; wind speeds, however, were an amazing 400 to 500 meters per second, and cloud layers were deeper, giving Saturn a more uniform appearance than Jupiter. In the nine months since Voyager 1 had visited Saturn, atmospheric activity had increased so that more storms, spots, and waves could be seen in the cloudtops. The ring images showed the three major rings easily visible from Earth, which are named A, B, and C from the outermost inward. In the B-ring, radial "spokes" which rotate with the planet were clearly visible. The detection of these spokes by Voyager 1 had been a surprise, because such structures cannot orbit Saturn as a result of the gravitational forces that shape the concentric, nearly circular rings. The Voyager 2 pictures helped to establish that the spokes are very tiny dust or haze layers suspended over larger ring particles by Saturn's magnetic field and, consequently, rotate with the field as the planet rotates.

Between the orbits of the moons Iapetus and Titan, Voyager 2 encountered Saturn's bow shock. As on its flyby of Jupiter, Voyager 2 crossed the bow shock many times, because the solar wind would alternately gust, compressing the magnetosphere, and relax, allowing the magnetosphere to expand. Because the solar wind's strength had increased since Voyager 1's encounter, Voyager 2 finally passed into Saturn's magnetopause, or the magnetosphere's boundary, just inside Titan's orbit. The spacecraft then proceeded to pass through three distinct regions of Saturn's magnetosphere. The first is dominated by Titan, whose orbit is surrounded by a cloud of hydrogen gas emanating from the moon's atmosphere and extending toward Saturn up to Rhea's orbit. Between Rhea and Mimas are intense radiation belts composed of charged particles that rotate with Saturn's magnetic field. Closer to the planet, the rings almost completely neutralize the charged particles, making

Saturn's rings one of the most radiation-free regions in the solar system.

The rings themselves were also very carefully studied by Voyager 2 scientists. Almost two and a half hours on the day of periapsis were devoted to a very careful photopolarimeter scan of the rings. This scan resolved objects as small as one hundred meters across and was done by measuring the change in intensity of starlight as the ring passed between the probe and the star Delta Scorpii.

On August 22, 1981, Voyager 2 began its survey of Saturn's moons as it flew by Iapetus. The moons, except for Phoebe and possibly Hyperion, have synchronous orbits around Saturn, so that one side of the moon always faces Saturn. Put another way, one side of the moon always faces ahead, leading the moon in its orbit, and the other side always faces behind, trailing the moon as it circles. In the case of Iapetus, the leading edge is darker than the trailing edge; the moons Dione and Rhea, however, have brighter leading faces and darker trailing faces crossed by bright streaks. After passing Iapetus, Voyager 2 flew by Hyperion. The probe returned pictures which revealed this moon to be irregularly shaped, with its long axis pointing out toward space instead of toward Saturn as had been expected. Just before the closest approach to Saturn, Voyager 2 turned its cameras toward the small satellites Telesto, Calypso, and Helene, and toward the larger moons Enceladus and Tethys, even though the closest approach to the larger moons would occur after periapsis.

The preliminary studies of Enceladus and Tethys proved fortunate, because fifty-five minutes after Voyager 2 crossed the plane of Saturn's rings, its camera platform's azimuth control became stuck. When the scan platform's back-and-forth motion stopped, Voyager 2 was behind Saturn and out of contact with Earth. The spacecraft was on automatic control and was recording its cameras' images for later relaying. Reviewing the images hours later, flight controllers and scientists watched as the cameras moved progressively off target so that first the high-resolution pictures were lost and then even the wide-angle pictures were blank.

As soon as contact was reestablished with Voyager 2 as it moved out of Saturn's shadow, flight controllers realized that the cameras and other sensitive instruments were pointed toward the Sun. If left in this position, the instruments would be destroyed, effectively blinding the spacecraft and making the rest of the mission practically useless. Quickly, commands were sent to rotate the entire spacecraft. Voyager 2 was so far from Earth, however, that an hour and a half would pass before these commands would be received. Adding to the danger was the possibility that Voyager 2 would not be able to decode the commands, as its primary receiver had failed soon after launch, and its backup receiver was faulty. If the flight engineers had not taken into account the fact that the spacecraft had cooled in the shadow of Saturn, and adjusted the commands accordingly, Voyager 2's last images would have recorded its cameras burning out in the Sun's glare.

Three days passed before the instrument platform was partially freed and a few final images of Saturn and the moon Phoebe were sent back to Earth. Unfortunately, the highest-resolution images of Enceladus and Tethys had been lost, along with three-dimensional pictures of the F-ring, a photopolarimeter scan of the F- and

A-rings, and images of the night side of Saturn with backlit rings. It was also clear that for future flybys, the entire spacecraft would have to be slowly rotated to keep time-exposed pictures from blurring.

## Knowledge Gained

During its flyby of Saturn, Voyager 2 conducted the first high-resolution reconnaissance of the moons Iapetus and Hyperion and of the two previously scanned moons, Tethys and Enceladus. The images of Iapetus revealed a dark leading edge surrounded by a concentric, dark circle. The trailing edge was much brighter, but the deepest craters showed dark bottoms. Voyager 2 flew so close to Iapetus that it was able to make the first direct measurement of this moon's mass as its gravity bent the spacecraft's trajectory.

The Hyperion pictures revealed an elongated moon, pockmarked by meteoric impacts, with its longest axis pointing away from Saturn. This dark, icy moon's orientation was seen to be so unusual that mission scientists suspected that Hyperion is not synchronously rotating about Saturn, as are all the other moons but Phoebe. Unfortunately, Voyager 2 could not observe Hyperion long enough to determine its exact orientation and rotation period.

Voyager 2's images of Tethys revealed a huge and ancient impact crater 400 kilometers wide—bigger than the moon Mimas. This crater, named Odysseus, is relatively shallow, because its floor rebounded after the initial meteoric impact; it now has nearly the same curvature as the rest of the moon. It was also discovered that the huge trench Ithaca Chasma, first photographed by Voyager 1, extends three-fourths of the way around Tethys.

The surface of Enceladus is incredibly bright, reflecting nearly all the light that reaches it. This extreme brightness suggested to the Voyager mission scientists that Enceladus' surface is very new and perhaps frequently restored by ice volcanoes. Voyager 2 detected no such ice volcanoes, but it did find a variety of terrain which indicates recent geological activity. Such activity was unexpected in such a small moon and is unknown among Enceladus' neighbors.

Voyager 2's high-resolution images of Saturn's rings showed much more detail than had ever been seen before. When various sections of the rings were compared, it was realized that the rings are very dynamic; their fine structure is constantly shifting and changing. The Cassini Division and the Keeler Gap (also called the Encke Division), which from Earth had appeared devoid of material, were shown to have small, dark ringlets. Scientists had expected to find small moons in the divisions sweeping away material, but none were detected. Voyager 2 also measured the rings' thickness and found it to be less than 300 meters; corrugations in the rings make them appear ten times thicker from Earth.

Weather patterns on Saturn proved to be remarkably stable. Storms identified by Voyager 2 as it approached Saturn were seen six weeks later at the same latitude and traveling with the same speed. Even more remarkable was that many storms appeared just where Voyager 1 data had predicted they would.

## Context

The third probe to fly by Saturn, Voyager 2 provided much detailed information that Pioneer 11 and Voyager 1 could not. Pioneer 11 had made several important discoveries, including Saturn's F-ring, but its imaging systems and other instruments could not match the resolution capabilities of the Voyager spacecraft. Voyager 1 had observed most of the previously unknown and in many cases unexpected aspects of the Saturnian system nine months before Voyager 2's passage, but a single flight through the Saturnian system could not capture every aspect for scrutiny. Also, to have a close look at Titan, which was the only moon in the solar system known to have a substantial atmosphere, Voyager 1 mission scientists had to give up the chance to send the probe on to Uranus and Neptune. The second Voyager craft's trajectory was calculated to take it past those two planets. Voyager 2 had slightly better instruments, as well; its imaging system had about 50 percent more sensitivity and produced sharper pictures. Finally, Voyager 1's photopolarimeter was destroyed by the intense radiation near Jupiter, and important details about Saturn's rings and the polarization of light scattered from Titan were left for Voyager 2 to record.

Voyager 1 provided information which greatly influenced the planning of Voyager 2's Saturn flyby. For example, Voyager 1's data on the complexity of Saturn's rings made scientists and flight controllers realize how important a high-resolution scan of the rings would be. Nevertheless, not all the guidance for the Voyager 2 mission was provided by Voyager 1. During 1966 and 1980, Saturn's rings' edges were facing Earth. Without the brighter rings to obscure them, a number of new satellites and rings were observed in the Saturnian system by several teams of astronomers. Voyagers 1 and 2 confirmed their existence, and these objects are now known as the two coorbital satellites Epimetheus and Janus; the satellite Helene, which shares an orbit with Dione; and the E-ring, near Enceladus. Another, much older, Earth observation was confirmed by Voyager 2 when it sent back images of Iapetus showing a dark leading surface and a bright trailing surface. In 1671, the astronomer Gian Domenico Cassini, who discovered Iapetus and the gap between the A- and B-rings which now bears his name, observed that Iapetus was easy to see when it was west of Saturn but could barely be seen when it was east of Saturn. These observations are consistent with a synchronously rotating satellite with a dark leading edge, which the Voyager 2 images revealed Iapetus to be.

Despite Voyager 2's successes, there was some sadness at the press conference held after the Saturn flyby. Everyone there knew that it would be the last such conference for quite some time. Even though Voyager 2 would eventually encounter Uranus, in 1986, that was five years in the future, and, more important, no new probes had been launched. The Voyager 2 flyby of Saturn not only marked the end of the Voyager program's formal objectives but also marked the end of a period of intense planetary exploration.

## Bibliography

Beatty, J. Kelly, et al., eds. *The New Solar System.* Cambridge, Mass.: Sky Publishing, 1982. A collection of articles by noted experts and authors. Several chapters are particularly relevant to Voyager 2's flyby of Saturn.

Cooper, Henry S. F., Jr. *Imaging Saturn: The Voyager Flights to Saturn*. New York: H. Holt and Co., 1985. A very readable, chronological account of the Voyager missions to Saturn.

Couper, Heather, and Nigel Henbest. *New Worlds: In Search of the Planets*. Reading, Mass.: Addison-Wesley Publishing Co., 1986. A summary of planetary exploration, including the exploration of Saturn. Also contains information about how to find and observe Saturn. Accessible to all readers.

Editors of Time-Life Books. *The Far Planets*. Alexandria, Va.: Time-Life Books, 1988. A volume in the Voyage Through the Universe series, this source is notable not only for its pictures and informative illustrations but also for its lively and complete account of the Voyager 2 mission.

Frazier, Kendrick. *Solar Systems*. Alexandria, Va.: Time-Life Books, 1985. A volume in the series Planet Earth, this work is attractively illustrated and understandable to the layman.

Hunt, Garry, and Patrick Moore. *Saturn*. New York: Rand McNally and Co., 1981. A succinct and complete treatment of almost all aspects of Saturn and the Voyager missions to that planet. Maps of some of the satellites and diagrams of the Voyager spacecraft and its instruments are included.

Morrison, David. *Voyages to Saturn*. NASA SP-451. Washington, D.C.: Government Printing Office, 1980. The official summary of the Voyager missions to Saturn, this work is notable for its chronological approach to both Voyager flybys of Saturn, its summaries, its pictures and tables, and its maps of Saturn's moons. The Voyager flybys of Jupiter are also summarized.

Morrison, David, and Tobias Owen. *The Planetary System*. Reading, Mass.: Addison-Wesley Publishing Co., 1987. A complete summary of all the Sun's known satellites by two members of the Voyager imaging team. Contains pictures and information never before published.

Murray, Bruce, ed. *The Planets*. New York: W. H. Freeman and Co., 1983. A collection of reprints of *Scientific American* articles. Includes discussions of Saturn, Saturn's moons, and planetary rings.

Smoluchowski, Roman. *The Solar System*. New York: W. H. Freeman and Co., 1983. A well-written and well-illustrated summary of mankind's understanding of the solar system.

Snow, Theodore P. *The Dynamic Universe: An Introduction to Astronomy*. 3d ed. St. Paul, Minn.: West Publishing Co., 1988. A well-written introduction to astronomy and astrophysics intended for nonscientists. The chapter on Jupiter contains a summary of the Voyager missions, and the chapter on Saturn discusses the use of Voyager 2's photopolarimeter to resolve Saturn's rings.

*Larry M. Browning*

## Cross-References

# VOYAGER 2
## Uranus

*Date:* November 4, 1985, to February 25, 1986
*Type of mission:* Unmanned deep space probe
*Country:* The United States

*Voyager 2 was the first spacecraft to collect and return data from the planet Uranus. This encounter was the third of four potential encounters made possible by a planetary alignment that occurs only once every 175 years.*

*Principal personages*
RICHARD P. LAESER, Voyager Project Manager for the Uranus
encounter
EDWARD C. STONE, Voyager Project Scientist and Principal
Investigator, cosmic ray experiment
ELLIS D. MINER, Assistant Project Scientist
CHARLES E. KOHLHASE, Principal Mission Designer
BRADFORD A. SMITH, Principal Investigator, imaging experiment
G. LEONARD TYLER, Principal Investigator, radio science
experiment
RUDOLF A. HANEL, Principal Investigator, infrared experiment
S. M. (TOM) KRIMIGIS, Principal Investigator, low-energy charged
particle experiment
NORMAN F. NESS, Principal Investigator, magnetometer
experiment
HERBERT S. BRIDGE, Principal Investigator, plasma science
experiment
ARTHUR L. LANE, Principal Investigator, photopolarimeter
experiment
JAMES W. WARWICK, Principal Investigator, planetary radio
astronomy experiment
FREDERICK L. SCARF, Principal Investigator, plasma wave
experiment
A. LYLE BROADFOOT, Principal Investigator, ultraviolet
spectrometer experiment

## Summary of the Mission

The Voyager 2 spacecraft first encountered the planet Uranus while the probe was on its way out of the solar system. This swing-by of Uranus was the third of four planetary encounters made possible by an alignment of the outer planets—Jupiter, Saturn, Uranus, and Neptune—which occurs only once every 175 years. This alignment allowed Voyager 2 to arrive at Uranus in nine years instead of sixteen by using the gravity of each planet to boost it on to the next.

In 1981, prior to Voyager 2's encounter with Saturn (but after Voyager 1's Saturn encounter), the National Aeronautics and Space Administration (NASA) approved the Voyager 2 Uranus mission. The gravity of Saturn would be used to direct the spacecraft's trajectory toward Uranus. The journey between these worlds would take more than four years and 1.5 billion kilometers, for a spacecraft that had already spent that long and traveled that distance in space.

The time between the Saturn and Uranus encounters was used by Voyager engineers to modify the craft's onboard computer programs. These modifications were needed to enable the probe to overcome the problems associated with visiting a planet that is twice as far from the Sun as is Saturn. One such problem was the decreasing light levels. At a distance of 3.2 billion kilometers from the Sun, the light at Uranus would be four hundred times dimmer than it is at Earth. This level of light made necessary longer photographic exposures, which would lead to blurred pictures if the spacecraft could not keep the target in the camera's field of view during the exposure. To address this need, a computer algorithm known as target motion compensation was written and sent to the spacecraft. This algorithm allowed Voyager to drift in such a way as to keep the target in the camera's sights. In essence, this routine allowed the spacecraft to "pan" the cameras, like a human photographer does to photograph a moving object.

The greater distance also forced ground engineers to reduce the rate at which the spacecraft transmitted data. This reduction compensated for the ever-decreasing signal strength as the spacecraft moved away from Earth. It also meant that as the spacecraft got farther away, more time would be required to send the same amount of information. At Jupiter, for example, one picture could be transmitted every 96 seconds; at Saturn, the rate had fallen to one picture every 3.2 minutes, and at Uranus, it would be one every 8.8 minutes. To reduce the impact of this problem during the cruise toward Uranus project managers made a bold decision. Instead of using one flight data subsystem computer to format the data to be sent and the other as a backup, the two would be used together with no backup. The primary subsystem would still format the data; the secondary subsystem, however, would be used to combine the data more efficiently. This combination routine, known as image data compression, could send a complete photograph using less than 40 percent of the information bits normally required. Thus, even with the slower transmission rates from Uranus, one picture could be transmitted every 4.8 minutes.

Many more changes were made to Voyager 2 to compensate for the greater distance from the Sun and Earth and the lack of knowledge of the outer solar system. These changes involved not only the spacecraft program but also procedures used to operate the spacecraft. The spacecraft that finally arrived at Uranus was far superior to the one that had passed by Jupiter and Saturn.

On November 4, 1985, the first phase of the Uranus encounter began. Known as the observatory phase, it started when the quality of data from the spacecraft instruments surpassed the quality of data from ground-based instruments. During this phase, systematic searches were made of the Uranian system for new satellites and rings. In addition, atmospheric measurements began to be taken to gain information regarding atmospheric structure and composition and wind patterns.

Twenty-five days prior to the spacecraft's closest approach to Uranus, on December 31, 1985, Voyager 2 discovered its first Uranian satellite, which was given the name Puck. Puck is 170 kilometers in diameter and is located between the outer Uranian ring, known as the epsilon ring, and the innermost satellite, known as Miranda. Very little information about Puck's surface was gained from the discovery pictures because of its small size and great distance from the spacecraft. Because of the importance of surface geology, however, the various Voyager teams worked quickly to modify the spacecraft's program to photograph Puck immediately before the busy near encounter phase.

To modify the program, ground controllers decided to eliminate a planned observation of Miranda and replace it with an observation of Puck, then known as 1985U1. The spacecraft photographed Puck successfully, but the receiving ground antenna station started to drift, producing a poor alignment of the ground antenna with the spacecraft and resulting in the loss of the spacecraft signal which contained the Puck photograph. Fortunately, the photograph had been recorded on the spacecraft's tape recorder and could be played again. The commands to replay the data had to be sent quickly, however, before new information was recorded over the Puck data. The second playback was successful, revealing the surface of the moon discovered only days earlier.

The next phase of the encounter was known as the far encounter. This phase started on January 10, 1986, when Uranus and its rings were too large to fit comfortably into one narrow-angle photograph. To capture the entire planet and its rings required that the observation be designed as a mosaic of four pictures. Each picture in the mosaic would contain one quarter view of the planet and its rings.

During the far encounter, the spacecraft experienced its first hardware failure since its encounter with Saturn. On January 18, 1986, six days prior to Voyager 2's closest approach to Uranus, unexpected gaps started appearing in the photographs. Engineers quickly reviewed both the ground data system and the multimission image processing laboratory for hardware failures or software problems. Two days later, convinced that the problem was on the spacecraft and not on the ground, spacecraft controllers sent commands to the spacecraft instructing it to transmit the contents of its flight data subsystem memory. After reviewing the information, analysts found that one memory location had an incorrect value. The following day, on January 21, a command was sent to the spacecraft to use one of the few remaining spare memory locations instead of the one that appeared to have failed. After the craft received the command, the gaps in the spacecraft photographs disappeared, proving that a memory location had indeed failed.

On January 22, 1986, the near encounter phase began. During this phase, which lasted only four days, the spacecraft would be closest to the planet and would be gathering most of the important scientific data of this part of its mission. Timing was critical during this phase. The spacecraft had to be in the correct place at the correct time if its commands were to execute properly. The Voyager project teams worked throughout the night of January 23 and early into the next morning, adjusting the spacecraft commands. The final commands were transmitted to the spacecraft less than eight hours prior to their execution.

On January 24, at 1759 Greenwich mean time, Voyager 2 passed 107,000 kilometers from the center of Uranus. The navigation team had done a superb job of directing the spacecraft to its destination. The spacecraft was off its schedule by only sixty-one seconds, and its placement was such that Voyager 2 would pass by Neptune several years later.

The last phase of the encounter, which began on January 26, 1986, was the post encounter. During this time, measurements resembled those which had been executed during the observation phase. Pictures showed Uranus as a crescent as Voyager 2 headed toward Neptune.

### Knowledge Gained

The visible atmosphere of Uranus was found to be composed predominantly of hydrogen and helium, with concentrations very similiar to those found in the Sun. Carbon, however, was found to be twenty times more abundant than in the Sun. This relatively large amount of carbon, which is combined with hydrogen to form methane, gives Uranus its blue-green color. Methane absorbs mainly in the red wavelengths, reflecting the blue light to the observer.

The infrared experiment found that almost the same amount of energy is emitted by the poles of Uranus as by the equator. This was surprising, for the poles are exposed to more sunlight during the eighty-four-year orbit of Uranus and thus should radiate more energy. In addition, the spin axis of Uranus was found to be tilted 98 degrees relative to its orbital plane. Thus, even though Uranus spins on its axis once every 17.24 hours, the south pole faced the Sun during the entire Voyager 2 encounter. It takes forty-two years (one-half of a Uranian orbit) for the Sun to rise and set at the planet's poles.

Few discrete clouds were observed in the atmosphere of Uranus. The motion of those few clouds seen, however, indicated that winds rotated with the planet at a maximum speed of about 200 meters per second at a southern latitude of 60°. The winds slowed on either side of this region until they became almost nonexistent at the pole and at 20° south latitude. Farther north at the equator, however, the radio science experiment found the winds to flow in a direction opposite the rotation, with speeds up to 100 meters per second.

The upper atmosphere of Uranus was found to extend far above the planet. This part of the atmosphere has an extremely high temperature of 500 degrees Celsius and may produce drag forces on the particles located in the rings. These forces may be responsible for removing dust-sized particles from the Uranian ring system. The extended atmosphere also interacts with sunlight, giving off emissions that were detected by the ultraviolet experiment.

The nine previously known rings were photographed by Voyager's cameras. They are very dark and contain few particles in the 1-to-10-centimeter range. The darkness may be the result of the bombardment of the methane-water ice particles by protons trapped in the Uranian magnetosphere. The result of this bombardment is a carbon residue on the ice, which makes the ring particles as dark as coal. Two additional rings were found as Voyager 2 approached Uranus. As the probe left, one single long-exposure photograph indicated that micrometer-sized dust exists throughout the entire ring system.

Voyager 2 discovered ten new satellites in all, increasing the total number of known Uranian satellites from five to fifteen. The new satellites range from 40 to 170 kilometers in diameter and are located between the outer part of the ring system and the orbit of Miranda. Compared to Saturn's icy moons, the five previously known moons of Uranus were found to be relatively dark. Ariel, the second moon out from Uranus, has a fractured surface, which may indicate that ice once flowed across it. It also possesses one of the most geologically active surfaces in the Uranian system. Yet the most distinctive surface was found on Miranda. This satellite may have broken apart and reformed during its early history.

The magnetic field experiment found that the axis of the Uranian magnetosphere was tilted at 59 degrees to the planet's rotational axis. In addition, instead of being generated at the planet's center, as on Jupiter and Saturn, the magnetic field was found to be offset one-third of a Uranian radius.

## Context

On March 13, 1781, Sir William Herschel discovered Uranus, the seventh planet in the solar system, from his home in Bath, England. At that time, Uranus was the first planet to be observed by modern astronomers which had not been known to the ancients; its discovery showed that the solar system's outer boundary was much farther than had been previously believed.

Since its discovery, many telescopes have been pointed at Uranus. Its extreme distance from the Sun, however, has made unraveling its secrets very difficult. If one counted all the photons of light collected from Uranus by all the telescopes in the years from its discovery up to the Voyager 2 encounter, the amount of light would equal that given off by a flashlight in one second. Thus, the Voyager encounter with Uranus greatly increased knowledge of the Uranian system.

As a result of the encounter, planetary scientists now have the ability to compare the system of Uranus with those of Jupiter and Saturn. This study, known as comparative planetology, will allow scientists to understand the physical characteristics of these worlds better. This knowledge can then be applied to Earth. For example, atmospheric studies of the outer planets can improve meteorologists' understanding of terrestrial atmospheric dynamics.

Study of the Uranian ring system showed that it had many similarities to the ring systems of both Jupiter and Saturn; nevertheless, models of ring dynamics cannot yet completely explain the thinness of the nine Uranian rings. In addition, there is much to learn from the interaction of the Uranian magnetosphere with the ring system. Better models need to be developed to improve the understanding of the Uranian magnetosphere as well as of the magnetic fields of Mercury, Earth, Mars, Jupiter, and Saturn.

The Voyager 2 mission, sometimes referred to as the Grand Tour mission (a grand tour past Jupiter, Saturn, Uranus, and Neptune), is truly one of the most remarkable missions of all time. At its completion, it will have observed all the gaseous giant outer planets and most of the major moons in the solar system. The design, engineering, and operation of such a spacecraft will remain a monument to the creativity and curiosity of humanity in its quest to understand the universe.

## Bibliography

Davis, Joel. *Flyby: The Interplanetary Odyssey of Voyager 2*. New York: Atheneum Publishers, 1987. This book, intended for general audiences, gives a behind-the-scenes look at the Voyager 2 encounter with Uranus. It describes the individuals responsible for making the encounter as successful as it was and the events in which they took part.

Gore, Rick. "Uranus: Voyager Visits a Dark Planet." *National Geographic* 170 (August, 1986): 178-195. This article, intended for general audiences, gives an overview of the Voyager 2 encounter of Uranus. It contains many photographs and drawings that are helpful in elucidating theories and physical characteristics of the Uranian system.

Hunt, Garry E., ed. *Uranus and the Outer Planets*. Cambridge: Cambridge University Press, 1982. This collection of papers, intended for college students, describes the history of the discovery of Uranus and the knowledge of the Uranian system prior to Voyager 2's swing-by.

Laeser, Richard P., et al. "Engineering Voyager 2's Encounter with Uranus." *Scientific American* 225 (November, 1986): 36-45. This article, written by the Voyager project manager, the manager, and the deputy manager for the Flight Engineering Office, is intended for high school and college students. It explains how Voyager 2 had to be modified in preparation for the Uranus encounter. Contains photographs and illustrations.

Morrison, David, and Tobias Owen. *The Planetary System*. Reading, Mass.: Addison-Wesley Publishing Co., 1987. This book, intended for first-year undergraduates, gives an overview of each planetary system in the solar system as well as a description of asteroids and comets. It contains many photographs, illustrations, graphs, and tables.

Radlauer, Ruth, and Carolyn Young. *Voyager 1 and 2: Robots in Space*. Chicago: Children's Press, 1987. This book, intended for elementary and junior high school students, describes the entire Voyager 1 and 2 program. It contains many photographs and includes Voyager 2 data from Uranus.

*Randii R. Wessen*

## Cross-References

# THE WEST GERMAN SPACE PROGRAM

*Date:* Beginning November 8, 1969
*Type of program:* National space program
*Country:* West Germany

Both as a member of the European Space Agency and in its own right, West Germany has become a space power. The country's space projects are exclusively nonmilitary and are carried out as part of a national program, as part of the European Space Agency's program, and under a cooperative agreement with the United States.

> *Principal personages*
> HERMANN OBERTH, a scientist who helped develop the theory of space travel and spaceship design
> WERNHER VON BRAUN, a pioneer in rocketry and space exploration
> EUGEN SÄNGER, a rocket propulsion engineer
> ULF MERBOLD, a mission specialist on STS 9
> REINHARD FURRER and
> ERNST MESSERSCHMID, mission specialists on STS 61A

## Summary of the Program

As early as the thirteenth century, a German monk named Albertus Magnus wrote about how to make a black powder that could be used for flying or "making thunder." It was the engineers from Germany, seven centuries later, who developed the rockets that sent humans to the Moon.

Founded in 1927, Germany's space society, Verein für Raumschiffsfahrt (VFR), experimented with small rocket engines. Wernher von Braun, a leading space travel researcher, imitated these experiments, developing a car driven by explosives. The project required that advanced mathematics be applied to contained, reactive forces.

After World War I, Germany began to develop rocketry for military purposes, giving von Braun the opportunity to produce liquid-fueled rockets such as the V-2. The Saturn 5 launch vehicle, which sent the United States' Apollo spacecraft to the Moon, was descended from the V-2.

Though he favored space applications, von Braun needed to emphasize military applications to proceed with German government research. He enlisted the best of his colleagues to assist him in his systematic studies. By 1935, von Braun's group had established themselves in an isolated peninsula near the Baltic Sea called Peenemünde, a secluded and remote resort ideal for secret and safe rocket testing. Because of the lack of funds caused by Germany's deep economic depression, von Braun and engineer Walter Dornberger, with their team of eighty, did not complete their goal until 1939; finally, however, they managed to develop the V-2 weapon from the A-4 rocket. The modest-sized missile was produced in a factory set up in tunnels under the Hartz Mountains near Mittelwerk.

Early in 1945, von Braun and many of his countrymen realized Germany was about to lose the war to the allied armies of the United States, the Soviet Union, Great Britain, and France. After much discussion, the rocketry team decided it would be best for them to transfer their allegiance to the United States. They judged the U.S. political climate to be more favorable for space ventures than that of the Soviet Union.

The group moved from Peenemünde to Harz. When Germany finally surrendered, the U.S. army's advance took them directly through Harz, where von Braun and his colleagues were waiting. Von Braun persuaded his captors that his team could be helpful to the United States, and the Americans realized that other members of the Allies were acquiring German technicians, patents, inventions, and equipment. A number of technical experts, including one hundred of the cream of Peenemünde, emigrated to the United States. Though no one knew it at the time, the space race had begun.

Fundamental aerospace development and interest in space travel continued in West Germany after World War II. The country set up a rocket test-bed at Trauen and a simulation center with a vacuum chamber at Ottobruunn. The varied laboratory studies included investigations into the methods and processes of rocket construction, the development of materials for space applications, and reliability control. The studies also involved building installations for the liquefaction of high-energy propellants, such as hydrogen and fluorine; designing supersonic and hypersonic wind tunnels; and conducting research in the fields of electronics and plasma physics.

Officially, space research in West Germany originated in 1962 with the enactment of a federal statute. Thereafter, certain research institutes undertook several satellite projects in collaboration with German industry. In 1963, this preliminary research led to the concept of a series of satellites, technically similar, but each having a different mission.

Azur was the first German-designed and -built research satellite. It was launched on November 8, 1969, from Vandenberg Air Force Base in California, in cooperation with the United States. The satellite's Sun-synchronous orbit (an orbit synchronous with the Sun's apparent path across the sky) enabled seven experiments to monitor Earth's radiation belts and solar particle flows. Its life expectancy was one hundred years.

Dial was launched by a Diamant B rocket from Kourou, French Guiana, on March 10, 1970. Its name was a combination of the words Diamant and *Allemand* (German). The launch created excessive vibration, making Dial's study of the hydrogen geocorona (a ring of colored light about Earth) and the ionosphere difficult to evaluate. Dial reentered the atmosphere in 1978.

Aeros 1, carrying four German experiments and one U.S. experiment, was launched by a Scout rocket from Vandenberg on December 16, 1972. The satellite dipped into Earth's upper atmosphere 3,844 times, measuring short-wave ultraviolet radiation from the Sun, before reentering on August 22, 1973.

Aeros 2 was also launched from Vandenberg by a Scout on July 16, 1974. It was designed to continue research on the upper atmosphere. Some of the data returned was satisfactory. It reentered the atmosphere on September 26, 1975.

Two other collaborative projects, Helios 1 and Helios 2, named after the Sun god of ancient Greece, were the largest bilateral projects in which the U.S. National Aeronautics and Space Administration had participated up to that time. West Germany paid $180 million of the $260 million required to fund the projects.

The U.S. space shuttle's Instrument Pointing System (IPS); the Active Magnetospheric Particle Tracer Explorers (AMPTEs), a three-satellite mission which included the German ion release module; and the German infrared laboratory (GIRL), a telescope cooled by super-liquid helium and designed to study origins of stars and active galaxies, were all projects of German design.

The West German Ground Space Operations Center at Oberpfaffenhofen was established in 1969 and employs thirty-five hundred scientists, technicians, and administrative personnel. Set up by the Federal German Aerospace Establishment, it was used for the first time in November, 1985, for the German-funded and -operated Spacelab D1 mission.

West Germany's contributions to the European Space Agency (ESA), in both financial and research support, are evidence of its dedication to aerospace science. The nation is the second largest contributor to ESA; it provides 17.9 percent of the agency's funds. West Germany's commitment to prospects for the industrial use·of space prompted the 1985 founding, with Italy's Aeritalia, of Intospace, the first international agency to provide information on microgravity activities. Within a year, nine European countries and a Japanese consortium had joined Intospace with contracts to place microgravity experiments on the Spacelab D1 mission.

## Knowledge Gained

Spacelab D1, launched on October 30, 1985, was the first manned mission managed by a country other than the United States or the Soviet Union. Earlier, West Germany had funded 53 percent of the twelve-year, U.S.-managed, ESA-NASA Spacelab project, which ended with Spacelab 2 in August, 1985.

The payload specialists that were to participate in the Spacelab program were selected in December, 1982. Ulf Merbold, the first West German in space, went into orbit aboard Spacelab 1 in November, 1983. The Spacelab 1 crew conducted some twenty-two separate international investigations comprising seventy-two experiments in five broad areas of scientific research: life sciences, atmospheric physics, Earth observations, astronomy, and solar physics.

Aboard Spacelab D1 were Wubbo Ockels, a scientist and astronaut, Reinhard Furrer, a physicist and university instructor, and Ernst Messerschmid, a physicist. West Germany had paid $175 million to fly its Spacelab D1 and an array of science experiments into orbit on the U.S. shuttle *Columbia*. The mission was managed from the control center in Oberpfaffenhofen.

A vestibular sled experiment on Spacelab D1 consisted of a moveable carriage on rails and a helmet that could provide various controlled stimuli and record the wearer's responses. The sled was designed to investigate contributions of the different sensory systems to spatial orientation in order to evaluate human sensory motor adaptation to weightlessness. The crew members were accelerated up and down a track as their eyes and ears were subjected to various stimuli in an effort to identify the activities and conditions that cause spacesickness. The results showed a gain in rapid, involuntary movement of the eyeball. Detection of this movement continued for forty-eight hours after the crew's return to Earth. The data suggested that in weightlessness the nervous system attaches greater significance to sight and other body senses and ignores information sent to the brain from the inner ear. Another experiment on Spacelab D1 was a sleeping bag which exerted some pressure on the body and so eliminated the sensation of continuous free-fall that had made sleeping in weightlessness so difficult for some astronauts.

Dornier, a West German space engineering corporation, has developed a recoverable, single-stage, liquid-fueled rocket. The vehicle is capable of long, high-altitude flights, made possible by flexible wings which enable it to glide after accomplishing its mission; it is also capable of using telemetry for communication. Guided from the ground, the rocket can return to and land at its departure point.

Germany's MBB/ERNO was the prime contractor for ESA's Exosat (European X-Ray Observatory Satellite), a science mission that carried out two thousand observations of various phenomena, including exotic objects such as neutron stars, quasars, and black holes. Exosat detected highly ionized iron in clusters of galaxies in the constellations Virgo, Coma, and Perseus, providing clues to the creation and evolution of some of the largest formations in the universe.

The Active Magnetospheric Particle Tracer Explorers, a joint U.S., West German, and British project, successfully monitored the effects of the solar wind (a stream of hot, ionized gas which emanates from the Sun) as it encountered Earth's magnetosphere, a magnetic field around Earth which extends about 60,000 kilometers toward the Sun. Of the three AMPTEs launched, West Germany contributed one, the ion release module, which was developed by the Max Planck Institute. Its orbits were monitored so that in an eight-month period, it could make seven releases of barium and lithium ions into the solar wind and into Earth's magnetic tail.

In 1984, the year of President Ronald Reagan's authorization for the development of the U.S. Space Station, West Germany made a proposition, seconded by Italy, that ESA authorize development of a manned laboratory facility, Columbus, that would become part of the station.

In 1986, there was a revival of interest in the Sänger/Horus spaceplane, indicating West Germany's determination to compete with France in the European space race. Nevertheless, West Germany also contributed 30 percent of the funds for ESA's preparatory development program for the French-initiated Hermes spaceplane.

Along with Britain, Israel, and Italy, West Germany has signed a memorandum of understanding with the United States providing for industrial and research groups to participate in the United States' Strategic Defense Initiative.

## Context

The space age is founded largely on the rocket research conducted by German scientists in the 1920's and 1930's. West Germany's interest in space exploration continues. In the 1980's, when France decided to make the Ariane launch vehicle the main focus of its space program, West Germany became the largest contributor to the Spacelab project. The Columbus module, the German-Italian contribution to the U.S. space station *Freedom*, represents a leap forward for the German space effort.

The extent of West Germany's space program is determined by budgetary considerations and by the importance of space-related developments relative to the importance of research in other areas of science and engineering.

The official West German space policy aims at the development of a completely autonomous European space capability operating through the European Space Agency. Such a capability would include transport systems, a heavy-lift launcher, a space station, a data-relay system, and military intelligence satellites. West German officials have stated that if ESA is unable to conduct this long-term project efficiently, West Germany will try to reach the goal alone.

## Bibliography

Braun, Wernher von, et al. *Space Travel: A History*. New York: Harper and Row, Publishers, 1985. A work by eminently qualified authors whose education and experience add impact to the philosophical and technical aspects of the evolution of astronautics. Black-and-white photographs illustrate this history of rocketry and space exploration through the era of the space shuttle. Includes a bibliography.

Furniss, Tim. *Manned Spaceflight Log*. Rev. ed. London: Jane's Publishing Co., 1986. The flights that took place between the launch of Vostok 1 on April 12, 1961, and the launch of Soyuz T-15 on March 13, 1986, are covered in this edition. The log summarizes thirteen missions by the X-15, a rocket-powered plane. At least one page is devoted to each spacecraft launch, and information is provided on the sequence, dates, crew, and achievements of each mission.

*The McGraw-Hill Encyclopedia of Space*. New York: McGraw-Hill Book Co., 1968. An exhaustive reference work on space. It documents the early space programs of the United States and the Soviet Union, as well as those of other countries. The contents include such topics as rocketry, satellites, space navigation and electronics, humans in space, extraterrestrial life, astronomy, planetary exploration, and the state of astronautics up until the Apollo Moon landing.

Osman, Tony. *Space History*. New York: St. Martin's Press, 1983. A conversational account of the development of space projects, this book covers the history of rocketry, lift-offs, Moon missions, the shuttle era, and possible future space settlements. Includes color illustrations, a glossary, and a bibliography of non-technical readings.

Turnill, Reginald, ed. *Jane's Spaceflight Directory*. London: Jane's Publishing Co., 1987. An oversized, encyclopedic volume covering such major topics as national and international space programs, military space, launch vehicles, world space centers, spacefarers, the solar system, and space industry. A separate section describes various experiments, space tools, and types of satellites. The addenda update the book's information on national space programs and satellite launches.

*Clarice Lolich*

## Cross-References

Active Magnetospheric Particle Tracer Explorers, 1; The European Space Agency, 372; European Space Agency Satellites, 379; European Launch Vehicles, 734; International Private Industry and Space Exploration, 1182; Space Centers and Launch Sites in the European Space Agency Nations, 1585; International Contributions to the U.S. Space Station, 1843; The Spacelab Program, 1884.

# WHITE DWARF STARS

*Type of phenomenon:* Stellar

*A white dwarf is a star that has a mass below 1.4 solar masses and has undergone gravitational collapse. White dwarfs represent the final phase in the evolution of a low-mass star. The Apollo-Soyuz Test Project, a joint Soviet-American manned mission, first detected discrete ultraviolet radiation from two of the hottest and most luminous white dwarfs known.*

*Principal personages*
ALVAN G. CLARK, the astronomer who detected the first
    white dwarf star
WALTER SYDNEY ADAMS, JR., the astronomer who first identified
    Sirius B as a white dwarf star
SIR ARTHUR STANLEY EDDINGTON, the astronomer who founded
    the theory of stellar structure
SUBRAMANYAN CHANDRASEKHAR, the astrophysicist who
    established the properties of white dwarf stars
CHESTER M. LEE, Apollo-Soyuz Test Project Program Director
GLYNN S. LUNNEY, Apollo-Soyuz Test Project Technical Director
STUART BOWYER, Principal Investigator, Extreme
    Ultraviolet Survey
BRUCE MARGON,
MICHAEL LAMPTON,
FRANCESCO PARESCE, and
ROBERT STERN, coinvestigators, Extreme Ultraviolet Survey

## Summary of the Phenomenon

A white dwarf represents one of the several possible end products of the stellar aging process. Its name refers to the fact that such stars are small and hot. "White" is misleading; these stars actually display a range of colors as they cool, from white to yellow, to red, to black, when they are called "black dwarfs." To understand the nature of a white dwarf, it is necessary to know how they can be formed.

The entire lifetime and fate of a star are ultimately determined by the force of gravity, which causes the initial formation of the star out of a cloud of interstellar gas and dust. In a stable, young star, the inward force of gravity must be balanced by outward pressure. High pressure in the interior of the star, called the core, results in high temperature, thus allowing nuclear reactions to take place. Temperatures of millions of Kelvins are required for these reactions. The energy generated is what allows a star to shine for millions, or perhaps billions, of years. First, hydrogen is converted into helium, then helium into carbon, and carbon into yet heavier elements. The greater the mass of the star, the higher will be the internal pressure and temperature and the further the chain of nuclear reactions will be able to progress. High-mass stars not only carry the chain of reactions further but also consume their nuclear fuel much more quickly than lower-mass stars do. (These nuclear reactions take place only in the hot interior of the star, not in the cooler outer envelope.)

No matter what a star's mass is, however, it eventually exhausts its store of nuclear fuel. When the energy supply is cut off, there is no longer anything to support the star's weight, and gravity causes it to contract. As the star contracts, the material is compressed to higher and higher density. Because of the high temperature, a star's core is not made up of atoms, but rather nuclei and free electrons. Eventually, the electrons get packed together as tightly as possible and form what is called a "degenerate electron gas." (Degenerate means simply that the material is packed to the minimum possible volume or maximum possible density. A particle is not able to move freely, as in an ordinary gas, but its motions are limited by the proximity of neighboring particles.) Degeneracy represents a high-pressure situation, and the pressure of a degenerate electron gas may be sufficient to halt the contraction of the star—a white dwarf has formed.

The incompressible material constituting a white dwarf resembles a solid or liquid but is far more dense. This is possible because in the hot interior of a white dwarf, the atoms are virtually completely ionized (that is, stripped of their electrons), and the bare ions can be packed much more closely together than can atoms in ordinary matter. As for the overall physical properties of a white dwarf, they typically have masses comparable to that of the Sun but compressed to roughly planetary dimensions. For example, if the Sun, whose mass is about 300,000 times that of Earth, were to be compressed to Earth's volume, the material would have an average density of about $10^9$ kilograms per cubic meter; a mere tablespoon would weigh about 1,000 tons at the surface of Earth.

White dwarfs are also among the hotter stars, with surface temperatures generally in the range of 6,000 to 30,000 Kelvins. The surface layers are nondegenerate, and the internal temperatures are considerably higher than at the surface. In fact, the stored thermal energy (the energy of motion of the nuclei) is the only source of a white dwarf's light, since the star is no longer contracting or undergoing nuclear reactions. Most white dwarfs have low luminosities (power outputs) compared to younger, nuclear energy-generating stars because of their small size, which makes them detectable at only relatively close distances. It is estimated, however, that approximately 10 percent of the stars in a given volume of space are white dwarfs.

Among the better-known white dwarfs are Sirius B, the faint companion to Sirius A, the brightest star in Canis Major (the Big Dog); Procyon B, the companion to Procyon A, the brightest star in Canis Minor (the Little Dog); and 40 Eridani B. Each of these white dwarfs is a member of a nearby (within twenty light-years), visual binary system, and the observations of their orbital motions can be used to compute their masses. Sirius B, the first white dwarf discovered, has a mass of about 1.1 solar masses and a radius of about 5,600 kilometers. (For comparison, the radius of Earth is about 6,400 kilometers.) The surface temperature is approximately 29,000 Kelvins, and the luminosity is about one three-hundredth that of the Sun. With a mass of 0.43 solar mass, 40 Eridani B has a radius of about 8,700 kilometers, a surface temperature near 16,900 Kelvins, and a luminosity about one two-hundredth that of the Sun. The mass of Procyon B is about 0.63 solar mass. All together, more than three hundred white dwarfs are known. Their average physical properties are a mass of about 0.7 solar mass, a radius of about 7,000 kilometers, and an average density of about $10^8$ kilograms per cubic meter.

The first white dwarf was detected in 1862 by Alvan G. Clark. Later called Sirius B, it was identified in 1915 as a white dwarf star by Walter Sydney Adams, Jr. Theoretical work on the physical state of white dwarfs began in earnest in the 1930's. Arthur S. Eddington had founded the theory of stellar structure in the 1920's, and later (in the mid-1930's) astrophysicist Subramanyan Chandrasekhar investigated the physics of a degenerate electron gas as it applied to stars, including the incorporation of the theory of relativity in his work. Although in an ordinary (nondegenerate) gas the pressure depends on both density and temperature, in a degenerate gas the pressure depends only on density. As a result, there is an inverse relation between the mass of a white dwarf and its radius: The larger the mass, the smaller the radius, and vice versa. This relation is readily understood in terms of the fact that more mass means stronger self-gravitation, which in turn requires higher pressure and higher density for stable equilibrium; increased density means a smaller volume, that is, a smaller radius.

Chandrasekhar also found that there is an upper limit to the mass of a star that can be supported by degenerate electron pressure. This is about 1.4 solar masses—the so-called Chandrasekhar limit—but the exact value depends on details of actual chemical composition and the extent to which relativity theory plays a role in the star's structure. The implication of the Chandrasekhar limit is that masses greater than that value are simply too heavy to be supported by the pressure of degenerate electrons; the contraction of the star would continue, perhaps to form a neutron star/pulsar or a black hole.

Although stars in the lower mass range, on the order of 1.5 solar masses or less, are by far the most common type, such stars age very slowly, and it is doubtful if any such stars could yet have consumed their nuclear fuel. From where then do the significant numbers of white dwarfs come? The answer must be that they evolve from more massive stars, since those stars age quickly as a result of their higher gravitational "squeeze."

Even though the details of the stellar aging process are not completely clear and do depend critically on the star's mass, it is known that most stars go through unstable phases in their later evolution—they become variable stars. These may take the form of periodic pulsations in size (and light output), or they may take a more violent, explosive form. In either case it is possible for mass loss to occur. The mass ejection may be quiescent, as in the case of a planetary nebula, in which an outer shell of stellar material simply lifts off and recedes from the hot inner core of the star. Alternatively, the mass loss may be more cataclysmic, as in the case of a nova or supernova. In these ways, more massive stars may shed sufficient material to get below the Chandrasekhar limit and thus become stable white dwarfs. Since all that remains is the hot inner core, this helps explain the relatively high surface temperatures of white dwarfs.

In their spectral features, white dwarfs tend to fall into two general classes: those with strong spectral lines because of hydrogen and those with strong helium lines. Stars with the strongest hydrogen lines are designated A-type stars; white dwarfs of this type are classified as DA (where D stands for dwarf). The non-DA stars have strong helium lines.

Because of their small size, the surface gravity of white dwarfs is large. This tends to make the spectral lines broad. Also the large surface gravity provides one test of Albert Einstein's general theory of relativity. According to that theory, radiation emitted in a strong gravitational field should be redshifted (that is, emitted at a somewhat longer wavelength or lower energy than would be the case in a weaker gravitational field). This effect is difficult to measure, but data from Sirius B and 40 Eridani B are consistent with the theory's predictions.

Another effect of the small size of white dwarf stars is that they often have intense magnetic fields compared to larger stars. A typical ordinary star such as the Sun has a fairly weak magnetic field—about $10^{-4}$ tesla. If it were to contract to the dimensions of a white dwarf, the magnetic-field lines would be highly compressed, making the magnetic field at the surface of the contracted star much stronger—on the order of 1 tesla. Some white dwarfs have magnetic fields 100 to 1,000 times stronger than that. This fact is inferred from the effect of the field on the spectral lines (called the Zeeman effect), which causes them to split.

Still another property that might be expected of white dwarfs is rapid rotation. Since rotating objects shrink in size, the rotation rate must increase in order to conserve angular momentum. There is no observational evidence, however, to suggest that white dwarfs are in fact rapidly rotating. Perhaps the mechanism of mass loss carries away most of the angular momentum, so that the remnant core rotates only slowly, if at all.

Eventually, a white dwarf, given sufficient time, will radiate away its store of thermal energy; that is, it will cool off. Cooling is a slow process, taking many billions of years, since the rate of cooling slows as the star's temperature drops. This gradual decrease in temperature is accompanied by a more rapid decrease in luminosity. The star thus dims and becomes known as a black dwarf.

## Knowledge Gained

Observations of white dwarf stars were made during the joint Soviet-American Apollo-Soyuz Test Project (ASTP) of July, 1975. Of the twenty-eight experiments conducted (five jointly and twenty-three unilaterally), several were of an astronomical nature, including soft X-ray observations and the Extreme Ultraviolet (EUV) Survey. The latter was an attempt to observe discrete (that is, pointlike) sources of ultraviolet radiation at wavelengths between 10 and 100 nanometers. Such radiation ought to be highly susceptible to absorption by diffuse hydrogen gas in the interstellar medium.

It had been previously supposed that the density of interstellar matter would not allow detectable amounts of EUV radiation to travel more than a few dozen light-years and that there were few potential sources within that range. By the mid-1970's, however, observations had suggested that EUV sources might be more numerous, and the density of interstellar hydrogen somewhat less, than previously thought. The EUV Survey instrument consisted of a grazing-incidence telescope and EUV detectors capable of resolving a 2.5-degree field of view.

The EUV Survey experiment achieved the first detection of discrete EUV sources outside the solar system. At least four stellar sources were identified, the two most intense being the white dwarfs HZ43 and Feige 24, both previously known from their visible light. Coincidentally, both objects are actually binary stars consisting of very blue DA white dwarfs with faint red-dwarf companions. (A red dwarf—not to be confused with a white dwarf—is an ordinary, unevolved star of low mass which is undergoing nuclear reactions in its core; it is denoted as an M-type star.)

HZ43 is an object of approximately thirteenth visual magnitude located in the direction of the constellation Coma Berenices (near the north galactic pole). Its distance from Earth is estimated from parallax data at about 200 light-years. Its white dwarf component, HZ43A, was the strongest of the EUV sources detected and was also observed as a soft X-ray source. The spectrum of data received indicates an effective temperature of about 110,000 Kelvins, which is considerably hotter than the temperature deduced from earlier data in the visible portion of the spectrum (about 50,000 ± 5,000 Kelvins). The high intensity of the radiation received also makes it more luminous than previously thought; in fact, it exceeds the luminosity of the Sun and is the hottest white dwarf known.

Feige 24, in the direction of the constellation Cetus, was the next most intense EUV source observed. Its indicated effective temperature is about 60,000 Kelvins, and it is also extremely luminous for such a compact object. Its distance is determined to be on the order of 300 light-years. In the case of Feige 24, the red-dwarf companion cannot be resolved as a separate image, but its presence and type are deduced from spectral features. Unlike HZ43, the spectrum shows some variability.

The spectra of both HZ43 and Feige 24 show them to be lacking in helium and heavy elements. Their atmospheres seem to consist of nearly pure hydrogen.

## Context

The luminosity of a star depends on two factors: the temperature, which determines the intensity of the spectrum radiated, and the radius of the star, which determines the surface area from which radiation can escape into space. Larger radii and/or greater temperatures correspond to larger luminosities.

If the distance to a star is known, the observed brightness (apparent magnitude) of the star may be used to estimate its luminosity (absolute magnitude). Then, if the temperature of the star is inferred from the spectrum received, the stellar radius may be calculated. In this way, it has been determined that the radius and luminosity of the white dwarf HZ43A are about 8,000 kilometers and 17 solar luminosities. For the white dwarf component of Feige 24, the radius is about 17,000 kilometers and the power output is roughly 7 solar luminosities. Although these are the only known white dwarfs whose power outputs exceed that of the Sun, these results are not inconsistent with the other previously known properties of white dwarfs.

The ASTP data could not be used to draw any conclusions about the masses of stars. Essentially, the only direct observational data concerning masses come from visual binary stars. These are binary systems in which both components can be observed, so that the orbital period and size can be determined and Kepler's laws applied. Because the low luminosity of white dwarfs makes them difficult to observe, direct data on masses are difficult to obtain. The few cases of known mass are consistent with theoretical expectations and with the Chandrasekhar limit. The evidence suggests that stars less than or equal to about 7 solar masses become white dwarfs, with some sort of mass ejection mechanism required to get the mass below the limit. It seems reasonably clear that white dwarfs are in fact objects with masses similar to that of the Sun but with dimensions on the order of planets; they are luminous by virtue of their stored thermal energy but are not undergoing nuclear reactions. The material in the interior of a white dwarf consists of a gas of degenerate electrons and nondegenerate nuclei, the pressure of which is able to support the star against further contraction.

Finally, one additional conclusion reached by the EUV Survey investigators should be mentioned. The EUV data were used to obtain more reliable estimates of the mean density of interstellar matter in the directions of the white dwarfs observed. The results indicate about 0.01 to 0.015 hydrogen atom per cubic centimeter (that is, fewer than 2 atoms per 100 cubic centimeters). This is somewhat less than had previously been expected and bodes well for the future of EUV stellar astronomy.

## Bibliography

Abell, George O. *Realm of the Universe*. 3d ed. New York: Saunders College Publishing, 1984. A brief, introductory, nonmathematical text for college students. Exceptionally well written, with numerous illustrations and excellent discussion of stellar evolution and its end products, including white dwarf stars, neutron stars, and black holes.

Angel, J. Roger P. "Magnetic White Dwarfs." *Annual Review of Astronomy and Astrophysics* 16 (1978): 487-519. This review article contains many references to original sources. Discusses similarities between magnetic white dwarf stars and magnetic neutron stars, evolution of magnetic fields in white dwarf stars, polarization, and the effects on magnetism of mass accretion in white dwarf binary systems.

Kaufmann, William J., III. *Universe*. New York: W. H. Freeman and Co., 1985. A beautifully illustrated, comprehensive introductory astronomy text. Contains some math, but is intended for general audiences. Good treatments of stellar evolution, white dwarf stars, neutron stars, pulsars, and black holes.

Liebert, James. "White Dwarf Stars." *Annual Review of Astronomy and Astrophysics* 18 (1980): 363-398. This review article contains almost no mathematics, but does make extensive use of technical terminology. Very well-written article covering all aspects of white dwarf stars, but for the serious rather than the casual reader. Especially valuable for its list of nearly two hundred references to books and articles on white dwarf stars.

National Aeronautics and Space Administration. *Apollo-Soyuz Test Project: Summary Science Report.* Vol. 1. Washington, D.C.: Government Printing Office, 1977. The official report of the joint Soviet-American mission of July, 1975, written in terms intelligible to the educated nonspecialist. Especially valuable are the chapters on the summary of scientific results and the Extreme Ultraviolet Survey.

Snow, Theodore P. *The Dynamic Universe.* St. Paul, Minn.: West Publishing Co., 1988. An introductory astronomy text for nonscience students, with excellent color pictures and diagrams. Good discussions of stellar properties, stellar evolution, and white dwarf stars.

Zeilik, Michael, and John Gaustad. *Astronomy: The Cosmic Perspective.* New York: Harper and Row, Publishers, 1983. Text is designed for an introductory, descriptive, comprehensive astronomy course. Contains an excellent chapter on the end products of the stellar aging processes. The section on white dwarf stars is especially useful.

Zeilik, Michael, and Elske V. P. Smith. *Introductory Astronomy and Astrophysics.* 2d ed. New York: Saunders College Publishing, 1987. Introductory text developed along physical rather than purely astronomical lines. Includes some math; good diagrams and tables.

*George W. Rainey*

## Cross-References

The Apollo-Soyuz Test Project, 132; Black Holes, 211; U.S. and Soviet Cooperation in Space, 259; The New Astronomy and the Study of Electromagnetic Radiation, 1066; Solar Radiation, 1359; Stellar Evolution, 1944; Supernovae and Neutron Stars, 1970.

# ZOND 1-8

*Date:* April 2, 1964, to October 27, 1970
*Type of program*: Unmanned spaceflight tests
*Country:* The Soviet Union

*The Zond program began as a series of interplanetary probe diagnostic flights to determine the cause of previous planetary probe failures. Later Zonds were unmanned precursors to man-rate the Soyuz reentry cabin and the Proton booster for circumlunar missions.*

### Principal personages

PAVEL I. BELYAYEV, the first cosmonaut scheduled to circumnavigate the Moon

ANATOLI A. BLAGONRAVOV, Chairman of the Commission for the Exploration and Use of Outer Space, Soviet Academy of Sciences

VALENTIN P. GLUSHKO, a leading designer of Soviet rocket engines

A. M. ISAYEV, a designer of sustainer engines for manned spacecraft and interplanetary probes

M. V. KELDISH, President of the Soviet Academy of Sciences

SERGEI P. KOROLEV, Chief Designer of the Soviet space program, 1957-1966

LEONID SEDOV, an academician and Chairman of the Interdepartmental Commission of Interplanetary Communications, Soviet Academy of Sciences

L. A. VOSKRESENSKY, Assistant to the Chief Designer, the designer of the Soyuz manned spacecraft used as the cabin for Zonds 4 through 8

MIKHAIL KUZMICH YANGEL, Chief Designer of the Soviet space program, 1966-1971

## Summary of the Program

The Zond program began in 1964 as a cover name for planetary probe diagnostic flights which were launched into deep space to determine the cause of failure in previous Venera and Mars missions. Beginning with the Zond 4 mission, the focus of the program changed. Instead of using the Zond craft as deep space probes, the Soviets, caught in the race for the Moon with the United States, used it to man-rate the Soyuz spacecraft and the Proton booster in preparation for a manned lunar landing. The first Zond (the Russian word for "probe") launch attempt was on November 11, 1963, but the spacecraft never left Earth orbit. A faulty rocket design prevented escape-stage ignition, and the marooned probe was named the Kosmos 21 satellite.

The 1964 Venus launch window (the period of time when planetary alignment and the booster's available energy allow a launch toward the planet) saw two flights. The first, on March 27, 1964, resulted in the Kosmos 27 satellite, another vehicle stranded in Earth orbit because of a launch failure. The second attempt to reach Venus in 1964, on April 2, placed the Zond 1 probe into a heliocentric orbit which passed Venus at a distance of 100,000 kilometers on July 19, 1964. Communication with Zond 1 was lost on May 14, 1964, at a distance of 14 million kilometers, while the vehicle was performing a midcourse correction maneuver.

Mars was the target for the Zond 2 probe, launched on November 30, 1964. Just after launch, however, it was noted that its power supply was about half of that expected. Efforts to correct the power shortage were unsuccessful, and contact with the probe was lost when it was 5 million kilometers from Earth. Yet before contact with Zond 2 was lost, three course corrections were completed which allowed the spacecraft to pass 1,600 kilometers from Mars on August 6, 1965.

Zond 3 had a dual mission after its July 18, 1965, launch. After 33 hours of flight, Zond 3 passed the Moon and took twenty-five photographs of the far side before continuing into deep space as another planetary probe diagnostic flight. The lunar photographs, however, were not transmitted to Earth immediately. It was not until the probe was 2,400,000 kilometers from Earth, nine days later, that the lunar photographs were first transmitted, using a 1,100-line facsimile scan system. In a test of the planetary photography gear to be used later aboard the Venera 2 and 3 probes, Zond 3 continued to transmit the photographs of the Moon until the space-craft was 31.5 million kilometers from Earth. At this distance, each frame required 34 minutes for transmission. Zond 3 was still functioning well when it reached the orbit of Mars. Yet, since the spacecraft was launched six months after the close of the previous Mars launch window, the planet was not within reach of the spacecraft.

All three of the early Zond probes were launched by an A-2 booster from the Tyuratam space center. The Zond program continued flight operations with launches in March and April, 1967. Yet booster failure prevented their success.

The new Zond flights were focused on man-rating the passenger cabin of the Soyuz spacecraft for circumlunar flight. The lunar flightplan called for the removal of the orbital module from the Earth-orbiting Soyuz spacecraft and launch of the passenger cabin and service module by a Proton booster into a circumlunar trajectory, looping the spacecraft around the Moon and returning it to Earth.

The first publicly acknowledged flight in the new Zond program came on March 2, 1968, when the 2,500-kilogram Zond 4 was launched from Tyuratam. The flight followed an unusual trajectory which carried it out to the distance of the Moon, but in an opposite direction from where the Moon was at the time of launch. Apparently this was to control the spacecraft's return to Earth, an easier task without the perturbations of the Moon's gravity.

Zond 5 was sent into a lunar trajectory from its Earth-parking orbit on September 15, 1968. A course correction on September 17, 1968, allowed Zond 5 to loop around the Moon at an altitude of 1,950 kilometers on September 18, 1968. The circumlunar spacecraft carried a cargo of cameras and biological specimens which included tortoises, insects, and plants. On the flight to the Moon, Zond 5 took photographs of Earth from a distance of 90,000 kilometers.

Photographs of the near and far sides of the Moon were taken using film which was returned to Earth for processing. For the first time, Soviet lunar photographs did not rely on facsimile transmission. As a result, each of the Zond 5 lunar photographs contained 134 million bits of information, compared to only 1.2 million bits in the Zond 3 photographs. Some stereo views of the Moon were also recorded. On the night of September 19-20, 1968, during Zond 5's return to Earth, the Jodrell Bank radio telescope in England monitored transmissions of a taped Russian voice calling off simulated instrument readings.

On September 21, 1968, Zond 5 reentered Earth's atmosphere over Antarctica at a velocity of 10,900 meters per second, exposing the heatshield to temperatures of 13,000 degrees Celsius. An atmospheric deceleration with a gravitational force of 10 to 16 times that of Earth slowed the reentry cabin to 200 meters per second. Parachutes deployed at an altitude of 7 kilometers, completing the landing of the first circumlunar flight. The seven-day flight of Zond 5 ended with the first Soviet ocean recovery when the reentry cabin splashed down in the Indian Ocean and was retrieved by a Soviet ship. Zond 5 was taken to Bombay, India, where the spacecraft was flown back to the Soviet Union.

The Tass news agency stated that the flight of the 2,720-kilogram Zond 6, launched November 10, 1968, was "to perfect the automatic functioning of a manned spaceship that will be sent to the Moon." After rounding the Moon on November 14, 1968, at an altitude of 2,420 kilometers, Zond 6 entered a return trajectory toward Earth. While still 256,556 kilometers from Earth, the Zond performed a course correction maneuver which aimed the craft precisely for a reentry corridor only 10 kilometers wide at an altitude of 45 kilometers above Earth.

Zond 6 used a skip-lob reentry trajectory in which the craft reentered the atmosphere over the Indian Ocean at 11 kilometers per second. After the vehicle slowed to 7.6 kilometers per second, its reentry cabin was oriented so its lift-generating heatshield catapulted the cabin back out of the atmosphere and into a ballistic reentry targeted for the Soviet Union. This skip-lob technique resulted in reduced reentry gravitational forces of only 4 to 7, a range tolerable by human passengers. Researchers admitted that while the skip-lob reentry reduced the gravitational load on the vehicle, the two periods of heating separated by a cold period put an increased thermal strain on the vehicle.

A Proton launch of August 7, 1969, placed the Zond 7 spacecraft on course for the Moon. The next day, at a distance of 70,000 kilometers, Zond 7 photographed Earth with color film instead of the black-and-white film used on previous Zond missions. The intent was to discern new features on Earth's surface using the color film. A midcourse correction on August 9, 1969, placed the craft on a trajectory which carried it around the Moon at an altitude of 2,000 kilometers on August 11, 1969. After a seven-day flight, Zond 7 used the same skip-lob reentry technique as its predecessor, landing near Kustanai, Kazakhstan, on August 14, 1969.

More than one year later, the final Zond flight was launched on October 20, 1970. Weighing an estimated 4,000 kilometers, Zond 8 took more color photographs of Earth and the Moon and carried biological specimens to the Moon and back. When it was 277,000 kilometers from Earth, Zond 8 was photographed against the stellar background to establish precisely its path to the Moon. Telescopes at the Sternberg Astrophysical Institute and the Crimean Astrophysical Observatory were aimed precisely at the Zond with the help of the spacecraft's onboard laser. Color photographs of Earth, the Moon, and the lunar far side—as well as three days' worth of live television photographs of Earth—were returned before the craft looped around the Moon at an altitude of 1,120 kilometers. More biological specimens were flown to the Moon aboard Zond 8.

The recovery of Zond 8 differed from those of the previous two flights in that it was a ballistic recovery, with the vehicle reentering over the North Pole instead of the South Pole. This trajectory was chosen so that the final phases of the flight could be controlled from Soviet ground stations. A nighttime splashdown occurred 725 kilometers southeast of the Chagos Archipelago in the Indian Ocean. Recovery crews watched the actual reentry, and the craft was retrieved immediately by the Soviet ship *Taman*. The spacecraft was taken to Bombay, India, for air transport to the Soviet Union.

## Knowledge Gained

Continuing Soviet difficulties to fly interplanetary probes successfully during the early 1960's prompted the creation of the Zond spacecraft series as engineering test-beds to perfect deep space probes. The Zond 1 and 2 probes failed to return data from their Venus and Mars targets but did provide valuable deep space operations experience and engineering data to help identify and correct ongoing problems. Zond 2 made the first space tests of ionic thrusters.

Previous Soviet deep space probes had encountered difficulties during the orientation changes needed to position the craft's course-correction rocket. By the time Zond 3 reached the orbit of Mars in 1965, the Soviets had finally overcome this obstacle. Though Zond 3 did not actually reach the planet Mars, because it was launched outside the normal planetary launch window, it was still functioning after traveling for the appropriate time and distance to have reached the planet and was, therefore, considered an engineering success.

Zond 3 tested photographic equipment to be used by later Venera probes as it passed the Moon on July 20, 1965. About 3 million square kilometers, from 90° west to 166° west, of the lunar far side were photographed, including the portion of the far side not detected by the Luna 3 reconnaissance vehicle six years earlier. Other lunar investigations by Zond 3 involved measuring the lunar spectra in the range of 2,500 to 3,500 angstroms as well as the ultraviolet and infrared ranges of 1,900 to 2,700 angstroms and 3 microns, respectively. Results from Zond 3 show that the Moon has an ultraviolet albedo of about 1 percent.

The Zond 4 unmanned test flight of the lunar version of the Soyuz spacecraft was apparently unsuccessful, as there was no announcement of the craft's recovery following its launch in 1968.

Zond 5, launched six months later, used a free-return trajectory (a trajectory requiring no further course changes after arriving at the Moon) to circumnavigate the Moon before safely returning to Earth. Engineering data gained from the lunar flight and subsequent atmospheric reentry at near-Earth escape velocity speeds were applied to the two following Zond lunar flights. Zond 6 and 7 flew special skip-lob reentry trajectories designed to test lower deceleration loads for the human passengers who were expected to fly the Soyuz spacecraft to the Moon.

Zond 8 was flown to the Moon more than one year after American astronauts had first set foot on the Moon. As with previous circumlunar Zonds, this one carried various biological specimens to test medical reactions to lunar flight. The passengers—tortoises, lower life-forms, and plants—proved as healthy as similar specimens which had flown in low-Earth orbit. Whether the later Zond series succeeded in its mission of man-rating the lunar Soyuz is not known, as no Soviet manned launch to the Moon was ever accomplished.

## Context

Some Western analysts believe that Zonds 4 through 8 were planned as tests for a serious man-around-the-Moon program. Certain Americans maintain that Premier Nikita Khrushchev was intent on surpassing the Americans at every major space goal even if it meant using unsophisticated technology. According to some observers, the plan was to maintain the image of Soviet space superiority while leaving the expensive science and engineering to the Americans. Both public and private statements by cosmonauts Vladimir Komarov, Gherman Titov, and Alexei Leonov left little doubt that the Soviet timetable called for perfecting the Soyuz spacecraft for a manned circumlunar flight before November 7, 1967, the fiftieth anniversary of the Bolshevik Revolution.

Paralleling the American Apollo plans under way at the same time, the Soviets found the road to the Moon to be very rocky. Bad luck and technical failure combined to deal Soviet manned lunar missions three serious setbacks. First, the head of the Soviet space program, Sergei Korolev, died while undergoing surgery in late 1966. Second, the 1967 Soyuz 1 disaster, in which cosmonaut Vladimir Komarov was killed, resulted in the diversion of manpower to correct design deficiencies in the Soyuz. Third, the Zond launch failures in March and April, 1967, delayed plans for Soviet manned lunar missions.

While unable to contribute to the Soviet festivities commemorating the Bolshevik Revolution, the Zond program persevered. The completion of the Zond 6 flight had all the appearances of being the final test before cosmonauts would be sent around the Moon.

This continuing Soviet progress with the Zond lunar flights forced the American political decision to fly the first manned Apollo-Saturn 5 mission into lunar orbit.

This decision resulted in the Christmas Eve, 1968, circumlunar mission of Apollo 8—a direct challenge to imminent Soviet plans to send a manned Soyuz spacecraft around the Moon. Three catastrophic launch failures involving the Proton booster, in January, April, and June of 1969, adversely affected its being man-rated in time for a circumlunar flight before the American Apollo 11 astronauts safely returned from the Moon in July, 1969. Had the Apollo 11 manned lunar landing failed and the Proton booster been cleared for manned flight, Zond 7 would most likely have carried cosmonauts on the first manned circumlunar flight.

On October 24, 1969, after the Apollo 11 manned lunar landing and continued technical problems with the Proton booster, M. V. Keldish, President of the Soviet Academy of Sciences, was reported as saying that the Soviet Union was setting aside its manned lunar program. Keldish said, "We no longer have a timetable for manned lunar trips."

With the conclusion of the Zond 8 flight in October, 1970, no further man-related Moon flights were launched by the Soviet Union. Indeed, by the end of 1970, the cosmonaut who had been selected for the first Soviet manned lunar flight was dead; Pavel Belyayev had died following surgery for a bleeding stomach ulcer.

## Bibliography

Gatland, Kenneth. *Robot Explorers*. London: Blandford Press, 1972. A chronology of Soviet and American lunar and planetary space exploration programs. Contains numerous color illustrations providing insights into the design and function of American and Soviet lunar and planetary spacecraft. The descriptive narrative provides details and results of all American and Soviet lunar and planetary exploration spacecraft and their missions.

McDougall, Walter. A. . . . *The Heavens and the Earth: A Political History of the Space Age*. New York: Basic Books, 1985. This well-researched and heavily footnoted historical text describes and analyzes the decisions by the leaders of both the United States and the Soviet Union and their effects on the respective space programs. Heavy emphasis on the key political and technological leaders of the time. Relates how the American and Soviet space programs became an integral part of Cold War politics.

Oberg, James E. *Red Star in Orbit*. New York: Random House, 1981. A comprehensive review of all phases of the Soviet space program, with equal emphasis given to both the failures in achieving Soviet spaceflight and the successes of ongoing research programs. Attention is given to the personalities and politics of the Soviet space program. An excellent overview of the canceled Soviet man-to-the-Moon program.

Smolders, Peter. *Soviets in Space*. New York: Taplinger Publishing Co., 1974. Covering all aspects of the Soviet space program, this book emphasizes manned activities. It concentrates on the successful aspects of Soviet space missions as they were reported by the Soviet Union. Contains numerous diagrams and photographs illustrating the technical details of Soviet spacecraft and their missions.

Stoiko, Michael. *Soviet Rocketry.* New York: Holt, Rinehart and Winston, 1970. An overview of the Soviet space program, tracing the evolution of Soviet rocketry and satellite technology and leading to planetary exploration and manned spaceflight. Emphasizes the pre-Sputnik technological development leading to the Soviet space program of the 1960's and speculates on future Soviet space programs. Suitable for the beginner. Illustrated.

Turnill, Reginald. *The Observer's Spaceflight Directory.* London: Frederick Warne, 1987. A lavishly illustrated summary of spaceflight activities by all nations. Lists chronologies of major manned and unmanned space missions. Technical narrative describes worldwide space activities by nation and program, providing details of spacecraft, mission summaries, and program results. One-third of the directory is devoted to Soviet programs.

U.S. Congress. Senate. Committee on Commerce, Science, and Transportation. *Soviet Space Programs: 1976-1980.* Part 2, *Manned Space Programs and Space Life Sciences.* Report prepared by Congressional Research Service, the Library of Congress. 98th Cong., 2d sess., 1984. Committee Print. This booklet provides a comprehensive description of all phases of Soviet manned spaceflight missions—including scientific investigations, medical research and results, and political effects of Soviet space activity.

*Robert Reeves*

## Cross-References

Apollo 8, 53; Apollo 11, 75; Biological Effects of Space Travel on Humans, 188; Cosmonauts and the Soviet Cosmonaut Program, 273; Soviet Launch Vehicles, 742; The Luna Orbiters, 786; The Soyuz-Kosmos Program, 1396; Soyuz 1, 1403; Space Centers and Launch Sites in the Soviet Union, 1592; The Soviet Spaceflight Tracking Network, 1877.

# GLOSSARY

*Ablative heatshield:* A heatshield which is composed of material that *ablates* (that is, melts and eventually vaporizes) as a spacecraft reenters Earth's atmosphere. The consequent removal of excess heat prevents the spacecraft from burning up.

*ABM.* See *Antiballistic missile.*

*Abort:* To terminate a launch or a mission, usually as the result of equipment failure. As a noun, the action of aborting.

*Absolute magnitude:* The brightness of a star or other celestial body measured at a standard distance of 10 parsecs. (See also *Apparent magnitude, Luminosity, Parsec.*)

*Absolute temperature scale:* A temperature scale which sets the lowest possible temperature (absolute zero, or the temperature at which molecular and atomic motion stops) at zero. (See also *Kelvin.*)

*Absorption spectrum:* An electromagnetic spectrum that shows dark lines which result from the passage of the electromagnetic radiation through an absorbing medium, such as the gases found in a star's atmosphere. The resulting *absorption lines* are characteristic of certain chemical elements and reveal much about the composition of the star's atmosphere. (See also *Electromagnetic spectrum, Emission spectrum, Spectrum.*)

*Acquisition:* The detection and tracking of an object, signal, satellite, or probe to obtain data or control the path of a spacecraft. (See also *Star tracker.*)

*Active experiment:* An experiment package carried by a satellite, usually in a canister, which typically has a control circuit, a battery-driven power system, data-recording instruments, and environmental control systems. (See also *Passive experiment.*)

*Active satellite:* A satellite equipped with onboard electrical power which enables it to transmit signals to Earth or another spacecraft. Most artificial satellites fit this description. (See also *Passive relay satellite.*)

*Advanced vidicon camera system (AVCS):* Spaceborne imaging systems made up of two 800-line cameras with nearly twice the resolution of a normal television camera. Capable of photographing a 3,000-kilometer-wide area with a resolution of 3 kilometers.

*Aerodynamics:* The study of the behavior of solid bodies, such as an airplane, moving through gases, such as Earth's atmosphere.

*Aerography:* The study of landfeatures on Mars.

*Aeronautics:* The study of aircraft and the flight of these man-made objects in the atmosphere.

*Aeronomy:* The study of the physics and chemistry of the atmospheres of Earth and other planets.

*Aerospace:* The space extending from Earth's surface outward to the farthest reaches of the universe.

*Air lock:* A small enclosed area (especially in the space shuttle and space stations) which is located between the interior of a spacecraft and outer space or another spacecraft, through which an astronaut or cargo can pass without depressurizing the spacecraft.

*Airbus (bus):* A spacecraft used to deliver payloads into orbit or to another spacecraft, such as a space station. The Soviet Progress carriers, as well as the space shuttle, perform airbus functions.

*Airglow:* A faint glow emitted by Earth which results from interaction between solar radiation and gases in the ionosphere, perceived from space as a halo around the planet. Airglow is known for interfering with Earth-based astronomical observations, making space-based telescopes desirable.

*Albedo:* The amount of electromagnetic radiation reflected from a nonluminous body, measured from 0 (perfectly black) to 1 (perfectly reflective).

*Altitude:* The distance of an object directly above a surface. Also, the arc or angular distance of a celestial object above or below the horizon.

*Angstrom:* One ten-thousand-millionth of a meter; a unit used to measure electromagnetic wavelengths.

*Angular momentum:* A property of a rotating body (or a system of rotating bodies) which is defined as the product of the distribution of the body's mass around the rotational axis (the *moment of inertia*) and the speed of the body around the axis (the *angular velocity*). Angular momentum remains constant; that is, an increase in one of the two factors is compensated by a decrease in the other. Hence, a spinning ice-skater will rotate faster as he pulls his arms toward his body; a planet or artificial satellite will move faster in its elliptical orbit as it approaches the point closest to the object around which it is orbiting (periapsis).

*Anemometer:* An instrument for measuring the force of wind.

*Antiballistic missile (ABM):* A missile designed to destroy a ballistic missile in flight.

*Antimatter:* Matter in which atoms are composed of antiparticles: positrons in place of electrons, antiprotons in place of protons, and so forth. The existence of such antiparticles is accepted, although their configuration as antimatter has yet to be discovered. Theoretically, the result of a meeting between matter and corresponding antimatter is mutual obliteration in a release of energy.

*Antisatellite (ASAT) system:* A weapons system used to destroy potentially hostile orbiting satellites.

*Aphelion:* The point in an object's orbit around the Sun at which it is farthest away from the Sun.

*Apoapsis:* The point in one object's orbit around another at which the orbiting object is farthest away from the object being orbited.

*Apocynthion:* The point in an object's orbit around the Moon at which it is farthest away from the Moon.

*Apogee:* The point in an object's orbit around Earth at which it is farthest away from Earth.

*Apolune:* Apocynthion of an artificial satellite.

*Apparent magnitude:* The brightness of a star or other celestial body as seen from a single point, such as Earth. The brightness is "apparent" only, because stars vary in their distance from Earth. (See also *Absolute magnitude*, *Luminosity*.)

*Apparent motion:* The path of movement of a body relative to a fixed point of observation.

*Applications technology satellite:* A satellite designed for developing applications (meteorology, navigation, communications, Earth resources, and the like). Also used as a relay between other satellites and Earth stations.

*APU.* See *Auxiliary power unit*.

*Arm.* See *Remote manipulator system*, *Robot arm*.

*Array:* A system of multiple devices (such as radio aerials or optical telescopes) situated so as to increase the strength of the data received.

*Artificial satellite:* A man-made satellite or object sent into orbit around a celestial body. Generally referred to simply as "satellites," these spacecraft are usually unmanned.

*ASAT.* See *Antisatellite system*.

*Ascent stage:* One of two stages of the Apollo lunar module; it carried the crew, their gear and samples, the life-support system, and fuel for lift-off from the Moon, orbit, and docking with the command and service module. (See also *Descent stage*.)

*Asteroid:* A small, solid body (also known as a *planetoid*), ranging in size from about 200 meters to 1,000 kilometers in diameter, which orbits the Sun. The solar system is home to thousands of these bodies, most of which occur in a region between the orbits of Mars and Jupiter.

*Asteroid belt:* The region between Mars and Jupiter (between 2.15 and 3.3 astronomical units from the Sun) where most of the solar system's asteroids have been found.

*Asthenosphere:* The layer of Earth below the lithosphere.

*Astronaut:* A space traveler, usually from the United States but also from other non-Communist nations. (See also *Cosmonaut*, *Spacenaut*.)

*Astronautics:* The science and technology of spaceflight, including all aspects of aerodynamics, ballistics, celestial mechanics, physics, and other disciplines as they affect or relate to spaceflight. (See also *Aerodynamics*, *Aeronautics*, *Celestial mechanics*.)

*Astronomical unit (AU):* The mean distance between the centers of Earth and the Sun: 92,955,630 miles or 149,597,870 kilometers. Used for measuring distance within the solar system.

*Astronomy:* The study of all celestial bodies and phenomena within the universe.

*Astrophysics:* The branch of astronomy dealing with the chemical and physical properties and behaviors of celestial matter and their interactions.

*Atmosphere:* Any gaseous envelope surrounding a planet or star. Earth's atmosphere consists of five layers: the troposphere, stratosphere, mesosphere, thermosphere (which roughly coincides with the ionosphere), and exosphere.

*Atmospheric pressure:* The force exerted by Earth's atmosphere, which at sea level is approximately 14.7 pounds per square inch, 101.325 newtons per square meter, or 1 bar. One "atmosphere" refers to any of these sea-level measures and can be used to refer to atmospheric pressure on other planets: Venus' surface pressure, for example, is 90 atmospheres.

*Atom:* The smallest particle of an element that can exist alone or in combination with other atoms. Most atoms consist of one or more electrons (negatively charged particles) orbiting a nucleus made of protons (positively charged particles) and neutrons (particles with no charge). The combinations of these particles determine the identity of the atom as a particular chemical element or isotope of that element.

*Attitude:* The orientation of a spacecraft or other body in space relative to a point of reference.

*Attitude control system:* The combined mechanisms working together to maintain or alter a spacecraft's position relative to its point of reference, including onboard computers, gyroscopes, star trackers, or a combination of these.

*AU.* See *Astronomical unit.*

*Aurora:* The colored lights appearing in the sky near the poles when charged particles issuing from the Sun become trapped in Earth's magnetic field. The arching, spiraling glows result from these particles interacting with atmospheric gases as they follow Earth's magnetic force lines.

*Aurora borealis:* The aurora occurring near Earth's North Pole.

*Aurora australis:* The aurora occurring near Earth's South Pole.

*Auxiliary power unit (APU):* A backup system on board a space shuttle, space station, or other spacecraft for generating non-propulsion electrical power in the event of a main-system failure.

*AVCS.* See *Advanced vidicon camera system.*

*Avionics:* The electronic devices used on board a spacecraft, or the development, production, or study of those devices.

*Axis:* The imaginary line around which a celestial body or man-made satellite rotates.

*Azimuth:* The arc, or angular distance, measured horizontally and moving clockwise, between a fixed point (usually true north) and a celestial object. (See also *Altitude.*)

*Backup crew:* A group of astronauts trained to perform the same functions as the crew members of a particular space mission (such as the commander, pilot, and flight engineer), in the event that an emergency requires replacement of the original crew.

*Ballistic missile:* A missile that is not self-guided but rather is aimed and propelled at the point of launch only, and hence follows the trajectory which is determined at launch.

*Ballistics:* The study of the motion of projectiles in flight, including their trajectories—especially important in the launching and course-correction maneuvers of spacecraft.

*Band.* See *Frequency, Hertz.*

*Bar.* See *Atmospheric pressure.*

*Barbecue maneuver:* The deliberately maintained slow roll of a spacecraft in orbit, so that all exterior surfaces will be evenly heated by the Sun.

*Barycenter:* The center of mass of a system of two or more bodies.

*Bhangmeter:* An optical-flash detector used to detect nuclear explosions from satellites.

*Big bang theory:* The cosmological theory, accepted by many scientists, that the universe has evolved from a gigantic explosion of a compressed ball of hot gas many billions of years ago. The theory holds that matter is still flying outward, uniformly, from the center of this explosion, and is therefore also referred to as the expanding universe theory. (See also *Steady state theory.*)

*Binary star:* A star system formed of two stars orbiting their combined center of mass. Three types of binaries include visual binaries, which emit radiation in the visible wavelength range (the most common binaries); spectroscopic binaries, detected by their Doppler shifts; and eclipsing binaries, in which one star periodically blocks light from the other as they rotate around each other. It is estimated that more than half of the stars in the Galaxy are binaries.)

*Biotelemetry:* The remote measurement and monitoring of the life functions (such as heart rate) of living beings in space, and the transmission of such data to the monitoring location, such as Earth.

*Biosatellite:* Formed from "biological" and "satellite," a biosatellite is an artificial satellite carrying life forms for the purpose of discovering their reaction to conditions imposed in the space environment.

*Black dwarf:* A star that has cooled to the point that it no longer emits visible radiation; the end state of a white dwarf star. (See also *White dwarf.*)

*Black hole:* A hypothetical celestial body whose existence is predicted by Albert Einstein's general theory of relativity and is accepted by many scientists. In a black hole, matter is so condensed and gravitational forces are so strong that not even light can escape. Black holes are thought to be either the product of a collapsed star (stellar black holes) or the result of the original big bang (primordial black holes).

*Blueshift:* An apparent shortening of electromagnetic wavelengths emitted from a star or other celestial object, indicating movement toward the observer. (See also *Doppler effect.*)

*Boom:* A long arm extending outward from a satellite or other spacecraft to hold an instrument or device such as a camera.

*Booster.* See *Rocket booster.*

*Bow shock:* The "wave" created by a planet's magnetic field when it forms an obstacle to the stream of ionized gases flowing outward from the Sun.

*Breccia:* A type of rock formed by sharp, angular fragments embedded in fine-grained material such as clay or sand. Among the "Moon rocks" returned by the Apollo astronauts, breccias were the most common.

*Burn:* As a noun, the term used to refer to the firing of a rocket engine, including any burn used during a spaceflight to set the spacecraft on a trajectory toward a planet or other target.

*Caldera:* A very large crater formed by the collapse of the central part of a volcano.

*Canopus:* The brightest star in the sky after Sirius, visible south of 37 degrees latitude. Canopus is often the target of a spacecraft's star tracker, which uses it as a reference point in steering a course toward the spacecraft's destination.

*Capsule communicator (capcom):* A ground-based astronaut who acts as a communications liaison between ground and flight crews during manned missions.

*Cassegrain telescope:* The most common type of reflecting telescope, named for its inventor, Guillaume Cassegrain (1672). The telescope contains two mirrors: a concave mirror near its base, which reflects light from the sky onto a convex mirror above it; the convex mirror, in turn, reflects the light back down through a hole in the middle of the convave mirror to the focal point. The Hubble Space Telescope is of Cassegrain design.

*C-band:* A radio frequency range of 3.9 to 6.2 gigahertz. (See also *Hertz.*)

*CCD.* See *Charge coupled device.*

*Celestial mechanics:* The branch of physics concerned with those laws which govern the motion (especially the orbits) of celestial bodies, both artificial and natural.

*Celestial sphere:* An imaginary sphere surrounding an observer at a fixed point in space (the sphere's center), with a radius extending to infinity, a *celestial equator* (a "belt" cutting the sphere into two even halves), and *celestial poles* (north and south). By reference to these points on the celestial sphere, the observer can describe the position of an object in space.

*Celsius scale:* A temperature scale, named for its inventor, Anders Celsius (1701-1744), which sets the freezing point of water at zero and the boiling point at 100. Also referred to as the centigrade scale, its increments correspond directly to Kelvins. To convert Kelvins to degrees Celsius, subtract 273.15. (See also *Kelvin.*)

*Centrifuge:* A device for whirling objects or human beings at high speeds around a vertical axis, exerting centrifugal force to test spacecraft hardware or train astronauts to withstand the forces of launch.

*Cepheid variable:* A star that has passed its main sequence phase (the greater part of its lifetime) and has entered a transitional phase in its evolution, during which the star expands and contracts, at the same time pulsating in brightness. By measuring the star's period of pulsation and extrapolating from that its absolute magnitude, then comparing the absolute magnitude to the apparent magnitude, astronomers find the distance of the star and nearby celestial objects.

*Chandrasekhar limit:* The maximum possible mass for a white dwarf star, calculated by Subramanyan Chandrasekhar in 1931 as approximately 1.4 solar masses (later modified upwards for rapidly rotating white dwarf stars). When the star's mass exceeds the Chandrasekhar limit, gravity compresses it into a neutron star.

*Charge:* A property of matter defined by the excess or deficiency of electrons in comparison to protons. Negative charge results from excess electrons; positive charge, from a deficiency of electrons.

*Charge coupled device (CCD):* A highly sensitive device, commonly one centimeter square, which is sensitive to electromagnetic radiation and contains electrodes and conductor channels, overlying an oxide-covered silicon chip, for collecting, storing, and later transferring the data to create images of celestial objects and other astronomical phenomena.

*Chromosphere:* The lower layer of the solar atmosphere (between the photosphere and the solar corona), several thousands of kilometers thick, which is composed mainly of hydrogen, helium, and calcium and is visible only when the photosphere is obscured, as during a solar eclipse. The term also applies to corresponding regions of other stars.

*Circular orbit:* An orbit in which the path described is a circle.

*Closing rate:* The speed of approach of two spacecraft preparing for rendezvous.

*Coma.* See *Comet.*

*Comet:* A luminous celestial object orbiting the Sun, consisting of a *nucleus* of water ice and other ices mixed with solid matter, and, as the comet approaches the Sun, a growing *coma* and *tail.* The coma is a collection of gases and dust particles that evaporate from the nucleus and form a glowing ball around it; the tail forms as these materials are swept away from the nucleus. Comets appear periodically, depending on the parameters of their solar orbits, and vary in size from a few kilometers to thousands.

*Command and service module:* The portion of the Apollo spacecraft consisting of the command module, in which the astronauts traveled to the Moon, and the service module, which contained the lunar module and main rocket engine.

*Communications satellite.* See *Telecommunications satellite.*

*Comsat:* An abbreviation for "communications satellite." (See also *Telecommunications satellite.*)

*Conjunction:* The alignment of two planets or other celestial bodies so that their longitudes on the celestial sphere are the same. *Inferior conjunction* occurs between two bodies whose orbits are closer to the Sun than Earth's; *superior conjunction* occurs between bodies whose orbits are farther from the Sun than Earth's.

*Constellation:* A collection of stars which form a pattern as seen from Earth. The stars in these groupings are often quite distant from one another, their main common characteristic being the illusory picture they form (such as the Big Dipper, or Ursa Major) against the backdrop of the night sky. Constellations are useful in that they provide points of reference for astronomers and other stargazers.

*Convection:* A process that results from the movement of unevenly heated matter— gases or liquids—whereby hotter matter moves toward and into cooler matter.

The resultant circular motion and transfer of heat energy is convection.

*Core:* The central portion of any celestial body, especially the terrestrial planets but also stars. Also, the central part of a launch vehicle, to which may be added strap-on boosters.

*Core sample:* A sample of rock and soil taken from Earth, the Moon, or another terrestrial planet by pressing a cylinder down into the planet's surface.

*Corona:* The outermost portion of the Sun's atmosphere, extending like a halo outward from the Sun's photosphere. The corona consists of extremely hot ionized gases that eventually escape as solar wind. The term is also used to refer to the corresponding region of any star's atmosphere.

*Coronagraph:* A device for viewing the solar (or another star's) corona, consisting of a solar telescope outfitted with an occulting mechanism to obscure the photosphere, as during a solar eclipse, so that the corona is more easily perceived.

*Cosmic dust:* Tiny solid particles found throughout the universe, thought to have originated from the primordial universe, the disintegration of comets, the condensation of stellar gases, and other sources. Also known as *interstellar dust*.

*Cosmic radiation:* Atomic particles that are the most energetic known, consisting mainly of protons, along with electrons, positrons, neutrinos, gamma-ray photons, and other atomic nuclei. These particles emanate from a number of sources, both within and beyond the Milky Way, and they bombard atoms in Earth's atmosphere to produce showers of secondary particles such as pions, muons, electrons, and nucleons. If a primary cosmic particle is sufficiently energetic when it hits an atmospheric atom, the secondary particles can reach Earth's surface and do, passing through matter.

*Cosmic ray detector:* A device for sensing, measuring, and analyzing the composition of cosmic radiation in an attempt to discover its sources and distribution.

*Cosmodrome:* Any Soviet launch site, one of the best known being Tyuratam/ Baikonur in Siberia.

*Cosmology:* The study of the origins and structure of the universe.

*Cosmonaut:* A Soviet astronaut.

*Countdown:* The tracking of the time immediately preceding a space launch, during which all conditions, both outside and inside the spacecraft, are closely monitored to ensure proper functioning of all systems. Usually expressed as "T" (time) "minus" so many minutes and seconds before engine ignition. (See also *Ground-elapsed time, Mission-elapsed time*.)

*Course-correction maneuver:* The firing of a rocket or the change of speed during a spaceflight to adjust the trajectory of a spacecraft, such as a probe, to ensure that it reaches its destination.

*Crater:* A depression in the surface of a planet or moon caused by the force of a meteorite's fall. Also, the depression that forms at the mouth of a volcano.

*Cruise missile:* A bomb-bearing missile which flies at low altitude by means of an onboard guidance system that senses terrain and identifies its target.

*Crust:* The outermost layer, or shell, of a planet or moon, such as Earth.

*Cryogenic fuels:* Liquid rocket propellants that operate at extremely low temperatures, such as liquid oxygen.

*Cyclotron radiation:* The radiation produced by charged particles as they spiral around magnetic lines of force at extremely high speeds.

*Data acquistion:* The detection, gathering, and storage of data by scientific instruments.

*DBS.* See *Direct broadcast satellite.*

*De-orbit:* To execute maneuvers, such as firing of retrograde rockets to reduce orbital speed and leave an orbit, usually in preparation for reentry into Earth's atmosphere or a change in course.

*Deep space:* Regions of space beyond the Earth-Moon system.

*Deep space probe:* A device launched beyond the Earth-Moon system that is designed to investigate other parts of the solar system or beyond. Sometimes called an *interplanetary space probe* in reference to spacecraft investigating the planets and the space between them.

*Density:* The ratio of an object's mass to its volume.

*Descent stage:* One of two stages of the Apollo lunar module; it carried fuel for landing as well as some scientific equipment. (See also *Ascent stage.*)

*Dewar:* A container, similar to a vacuum bottle, with inner and outer walls between which is evacuated space to prevent transfer of heat. Used to store cryogenic fuels at very low temperatures.

*Dielectric:* Used to characterize any device, substance, or state (insulating materials, a vacuum) that is a nonconductor of electricity.

*Digital imaging.* See *Imaging.*

*Direct broadcast satellite (DBS):* A telecommunications satellite designed to broadcast television signals directly into private residences equipped with dish antennae, particularly useful where television reception is difficult.

*Dirty snowball theory:* The model of comets, accepted by most astrophysicists, that considers a comet's nucleus to be composed of a small sphere of ice and rock.

*Diurnal:* Occurring daily. The *diurnal motion* of a planet or other celestial body is its daily path across the sky as seen from a fixed point such as Earth, which depends on the position of the observer.

*Dock:* To link one spacecraft with another or others while in space, first achieved in 1965 by Geminis 6A and 7.

*Doppler effect:* First described in 1842 by Christiaan Doppler, the principle that describes the effect, from the perspective of an observer, of an object's movement on the electromagnetic or sound energy that it emits. The wavelength or frequency of this energy appears to increase (shorten) if the energy source is approaching the observer, and the rate (speed) of approach will determine the rate of increase. The opposite is true as the energy source moves away from the observer. Hence, the sound from an ambulance streaking past a motorist seems to rise sharply as it approaches, then fall as it rushes away: The motorist perceives increasingly "compressed" (shortened) wavelengths of sound as the ambulance approaches, then increasingly "stretched" (elongated) wavelengths as the ambulance speeds down the road. Electromagnetic (light) energy behaves similarly. Red and infrared rays have longer wavelengths, while the wavelengths of blue and ultraviolet rays are shorter. A source of light that is moving away from an observer will appear to get "redder" (called the *redshift*). If the light source is approaching, it will get "bluer" (*blueshift*). These phenomena are measured by observing the spectral lines of the energy source over time. The Doppler effect is at the base of much of our understanding of the universe, providing strong support for the theory of the expanding universe.

*Downlink:* Transmissions to Earth from a spacecraft; often used in reference to telecommunications satellites.

*Drogue chute:* A small parachute designed to pull a larger parachute from stowage or to decrease the velocity of a free-falling spacecraft during reentry.

*Early-warning satellite:* A satellite designed to detect launches of ballistic missiles and tests of nuclear weapons.

*Earth day:* Twenty-four hours, or the time required for Earth to complete one rotation on its axis. Scientists measure the planets' periods of rotation in Earth days.

*Earth-orbital probe:* An unmanned spacecraft carrying instruments for obtaining information about the near-Earth environment.

*Earth resources satellite:* A satellite designed to detect and store data on Earth resources and their conditions, such as mineral deposits, forests, crops and crop diseases, and pollution. The Landsat series of satellites is a preeminent example.

*Eccentricity:* The degree to which an ellipse (or orbital path) departs from circularity. Eccentricity is characterized as "high" when the ellipse is very elongated.

*Eclipse:* The obscuring of one celestial body by another. In a *lunar eclipse*, Earth's shadow obscures the Moon when Earth is situated directly between the Sun and Moon. In a *solar eclipse*, the Moon is situated between the Sun and Earth in such a way that part or all of the Sun's light is blocked; the total blockage of sunlight (with the exception of the Sun's corona) is called a *total eclipse* of the Sun.

*Ecliptic plane:* The plane in which Earth orbits the Sun. From Earth, the ecliptic plane is perceived as the Sun's yearly path through the sky.

*Ejecta:* Material thrown out from a volcano.

*Electromagnetic radiation:* Radiation, or a series of waves of energy, consisting of electric and magnetic waves, or particles (photons), vibrating perpendicularly to each other and traveling at the speed of light. Electromagnetic radiation varies in wavelength and frequency as well as source (which may be thermal or nonthermal) and whether or not it is polarized. (See also *Electromagnetic spectrum*.)

*Electromagnetic spectrum:* The continuum of all possible electromagnetic wavelengths, from the longest, radio waves (longer than 0.3 meter), to the shortest, gamma rays (shorter than 0.01 nanometer). The shorter the wavelength, the higher the frequency and the greater the energy. Within the electromagnetic spectrum is a range of wavelengths that can be detected by the human eye, visible light. Its wavelengths correspond to colors: Red light emits the longest-wavelength visible radiation; violet light, the shortest-wavelength radiation. None of these types of electromagnetic radiation is discrete; each blends into the surrounding forms. Detection of nonvisible radiation by special instruments (used in such branches of astronomy as infrared astronomy and X-ray astronomy) reveals much about the behavior of celestial bodies and the origins of the universe.

*Electron:* An atomic particle which carries a negative charge and a mass about one eighteen-thousandth of a proton. One or more electrons whirl around the nuclei of all atoms and can also exist independently.

*Electronic intelligence satellite (ELINT):* A satellite designed to identify sources of radar and radio emissions, primarily used in military applications. (See also *Ferret.*)

*Electrophoresis:* A process for separating cells using a weak electric charge, more easily accomplished in space than on Earth.

*Elementary particles:* The smallest units of matter or radiation, characterized by electrical charge, mass, and angular momentum. Among elementary particles are electrons, neutrons, protons, neutrinos, the various mesons, and their corresponding antiparticles (which form antimatter). Photons, the smallest units of electromagnetic radiation, are also considered as elementary particles.

*ELINT.* See *Electronic intelligence satellite.*

*Ellipse:* An oval-shaped geometric curve formed by a point moving so that the sum of the distances between two points around which it moves is always the same. The planets trace out ellipses in their orbits around the Sun.

*ELV.* See *Expendable launch vehicle.*

*Elliptical orbit:* An orbit which departs from circularity, as most orbits do. A *highly elliptical orbit* is one whose apoapsis is much greater than its periapsis, resulting in an orbit that traces out an elongated ellipse.

*Emission spectrum:* A spectrum showing the array of wavelengths emitted by a thermal source of electromagnetic radiation, such as a star. Atoms in this source subjected to thermal (heat) energy will emit energy as their electrons move from one energy level to another. The wavelengths that characterize these energy jumps correspond to specific elements (such as hydrogen), and appear as a characteristic line on the emission spectrum. The relationships of these lines to one another tell astronomers much about the composition, density, temperature, and other conditions in the energy source.

*EMU.* See *Spacesuit.*

*Equatorial orbit:* An orbit that follows the equator of the body orbited.

*Escape velocity:* The speed at which an object must travel to escape the gravitational attraction of a celestial body. In order for a spacecraft to leave Earth orbit, for example, its engines must exert enough in-orbit thrust to achieve escape velocity.

*EVA.* See *Extravehicular activity.*

*Event horizon:* The boundary beyond which an observer cannot see. Also, the boundary beyond which nothing can escape from a black hole, where escape velocity equals the speed of light and thus nothing, not even light, can escape. Therefore, the event horizon is theoretically the spherical delineation of a black hole. (See also *Escape velocity.*)

*Exobiology:* The study of the conditions for and potential existence of life-forms beyond Earth.

*Exosphere:* The outermost layer of Earth's atmosphere.

*Expendable launch vehicle (ELV):* A launch vehicle not intended for reuse. The Altas, Delta, Titan, and Saturn launch vehicles fall into this category.

*External tank:* The large tank that stores liquid fuel for the three space shuttle main engines; it separates from the shuttle after all the fuel has been used (about 8.5 minutes after lift-off) and burns up in the atmosphere.

*Extraterrestrial life.* See *Exobiology.*

*Extravehicular activity (EVA):* Popularly known as a "space walk," any human maneuver taking place partially or fully outside the portion of a spacecraft that houses the astronauts.

*Extravehicular mobility unit (EMU).* See *Spacesuit.*

*F region.* See *Thermosphere.*

*False-color image:* An image resembling a photograph, created from data collected by instruments (such as an infrared sensor) aboard a spacecraft and deliberately assigned unnatural colors in order to make nonvisible radiation visible or to highlight distinctions. (See also *Imaging.*)

*Ferret:* An electronic intelligence satellite designed to detect hostile electromagnetic radiation. (See also *Electronic intelligence satellite.*)

*Fission (atomic):* The breaking of an atomic nucleus into two parts, resulting in a great release of energy.

*Flightpath:* The trajectory of an airborne or spaceborne object relative to a fixed point such as Earth.

*Fluid mechanics:* The study of the behavior of fluids (gases and liquids) under various conditions, including that of microgravity in spaceflight. Understanding fluid mechanics in space is important to the technology of spaceflight and may have applications on Earth as well.

*Flyby:* A close approach to a planet or other celestial object, usually made by a probe for the purpose of gathering data; the maneuver does not include orbit or landing. Also used to refer to a mission which undertakes a flyby.

*Fluorescence:* The property of emitting visible light absorbed from an external source.

*Focal ratio (f-number):* The ratio of (1) the distance between the center of a lens or mirror and its point of focus (focal-length) and (2) the aperture, or diameter, of the mirror lens. The focal ratio of a telescope determines its power of magnification.

*Footprint:* An area on Earth's surface where a spacecraft is expected to land. Also, an area served by a telecommunications satellite.

*Frauenhofer lines:* Prominent absorption lines in the Sun's spectrum, first observed by Joseph von Frauenhofer in 1814, indicating the presence of certain elements in the Sun's corona. Also used to refer to such absorption lines in other stars' spectra.

*Free-flyer:* Any spacecraft capable of solitary flight, and not attached to another for electrical power.

*Free return trajectory:* An orbital flight path which allows a disabled spacecraft to reenter Earth's atmosphere without assistance.

*Frequency:* The number of times an event recurs within a specific period of time. Frequency characterizes both sound and electromagnetic radiation and is defined as the ratio of its wavelength to its speed. Frequency is measured in hertz or multiples of hertz.

*Fuel cell:* A device that joins chemicals to produce electric energy, different from a battery in that the chemicals are joined in a controlled fashion depending on electrical load. A by-product of fuel cells that use oxygen and hydrogen is potable water. Used on Apollo and space shuttle missions.

*Fusion:* A thermonuclear reaction in which the nuclei of light elements are joined to form heavier atomic nuclei, releasing energy. The process can be controlled to produce power. It is also the process whereby the stars formed the elements with atomic numbers up to iron.

*Gabbro:* A dark-colored, igneous, crystalline rock.

*Gain:* The increase in power of a transmitted signal as it is picked up by an antenna.

*Galaxy:* A collection of stars, other celestial bodies, interstellar gas and dust, and radiation rotating or clustered around a central hub, classified by Edwin Hubble in 1925 as one of four shapes: spiral, elliptical, lenticular, or irregular. Galaxies are thousands of light-years across and contain billions of stars, and there are thousands of galaxies in the universe.

*Gamma radiation:* Electromagnetic radiation with wavelengths less than 0.01 nanometer, the most energetic known in the universe outside cosmic radiation. The ability of gamma rays to penetrate the interstellar matter and radiation of the universe makes them especially valuable to astronomers.

*Gamma-ray astronomy:* The branch of astronomy which investigates gamma radiation and its sources by detectors sent aloft in satellites such as Orbiting Solar Observatory 3, SAS 2, and COS-B. Among the sources of gamma rays are pulsars and neutron stars.

*Gegenschein:* A patch of faint light about twenty degrees across, visible from the night side of Earth at a point opposite the Sun in the ecliptic plane, and possibly caused by the reflection of sunlight from a dust "tail" swept away by the solar wind. (See also *Zodiacal light*.)

*Geiger counter:* A device that detects high-energy radiation (including cosmic rays) by means of a tube containing gas and an electric current. The radiation causes the gas to ionize, which is transmitted to the current and detected as a sound or a needle jump.

*Geocentric orbit:* An orbit with Earth as the object orbited.

*Geodesy:* The science concerned with the size and shape of Earth and its gravitational field.

*Geostationary orbit:* A type of geosynchronous orbit which is circular and lies in Earth's equatorial plane, at an altitude of approximately 36,000 kilometers. As a result, a satellite in geostationary orbit appears to hover over a fixed point on Earth's surface. (See also *Geosynchronous orbit*.)

*Geosynchronous orbit:* A geocentric orbit with a period of 23 hours, 56 minutes, 4.1 seconds, equal to Earth's rotational period. Such an orbit is also *geostationary* if it lies in Earth's equatorial plane and is circular. If inclined to the equator, a geosynchronous orbit will appear to trace out a figure eight daily; the size of the figure eight will depend on the angle of inclination. These orbits are used for satellites whose purpose it is to gather data on a particular area of Earth's surface or to transmit signals from one point to another. Communications satellites are geosynchronous.

*GET*. See *Ground-elapsed time*.

*Gigahertz*. See *Hertz*.

*Glide path:* The path of descent of an aircraft under no power.

*Globular clusters:* Spherically shaped congregations of thousands, sometimes millions, of stars, which occur throughout the universe, although more often near elliptical galaxies than spiral galaxies such as the Milky Way. It is believed that globular clusters contain the oldest stars, and because they also contain a variety of stars of different sizes, all occurring at relatively the same distance from Earth, it is possible to learn much from them about the history of stars and the size of the Galaxy.

*Gravitation:* The force of attraction which exists between two bodies, such as Earth and the Moon. In 1687, Sir Isaac Newton described this force as proportional to the product of the masses of the two bodies and as inversely proportional to the distance between them squared. Although gravitation is the weakest of the naturally occurring forces (the others being electromagnetic and nuclear in nature), it has the broadest range and is responsible for much celestial movement, including orbital dynamics.

*Gravitational constant:* The universal constant defined as the force of attraction between two bodies of 1 kilogram mass separated by 1 meter.

*Gravitational field:* A force field of attraction exerted around a mass, such as a celestial body.

*Gravity assist:* A technique, first used with the Mariner 10 probe to Mercury, whereby a spacecraft uses the gravitational and orbital energy of a planet to gain energy to achieve a trajectory toward a second destination or to return to Earth.

*Great Red Spot:* A vast, oval-shaped cloud system occurring at 22 degrees south latitude in Jupiter's atmosphere, rotating counterclockwise. Its name comes from an unknown substance which the convection of the phenomenon pulls to the surface; the substance absorbs violet and ultraviolet radiation and consequently delivers a red hue to the Spot. The Great Red Spot has been observed for more than three centuries.

*Greenhouse effect:* The heating of a planet's surface and lower atmosphere as a result of trapped infrared radiation. Such radiation becomes trapped when there is an excess of carbon dioxide in the atmosphere, which absorbs and reemits infrared radiation rather than allowing it to escape. As a result, the atmosphere acts like a greenhouse, heating the planet. The effect on Earth is exacerbated by the burning of fossil fuels, which releases carbon dioxide into the atmosphere.

*Ground station:* A location on Earth where radio equipment is housed for receiving and sending signals to and from satellites, probes, and other spacecraft.

*Ground test:* To test, on Earth, craft, devices, and instruments designed for operation in space.

*Ground-elapsed time (GET):* The time that has elapsed since lift-off.

*Gyroscope:* A device which uses a rapidly spinning rotor to assist in stabilization and navigation.


*Hard landing:* A crash landing. Early probes to the Moon, for example, were designed to take pictures of the lunar surface during free fall before impacting the surface.

*Hatch:* A tightly sealed door to the outside or to another module of a spacecraft.

*Heatshield:* A layer of material which protects a space vehicle from overheating, especially upon reentry into Earth's atmosphere. (See also *Ablative heatshield.*)

*Heliocentric orbit:* An orbit with the Sun at its center.

*Heliopause:* The border between the solar system and the surrounding universe, where the solar wind gives way to interstellar matter and winds.

*Hertz:* An SI unit of frequency, equaling one cycle per second. Multiples include kilohertz ($10^3$ hertz), megahertz ($10^6$ hertz), and gigahertz ($10^9$ hertz).

*High-Earth orbit:* Any Earth orbit at a relatively great distance from Earth, such as the geosynchronous orbits of telecommunications satellites.

*High-gain antenna:* A single-axis, strongly directional antenna that is able to receive or transmit signals at great distances.

*Horizon:* The line formed where land meets sky, from the perspective of an observer. In astronomy, the horizon also means the circle on the circumference of the celestial sphere which is formed by the intersection of the observer's horizontal plane with the sphere. The *particle horizon* is the theoretical horizon on the celestial sphere at a distance beyond which particles cannot yet have traveled.

*Hubble's law:* The principle, articulated in 1929 by Edwin Hubble, that the galaxies are moving away from one another at speeds proportional to their distance—that is, uniformly across time. Hubble deduced this principle from observations of the redshifts in galactic spectra. Along with the discovery of the cosmic microwave background radiation by Arno Penzias and Robert Wilson in 1965, Hubble's law forms the basis for the "big bang" theory of the expanding universe. (See also *Big bang theory*, *Doppler effect*, *Redshift*.)

*Hypergolic fuel:* Rocket fuel that ignites spontaneously when its components are mixed with an oxidizer. As a result, such a fuel can be stored in place for ignition.

*ICBM.* See *Intercontinental ballistic missile*.

*IGY.* See *International Geophysical Year*.

*Imaging:* The process of creating a likeness of an object by electronic means.

*Impact basin:* A large depression in the surface of a planet or a moon, created by the force of meteorite impact.

*Inclination.* See *Orbital inclination*.

*Inertial Upper Stage (IUS):* A rocket engine, used on the space shuttle, which boosts satellite payloads from the shuttle's payload bay into higher Earth orbit.

*Infrared astronomy:* The branch of astronomy which examines the infrared emissions of stars and other celestial phenomena. Studying the infrared emissions tells astronomers much about the composition and dynamics of their sources. Because infrared rays cannot readily penetrate most of Earth's atmosphere, infrared astronomy has burgeoned with space age technology such as the Infrared Astronomical Satellite and the Kuiper Airborne Observatory.

*Infrared radiation:* Electromagnetic radiation of wavelengths from 1 to 1,000 micrometers, wavelengths that occur next to visible light at the red end of the electromagnetic spectrum.

*Infrared scanner:* An imaging instrument which is sensitive to the infrared spectrum or to heat.

*Infrared spectrometer:* A spectrometer that takes spectra of infrared radiation emitted by celestial bodies.

*Intercontinental ballistic missile (ICBM):* A ballistic missile with a range of more than 10,000 kilometers, designed to carry a warhead.

*Interferometry:* A data acquisition technique which uses more than one signal receiver (such as a series of radio telescopes). Signals are combined to form one highly detailed image. (See also *Very long-baseline interferometer*.)

*Intergalactic medium:* Matter that exists between galaxies. Although space between galaxies is generally transparent and apparently empty, intergalactic matter must exist, because the combined mass of the galaxies in a galaxy cluster (of which there are many) is much less than that required to exert the gravitational force that forms the cluster. Hence, not only must intergalactic matter exist, but there must be enough of it to account for the missing mass. Postulations include invisible masses, such as black holes and other forms of dead stars, as well as the intergalactic gases.

*Intermediate range ballistic missile (IRBM):* A ballistic missile with a range of approximately 2,800 kilometers.

*International Geophysical Year (IGY):* The eighteen-month period from July, 1957, to December, 1958, during which many countries cooperated in the study of Earth and the Sun's effect on it. During this time, the space age can be said to have begun with the launch of Sputnik 1 on October 4, 1957.

*Interplanetary space probe.* See *Deep space probe.*

*Interstellar dust.* See *Cosmic dust.*

*Interstellar wind.* See *Solar wind, Stellar wind.*

*Ion:* An atom that is not electrically balanced but rather has either more electrons than protons or more protons than electrons. Such atoms are unstable and thus in search of the particles (missing electrons or protons) that will return them to electric balance.

*Ionization:* The process whereby atoms are made into ions, by removal or addition of electrons or protons. Such a process often occurs as a result of excitation of atoms into an energy state whereby they lose electrons.

*Ionosphere:* The ionized layer of gases in Earth's atmosphere, occurring between the thermosphere (below) and the exosphere (above), between about 50 and 500 kilometers above the planet's surface. Within the ionosphere, ionized gases are maintained by the Sun's ultraviolet radiation. The resulting free electrons reflect long radio waves, making long-distance radio communication possible. Other planets are known to have ionospheres, including Jupiter, Mars, and Venus.

*IRBM.* See *Intermediate range ballistic missile.*

*IUS.* See *Inertial Upper Stage.*

*K-band:* A radio frequency range of about 11 to 15 gigahertz. (See also *Hertz.*)

*Kelvin:* A unit of temperature on the Kelvin temperature scale, which begins at absolute zero ($-273.15°$ Celsius). One unit Kelvin is equal to one degree Celsius. The Kelvin scale is particularly suited to scientific (especially astronomical) measurement. (See also *Absolute temperature scale.*)

*Kepler's laws of motion:* Three laws of motion discovered by Johannes Kepler and published by him in 1618-1619: (1) Each planet moves in an ellipse around the Sun, with the Sun at one of the two foci of that ellipse. (2) A line from the sun to the planet sweeps out equal areas in equal times. (3) The square of the period of a planet's orbit is proportional to the cube of its mean distance from the Sun. (See also *Angular momentum.*)

*Kick motor:* A rocket motor on a spacecraft designed to boost it, or a payload, from parking orbit into a higher orbit or a different trajectory. Also known as an *apogee motor.*

*Kilogram:* A metric unit of weight, the equivalent of 1,000 grams or approximately 2.25 pounds.

*Kilometer:* A metric unit of distance, the equivalent of 1,000 meters or approximately 0.62 mile.

*Lander:* A spacecraft or module designed to make a soft landing on the surface of a planet; it carries scientific instruments to measure surface conditions.

*Laser:* Originally an acronym for "light amplification by stimulated emission of radiation." A beam of infrared, visible, ultraviolet, or shorter-wavelength radiation produced by using electromagnetic radiation to excite the electrons in a suitable material to a higher energy level in their cycles around their atomic nuclei. These electrons are then stimulated in such a fashion that they jump back down to their normal energy levels. When they do, they emit a stream of "coherent" radiation: photons with the same wavelength and direction as the originating radiation. This results in a narrow, intense beam of light (or nonvisible radiation), which bounces off a reflector and directly back to the propagating material, where the process is repeated and thus the laser is maintained. Laser technology has a vast range of applications in telecommunications, medicine, and astronomical measurements.

*Laser-ranging:* A technique whereby scientists at two different Earth stations can determine, very precisely, their distance from each other by bouncing a laser beam off a satellite retroreflector. The time it takes to receive an "echo" allows each scientist to calculate his distance from the satellite; knowing both distances allows calculation of the distance between the two points on Earth. Over time, these measurements are repeated; changes in the distance between the two Earth locations are noted, providing much information about crustal movements and the likelihood of earthquakes.

*Laser reflector:* An instrument off which a scientist can "bounce," or reflect, a laser beam in order to measure (usually great) distances.

*Latitude:* The angular distance from a specified horizontal plane of reference. On Earth, the distance north or south of the equatorial plane; in the solar system, the angular distance of a celestial body from the ecliptic plane. (See also *Longitude*.)

*Launch:* To boost a body, such as a spacecraft, from Earth into space or from one orbit into another orbit or a trajectory. Also, the act of doing so.

*Launch escape system (LES):* A mechanism used during the Apollo Moon missions, consisting of a solid-fueled rocket booster set atop the command module at launch. After lift-off, the LES could fire, to remove the module to safety in the event of an emergency. The mechanism proved successful at both low and high altitudes.

*Launch site:* A location housing a facility designed to handle preparations for launch as well as the launch itself.

*Launch vehicle.* See *Expendable launch vehicle*.

*Launch window:* A period of time (usually days or hours) during which conditions, such as weather and planetary alignment, are in sync for meeting the goals of a particular space mission and launch is therefore possible.

*Launchpad:* The physical platform from which a spacecraft is launched.

*LES.* See *Launch escape system*.

*Life-support system:* The combined mechanisms that maintain an environment capable of sustaining life, including devices that control air pressure, oxygen, temperature, and the like.

*Lift-off:* The point at which a launch vehicle or spacecraft separates from the ground or from another spacecraft on its way into space.

*Light-year:* The distance that light travels in one year, or approximately $9.5 \times 10^{12}$ kilometers.

*Limb:* The outer edge of the visible disk of the Sun, Moon, planets, or other celestial body.

*Liquid-fueled rocket booster:* A rocket booster that uses a liquid, or cryogenic, propellant. Expendable launch vehicles from Redstone through Titan have used liquid-fueled rockets.

*Lithosphere:* Earth's crust and the top layer of the underlying mantle, about 80 kilometers thick. The term can be used in reference to the solid part of any planet.

*Long-range intercontinental ballistic missile (LRICBM):* An intercontinental ballistic missile with a range greater than approximately 4,630 kilometers.

*Longitude:* The angular distance from a specified vertical plane of reference: on Earth, the angular distance east or west of the plane that dissects Earth through the poles at the meridian.

*Look angle:* Angular limits of vision.

*Low-Earth orbit:* Generally, any orbit at an altitude of about 300 kilometers or less. Such an orbit has a period (time required to complete one orbit around Earth) of 90 minutes or less.

*LRICBM.* See *Long-range intercontinental ballistic missile.*

*LRVs.* See *Lunar Rover Vehicles.*

*Luminosity:* The brightness of a celestial object.

*Lunar day:* The time it takes the Moon to complete one rotation on its axis, or approximately 27.33 days.

*Lunar module:* The portion of the Apollo spacecraft, housed in the service module during the trip to the Moon, which made a controlled descent to the Moon's surface and later lifted off to rejoin the command module. (See also *Command and service module.*)

*Lunar Rover Vehicles (LRVs):* The Moon vehicles used on Apollo missions 15, 16, and 17 to transport the astronauts several kilometers over the lunar surface. Battery-powered with four wheels and a television camera, these lunar "cars" enabled the astronauts to transmit their observations to Earth.

*Mach:* The ratio of the speed of a moving object to the speed of sound in the surrounding medium. At Mach 1, the speed of an aircraft equals the speed of sound.

*Magellanic Clouds:* The two nearest galaxies outside the Milky Way, visible from the Southern Hemisphere as the Large Cloud and the Small Cloud, respectively 160,000 and 185,000 light-years away. The Magellanic Clouds have been instrumental in establishing an extragalactic distance scale.

*Magnetic field:* Any force field of attraction created by the mass of a body or the combined masses of multiple bodies. Magnetic fields are responsible for much of the shape of the universe, from the orbits of planets in the solar system to the shapes of galaxies and clusters of galaxies. (See also *Gravitation*.)

*Magnetometer:* An instrument that detects disturbances in a magnetic field.

*Magnetopause:* The boundary between a magnetic field, or magnetosphere, of a planet and the outflowing solar wind.

*Magnetosphere:* The region encompassed by a body's magnetic field, within which the body's magnetic lines of force control the movement of ionized particles.

*Magnetotail:* A "tail" of nearly parallel lines of magnetic force extending from Earth in the direction away from the Sun.

*Magnitude:* The brightness of a celestial body expressed numerically. (See also *Absolute magnitude*, *Apparent magnitude*.)

*Main sequence star:* A star, such as the Sun, which produces energy mainly by a hydrogen-to-helium fusion reaction. Most stars spend the greater part of their lifetimes in this state.

*Manned Maneuvering Unit (MMU).* See *Spacesuit*.

*Man-rating:* Approval for use during a manned mission. A device that is *man-rated* is deemed safe for use by or around humans.

*Mantle:* The section of Earth between the lithosphere and the central core.

*Mare (pl. maria):* A large flat area on the Moon or Mars, so named (after the Latin for "sea") because these areas appear dark, thus sealike, to the Earth observer.

*Maritime satellite:* A satellite designed for telecommunications by and for shipping industries. These satellites occupy geostationary orbits over oceans to transmit ship-to-shore communications and data.

*Mascon:* One of several concentrations of mass located beneath lunar maria, which causes a distortion in the orbit of a spacecraft around the Moon.

*Maser:* An acronym for "microwave amplification by stimulated emission of radiation." A device similar to a laser in which energy is generated as in a laser, but at microwave levels. A maser can exist in nature as a celestial object. Artifical masers are used to amplify weak radio signals. (See also *Laser*.)

*Mass:* The amount of matter contained within a body, which determines the amount of gravitational force it exerts. Mass is measured in such units as kilograms and pounds; it differs from weight, however, which is the force exerted on a mass by gravity.

*Mass spectrometer:* An instrument that identifies the chemical composition of a substance by separating ions by mass and charge.

*Materials processing:* The manufacture of crystals and other materials in the microgravity environment of a spacecraft, whereby uniform crystal growth and other processes that are difficult on Earth can by accomplished to improve space technology and for industrial applications.

*Matter:* A substance that has mass and occupies space, which along with energy is responsible for all observable phenomena.

*Maunder minimum:* Named for E. W. Maunder, who in 1890 discovered a period in the 300-year history of sunspot observations when few sunspots were recorded. Confirmed independently in 1976 by evidence from tree rings, the Maunder minimum covers the years 1645 to 1715, a period also known as the Northern Hemisphere's "Little Ice Age."

*Megahertz.* See *Hertz.*

*Mesosphere:* The layer of Earth's atmosphere occurring above the stratosphere and below the thermosphere, from about 40 kilometers to 85 kilometers above sea level. This is the coldest layer of the atmosphere.

*MET (Mission-elapsed time).* See *Ground-elapsed time.*

*Meteor:* A streak of light in Earth's upper atmosphere caused by the burning of a meteoroid.

*Meteorite:* A meteoroid that does not burn completely and reaches Earth.

*Meteoroid:* A particle of interplanetary dust greater than 0.1 millimeter which enters Earth's atmosphere and burns as a result of friction, creating a "shooting star."

*Meteorological satellite:* A satellite that collects data on weather systems for forecast and other analysis.

*Meter:* The metric unit of length, equivalent to approximately 39.37 inches, or a little more than 1 yard.

*Metric system:* The decimal system of weights and measures, which forms part of the *Système International d'Unités.* (See also *SI units.*)

*Metric ton:* A metric unit of weight equivalent to about one short ton (2,205 pounds). Just as thrust is often measured in pounds in the United States, metric tons are often used as units of thrust in the Soviet Union and other countries. (See also *Newton, Pound.*)

*Microgravity:* Nearly zero gravity. Microgravity exists in a space vehicle because of the minute gravitational forces exerted by objects on one another. The microgravity environment is of great importance as an ideal environment for certain types of materials processing.

*Micrometeorite:* A micrometeroid that has reached Earth's surface.

*Micrometeoroid:* A meteoroid with a diameter of less than 0.1 millimeter. Because of their size, micrometeoroids rarely burn up but reach Earth's surface instead, as spherules or as cosmic dust particles.

*Micropaleontology:* The study of microscopic fossils, of potential importance in exobiology as well as life sciences on Earth.

*Microwaves:* A form of electromagnetic radiation with wavelengths ranging between 1 millimeter and 30 centimeters, located between infrared and long-wave radio on the electromagnetic spectrum.

*Milky Way:* The galaxy in which our solar system is located, of the spiral variety, containing about $10^{11}$ stars and about 100,000 light-years across. (See also *Galaxy.*)

*Mission-elapsed time (MET)*. See *Ground-elapsed time*.

*Mission specialist:* An astronaut who has overall responsibility for a mission payload.

*MLR*. See *Monodisperse latex reactor*.

*MMU*. See *Spacesuit*.

*Molecule:* The smallest unit of a substance, formed by a characteristic complex of atoms joined together. The smallest unit of the substance water, for example, is a molecule formed by two hydrogen atoms and one oxygen atom.

*Monodisperse latex reactor (MLR):* A device designed to develop monodisperse, or identically sized, beadlike rubber particles for use in medical and industrial research.

*Moon:* Any natural satellite orbiting a planet, especially Earth's Moon.

*MSS*. See *Multispectral scanner*.

*Multispectral scanner (MSS):* A type of radiometer, used on such satellites as Landsat, which produces detailed false-color images of a planet's surface.


*Nanometer:* One thousand millionth of a meter; a unit used to express electromagnetic wavelengths.

*Navigation satellite:* A satellite which provides positional information for any moving object on land, sea, or in the air, including inner space.

*Navsat:* An abbreviation for "navigation satellite."

*Near-Earth space:* Roughly defined as the space environment from the outer reaches of Earth's atmosphere to the path of the Moon's orbit, the area beyond which is known as deep space.

*Nebula:* A celestial body composed of aggregated gas and dust, which may be either luminous, reflecting or emitting light under the influence of nearby stars (an emission nebula), or dark, obscuring the light of distant stars and appearing as a silhouette.

*Neutral gas analyzer:* An instrument that determines the chemical composition of the atmosphere.

*Neutrino:* An elementary particle of enormous penetrating power as a result of its lack of electric charge and its nearly total lack of mass. Traveling directly out from the cores of stars as a by-product of nuclear reactions, neutrinos have enormous potential as a source of information on the stars and other astrophysical phenomena.

*Neutron:* An uncharged elementary particle found in atomic nuclei; its mass is approximately equal to that of a proton.

*Neutron stars:* The smallest stars known, with diameters of about 20 kilometers and densities matching that of the Sun, consisting of a thin iron shell enclosing a liquid sea of neutrons. The properties of neutron stars are beyond scientists' complete understanding, but they are thought to originate from main sequence stars much larger than the Sun, which become supernovae. Rapidly spinning neutron stars are observable as pulsars.

*New Astronomy:* A term used collectively to refer to the areas of astronomy (such as gamma-ray astronomy, infrared astronomy, and X-ray astronomy) investigating electromagnetic emissions by celestial phenomena. The application of space technology and electronics to the development of instruments capable of detecting such data has greatly increased astronomers' understanding of the universe.

*Newton:* An SI unit of force used to measure thrust.

*Northern lights.* See *Aurora.*

*Nose cone:* The conically shaped front end of a launch stack, missile, or other spacecraft, built for aerodynamic efficiency and as a protective shield.

*Nova:* A star which emits a sudden radiation of light and quickly (over months or years) returns to its former brightness. (See also *Supernova.*)

*Nuclear energy:* Energy that is released as a result of interactions between elementary particles and atomic nuclei.

*Nuclear reactor:* A device, usually located at a nuclear power station, designed to contain nuclear fission reactions during the production of nuclear energy.

*Nucleus:* The central part of an atom, around which electrons rotate. An atomic nucleus can consist of one proton (in a hydrogen atom) or many protons and neutrons (as in an atom of uranium).


*Oblate:* Flattened at the poles.

*Occultation:* The obscuring of one celestial body by another, such as occurs during a solar eclipse.

*OMS.* See *Orbital maneuvering system.*

*Oort Cloud:* A theoretical cloud of millions of comets orbiting the Sun between 30,000 and 100,000 astronomical units from the Sun, postulated by Dutch astronomer Jan Oort in 1950.

*Opposition:* The alignment of Sun, Earth, and a superior planet (one whose orbit is farther from the Sun than Earth's) in a straight line; that is, the superior planet appears in the sky at 180 degrees celestial longitude from the Sun. In this position, the planet is closest to Earth and therefore most easily observed by ground-based instruments.

*Orbit:* The path traced out by one celestial or artificial body as it moves around another that exerts greater gravitational force. The distinguishing characteristics of an orbit are called its *orbital parameters* and include apoapsis, periapsis, inclination to the ecliptic of the body orbited, eccentricity, and period. All orbits trace out an ellipse, of which the body orbited forms at least one of two foci. (See also *Apoapsis, Circular orbit, Eccentricity, Ellipse, Elliptical orbit, Equatorial orbit, Geocentric orbit, Geostationary orbit, Geosynchronous orbit, Heliocentric orbit, Orbital inclination, Parabolic orbit, Parking orbit, Periapsis, Period, Polar orbit, Prograde orbit, Retrograde orbit, Synchronous orbit, Transfer orbit.*)

*Orbital inclination:* The angle formed between the orbital plane of a satellite and the equatorial plane of the object orbited.

*Orbital maneuvering system (OMS):* A system of rocket engines, located on the space shuttle's aft fuselage, which provide small amounts of thrust for fine maneuvers in orbit.

*Orbital transfer vehicle (OTV):* A liquid-fueled thrusting mechanism designed to boost satellites into orbit from the U.S. Space Station. The OTV will be housed at the Space Station for regular use.

*Orbiter:* A spacecraft intended to orbit, rather than land on, a planet or other celestial body, often used to relay signals from a lander to Earth. (See also *Lander*.)

*O-ring:* A ringed rubber gasket, one-quarter inch in width, which acts as a sealant between the bottom and next to bottom segments of a shuttle solid-fueled rocket booster. Failure of an O-ring or the insulating putty which surrounds it can allow combustible gases to escape through the joint from within the rocket, as apparently occurred to cause the *Challenger* disaster of January, 1986.

*OTV.* See *Orbital transfer vehicle*.

*Outer space:* All space beyond Earth's atmosphere. (See also *Deep space*.)

*Outgassing:* The process whereby gases are emitted from solids into a vacuum, referring mainly to the exudation of gases from terrestrial bodies into space, a remnant of the way these bodies were formed.

*Ozone layer:* The thin layer of Earth's atmosphere, located between 12 and 50 kilometers above Earth's surface (in the stratosphere), in which ozone ($O_3$) is found in its greatest concentrations. This layer, which absorbs most of the ultraviolet radiation entering the atmosphere, forms a protective blanket around the planet, shielding it from excess radiation.

*PAM.* See *Payload Assist Module*.

*Panspermia:* A theory proposed by chemist Svante Arrhenius in 1906, and later modified by Sir Fred Hoyle, which holds that organic molecules (hence the beginnings of life) were transported to Earth by means of comets. The organic material found in Halley's comet supports the theory, which is further supported by the argument that each process on the road to a life-form is so improbable as to require a greater combination of conditions than those possible on Earth alone. Nevertheless, the theory is far from accepted by most scientists.

*Parabolic orbit:* An orbit that describes a parabola around the object orbited and hence escapes from the gravitational field of that object. A comet's orbit "around" the Sun is parabolic.

*Parallax:* The apparent displacement of a celestial object as seen from two different points on Earth. Knowing this angle allows astronomers to calculate the object's distance from Earth.

*Parking orbit:* An interim orbit around a celestial body between launch and injection into another orbit or into a trajectory toward another destination.

*Parsec:* A unit for measuring astronomical distances equivalent to 3.26 light-years.

*Particle.* See *Elementary particles*.

*Passive experiment:* An experiment package which requires only exposure to the space environment to perform its investigations.

*Passive relay satellite:* An early telecommunications satellite, such as Echo, which relayed radio signals from one point to another by bouncing them off its surface.

*Payload:* Any experiment package, satellite, or other special cargo carried into space by a spacecraft.

*Payload Assist Module (PAM):* A solid-fueled rocket engine designed to boost satellites into geostationary orbit from the space shuttle's payload bay.

*Payload bay:* The portion of the space shuttle that carries satellites into space, approximately 18 by 4 meters. Hinged doors at the top of the fuselage open to expose the satellite, which can then be boosted into orbit from the bay by a Payload Assist Module.

*Payload specialist:* An astronaut who assists a mission specialist in conducting an experiment aboard the space shuttle.

*Periapsis:* The point in one object's orbit around another at which the orbiting object is closest to the object being orbited.

*Pericynthion:* The point in an object's orbit around the Moon at which it is closest to the Moon.

*Perigee:* The point in an object's orbit around Earth at which it is closest to Earth.

*Perihelion:* The point in a solar orbit at which the orbiting object is closest to the Sun.

*Perilune:* Pericynthion of an artificial satellite.

*Period:* The time span between repetitions of a cyclic event. An *orbital period* is the time required for a satellite or moon to make one complete orbit around a planet, a moon, the Sun, or another celestial body.

*Photometer:* An instrument that measures the brightness of a light source.

*Photon:* The smallest theoretical quantity of radiation, visualized as both wavelength energy and an elementary particle.

*Photomultiplier:* An instrument for increasing the apparent brightness or strength of a source of light by means of secondary excitation of electrons; effectively, a light (or other radiation) amplifier.

*Photopolarimeter:* An instrument for producing an image of a celestial body (or other light source) by means of polarized light.

*Photoreconnaissance:* The gathering of information, especially on enemy installations, by means of photography from the air or from space.

*Photosphere:* The region of the Sun that separates its exterior (the chromosphere and corona) from its interior, forming the boundary between the transparent and opaque gases. The photosphere appears as the bright central disk from Earth, and it is the source of most of the Sun's light.

*Photovoltaic cell:* A solid state energy device that converts sunlight into electricity.

*Pitch, roll, and yaw:* Movements that a spacecraft undergoes as a result of launch or other stresses. *Pitch* is up-down movement; *roll* is longitudinal rotation; *yaw* is side-to-side movement.

*Pixel:* A small unit arranged with others in a two-dimensional array which contains a discrete portion of an image (as on a television screen) or an electrical charge (as on a charge coupled device). Together, these pixels form an image or other meaningful information.

*Planets:* A planet is a nonluminous natural celestial body that orbits the Sun (or another star) and is not categorized as an asteroid or comet. There are nine known planets in the solar system: Mercury, Venus, Earth, Mars, Jupiter, Saturn, Uranus, Neptune, and Pluto.

*Plasma:* Ionized gas, consisting of roughly equal numbers of free electrons and positive ions. Plasma forms the atmospheres of stars, interstellar and intergalactic matter, nebulae—in fact, most of the matter in the universe. The extremely high excitation of its constituent particles has earned for it the label "fourth state of matter," after solid, liquid, and gas.

*Plasma sheath:* The definite outer boundary of Earth's ionosphere, identified by Orbiting Geophysical Observatory 1.

*Plate tectonics:* The study of the continental drift, seafloor spreading, and other dynamics of Earth's lithosphere, which is divided into seven major sections, or "plates."

*Pogo effect:* The up-and-down vibrating motion that occurs during the launch of a spacecraft.

*Polar orbit:* An orbit in which a satellite passes over a planet's or moon's poles.

*Polarimeter:* An instrument for measuring the degree to which electromagnetic radiation is polarized.

*Pole:* One of two points on the surface of a planet where it is intersected by its axis of rotation. In a magnetic field, one of two or more points of concentration of the lines of magnetic force.

*Posigrade:* Moving in the direction of travel.

*Pound:* A unit used to measure thrust in the United States and some other English-speaking nations.

*Precession:* A type of motion that occurs in a rotating body in response to torque: A planet or other rotating body orbiting around a gravitational force, such as the Sun, slowly turns in the direction of its rotation so that, over a long period, each of the planet's poles describes a circle. The fact that precession is exhibited by many planets and moons means that adjustments must be made in the locations to which astronomers look to observe stars and other celestial phenomena. Earth's period of precession is approximately 25,800 years.

*Probe.* See *Deep space probe*.

*Prograde orbit:* An orbit that moves in the same direction as the rotation of the body orbited.

*Propellant.* See *Cryogenic fuels*, *Hypergolic fuel*, *Solid propellant*.

*Propulsion system:* The combined mechanisms that propel a space vehicle, including engines and fuel systems.

*Proton:* An elementary particle of matter that carries positive charge and forms the nucleus of the hydrogen atom, as well as the nuclei of other chemical elements in combination with protons and neutrons.

*Pulsar:* A rapidly spinning neutron star that emits a narrow beam of electromagnetic radiation in the form of visible light and radio waves (single pulsars), as well as X rays and gamma rays (pulsars occurring in binary star systems). The regular emission of radio waves can be detected on Earth by radio telescopes, and the pulsar's distance from Earth can be detected by the difference in the arrival time of radio waves at different wavelengths.

*Quarks:* Subparticles hypothesized to form the known elementary particles (electrons, protons, neutrons, and their antiparticles), characterized by electric charge, "flavor," and "color." The forces required to break elementary particles into their component quarks is so great that quarks do not exist as free particles in nature, although it is thought that neutron stars may consist of a "quark soup" within a solid iron shell.

*Quasar:* An acronym for "quasi-stellar" or "quasi-stellar object." An object continuously releasing a tremendous amount of energy, equivalent to the output of between one million and 100 trillion suns, which includes virtually all kinds of electromagnetic radiation (gamma rays, X rays, ultraviolet, optical, and infrared radiation, microwaves and radio waves) from a very small volume of space about the size of the solar system. As far as is known, all objects satisfying these criteria are located in the nuclei of galaxies, although it is thought that they may be galaxies themselves, with black holes at their centers. Discovered in 1963, the first quasar caused much excitement among astronomers, and these phenomena continue to be among the most fascinating and mysterious in the universe.

*Radar:* An acronym for "radio detection and ranging." A means of locating and determining the distance of objects by bouncing radio waves off them and measuring the time required to receive the echo.

*Radiation.* See *Electromagnetic radiation.*

*Radio astronomy:* The branch of astronomy that examines the radio emissions of celestial objects. Because radio radiation, along with visible radiation, can penetrate Earth's atmosphere, radio receivers have provided much of the data detectable by ground-based, as well as space-based, instruments. Radio emissions also form a significant portion of certain celestial phenomena, such as radio galaxies, quasars, and pulsars.

*Radio telescope:* A radio receiving aerial, either a dish or a dipole, connected to recording devices, whereby distant radio emissions can be detected.

*Radioisotope thermoelectric generator (RTG):* A device for creating power from a radioactive substance, used on spacecraft to supplement the power generated by the solar-energy-collecting solar panels. The RTG is especially important when access to sunlight is weak or nonexistent.

*Radiometer:* An instrument, used by meteorological and other satellites, that measures Earth's infrared and reflected solar radiance and uses small, selected wavelengths (ultraviolet to microwave) to measure temperature, ozone, and water vapor in the atmosphere. Radiometers are sensitive to one or more wavelength bands in the visible and invisible ranges. If visible wavelengths are used, the satellite can detect cloud vistas from reflected sunlight, resulting in a slightly blurred version of those images photographed directly by astronauts. Using the invisible range, satellites can capture terrestrial radiation, producing images from Earth's radiant energy.

*RBV*. See *Return beam vidicon*.

*Real time:* Referring to the transmission of signals or other data at the same time that they are used.

*Reconnaissance satellite:* A satellite that gathers information about enemy military installations.

*Red giant:* Stars with surface temperatures less than 4,700 Kelvins and between 10 and 100 times the diameter of the Sun.

*Red Planet:* Mars, so named because of its color as seen through Earth-based telescopes.

*Redshift:* The apparent lengthening of electromagnetic wavelengths issuing from a celestial object or other source as a result of the object's movement away from the observer. As a result, the spectral lines in the spectra of such an object will shift toward the red end of the electromagnetic spectrum. (See also *Doppler effect*.)

*Reentry:* The return of a spacecraft into Earth's atmosphere.

*Reflecting telescope:* An optical telescope that uses a mirror or mirrors to capture, magnify, and focus light from the object observed. These telescopes, such as the 200-inch reflecting telescope on Palomar Mountain in Southern California, are widely used for Earth-based as well as space-based optical astronomy. (See also *Cassegrain telescope*, *Refracting telescope*.)

*Refracting telescope:* An optical telescope that uses a lens to magnify and focus light from the object observed. Refracting telescopes were used by the earliest astronomers. When reflecting telescopes were perfected in the twentieth century, refracting telescopes became less important in astronomy, although they are still widely used for guided and amateur observations. (See also *Reflecting telescope*.)

*Regolith:* A thick layer of broken rock that overlies the surface of a moon or planet, caused by the impact of a meteoroid.

*Relativity:* The physical law, first proposed by Albert Einstein, that states that measurements of time and space are dependent upon the frame of reference in which they are measured. The *general theory of relativity* applies this law to gravity and mass; the *special theory of relativity* applies it to the propagation of electric and magnetic phenomena in space and time.

*Remote manipulator system (RMS):* The space shuttle's 15-meter-long robot arm. Operated from within the shuttle by an astronaut, the arm duplicates the operator's hand and wrist movements, allowing payloads to be moved and repairs to be made without extravehicular activity. Because the RMS was manufactured by a

Canadian aerospace company, it is sometimes called the "Canada arm."

*Remote sensing:* Acquiring data at a distance by electronic or mechanical means.

*Rendezvous:* The planned meeting of two spacecraft in orbit and often their maneuvering into proximity of each other in preparation for docking.

*Resolution:* The degree to which a photographic or other imaging system, or the image produced, clearly distinguishes objects of a certain size. In a photograph with a resolution of 200 meters, for example, the smallest distinguishable objects are 200 meters across.

*Restart:* Reignition of a rocket engine after it has been inactive during orbit.

*Retrofire:* The firing of a rocket to slow down or change the orbit of a spacecraft.

*Retrograde orbit:* An orbit that moves opposite to the rotational direction of the body orbited.

*Retroreflector:* A device, carried by a satellite, used to reflect laser beams directed at the satellite from Earth. (See also *Laser ranging*.)

*Retro-rocket:* A rocket that exerts thrust to slow down or change the orbit of a spacecraft.

*Return beam vidicon (RBV):* A camera, used by Earth resources satellites, that takes very high-resolution photographs of the planet's surface from space.

*Revolution:* One complete orbit of a planet around the Sun or of a natural or artificial satellite around another celestial body.

*Rille:* A long, narrow valley on the Moon.

*RMS.* See *Remote manipulator system.*

*Robot arm:* A mechanical arm extending from many spacecraft which can be remotely controlled to manipulate instruments and repair equipment. (See also *Remote manipulator system.*)

*Robotics:* The development, construction, and use of computerized machines to replace humans in a variety of tasks requiring precise "hand-eye" coordination.

*Roche limit:* Named for Édouard Roche, who discovered it in 1848, the minimum distance from a planet at which a natural satellite can form by accretion: roughly 2.44 times the planet's radius. Within this limit an existing satellite will be torn apart by gravitational stresses. Saturn's rings, which lie within the planet's Roche limit, may be the remnants of a former moon.

*Rocket booster:* A propulsion engine used to launch a spacecraft into orbit from Earth or into a different orbit or trajectory from space.

*Roll.* See *Pitch, roll, and yaw.*

*Rollout:* The termination of a flight, occurring after touchdown on the landing site and before brakes are set, during which an aircraft or space shuttle rolls to decrease speed.

*RTG.* See *Radioisotope thermoelectric generator.*

*Sample return mission:* A mission designated to collect soil and rock samples from another body and return them to Earth.

*Satellite:* Any body that orbits another of larger mass, usually a planet. Satellites include moons, the small bodies that form planetary rings, and man-made satellites. (See also *Artificial satellites*.)

*Scanning radiometer:* An instrument used on meteorological satellites to measure radiation emitted by the atmosphere, especially in the infrared region, building up a picture of atmospheric conditions and temperature that can be used in forecasting.

*Scarp:* A broken slope or a line of cliffs caused by a fault line or by erosion.

*Schwarzschild radius:* The radius of a collapsing mass, such as a degenerating star, at which it becomes a black hole—that is, at which its gravitational force will not allow light to escape. The length of this radius depends on the body's mass, and the formula for calculating it was established by Karl Schwarzschild in 1916.

*Scientific satellite:* A broad term for any satellite dedicated primarily, if not solely, to collecting scientific data, especially data on astrophysical phenomena. Although most satellites can be described as "scientific" in some sense, the main purpose of a scientific satellite is to broaden our knowledge of the universe, rather then serve a practical (e.g., telecommunications), military (e.g., reconnaissance), or commercial purpose.

*Seismic activity:* Any movement in the outer layer of a planet or moon.

*Seismometer:* A sensitive electronic instrument that measures movements in the outer layer of a planet or moon. The graphs produced by this instrument can be interpreted—on the Richter scale, generally—to determine the magnitude and intensity of seismic activity.

*Selenography:* The study of lunar surface features; the counterpart of geography on Earth.

*Selenology:* The study of the Moon, analogous to geology on Earth.

*Service propulsion system:* A large rocket engine which propelled the Apollo command and service module, slowing it as it neared the Moon, and later sending it back on a trajectory toward Earth.

*Shuttle imaging radar (SIR):* A high-resolution radar imaging system, used aboard the space shuttle, which operates at frequencies high enough to penetrate not only Earth's atmosphere but at times a few feet beneath its surface as well.

*Shroud:* A heat-resistant covering used to protect a spacecraft, payload, or missile, especially during launch.

*SI units:* The collective units of measurement used in the *Système International d'Unités*, the system of measurement most widely accepted by scientists. Its fundamental, or *base* units are seven: the meter (the base unit of length), kilogram (mass), second (time), ampere (electric current), Kelvin (temperature), mole (amount of substance), and candela (luminosity). From these seven base units, other units are *derived*, which are multiples, fractions, or powers of the base units such as the kilometer (1 meter $\times$ $10_3$) and the square meter (the unit of area). Further derived units are derived from combinations of the base units and have their own names: hertz (the unit of frequency, which is cycles per second), newton (force or thrust, kilogram-meters per second squared), pascal (pressure, newtons per square meter), joule (energy, the kilogram-meter), watt (power, joules per second), coulomb (quantity of electricity, the ampere-second), volt (electric potential, watts per ampere), farad (capacitance, or the ability to store energy, coulombs per volt), and ohm (electrical resistance, volts per ampere). In the United States, the base SI units are coming into increasing use. Some measures, however, remain more familiarly rendered by English units of measure, even in scientific use: It is common, for example, to refer to rocket thrust in pounds or even metric tons rather than newtons, and atmospheric pressure is often measured in pounds per square inch (or bars and millibars in the centimeter-gram-second system).

*SIR.* See *Shuttle imaging radar*.

*Soft landing:* A controlled landing on a planet's or moon's surface, designed to minimize damage to the spacecraft and its instrument payload.

*Solar array:* An assembly of solar cells, as on a solar panel extending from a satellite.

*Solar cell:* A photovoltaic device that converts solar energy directly into electricity for use in powering a spacecraft.

*Solar constant:* The amount of solar energy received by a square meter per second on Earth (or one astronomical unit from the Sun), approximately 1,370 watts per square meter per second.

*Solar cycle:* A period of approximately eleven years during which the number of sunspots visible near the Sun's equator increases to a maximum and then decreases. Other solar activity follows the solar cycle. (See also *Sunspots*.)

*Solar flare:* A large arc of charged particles and electromagnetic radiation ejected from the Sun's surface (in the low corona and upper chromosphere) and lasting from a few minutes to several hours. Solar flare activity affects radio transmission on Earth and can produce auroras in Earth's atmosphere.

*Solar mass:* A unit equivalent to the mass of the Sun, or $1,989 \times 10^{33}$ grams. Masses of other stars are sometimes given in solar masses.

*Solar system:* The Sun, the planets, asteroids, comets, and other matter that orbit the Sun, and the satellites of those bodies, along with interplanetary space, radiation, and gases. (See also *Planets*.)

*Solar wind:* The hot ionized gases, or plasma, that escape the Sun's gravitational field and flow in spirals outward at about 200 to 900 kilometers per second. It consists primarily of free protons, electrons, and alpha particles escaping from the Sun's corona. (See also *Stellar wind*.)

*Solid propellant:* Rocket propellant in solid form: cast, extruded, granular, powder, or other.

*Solid-fueled rocket booster (SRB):* One of two rocket boosters, fueled by solid propellants, which assists the main engines of the space shuttle during the first two minutes of ascent. The SRBs then separate from the external tank; their descent is slowed by drogue chutes issuing from nose caps, the SRBs splash down, and they are recovered for later reuse. (See also *External tank*.)

*Sonar:* An acronym for "sound navigation ranging." A system for bouncing sonic and supersonic waves off a submerged object in order to determine its distance.

*Sounding rocket:* A suborbital rocket carrying scientific instruments which take measurements of Earth's atmosphere. Sounding rockets were used before satellites came into prominence.

*Sounding sensor:* A sonarlike device that probes the atmosphere to detect data about temperature, moisture, and other conditions.

*Space adaptation syndrome.* See *Spacesickness.*

*Space age:* The age of space exploration, whose beginning is generally dated from October 4, 1957, the day on which the first artificial satellite, Sputnik 1, was launched into Earth orbit.

*Space capsule:* A small, manned or unmanned, spacecraft, such as those used on the Mercury and Gemini missions, which is pressurized and otherwise environmentally controlled.

*Space center:* A complex that houses a variety of facilities for development of space technology and preparations for or monitoring of space missions, such as launch facilities.

*Space medicine:* The study of human health in microgravity and other conditions surrounding space travel, including systems for maintaining health.

*Space race:* A term applied primarily to the early years of space exploration (1957 through the 1960's), during the Cold War between the United States and the Soviet Union. Space "firsts" were a preoccupation of the space programs of both countries, becoming a matter of public concern and national pride, culminating in the race to place the first man on the Moon—achieved in 1969 by the United States. The achievements of both nations in space have been impressive; it is arguably impossible to quantify them in any meaningful fashion.

*Space shuttle main engine (SSME):* A reusable, liquid-fueled engine which generates 70,000 horsepower. Three SSMEs are clustered in the tail of the U.S. space shuttle, supplying a total thrust of about 5 kilonewtons, somewhat less than the F-1 engines of a Saturn 5.

*Space station:* A large, Earth-orbiting structure designed to provide an environment in which atmospheric and gravitational conditions on Earth can be duplicated for long-term habitation. Space stations will serve a variety of purposes: as way stations on the way to Mars and other destinations, as materials processing plants, as sites for scientific and biological studies. Skylab, Spacelab, and Salyut were early versions of the Mir and U.S. space stations, which in turn are prototypes of the larger space stations described above.

*Spacecraft:* Any self-contained, manned or unmanned, space vehicle; more specifically, a deep space probe.

*Spacenaut:* Any space traveler; specifically, one who is neither an American nor a Soviet.

*Spacesickness:* Any health problem experienced as a result of space travel, which varies with individual and spacecraft environment. Specifically, however, spacesickness is the nausea and other symptoms associated with adjustment to microgravity. Also known as *space adaptation syndrome*.

*Spacesuit:* The pressurized garment worn by an astronaut during extravehicular activity, and sometimes within a spacecraft. The spacesuit worn by space shuttle astronauts outside the spacecraft, called an *extravehicular mobility unit*, incorporates a portable life-support system, a manned maneuvering unit, a displays and controls module, a liquid cooling and ventilation garment, a urine collection device, and a delivery system for drinking water.

*Spacewalk.* See *Extravehicular activity*.

*Spacionaute:* A French astronaut.

*Spectrograph:* A type of spectrometer that splits light into its component wavelengths and records the separated wavelengths photographically or by means of a charge coupled device.

*Spectrometer:* An instrument that splits electromagnetic radiation into its component wavelengths for viewing or electronic recording of the emitting body's spectrum.

*Spectroscope:* A device that splits electromagnetic radiation into its component wavelengths, which can then be "read" by a spectrometer or a spectrograph.

*Spectroscopy:* The creation and interpretation of spectra using a variety of instruments, including spectrographs and a variety of spectrometers. By analyzing the spectra of celestial bodies, scientists are able to discover much about their composition and the chemical reactions taking place in them.

*Spectrum:* An image that represents the distribution and intensity of electromagnetic radiation from a body. This image can be photographic or a "map" of lines showing all or selected wavelengths.

*Spin axis:* The line around which a body rotates.

*Spin stabilization:* The method whereby an artificial satellite is made to spin at a constant rate about a symmetry axis, relying on gyroscopic effects to keep that axis relatively fixed in space.

*Spiral galaxy:* A galaxy consisting of a bulge of gas and stars at the center, around which "arms" of stars and other celestial bodies, matter, and radiation rotate in a spiral fashion. Spiral galaxies, of which the Milky Way is one, are by far the most common in the universe.

*Splashdown:* The free-fall landing of a space capsule or other spacecraft in one of Earth's oceans.

*SRB.* See *Solid-fueled rocket booster*.

*SSME.* See *Space shuttle main engine*.

*Stage:* A self-contained section of a space vehicle, used for propulsion of a spacecraft into orbit and separated from the launch stack after use.

*Standby:* A piece of equipment available to replace its counterpart on short notice.

*Star:* A large, nearly spherical mass of extremely hot gas bound together by gravity.

*Star tracker:* An electronic device programmed to detect and lock onto a celestial body, such as the star Canopus, to provide a spacecraft with a fixed point of reference for purposes of navigation.

*Steady state theory:* A model of the universe, proposed by Hermann Bondi, Thomas Gold, and Fred Hoyle, which posits that the density of matter in the universe remains constant in an expanding universe, being created at the same rate as that at which old stars die. The theory is less widely subscribed to than the big bang theory, because it does not explain the presence of the cosmic microwave background radiation. (See also *Big bang theory*.)

*Stellar wind:* The ionized gases, or plasma, that flow out from stars at high speeds, composed mainly of free protons and electrons. (See also *Solar wind*.)

*Stratosphere:* The layer of Earth's atmosphere between the troposphere and the mesosphere, extending from about 15 to 50 kilometers above Earth's surface, roughly coinciding with the ozone layer, which absorbs the Sun's ultraviolet radiation and heats the stratosphere from a low of about $-60°$ Celsius at the bottom to about $0°$ Celsius at its top. There is no meteorological activity or vertical air movement in this region of the atmosphere.

*Suborbital flight:* A spaceflight comprising less than one orbit of Earth or not intended to reach orbit.

*Subsatellite:* A satellite carried into orbit by another satellite. Also, a satellite of a moon.

*Sunspots:* Dark spots that appear on the Sun's surface in cycles, increasing and decreasing with the eleven-year solar cycle. These dark spots are about 500 Kelvins cooler than a surrounding lighter area of the spot, which in turn is another 500 Kelvins cooler than the surrounding photosphere. These cooler regions result from magnetic fields.

*Supergiant:* The brightest stars in the universe, which also include the largest: Red supergiants are 1,000 times the size of the Sun.

*Supernova:* A nova resulting from the explosion of any star whose mass is 1.4 times the Sun's. (See also *Nova*.)

*Surveillance:* Ongoing monitoring of enemy territory or military installations by aircraft or satellites carrying any of a variety of sensors.

*Swing-by:* The close approach of a spacecraft as it passes a planet on a tour of the solar system. (See also *Flyby*.)

*Synchronous orbit:* Any orbit whose period equals the rotational period of the object orbited.

*Système International d'Unités.* See *SI units*.

*Tectonics:* The branch of geology that examines folding and faulting in Earth's crust. (See also *Plate tectonics*.)

*Telecommunications satellite:* An artificial satellite dedicated to the receiving and transmission of radio, television, and other communications signals. Such satellites are usually placed in geostationary orbits so that they remain over a fixed point on Earth.

*Telemetry:* Real-time transmission of data from a distance via radio signals.

*Teleoperations:* Manipulation of an orbiter, booster, or instruments in space from Earth via remote control.

*Terminator:* The line, on a planet or moon, between dark and light that forms the boundary between day and night.

*Terrestrial planets:* In addition to Earth, Mercury, Venus, and Mars, so called because they resemble Earth in certain fundamental features such as density and composition.

*Test flight:* Experimental operation of an aircraft or spacecraft to determine whether it functions as designed and to identify systems in need of adjustment.

*Test range:* A site dedicated to the testing of aircraft or spacecraft.

*Thermal mapping:* Gathering data from which to construct maps by means of instruments capable of sensing heat-producing electromagnetic radiation.

*Thermal tiles:* Heat-resistant tiles glued to the underside of the space shuttle to protect it from overheating upon reentry into Earth's atmosphere. They are favored over ablative material because they are lighter.

*Thermosphere:* The highest layer of Earth's atmosphere except for the exosphere, beginning at 85 kilometers above sea level. The oxygen and nitrogen that compose the atmosphere at this level are extremely rarefied, and are heated by the Sun's ultraviolet radiation to the point of ionization; hence the ionosphere (which lies between 50 and 500 kilometers above sea level) roughly coincides with the thermosphere. This is also the region in which auroras and meteors occur.

*Three-axis stabilization:* Stabilization of a satellite against pitch, roll, and yaw. (See also *Pitch, roll, and yaw.*)

*Thrust:* The force required to propel a vehicle, especially that force exerted by a rocket engine to launch a space vehicle into orbit or a deep space trajectory. Measured in newtons (SI), metric tons, or pounds.

*Time dilation:* The phenomenon, predicted by Albert Einstein's special theory of relativity, whereby time appears to slow down in a system moving near the speed of light from the vantage point of an observer outside that system.

*Topside observation:* Electronic scanning of Earth's (or another) atmosphere from above. Used mainly in reference to meteorological satellites.

*Tracking network:* A network of tracking stations at different points on the globe which send and receive radio signals to and from spacecraft, via large dish antennae, allowing continuous communications with spacecraft. Examples are the Spaceflight Tracking and Data Network and the Deep Space Network.

*Trajectory:* The path traced out by a ballistic missile or by a spacecraft launched from Earth or from orbit toward the Moon or other destination.

*Transducer:* Any device that transforms one type of energy into another, such as a solar cell (sunlight into electrical power), a thermocouple (thermal energy into electric signal), or a Geiger counter (radioactive into sound energy).

*Trans-Earth injection:* A boost from lunar (or other planetary) orbit which places a spacecraft on a trajectory toward Earth.

*Transfer orbit:* The orbit into which a spacecraft is boosted from Earth orbit on its way to orbit around another celestial body. Since the spacecraft does not complete a full revolution of the transfer orbit, but only part of the ellipse, the path it follows describes a trajectory which intersects the final orbit.

*Transit:* The passage of one celestial body across the face of another or across the observer's meridian.

*Translunar injection:* The process whereby a spacecraft in orbit around Earth is boosted into a trajectory that heads it toward the Moon.

*Transponder:* A device that receives radio signals and automatically responds to them using the same frequency.

*Triangulation:* A means of determining the position of an object by calculation from known quantities: The distance between two fixed points and the angles formed between the line described by those points and the line between a third point. Triangulation is the oldest method of determining distances, both on Earth and in space.

*Troposphere:* The layer of Earth's atmosphere that lies closest to Earth's surface, extending upward to about 8 kilometers. The troposphere is the densest region of the atmosphere and the region in which all meteorological phenomena occur.

*Ultraviolet astronomy:* The branch of astronomy that examines the ultraviolet emissions of celestial phenomena. Ultraviolet astronomy has developed with the advent of the space age; since ultraviolet rays are unable to penetrate Earth's atmosphere, instruments carried aloft by satellites such as the International Ultraviolet Explorer have enabled scientists to learn much about celestial bodies, since many of the elements of which they are composed are most evident in the spectroscopic measurements taken of them.

*Ultraviolet radiation:* Electromagnetic radiation which is emitted between the wavelengths of 900 and 3,000 angstroms (between 400 and 2 nanometers), which is the band lying between visible violet light and X-radiation on the electromagnetic spectrum.

*Ultraviolet spectrometer:* An instrument that measures electromagnetic wavelengths in the ultraviolet range, used on satellites such as the International Ultraviolet Explorer and the Extreme Ultraviolet Explorer.

*Uplink:* Signals sent up to a satellite from an Earth station.

*Vacuum:* An area in which absolutely nothing exists. Although a true vacuum never occurs in nature, the behavior of bodies within a vacuum is of concern to physicists studying interplanetary and deep space, in which near-vacuum conditions exist.

*Van Allen radiation belts:* The two layers of Earth's magnetosphere, discovered by James Van Allen in the late 1950's, in which ionized particles spiral back and forth between Earth's magnetic poles. These zones are of importance for the potential hazards they pose to electronic instruments aboard spacecraft.

*Variable star:* A star whose brightness varies over time, as a result of several intrinsic or extrinsic factors. There are thousands of such stars, and they can be categorized into seven classes based on the causes of their variation. (See also *Cepheid variable*.)

*Vernier rocket:* A small thruster rocket used in space to make fine corrections to a spacecraft's orientation or trajectory.

*Very long-baseline interferometry:* A technique used by radio astronomers to increase the sharpness (resolution) of received signals by using several or many radio telescopes at widely spaced locations. Unlike ordinary *radio interferometry*, in which two or only a few radio telescopes are used, this more advanced technique allows highly accurate mapping of celestial bodies that emit radio signals. (See also *Interferometry*.)

*Vidicon:* A video camera, or a device that converts light into electronic signals that can be transmitted or recorded as pictures.

*Volcanism:* The dynamic process in which molten material from the interior of a planet is transferred to the planet's solid surface, issuing forth explosively from cracks or other openings.

*Wavelength:* A characteristic that in part defines sonic waves and electromagnetic radiation: the length (measured in angstroms or nanometers in the electromagnetic range) between successive crests in a photon's wave pattern as it moves up and down in a direction of propagation.

*Weather satellite.* See *Meteorological satellite*.

*Weightlessness.* See *Zero gravity*.

*White dwarf:* A dying star (one that is collapsing in on itself) with a mass 1.4 times that of the Sun or less, and with a radius approximately that of Earth. Such stars are destined to end their lives as cold, dark spheres, having expended all of their energy but not initially massive enough to end life as neutron stars or black holes.

*Wind tunnel:* A large tubular structure through which air is forced to flow at high speeds for the purpose of testing the behavior of aircraft and other structures that travel through the atmosphere.

*Window.* See *Launch window*.

*X-band:* The range of radio frequencies between 5.2 and 10.9 gigahertz.

*X-radiation:* Electromagnetic radiation with wavelengths between 0.1 and 10 nanometers, the range lying between gamma and ultraviolet radiation on the electromagnetic spectrum.

*X-ray astronomy:* The branch of astronomy that examines the X-ray emissions of celestial phenomena. This radiation cannot be studied from the ground, since Earth's atmosphere absorbs most X-radiation, and therefore has blossomed with the advent of spacecraft that can carry X-ray telescopes and other detectors into space. The examination of celestial X-ray sources has led, among other things, to the discovery of neutron stars and black holes as members of binary star systems. The Einstein Observatory launched by NASA in 1978 revealed that nearly all stars, not a few, emit X-radiation. The importance of X-ray astronomy was therefore established.

*Yaw.* See *Pitch, roll, and yaw.*

*Zero gravity:* The condition of absolute weightlessness, which occurs in free-fall and is approached in deep space, far from massive bodies. Because all masses exert gravitational force on one another, the condition of zero gravity does not occur in nature. (See also *Microgravity.*)

*Zodiacal light:* The glow seen in the west after sunset and in the east before dawn, caused by sunlight reflecting off microscopic dust particles.

# CHRONOLOGICAL LIST

The following list includes all articles covering topics that can be identified with a date of inception, followed by the page number on which the article opens. Articles are dated as specifically as possible: Those covering missions or a series of missions, for example, are listed by month and day of launch; those treating topics less susceptible to specific dating, such as entire programs, socioeconomic phenomena, or areas of research, are dated by month or year. The abbreviation "ff" indicates that the article covers an event, program, discipline, or technology that is ongoing.

## 1964

| | |
|---|---|
| April 2 | Zond 1-8, 2275 |
| May | The Apollo Program, 28 |
| August 28 | Nimbus Meteorological Satellites, 1072 |
| September 5 | The Orbiting Geophysical Observatories, 1099 |
| October | The Voskhod Program, 2170 |
| November 5 | Mariner 3 and 4, 842 |

## 1965

| | |
|---|---|
| March 23 | Gemini 3, 494 |
| April 6 ff | Insuring Spacecraft and Human Life, 608 |
| April 6 ff | The Intelsat Communications Satellites, 613 |
| April 23 ff | Soviet Telecommunications Satellites, 2003 |
| June 3 | Gemini 4, 501 |
| June 3 ff | The Manned Maneuvering Unit, 829 |
| August | The Skylab Program, 1285 |
| August 21 | Gemini 5, 507 |
| November ff | The French Space Program, 461 |
| November 19 | Solar Explorers, 440 |
| December 4 | Gemini 6A and 7, 514 |
| December 16 ff | Pioneer Missions 6-E: The Delta Launches, 1123 |

## 1966

| | |
|---|---|
| February 3 | Environmental Science Services Administration Satellites, 367 |
| February 3 ff | Lunar Soil Samples, 823 |
| March 16 | Gemini 8, 520 |
| March 31 | The Luna Orbiters, 786 |
| April 8 | The Orbiting Astronomical Observatories, 1092 |
| May | The Surveyor Program, 1978 |
| June 3 | Gemini 9, 9A, and 10, 527 |
| August 10 | The Lunar Orbiter, 816 |
| September 9 ff | Attack Satellites, 167 |
| September 12 | Gemini 11 and 12, 533 |
| November | The Soyuz-Kosmos Program, 1396 |
| December 6 | Applications Technology Satellites, 138 |
| December 14 | U.S. Biosatellites, 204 |

## 1967

| | |
|---|---|
| January 1 | Apollo 1-6, 37 |
| April 23 | Soyuz 1, 1403 |
| June 14 | Mariner 5, 849 |
| September 18 ff | Ocean Surveillance Satellites, 1085 |

## 1972

## 1973

## 1974

## 1975

## 1976

## 1977

# ALPHABETICAL LIST

SPACE EXPLORATION

# CATEGORY LIST

**PROBES**

**EARTH RESOURCES SATELLITES**

**METEOROLOGICAL SATELLITES**

# CATEGORY LIST

# SPACE EXPLORATION

C

# MAGILL'S
# SURVEY
# OF
# SCIENCE

# INDEX

Page ranges appearing in boldface type indicate that an entire article devoted to the topic appears on those pages; a single page number in bold denotes definition of a term in the Glossary.